HP NonStop™ Server Security

A Practical Handbook

Computer Security Titles from Digital Press

Internet Security, Tim Speed and Juanita Ellis, 1555582982, 2003

Cybersecurity Operations Handbook, John Rittinghouse and William Hancock, 1555583067, 2003

Mobile Security, John Rhoton, 1555582842, 2004

HP NonStop Server Security, XYPRO, 1555583148, 2003

Implementing Homeland Security Initiative for Enterprise IT, Michael Erbschloe, 1555583121, 2004

Firewalls, John Vacca, 1555582974, 2004

Microsoft Windows Server 2003 Security Infrastructure, Jan De Clercq, 1555582834, 2003

Implementing Network Security, Tony Kenyon, 1555582915, 2004

Other titles from Elsevier Science

The Information Systems Security Officer's Guide: Establishing and Managing an Information Protection Program, Second Edition, Gerald Kovacich, ISBN 0-7506-7656-6

Investigative Data Mining for Security and Criminal Detection, Jesus Mena, ISBN: 0-7506-7613-2

Information Assurance: Managing Organization IT Security Risks, Joseph Boyce, Daniel Jennings, ISBN: 0-7506-7327-3

Handbook of Computer Crime Investigation: Forensic Tools and Technology, Eoghan Casey, ISBN: 0-12-163103-6

Digital Evidence and Computer Crime: Forensic Science, Computers, and the Internet, Eoghan Casey, ISBN: 0-12-162885-X

High-Technology Crime Investigator's Handbook, Gerald Kovacich, William Boni, ISBN: 0-7506-7086-X

I-Way Robbery: Crime on the Internet, William Boni, Gerald Kovacich, ISBN: 0-7506-7029-0

FINDsomeone.com, R. Scott Grasser, ISBN: 0-7506-7020-7

Information Security Best Practices: 205 Basic Rules, George Stefanek, ISBN: 1-878707-96-5

Netspionage: The Global Threat to Information, William Boni, Gerald Kovacich, ISBN: 0-7506-7257-9

For listings of these and other titles go to:

http://www.books.elsevier.com/security and
http://www.books.elsevier.com/forensics

HP NonStop™ Server Security

A Practical Handbook

Terri Hill
Ellen Alvarado

ELSEVIER
DIGITAL
PRESS

Amsterdam • Boston • Heidelberg • London • New York • Oxford
Paris • San Diego • San Francisco • Singapore • Sydney • Tokyo

Digital Press™

An Imprint of Elsevier

Copyright © 2004, XYPRO Technology Corporation.

No part of this publication may be reproduced, stored in a retrieval system, or transmitted in any form or by any means, electronic, mechanical, photocopying, recording, or otherwise, without the prior written permission of the publisher.

Permissions may be sought directly from Elsevier's Science and Technology Rights Department in Oxford, UK. Phone: (44) 1865 843830, Fax: (44) 1865 853333, e-mail: permissions@elsevier.co.uk. You may also complete your request on-line via the Elsevier homepage: http://www.elsevier.com by selecting "Customer Support" and then "Obtaining Permissions".

 Recognizing the importance of preserving what has been written, Elsevier prints its books on acid-free paper whenever possible.

Library of Congress Cataloging-in-Publication Data

British Library Cataloguing-in-Publication Data

A catalogue record for this book is available from the British Library.

ISBN-13: 978-1-55558-314-9
ISBN-10: 1-55558-314-8

The publisher offers special discounts on bulk orders of this book. For information, please contact:

Manager of Special Sales
Elsevier
200 Wheeler Road
Burlington, MA 01803
Tel: 781-313-4700
Fax: 781-313-4882

For information on all Digital Press publications available, contact our World Wide Web home page at: http://www.digitalpress.com or http://www.bh.com/digitalpress

Transferred to Digital Printing 2009

For Dale and Sheila

Key Contributors: Terri Hill, Ellen Alvarado, Scott Uroff—XYPRO Technology Corporation

Contributors and Editors: Bob Alvarado, Antonio Arizo, Sean Bicknell, Dale Blommendahl, Tracy Ding, Barry Forbes, Ellen Gershev, Harriet Hood, Sheila Johnson, Steven Liu, Noel Mabugat, Ajay Nair, Sini Nair, Sandra Parry, Lisa Partridge, Kristie Rusk, Lauren Uroff—XYPRO Technology Corporation

Diagram Designer: Harriet Hood—XYPRO Technology Corporation

Comments and Errata: Please visit www.xypro.com/securitybook

About XYPRO: With over 200 years of collective experience, XYPRO Technology Corporation has specialized in the HP NonStop Server Platform since being founded in 1983. Beginning with the initial release of the XYGATE Security and Access Control Software in 1990, XYPRO has focused exclusively on HP NonStop Server Security and Cross-Platform Encryption. XYPRO is proud to be recognized as one of the leading providers of HP NonStop Server security software and is regarded as expert in the field.

Contents

Foreword   **xxxiii**

Preface   **xxxv**

Introduction   **xxxvii**

About This Handbook   xxxviii
  Disclaimer   xxxviii
  How this handbook is organized   xxxviii
  Parts of the handbook   xxxix
    Discovery   xxxix
    Best Practice   xxxx
    Advice and Policy Suggestions   xxxx
    RISK Identification   xxxxi
  Applying the Security   xxxxi
    Highly Secure   xxxxii
    Commercially Secure   xxxxii
    Moderately Secure   xxxxii
    Determining Security Level   xxxxiii
    Assumptions   xxxxiii

1   Security Basics   **1**

Importance of Corporate Security Policies and Standards   1
  Adapting Best Practice to the Corporate Security Policy   3

Information Security   3
   Three requirements for information security   3
      Integrity   3
      Availability   4
      Confidentiality   4
   Categories of Information   5
      Confidential   5
      Restricted   6
      Internal-Use   6
      Non-Restricted   6
   How To Go About Securing An Organization's Information   6
Controlling Access to Systems and Resources   7
   Physical Controls   8
   Logical Controls   8
      Accountability   9
      Authentication   9
      Authorization   10
      Auditability   10
Compliance Monitoring and Documentation   10
      Monitoring for Breaches   11
      Frequency of Compliance Review   11

2   The HP NonStop Server Architecture and Environment   13

Understanding the Architecture   13
   Scalability and Availability   13
   Software and Application Characteristics   13
   Networking   14
   Two Personalities   15
HP NonStop Networking   15
   The Expand Network   15
      Understanding the Expand Network   15
      Controlling Access Within the Expand Network   17
   TCP/IP   19
      Addressing Remote Hosts   20
      Configuring TCP/IP   20

Telnet   21

Dial Access   22

Interactive Access To The Operating System   22

Hardware and Software Involved   22

Physical Control   22

Additional Authentication   23

Logical Port/User Restriction   24

Encryption   24

Auditing   25

Best Practice Recommendations: 25

Guardian Personality   26

Security and Audit Controls in Guardian Systems   26

Security Components   26

Users   26

Objects   27

Authentication   31

Authorization   31

Auditing and Controls   32

Sanitizing an HP NonStop System   32

User Management   33

Secure the Operating System Software   33

Reserve the System Disk for HP Operating System Files   33

Configuring the Safeguard Subsystem   34

Safeguard Global Configuration   35

SUPER.SUPER Undeniable   36

Safeguard Global Authentication Controls   37

Safeguard Global Password Controls   37

Safeguard Global Warning-Mode Controls   38

Safeguard Global Device Controls   38

Safeguard Global Process Controls   38

Safeguard Global Diskfile Controls   39

Safeguard Global CMON Controls   39

Safeguard Global Command Interpreter Controls   40

Safeguard Global Audit Controls   40

The Concept of Ownership in the Safeguard Subsystem   42

Primary Owner   42

Secondary Owner(s)   43

Ownership Recommendations   43

Safeguard Objects   43

Object Protection Records   44

Owner   44

Access Control List (ACL)   45

Audit Parameters   47

Safeguard OBJECTTYPES   48

OBJECTTYPE OBJECTTYPE   48

OBJECTTYPE Protection Records   49

OBJECTTYPE ACL   51

OBJECTTYPE Status   51

OBJECTTYPE Audit Attributes   52

Non-Object Safeguard Entities   53

Configuring Safeguard Audit Pools   54

SECURITY-GROUPs   59

SECURITY-ADMINISTRATOR GROUP   60

Safeguard-Controlled Terminals   63

Security Event-Exit Process (SEEP)   63

Safeguard Warning Mode   68

WARNING-MODE   69

WARNING-FALLBACK-SECURITY   69

Safeguard Auditing   72

Configuring What Will Be Audited   73

How the Safeguard Subsystem Determines What to Audit   76

Safeguard Globals and Configuration Recap   77

3   Authentication; User Administration   81

User Administration   81

Userids   81

Groups   81

Members   82

Aliases   83

Single SignOn   84

Privileged IDs   84
   Userids With Inherent Guardian privileges   84
     NULL.NULL   85
     Group Manager IDs   85
     SUPER Group IDs   86
     SUPER.SUPER   86
   Application-Owner IDs   90
   Job-Function IDs   91
   Securing Privileged Userids   92
Personal Userids   94
   Administering Userids   95
     Procedures To Request New Userids   95
     Procedures To Delete Obsolete Userids   95
   Who Can Manage Userids   96
Managing Userids In the Guardian System   97
     ADDUSER and DELUSER   97
     RPASSWRD   97
     The DEFAULT Program   97
     The USERS Program   98
Managing Userids With the Safeguard Subsystem   98
   The USER OBJECTTYPE   98
   Userid/Alias-Related Safeguard Global Parameters   99
     Command Interpreter Attributes   100
   Userid/Alias Record Attributes   102
     User Record Ownership   102
     USER-EXPIRES   102
     Frozen/Thawed   103
     Guardian Default Volume   103
     Guardian Default Security   103
     Subject Default Protection   104
     Command Interpreter Attributes   104
     OSS-Specific Attributes   105
     PRIMARY-GROUP   106

Auditing Users   106

    What Can Be Audited   106

        Without the Safeguard Subsystem or CMON   107

        With CMON   107

        With the Safeguard Subsystem   107

        With Third Party Products   107

    Auditing Users With the Safeguard Subsystem   107

        Audit-Related Global Parameters   107

        Audit-Related User Record Parameters   108

Password Administration   110

    "Hardened" Passwords   111

        Content Rules   111

Password-Related Logon Controls   112

        With the Safeguard Subsystem   113

    Password Quality Controls   114

        Without the Safeguard Subsystem   114

        With the Safeguard Subsystem   114

        With Third Party Software   116

    Password Expiration   116

        Without the Safeguard Subsystem   117

        With the Safeguard Subsystem   117

        Password-Expiration With Third Party Products   121

    Who Can RESET Passwords   121

        Without the Safeguard Subsystem   122

        With the Safeguard Subsystem   122

        With Third Party Password Products   122

    Administering Passwords for Sensitive Userids   122

4   Authentication, Granting Access to the HP NonStop Server   125

Guardian Authentication   127

        Logon-Related TACLCONF Configuration   127

        Logon-Related CMON Configuration   130

        Logon-Related Password Issues   130

        Logon-Related Safeguard Global Parameters   130

OSS Authentication | 132
Safeguard-Controlled Terminals | 132
   Dynamic Safeguard-Controlled Sessions | 132
   Static Safeguard Terminals | 132
      The Terminal Definition Record | 133
   TERMINAL-EXCLUSIVE-ACCESS | 135
Granting Access to the Remote Nodes | 136
   REMOTEPASSWORDs | 136
CMON | 137
   CMON Can Control Access To Privileged Ids | 138
   CMON Can Control Remote Access | 138
   CMON Can Control Access To Utilities Based on Port and Userid | 138
   CMON Can Perform Load Balancing | 138
   CMON in a Non-Safeguard Environment | 138
      CMONREQUIRED | 139
      CMONTIMEOUT | 139
      REMOTECMONREQUIRED | 140
      REMOTECMONTIMEOUT | 140
   CMON in a Safeguard Environment | 141
      CMON | 141
      CMONERROR | 141
      CMONTIMEOUT | 142

5 Authorization—Object Security | **143**

Defining User Access to System Resources | 143
   Principles for Granting Access to System Resources | 143
   A Typical Access Matrix | 144
Guardian Process Security | 144
   Programs | 145
   Process Identifiers | 145
      Process Names | 146
      Process Identification Number (PIN) | 147
   Process Properties | 147
      Unnamed Processes | 147

PRIORITY   148

STATE   149

Process Structure   150

Securing Processes   151

With CMON   152

Without the Safeguard Subsystem   152

How the Guardian System Evaluates Process Access Attempts   152

Securing Processes With the Safeguard Subsystem   153

Process-Related Safeguard OBJECTTYPES   153

Securing NAMED and UNNAMED Processes   154

How the Safeguard Subsystem Evaluates Process Management Requests   156

A User Creating a Protected Process   156

A Process Opening a Protected Process or Subprocess   156

Stopping a Protected Process   156

Process-Related Safeguard Global Parameters   156

ACL-REQUIRED-PROCESS   157

CHECK-PROCESS   157

CHECK-SUBPROCESS   158

COMBINATION-PROCESS   158

DIRECTION-PROCESS   159

Process And Subprocess Protection Records   159

Process Protection Record Ownership   160

Auditing Process And Subprocess Access and Management   160

AUDIT-PROCESS-ACCESS{ -PASS | -FAIL }   161

AUDIT-PROCESS-MANAGE { -PASS | -FAIL }   161

Device Security   163

Identifying Devices   163

Device Name   163

Qualifier   163

Subqualifier   163

LDEV-Number   163

Without the Safeguard Subsystem   163

With the Safeguard Subsystem   163

DEVICE-Related Safeguard OBJECTTYPES   164

DEVICE-Related Safeguard Global Parameters   165

Device And Subdevice Protection Records   167
Auditing Device And Subdevice Access and Management   168
AUDIT-DEVICE-ACCESS{ -PASS | -FAIL }   169
AUDIT-DEVICE-MANAGE { -PASS | -FAIL }   169
The File Subsystem   170
File Names   171
Types of Files   171
Enscribe Database   172
Format 1 Files   173
Format 2 Files   173
NonStop SQL   173
Securing Diskfiles In the Guardian Environment   173
The Default Program   175
Securing Disk Files With the Safeguard Subsystem   175
Diskfile-Related User Record Settings   176
Guardian Default Volume   176
Guardian Default Security   176
Subject Default-Protection   176
Disk-Related Safeguard OBJECTTYPES   176
Disk-Related Safeguard Global Settings   177
ACL-REQUIRED-DISKFILE   178
CHECK-VOLUME   178
CHECK-SUBVOLUME   179
CHECK-FILENAME   180
CLEARONPURGE-DISKFILE   180
COMBINATION-DISKFILE   181
DIRECTION-DISKFILE   182
Diskfile-related Protection Records   182
VOLUME Protection Records   183
SUBVOLUME Protection Records   184
DISKFILE Protection Records   185
How the Safeguard Subsystem Evaluates Diskfile CREATE Attempts   187
How the Safeguard Subsytem Evaluates File Access Attempts   188
Auditing Disk File Access and Management Attempts   191
Disk File-Related Global Audit Parameters   191

AUDIT-DISKFILE-ACCESS{ -PASS | -FAIL }   191
AUDIT-DISKFILE-MANAGE { -PASS | -FAIL }   192
Disk File-Related Protection Record Audit Parameters   193
AUDIT-ACCESS{ -PASS | -FAIL }   193
AUDIT-MANAGE { -PASS | -FAIL }   194

6   Gazette A to Z   197

ADDUSER User Program   197
Securing ADDUSER   197
Without the Safeguard Subsystem   198
With the Safeguard Subsystem   199
AUDSERV System Program   200
Securing AUDSERV   200
AXCEL User Program   201
Securing AXCEL   201
BACKCOPY System Utility   202
Securing BACKCOPY   202
BACKUP User Program   203
Securing BACKUP   204
Binder Subsystem   205
BINSERV   206
BIND   206
VPROC   208
Securing BINDER Components   208
BUSCMD System Utility   211
Securing BUSCMD   211
$CMON System Program   212
The CMON Program   212
CMON and TACL   213
CMON and the Safeguard Subsystem   214
Securing CMON   214
Compilers   215
Securing Compiler Components   216
C/C++   216

COBOL85	218
FORTRAN	219
NMC/NMCPLUS	220
NMCOBOL	221
Pascal	222
PTAL	222
SCOBOL	223
SQL	224
TAL	224
COUP System Utility	225
Securing COUP	226
CROSSREF User Program	227
CROSSREF	228
SYMSERV	228
Securing CROSSREF	228
*CSTM Customization Files	229
DSAPCSTM Configuration File	230
EMSACSTM Configuration File	231
FTPCSTM Configuration File	232
FUPCSTM Configuration File	233
INSPCSTM Configuration File	235
SCFCSTM Configuration File	236
SEECSTM Configuration File	237
TACLCSTM Configuration File	238
VHSCSTM Configuration File	240
Data Build User Program	241
Securing Data Build Components	242
DATA Loader/MP User Program	243
Securing DataLoader/MP Components	243
DCOM System Utility	244
Securing DCOM	245
Data Definition Language (DDL) Subsystem	245
Using DDL Definitions	245
Enscribe DBMS	246

Enscribe Application Dictionaries	247
Securing DDL Components	247
DEFAULT User Program	248
Setting Default Volume	249
Setting Default File Security	249
Securing DEFAULT	249
DELUSER User Program	250
Securing DELUSER	250
Without the Safeguard Subsystem	251
With the Safeguard Subsystem	252
Disk Processes	253
Disk Process Security	253
DISKGEN System Utility	254
Securing DISKGEN	254
Distributed Name Service (DNS) Subsystem	255
DNS Components	255
DNSCOM	256
DNSCONF	257
DNSEXP	257
DNSHELP	257
DNSMGR	257
LOAD	257
DBDDLS & ENFORM Reports	257
DNS Database Configuration	257
Securing DNS Components	258
DIVER System Utility	259
Securing DIVER	260
DSAP User Program	260
DSAP	261
DSAPDDL	261
DSAPCSTM	261
Securing DSAP	261
DSM/SCM Subsystem	262
DSM/SCM Methodology	262

Securing DSMSCM Components   265

DSM/TC Subsystem   267

   MEDIACOM   268

   MEDIADBM   268

   MEDIAMSG   268

   MEDIASRV   268

   MEDDEM   269

   SQL Tape Catalog and Database   269

   ZSERVER   269

   Securing DSM/TC Components   269

      MEDIACOM Commands with Security Implications   271

ECHO User Program   273

   ECHO   273

   ECHOSERV   273

   Securing ECHO   273

EDIT User Program   274

   EDIT   275

   TEDIT   275

   VS   275

   Securing EDITORS   275

EMS Subsystem   276

   EMS Components   277

      Event Message Collectors   277

      Event Message Distributors   279

      EMS Filters   280

      EMS Object Programs   280

      EMS Utilities   281

   Securing EMS Components   281

EMSA Subsystem   282

   Customizing the EMSA environment   283

   Securing EMSA Components   283

ENABLE User Program   285

   Securing ENABLE Components   286

ENFORM Subsystem   287
  ENFORM Components   288
    Query Specification with ENFORM   288
    The Query Processor (QP)   290
    Optional User-provided Components   290
    Optional ENFORM Plus Components   290
  Securing ENFORM Components   291
ERROR User Program   294
  ERROR Security   295
Expand Subsystem   295
  NCPOBJ   295
  OZEXP   296
  $ZNUP   297
  Expand Profile Templates   297
  Securing Expand Components   297
FINGER System Utility   298
  FINGER   299
  FINGSERV   299
  Securing FINGER   299
File Transfer Protocols   300
  FTP   301
  FTPSERV   301
  FTP CUSTOM Files   301
  FTP Systems   301
  FTP Userids   301
  Securing the Anonymous FTP Userid and Environment 301
  With CMON   303
  Without the Safeguard Subsystem   303
  With the Safeguard Subsystem   304
  With Third Party Products   304
  Securing FTP Components   305
  Trivial File Transfer Program (TFTP) User Program   306
  TFTP Components   307
  Securing TFTP Components   308
  Information Exchange Facility (IXF) User Program   309

Securing IXF Components   309

FUP System Utility   310

FUP   311

ORSERV   311

FUP Customization Files   311

FUPLOCL Files   311

Securing FUP Components   312

FUP Commands with Security Implications   313

GOAWAY System Utility   316

Securing GOAWAY   316

INSPECT Subsystem   317

INSPECT User Program   318

IMON System Program   318

DMON System Program   319

INSPECT Customization Files   319

INSPSNAP   319

INSPECT SAVEABEND Files   320

VISUAL INSPECT SOFTWARE   320

INSPECT and Pathway   320

Securing INSPECT Components   320

INSPECT Commands With Security Implications   321

Libraries, SRLs and Common Routines   322

System Libraries   323

Resolving System Libraries with BINDSERV   323

User Libraries   323

Shared Run-Time Libraries (SRLs)   324

Public SRLs   324

Private SRLs   324

Resolving SRLs with NLD   325

Loading SRLs with LTILT   325

Verifying SRLs with VTILT   325

Loading SRLs with ZTILT   326

Securing Libraries Components   326

Licensed Files   327
    Securing LICENSED Files   328
        Documentation and Authorization of Licensed Programs   329
        Securing Licensed Files   330
        Licensed Operating System Programs   330
        Controlling the LICENSE command   334
        Scheduled Review for Unauthorized Licensed Files   335
LISTNER System Utility   336
    PORTCONF   337
    TCP/IP Services File   338
    Securing LISTNER   338
LOGIN System Program   339
    Securing LOGIN   339
LOGON User Program   340
    Securing LOGON   340
MEASURE Subsystem   341
    MEASCOM   342
    MEASCTL   343
    MEASFH   343
    MEASCHMA, MEASDDLB, MEASDDLF, MEASDDLS, MEASDECS   343
    MEASDECS   343
    MEASIMMU   343
    MEASMON   343
    MEASTCM   344
    MEASZIP   344
    OUTPUT DATA FILES   344
    Securing MEASURE Components   344
Native Link Editor (NLD) User Program   347
    Securing NLD   347
Native Object File Tool (NOFT) User Program   348
    Securing NOFT   349
NETBATCH Subsystem   349
    NETBATCH   350
    BATCHCOM   351

BATCHCAL 351

BATCHCTL 351

NBEXEC 351

NetBatch Plus 351

ATTACHMENT-SETs 351

Securing NETBATCH Components 352

NSKCOM System Utility 354

NSKCOM 354

ZSYSCFG File 355

Managed SWAP Files 355

Securing NSKCOM 355

Operating System 356

Securing the SYSTEM Disk 356

Current Operating System - $SYSTEM.SYSnn 358

Communication OS - $SYSTEM.CSSnn 360

Old Operating System - $SYSTEM.SYS++ 360

$SYSTEM.SYSTEM 362

Z Subvolumes 363

PAK/UNPAK User Programs 364

PAK 364

UNPAK 364

Securing PAK/UNPAK 365

Password User Program 366

Configuring the PASSWORD Program 366

BLINDPASSWORD 367

ENCRYPTPASSWORD 368

MINPASSWORDLEN 369

PROMPTPASSWORD 369

Third Party Password Products 370

Securing PASSWORD 370

Pathway Subsystem 371

PATHCOM 372

PATHMON 373

LINKMON 375

     PATHTCP2   375
     PATHCTL   376
     {}PATHTCPL   376
     POBJDIR/POBJCOD   376
     Server Programs   377
   Securing Pathway Components   377
PCFORMAT User Program   379
   Securing PCFORMAT   380
PEEK System Utility   381
   Securing PEEK   381
PING User Program   381
   Securing PING   382
PROGID'd Files   382
   Securing PROGID'd Files   384
     Documentation and Authorization   384
     Protecting Against Authorized Use   385
     Controlling Use of the PROGID Command   386
     Scheduled Review for Unauthorized PROGID'd Files   387
PUP System Utility   389
   Securing PUP   389
     PUP Commands With Security Implications   389
NonStop RDF Subsystem   391
   RDF Components   392
     NonStop RDF User Programs   392
     NonStop RDF Processes   394
     Other NonStop RDF Components   396
   Interaction of NonStop RDF Components   397
   Securing NonStop RDF Components   399
     NonStop RDF Commands with Security Implications   401
RESTORE User Program   403
     File Mode   403
     Listonly Mode   404
     Volume Mode   404
     How RESTORE Interacts With NonStop TMF Software   404

Securing RESTORE 405

RPASSWRD User Program 407

Securing RPASSWRD 408

Safeguard Subsystem 408

Security Considerations of Safeguard Software Installation 409

Safeguard Subsystem Components 410

Securing Safeguard Components 411

SAFECOM Command Commands With Security Implications 411

Subsystem Control Facility (SCF) 414

Subsystems Controlled Via SCF 415

On D-Series Operating Systems 415

On G-Series Operating Systems 415

SCF 416

SCF Custom Files 416

SCF LIBRARIES 416

SCFTEXT 416

Subsystem-specific servers 416

Securing SCF Components 417

SCF Commands with Security Implications 418

Subsystem Control Point (SCP) 420

Securing SCP Components 422

SEEVIEW User Program 423

Securing SEEVIEW 423

SERVICES Configuration File 425

Securing SERVICES/HOSTS Files 425

SORT Subsystem 426

RECGEN 427

SORT 427

SORTPROG 427

Securing SORT Components 428

Subsystem Programmatic Interface (SPI) 429

SPI Components 430

Definition Files 430

Securing SPI Components 431

Spooler Subsystem   432
    Spooler Subsystem Components   433
        Collectors   434
        FONT   434
        PERUSE   434
        Print Processes   435
        RPSETUP Utility   436
        SPOOLCOM   436
        Supervisors   437
        Spooler Data Files   438
    Securing Spooler Components   438
Storage Management Foundation (SMF) Software   441
    Securing SMF Components   444
NonStop SQL Subsystem   447
    Two Versions of NonStop SQL Database   447
        NonStop SQL/MP Database   447
        NonStop SQL/MX Database   447
        SQLCAT   449
        SQLCI / SQLCI2 / SQLUTIL   449
        Licensed SQLCI2   455
        SQLCOMP / NLCPCOMP   455
        SQLCFE / SQLH   456
        SQLESP / SQLESMG   456
        SQLMSG / NLCPMSG   456
        SQLUTIL   456
        AUDSERV   456
    Securing SQL Components   456
SWID System Utility   459
    Securing SWID   460
SYSGENR System Utility   461
    Securing SYSGENR Components   461
System Configuration Files   462
        CONFALT File   463
        CONFAUX File   463
        CONFBASE File   464

CONFLIST File   464
CONFTEXT File   464
Command Interpreter Input File (CIIN)   466
CUSTFILE File   467
RLSEID File   468
OSCONFIG File   468
Securing the SYSTEM CONFIGURATION Files   469
System Processes   471
Securing System Processes   473
System Startup Files   475
System Startup Files   476
Securing the System Startup Files   476
System Utilities   477
TFD Data System   477
DUMPUTIL   478
RCVDUMP   478
RELOAD   478
PRDUMP   478
TFDS monitor   478
TFDSCOM   478
TFDSCONF   479
Securing TFDS   479
Failure Utilities   481
COPYDUMP   481
CRUNCH   481
GARTH   481
RECEIVEDUMP/RCVDUMP   481
Securing Failure Tools   481
TACL Tool Utilities   482
FCHECK   483
FILCHECK   483
TANDUMP   483
Securing TACL Tools   484

TACL Subsystem   485
    TACL Subsystem Components   485
    Securing TACL Components   492
TAPECOM System Utility   494
    Securing TAPECOM   495
        TAPECOM Commands With Security Implications   495
Telnet Subsystem   497
    Securing Telnet Components   498
TGAL User Program   498
    Securing TGAL   499
NonStop TMF Subsystem   499
    NonStop TMF Software and Database Recovery   500
        NonStop TMF Configuration   501
        NonStop TMF Auditing   501
        Database Recovery Methods   502
    NonStop TMF Subsystem Components   503
        NonStop TMF Audit Trails   504
        NonStop TMF Configuration   504
        TMFCOM   505
    Securing NonStop TMF Components   506
TRACER (TRACE ROUTE) System Utility   511
    Securing TRACER   511
USERS User Program   512
    Securing USERS   512
VIEWPOINT Application   513
    Securing VIEWPOINT Components   514
VIEWSYS User Program   514
    Securing VIEWSYS   515
Virtual Hometerm Subsystem (VHS)   515
    The VHS Components   516
        VHS   517
        VHSCSTM   517
        VHS Conversational Interface   517
        VHS Primary Log File Set   517

VHS Prompt File	517
VHS Browser	518
Securing VHS Components	518
7 Securing Applications	**521**
Understanding Application Development	521
In House Application Development	521
Source Control	522
Application Configuration Source Files	523
Object Release Control	523
Application Security Considerations	524
Third-Party Vendor Applications	524
Legacy Applications	524
In-House System Tools	525
Third-Party System Tools	525
Securing the Production Applications	526
Platforms	527
The Pathway Subsystem	528
Configuring Pathways	530
Communication Between Pathway Environments	531
Securing a Pathway Application	532
Binder	534
Non-Pathway Applications	534
Batch	535
Tools	535
Database Management Systems (DBMS)	536
Enscribe Databases	536
NonStop SQL Databases	537
SQL Objects	540
Sanitizing Test Data	544
DEFINEs, ASSIGNs, PARAMs	545
DEFINEs	545
DEFINE Format	546
_DEFAULTS DEFINE	547
ASSIGNs	547

PARAMs   548

Application Management and Support   548

System Management   548

Database Management   549

Communications   549

Protection and Recovery   549

A   Gathering The Audit Information   **553**

Legend   553

Guardian Wildcarding   553

CUSTFILE   554

DSAP Commands   556

Fileinfo Commands   557

FUP (File Utility Program) Commands   558

Pathway Commands   559

Status Command   560

Safeguard Commands   561

Gathering Information about Objects Protected by the Safeguard Subsystem   561

Gathering Information about the Safeguard Audit Trail   565

SQL Commands   566

Gathering System Information   569

SYSINFO   569

RLSEID File   569

Researching TACL Configuration   570

ASSIGNs   570

ASSIGNs and DEFINEs In NETBATCH   570

DEFINEs: 572

PARAMs: 573

Viewing the TACLCONF Parameters   573

PASSWORD BIND Settings   574

SCF (Subsystem Control Facility) Commands   575

NonStop TMF Software   578

USERS Program   582

SPOOLCOM   582

PERUSE   583

BATCHCOM   584

B   **HP NonStop File Codes**   **587**

C   **Third Party HP NonStop Server Security Vendors**   **589**

About the Authors   **591**

Index   **593**

Foreword

In the early part of my career, I attended a forum on information security convened by the Office of Technology Assessment for the United States Congress. As a cryptography researcher, I was expecting extensive technical discussion about encryption and digital signature algorithms. Instead, I was reminded that cryptographic algorithms played only a part in solving a bigger problem, one with multiple aspects represented by the various participants: how to make a full system secure.

HP NonStop Server Security again renews this perspective, and takes it one step further.

Cryptography researchers have identified many good design principles for algorithms, which have resulted in a number of remarkable algorithms over the years. Information security experts have likewise identified good design principles for secure systems.

To make a full system secure, however, administrators need more than good ideas. While there may be only a few algorithms in use, a system has many components and programs, and every component is a potential avenue for attack, moreover, each component is unique. Administrators therefore need not only to know the principles, but also guidance on how to apply them in each situation.

HP NonStop Server Security provides that kind of information. Direct and concise, it provides readable advice on the key decisions in safeguarding the numerous components of the HP NonStop environment—just the kind of approach that administrators can use to put security principles into practice.

HP NonStop Servers protect critical resources for organizations worldwide, so it is no surprise that they would be potential targets of attack. *HP NonStop Server Security* is a helpful addition to organizations' tools for managing these systems, and in their panoply in the continuing battle for information security.

Burt Kaliski
RSA Laboratories
Bedford, Massachusetts, USA
August 12, 2003

Preface

This handbook represents the efforts of many individuals at XYPRO, who collectively have over 200 years of experience with the HP NonStop platform. As a vendor of third party security software for the HP NonStop platform, we were very careful to ensure that this handbook was useful for security administrators, system resource personnel, auditors and the general HP NonStop server community whether or not they chose to use our suite of software tools.

There hasn't been a comprehensive publication on this topic since the early 1990's. The lack of reference material for the Guardian Operating system prompted us to author this book in the hopes that it would facilitate securing the HP NonStop server. We at XYPRO believe in this platform and have dedicated 20 years to developing software to take advantage of its unmatched functionality, reliability and scalability.

Plenty of other companies believe in NonStop servers too. According to a 1999 Research Note from D. H. Brown Associates, Inc., NonStop servers process 66 percent of the credit card transactions, 95 percent of securities transactions, and 80 percent of automated teller machine (ATM) transactions. They also participate in 75 percent of electronic funds transfers (EFT) networks. According to the Gartner Group, NonStop servers are the only out of the box ultra high-availability system on the market today.

This handbook seeks to familiarize auditors and those responsible for security configuration and monitoring, with the aspects of the HP NonStop server operating system that make the NonStop Server unique, the security risks these aspects create, and the best ways to mitigate these risks.

Please remember that the needs of the corporation, computer center, applications and customers must always take precedence over our recommended Best Practices in the environment. Use this handbook as a guideline, not a rule.

This handbook has been organized to address topics as units. This is particularly true for discussions about Safeguard.

Each section also includes Discovery, Best Practices, and Recommendations.

The HP NonStop server's subsystems have been presented in a logical manner, beginning with the subsystems that make up the Operating System itself, native Guardian security, and Safeguard and continuing through user administration, how users are authenticated when attempting to access the HP NonStop server and how each user is granted access to information and programs as appropriate to job function.

Because securing the information on an HP NonStop server is primarily implemented via the principles of access control, the handbook is organized based on these principles.

We hope you enjoy this handbook and find the information interesting and useful. We had a great time writing it.

Acknowledgments

Without the assistance of individuals outside of XYPRO this book simply wouldn't have been published.

We are very grateful to have met and had the opportunity to work with the fine folks at Digital Press, including Theron Shreve. Thanks also to Alan Rose of Multiscience Press, and Darrell Judd. They said it was impossible to publish this book within the timeframe. It turns out their specialty is making the impossible possible. It has been a distinct pleasure working with all of them.

Very special thanks go to Mark Chapman for his impeccable editing skills as well as to Walter Bruce and Ron La Pedis for their encouragement. Their feedback proved invaluable.

And finally, thanks to the originators of the HP NonStop Server.

Introduction

"To have the same number of takeoffs and landings and never have my name in the paper".

I received that well-practiced answer when I asked a commercial wide-body pilot nearing retirement what his goals had been during his nearly 30 years flying.

I thought—vendors of key IT infrastructure should have the same goals—no major crashes and staying out of the headlines. My pilot friend understood implicitly that he was part of the transportation infrastructure and that "boring was beautiful." Every element of the aircraft, the flight procedures and even personnel assignment, were centered on maximizing reliability and thus safety. IT infrastructure vendors need to be thinking the same way.

By Kevin Tolly
Network World, 02/03/03

If a company's software applications are the 'castle', then access control is the moat or first level of defense. Logon controls are the outer gate and dial up and FTP access are the postern gates, CMON and HP Safeguard software are the gatekeepers, lookouts and tattletales. Safeguard Protection Records and HP Guardian Security vectors are the bricks in the castle wall encircling all the application objects files, source files and data files. Other subsystems such as NonStop TMF software and SCF and the operating system in general are the underpinnings or foundation that support the applications and also 'live' within the walls. Application databases and reports, proprietary corporate data and personal employee data are the treasures that must be protected.

Application users are the tenants of the castle. The security, operations and technical support groups are the staff that assist the tenants and keep the castle's systems functioning.

Security's mission is to protect the castle, its tenants and its contents. Their job is four-fold. First, to minimize the likelihood of damaging mistakes by the tenants or staff. Second, to prevent plots, intrigues and pilfering by the castle's tenants and staff. Third, to prevent invasion by outsiders. Fourth, to mitigate the damage possible in the event of mistakes or breaches.

The Auditor's job is both to monitor the Security Department's effectiveness and to provide the 'hammer' that enables the Security Department to change company procedures and culture, when necessary, to effectively secure the castle.

About This Handbook

This handbook seeks to familiarize auditors and those responsible for security configurations and monitoring, with the aspects of the HP NonStop server operating system that make the NonStop server unique, the security risks these aspects create, and the best ways to mitigate these risks.

Disclaimer

This handbook represents the efforts of many individuals, who collectively have over 200 years of experience, in an effort to provide a practical handbook for security administrators, system resource personnel, auditors and the general HP NonStop server community.

A lot of hard work has gone into this handbook to ensure that the information presented herein is accurate, but errors and omissions may be found.

Please remember that the needs of the corporation, computer center, applications and customers must always take precedence over our recommended Best Practices in the environment. Use this handbook as a guideline, not a rule.

How this handbook is organized

The HP NonStop server's subsystems have been presented in a logical manner, beginning with the subsystems that make up the Operating System itself, native Guardian security, and Safeguard subsystem and continuing through user administration, how users are authenticated when attempting to access the HP NonStop server and how each user is granted access to information and programs as appropriate to job function.

Because securing the information on an HP NonStop server is primarily implemented via the principles of access control, the handbook is organized based on these principles.

Access Control is the overall term for the set of manual and automated procedures designed to provide individual accountability by:

User authentication to ensure that only authorized users access the system

Object-centric access control that maps the subject user and operation to the object resource

Auditing that records when who did what to which object

This section provides an overview of these principles.

For detailed information regarding Authentication procedures on the HP Non-Stop server, see this handbook's Parts Two and Three, *Administering Users* and *Granting Access to the HP NonStop Server*.

For detailed information regarding Authorization procedures on the HP NonStop server, see Parts Four and Five, *Controlling Access to Objects* and *Controlling Access to Utilities*.

Parts of the handbook

This handbook has been organized to address topics as units. This is particularly true for discussions about the Safeguard subsystem. Safeguard configuration is discussed separately from the discussion on User Management with Safeguard.

Part Six is the Gazette: an alphabetical series of sections addressing specific utility programs or subsystem's software security. The Gazette is more "how to secure the components of a subsystem," not "how to use a subsystem."

Each section also includes Discovery, Best Practices, and Recommendations.

Discovery

Each Discovery subsection includes a list of questions that, when answered, provides the information necessary for evaluating the risk posed by the particular subsystem in the environment. Each question is 'numbered'; the numbers correspond with the Risk Identifiers and the Best Practice recommendations.

In the Discovery tables, each question also has a reference to the kind of method used to gather the data needed to respond to the question. The data-collection methods are detailed in *Appendix A: Gathering the Information*.

Best Practice

Each Best Practice identification discusses the recommended methods of mitigating each risk present in the particular subsystem. Each Best Practice item is numbered; the numbers correspond with those in the Discovery tables.

About the Numbering Convention

The Best Practice (BP) numbering convention is designed to uniquely identify each Best Practice item.

To provide a shorthand means of referring to a practice and to support a checklist for security review summaries, there is an identifier associated with each item in every Best Practice subsection throughout the handbook. The identifiers are based on the Best Practice points for each subsystem or subsystem component. The Best Practice numbers correspond with the stipulated risks and the discovery questions.

The identifiers are made up of four parts:

Part 1   BP (this part is dropped in the Discovery listings)

Part 2   The subsystem identifier. Each section has a Subsystem Identifier. For example, the Safeguard Subsystem is abbreviated to SAFE.

Part 3   The category identifier within each subsystem. In general, each subsection has a category identifier. For example, OBJT is the category for the Safeguard OBJECTTYPE related items. For example, BP-SAFE-OBJT

Part 4   A number identifying each particular question. Within each subsystem (Section), the primary numbers begin with 01. For example, BP-SAFE-OBJT-01.

Example:
`BP-FILE-DELUSER-01`   DELUSER should be secured "- - - -".

Advice and Policy Suggestions

Advice and policy recommendations are noted throughout the handbook. These are ideas or suggestions that may or may not be important to a specific company.

Some advice topics may recommend the use of third party products to enhance the 'native' security provided by HP's Guardian and Safeguard security mechanisms.

About the Numbering Convention

Policy, advice and recommendations are uniquely identified throughout the handbook.

The identifiers are made up of four parts:

Part 1   AP for advice or recommendations or 3P for a recommendation that is best supported by a third party tool (this part is dropped in the Discovery listings)

Part 2   The subsystem identifier or ADVICE.

Part 3   The category identifier within each subsystem. In general, each subsection has a category identifier. For example, PASSWORD is the category for the User Password related items. For example, AP-ADVICE-PASSWORD

Part 4   A number identifying each particular question. Within each subsystem (Section), the primary numbers begin with 01. For example AP-ADVICE-PASSWORD-01.

```
Example:
AP-ADVICE-CMON-03    Put procedures in place to keep CMON up-to-date
with new Operating System releases.
```

RISK Identification

Risks are addressed throughout the handbook. To bring these to the reader's attention, they are italicized.

RISK   Adding users to the system is a primary gateway through which unauthorized users could gain access.

Applying the Security

Throughout this handbook, specific security vectors and configuration settings are suggested. Each HP NonStop server may have unique security requirements. In researching those requirements, three distinct types of security levels were identified:

Highly secure system

Commercially secure system

Moderately secure system

Highly Secure

A highly secure system contains both strict user authorization and enforced user-operation-object restrictions (Access Control Lists).

When corporate needs require this level of security, only the most complete implementation of Safeguard software or a third party equivalent will suffice. Each user's identity must be positively verified, often with an additional identification mechanism such as a cryptographic token. There must be explicit permission for each user to access each object necessary for the user's job function, with no implicit security measures acceptable. All access attempts not explicitly permitted must be denied.

Authorized system activity and audit reports must be reviewed often and violations must be aggressively and rapidly pursued to a resolution.

Commercially Secure

A commercially secure system has strict user authorization and user-operation-object restrictions, ensuring that the system is functionally secure.

When a corporation uses this level of security, the amount of time spent on security implementation is balanced against the chance of loss. The user must be positively identified, though an additional identification mechanism such as a cryptographic token is unusual. Both implicit and explicit user-operation-object controls are acceptable. All user access attempts that are not explicitly permitted are denied, but users who are otherwise authorized may depend on implicit access.

System activity that has been authorized is reviewed as necessary. Failed activity reports are reviewed often and violations must be pursued to a resolution.

Moderately Secure

A moderately secure system is one that does not handle confidential information and has all resources generally available to all users on the system. The user is positively identified when logging on to the system, but there are generally few or no user-operation-object controls. Many general users have access to system tools, configuration files, and applications. While these systems may be secured from external entry, the internal security is very open to the users of the system.

With this level of security, the system must be available only to internal personnel; external access to the system must be restricted. If external access to such a system is permitted, the system must be considered insecure and cut off from accessing more highly secured systems.

Failed activity reports are reviewed on this system on a regular basis. External violations must be pursued, but internal violations are often handled by direct contact.

Determining Security Level

The Corporate Security Policy and/or Security Standards should specify how the HP NonStop server should be secured in the environment. The following questions can help determine a general security level:

Is this system connected via an interactive network to other systems?

Does this system supply data to another system?

Will users from networked systems have access to this system?

What is the primary use of the system?

Production
Development
Backup
Testing
Communications
Other

What is the level of sensitivity of the data contained on the system?

What is the level of confidentiality of the data contained on the system?

What methods are used to physically secure the system?

What methods are used to secure user access to the system?

Guardian system
Safeguard subsystem
Third party tools
Other tools

Are there outside security requirements that must be met, such as governmental regulations?

Assumptions

For the purpose of reading this handbook, the security standards that are implied are those for the "commercially secure" system.

This book primarily addresses the security of HP NonStop server system files, processes, users, security controls, and security products.

Please note that while addressing the higher level issues surrounding the security requirements for applications, this book cannot address specific application security needs since each application has unique security needs. In addition, methods of physical security are not directly addressed in this handbook, but are very important to the overall security of any computer system.

Security Basics

Part One discusses Security Principles, including:

> Importance of Corporate Security Policies and Standards
>
> Adapting Best Practice to Corporate Security Policy
>
> Information Security
>
> Controlling Access to Systems and Resources
>
> Compliance Monitoring and Documentation

Importance of Corporate Security Policies and Standards

> Information security policies underpin the security and well being of information resources. They are the foundation, the bottom line, of information security within an organization.
> —*Information Security Policy World*

People frequently use the terms "policy," "standard," and "guidelines" to refer to documents that establish the security stance of an organization. For the purposes of this handbook, the following definitions will apply:

> A Security Policy is a concise statement, by senior management, of the corporate commitment to take responsibility for protecting information. The policy is then implemented by taking specific actions, utilizing the specific security standards, procedures and mechanisms that are most effective.
> —*SANS Institute, website*

A CORPORATE SECURITY **POLICY** is a document that outlines specific requirements or rules that must be met within the organization. In the information security realm, policies are usually goal-specific, and usually cover more than one platform or area. An example of a policy is "Users must be authorized to access the system by using at least a userid and password. Users who will have access to restricted applications must use an additional form of authentication such as a secure token or a biometric identification."

A **STANDARD** is a collection of system-specific and procedure-specific requirements that must be met by everyone. For example, an HP NonStop server policy would cover the security rules and regulations that harden the NonStop server. People must follow this standard exactly if they wish to add new servers or add applications to existing servers. An example of an HP NonStop server specific policy is:

"Users must have a unique Guardian userid that is assigned only to this user. The password for this userid must be at least six characters long, contain both alphanumeric and special characters and must be changed every 60 days."

This handbook uses **BEST PRACTICES** rather than **GUIDELINES** to mean a collection of system specific and procedure specific "suggestions" for best practice. They are not requirements to be met, but are strongly recommended to adequately secure the HP NonStop server.

Effective **SECURITY POLICIES** make frequent references to **STANDARDS** and **BEST PRACTICES** that exist within an organization.

Good security practices require the creation of both a corporate-wide **SECURITY POLICY** and platform-specific **SECURITY STANDARDS**. Without both, the group responsible for Information Security (Security) has no means to justify the enforcement of good security practices and the group responsible for Internal Audit (Audit) has nothing against which to judge the corporate security environment.

Because securing an HP NonStop server consists primarily of implementing access controls, discussions in this book concentrate on the principles of access control and how they are put into effect on the HP NonStop server.

Good security practices also include monitoring the system for compliance to the Corporate Security Policy and Standards. The Corporate Security Policy and Standards should dictate what is monitored and the frequency of audit reports and reviews.

Adapting Best Practice to the Corporate Security Policy

It is unlikely that any given organization will exactly match every Best Practice recommendation. Those recommendations that absolutely cannot be put into use at a company should be documented. Documentation should include:

The reason the objective cannot be met in the environment

The steps taken to mitigate the risk caused by not meeting the objective

The signature of a person of authority who undertakes responsibility for the risk assumed by not meeting the objective.

This information should be made available to both Internal and External Audit, when requested or when the security staff responds to audit issues.

Information Security

Information is an asset to the corporation. It might be extremely sensitive, such as a company that provides financial services or it might be business sensitive, such as a company that provides material goods, but in either case the need to use the data is ever-present. Information security is the field that defines, designs, and monitors mechanisms and procedures that secure information.

Three requirements for information security

In order for information to be meaningful, it must be accurate. To be useful, it must be available for queries, as appropriate. To be safe from prying eyes or misuse, sensitive information must be kept confidential. Thus, the three principles of information security are:

Integrity

Availability

Confidentiality

Integrity

Integrity is the assurance that the information and programs can be changed only when authorized and in a controlled manner that completes without error.

The security policy addressing integrity should identify types of events that might disrupt information and program usage, and address the extent to which mitigation of these threats is deemed important. Some risks might be:

Malicious action

Incorrect program code

Power failure during a transaction

Hardware failure

Mitigation of these risks can include measures such as:

Requiring multiple authorized users to perform the transaction

Quality testing and change control procedures

Battery backups

Redundant equipment implementation

Availability

Availability is the assurance that authorized users have uninterrupted access to information and resources. From a system management standpoint, this refers to adequate response time and guaranteed bandwidth.

From a security standpoint, availability refers to the ability to protect against breaches and to recover from them. Availability can be divided into "normal operations" and "contingency planning," which deal with day-to-day operations and disaster recovery, respectively.

The security policy addressing availability should identify each event that might make a system unavailable and address the extent to which resistance to that threat is deemed important. Some risks might be:

Malicious or incompetent acts by authorized users

Cut phone lines

Denial of service attack

Mitigation of these risks can include measures such as:

Increased levels of user authorization

Multiple communication channels

Stringent network access controls

Confidentiality

Confidentiality is the need to keep sensitive information from being disclosed to unauthorized recipients. The need might be corporate, such as new product information or marketing strategies. The need might be regulatory, such as privacy of information belonging to or about customers, such as social security numbers and PINs, financial or health-related data. From a management standpoint, it can be summarized as ensuring that no data is revealed without appropriate authorization.

The security policy addressing confidentiality should identify each event that might put information at risk and address the extent to which resistance to the revelation of information is deemed important. Some risks might be:

Exposure of confidential transactions over a communication medium

Unauthorized personnel downloading restricted information to an unprotected computer system

Malicious theft of confidential information

Mitigation of these risks can include measures such as:

Encryption of communication lines

Securing restricted information using a system security package

Monitoring access attempts to confidential information

Categories of Information

There are four classes of information:

Confidential

Restricted

Internal-Use

Non-Restricted

Confidential

Confidential information is information that is only for use within the corporation. It is usually corporate specific, not addressing private information about clients. Confidential information might have an *extremely high* negative impact on the corporation if disclosed. Examples are: information concerned with activities such as strategic planning, mergers and acquisitions, product development, marketing strategy, financial forecasts and financial results. All passwords and encryption keys, as well as all information addressing vulnerabilities within the corporation, such as audits and security incident reports, are considered confidential. There may be regulatory restrictions on the protection of confidential information.

Restricted

Restricted information is usually customer or client specific. Restricted information might have a *high* negative impact on the corporation if disclosed. One example is information of a personal nature about corporate staff members or customers, which the corporation, as custodian of that information, is obligated to protect. Production data and software are also in this category. There are often regulatory restrictions on the protection of restricted information.

Internal-Use

Internal-use information might have a *moderately* negative impact on the corporation if disclosed. Information commonly shared within the company, including operating procedures, policies, interoffice memoranda and internal directories are common examples.

Non-Restricted

Nonsensitive information is designed to be available for public use, such as published annual reports, marketing material, special company programs, etc.

How To Go About Securing An Organization's Information

Once all the various types of information the organization must protect are categorized, the appropriate controls necessary to protect them must be put in place. The controls should reflect the sensitivity of the information and the cost of the loss or exposure of information.

How an organization meets these information security requirements is codified in its Corporate Security Policy and Standards.

The Policy must not only state the particular security need, confidentiality, for example, but also address the range of circumstances under which the need for confidentiality must be met and the associated operating standards. Without this, the policy will be so general as to be useless. The policy must:

List the expected risks and give guidelines for recognizing new risks

Assign a level of concern to each risk

State how the risks are to be mitigated

Document how to recover from breaches of security

Mandate training to instill security awareness and acceptance by users

Management controls, whether administrative, procedural or technical, are the mechanisms and techniques instituted to implement a security policy. Some controls are explicitly concerned with protecting information and information systems, but the concept of management controls includes much more than a computer's specific role in enforcing security.

Controls have 3 functions:

Prevent the unauthorized disclosure, modification or destruction of information.

Detect the unauthorized disclosure, modification or destruction of information.

Correct the unauthorized disclosure, modification or destruction of information.

Controls should be required for:

Physical protection of information in all forms (written, backup tapes, disks, communication lines, online and so on).

Procedures to handle information within the organization or between organizations (FTP authorization, high speed bulk transmission, and so on).

Software development and maintenance practices for the applications that generate and manage the information.

Administration of personnel who handle the information.

Logical protection of information residing on the HP NonStop server.

Technical measures alone cannot prevent security violations. Technical measures may prevent people from doing unauthorized things, but cannot prevent them from doing inappropriate things that their job functions entitle them to do.

Even a technically sound system with informed watchful management and users cannot be free of all possible vulnerabilities. The residual risk must be managed with auditing, backup, and recovery procedures, supported by general alertness and creative responses. Moreover, organizations must have administrative procedures in place to bring unusual activity to the attention of someone who can legitimately inquire into the appropriateness of such activity, and ensure that the appropriate inquiry and possible actions are taken.

Controlling Access to Systems and Resources

Access to the sensitive data and the computers where it resides is limited by both physical controls and logical controls.

Physical Controls

Sensitive information and computers must be stored in locked areas with restricted access, controlled by electronic card readers, escorts, or security guards. Users should be granted access only if they have a genuine need to access information. Keep a database of authorized people, including what each user is allowed to access. Also, keep a log of the time and date that each person enters secure areas.

Physical security includes more than just user access. The following subjects must also be considered:

Physical protection of equipment and personnel
> Barriers
> Surveillance

Fire protection and prevention
> Prevention
> Detection
> Extinguishers

Flood prevention
> Proximity to water hazard
> Detection of leaks

Utilities
> Continuity of power supplies
> Air conditioning
> Prevention
> Detection of loss

Communications lines
> Continuity of service
> Detection of taps

Physical security generally falls outside the scope of an audit of the HP NonStop server and is therefore not covered in this handbook. For more information, refer to the commercially available texts about physical security.

Logical Controls

Computer-based protections consist of:

Access control software

User authentication methods

Encryption techniques

Access Control is the whole array of tools and procedures used to limit, control, and monitor access to information and utilities. Access control is based on a user's identity and membership in predefined groups. Access control makes it possible to control the use, availability, integrity, and confidentiality of objects and information on the HP NonStop server.

Access Control has four major components:

Accountability

Authentication

Authorization

Auditability

This section provides an overview of these principles.

For detailed information regarding Authentication procedures on the HP Non-Stop server, see Parts Three and Four, *Authentication; User Administeration* and *Granting Access to the HP NonStop Server.*

For detailed information regarding Authorization procedures on the HP NonStop Server, see Parts Four and Five, *Authentication, Granting Access to the HP NonStop Server and Authorization; Object Security.*

Accountability

Accountability means ensuring that only a specific user can perform a specific action and being able to prove that a specific user performed a specific action. It also ensures that the user will not later be able to claim that they never made the action. This is called *nonrepudiation.*

In order to provide individual accountability, user authentication is required. Without reliable authentication, there can be no accountability.

In order to provide individual accountability, auditing is also required. Every authentication and every attempted access must be recorded and not modifiable.

Authentication

Authentication is the process of ensuring accurate user identification. Users must be given userids in appropriate administrative groups and be uniquely identified to the system.

On the HP NonStop server, there are two types of user groups:

Administrative Groups   The group that is part of the userid. This group is the primary unit that categorizes a given user's job function.

File-sharing Groups   Groups created in Safeguard software to grant access to diskfiles and other objects on the system. File-sharing groups are primarily relevant in the OSS environment.

A personal, unique userid identifies the user to the system. When combined with a strong password, it enables the system to authenticate the user's identity.

Authorization

Authorization is the process of controlling access to system resources. See Part Five, *Authorization; Object Security*, for audit procedures relating to Authorization.

Access to system resources is based on individual userids and group memberships. Therefore, userids must be carefully assigned based on the principles of Least Privilege and Separation of Duties.

User access to system OBJECTS (files, processes and devices) should be granted based on job function, mediated by the principles of Least Privilege and Separation of Duties.

Auditability

Monitoring complements the three previously described controls by showing how the controls have controlled the system. Without monitoring, individual accountability, authentication and authorization cannot be shown to have worked.

Monitoring must discover all occurrences of unusual authorized activities such as changing the security implementation or adding a user and all occurrences of unauthorized activity such as a bad logon or a denied file access.

Compliance Monitoring and Documentation

Compliance monitoring encompasses two activities:

Managing residual risks

Assuring compliance to the Security Policy

Monitoring for Breaches

Technical measures alone cannot prevent security violations. The mechanisms and techniques, administrative, procedural and technical, may prevent people from doing unauthorized things, but cannot prevent them from doing inappropriate things that their job functions entitle them to do.

Even a technically sound system with informed, vigilant management and users cannot be free of all possible vulnerabilities. The residual risk must be managed by auditing and thorough backup and recovery procedures, including disaster recovery.

In order to provide individual accountability, auditing is required. For complete accountability, every authentication and every attempted access must be recorded.

Frequency of Compliance Review

Compliance review consists of three parts – the security administration staff monitoring its own efforts, the internal audit division of the corporation monitoring compliance with the Security Policy and Standards and external independent auditors monitoring the corporation in light of all appropriate regulatory and internal standards.

Self-Monitoring

The security administration group must have a self-monitoring process that periodically reviews the standards and procedures used in the department. Some items to review regularly are:

Are users and their managers adhering to the standards on a regular basis with few exceptions found when the day-to-day activity is audited for unauthorized security events?

Does the installation fully implement the capabilities of the security system?

Have new features been added or new products been created that could enhance the security of the information assets?

Are the appropriate managers aware of the self-monitoring process and do they respond appropriately when managerial decisions are required?

Are methods in place to address all audit exceptions?

The HP NonStop Server Architecture and Environment

Understanding the Architecture

The HP NonStop server is unique in both hardware and software components. It is the combination of these two components that make the HP server continuously available.

This section will give a brief overview of the HP NonStop server architecture as a basis for other discussions in this book.

Scalability and Availability

The HP NonStop server platform is a scalable, shared nothing, multiple processor, multiprocessing environment equipped with both hardware and software configured to provide continuously available service, that is, a computing environment where failures can be tolerated without eliminating the services provided.

The heart of the NonStop platform is the multiple processor, multiple interprocessor-bus, multiple controller and multiple disk hardware configuration. No single hardware failure should eliminate processing—all paths are configured as redundant by default. Since the hardware is scalable, additional resources such as CPUs and disks can be added as necessary without requiring systems engineering to redesign the machine.

Software and Application Characteristics

The software, both operating system and application, is designed to support the fault-tolerant hardware. The operating system continually monitors the status of all components, switching control as necessary to maintain operations. There are also features designed into the software to allow programs to be written as continuously available programs, that is, a pair of processes where one process performs all the primary processing and the other serves as a "hot backup", receiving updates to all data elements whenever the primary reaches a critical point in processing. Should the primary stop, the backup steps in to resume execution with the current transaction.

In addition, the application environment is designed for scalability and fault-tolerance. The primary application monitor for the HP NonStop server is "Pathway", a system of monitor processes and control programs that support a client/server environment. A Pathway is fault-tolerant at the transactional environment level—that is, if a component of the application fails, the transaction in process is backed-out, the environment is modified to deal with the failed component and the user is returned to service with only a small amount of downtime (see Figure 2-1).

Networking

The HP NonStop server supports networking. Any individual system can have up to 16 processors on a single system, and up to 255 systems can be connected into a single network. Each system, called a "node", has a unique name and number, but can otherwise be used by all other systems for processing as necessary and as permitted by operating system security. The systems are connected with a high speed proprietary link called HP Expand software, which can run over many different communication

Figure 2-1
NonStop
Application
Environment

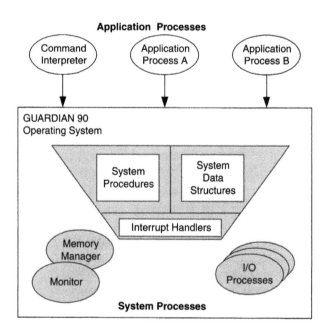

media, such as dedicated fiber optic cable, TCP/IP or SNA for systems that rely on an IBM-mainframe based backbone for communications.

Two Personalities

The NonStop server platform offers two personalities for interaction with programming and management staff. The "Guardian" personality is the original personality, currently used by most NonStop installations. The Open System Services "OSS" or "POSIX" personality is a UNIX-compatible implementation that is beginning to gain in popularity. When discussing security on the NonStop platform, it is important to distinguish between the two personalities as they support different security features.

In this handbook, OSS is treated both as a Subsystem and as an Environment within individual Subsystems. For example, $CMON can perform both logon mediation and LOAD BALANCING in the Guardian environment, but can only perform logon mediation in the OSS environment. So the advantages that a company can derive from $CMON depend on whether or not the company develops or runs its applications in OSS.

HP NonStop Networking

The Expand Network

The Expand subsystem enables connection of as many as 255 geographically dispersed HP NonStop servers to create a network with the reliability and capacity to preserve data integrity, and potential for expansion of a single HP server.

Understanding the Expand Network

Expanding (networking) two or more HP NonStop servers, configured through one of several network protocols, makes each remote system as accessible as the local system. When Expand software is configured and users and files have appropriate network accessibility, resources on remote systems can be as easily referenced and used as local resources (see Figure 2-2).

Nodes

Each HP NonStop server system in the network is referred to as a "node." It has a unique serial number assigned by HP for sales and service purposes. Each node is also assigned a unique name and number by the customer for internal use. Names begin with a "\", such as \CUST1. The node is also assigned a number in the network between 0 and 254. Users reference the node by its name.

Figure 2-2
*Expand System
Environment*

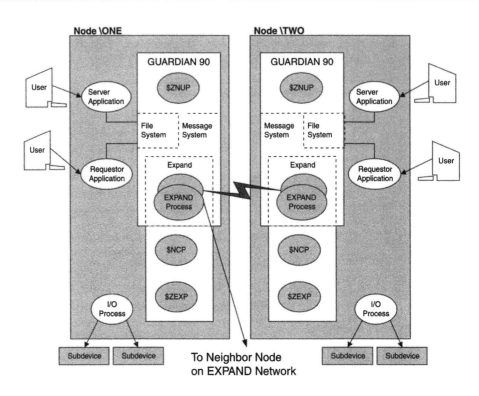

To Neighbor Node
on EXPAND Network

Nodes can be added without disturbing other nodes. When done online, the new node queries its neighbors to determine other accessible nodes on the network. Likewise, when a node is disabled, the other nodes recognize this fact.

AP-ADVICE-NETWORK-01   Use SCF maps to list all nodes on the network. Compare list to network diagram provided by operations.

Unattended Sites

Due to the reliability of HP NonStop servers, they can be installed at unattended sites. Such sites present extra risks. The Corporate Security Policy and Standards should dictate the physical security for the unattended sites and how the resources and data on the unattended systems will be secured to prevent unauthorized access.

Security issues that must be addressed are:

AP-ADVICE-NETWORK-02   Network access makes the data more vulnerable to disclosure or corruption.

AP-ADVICE-NETWORK-03   Secure 'dangerous' utilities at the unattended site for local access only. See the Gazette for information about all utilities.

AP-ADVICE-NETWORK-04   Secure SUPER.SUPER at the unattended site to both local and remote access.

Controlling the Addition of Nodes to the Network

There are several security issues concerned with network configuration. Nodes can be added to the network without disruption of the network.

All Corporate Security Policy and Standards should mandate the creation of an up-to-date diagram of the HP NonStop server Expand network.

AP-ADVICE-NETWORK-05   Procedures to review the network periodically and monitoring to verify that only proper connections exists

Max System Number

The MAX SYSTEM NUMBER defines the maximum number of nodes that the local node will 'recognize' on the network. On pre-G-series systems this value is set during a COLD LOAD or SYSGEN. The default (and maximum value) is 254.

If the MAX SYSTEM NUMBER on each node matches the exact number of authorized systems on the network, additional nodes cannot be easily be added.

RISK   The downside of such a requirement is that when a legitimate node must be added to the network, each existing system will require a SYSGEN to recognize the new node.

If the MAX SYSTEM NUMBER on each node is greater than the number of authorized systems on the network, additional nodes can be added.

RISK   Adding an IP address to the network is easy; however, it would require collusion with an inside employee to configure the network to recognize the unauthorized node. The risk of an unauthorized node being added to a network can be mitigated by:

AP-ADVICE-NETWORK-06   Reviewing the Network Map regularly to verify that only authorized nodes are configured according to the Network Map.

AP-ADVICE-NETWORK-07   Restricting physical access to the Expand network cabling.

AP-ADVICE-NETWORK-08   Restrict access to the SCF commands that configure the Expand network.

Controlling Access Within the Expand Network

Four factors can be used to control whether or not a user can access files or resources on a remote node:

Expand   Can be configured to prevent PASSTHRU access from one node to others.

CMON*   Can be used to control user logons by IP address.

For information on using CMON to control remote access to a node, see the Part Four section on CMON.

File Security*   Remote access to individual files can be restricted by Guardian Security vectors or Safeguard DISKFILE, SUBVOLUME or VOLUME Protection Records on each node.

For information on securing files against remote access, see Securing Diskfiles in Part Five.

REMOTEPASSWORD*   REMOTEPASSWORDS in individual User Records on each node determine whether or not the users have remote access.

For information on REMOTEPASSWORDS, see Defining User Access in Part Five. (* These topics are discussed later in other sections).

Figure 2-3
Expand and Network Security

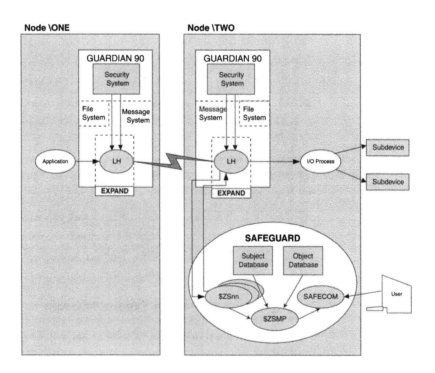

PASSTHRU_<ON | OFF>

PASSTHRU is an Expand Profile parameter used to control 'pass through' access from one node to one or more other nodes. When a user on a node that is configured PASSTHRU_OFF attempts to access resources on another node, the attempt will be denied. But users on other nodes that are configured PASSTHRU_ON will be able to access the restricted node resources. In this manner, PASSTHRU_ON is a one-way street.

PASSTHRU_ON allows access to networked nodes when they are accessed via the current node. PASSTHRU_ON is the default setting.

PASSTHRU_OFF prevents access to adjacent nodes when that access is attempted via the current node.

For example, if a company allows its customers to logon to one node in their network, call it \CUST, but does not want these same users to be able to access files or resources on any other node on their network, \CUST can be configured PASSTHRU_OFF, which prevents these users from specifying resources on other nodes at the TACL prompt. If the users have userids on the other nodes, they can logon to those nodes directly, but not via \CUST.

AP-ADVICE-NETWORK-09   Restrict access to the SCF commands that configure the Expand network.

	Discovery Questions	Look here:
NETWORK-NODES-01	How many systems in the network?	SCF
NETWORK-NODES-02	What are the network nodes names?	SCF
NETWORK-NODES-03	What are the network node numbers?	SCF
NETWORK-NODES-04	What is the MAX SYSTEM NUMBER?	SCF
NETWORK-NODES-05	Is the max number of nodes used?	SCF
NETWORK-NODES-06	Is PASSTHRU_ON?	SCF

TCP/IP

The TCP/IP protocols are a family of data communications protocols that allow communication between heterogeneous systems in a multi-network environment. This allows for communication between HP NonStop servers and other systems.

The HP NonStop TCP/IP subsystem actually consists of a variety of products in the TCP/IP protocol family and provides services at the Network through Application Layers of the OSI Reference Model. The TCP/IP subsystem is the base subsystem for all the other components of the TCP/IP software. It provides a file-system interface to the TCP, User Datagram Protocol (UDP), and IP protocol. The TCP/IP subsystem runs as a single or dual process on the NonStop server.

The ONLY real requirement for Network security (from an end user point of view) is that the data sent across the network be ENCRYPTED. There are administrative security issues such as with any functional application, authenticating who is logging on to control the network and make changes to configurations, routing, encryption key management, etc. Everything else must be handled by the platform and application in question. If each node took good care of its own security, then the risk from all the intrusions would be mitigated. About the only things that are legitimate "network security issues" for HP NonStop server networks are:

1. Network administration and configuration security
2. Communication path encryption and key management (a shared concern between the network and production nodes)
3. Denial of service detection and prevention

All the firewall issues should be handled by securing production nodes appropriately REGARDLESS of whether or not the node is part of a network.

Addressing Remote Hosts

To address a remote host, specify either a host internet address or a host name.

Host Internet Address

A host can have one or more internet addresses on each network to which it is attached. The address is known as the IP address. For example, the class A address 38.3.9.24 identifies the network address as 38 and the local host address as 3.9.24.

Host Name

A host name is the official name by which the host system is known to the internet. On an HP NonStop server, the host name can be associated with the system's internet address in the TCP/IP HOSTS configuration file, or the name can be mapped to an address through a name server.

Configuring TCP/IP

SCF is an interactive interface that allows operators and system managers to configure, control, and monitor the HP NonStop TCP/IP subsystem. SCF is part of DSM. The Subsystem Control Point (SCP) provides an interface to the I/O processes of the various subsystems.

The TCP/IP subsystem can be managed programmatically or interactively by sending commands that act on one or more DSM-related objects. The TCP/IP subsystem defines three types of objects:

Processes

Subnets

Routes

	Discovery Questions	Look here:
TCPIP-NETWORK-01	Is TELSERV configured on the node?	SCF
TCPIP-NETWORK-02	Is Telnet run on the system to support terminals?	SCF
PROCESS-TCPIP-01	Is the TCP/IP object file running on the system?	Status

Telnet

The Telnet protocol is a general, bidirectional, eight-bit byte-oriented protocol in the TCP/IP protocol suite that provides a standard method of interfacing terminal devices and terminal-oriented processes to each other. A Telnet connection is a TCP connection that contains Telnet control information.

On HP NonStop servers, the Telnet application allows users to emulate a virtual terminal connected to a remote host. Users can connect to any remote host on the network that has a Telnet server.

The Telnet subsystem is a server and uses the sockets library routines of the TCP/IP subsystem for TCP access to accommodate the incoming Telnet applications.

AP-ADVICE-NETWORK-12   Determine if TELSERV is configured for communications on this node.

AP-ADVICE-NETWORK-13   Determine if any virtual terminals or applications use the Telnet communication method.

	Discovery Questions	Look here:
TELNET-NETWORK-01	Is TELSERV configured on the node?	SCF
TELNET-NETWORK-02	Is Telnet run on the system to support terminals?	SCF
PROCESS-TELSERV-01	Is the TELSERV object file running on the system?	Status

Dial Access

Dial access uses modems and a phone line to provide access to interactive computers. Banks of dial access modems provide access for many different types of users using many different types of applications.

People with dial access needs are typically:

HP service personnel doing remote support

Vendors providing off-site customer service

System managers and other key employees working from home

Interactive Access To The Operating System

The goal in providing dial access is to give the user access to TACL or another command interpreter in a secure manner.

RISK   An unauthorized user can repeatedly attack the dial access userid and password without physically being present.

RISK   A modem disconnect can leave a dial access session incomplete, ready to be acquired by the next user using the modem.

RISK   Clear-text transmissions are extremely easy to monitor and interpret.

The mitigation of risk includes adding physical control over the dial access port, increasing authentication methods, providing transmission security and aggressive auditing of dial access activity.

Hardware and Software Involved

Use of a dial access port requires:

A modem called the Host Modem connected to the host computer

A modem called the Remote Modem connected to the computer being used by the person who wants dial access

Software in the destination computer that emulates a terminal on the host computer

Physical Control

Physical controls can be used to ensure that the dial access port is only available when there is a need for its use.

Dial Port Enabling

Physical enabling requires human intervention to enable the modem. To use the dial access port requires calling the computer room and asking an operator to plug in the modem and start the command interpreter process. Another call is needed afterwards to request that the operator disable the dial access port.

This level of security can be quite high, since human authorization and action is required to enable the system. It is also inefficient, since a human is required, and may be open to error when the disabling operation is not performed in a timely manner.

Dial Back Modem

Dial back modems are used to secure dial access ports. The user dials a dedicated processing facility and enters a userid and password. That userid is used by the dedicated facility to look up which number to call back. When the return call is made, the command interpreter would be created on the NonStop server.

RISK   This security method is unreliable because of the advent of call forwarding services from the user's local telephone company. It is possible for a malicious user to set the call forwarding feature on the authorized user's home phone number in order to force the call back to be transferred to the malicious user's location.

This method was used successfully by hackers in the 1980s. The use of dial back modems declined at that time.

Additional Authentication

Once a person has access to the dial access ports, the user must be authenticated. For many purposes, the userid and password can serve as sufficient authentication, but specific Corporate Security Policies and Standards may require a more thorough authentication process.

Using A Cryptographic Token

A cryptographic token adds additional authentication using the concept of token ownership. If the token is unavailable through theft or fraud, the logon cannot occur. The cryptographic token authentication may take place at the point at which the modem connects or as part of the logon process.

Logical Port/User Restriction

Communications Control

Logical communications control software on the HP NonStop server must reset the dial access port's command interpreter whenever the host modem detects a disconnection.

$CMON Control

The HP NonStop server operating system has provisions for a process called $CMON. The $CMON process (refer to section on $CMON) can support PORT and USER based restrictions, which can be used to limit which userids can be used with a dial access modem. For example, $CMON can be setup to allow technical support to use a dial access modem without permitting any other userids access.

> **3P-CMON-DIALUP-01**   Use a CMON product that allows users to be identified and restricted for dialup access.

Firewall

An external firewall can be used to limit access to the HP NonStop server to only those parties that can successfully pass the firewall. This supports and enhances the network security. The firewall machine can protect multiple HP NonStop server installations.

The firewall must limit access to the NonStop servers using PORT address limitations. The firewall itself must be secured to prevent unauthorized modification and fraudulent use.

Encryption

If the contents of the dialup access session are sensitive, those contents should be encrypted to avoid communication sniffing.

Encrypting Modems

Encrypting modems use hardware to perform the encryption function. Their use requires each user who might have access to the dial access port to have an encrypting modem that is keyed identically with the host side.

Session Encryption

Session encryption uses software on both the host and on the personal computer that the person dialing in is using. The software encrypts information before transmission and then decrypts when receiving information.

Auditing

All dial access activity must be audited. The degree of auditing used is dependent on the Corporation Security Policy and Standards.

> *RISK*   At a minimum, a record of every failed attempt to access the dial access port must be kept. When a pattern of attack or abuse is discovered, it must be handled immediately according to the Security Policy and Standards.

Safeguard Auditing

In a less-secure environment, Safeguard auditing of logons and logoffs at the dial access port can suffice. With increasing need for security, auditing of transactions such as program execution and file opens/closes becomes necessary.

Third Party Key-Stroke Level Auditing

A third-party package that provides keystroke auditing can be used. The characters of every command are recorded to an audit file and reviewed on a regular basis, usually daily, to detect unexplained or unauthorized entries.

> **3P-ACCESS-AUDIT-01**   Use a third-party access product that can perform keystroke audits on communication lines.

Best Practice Recommendations:

Use port controls on the host side to ensure that only authorized personnel can use the dial access port

Use communication control software that ensures that the port command interpreter is reset whenever a host modem disconnection occurs

Use additional authentication to ensure that the person attempting to use the system is authorized

Use session encryption to ensure that the contents of the session cannot be revealed

Use keystroke auditing to monitor the session's activities

	Discovery Questions	Look here:
DIALUP-NETWORK-01	Is Dial Access configured on the node?	SCF
DIALUP-NETWORK-02	How is Dialup access used on the system?	SCF

Guardian Personality

Guardian operating system security is a matrix composed of subject, object and access rules defined at the object level. Extensions have been made over time to accommodate a more sophisticated access control system. In Guardian terminology, subjects are users, objects are diskfiles and the access is defined by the diskfile security vector.

The command interpreter is called Tandem Advanced Command Language (TACL). It is both a command interpreter and the interpreter for the TACL Control Language, which supports a job control language. There are two security issues presented in TACL. First, TACL can be used to write job control language programs called "macros" that can change underlying command interpreter basics such as the act of logging off or the act of starting a program. Second, during the logon process, TACL executes existing TACL macros named according to a certain standard.

Security and Audit Controls in Guardian Systems

Security Components

The Guardian security components are:

> Users (Subjects)
> Objects
> File Security

Users

Guardian defines users (subjects) by assigning a unique user name and number to each user:

> <GroupName>.<MemberName>
> <Group Number>,<Member Number>

The combination of GroupName.MemberName must be unique for a single system and unique over the network of Guardian systems if the user will have access to any system other than that user's local system.

There is also an alphanumeric user name assigned based on the group and user number combination. The group numbers range from 0 to 255. Group 255 is reserved and has many inherent privileges. This group is usually called the "SUPER" group. User numbers range from 0 to 255, also. The user number 255 is referred to as the "group manager" and has many inherent privileges. The userid 255,255 is commonly referred to as the "SUPER.SUPER" userid and has full and unrestricted access to the system.

Userids	User Names	Notes
0,0	NULL.NULL	Used for command interpreters that have not been authorized for any user ("logged off")
,	<groupname>.<username>	A standard userid
*,255	<groupname>.<manager>	The manager of the group with many inherent privileges
255,*	SUPER.<username>	A userid in the SUPER group with many inherent privileges
255,255	SUPER.SUPER	The super or root userid for the system

A userid is "local" to the system where it is created. It can be "networked" with the same userid on another system by means of the "remote password," which is not really a password, but instead, a simple yes/no permission to use another Guardian system in the network. A userid that was created on a different system and has traversed the Expand network to use the local system is called a "remote" user.

There are privileges inherent in certain userids. These, and all aspects of secure user management are discussed in detail in the section on User Administration in Part Three.

Objects

All devices, processes and diskfiles are considered objects on the HP NonStop server, but the basic operating system, known as the Guardian system, only provides user definable security for diskfile objects. This section contains only a brief overview. All aspects of securing NonStop objects are discussed in the section on Object Security in Part Five.

Diskfiles

DISKFILES have four-part names.

Standard NonStop Diskfile Naming Convention:

\SYSTEM.$DISKVOL.SUBVOLUM.DISKFILE *

\SYSTEM   Up to 7 characters, name of Guardian system where disk is physically attached

$VOLUME   Up to 7 characters, logical name of the disk where file is
              physically located.

SUBVOLUME   Up to 8 characters, a collection of diskfiles

DISKFILE   Up to 8 characters, the final component of the filename.

Example:
`\CUST1.$DATA3.MYAPP.MYFILE`

> * Partially qualified names are assumed to be located on the current default location of any part
> that is not explicitly qualified.

The Guardian Diskfile Security String

DISKFILES have an owner, that is, the userid of the user who created or is assigned
ownership of the diskfile.

Each diskfile has a security vector. By default, the security vector is the owner's
default security as defined in the owner's User Record.

NOTE: A file owner or the owner's group manager or SUPER.SUPER can give his or
her files to another user, using the FUP GIVE command, and can also change the file's
security vector using the FUP SECURE command.

The security vectors control the following:

READ   Determines who can read or copy any kind of file or who can
            execute a macro or OBEY an obey file.

WRITE   Determines who can modify the contents of a file.

EXECUTE   Determines who can execute a code 100 or 700 (object) file with
            the TACL RUN command.

PURGE   Determines who can delete, rename or FUP GIVE a file.

The operations are always displayed in this order: READ, WRITE, EXECUTE,
PURGE sometimes abbreviated as RWEP.

There are seven possible values for each vector. These values reflect who is allowed
to perform the operation and whether or not the operation can be performed by someone on a remote node. The value is always a single character. The values are:

WHO CAN PERFORM THE OPERATION	LOCAL	REMOTE
File Owner	O (owner)	U (user)
File Owner's Group	G (group)	C (community)
Everyone	A (all local users)	N (all network users)
Local SUPER.SUPER only	- (hyphen)	

A—All local users can access the file.

N—All network users can access the file.

G—Only local members of the owner's group can access the file.

C—Only network members of the owner's group can access the file.

O—Only the local file owner or group manager can access the file.

U—Only the remote and local file owner or group manager can access the file.

—Only the local SUPER.SUPER.

```
Example:
$SYSTEM.SYS00
               CODE       EOF  LAST MODIFIED  OWNER    RWEP  PExt  SExt
   LOGON       100     435254 17APR2001 7:53 255,255 UUNU    74   16
   DEFAULT     100     559588 17APR2001 7:53 255,255 UUNU   188   32
```

This example shows two of Safeguard software's object files. They are both owned by SUPER.SUPER. The security strings are the same:

```
RWEP
UUNU
```

Only SUPER.SUPER can READ, WRITE or PURGE these files. Everyone, whether logged onto a remote node or the local node, can EXECUTE the file.

Processes

All running processes have an owner. In most cases the owner is the userid of the user who executed the object file. This is true unless the object file is PROGID'd. For a PROGID'd process, the owner of the process is the owner of the object file. See the section on PROGID in the Gazette portion of this book.

On the HP NonStop server, most objects, including processes, are considered to be files. The file name for a process is known as a process file name. The process file name can be used to communicate with the process. Process file names must begin with a dollar sign ($). Subprocess names must begin with a hash or pound sign (#) and be preceded by the parent process name.

Running processes are also identified numerically on a list known as the Process Control Table, which is allocated in the system data space and protected.

> The process' **PIN** (Process Identification Number) is its number within a CPU. The process' **PID** (Process ID) is a combination of the CPU number and the PIN, separated by a comma.

```
Syntax:
<cpu #>,<process #>

Examples:
03,211
12,377
```

The example shows process number 211 running in CPU 03. This is a LOW PIN process. The second example shows process number 377 running in CPU 12, which is a HIGH PIN process (>255).

Process Security

Each Guardian process is assigned a creator access ID (sometimes known as the CAID), a process access ID (or PAID), and a stop mode. The following paragraphs describe how the creator access ID, process access ID, and stop mode work together to provide process security.

The CAID is the userid of the process or TACL that started this process.

The PAID is the same as the CAID unless the program is PROGID'd or the process has switched ownership programmatically, and is used to determine whether restricted actions against a process (such as stopping the process or invoking the debugger) are possible.

The security of processes is not configurable in the Guardian system. Only the following users are able to stop, suspend, activate or alter the priority of a process:

The owner

The owner's Group manager

SUPER.SUPER

For more detailed information, refer to the section on Guardian Process Security in Part Five.

Devices

In the Guardian environment, any process can open any device for input or output. All devices are addressed in the same way that a diskfile is addressed, by name.

Standard NonStop Device Naming Convention:

\SYSTEM.$DEVICE.#SUBDEV

```
Example:
\CUST1.$TAPE
```

For more detailed information, refer to Guardian Object Security in Part Five.

Authentication

Basic Guardian authenticates a user by prompting a user for a userid and the password for that userid when logging on to the TACL command interpreter. The password can be up to 8 characters long, has no restrictions on value and is stored using a one-way encryption algorithm in the system's USERID file.

In the Guardian personality, a user attempting access to a file or process on a remote node must pass at least three levels of security.

The first level authenticates the user as they log onto the local node. The target userid or alias must exist on the node, it must not be frozen or expired. (If Safeguard software is present, it performs this authentication. If Safeguard software is not present, the Guardian environment performs the authentication.)

The second level authenticates the userid on the remote node. The user name and user number must both be the same on both the originating node and the target node. (If Safeguard software is present, it performs this authentication. If Safeguard software is not present, the Guardian environment performs the authentication.)

The third level validates the REMOTEPASSWORDs on each node. The Guardian environment performs the validation.

In the Safeguard personality, an additional level of security is evaluated.

If all three security checks are passed, in the fourth level of security, the file or process access request is passed to the Safeguard Monitor process on the target node which then grants or denies the access based on the Safeguard Protection Record securing the file or process. If there is no Safeguard Protection Record, then the Guardian security vector determines whether or not the remote user is granted access to the file. The access request is *only sent to the Monitor at the destination node* NOT the originating or any intermediary nodes.

Authorization

Authorization is based on the Guardian diskfile security string. The combination of user, object and access requested is granted or denied based solely on the Guardian security string, without regard to context or history. Part Five of this handbook includes topics on authorizing access to all types of NonStop objects.

Auditing and Controls

Basic Guardian operating system security has no intrinsic auditing available. There is an exit available for the implementation of custom software that can monitor user logons and logoffs, process run commands and process priority alteration. This exit communicates with a process named $CMON. HP does not supply $CMON. There is a limited, unsupported implementation available free with a membership in ITUG, international user group for the HP NonStop server. This version can be modified in-house.

> **3P-CMON-PROCESS-01**   Several third party software suppliers offer supported and enhanced versions of a program to run as $CMON.

Controls for the Guardian personality are limited solely to the userid, security vector, PROGID and LICENSE for each diskfile.

> *RISK*   No controls are available to limit the activities of any group manager or SUPER.SUPER users.

> *RISK*   No auditing is available on what actions have been taken by these users.

Audits and controls are discussed throughout this handbook in Parts 3, 4, and 5 where they apply.

Sanitizing an HP NonStop System

This section is concerned with preparing the HP NonStop server for use. Many aspects of security will be covered in much greater detail in later sections on specific objects or programs.

By *sanitize*, we mean putting adequate security measures into place to keep the system secure as it evolves. Security policies and procedures should be followed from the moment the HP software is installed and while applications are being developed, tested, and put into production.

It must be assumed that any newly delivered system is not secure. General access should not be allowed until the security administrator and the system manager have put security measures into place.

User Management

The user community should be set up so that users who need to share certain files are in the same administrative groups.

No individuals should have a userid in the SUPER group. SUPER group privileges should be granted sparingly, limited to a small set of trusted users who must perform the privileged tasks associated with the SUPER group.

Delete the NULL.NULL userid.

Delete all SUPER group members. Delete the SUPER.SUPER and re-add the 255,255 userid under a different name, such as SYS.SYS. Then re-add SYS group ids. This reduces the risk of users knowing the SUPER.SUPER name combination and guessing the password. This can most easily be done when the system is being sanitized.

Secure the Operating System Software

Securing the operating system involves the protection of the software provided by its manufacturer, including the operating system, utilities, compilers, libraries and other such programs.

The Corporate Security Policy and Standards should specify how the HP software is to be secured. HP makes the following general recommendations:

HP Recommended Security of System Files

Security	Description
?OOO	General libraries (including runtime libraries, sourced files, error message files)
OO?O	User tools (including editors and compilers)
OO?O	System tools (including FUP, NETMON, DSAP, TACL, BACKUP, RESTORE,PATHWAY, TMFCOM, TRANSFER, MAIL)
?OOO	Microcode (macro) files
- - - -	Special files (including TANDUMP, DIVER, USERID, and USERIDAK)
Owner	**Description**
255,255	SUPER.SUPER should own all the operating system files

Reserve the System Disk for HP Operating System Files

No unauthorized and undocumented files, especially object files, should reside in $SYSTEM.SYSTEM or $SYSTEM.SYSnn subvolumes. Files that reside in 'system' subvolumes are generally included in the program search list. Programs that reside in subvolumes within the search list do not need to be fully qualified in order to be invoked.

Any non-HP programs that must reside on $SYSTEM should not be located in $SYSTEM.SYSnn. This is the subvolume containing the operating system that will be replaced upon upgrades.

Configuring the Safeguard Subsystem

Safeguard software was developed to enhance the security provided by the Guardian system. It provides more comprehensive security. Safeguard software works with the Guardian environment to apply more extensive and more specific security controls.

Safeguard and Guardian Compared

	Guardian System	Safeguard System Without OBJECTTYPE	Safeguard System With OBJECTTYPE
Default file security	User with DEFAULT PROGRAM access - User's Grp Mgr - SUPER.SUPER	User's Group Manager User Record Owner SUPER.SUPER (2) User	
Default subvolume	User with DEFAULT PROGRAM access - User's Grp Mgr - SUPER.SUPER	User's Group Manager User Record Owner SUPER.SUPER (2) User	
Aliases supported	No.	Yes, for auditing No, for Protection Records (Underlying userid used for all access rulings)	
Who can add a user	SUPER.SUPER Group Managers	User's Group Mgr. SUPER.SUPER.(2)	OBJECTTYPE Record members with CREATE SUPER.SUPER (2)
Who can alter user information	N/A	SUPER.SUPER.(2) User Record Owner	
Who can Change Password	User User's Grp Mgr. (1) SUPER.SUPER	User User's Group Mgr. SUPER.SUPER (2) User Record owner	
Auditing	No	Yes	
Terminal Control	No	Yes	

Safeguard and Guardian Compared

	Guardian System	Safeguard System Without OBJECTTYPE	Safeguard System With OBJECTTYPE
Objects protected	Diskfiles Processes,Subprocesses	Volumes, Subvolumes, Diskfiles Processes, Subprocesses Devices, Subdevices Users Aliases	
Objects with *configurable* **security**	Diskfiles	Volumes, Subvolumes, Diskfiles, Processes, Subprocesses Devices, Subdevices Users Aliases	
Who can ADD diskfile security	Owner Owner's Grp Mgr. SUPER.SUPER	File owner File owner's Grp Mgr. SUPER.SUPER(2)	OBJECTTYPE Record members with CREATE SUPER.SUPER (2)
Who can ALTER diskfile security	Owner Owner's Grp Mgr SUPER.SUPER	Protection Record Owner. Primary Owner's Grp Mgr. Secondary Owner(s) SUPER.SUPER(2)	
Process Control	Owner Owner's Grp Mgr SUPER.SUPER	Protection Record members granted R,W,P,C	
Device Control	None.	Protection Record members granted R,W	

1 - If PASSWORD program binding changes have not been made to force entry of old password before entering new password.
2 - If SUPER.SUPER is configured as UNDENIABLE

Safeguard controls fall into three categories:

    User authentication
    Authorization of object access attempts
    Auditing

Configuration within each of these categories is affected by global parameters and attributes within individual Protection, User or Alias Records.

Safeguard Global Configuration

The following aspects of Safeguard software can be configured globally:

    User authentication controls

Password controls

Priority of Protection Records between DEVICES and SUBDEVICES

Priority of Protection Records between PROCESSES and SUBPROCESSES

Priority of Protection Records between VOLUMES, SUBVOLUMES, and DISKFILES

Auditing, both system-wide and for individual objects

Logon controls

The Command Interpreter to be started after a user logs on *at a Safeguard terminal*

Exclusive access for the user logged on *at a Safeguard terminal*

Client subsystem auditing

System-level warning mode

SUPER.SUPER Undeniable

Local SUPER.SUPER is made undeniable with an entry in the CONFTEXT file.

When Safeguard is configured so that SUPER.SUPER is undeniable, Safeguard software ignores explicit denials of access authorities for SUPER.SUPER.

This parameter takes effect when the system is cold loaded with the OSIMAGE file that was produced from the CONFTEXT file containing this parameter. See the *Security Considerations of Safeguard Software Installation* subsection immediately above for more information.

BP-SAFEGARD-CONFIG-01   Safeguard should be configured SUPER.SUPER UNDENIABLE so that, in an emergency, SUPER.SUPER can perform any required task, including modifying a Safeguard Protection or User Record.

RISK   Users logged on as SUPER.SUPER, or as an alias to SUPER.SUPER, will be able to alter the Safeguard configuration, possibly compromising system security.

To mitigate the risks of SUPER.SUPER UNDENIABLE:

AP-ADVICE-SAFEGARD-01   Do not allow users to logon as SUPER.SUPER except in emergencies or for pre-approved maintenance such as operating system upgrades.

3P-ACCESS-SAFEGARD-01   Use a third party access control product to grant users granular access to SUPER.SUPER privileges. If a third party access control product is in use:

3P- ACCESS-SAFEGARD-01A   If users are granted access to a SAFECOM running as SUPER.SUPER, it is recommended that the ADD command be denied to prevent any Protection, User or Alias Records from being added (and therefore owned) by SUPER.SUPER, which would prevent the Security Admin userid the ability to even see the added records.

3P- ACCESS-SAFEGARD-01B   If the system management group needs to add Safeguard records, provide them a secure SAFECOM running as the Security Admin userid.

AP-ADVICE-SAFEGARD-02   Whether or not SUPER.SUPER is UNDENIABLE and whether or not a third party access control product is in use, a Safeguard audit report, which includes the addition or alteration of any Safeguard objects, should be reviewed daily.

Safeguard Global Authentication Controls

The following global attributes are discussed in User Administration in Part Three.

BP-SAFEGARD-GLOBAL-53   BLINDLOGON = ON

BP-SAFEGARD-GLOBAL-54   NAMELOGON = ON

BP-SAFEGARD-GLOBAL-55   TERMINAL-EXCLUSIVE-ACCESS = OFF

BP-SAFEGARD-GLOBAL-03   AUTHENTICATE-FAIL-FREEZE = OFF

BP-SAFEGARD-GLOBAL-02   AUTHENTICATE-FAIL-TIMEOUT = 60 seconds

BP-SAFEGARD-GLOBAL-01   AUTHENTICATE-MAXIMUM-ATTEMPTS = 3

Safeguard Global Password Controls

The following global attributes are discussed in Password Management in Part Three.

BP-SAFEGARD-GLOBAL-06   PASSWORD-ENCRYPT = ON

BP-SAFEGARD-GLOBAL-05   PASSWORD-HISTORY = 10

BP-SAFEGARD-GLOBAL-07   PASSWORD-MINIMUM-LENGTH = 6 to 8

BP-SAFEGARD-GLOBAL-04   PASSWORD-REQUIRED = OFF

BP-SAFEGARD-GLOBAL-09   PASSWORD-EXPIRY-GRACE = between 7 and 15

BP-SAFEGARD-GLOBAL-08   PASSWORD-MAY-CHANGE = 7

Safeguard Global Warning-Mode Controls

The following global attributes determine whether or not Safeguard software is in Warning Mode and how it will behave when it is. These are discussed in the Warning Mode section of this section.

BP-SAFEGARD-GLOBAL-10   WARNING-MODE = OFF

BP-SAFEGARD-GLOBAL-11   WARNING-FALLBACK-SECURITY = GUARDIAN

Safeguard Global Device Controls

The following global attributes determine how Device Protection Records will be processed. These are discussed in the Authorization and Object Security in Part Five.

BP-SAFEGARD-GLOBAL-12   DIRECTION-DEVICE parameter should be SUBDEVICE-FIRST

BP-SAFEGARD-GLOBAL-13   CHECK-DEVICE parameter should be ON

BP-SAFEGARD-GLOBAL-14   COMBINATION-DEVICE parameter should be FIRST-ACL

BP-SAFEGARD-GLOBAL-15   CHECK-SUBDEVICE parameter should be ON

BP-SAFEGARD-GLOBAL-16   ACL-REQUIRED-DEVICE parameter should be OFF

Safeguard Global Process Controls

The following global attributes determine how Process Protection Records will be processed. These are discussed in Securing Processes with the Safeguard Subsystem in Part Five.

BP-SAFEGARD-GLOBAL-17   DIRECTION-PROCESS parameter should be SUBPROCESS-FIRST

BP-SAFEGARD-GLOBAL-18   CHECK-PROCESS parameter should be ON

BP-SAFEGARD-GLOBAL-19   COMBINATION-PROCESS parameter should be FIRST-ACL

BP-SAFEGARD-GLOBAL-20   CHECK-SUBPROCESS parameter should be ON

BP-SAFEGARD-GLOBAL-21   ACL-REQUIRED-PROCESS parameter should be OFF

Safeguard Global Diskfile Controls

The following global attributes determine how disk file access attempts will be processed. These are discussed in the Securing Diskfiles with Safeguard Part Five.

BP-SAFEGARD-GLOBAL-22   DIRECTION-DISKFILE parameter should be FILENAME-FIRST

BP-SAFEGARD-GLOBAL-23   CHECK-VOLUME parameter should be OFF

BP-SAFEGARD-GLOBAL-24   COMBINATION-DISKFILE parameter should be FIRST-ACL

BP-SAFEGARD-GLOBAL-25   CHECK-SUBVOLUME parameter should be ON

BP-SAFEGARD-GLOBAL-26   ACL-REQUIRED-DISKFILE parameter should be OFF

BP-SAFEGARD-GLOBAL-27   CHECK-FILENAME parameter should be ON

BP-SAFEGARD-GLOBAL-28   CLEARONPURGE-DISKFILE parameter should be OFF

Safeguard Global CMON Controls

The following global attributes determine how Safeguard software will interact with CMON. These are discussed in the CMON in Part Four.

RISK   Safeguard software will not consult $CMON when starting a Safeguard terminal TACL if CMON is OFF.

RISK   When Safeguard processes a logon and the Safeguard global CMON is set to OFF, then neither LOGON nor LOGOFF messages are sent to $CMON.

BP-SAFEGARD-GLOBAL-50   CMON parameter should be ON

BP-SAFEGARD-GLOBAL-51   CMONERROR parameter should be ACCEPT.

BP-SAFEGARD-GLOBAL-52   CMONTIMEOUT parameter value depends on the speed of the system or = 30 sec

RUN messages that are sent to $CMON will be processed normally by CMON, regardless of the Safeguard CMON settings.

Safeguard Global Command Interpreter Controls

The following Command Interpreter (CI) attributes determine whether or not Safeguard software will start a Command Interpreter after it has authenticated the user *at a Safeguard-controlled terminal* and how that program will be configured. The defaults should be used if Safeguard controlled terminals are not implemented.

These globals are discussed in Managing Userids with the Safeguard Subsystem in Part Three.

CI-PROG

CI-LIB

CI-CPU

CI-NAME

CI-SWAP

CI-PRI

CI-PARAM-TEXT

Safeguard Global Audit Controls

The following Audit Control attributes determine whether or not attempts to ACCESS the object the record is protecting will be audited.

These globals are discussed in Managing Userids with the Safeguard Subsystem in Part Three.

BP-SAFEGARD-GLOBAL-34   AUDIT-AUTHENICATE-PASS should be ALL

BP-SAFEGARD-GLOBAL-35   AUDIT-AUTHENTICATE-FAIL should be ALL

BP-SAFEGARD-GLOBAL-29   AUDIT-CLIENT-SERVICE should be OFF

These globals are discussed in Managing Devices with the Safeguard Subsystem in Part Five.

BP-SAFEGARD-GLOBAL-38   AUDIT-DEVICE-ACCESS-PASS should be NONE

BP-SAFEGARD-GLOBAL-39   AUDIT-DEVICE-ACCESS-FAIL should be ALL

BP-SAFEGARD-GLOBAL-40   AUDIT-DEVICE-MANAGE-PASS should be ALL

BP-SAFEGARD-GLOBAL-41   AUDIT-DEVICE-MANAGE-FAIL should be ALL

These globals are discussed in Managing Diskfiles with the Safeguard Subsystem in Part Five.

BP-SAFEGARD-GLOBAL-46   AUDIT-DISKFILE-ACCESS-PASS should be NONE

BP-SAFEGARD-GLOBAL-47   AUDIT-DISKFILE-ACCESS-FAIL should be ALL

BP-SAFEGARD-GLOBAL-48   AUDIT-DISKFILE-MANAGE-PASS should be ALL

BP-SAFEGARD-GLOBAL-49   AUDIT-DISKFILE-MANAGE-FAIL should be ALL

These globals are discussed in Managing Objects with the Safeguard Subsystem in Part Five.

BP-SAFEGARD-GLOBAL-30   AUDIT-OBJECT-ACCESS-PASS should be NONE

BP-SAFEGARD-GLOBAL-31   AUDIT-OBJECT-ACCESS-FAIL should be ALL

BP-SAFEGARD-GLOBAL-32   AUDIT-OBJECT-MANAGE-PASS should be ALL

BP-SAFEGARD-GLOBAL-33   AUDIT-OBJECT-MANAGE-FAIL should be ALL

These globals are discussed in Managing Processes with the Safeguard Subsystem in Part Five.

BP-SAFEGARD-GLOBAL-42   AUDIT-PROCESS-ACCESS-PASS should be NONE

BP-SAFEGARD-GLOBAL-43   AUDIT-PROCESS-ACCESS-FAIL should be ALL

BP-SAFEGARD-GLOBAL-44   AUDIT-PROCESS-MANAGE-PASS should be ALL

BP-SAFEGARD-GLOBAL-45 AUDIT-PROCESS-MANAGE-FAIL should be ALL

These globals are discussed in Managing Userids with the Safeguard Subsystem in Part Three.

BP-SAFEGARD-GLOBAL-36 AUDIT-SUBJECT-MANAGE-PASS should be ALL

BP-SAFEGARD-GLOBAL-37 AUDIT-SUBJECT-MANAGE-FAIL should be ALL

The Concept of Ownership in the Safeguard Subsystem

Safeguard software introduces a concept of a Protection Record owner for all types of records.

RISK Safeguard software will not allow any userid to manage any Protection Record, User Record or Alias Record that the userid doesn't own, unless the userid is SUPER.SUPER and SUPER.SUPER is undeniable. The record owner's Group Manager can also manage the record.

RISK Even the INFO command will not display information about Protection Records, Users or Aliases that the userid doesn't own, which can essentially "mask" records.

There are two types of owners:

Primary Owners
Secondary Owners

Primary Owner

The Primary Owner is the owner of the Protection or User Record. The Primary Owner can do anything to the record.

The Primary Owner can be a local user or network user.

AP-ADVICE-SAFEGARD-03 If the Security Staff manages Safeguard software on more than one node, it is recommended that the Primary Owner of all userids be entered as a network user. A network owner can perform administrative tasks across the network.

```
Example 1:
GROUP.USER      USER-ID  OWNER    LAST-MODIFIED   LAST-LOGON     STATUS
FTP.MANAGER     200,255  253,1    17OCT02, 10:14 17OCT02, 10:15  THAWED
```

Example 1 shows a user record with a local owner.

```
Example 2:
5> Safecom info user 222,77

GROUP.USER     USER-ID  OWNER    LAST-MODIFIED LAST-LOGON   STATUS
ABCO.BRYAN     222,177 \*.253,1  12APR02, 11:00 21JAN03, 9:58 THAWED
```

Example 2 shows a user record with a network owner.

Secondary Owner(s)

Secondary ownership is defined by the owner access (O) authority in the ACL of a Protection Record.

The Primary Owner can add Secondary Owners to any Object Protection Record's ACL.

Secondary owners can do anything that the Primary Owner is permitted to do. They are equal, in every way, to the Primary Owner.

```
Example:
$DATAA.BRYAN
 DATAFILE     5NOV02, 9:22 \*.253,1 THAWED
    \*.122,177    R,W,E,P, O
 GROUP \*.00122     R
 GROUP \*.00300     R
```

This example shows a DISKFILE Protection Record. The Primary Owner is network user 253,1. Network user 122,177 is a Secondary Owner.

Ownership Recommendations

In order to simplify Safeguard management, it is highly recommended that a single user owns all the Protection Records.

AP-ADVICE-SAFEGARD-04   All Protection Records, all User Records and all Alias Records should be owned by a single Security Manager userid. This is the only way to guarantee that the Security Manager can view all existing User, Alias and Object Protection Records.

Safeguard Objects

Users, Diskfiles, Devices and Processes are commonly referred to as OBJECTs on the HP NonStop server. Safeguard software secures the following objects:

USER

ALIAS

GROUP

VOLUME

SUBVOLUME

DISKFILE

PROCESS

SUBPROCESS

DEVICE

SUBDEVICE

OBJECTTYPE

Each type of object can be secured via Protection Records. That is, diskfiles may be secured with DISKFILE Protection Records, VOLUME Protection Records and SUBVOLUME Protection Records. Processes are secured with PROCESS and SUBPROCESS Records.

This Protection Record determines:

Who can MANAGE the object, that is ALTER or DELETE the object's Protection Record

Who can ACCESS the object, that is READ, WRITE, EXECUTE or PURGE it

Object Protection Records

Protection Records for the various types of Objects contain several common attributes. They are:

Owner

Access Control List (ACL)

Status

Audit Configuration

These common attributes are discussed here. The attributes specific to certain types of objects will be discussed in detail in the appropriate sections. For example, DISKFILE Protection Records have several unique attributes. These will be discussed in Securing Diskfiles with the Safeguard Subsystem in Part Five.

Owner

All OBJECTTYPE Protection Records have a Primary Owner. They may also have one or more optional Secondary Owners.

Access Control List (ACL)

The ACL portion of the Protection Record is where users are granted or denied specific access privileges to the underlying object.

When an attempt is made to access a protected object, Safeguard software checks the Protection Record(s) for the target object to determine whether the user or File-Sharing Group (identified by the PAID) has the required authority to access the object. Some types of objects, such as files, may be protected by more than one Safeguard Rule.

The privileges relevant to the various types of objects vary, as shown in the table below.

Operations / Privileges Granted in Safeguard Protection Records

Operation	Diskfile	Volume & Subvolume	Process & Subprocess	Device & Subdevice	Objecttype	Security-Grps
READ	OPEN for input	OPEN for input	OPEN for input and output	OPEN for input and output		
WRITE	OPEN for input and output	OPEN for input and output	OPEN for input and output	OPEN for input and output		
EXECUTE	EXECUTE the object file	EXECUTE any object file not protected by another record				EXECUTE the restricted Safeguard commands
PURGE	PURGE the file	PURGE any file not protected by another record	STOP the process			
CREATE	*1	CREATE a file in any subvol not protected by a SUBVOL Record	CREATE a process with a given name.		CREATE records for individual objects of the same Object Class	
OWN	ALTER or PURGE the Record	ALTER or PURGE the Record	ALTER or PURGE the Record	ALTER or PURGE the Record	ALTER or PURGE the Objecttype Record	ALTER or PURGE the Security Group Record

*1 CREATE authority for a disk file has no meaning unless the PERSISTENT attribute is ON for that file name.

RENAMING Considerations

The RENAME operation requires special evaluation of access authorities as shown in the table below.

Access Authorities Required to Rename a File					
Current File Name			New File Name		Result
Safeguard Record Exists?	Safeguard Purge Allowed?	Guardian Purge Allowed?	Safeguard Vol/Subvol/ Disk Record Exist?	Safeguard Create Allowed?	Rename Allowed?
No	-	Yes	No	-	Yes
No	-	Yes	Yes	Yes	Yes
No	-	Yes	Yes	No	No
No	-	No	-	-	No
Yes	Yes	-	No	-	Yes
Yes	Yes	-	Yes	Yes	Yes
Yes	Yes	-	Yes	No	No
Yes	No	-	-	-	No

The PERSISTENT Attribute and Renaming:

If the original file *does not have* a PERSISTENT Protection Record, the new file *assumes* the original file's Protection Record.

If the original file has a PERSISTENT Protection Record, the new file *does not assume* the original file's Protection Record.

If the new file name *has* a PERSISTENT Protection Record, the new file assumes the PERSISTENT Record.

Defining Users In Protection Record ACLs

Only userids and File-Sharing Groups can be used in Safeguard Protection Records. Aliases cannot be used in Safeguard Protection Records.

RISK   Aliases gain all the access authority defined for their underlying userid or File-Sharing Group membership.

3P-SAFEGARD-CONFIG-01   Instead of aliases, a third party access control product should be used to grant granular access to the privileges of functional and application userids.

Remote access is defined as an access attempt made by a user authenticated on a different node. If remote access is appropriate for a given object, the users must be defined as network users (*.) when granting privileges in the ACL or Safeguard software will deny the access requests from another node.

Users defined as network users are automatically granted the appropriate local access privileges as well.

RISK   Ownership * gives global rights to all nodes.

3P-OBJECT-ACCESS-01   A third party tool can provide additional security to identify and restrict * for specific nodes.

Audit Parameters

The individual Protection Records for each object determines whether or not attempts to ALTER or DELETE the Protection Record (i.e., MANAGE) will be audited and whether or not attempts to ACCESS the object the record it is protecting will be audited. See the following discussion for the variations of AUDIT-ACCESS and AUDIT-MANAGE parameters that apply to the object types.

AUDIT-ACCESS-{PASS | FAIL}

The AUDIT-ACCESS-PASS and AUDIT-ACCESS-FAIL attributes determine whether or not Safeguard software will write audits when someone attempts to access the object to which the Protection Record applies.

The valid entries are:

ALL   All successful / failed attempts to access the protected object will be audited.

NONE   No successful / failed attempts to access the protected object will be audited.

LOCAL   Only successful / failed local attempts to access the protected object will be audited.

REMOTE   Only successful / failed remote attempts to access the protected object will be audited.

AUDIT-MANAGE{-PASS | -FAIL}

The AUDIT-MANAGE-PASS and AUDIT-MANAGE-FAIL attributes determine whether or not Safeguard will write audits when someone attempts to ALTER or DELETE the particular Protection Record.

The valid entries are:

ALL   All successful / failed attempts to ALTER or DELETE the
            object's Protection Record will be audited.

NONE   No successful / failed attempts to ALTER or DELETE the
            object's Protection Record will be audited.

LOCAL   All successful / failed local attempts to ALTER or DELETE
            the object's Protection Record will be audited.

REMOTE   All successful / failed remote attempts to ALTER or
            DELETE the object's Protection Record will be audited.

Safeguard OBJECTTYPES

Each type of object has an associated OBJECTTYPE Protection Record that controls who is allowed to CREATE Protection Records for individual objects of that particular Object Class. For example, the ability to CREATE Protection Records for diskfiles is controlled by the DISKFILE OBJECTTYPE.

The Object Class is made up of all objects of the type protected by an OBJECTTYPE Protection Record, for example diskfiles make up the Object Class of the DISKFILE OBJECTTYPE.

Safeguard software supports Protection Records for the following OBJECT-TYPEs:

USER (includes aliases)

VOLUME

SUBVOLUME

DISKFILE

PROCESS

SUBPROCESS

DEVICE

SUBDEVICE

OBJECTTYPE

Each OBJECTTYPE Protection Record will be discussed in the appropriate section, for example, the DISKFILE OBJECTTYPE will be discussed in Securing Diskfiles with the Safeguard Susbsystem in Part Five.

OBJECTTYPE OBJECTTYPE

The OBJECTTYPE Protection Records are in themselves "pseudo-objects," therefore, an additional OBJECTTYPE record exists to control the creation of new

OBJECTTYPE Protection Records. This is called the OBJECTTYPE OBJECTTYPE record.

Only the owner and other users granted CREATE (C) authority on the OBJECTTYPE OBJECTTYPE ACL (if present) can create other OBJECTTYPE records.

Only the owner and other users granted OWNER (O) authority on the OBJECTTYPE OBJECTTYPE ACL can MANAGE the OBJECTTYPE OBJECTTYPE Protection Record.

BP-SAFEGARD-CONFIG-02   The OBJECTTYPE OBJECTTYPE Protection Record should be used to restrict who can create the remaining OBJECT-TYPE Records.

AP-ADVICE-SAFEGARD-05   In general, only members of the Security Group should be authorized to CREATE, ALTER or DELETE Safeguard Protection Records.

Note: The OBJECTTYPE DISKFILE has no effect on the Guardian default protection for a user's disk files. It only controls who can execute the Safecom ADD DISKFILE command to add a Diskfile Protection Record.

OBJECTTYPE Protection Records

OBJECTTYPE Protection Records determine who can MANAGE the particular OBJECTTYPE Protection Record, that is, ALTER or DELETE the Protection Record and who can CREATE or MANAGE Protection Records for individual objects of the same Object Class.

When a user attempts an ADD command (for example, ADD DISKFILE), Safeguard software first checks for the presence of a Protection Record for the corresponding OBJECTTYPE.

If no record exists, Safeguard software proceeds according to the default rules shown in the Table *Who Can Place Objects Under Safeguard Control.*

If a record exists for the corresponding OBJECTTYPE, Safeguard software consults its ACL and makes the appropriate ruling:

If the user has CREATE authority on the OBJECTTYPE ACL, the ADD succeeds.

If the user doesn't have CREATE authority on the OBJECTTYPE ACL, the ADD command fails.

Each OBJECTTYPE Protection Record contains the following attributes:

Owner

ACL

Status

Audit Configuration

OBJECTTYPE Ownership

OBJECTTYPE Protection Records respect the standard Primary and Secondary ownership privileges and processing.

RISK   In addition to the Primary Owner, the Primary Owner's group manager, and local SUPER.SUPER, any user ID that has an ACL entry granting OWNER authority can also modify the OBJECTTYPE Protection Record.

Who can Manage Object-Class Protection Records?

The following table summarizes who is allowed to CREATE, ALTER or DELETE Protection Records for the relevant Object-class.

Who Can Place Objects Under Safeguard Control		
OBJECTTYPE	Who Can Create ACLs *Without* Objecttype Records?	Who Can Create ACLs *With* Objecttype Records
USER	Local SUPER.SUPER and local grp mgrs	Only userids specifically granted CREATE privileges and SUPER.SUPER if not undeniable
ALIAS	Local owner of the underlying ID or the owner's Grp mgr or SUPER.SUPER	Only userids specifically granted OWN and CREATE privileges and the OBJECTTYPE Record's Primary Owner and his Group Manager.
GROUP	Local SUPER group	Only userids specifically granted CREATE privileges and SUPER SUPER if not deniable
OBJECTTYPE	Local SUPER group	Only userids specifically granted CREATE privileges and SUPER SUPER if not deniable
VOLUME	Local SUPER group	Only userids specifically granted CREATE privileges and SUPER SUPER if not deniable
SUBVOLUME	Any local user	Only userids specifically granted CREATE privileges and SUPER SUPER if not deniable
DISKFILE	Local file owner Local SUPER.SUPER Owner's local grp mgr	Only userids specifically granted CREATE privileges and SUPER SUPER if not deniable
PROCESS	Any local user	Only userids specifically granted CREATE privileges and SUPER SUPER if not deniable

Who Can Place Objects Under Safeguard Control

OBJECTTYPE	Who Can Create ACLs *Without* Objecttype Records?	Who Can Create ACLs *With* Objecttype Records
SUBPROCESS	Any local user	Only userids specifically granted CREATE privileges and SUPER SUPER if not deniable
DEVICE	Local SUPER group	Only userids specifically granted CREATE privileges and SUPER SUPER if not deniable
SUBDEVICE	Local SUPER group	Only userids specifically granted CREATE privileges and SUPER SUPER if not deniable
SECURITY GROUPS	Local SUPER group	Members of the SECURITY-ADMINISTRATOR SECURITY GROUP
TERMINAL	Local SUPER group	Members of the SECURITY-ADMINISTRATOR SECURITY GROUP
SEEP	Local SUPER group	Members of the SECURITY-ADMINISTRATOR SECURITY GROUP

OBJECTTYPE ACL

The following access authorities can be granted to users and user groups:

CREATE   ADD a Protection Record for an object in the Object-Class

OWNER   ALTER or DELETE the OBJECTTYPE Protection Record itself

BP-SAFEGARD-CONFIG-03   All OBJECTTYPE Protection Records should be owned by a single Security Manager userid.

OBJECTTYPE Status

Each OBJECTTYPE Protection Record can be FROZEN or THAWED. Freezing an OBJECTTYPE Protection Record temporarily suspends the authorities granted by the record's ACL. While the OBJECTTYPE Protection Record is frozen, only the following users can CREATE Protection Records for the relevant Object Class:

The Primary Owner of the OBJECTTYPE Protection Record

The Primary Owner's group manager

The Primary or Secondary Owner of an individual Object class Protection Record

Local SUPER.SUPER

For example, if the VOLUME OBJECTTYPE Protection Record is frozen, the Primary Owner of the Protection Record for $SYSTEM can alter the $SYSTEM Protection Record, but could not add a new Protection Record for the $USER volume, unless he was also the Primary Owner of the VOLUME OBJECTTYPE Protection Record (or that Primary Owner's Group Manager or SUPER.SUPER).

RISK When an OBJECTTYPE Protection Record is FROZEN, authorities granted to users in the OBJECTTYPE's ACL are changed. Users granted CREATE but not OWNERSHIP authority cannot create new PROCESS Protection Records while the PROCESS OBJECTTYPE is FROZEN.

Consider the following example:

```
Example:
OBJECTTYPE PROCESS
253,1         O
220,250       C
```

When the PROCESS OBJECTTYPE shown above is THAWED, user 220,250 can CREATE Protection Records for individual processes, but user 253,1 cannot.

When the PROCESS OBJECTTYPE shown above is FROZEN, user 220,250 cannot CREATE Protection Records for individual processes, but user 253,1 can.

OBJECTTYPE Audit Attributes

OBJECTTYPE Audit Attributes follow the same standards as other Protection Record Audit Attributes. The OBJECTTYPE Audit Attributes are:

AUDIT-ACCESS-PASS

AUDIT-ACCESS-FAIL

AUDIT-MANAGE-PASS

AUDIT-MANAGE-FAIL

AUDIT-ACCESS{-PASS | -FAIL}

The AUDIT-ACCESS-PASS and AUDIT-ACCESS-FAIL attributes determine whether or not Safeguard software will write audits when someone attempts to CREATE a Protection record for an object in the relevant object class.

The valid entries are:

ALL   All successful / failed attempts to CREATE a Protection Record for an object in the relevant object-class will be audited.

NONE   No successful / failed attempts to CREATE a Protection Record for an object in the relevant object-class will be audited. The default value is NONE.

LOCAL   Only successful / failed local attempts to CREATE a Protection
           Record for an object in the relevant object-class will be audited.

REMOTE   Only successful / failed remote attempts to CREATE a Protection
           Record for an object in the relevant object-class will be audited.

AUDIT-MANAGE{-PASS | -FAIL}

The AUDIT-MANAGE-PASS and AUDIT-MANAGE-FAIL attributes determine
whether or not Safeguard software will write audits when someone attempts to ALTER
or DELETE this OBJECTTYPE Record.

The valid entries are:

ALL   All successful / failed attempts to ALTER or DELETE this OBJECT-
           TYPE Record will be audited.

NONE   No successful / failed attempts to ALTER or DELETE this OBJECT-
           TYPE Record will be audited. The default value is NONE will be
           audited.

LOCAL   Only successful / failed local attempts to ALTER or DELETE this
           OBJECTTYPE Record will be audited.

REMOTE   Only successful / failed remote attempts to ALTER or DELETE
           this OBJECTTYPE Record will be audited.

Non-Object Safeguard Entities

Besides the Protection Records for all types of objects, Safeguard includes four other
entities:

Audit Pools

Security Groups

Terminal Definition Records

Security Event Exit Processes (SEEPs)

Who Can Create/Manage Non-Object Safeguard Entities

OBJECTTYPE	Who Can Create or Alter *Without* OBJECTTYPE Records?	Who Can Create or Alter *With* OBJECTTYPE Records
Audit Service	Local SUPER group	Members of the SECURITY-ADMINISTRATOR SECURITY GROUP
Security Groups	Local SUPER group	Members of the SECURITY-ADMINISTRATOR SECURITY GROUP
Terminals	Local SUPER group	Members of the SECURITY-ADMINISTRATOR SECURITY GROUP
SEEPs	Local SUPER group	Members of the SECURITY-ADMINISTRATOR SECURITY GROUP

Configuring Safeguard Audit Pools

Audit records are written to the Audit Trail as they are received by the Safeguard Audit Service. The Audit Trail is composed of one or more Audit Pools. The term Audit Pool refers to the subvolume where the audit files reside. The Audit Pool name is always the same as the subvolume name.

By default, Safeguard software creates the current Audit Pool in $SYSTEM.SAFE.

BP-SAFEGARD-CONFIG-04   The Safeguard audit trail should be moved off $SYSTEM to another, less busy, volume.

The first file in an audit pool will be named A0000001; the second file, A0000002, etc. Safeguard software configures all the files at once, then writes to each one until it fills up. Once a file is full, Safeguard software opens the next file in the series. When the last file is full, Safeguard software's behavior is determined by the AUDIT SERVICE RECOVERY setting described below.

The Safeguard Audit Service can maintain multiple Audit Pools, but only one can be active at a time.

Determining the Size of Audit Pools

The size of an Audit Pool is determined by the number of individual files it will contain and the size of the files. These are configured using the AUDIT POOL command, which determines:

MAXFILES

EXTENTSIZE

MAXEXTENTS

Once these values are entered, the disk space is allocated and the files created.

MAXFILES

The MAXFILES parameter determines the maximum number of files that will be allocated to the Audit Pool.

The default value is 2 files.

EXTENTSIZE

The EXTENTSIZE parameter determines the space on a disk allocated for a file. These parameters set the size of the first and secondary extents, in 2048-byte pages.

The default value is 128 pages.

MAXEXTENTS

The MAXEXTENTS parameter determines the maximum number of disk file extents for each audit file.

The default value is 16 extents.

Sizing the Audit Files

The length of time that the Corporate Security Policy and Standards requires that Safeguard audits must be saved online will determine the number of Audit Pools required and the size and number of the files in each Audit Pool.

The method of generating Safeguard audit reports will have an impact on the size of Safeguard audit files. In general, the smaller the file, the faster a report can be generated, but many products, including Safeart, the audit tool provided by HP, can only generate a report on one audit file at a time. If research is needed for an event in a time period that spans two audit files, two reports must be run, one per audit file.

Many companies size the files so that one file will contain approximately one day's audit. Some size the files for a week's worth of audit. Some companies 'manually' roll the files at midnight every night, whether the files are full or not.

Some companies have a single Audit Pool, some use multiple audit pools as a method of retaining more audits online, while each individual audit file is relatively small.

AP-ADVICE-SAFEGARD-06   Use the method that best meets the requirements stated in the Corporate Security Policy.

3P-SAFEGARD-AUDIT-01   Use a third party product to produce Safeguard audit reports.

How Long Should Safeguard Audit Trails Be Saved

The Corporate Security Policy should mandate how long Safeguard audit trails must be kept online, how often they should be backed up to tape, and how long the archived files must be saved. This may depend on Industry Standards created by such agencies as the Securities and Exchange Commission or the Federal Banking System.

Configuring How the Safeguard Subsystem Writes Its Audits

Two AUDIT SERVICE attributes determine the manner in which audit records are written to disk. These are:

WRITE-THROUGH CACHE

EOF REFRESH

WRITE-THROUGH CACHE

The WRITE-THROUGH CACHE attribute determines whether or not audit records can be retained in memory or are written immediately to disk.

If WRITE-THROUGH CACHE is ON, after each audit record is written to memory, it is immediately written to disk.

If WRITE-THROUGH CACHE is OFF, audit records written to memory may be cached and not written to disk immediately.

RISK   If OFF, a CPU crash will lose audit.

BP-SAFEGARD-CONFIG-05   The default and best practice value is WRITE-THROUGH CACHE OFF for performance reasons.

EOF REFRESH

The EOF REFRESH attribute determines whether or not the End Of File (EOF) marker will be updated after each audit record is written, even if the record is retained in memory.

If EOF REFRESH is OFF, the EOF will not be updated until the record is actually written to disk.

If EOF REFRESH is ON, the EOF will be updated.

If WRITE-THROUGH CACHE is ON, EOF REFRESH is automatically set ON.

But, if WRITE-THROUGH CACHE is then turned off,

EOF REFRESH remains ON.

BP-SAFEGARD-CONFIG-06 The default and best practice value is EOF REFRESH OFF.

Configuring AUDIT SERVICE RECOVERY Mode

The AUDIT SERVICE RECOVERY attribute determines how Safeguard software will behave if the current audit pool is either unassigned or becomes unavailable for any reason. Note that Safeguard software will always attempt to use the *next* audit pool if one is configured. Only if the next audit pool is also undefined or unavailable will Safeguard software go into the specified RECOVERY Mode when the current audit pool is unavailable.

There are three RECOVERY modes:

RECYCLE

SUSPEND AUDIT

DENY GRANTS

RECYCLE

When RECYCLE is selected, the oldest unreleased audit file will be reused. The file will be purged and a new file with the next sequence number created. For example, if the Audit Pool is configured to have a maximum of 10 files, when the 10th file is full, Safeguard software will delete A0000001 and open a new file named A0000011.

If a disk fails, Safeguard must suspend auditing, because it can't create a new audit file.

RECYCLE does not apply to the audit pool $SYSTEM.SAFE whether it is the primary audit pool or the 'fallback' audit pool.

BP-SAFEGARD-CONFIG-07 RECYCLE is the recommended RECOVERY setting.

If RECOVERY mode is RECYCLE and the Corporate Security Policy and Standards require that Safeguard software audits be retained online for a specific time period, steps must be taken to prevent the loss of data due to Safeguard purging old audit files:

The Audit Trail must be large enough to retain the required amount of data.

The individual Audit Pools may require more and/or larger files.

AP-ADVICE-SAFEGARD-07   If RECOVERY mode is RECYCLE and the Corporate Security Policy and Standards require that Safeguard software audits be retained online for a specific time period, it is highly recommended that at least one secondary Audit Pool be configured and set as the NEXT AUDIT POOL. This will prevent the loss of data due to Safeguard software purging old audit files.

SUSPEND AUDIT

Safeguard software suspends auditing as long as the current audit pool is unavailable. This value guarantees that processing will continue even when Safeguard software cannot write its audits.

RISK   During the time the audit is suspended, there will be no audit trail to provide accountability in case of a security breach.

DENY GRANTS

If the current audit pool becomes unavailable, and RECOVERY is configured to DENY GRANTS, Safeguard software will deny any authorization (object access attempts) and any authentication (logon) requests that require auditing. In this case:

RISK   Only successful access attempts by members of the Security Groups will be granted.

RISK   What auditing does occur will be redirected to $SYSTEM.SAFE. If there is no available space on $SYSTEM, no activity that requires auditing will be allowed. It will not even be possible to switch to another Audit Pool.

AP-ADVICE-SAFEGARD-08   If AUDIT SERVICE is configured to DENY GRANTS, make sure that $SYSTEM always has enough space for 'fallback' auditing or risk disruption of service.

AP-ADVICE-SAFEGARD-09   If AUDIT SERVICE is configured to DENY GRANTS, it is especially important to configure at least one secondary Audit Pool or risk disruption of service.

NOTE: If the RECOVERY setting is DENY GRANTS and Safeguard software is included with system generation then, before shutting down the system, the current Audit Pool must be moved to a disk that is connected to the same CPU as $SYSTEM.

Otherwise, auditing will be suspended during the cold load and Safeguard software will DENY access attempts that require audits. Once the Cold Load is complete, Safeguard software should be reconfigured to use the normal audit pool.

Managing Multiple Audit Pools

It is possible to have multiple audit pools on different volumes and subvolumes, but only one can be current at a time. When there are multiple audit pools:

Define which audit pool is to be used as the current audit pool; that is, which audit pool is to receive audit records.

Define the next audit pool to be used when the current audit pool is filled. Because an audit pool can contain several audit files, a system may have several different volumes and subvolumes containing multiple audit files.

Within an audit pool, when the current audit file is filled, Safeguard software automatically switches to the next available file in that audit pool. Alternatively, users can monitor usage of the audit files and manually switch to the next file or switch to another audit pool, as necessary.

As long as unused or released audit files remain available in the current audit pool, there is no danger of audit data being lost; even that danger is minimized if the NEXT AUDIT POOL has been specified. Therefore, part of the task of monitoring the audit service activity is to release (allow the purging of) audit files that are no longer needed so that Safeguard software can reuse them.

NOTE: The Safeguard subsystem writes a message to the system console each time it switches from one audit file to another. These messages can be used to determine when to extract data from a used audit file before it is recycled.

SECURITY-GROUPs

The Safeguard SECURITY GROUPS make it possible to delegate to specific users the authority to execute certain restricted Safeguard commands. **The SECURITY GROUPS do not exist until they are added.**

The restricted commands are shown in the tables below.

RISK   Until the SECURITY-GROUPS are added, the restricted Safeguard commands can be executed by all SUPER group members. Once the SECURITY GROUPS are created, only those users with EXECUTE authority on each SECURITY-GROUP's ACL (and SUPER.SUPER if configured UNDENIABLE) can use the commands restricted to that the group.

There are two valid SECURITY-GROUPS:

SECURITY-ADMINISTRATOR GROUP

SYSTEM-OPERATOR GROUP

Safeguard software does not treat SECURITY-GROUPS as objects. They are not affected by the Safeguard Warning Mode.

SECURITY-ADMINISTRATOR GROUP

Members of this group can manage (configure) all aspects of Safeguard and Safeguard auditing except releasing and 'rolling' Safeguard audit files.

BP-SAFEGARD-SECADMIN-01   The SECURITY-ADMINISTRATOR GROUP should be defined.

BP-SAFEGARD-SECADMIN-02   The User Record for the Security Admin userid itself, should be owned by SUPER.SUPER, so that SUPER.SUPER can restore access to the Security Admin userid if something goes wrong. For example, if the Security Admin userid is frozen or its password expires.

Command	Without Sec Groups	SEC-ADMIN	SYS-OPER
ADD AUDIT POOL	SUPER group	Yes	Yes
ALTER AUDIT POOL	SUPER group	Yes	Yes
ALTER AUDIT SERVICE	SUPER group	Yes	No
DELETE AUDIT POOL	SUPER group	Yes	Yes
SELECT	SUPER group	Yes	Yes
ADD TERMINAL	SUPER group	Yes	No
ALTER TERMINAL	SUPER group	Yes	No
DELETE TERMINAL	SUPER group	Yes	No
FREEZE TERMINAL	SUPER group	Yes	Yes
THAW TERMINAL	SUPER group	Yes	Yes
ADD EVENT-EXIT-PROCESS	SUPER group	Yes	No
ALTER EVENT-EXIT-PROCESS	SUPER group	Yes	No
DELETE EVENT-EXIT-PROCESS	SUPER group	Yes	No
ALTER SAFEGUARD	SUPER group	Yes	No
STOP SAFEGUARD	SUPER group	Yes	No

SYSTEM-OPERATOR GROUP

Members of this group can only FREEZE and THAW Safeguard-controlled terminals and manage the Safeguard audit trails.

BP-SAFEGARD-SYSOPR-01   The SYSTEM-OPERATOR GROUP should be defined.

BP-SAFEGARD-SYSOPR-02   The User Record for the System Operator should be owned by the Security Administrator user.

The SECURITY-GROUP Definition Records

Only a member of the local SUPER group can ADD Security-Group Definition Records. Once the groups have been created, each group definition record determines who is allowed to ALTER or PURGE it. Please refer to Managing Userids with the Safeguard Subsystem in Part Three.

The Security-Group Record attributes are:

Owner

ACL

Status

Audit Configuration

Security-Group Ownership

SECURITY-GROUP Protection Records respect the standard Primary and Secondary ownership privileges and processing.

In addition to the Primary Owner, the Primary Owner's group manager, and local SUPER.SUPER, any userid with OWNER authority in the SECURITY-GROUP Definition Record can also modify the Record.

Security-Group Access Control List

The following access authorities can be granted to users and user groups in a SECURITY-GROUP:

EXECUTE   EXECUTE the appropriate restricted Safeguard commands

OWNER   ALTER or DELETE the Security-Group Record itself

STATUS

The STATUS is either FROZEN or THAWED. If a SECURITY-GROUP Record is frozen, the authorities granted to userids listed on a security group ACL are temporarily suspended.

While the SECURITY-GROUP is frozen, only the primary owner, the primary owner's group manager, and local SUPER.SUPER can execute the commands restricted to that SECURITY-GROUP.

BP-SAFEGARD-SECADMIN-03   STATUS = THAWED

BP-SAFEGARD-SYSOPR-03   STATUS = THAWED

Security-Group Audit Attributes

SECURITY-GROUP audit attributes follow the same standards as other Protection Record audit attributes. The SECURITY-GROUP audit attributes are:

AUDIT-ACCESS-PASS

AUDIT-ACCESS-FAIL

AUDIT-MANAGE-PASS

AUDIT-MANAGE-FAIL

BP-SAFEGARD-SECADMIN-04   AUDIT- ACCESS-PASS = ALL

BP-SAFEGARD-SECADMIN-05   AUDIT- ACCESS-FAIL= ALL

BP-SAFEGARD-SECADMIN-06   AUDIT- MANAGE-PASS = ALL

BP-SAFEGARD-SECADMIN-07   AUDIT- MANAGE-FAIL= ALL

BP-SAFEGARD-SYSOPR-04   AUDIT- ACCESS-PASS = ALL

BP-SAFEGARD-SYSOPR-05   AUDIT- ACCESS-FAIL= ALL

BP-SAFEGARD-SYSOPR-06   AUDIT- MANAGE-PASS = ALL

BP-SAFEGARD-SYSOPR-07   AUDIT- MANAGE-FAIL= ALL

```
LAST-MODIFIED   OWNER  STATUS
SECURITY-ADMINISTRATOR
        7JAN03, 11:12    255,255 THAWED

     222,233      E,  O
     222,250      E,  O
     253,001      E,  O
   AUDIT-ACCESS-PASS = ALL     AUDIT-MANAGE-PASS = ALL
   AUDIT-ACCESS-FAIL = ALL     AUDIT-MANAGE-FAIL = ALL
```

Safeguard-Controlled Terminals

Safeguard software can be configured to take over control of the logon dialog at specific terminals. Some or all of the terminals on the system can be controlled by Safeguard. They are put under Safeguard software control by creating a Terminal Definition Record or dynamic TCP/IP ports configured to start LOGON.

Terminal Definition Records differ from Safeguard Object Protection Records in that there is no ACL portion. To control access to a Safeguard terminal, create a DEVICE (or SUBDEVICE) Protection Record based on the terminal's device name. See Device Security in Part Five.

The Terminal Definition Record also allows specification of a particular command interpreter to be started automatically at the terminal after user authentication.

NOTE: Safeguard software can start a specific command interpreter only at a Safeguard terminal, that is, one put under Safeguard control with a Terminal Definition Record or LOGON program. Though the CI can be specified in a User Record and in a Safeguard Globals, it is enforced only at terminals controlled by Safeguard software.

Safeguard-controlled terminals can also be configured for exclusive access, which ensures that any user who is logged on to a Safeguard terminal has exclusive access to the terminal until the user logs off. This feature is configured with the TERMINAL-EXCLUSIVE-ACCESS parameter.

Please see LOGON in Part Four for a detailed discussion of Safeguard-controlled terminals.

Who Can Add or Manage Safeguard-Controlled Terminals

If the SECURITY-ADMINISTRATOR group has been defined on the system, only SECURITY-ADMINISTRATOR GROUP members (and SUPER.SUPER if configured UNDENIABLE) can access terminal commands, other than INFO, which any user can execute.

RISK If the SECURITY-ADMINISTRATOR has not been defined on the system, any SUPER group member can execute the terminal commands.

Security Event-Exit Process (SEEP)

A SEEP is a process that participates in security policy enforcement. Depending on how the event-exit process is configured, Safeguard software passes it requests for Authorization Events, Authentication Events, and Password Change Events. The SEEP rules on the request and returns the ruling to Safeguard software for interpretation and enforcement. The SEEP commands allow a security administrator to configure and manage the security event exit process.

RISK   A poorly written SEEP can prevent Safeguard software from functioning correctly.

AP-ADVICE-SAFEGARD-10 SEEPs should only be created by extremely knowledgeable programmers.

3P-OBJSEC-SEEP-01   Use a third party Safeguard SEEP product to enhance Safeguard capabilities for object security.

3P-PASSWORD-SEEP-01   Use a third party Safeguard SEEP product to enhance Safeguard capabilities of password quality.

The SEEP Configuration Record

SEEP Configuration Records have the following parameters:

EVENT-EXIT-PROCESS (Name)
ENABLED
RESPONSE-TIMEOUT
ENABLE-AUTHENTICATION-EVENT
ENABLE-AUTHORIZATION-EVENT
ENABLE-PASSWORD-EVENT
PROG
PNAME
LIB
CPU
SWAP
PRI
PARAM-TEXT

Safeguard software does not treat SEEP Configuration Records as objects. They are not affected by the Safeguard Warning Mode.

The EVENT-EXIT-PROCESS

The EVENT-EXIT-PROCESS parameter determines the name of the SEEP Configuration Record.

ENABLED

The ENABLED parameter determines whether or not the SEEP is ruling on security events relayed from Safeguard software:

If ENABLED is ON, Safeguard software will start the process and send designated SEEP messages to the process.

If ENABLED is OFF, Safeguard software will not start the designated SEEP and will not send it any messages.

The default value is OFF. If this attribute is omitted, it is set to the default.

RESPONSE-TIMEOUT

The RESPONSE-TIMEOUT parameter determines the time, in seconds, which Safeguard software will wait for the SEEP to respond to an event.

The Safeguard's Subsystem response to a TIMEOUT depends on the type of SEEP:

If a Password-Quality SEEP times out and the user attempting the access is NOT a local member of the SUPER group, Safeguard software denies the password change request.

If an Authorization SEEP times out Safeguard software denies the access request.

If an Authentication SEEP times out for *any* user, Safeguard software denies the authentication request.

The default value is five seconds. If this attribute is omitted, it is set to the default.

ENABLE-AUTHENTICATION-EVENT

The ENABLE-AUTHENTICATION-EVENT determines whether or not authentication events will be sent to the SEEP:

If ENABLE-AUTHENTICATION-EVENT is ON, authentication events will be sent to the SEEP when it is enabled.

If ENABLE-AUTHENTICATION-EVENT is OFF, authentication events will not be sent to the SEEP.

The default value is OFF. If this attribute is omitted, it is set to the default.

ENABLE-AUTHORIZATION-EVENT

The ENABLE-AUTHORIZATION-EVENT determines whether or not authorization events will be sent to the SEEP.

If ENABLE-AUTHORIZATION-EVENT is ON, authorization events will be sent to the SEEP.

If ENABLE-AUTHORIZATION-EVENT is OFF, authorization events will not be sent to the SEEP.

The default value is OFF. If this attribute is omitted, it is set to the default.

ENABLE-PASSWORD-EVENT

The ENABLE-PASSWORD-EVENT determines whether or not password change events will be sent to the SEEP.

The PASSWORD SEEP behaves differently, depending on whether or not the AUTHENTICATION SEEP is also enabled:

If both the PASSWORD and AUTHENTICATION SEEPs are enabled, password changes that occur during login on are not sent to the Password SEEP, only password changes from the PASSWORD program and from the Safeguard ADD USER, ALTER USER, ADD ALIAS, and ALTER ALIAS commands will be sent to the Password SEEP

If the PASSWORD SEEP is enabled but the AUTHENTICATION SEEP is disabled, all password change events, included those that occur at login, are sent to the PASSWORD-SEEP for evaluation.

If ENABLE-PASSWORD-EVENT is OFF, password events will not be sent to the SEEP.

The default value is OFF. If this attribute is omitted, it is set to the default.

PROG

The PROG parameter specifies the object file Safeguard software will start when the SEEP is enabled. The object file must be a local file.

If no object file is entered, no program will be started. There is no default value.

LIB

The LIB parameter defines the library file, if any, is to be used with the SEEP.

If no library is specified, no library file will be used.

CPU

The CPU parameter determines the CPU in which the SEEP will be run. The valid entries are the word "any" or a two-digit number representing the CPU desired. If the value is ANY, any available CPU will be used.

If no CPU is specified, any available CPU will be used.

PNAME

The PNAME parameter determines the process name that will be assigned to the SEEP.

If no PNAME is specified, Safeguard software will generate a process name when it starts the SEEP.

RISK The PNAME should be unique. If a process of the same name already exists, Safeguard software will stop it before starting the SEEP.

SWAP

The SWAP parameter determines the location of the SEEP's swap space. The value must be a valid volume name. The subvolume and file names are optional.

The NonStop S series systems, the swap space can be controlled via the NSKCOM program.

PRI

The PRI parameter determines the priority at which the SEEP runs.

The default value is 155. If no PRI is entered, Safeguard software starts the SEEP at the default priority.

PARAM-TEXT

The PARAM-TEXT determines the data (if any) to be supplied as the startup message for the SEEP.

The PARAM-TEXT must be the final attribute in the command string.

If no PARAM-TEXT is entered, no startup text is used.

Who Can Manage SEEPs

SEEPs are managed with the EVENT-EXIT-PROCESS commands:

INFO

ADD

ALTER

DELETE

The INFO command can be executed by any user.

The ADD, ALTER, and DELETE commands can only be executed by members of the SECURITY-ADMINISTRATOR Security Group (and SUPER.SUPER if configured UNDENIABLE), if defined on the system.

If the SECURITY-ADMINISTRATOR Security Group is not defined, any SUPER group member can use these commands.

AP-ADVICE-SEEP-01   Only select users should be allowed to ADD, ALTER or DELETE SEEPs.

Safeguard Warning Mode

Warning Mode is intended for use as a tool for testing new Safeguard Protection Records as they are put into use on the system. When in Warning Mode, Safeguard software allows access to any object that has a Protection Record, even in those instances in which the ACL would deny the attempted access if it was in production. Safeguard audits any access attempt that would normally have been denied. Warning Mode makes it possible to test the effectiveness and accuracy of the new Protection Records. Once the Protection Records are implemented satisfactorily, change WARNING MODE to OFF to disable Warning Mode and enforce all Safeguard rules.

It is important to note the following facts about Warning Mode:

RISK   Warning Mode is system-wide, the entire node is vulnerable as long as WARNING-MODE is ON.

RISK   When WARNING-MODE is ON, Safeguard software allows access to all objects.

Objects that are not protected by Safeguard software are unaffected in Warning Mode. For example, if a disk file does not have a Safeguard Protection Record *and ACL-REQUIRED-DISKFILE is OFF*, access to that disk file will be unaffected by Warning Mode.

OBJECTTYPES, SECURITY GROUPS, Terminal Definition Records and SEEP Configuration Records are not affected by Warning Mode. Safeguard software does not treat them as objects.

If the Safeguard Global parameters ACL-REQUIRED-xxx (for example, DISKFILE, PROCESS or DEVICE) are configured ON, access is normally denied for any object that does not have a Protection Record. In Warning Mode, however, access to all such objects will be granted.

3P-OBJSEC-SEEP-02   Use a third party Safeguard SEEP product to enhance Safeguard capabilities for object security with the ability to perform rule-by-rule WARNING MODE

WARNING-MODE

The WARNING-MODE attribute determines whether or not the Safeguard subsystem is in Warning Mode:

If WARNING-MODE is ON, Warning Mode is enabled.

If WARNING-MODE is OFF Warning Mode is disabled.

The default value is OFF.

Warning Mode Rulings on Object ACLs				
Safeguard ACL Ruling	Guardian Security	Access Result	Audit Generated	Outcome in Audit Record
Std Mode – Grant	N/A	Yes	As specified	Granted
Std Mode - Fail	N/A	No	As specified	Denied
Warn Mode – Grant	N/A**	Yes	As specified	Granted
Warn Mode - Fail	N/A**	Yes*	Always	Warning*

* Indicates that access result is due to Warning Mode evaluation of the ACL .
** Depends upon Fallback setting

BP-SAFEGARD-GLOBAL-10   WARNING-MODE = OFF

WARNING-FALLBACK-SECURITY

Diskfiles and processes differ from other Safeguard objects in that they have Guardian security associated with them. The WARNING-FALLBACK-SECURITY is a Global attribute that determines how Safeguard software will rule on access attempts to these objects while it is in WARNING MODE.

WARNING-FALLBACK-SECURITY can be set to either GUARDIAN or GRANT:

If WARNING-FALLBACK-SECURITY is set to GUARDIAN, Safeguard software bypasses the Protection Record and bases it's ruling on the diskfile's

Guardian Security String. This allows testing of the Safeguard software security settings while maintaining Guardian protection.

If WARNING-FALLBACK-SECURITY is set to GRANT, Safeguard bypasses both the Protection Record *and* the Guardian security string and grants the access that it would otherwise deny. This can be useful when the Guardian security has not been kept current with the security policy. This method of operation may also be useful in certain extreme emergency situations when routine security measures need to be suspended.

The default value is GUARDIAN.

RISK   When WARNING-FALLBACK-SECURITY is set to GRANT, the system is vulnerable; all security is bypassed, granting users access that would otherwise be denied even by Guardian security.

BP-SAFEGARD-GLOBAL-11   WARNING-FALLBACK-SECURITY = GUARDIAN

Evaluating Disk File Access in Warning Mode

Diskfiles have Guardian Security Strings that affect the access granted while Safeguard software is in Warning Mode. In Warning Mode with the fallback option set to GUARDIAN, Safeguard software checks the Guardian disk file Security String before granting access:

If the Guardian security string grants the access, Safeguard allows the access and writes an audit record with the outcome WARNING.

If the security string does not grant the access, Safeguard denies the access. No audit record is written in this instance unless auditing is specified for the disk file.

Warning Mode Rulings on Diskfile ACLs				
Safeguard ACL Ruling	Guardian Security	Access Result	Audit Record Generated	Outcome in Audit Record
Prod Mode – Grant	N/A	Yes	As specified	Granted
Prod Mode - Fail	N/A	No	As specified	Denied
Prod Mode – No Record	Use Guardian	Yes / No #	No	N/A
Grant	Grants	Yes	As specified	Granted
Grant	Denies	No	As specified	Granted

Warning Mode Rulings on Diskfile ACLs				
Safeguard ACL Ruling	Guardian Security	Access Result	Audit Record Generated	Outcome in Audit Record
Deny	Grants	Yes*	Always	Warning*
Deny	Denies	No	As specified	Denied
No Record	Use Guardian	Yes / No #	No	N/A
Warning Mode With Grant Fall Back				
Grant	N/A	Yes	As specified	Granted
Deny	N/A	Yes*	Always	Warning*
NoRecord	Use Guardian	Yes / No #	No	N/A

* Indicates that access result is due to Warning Mode evaluation of the Protection Record.
\# Indicates that access result is determined by Guardian settings.

Evaluating Process Access in Warning Mode

Processes differ from other objects; they have default Guardian security rules and they have stop modes, which influence whether or not a process can be stopped by another process. There are three stop modes:

Mode 0   Process can be stopped by any other process.

Mode 1   Process can only be stopped by:

- SUPER.SUPER

- A process whose PAID is the same as the target process's PAID or CAID.

- A process whose PAID is the same as the PAID or CAID of the target process owner's Group Manager.

Mode 1   is the default.

Mode 2   Process cannot be stopped by any other process.

NOTE: If a process has stop mode 2 and the access attempt is granted, Safeguard software writes an audit record with the outcome of either WARNING or GRANTED, however, the process will not actually be stopped because the Guardian stop mode of 2 always takes precedence over the Safeguard ruling. The request will be pending until the process sets itself to a lower stop mode.

Warning Mode Rulings on Process and Subprocess ACLs

Safeguard ACL Ruling	Guardian Security	Access Result	Audit Record Generated	Outcome in Audit Record
Std Mode – Grant	Mode 0,1 Mode 2	Yes No**	As specified As specified	Granted Granted/Warning**
Std Mode - Fail	Mode 0,1,2	No	As specified	Denied
Std Mode – No Record	Use Guardian	Yes / No	No	N/A
Warning Mode With Guardian Fall Back				
Grant	Mode 0,1 Mode 2	Yes No**	As specified As specified	Granted Granted
Deny	Mode 0,1 Mode 2	Yes* No**	Always* Always*	Warning* Warning*
No Record	Use Guardian	Yes / No#	No	N/A
Warning Mode With Grant Fall Back				
Grant	Mode 0,1 Mode 2	Yes No**	As specified As specified	Granted Granted
Deny	Mode 0,1 Mode 2	Yes* No**	Always* Always*	Warning* Warning*
NoRecord	Use Guardian	Yes / No #	No	N/A

* Indicates that access result is due to Warning Mode evaluation of the ACL .

** Attempts to stop a process at mode 2 do not produce a security violation message, but the process will not stop until the process sets itself to a lower stop mode. These requests are treated as pending and are audited as GRANTED or WARNING.

\# Indicates that the access result is determined by Guardian settings.

Safeguard Auditing

The ability to track security events on the system is one of the most important aspects of Access Control. On the HP NonStop server, Safeguard software audits information about a wide range of events in its audit files. The Safeguard audit files are collectively referred to as the Audit Trail.

Audit records are written to the Audit Trail as they are received (see the section: *Configuring How Safeguard Writes Its Audits*) by the Safeguard Audit Service.

The Safeguard subsystem generates audit records for the events it controls. Some events are recorded regardless of Safeguard settings and other events will not be recorded unless specifically configured for auditing.

Configuring What Will Be Audited

Some Safeguard events are always audited. Most must be configured to enable auditing.

Safeguard Events That Are Always Audited

The following types of events are always audited, regardless of any Safeguard audit settings and regardless of whether or not the commands executed successfully:

Attempts to execute the Safeguard ALTER or STOP commands

Attempts to execute Safeguard AUDIT SERVICE commands other than INFO

Attempts to execute Safeguard TERMINAL commands other than the INFO

Attempts to execute EVENT-EXIT-PROCESS commands other than INFO

Safeguard Events That Must Be Configured For Auditing

The following types of events must have auditing specified to be recorded in the Safeguard audit trail:

Attempts to AUTHENTICATE users

Attempts to ACCESS objects

Attempts to CREATE or MANAGE Safeguard User/Alias Records

Attempts to CREATE or MANAGE Safeguard Protection Records

Attempts to CREATE or MANAGE Safeguard OBJECTTYPE Records

Automatic LOGOFFS that occur if a user logs on at an already logged on terminal

This section discusses how Safeguard auditing works and how to configure auditing in general. However, the recommended audit settings for each of the Object-classes is discussed in the sections devoted to the individual object types. For example, recommended audit settings for User Records are discussed in Part Three.

Configuring Global or System-wide Auditing

Normally, Safeguard software audits only those items that have auditing specified in their Protection Records. However, system-wide auditing can be configured so that auditing is performed even if it is not specified in individual Protection Records.

Auditing specified by Safeguard Global parameters *supplements* the settings in the individual Protection Records (provided that Safeguard software is configured to check the individual record). For example, if an individual record is set to audit local attempts and the Safeguard Global configuration is set to audit remote attempts, both local and remote attempts are audited.

To configure system-wide auditing of all system objects, in addition to the audit settings in the individual Protection Records, the Global parameters are:

AUDIT-CLIENT-SERVICE

AUDIT-OBJECT-ACCESS-PASS

AUDIT-OBJECT-ACCESS-FAIL

AUDIT-OBJECT-MANAGE-PASS

AUDIT-OBJECT-MANAGE-FAIL

AUDIT-CLIENT-SERVICE

HP privileged subsystems such as FUP and SCF are known as Clients. The AUDIT-CLIENT-SERVICE parameter determines whether or not Safeguard will accept event information from these clients and write the event records into the Safeguard audit trail on their behalf.

It is important to note the following facts about client auditing:

Audit records from clients are not standardized. Each client's audit records have different content and a different format.

Clients might not create the same audit records with the same content from release to release.

Auditing HP clients will consume considerable system resources and add a large number of records to the Safeguard audit files.

Some of the Safeguard Global audit parameters also affect client auditing. When AUDIT-CLIENT-SERVICE is ON:

The Global AUDIT-PROCESS-ACCESS-PASS or AUDIT-PROCESS-ACCESS-FAIL attribute values determine whether or not Safeguard software will write audit records not only for Safeguard-protected process objects but also for client operations that pertain to processes and subprocesses.

The Global AUDIT-DEVICE-ACCESS-PASS or AUDIT-DEVICE-ACCESS-FAIL attribute values determine whether or not Safeguard software will write audit records not only for Safeguard-protected device objects but also for client operations that pertain to devices and subdevices.

BP-SAFEGARD-GLOBAL-29   AUDIT-CLIENT-SERVICE = OFF if OSS is *not* in use on the system.

In order to enable Safeguard auditing of OSS activity, the AUDIT-CLIENT-SERVICE parameter must be ON.

BP-SAFEGARD-GLOBAL-29   AUDIT-CLIENT-SERVICE = ON if OSS is in use on the system.

RISK   Turning AUDIT-CLIENT-SERVICE ON will generate a greatly increased number of auditable events and require more system resources to write the audit records.

AP-ADVICE-SAFEGARD-11   The system must have sufficient disk space to accommodate the increased size of the Safeguard audit trail(s)

AP-ADVICE-SAFEGARD-12   The system must have adequate system resources such as CPUs and memory to handle the increased amount of audit activity.

AUDIT-OBJECT-ACCESS{ -PASS | -FAIL }

The AUDIT-OBJECT-ACCESS-PASS and AUDIT-OBJECT-ACCESS-FAIL parameters determine whether or not successful or unsuccessful attempts to access *any* object will be audited. The value can be ALL, NONE, LOCAL, or REMOTE.

This global attribute *supplements* the audit parameters for the individual objects. If the parameter in the individual object's Protection Record is LOCAL and the Global Attribute is REMOTE, then both LOCAL and REMOTE access attempts will be audited.

The default value for both PASS and FAIL is NONE.

BP-SAFEGARD-GLOBAL-30   AUDIT-OBJECT-ACCESS-PASS = NONE

BP-SAFEGARD-GLOBAL-31   AUDIT-OBJECT-ACCESS-FAIL = ALL

RISK   Configuring Safeguard software to audit all system objects could cause system performance problems.

AP-ADVICE-SAFEGARD-13   The system must have adequate system resources such as CPUs and memory to handle the increased amount of audit activity.

AUDIT-OBJECT-MANAGE{ -PASS | -FAIL }

The AUDIT-MANAGE-PASS or AUDIT-MANAGE-FAIL parameters determine whether or not successful or unsuccessful attempts to create or manage Protection Records for any object will be audited. The value can be ALL, NONE, LOCAL, or REMOTE.

This global attribute *supplements* the audit parameter for the individual objects. If the parameter in the individual object's Protection Record is LOCAL and the Global Attribute is REMOTE, then both LOCAL and REMOTE management attempts will be audited.

The default value for both PASS and FAIL is NONE.

BP-SAFEGARD-GLOBAL-32   AUDIT-OBJECT-MANAGE-PASS = ALL

BP-SAFEGARD-GLOBAL-33   AUDIT-OBJECT-MANAGE-FAIL = ALL

How the Safeguard Subsystem Determines What to Audit

Auditing is specified with either Global attributes or in Protection Records for individual objects. For example, auditing for an individual disk file is specified in the disk file's Protection Record, but auditing for all disk files on the system is specified with global attributes. Settings specified in individual Protection Records *supercede* those in the Safeguard Globals in some instances and *supplement* them in others:

If a Global AUDIT attribute is NONE but ALL in an individual Protection Record, then events for the object being protected will be audited.

If a Global AUDIT attribute is ALL but NONE in an individual Protection Record, then events for the object being protected will not be audited.

However, if a Global AUDIT attribute is REMOTE but LOCAL in an individual Protection Record, or vice versa, then both LOCAL and REMOTE events will be audited.

Individual	Global→ ALL	LOCAL	REMOTE	NONE
ALL	Audit ALL	Audit ALL	Audit ALL	Audit ALL
LOCAL	Audit LOCAL	Audit LOCAL	Audit ALL	Audit LOCAL
REMOTE	Audit REMOTE	Audit ALL	Audit REMOTE	Audit REMOTE
NONE	No audit	No audit	No audit	No Audit

When an attempt is made to access a protected object, Safeguard software first checks the Protection Record for the target object to determine whether the user has the required authority to access the object.

If the user has the required permissions, the Safeguard subsystem allows the requested access and checks the value of the AUDIT-ACCESS-PASS attribute. If

AUDIT-ACCESS-PASS is specified, the successful access is recorded in the current audit file.

If the user lacks the required permissions, the Safeguard subsystem issues a security violation and checks the value of the AUDIT-ACCESS-FAIL attribute. If AUDIT-ACCESS-FAIL is specified, the unsuccessful access is recorded in the current audit file.

Safeguard Globals and Configuration Recap

The following is a recap of the Safeguard configurations that have been discussed throughout this section and may be addressed in other sections of this book. In order to locate these important settings for the Safeguard environment, this table has been placed here for reference.

Safeguard Global or Configuration	Safeguard Setting or Keyword	Value
SAFEGARD-CONFIG-01	SUPER.SUPER UNDENIABLE	YES
SAFEGARD-CONFIG-02	OBJECTTYPE OBJECTTYPE Exists	YES
SAFEGARD-CONFIG-03	OBJECTTYPE OBJECTTYPE owner should be SUPER.SUPER	YES
SAFEGARD-CONFIG-04	Audit Trail not on $SYSTEM	<> $SYSTEM
SAFEGARD-CONFIG-05	WRITE-THROUGH-CACHE	OFF
SAFEGARD-CONFIG-06	EOF-REFRESH	OFF
SAFEGARD-CONFIG-07	RECYCLE Audit Trails Mode	RECOVERY
SAFEGARD-GLOBAL-01	AUTHENTICATE-MAXIMUM-ATTEMPTS	3
SAFEGARD-GLOBAL-02	AUTHENTICATE-FAIL-TIMEOUT	60 sec
SAFEGARD-GLOBAL-03	AUTHENTICATE-FAIL-FREEZE	OFF
SAFEGARD-GLOBAL-04	PASSWORD-REQUIRED	OFF
SAFEGARD-GLOBAL-05	PASSWORD-HISTORY	10
SAFEGARD-GLOBAL-06	PASSWORD-ENCRYPT	ON
SAFEGARD-GLOBAL-07	PASSWORD-MINIMUM-LENGTH	6
SAFEGARD-GLOBAL-08	PASSWORD-MAY-CHANGE	7
SAFEGARD-GLOBAL-09	PASSWORD-EXPIRY-GRACE	15
SAFEGARD-GLOBAL-10	WARNING-MODE	OFF
SAFEGARD-GLOBAL-11	WARNING-FALLBACK-SECURITY	GUARDIAN

Safeguard Global or Configuration		
	Safeguard Setting or Keyword	**Value**
SAFEGARD-GLOBAL-12	DIRECTION-DEVICE	SUBDEVICE-FIRST
SAFEGARD-GLOBAL-13	CHECK-DEVICE	ON
SAFEGARD-GLOBAL-14	COMBINATION-DEVICE	FIRST-ACL
SAFEGARD-GLOBAL-15	CHECK-SUBDEVICE	ON
SAFEGARD-GLOBAL-16	ACL-REQUIRED-DEVICE	OFF
SAFEGARD-GLOBAL-17	DIRECTION-PROCESS	SUBPROCESS-FIRST
SAFEGARD-GLOBAL-18	CHECK-PROCESS	ON
SAFEGARD-GLOBAL-19	COMBINATION-PROCESS	FIRST-ACL
SAFEGARD-GLOBAL-20	CHECK-SUBPROCESS	ON
SAFEGARD-GLOBAL-21	ACL-REQUIRED-PROCESS	OFF
SAFEGARD-GLOBAL-22	DIRECTION-DISKFILE	FILENAME-FIRST
SAFEGARD-GLOBAL-23	CHECK-VOLUME	OFF
SAFEGARD-GLOBAL-24	COMBINATION-DISKFILE	FIRST-ACL
SAFEGARD-GLOBAL-25	CHECK-SUBVOLUME	ON
SAFEGARD-GLOBAL-26	ACL-REQUIRED-DISKFILE	OFF
SAFEGARD-GLOBAL-27	CHECK-FILENAME	ON
SAFEGARD-GLOBAL-28	CLEARONPURGE-DISKFILE	OFF
SAFEGARD-GLOBAL-29	AUDIT-CLIENT-SERVICE	OFF
SAFEGARD-GLOBAL-30	AUDIT-OBJECT-ACCESS-PASS	NONE
SAFEGARD-GLOBAL-31	AUDIT-OBJECT-ACCESS-FAIL	ALL
SAFEGARD-GLOBAL-32	AUDIT-OBJECT-MANAGE-PASS	ALL
SAFEGARD-GLOBAL-33	AUDIT-OBJECT-MANAGE-FAIL	ALL
SAFEGARD-GLOBAL-34	AUDIT-AUTHENTICATE-PASS	ALL
SAFEGARD-GLOBAL-35	AUDIT-AUTHENTICATE-FAIL	ALL
SAFEGARD-GLOBAL-36	AUDIT-SUBJECT-MANAGE-PASS	ALL
SAFEGARD-GLOBAL-37	AUDIT-SUBJECT-MANAGE-FAIL	ALL
SAFEGARD-GLOBAL-38	AUDIT-DEVICE-ACCESS-PASS	NONE
SAFEGARD-GLOBAL-39	AUDIT-DEVICE-ACCESS-FAIL	ALL
SAFEGARD-GLOBAL-40	AUDIT-DEVICE-MANAGE-PASS	ALL
SAFEGARD-GLOBAL-41	AUDIT-DEVICE-MANAGE-FAIL	ALL

Safeguard Global or Configuration

	Safeguard Setting or Keyword	Value
SAFEGARD-GLOBAL-42	AUDIT-PROCESS-ACCESS-PASS	NONE
SAFEGARD-GLOBAL-43	AUDIT-PROCESS-ACCESS-FAIL	ALL
SAFEGARD-GLOBAL-44	AUDIT-PROCESS-MANAGE-PASS	ALL
SAFEGARD-GLOBAL-45	AUDIT-PROCESS-MANAGE-FAIL	ALL
SAFEGARD-GLOBAL-46	AUDIT-DISKFILE-ACCESS-PASS	NONE
SAFEGARD-GLOBAL-47	AUDIT-DISKFILE-ACCESS-FAIL	ALL
SAFEGARD-GLOBAL-48	AUDIT-DISKFILE-MANAGE-PASS	ALL
SAFEGARD-GLOBAL-49	AUDIT-DISKFILE-MANAGE-FAIL	ALL
SAFEGARD-GLOBAL-50	CMON	ON
SAFEGARD-GLOBAL-51	CMONERROR	ACCEPT
SAFEGARD-GLOBAL-52	CMONTIMEOUT	30 SEC
SAFEGARD-GLOBAL-53	BLINDLOGON	ON
SAFEGARD-GLOBAL-54	NAMELOGON	ON
SAFEGARD-GLOBAL-55	TERMINAL-EXCLUSIVE-ACCESS	OFF
SAFEGARD-GLOBAL-56	CI-CPU	default
SAFEGARD-GLOBAL-57	CI-LIB	default
SAFEGARD-GLOBAL-58	CI-PROG (it will default to $SYSTEM.SYSTEM.TACL)	default
SAFEGARD-GLOBAL-59	CI-SWAP	default
SAFEGARD-GLOBAL-60	CI-PRI	145
SAFEGARD-GLOBAL-61	CI-PARAM-TEXT	default

3

Authentication; User Administration

The joke goes that the only secure computer is the one without users. This section outlines the principles for securing the system, even with users! These principles include a good user schema based on the principles of Least Privilege, Separation of Duties and Individual Accountability.

User Administration

This chapter discusses administering userids and aliases on an HP NonStop server.

Userids

Users are defined by assigning a unique user name and number to each user:

<GroupName>.<MemberName>

<GroupNumber>,<MemberNumber>

The Group Name or Number identifies the user's administrative group. The Member Name or Number identifies the user within the group. The combination must be unique for a single system and unique over the network of systems if the user will have access to multiple nodes.

Groups

On the HP NonStop server, there are two types of user groups:

Administrative

File-sharing

Administrative Groups

Administrative Groups exist primarily for user management but can also be used for file-sharing in Safeguard software . Administrative Groups are used in both the Guardian and Safeguard environments.

Administrative Group Names are made up of 1 to 8 alphanumeric characters. The first character must be a letter. Groups with numbers ranging from 0 to 255 may be used as Administrative Groups.

Administrative Groups can be thought of as Job Function Groups because they are the primary unit that categorizes a given user's job function. Users with similar job descriptions and tasks require the same access to system resources. They should be given userids in the same Administrative Group.

File-sharing Groups

File-Sharing Groups can only be created in the Safeguard software. They are used to grant access to disk files and other objects on the system. They are used primarily in the OSS environment but can be used in the Guardian environment.

Groups numbered above 255 exist solely for file-sharing purposes.

Members

Member Names are made up of 1 to 8 alphanumeric characters. The first character must be a letter. Member Numbers must be between 0 and 255.

A secure system requires a well organized and well thought out userid schema. Users must be given userids in appropriate administrative groups and uniquely identified to the system.

In general, userids can be broken down into two categories:

>   Personal IDs
>   Privileged IDs

Privileged IDs fall into 3 categories:

>   IDs with inherent Guardian privileges
>   Application Owner IDs
>   Job-Function IDs

Privileged IDs will be discussed later in this section.

Aliases

Aliases are only available in Safeguard environments.

An alias is an alternate user name that can be used to log on to the system. Each alias has its own Alias Authentication Record and set of user attributes. Users may be assigned one or more aliases.

Alias names can contain between 1 and 32 alphanumeric characters. Some special characters such as dots (.), hyphens (-) and underscores (_) can also be included in alias names.

Unlike userids, which TACL automatically upshifts, aliases are *case sensitive*.

AP-ADVICE-ALIAS-01   Use good naming conventions when creating aliases. If a two or three character job-function descriptor is used at the beginning of each alias name, researching alias configuration and audit activity is easier.

AP-ADVICE-ALIAS-02   Don't create alias names that look like Guardian userids. It makes it difficult to read audit and other user-related reports. In general, don't make aliases all upper case and don't include dots (.).

For example, use oper-joe or operjoe instead of OPER.JOE.

Each alias has a specific underlying userid, for example oper-joe is mapped to 210,5. Each underlying userid can have multiple aliases mapped to it.

RISK   Aliases *cannot* be included in Safeguard Protection Records. An alias's access to system resources is based solely on that of the underlying userid.

RISK   An alias gains all of its underlying userid's privileges.

RISK   Safeguard software provides limited auditing of alias activity.

Aliases to privileged userids such as SUPER.SUPER or the application owner IDs should be used only as a last resort. The most secure way to grant the necessary access to users who must 'act' as a privileged userid in order to perform their job function is with a third party access control product which can make access to resources much more granular and provide comprehensive auditing.

3P-ADVICE-ALIAS-01   If aliases are required, use third party products to both limit their privileges and provide more extensive auditing.

Single SignOn

Single-SignOn provides an employee with a single userid that is valid on multiple platforms. In this instance, the userid on the NonStop server would need to match some corporate standard, such as an employee number.

Because such userids are unlikely to fit the NonStop server's userid naming conventions, the only way to implement Single-SignOn is with aliases. Such aliases can be only be implemented securely if:

Each alias has a unique underlying userid.

The underlying userids are assigned to appropriate administrative groups based on the job function.

The underlying userids are not Privileged IDs such as SUPER.SUPER or an Application Owner.

If the alias will be the primary ID, the underlying userid can be frozen.

Safeguard rules are used to grant the underlying userids appropriate access.

Such aliases can be implemented securely by creating an individual userid, in the appropriate administrative group, for each user. The alias is then created for this individual userid. The underlying userid can then be frozen to prevent anyone logging onto it, and the alias used as the primary ID. This way, the user's privileges can be restricted, based on the underlying userid, which can be used in Safeguard Protection Records.

Privileged IDs

Certain userids have special privileges which make them more powerful and, therefore, potentially more dangerous:

IDs with inherent Guardian privileges

Application Owner Userids

Job Function Userids

On secure systems, use of these Privileged IDs by individual users should be tightly controlled.

Userids With Inherent Guardian privileges

The HP NonStop server Guardian operating system grants special privileges to several userids. These privileges will be granted the moment the userids are created. The privileges can only be limited by implementing Safeguard software. These IDs are:

NULL.NULL (0,0)

NULL.FTP (0,15)

anonymous (0,15)

FTP (0,15)

Group Manager IDs (*,255)

SUPER group IDs (255,*)

SUPER.SUPER (255,255)

NULL.NULL

The NULL.NULL's user number is 0,0. This userid is provided on the HP SUT tapes as an owner of a logged off TACL process.

RISK   NULL.NULL can stop any process with PAID of 0,0, i.e. a logged off TACL.

If NULL.NULL cannot be deleted, mitigate the risk of having it on the system by taking the following steps:

BP-USER-NULLNULL-01   Rename the 0,0 userid to something other than NULL.NULL.

BP-USER-NULLNULL-02   Expire or FREEZE the 0,0 userid so it can't be used to logon to the system.

Group Manager IDs

The Group Manager is the 255 member of any group. Some of the risks associated with Group Manager IDs are:

RISK   Group Managers can ADD, ALTER and DELETE userids in their own group if Safeguard software it not present.

RISK   Group Managers can 'log down' to the userid of any member of the same group without a password unless prevented by Safeguard software.

RISK   Group Managers can PROGID any program owned by a group member.

RISK   In Safeguard, the group manager of the Primary Owner of any object's Protection Record can also modify any Safeguard Protection Records owned by members of the same group.

It is not unusual for a Group Manager userid to be either an Application Owner or Job Function ID. Please refer to the section on Application Owner IDs later in this chapter.

SUPER Group IDs

A SUPER group member is any userid in group number 255. Some of the risks associated with SUPER Group member userids are:

RISK   SUPER Group members can set and reset the system time.

RISK   SUPER Group members can typically manage all jobs in the SPOOLER, regardless of who owns them.

RISK   SUPER Group members can typically manage all jobs in PERUSE, regardless of who owns them.

RISK   SUPER Group members can perform all commands within SCF.

SUPER.SUPER

The SUPER group number is 255. The Group Manager's member number is 255, therefore, 255,255 is commonly referred to as SUPER.SUPER or the SUPERID. When an HP NonStop server is shipped, the SUT tape assumes the existence of SUPER.SUPER. If the userid doesn't exist when the tape is used, it is created.

The SUPER.SUPER userid is provided on the HP SUT tapes

RISK   SUPER.SUPER can log on as any other userid *without a password* unless explicitly denied in SAFEGUARD.

RISK   SUPER.SUPER can ADD, ALTER or DELETE any userid in the Guardian and Safeguard environments if SUPER.SUPER is configured UNDENIABLE.

RISK   SUPER.SUPER can READ, WRITE, EXECUTE, or PURGE any file on the system.

RISK   SUPER.SUPER can stop any process.

RISK   SUPER.SUPER can debug any process.

RISK   SUPER.SUPER can run any program or utility.

RISK   SUPER.SUPER can bring up or take down any device.

RISK   SUPER.SUPER can LICENSE any program.

RISK   SUPER.SUPER can PROGID any program.

RISK   SUPER.SUPER can manage all jobs in the Spooler, regardless of ownership.

RISK   SUPER.SUPER can manage all jobs in PERUSE, regardless of owner.

RISK   The operating system runs as SUPER.SUPER.

RISK   Safeguard, Expand and most other system processes run as
SUPER.SUPER.

By default, the inherent abilities of SUPER.SUPER are local only. Privileges on
one system do not extend to another system. A user logged on to a local system as
SUPER.SUPER is not automatically accorded SUPER.SUPER privileges on a remote
system.

The user name SUPER.SUPER is not required. Some Corporate Security Policies
and Standards mandate that the name be changed to a name not readily known to
potential hackers. On a new system, the name should be changed:

After the Security Admin userid has been created

Before any other userids have been created in the SUPER Group

Before any major processes are started.

On an existing system, the change is more problematic because all SUPER group
IDs must be deleted before the group name can be changed. This should only be
undertaken after extensive thought and preparation.

Considerations for Reducing the Risks Associated with SUPER.SUPER

The SUPER.SUPER ID is used for system configuration and to resolve system emergencies. It is not intended for routine operational use. Without special mechanisms
provided by Safeguard software, SUPER.SUPER has unlimited access to all resources
on a local system.

Although SUPER.SUPER is not required for day-to-day operations,
SUPER.SUPER might be required to:

LICENSE object files

PROGID object files to SUPER.SUPER

Manage userids if Safeguard software is not installed

Run BACKUP and RESTORE

Resolve certain emergencies

Perform System INSTALLs

LICENSE or PROGID Object Files

3P-ACCESS-USER-01   A third party access control product can be used to
grant authorized users access to FUP running as SUPER.SUPER. The use of the

LICENSE and PROGID commands should be restricted for all but authorized users.

3P-OBJSEC-USER-01   A third party object security product can grant the LICENSE and PROGID authorities to other users on a file-by-file basis.

Please refer to the Gazette section on LICENSED Files and PROGID'd Files for detailed information on securing these files.

Manage Userids

If Safeguard is not used to manage userids, SUPER.SUPER is needed to:

ADD new user groups

ADD userids to administrative groups that do not have a group manager ID

DELETE userids from administrative groups that do not have a group manager ID.

RISK   If Safeguard software is not installed, recovering the SUPER.SUPER userid if it is deleted from the system can be difficult. There are only two options:

If no CIIN file was specified when the system was generated, a system load can be performed from the System Console. The operator becomes SUPER.SUPER and can then ADD the SUPER.SUPER userid to the USERID file.

If a CIIN file was specified when the system was generated, a system load from a tape might need to be performed. The USERID file on the tape contains an entry for SUPER.SUPER.

BP-USER-POLICY-01   Use Safeguard software to manage userids.

Managing Processes

AP-PROCESS-SAFE-01   Use Safeguard software to selectively grant the ability to stop processes (both NAMED and UNNAMED) to an appropriate set of users.

3P-PROCESS-SPECIAL-01   Third party process control products provide the capability of delegating to the appropriate users, such as an operator, the ability to manage processes owned by other users, such as application Pathway servers. These products also provide auditing of the process management activities they control.

Resolve Emergencies

> **3P-ACCESS-USER-01**   A third party access control product can be used to grant authorized users granular access to utilities running as SUPER.SUPER. These products also provide auditing of the activities they control.

BACKUP and RESTORE

Because only SUPER.SUPER has inherent READ access to every file on the system, BACKUP and RESTORE are usually run as SUPER.SUPER. There are three solutions to running BACKUP and RESTORE without users logging on as SUPER.SUPER. They are listed in order of preference:

1. Third party access control product:

    3P-ACCESS-BACKUP-01   Use a third party access control product to allow the users responsible for creating backups the ability to run BACKUP as SUPER.SUPER.

    3P-ACCESS-RESTORE-01   Use a third party access control product to allow the users responsible for restoring files the ability to run RESTORE as SUPER.SUPER.

2. PROGID'd BACKUP and RESTORE object files:

    Create copies of the BACKUP and RESTORE and PROGID these copies to SUPER.SUPER.

    RISK   PROGID'd programs must be secured against unauthorized use.

    AP-ADVICE-BACKUP-01   The PROGID'd copies of BACKUP and RESTORE should not reside in $SYSTEM.SYSTEM, $SYSTEM.SYSnn or any subvolume in the PMSEARCHLIST that is shared by all users.

    AP-ADVICE-RESTORE-01   The PROGID'd copies of BACKUP and RESTORE should be secured so that only users authorized to create backup tapes can execute them.

3. Safeguard Protection Records that grant read access to every file:

    Create a Job Function ID, such as SUPER.BACKUP, that will be used to run the BACKUP and RESTORE programs. Grant this ID READ access to every file on the system via Safeguard software .

    RISK   Maintenance of Safeguard Protection Records for every file on the system is impractical.

System Install

Normally SUPER.SUPER is required to perform a system installation or update. However, if the INSTALL program has PROGID set to the SUPER.SUPER, other users can run INSTALL.

On pre-G-series systems, secure the PROGID'd INSTALL so only the appropriate SUPER Group members have EXECUTE authority. (Remember that, in this instance, file-sharing members of the SUPER Group also receive EXECUTE authority).

Application-Owner IDs

Application-Owner IDs provide the "place holder" ownership of all application objects on a system. Each application should be assigned the following four userids:

AP-USER-APPOWNER-01   An Object code owner

AP-USER-APPOWNER-02   A Source code owner

AP-USER-APPOWNER-03   A Database owner

AP-USER-APPOWNER-04   An Executing (Pathway) owner which runs the application and generates batch jobs.

This schema provides clear separation of ownership for the file-based entities as well as the running application processes that make up the on-line and batch. Under this configuration, control over each component of an application is divisible along the lines of those four userids, each restricted to the required privileges based on Least Privilege and Separation of Duties.

For example, the Executing ID WRITES to the database, but the database files are owned by the Database Owner, who alone can configure them. The Executing ID executes the object code but can't PURGE or ALTER it, and has no access to source code.

Some companies choose to have a single userid own the source code for *all* the applications.

RISK   Having a single source code owner makes it more likely that the source code files for one application might be inadvertently accessed by developers for another application.

AP-ADVICE-APPOWNER-01   Use consistent naming conventions to make the separate source code files more obvious to the users and easier to secure.

Some companies choose to have a single userid own (configure) the databases for *all* applications.

RISK   Having a single database owner makes it more likely that the databases for one application might be inadvertently accessed by another application.

AP-ADVICE-APPOWNER-02   Use consistent naming conventions to make the separate databases more obvious to the users and easier to secure.

All user access to the production data, the production Pathway, and the Production jobstreams must be limited in scope and audited.

Job-Function IDs

Access rights to system objects are allocated to the Job Function userids. Job Function userids are created for each functional area defined within the organization, and access for each Job Function userid is assigned to System and Application Owner objects based on their Job Function definition and specific needs. Some appropriate Job Functions might be:

AUDIT

CHANGE CONTROL

DEVELOPMENT (by application area)

FILE TRANSFER ANALYSTS

FILE TRANSFER OPERATORS

NETWORK/COMM SUPPORT

OPERATIONS MANAGEMENT

QUALITY ASSURANCE (by application area)

JOB SCHEDULING

SECURITY

SYSTEM MANAGEMENT

For example:

The Security Admin userid exists to own security tools and security objects such as USER Records and Safeguard Protection Records.

The RDF manager ID exists to own all the RDF programs, processes and databases.

The Change Control manager ID exists to transfer application code and configuration files from development to production.

The NonStop TMF manager ID exists to own all the TMF programs, processes and databases.

Securing Privileged Userids

AP-USER-PRIVLEGE-01   No users should be assigned a Privileged ID as a personal userid

RISK   If users can log directly on as a shared Privileged ID, there is no accountability for any of their actions. The audit trails for Safeguard software and any third party Security products will show only that the activity was performed by a Privileged ID, not the user who was working as SUPER. SUPER.

AP-USER-PRIVLEGE-02   No user should be assigned NULL.NULL as a personal userid. NULL.NULL should not exist or be FROZEN.

AP-USER-PRIVLEGE-03   No users should be assigned a Group Manager ID as a personal userid.

AP-USER-PRIVLEGE-04   No users should be assigned userid in the SUPER Group as a personal userid.

AP-USER-PRIVLEGE-05   No users should be assigned SUPER.SUPER as a personal userid.

AP-USER-PRIVLEGE-06   No users should be assigned an Application Owner ID as a personal userid.

AP-USER-PRIVLEGE-07   No users should be assigned a Job-Function ID as a personal userid.

AP-USER-PRIVLEGE-08   Privileged IDs should never be shared.

AP-USER-POLICY-01   Users should not be able to logon as any Privileged ID except for emergencies or pre-approved reasons.

AP-USER-PRIVLEGE-09   Privileged IDs should be FROZEN unless applications will not run with a FROZEN owner.

AP-USER-PRIVLEGE-10   All Privileged IDs should be treated as 'check out' or 'firecall' IDs.

AP-USER-PRIVLEGE-11   When the Privileged ID userid has been 'checked out,' the password should be set to expire after a short but reasonable time.

AP-USER-PRIVLEGE-12   When the Privileged ID userid has been 'checked in,' the password should be reset and locked up again.

AP-USER-POLICY-02   Privileged ID's passwords must expire and be changed at regular intervals.

AP-USER-POLICY-03   The only written copy of any Privileged ID's password must be kept under lock and key.

3P-CMON-PRIVLEGE-01   Use CMON to prevent users from directly logging onto the system as a Privileged ID.

3P-ACCESS-PRIVLEGE-01   Third party access-control software should be used to grant granular access to any Privileged ID for users who require these privileges in order to perform their jobs. These products provide command restrictions within utilities and programs as well as comprehensive auditing of the activities they mediate.

3P-PROCESS-PRIVLEGE-01   Third party process control software should be used to grant granular management of processes running as any Privileged ID for users who require these privileges in order to perform their jobs. These products provide comprehensive auditing of the activities they control.

BP-SAFEGARD-OBJTYPE-02   Safeguard OBJECTTYPE Records should be created to control the user management privileges of any Group Managers.

	Discovery Questions	Look here:
USER-POLICY-01	Is Safeguard software used to Manage userids?	Policy
USER-POLICY-02	Are procedures in place to authorize and document the use of all the Privileged IDs as "check out" or "firecall" IDs?	Policy
USER-POLICY-03	Are the Privileged IDs passwords changed at regular intervals?	Policy
USER-POLICY-04	Are the Privileged IDs passwords stored in a safe or other secure place?	Policy
CMON-PRIVILEGE-01	If users are allowed to logon as any Privileged ID, are 'stepped' logons enforced with CMON?	Policy
USER-PRIVLEGE-01	Are any Privileged IDs personal userids?	Policy USERS
USER-PRIVLEGE-02	If the 0,0 userid exists, is it called NULL.NULL?	USERS Safecom
USER-PRIVLEGE-03	Are any Group Manager ids used as personal userids?	USERS Safecom
USER-PRIVLEGE-04	Are any Super Group Manager ids used as personal userids?	USERS Safecom
USER-PRIVLEGE-05	Is SUPER.SUPER used as a personal userid?	USERS Safecom
USER-PRIVLEGE-06	Are any Application Group Owner ids used as personal userids?	USERS Safecom

	Discovery Questions	Look here:
USER-PRIVLEGE-07	Are any Job Function ids used as personal userids?	USERS Safecom
USER-PRIVLEGE-08	Are any of the Privileged IDs shared IDs?	USERS Safeguard
USER-PRIVLEGE-09	Are all the Privileged IDs on the system FROZEN?	USERS Safeguard
USER-PRIVLEGE-10	Are all the Privileged IDs 'checkout' IDs?	USERS Safeguard
USER-PRIVLEGE-11	Are all the Privileged ID's passwords set to expire after a short interval?	USERS Safeguard
USER-PRIVLEGE-12	Are all the Privileged ID's passwords reset after 'checkin'?	USERS Safeguard

Personal Userids

Every user who needs to access the HP NonStop server must have a personal userid. The userids should be assigned based on their responsibilities and the tasks they must perform.

AP-USER-POLICY-04   Each individual who must access the HP NonStop server should be provided with a personal userid.

AP-USER-POLICY-05   In order to provide proper individual accountability, users must only logon to the HP NonStop server with their individual userid.

AP-USER-POLICY-06   If a user's job requires access to the privileges of more than one job function group, he must be assigned a userid in each of the appropriate administrative groups.

RISK   Managing passwords for multiple userids is cumbersome and time consuming for users.

RISK   Users frequently write down their passwords if there are too many to remember.

3P-USER-ADMIN-01   Third party password quality programs can help to keep passwords for multiple systems in sync.

3P-USER-ADMIN-01   Third party access-control products make it possible for users who 'wear several hats' to do their jobs with a single userid. The products can be used to grant any extended privileges necessary to users such as operators or system support. The products also provide auditing of the activities they mediate.

	Discovery Questions	Look here:
USER-POLICY-05	Does each user have an individual userid?	Policy
USER-POLICY-05	Do users log on with shared userids?	Policy
USER-POLICY-06	Do users logon with their specified userid?	Policy
USER-POLICY-07	Do users with multiple job functions use separate and distinguishable userids for those functions?	Policy

Administering Userids

Procedures To Request New Userids

AP-USER-POLICY-07   The security department should design and distribute forms for new userid or alias requests. The forms should be filled out by the manager who will be directing the new user's work. The request should include the new user's job description and the access they will need to the HP NonStop servers. This will help the security staff to create the new userid in the correct User Group with the correct access to system resources.

Procedures To Delete Obsolete Userids

AP-USER-POLICY-08   The security department should work with the Human Resources department to create a mechanism for notifying the security staff when personnel with access to the HP NonStop server leave the company or transfer to a new job requiring different access, so that the now obsolete userid can be deleted from the system as soon as possible.

Orphaned files

RISK   Orphaned files take up disk space.

RISK   If userids are recycled, any files owned by an obsolete userid that are left on the system will automatically be accessible to the next user to be assigned the recycled userid.

The security department should work with the System Manager and department managers to create a mechanism for eliminating orphaned files.

AP-USER-POLICY-09   The Corporate Security Policy and Standards should mandate a periodic review of the system for orphaned files.

When a userid is deleted from the system, a list of all the files owned by the userid should be generated and sent to the user's manager who should determine the disposition of the files:

The manager should indicate which files can be deleted and which should be retained and indicate the userid that should take ownership of the files being retained.

The security department should set a time limit for department managers to reply to the request about the disposition of the files.

Procedures should be in place for a 'default' disposition of the files if the department managers don't reply.

Procedures should be in place to follow up on the disposition of orphaned files to be sure that they have either been removed or given to another userid.

AP-USER-POLICY-10   The Corporate Security Policy or Standards should determine whether the security department or the system manager group will be responsible for performing the task of giving the files to the designated userid.

	Discovery Questions	Look here:
USER-POLICY-08	Is the creation of alias names controlled?	Policy
USER-POLICY-09	Is the Security Administrator notified when a person leaves the company or is transferred in job function?	Policy
USER-POLICY-10	Is the system periodically reviewed for orphaned files?	Policy Fileinfo
USER-POLICY-11	Who is responsible for performing the disposition of the orphaned files?	Policy

Who Can Manage Userids

The Security products in place on the system determine who can manage users.

	Guardian	Safeguard *Without* OBJECTTYPE USER	Safeguard *With* OBJECTTYPE USER
ADD	255,255 and user's group mgr	255,255, grp mgr[1]	Any user with CREATE authority in OBJECTTYPE record
ALTER	255,255 user's group mgr	255,255, User Record owner, owner's grp mgr	255,255, User Record owner, owner's grp mgr
DELETE	255,255 user's group mgr	255,255, User Record owner, owner's grp mgr	255,255, User Record owner, owner's grp mgr

	Guardian	Safeguard *Without* OBJECTTYPE USER	Safeguard *With* OBJECTTYPE USER
FREEZE	N/A	255,255, User Record owner, owner's grp mgr	255,255, User Record owner, owner's grp mgr
THAW	N/A	255,255, User Record owner, owner's grp mgr	255,255, User Record owner, owner's grp mgr
INFO	Users who can EXECUTE the Users Program	255,255, User Record owner, owner's grp mgr	255,255, User Record owner, owner's grp mgr

[1] - Once the userid's Administrative Group exists. (Only 255,255 can add a group.mgr.)

Managing Userids In the Guardian System

Guardian security allows only local Group Managers and SUPER.SUPER to ADD, DELETE or ALTER userids. SUPER.SUPER can ADD members to any GROUP whether it already exists or not. Group Managers are restricted to managing userids in their own GROUP.

ADDUSER and DELUSER

If Safeguard software is not in use on the system, then the ADDUSER program is used to create userids and DELUSER is used to delete them.

How the ADDUSER and DELUSER programs are secured depends on who is allowed to perform this function as defined by the Corporate Security Policy. See ADDUSER and DELUSER sections in the Gazette for a detailed discussion on securing these programs.

RPASSWRD

If Safeguard software is not in use on the system, then the RPASSWRD program is used to create remote passwords for userids.

How this program is secured depends on the Corporate Security Policy and whether or not Safeguard software is in use on the systems. See the RPASSWRD section in the Gazette for a detailed discussion on securing the program.

The DEFAULT Program

The DEFAULT program is used to set the default subvolume and default file security vector for each userid.

How the DEFAULT program is secured depends on the Corporate Security Policy and Standards. See the DEFAULT section in the Gazette for a detailed discussion on securing the program.

The USERS Program

The USERS program is used to view information about userids.

How the USERS program is secured depends on the Corporate Security Policy and Standards. See the USERS section in the Gazette for a detailed discussion on securing the program.

Managing Userids With the Safeguard Subsystem

Safeguard software enhances control of userids and adds the ability to configure aliases on the HP NonStop server.

Safeguard software considers userids to be objects. Like other objects, the characteristics of individual userids are maintained in USER Protection Records, referred to hereafter as User Records. The following items affect Safeguard user configuration:

User OBJECTTYPE

User-related Safeguard Global Parameters

User Records

The USER OBJECTTYPE

An OBJECTTYPE Protection Record controls who is allowed to CREATE Protection Records for individual objects of that particular Object Class. The User OBJECTTYPE, therefore, is used to restrict who is allowed to CREATE User and Alias Records. Please refer to Part Two: Safeguard Subsystem for more information on OBJECTTYPES.

Any local SUPER Group member can create the User OBJECTTYPE record unless a specific list of users has been specified within the Protection Record for the OBJECTTYPE OBJECTTYPE Protection Record.

BP-SAFEGARD-CONFIG-02   The OBJECTTYPE OBJECTTYPE Protection Record should be used to restrict who can create the other OBJECTTYPE Records.

Any user granted create (C) in the Protection Record of the USER OBJECTTYPE record can ADD userids.

Any user granted ownership (O) in the Protection Record of a USER can ALTER or DELETE the user.

BP-SAFEGARD-CONFIG-04 Only members of the Security Group and SUPER.SUPER should be authorized to CREATE, ALTER or DELETE userids.

BP-USER-OBJTYPE-01 The USER OBJECTTYPE should be created.

BP-USER-OBJTYPE-02 Security.Admin should be granted both OWN and CREATE in the USER OBJECTTYPE Protection Record.

Userid/Alias-Related Safeguard Global Parameters

The User-related Global Parameters not discussed elsewhere in the handbook are:

Audit Parameters

Command Interpreter Parameters

OSS Parameters

The following user-related Safeguard Globals are discussed in Part Four under LOGON.

NAMELOGON

BLINDLOGON

TERMINAL-EXCLUSIVE-ACCESS

AUTHENTICATE-MAXIMUM-ATTEMPTS

AUTHENTICATE-FAIL-TIMEOUT

AUTHENTICATE-FAIL-FREEZE

The following user-related Safeguard Globals are discussed in Password Management.

PASSWORD-REQUIRED

PASSWORD-HISTORY

PASSWORD-ENCRYPT

PASSWORD-MINIMUM-LENGTH

PASSWORD-MAY-CHANGE

PASSWORD-EXPIRY-GRACE

Command Interpreter Attributes

The Command Interpreter (CI) parameter determines the program that Safeguard software will start after it has authenticated the user *at a Safeguard-controlled terminal.* The remaining CI parameters set specific characteristics of the program. *If no entry is made for CI-PROG, the other CI-parameters will be ignored.*

CIs can be configured in three places:

> User Records
>
> Safeguard Terminal Records
>
> Safeguard Global Parameters

Safeguard software searches for a CI specification in the following order: User Record, Terminal Definition Record and, finally, the Safeguard Globals. The *first* specification found during the search is the CI that is started after user authentication. Therefore, *a command interpreter specified in a user authentication record always takes precedence* over one specified in a Terminal Definition Record or the Safeguard global record.

If no CI is specified in the user authentication record or in the Terminal Definition Record, the CI defined in the Safeguard Globals is used. If no CI is specified globally, then the CI started is $SYSTEM.SYSTEM.TACL.

CI-PROG [<program-file name>]

The CI-PROG parameter determines the command interpreter that Safeguard software will start after it has authenticated the user at a Safeguard-controlled terminal. The <program-file name> is the name of the command interpreter's object file. It must be a local file. This value is frequently $SYSTEM.SYSTEM.TACL.

If no entry is made for CI-PROG, the rest of the CI parameters will be ignored.

CI-LIB [lib-filename]

The CI-LIB parameter determines the library file to be used with the command interpreter that is started when this user is authenticated at a Safeguard terminal. The <lib-filename> must be a local file name. If <lib-filename> is omitted, no library file is used.

If no entry is made for CI-PROG, the CI-LIB parameter will be ignored.

CI-CPU [cpu-number | ANY]

Determines the CPU in which Safeguard software will start the command interpreter. If ANY is specified, any available CPU may be used. If <cpu-number> is omitted, any CPU may be used.

If no entry is made for CI-PROG, the CI-CPU parameter will be ignored.

CI-NAME [process-name]

Determines the process name that Safeguard software will apply to the specified command interpreter process. The <process-name> must be a local process name. If the <process-name> is omitted, Safeguard software will generate the process name.

If no entry is made for CI-PROG, the CI-NAME parameter will be ignored.

CI-SWAP [$ <volume name> [.<subvol.filename>]]

Determines the name of the volume or file to be used as the swap volume or file for the specified command interpreter. The <volume name> must be a local volume name. If <volume name> is omitted, the configured system volume is used.

If no entry is made for CI-PROG, the CI-SWAP parameter will be ignored.

CI-PRI [priority]

Determines the priority at which Safeguard software will start the specified command interpreter. If the priority is omitted, the process will run at the same priority as Safeguard, which is determined by the value of the CI-PRI parameter in the Safeguard's configuration record.

RISK If this parameter is not set, or the Safeguard global for CI-PRI is not set, then the process will be started at 199.

BP-SAFEGARD-GLOBAL-60 CI-PRI should be 150 or less

CI-PARAM-TEXT [startup-param-text]

Determines the data to be supplied as the startup message text for the command interpreter specified by CI-PROG. If the CI-PARAM-TEXT attribute is specified, it must be the last attribute in the command string. If <startup-param-text> is omitted, the string is set to null (no text supplied in the startup message).

If no entry is made for CI-PROG, the CI-PARAM-TEXT parameter will be ignored.

Userid/Alias Record Attributes

Numerous parameters in the User Record have security implications and the settings should be determined by the Corporate Security Policy and Standards. These are:

OWNER

USER EXPIRES

USER STATUS

GUARDIAN DEFAULT VOLUME

GUARDIAN DEFAULT SECURITY

SUBJECT DEFAULT PROTECTION

Command Interpreter Attributes

OSS-Specific Attributes

Audit-Related Parameters

The following password-related User Parameters are discussed later in Password Administration:

PASSWORD-EXPIRES

PASSWORD-EXPIRY-GRACE

PASSWORD-MAY-CHANGE

PASSWORD-MUST-CHANGE

User Record Ownership

BP-USER-ADMIN-02   All Safeguard User and Alias Records should be owned by a single Security Admin userid. This is the only way to guarantee that the Security Admin userid can view all existing Users and Aliases on the system.

RISK   If only Security.Admin is allowed to ALTER userids, there is a risk that the Security.Admin's User Record might be frozen or expired, making it impossible for someone to logon with the userid in an emergency.

BP-SAFEGARD-CONFIG-03   The Security Admin ID itself should be owned by SUPER.SUPER, so that SUPER.SUPER can reset Security.Admin's password, thaw the user record, or alter its expiration date if it should become necessary.

USER-EXPIRES

The USER-EXPIRES parameter determines the date that the userid or alias will expire. Once a userid is expired, no one can use it to access the system.

The userid can be reactivated by changing the USER-EXPIRES attribute to a future date.

RISK If both date and time are omitted when the ALTER command is issued, the USER- EXPIRES date is set to NONE, and the userid will never expire.

AP-USER-CONFIG-01 All non-employees should have a value set in the USER-EXPIRES parameter that corresponds with their need.

Frozen/Thawed

When a userid or alias is frozen, it cannot be used to logon.

RISK If Safeguard software is down for any reason, FROZEN userids (though still frozen) behave as if they are thawed.

Guardian Default Volume

The Guardian Default Volume parameter determines the volume and subvolume where the user's TACL session will begin.

RISK If no GUARDIAN DEFAULT VOLUME is entered when a user record is added, Safeguard software assigns the default value of $SYSTEM.NOSUBVOL.

BP-USER-CONFIG-01 Each user should have a unique GUARDIAN DEFAULT VOLUME to prevent the sharing of TACLCSTM and other *CSTM files.

BP-USER-CONFIG-02 The GUARDIAN DEFAULT VOLUME should not be on the $SYSTEM disk. No personal files should exist on the $SYSTEM disk.

Guardian Default Security

This attribute is used to designate the default security for files created by the user.

Such assignments should be consistent with the organization's policies. The safest (and most restrictive) approach in the Guardian environment is to set all user defaults to local owner for all permissions (that is, OOOO). Then only deliberate action can make a new file available to users other than the owner, the owner's group manager, or SUPER.SUPER (if SUPER.SUPER is not configured UNDENIABLE).

Often, however, certain groups of users, such as the security staff, developers and system technical support, share many of their files. For these users, the Guardian Default Security might allow their group read and/or execute (GOGO or NUNU).

AP-USER-CONFIG-02   The Security Policy should include the appropriate Guardian Default Security settings for each user group in the organization.

Changing Default Security

Whether or not Safeguard software is installed, users can change their default security using the DEFAULT program if they have execute access to the DEFAULT object file. A user's group manager or SUPER.SUPER can also change the user's default security string, by logging onto that user's userid if the Safeguard Global PASSWORD-REQUIRED is OFF.

AP-USER-CONFIG-03   The Security Policy should dictate whether or not users are allowed to alter their default security.

Subject Default Protection

The DEFAULT PROTECTION parameter defines the Safeguard Diskfile Protection Record that will be automatically created for each file the user creates.

The default Protection Record is defined like any other diskfile Protection Record, specifying the Protection Record owner, ACL and audit parameters.

If no DEFAULT PROTECTION parameter is specified, then any files the user creates will be assigned the Default Security String. There will be no Safeguard Diskfile Protection Record, unless added by an authorized user. The file may, however, be protected under a VOLUME or SUBVOLUME rule.

RISK   Not all files that a user creates may need a Protection Record, such as edit files, temporary files, etc.

RISK   An excessive number of Protection Records can be automatically created.

RISK   If the protection record of the 'auto'-protection record does not give the Security.Admin userid ownership access, Security.Admin will not be able to 'see' these records. This makes it very difficult to research access problems and to clean up orphaned protection records.

BP-USER-CONFIG-03   Do not use SUBJECT DEFAULT PROTECTION in User Records.

Command Interpreter Attributes

The Command Interpreter (CI) parameter determines the program that Safeguard software will start after it has authenticated the user at a Safeguard-controlled terminal.

Please refer to the discussion on Command Interpreter parameters as discussed previously in this section.

OSS-Specific Attributes

Two of the three OSS-specific settings represent the OSS equivalents of Guardian-specific User Record attributes:

INITIAL-DIRECTIORY is the OSS equivalent of the GUARDIAN-DEFAULT-VOLUME

INITIAL-PROGRAM is the OSS equivalent of CI-PROG.

The third OSS Specific setting is INITIAL-PROGTYPE.

The INITIAL-PROGRAM and INITIAL-PROGTYPE attributes are not currently implemented; they are reserved for future use.

INITIAL-DIRECTORY [directory-path]

This parameter determines the user's 'home directory', within the OSS file system. The <directory-path name> is a case-sensitive text string of up to 256 characters. It must be a syntactically valid OSS pathname. The directory must exist or the user will not be permitted to logon.

If the INITIAL-DIRECTORY attribute is specified, it must be the last attribute in the command string.

RISK If directory-path is omitted, the string is set to null (no pathname) and the Guardian default directory is assumed.

INITIAL-PROGRAM [prog-path]

Note that this feature is not currently implemented on HP NonStop™ systems. It is reserved for future use.

This parameter will determine the OSS program that Safeguard software will start after it has authenticated the user at a Safeguard-controlled terminal. The <prog-path > is a case-sensitive text string of up to 256 characters. It must be a syntactically valid OSS pathname. If <prog-path> is omitted, the string is set to null (no pathname).

INITIAL-PROGTYPE [prog-type]

Note that this feature is not currently implemented on HP NonStop™ systems. It is reserved for future use.

Determines the type of the initial program within the OSS environment for the user. The valid <prog-types> are:

PROGRAM

SERVICE

WINDOW

If <prog-type> is omitted, the initial program type is set to PROGRAM.

PRIMARY-GROUP

Represents the user's PRIMARY GROUP. When a userid is added, the administrative group for the user is also that user's primary group. To change the primary group, use the ALTER USER command to alter the PRIMARY-GROUP attribute.

If a second PRIMARY-GROUP is added, the Safeguard software does not implicitly add this group to the user's group list if the user does not already belong to this group. The previous primary group remains on the user's group list, but not as the primary group.

ADDING a PRIMARY-GROUP without <group-name> or <group-num>, PRIMARY GROUP clears the primary group setting, and the user's administrative group becomes the primary group.

How Groups Are Processed When Logging On

Logon sets the group list of a process to contain the user's entire group list, and also copies the user's primary group to the real group ID, effective group ID, and saved set-group-ID of the process. Because a user's primary group may differ from that user's administrative group, the effective group ID of a process may differ from the administrative group of the process as defined by the PAID.

Auditing Users

The principles of good security mandate Individual Accountability. It must be possible to link each action on the system to the user who actually performed the action. In other words, accurate and complete auditing is necessary.

What Can Be Audited

The amount of auditing available depends on whether or not Safeguard software or third party security products are in use on the system.

Without the Safeguard Subsystem or CMON

Without Safeguard software or CMON or a third party access control product, user activity and maintenance cannot be audited.

With CMON

If $CMON is running, it can be configured to audit LOGONs, LOGOFFs, PROCESS starts, user adds, user deletes, and process priority changes.

With the Safeguard Subsystem

Safeguard software can be configured to audit the following user-related activities:

Logons and Logoffs

Changes to Safeguard User Records

Process Creates and Opens

Attempts to access objects such as files, processes and devices

BP-USER-ADMIN-05 To provide accountability of user activities, Safeguard software should be configured to perform the auditing mandated by the Corporate Security Policy and Standards.

With Third Party Products

3P-ACCESS-AUDIT-01 Third party access control products can provide audits of user activities, capturing not just file opens but the commands issued within utilities, with or without Safeguard.

3P-PROCESS-AUDIT-01 Third party process control products can audit the commands such as ALTPRI, SUSPEND or STOP requests with or without Safeguard software .

Auditing Users With the Safeguard Subsystem

The amount and type of auditing is determined by both Safeguard Global and/or User Record audit parameters.

User-Related Global Audit Parameters

The Global parameters that affect user management auditing are:

AUDIT-AUTHENTICATE-PASS / FAIL

AUDIT-SUBJECT-MANAGE-PASS / FAIL

AUDIT-AUTHENTICATE-PASS | FAIL

The AUDIT-AUTHENTICATE-PASS and AUDIT-AUTHENTICATE-FAIL global parameters determine whether or not Safeguard software will write audits when someone attempts to logon. Valid entries are: ALL, NONE, LOCAL and REMOTE.

How the AUDIT-AUTHENTICATE-PASS and AUDIT-AUTHENTICATE-FAIL parameters are configured depends on the Corporate Security Policy and Parameters.

BP-SAFEGARD-GLOBAL-34   The AUDIT-AUTHENTICATE-PASS global parameter should be ALL.

BP-SAFEGARD-GLOBAL-35   The AUDIT-AUTHENTICATE-FAIL global parameter should be ALL.

AUDIT-SUBJECT-MANAGE-PASS | FAIL

The AUDIT-SUBJECT-MANAGE-PASS and AUDIT-SUBJECT-MANAGE-FAIL global parameter determines whether or not Safeguard software will write User Record changes to the Safeguard Audit Trail. Valid entries are: ALL, NONE, LOCAL and REMOTE.

BP-SAFEGARD-GLOBAL-36   The AUDIT-SUBJECT-MANAGE-PASS global parameter should be ALL.

BP-SAFEGARD-GLOBAL-37   The AUDIT-SUBJECT-MANAGE-FAIL global parameter should be ALL.

Audit-Related User Record Parameters

The parameters in the User Record that determine which actions related to the record will be audited are:

AUDIT-USER-ACTION-PASS / FAIL

AUDIT-AUTHENTICATE-PASS / FAIL

AUDIT-MANAGE-PASS / FAIL

AUDIT-AUTHENTICATE{ -PASS | -FAIL }

The AUDIT-AUTHENTICATE-PASS and AUDIT-AUTHENTICATE-FAIL parameters determine whether or not successful or unsuccessful logon attempts will be audited. The value can be ALL, NONE, LOCAL, or REMOTE.

This global attribute *supplements* the audit parameter for the individual User Record. If the parameter in the individual object's Protection Record is LOCAL and the Global Attribute is REMOTE, then both LOCAL and REMOTE management attempts will be audited.

The default value for both PASS and FAIL is NONE.

BP-USER-CONFIG-04   AUDIT-AUTHENTICATE-PASS = ALL

BP-USER-CONFIG-05   AUDIT-AUTHENTICATE-FAIL = ALL

The conditions specified for this attribute also apply to the system-wide auditing of automatic logoffs

AUDIT-MANAGE{ -PASS | -FAIL }

The AUDIT-MANAGE-PASS and AUDIT-MANAGE-FAIL User Record parameters determine whether or not Safeguard software will write audits when someone attempts to change this particular User Record. The value can be: ALL, NONE, LOCAL and REMOTE.

BP-USER-CONFIG-06   If the Global AUDIT-SUBJECT-MANAGE-PASS attribute is not ALL, then each user record should be configured AUDIT-MANAGE-PASS ALL.

BP-USER-CONFIG-07   If the Global AUDIT-SUBJECT-MANAGE-FAIL attribute is not ALL, then each user record should be configured AUDIT-MANAGE-FAIL ALL.

AUDIT-USER-ACTION{ -PASS | -FAIL }

The AUDIT-USER-ACTION-PASS and AUDIT-USER-ACTION-FAIL User Record parameters determine whether or not Safeguard software will write audits when the user accesses objects such as files, processes or devices, *regardless of whether or not a Safeguard Protection Record for the target object exists*. The value can be: ALL, NONE, LOCAL and REMOTE.

BP-USER-CONFIG-08   If the AUDIT-USER-ACTION-PASS attribute is not NONE, then each user record should be configured AUDIT-USER-ACTION-PASS NONE.

BP-USER-CONFIG-09   If the AUDIT-USER-ACTION-FAIL attribute is not ALL, then each user record should be configured AUDIT-USER-ACTION-FAIL ALL.

NOTE: It is also important to realize that a single user action will generate multiple underlying events, each of which generates a Safeguard audit record. For example, if a user issues a SAFECOM INFO USER command it causes the following three underlying events:

The attempt to run SAFECOM

The attempt to open the user's terminal

The attempt to open the $ZSMP process

Simply logging on to the system will generate Safeguard audits not only as Safeguard software reads the USERID file and authenticates the user, but as the user reads the TACLLOCL and TACLCSTM files and opens any files or macros run from within these files.

RISK   Setting AUDIT-USER-ACTION-PASS to ALL can increase the amount of auditing enough to cause an impact on system performance, especially if the SUPER.SUPER user record is configured to audit all activity.

Password Administration

The use of passwords for user identification and authentication is one of the foundations supporting the security structure of the HP NonStop server operating system.

BP-PASSWORD-POLICY-01   Passwords must be required.

Passwords are also the most easily compromised method of user identification. Detection of their fraudulent use is difficult because the compromised passwords are still available to the authorized user.

RISK   A user working on a number of systems, using more than one userid and, perhaps, one or more aliases, and faced with keeping passwords for each one up-to-date across multiple nodes tends to choose easy-to-remember passwords and to use them over and over again. Hackers make use of this and base their attacks on passwords using personal information about the users. Passwords should, therefore, be "strengthened" by ensuring that they don't contain personal information. Easily compromised values such as names or important dates cannot be used.

RISK   Another common password attack is a 'dictionary attack,' which compares encrypted passwords to a list of words encrypted using the same algorithm. Again, the imposition of rules that govern the contents of the password strengthen the password by making it less likely to contain a common word that will be found in the encrypted dictionary.

RISK   Finally, there are some userids that are so sensitive that restricted knowledge of their passwords is essential to prevent deliberate or inadvertent damage to corporate systems. The preferred method of protecting these sensitive passwords is to split the password into two or more parts and have different people create and enter the separate parts and then seal the password in an envelope, which can be locked up if desired.

"Hardened" Passwords

Content Rules

AP-PASSWORD-POLICY-01   The Corporate Security Policy should mandate the use of Strong Passwords.

When a password contains different types of characters, it is much harder for the password to be compromised based on personal knowledge or dictionary attack.

BP-PASSWORD-POLICY-02   Passwords should be stored encrypted.

BP-PASSWORD-POLICY-04   When passwords are sent, propagated, or otherwise transmitted across networks they should be encrypted.

BP-PASSWORD-QUALITY-01   Passwords should be 6-8 characters in length.

BP-PASSWORD-QUALITY-02   Passwords should contain at least one number

BP-PASSWORD-QUALITY-03   Passwords should contain at least one upper case and one lower case character

BP-PASSWORD-QUALITY-04   Passwords should contain at least one special character.

3P-PASSWORD-CONTROL-01   Use a third party product that can control the length, character string and other limitations on the password.

Safeguard software has the added capability of expiring passwords at regular intervals. This feature will be discussed separately, in the subsection of the Safeguard password discussion that follows.

Other procedural rules can be used to harden passwords:

Generating random passwords that conform to password quality rules ensure that dictionary attacks are ineffective.

AP-ADVICE-PASSWORD-01   Splitting passwords for sensitive userids into two or more parts ensures that no single person knows the entire password.

Password Quality Parameters may be set in a variety of ways. These are summarized in the table below

Where PASSWORD PARAMETERS May Be Set

	TACL Program (TACLCONF)	PASSWORD Program bind settings	SAFEGUARD GLOBAL SETTINGS	SAFEGUARD USER RECORD	
Required	NOCHANGEUSER		PASSWORD-REQUIRED		
Encryption		ENCRYPTPASSWORD	PASSWORD-ENCRYPT		
Length		MINPASSWORDLEN	PASSWORD-MINIMUM-LENGTH		
Password pgm prompts for OLD and NEW passwords		PROMPTPASSWORD			
Name vs Number	NAMELOGON		NAMELOGON		
Password chg parameters			PASSWORD-MAY-CHANGE PASSWORD-EXPIRY-GRACE	PASSWORD-MAY-CHANGE PASSWORD-EXPIRY-GRACE	
Periodic Password Expiration			PASSWORD-MUST-CHANGE PASSWORD-FAIL FREEZE	PASSWORD-EXPIRES	
Password echo to screen	BLINDLOGON	BLINDPASSWORD	BLINDLOGON	Safeguard	THIRD PARTY
Numbers Required				NO	YES
Upper and lower Case required				NO	YES
Special Characters Required				NO	YES
Control Characters required				NO	YES
'Immediate' Expiration				Yes (if date is set manually)	YES

Password-Related Logon Controls

Some of the password-related logon controls available depend on whether or not Safeguard software or a third party password product is installed on the system.

> At Safeguard terminals, the LOGON program processes logons.

The following chart summarizes the logon control settings with and without Safeguard software. Refer to the PASSWORD Program in the Gazette for a detailed discussion on its configuration and security.

Parameter Keyword	With Safeguard Software	Without Safeguard Software
BLINDPASSWORD	ON	Depends on TACLCONF Settings
PROMPTPASSWORD	ON	Depends on TACLCONF Settings

With the Safeguard Subsystem

Control parameters that are used when logging on are configured in the Safeguard Globals. The parameters are:

BLINDLOGON

NAMELOGON

PASSWORD-REQUIRED

BLINDLOGON

The BLINDLOGON Global parameter determines whether or not passwords can be typed on the same line as the user name.

RISK When passwords are entered on the same line as the user name, they will be displayed, in the clear, on the screen.

BP-SAFEGARD-GLOBAL-53 BLINDLOGON should be ON.

NAMELOGON

The NAMELOGON Global parameter determines whether on not a user can logon using a userid (group number,member number).

RISK Because there are a finite number of userids available on an HP Non-Stop server, it is easier for a hacker to guess a userid than a user name.

If NAMELOGON is ON, only a user name (group name.member name) will be accepted when a user logs on.

If NAMELOGON is OFF, a user may enter either a user name (group name.member name) or a userid (group number,member number).

The default value is ON.

BP-SAFEGARD-GLOBAL-54 NAMELOGON should be ON

PASSWORD-REQUIRED

The PASSWORD-REQUIRED parameter determines whether or not a password is required when SUPER.SUPER or a group manager userid 'logs down' to another userid.

If PASSWORD-REQUIRED is ON, users logged on as SUPER.SUPER or a group manager userid must enter the password of the userid they are 'logging down' to.

If PASSWORD-REQUIRED is OFF, users logged on as SUPER.SUPER or a group manager userid need not enter the password of the userid they are 'logging down' to.

The default value is OFF; no password is required.

BP-SAFEGARD-GLOBAL-04   PASSWORD-REQUIRED = OFF

Password Quality Controls

The ability to 'strengthen' users' passwords is controlled within the PASSWORD program and with Safeguard Global parameters.

Refer to the PASSWORD Program in the Gazette for a detailed discussion on its configuration and security.

Without the Safeguard Subsystem

In the Guardian environment, the Password parameters must be configured by binding them in the PASSWORD program.

The parameters that can be bound into the PASSWORD program are:

BLINDPASSWORD
ENCRYPTPASSWORD
MINPASSWORDLEN
PROMPTPASSWORD

These parameters should be bound to the PASSWORD program even if Safeguard software is installed on the system. To determine the current value, see Viewing the PASSWORD BIND Parameters in Appendix A.

With the Safeguard Subsystem

The quality and protection of passwords is configured in the Safeguard Globals. The parameters are:

PASSWORD-ENCRYPT

PASSWORD-HISTORY

PASSWORD-MINIMUM-LENGTH

PASSWORD-ENCRYPT

The PASSWORD-ENCRYPT parameter determines whether or not passwords will be encrypted when they are stored in the USERID and LUSERID files. If the passwords are stored in encrypted form, they are unreadable even if someone gains access to the files.

A value of ON, causes passwords to be encrypted when stored in the file.

A value of OFF, means that passwords are not encrypted.

The default value is OFF.

BP-SAFEGARD-GLOBAL-06   PASSWORD-ENCRYPT should be ON

Just setting this parameter to ON does not cause existing passwords to be encrypted; they will be encrypted the next time they are changed. Therefore, all users should change their passwords after setting this parameter.

PASSWORD-HISTORY

The PASSWORD-HISTORY parameter determines the number of previously used passwords that will be retained in the 'password database' for each user. Passwords in the database cannot be reused. Each time the user creates a new password it is added to the database. Only the most recent passwords are retained. If PASSWORD-HISTORY is set to ten, then the ten most recent passwords will be retained. When the user creates the eleventh new password, the oldest will be deleted from the database.

The value can be a number between 1 and 99. The default is 0.

RISK   A value of zero means that passwords will not be retained; users will be able to reuse passwords.

RISK   The longer a password is in use, the more likely that other people will learn it.

BP-SAFEGARD-GLOBAL-05   PASSWORD-HISTORY should be 10 (or greater)

PASSWORD-MINIMUM-LENGTH

The PASSWORD-MINIMUM-LENGTH parameter determines the minimum number of characters users must include in their passwords.

The value must be a number between zero and eight. The default is zero.

RISK   A value of zero means that passwords are not required.

RISK   The default is zero, no password required. If no password is required, anyone can logon to the system with a valid userid. Lists of userids may be easy to obtain.

BP-SAFEGARD-GLOBAL-07   The PASSWORD-MINIMUM-LENGTH value should be between 6 and 8.

> At the time that this attribute is set, it does not invalidate existing passwords. It affects passwords the next time they are changed. Therefore, all users should change their passwords after this attribute is reset.

RISK   Safeguard software can only validate PASSWORD-MINIMUM-LENGTH if the PASSWORD program is not set for ENCRYPTION.

With Third Party Software

Strong passwords should be at least 6 characters in length and contain at least one number, one upper case and one lower case character and perhaps at least one special character. When a password contains different types of characters, it is much harder for the password to be compromised based on personal knowledge or dictionary attack.

3P-PASSWORD-QUALITY-01   Third party products can provide quality rules and enforce those rules for passwords.

Password Expiration

The ability to expire users' passwords is determined by whether or not Safeguard software or a third party password product is in use on the system.

AP-PASSWORD-EXPIRE-01   Users must change their password at regular intervals.

The interval should be as short as possible without being unmanageable. The Corporate Security Policy should dictate how often users must change their password and how often the passwords for the powerful userids should be changed and how they are stored.

The Corporate Security Policy should dictate that whenever a password is created by anyone other than the user himself, the affected user should be forced to change their password the first time they log on after the password change. This minimizes the length of time that the security staff or Help Desk knows any individual's passwords.

AP-PASSWORD-EXPIRE-02 Immediate expiration of passwords when they are reset by someone other than the user minimizes the length of time that the security staff knows a user's password.

3P-PASSWORD-EXPIRE-01 Third party products can be utilized to immediately expire passwords if they are reset by someone other than the user.

Without the Safeguard Subsystem

RISK It is not possible to expire passwords before the user is logged on to a TACL without Safeguard software unless a third party Password Quality program is in use.

AP-PASSWORD-EXPIRE-03 It is possible to force users to change their password, even without Safeguard software, by writing an in-house macro that can be run from the TACLLOCL file.

RISK The TACLLOCL file approach is not as secure as password-expiration enforced by Safeguard software or a third party product because the user's password has already been accepted, the user authenticated, and TACL started.

With the Safeguard Subsystem

Safeguard can be configured to automatically expire passwords at regular intervals. This feature is set in the Safeguard Globals. The date the password will expire is calculated each time the user's password is changed. The date in the User Record may be overwritten by anyone who is authorized to ALTER the User Record.

The Global parameters are:

PASSWORD-EXPIRY-GRACE
PASSWORD-MAY-CHANGE

Password-Expiration Related Safeguard Global Parameters

The Safeguard Global parameters that affect password expiration are:

PASSWORD-EXPIRY-GRACE
PASSWORD-MAY-CHANGE

PASSWORD-EXPIRY-GRACE

The PASSWORD-EXPIRY-GRACE parameter determines the number of days after a user's password expires that the user will still be able to logon with the old password and create a new password during the logon process.

This parameter may be configured both in the Global Settings and the User Record. If defined in both places, the User Record setting takes precedence.

The default value is zero, no PASSWORD-EXPIRY-GRACE.

BP-SAFEGARD-GLOBAL-09   PASSWORD-EXPIRY-GRACE should be between 7 and 15 days

PASSWORD-MAY-CHANGE

The PASSWORD-MAY-CHANGE parameter defines the number of days before a user's password expires and if the user may change his password.

The following facts apply:

RISK   If no PASSWORD-MAY-CHANGE value is set, the user may change his password at any time and repeatedly. Users can cycle the password to overcome the history limit.

RISK   A value of 0 also allows the password to be changed at any time.

RISK   The default value is 0; no restrictions on password change date.

RISK   If the PASSWORD-MAY-CHANGE period is greater than the PASSWORD-MUST-CHANGE period in a user authentication record, that user's password can be changed at any time.

BP-SAFEGARD-GLOBAL-08   PASSWORD-MAY-CHANGE should be at least one day less than the MUST-CHANGE value.

Password-Expiration Related User-Record Parameters

The User Record attributes that affect password expiration are:

PASSWORD-EXPIRES
PASSWORD-EXPIRY-GRACE
PASSWORD-MAY-CHANGE (display only)
PASSWORD-MUST-CHANGE

PASSWORD-EXPIRES

The PASSWORD-EXPIRES attribute specifies the date that the user's current password will expire. The date is calculated based on the PASSWORD-MUST-CHANGE global attribute.

> **RISK** If the PASSWORD-EXPIRES field in the User Record is set 'manually', it takes precedence over the PASSWORD-EXPIRES date calculated as a result of the PASSWORD-MUST-CHANGE Global parameter.

> **RISK** If the PASSWORD-EXPIRES value is NONE, the user will not be forced to reset the password.

PASSWORD-EXPIRY-GRACE

The PASSWORD-EXPIRY-GRACE attribute specifies the number of days after a user's password expires that the user may still change the password. The user will be forced to change the password at logon. For example if a user's password expires on January 5, and PASSWORD-EXPIRY-GRACE is 5, they will be able to logon and choose a new password until January 10. After January 10, the security staff or another user who has been authorized to reset passwords, will have to reset the user's password before logon is allowed.

This parameter may be configured both in the Global Settings and the User Record. If defined in both places, the User Record setting takes precedence.

> **RISK** The default value is zero, no EXPIRY-GRACE. This generates a lot of password reset requests.

> **BP-USER-CONFIG-10** PASSWORD-EXPIRY-GRACE should be between 7 and 15 days.

PASSWORD-MAY-CHANGE

The PASSWORD-MAY-CHANGE attribute is a 'display only' field in the User Record. This value is calculated by Safeguard software and cannot be changed at the user level.

The attribute defines the number of days before the password expiration date within which a password may be changed by its user.

The following facts apply:

> **RISK** If no password expiration date set, the password may be changed at any time.

RISK   A value of 0 also allows the password to be changed at any time.

RISK   The default value is 0; no restrictions on password change date.

RISK   If the PASSWORD-MAY-CHANGE period is greater than the PASSWORD-MUST-CHANGE period in a user authentication record, that user's password can be changed at any time, unless set globally.

BP-USER-CONFIG-11   PASSWORD-MAY-CHANGE should be (MUST-CHANGE) minus 1

PASSWORD-MUST-CHANGE

The PASSWORD-MUST-CHANGE parameter determines the number of days that the user may use the same password.

If the PASSWORD-EXPIRES field in the User Record is set 'manually,' it takes precedence over the PASSWORD-EXPIRES date calculated as a result of setting the PASSWORD-MUST-CHANGE Global attribute.

RISK   The default value is NONE, the user will not be forced to change the password, unless set globally.

BP-USER-CONFIG-12   PASSWORD-MUST-CHANGE should be set to a value between 30 and 60 days

How the Safeguard Password Expiration-Related Parameters Interact

Use the configuration of Password Expiration-Related Parameters to enforce the Corporate Security Policy:

How PASSWORD-HISTORY and MAY-CHANGE Interact

Use PASSWORD-HISTORY in combination with PASSWORD-MAY-CHANGE to prevent users from re-using passwords over and over.

If PASSWORD-HISTORY is set to 10 and PASSWORD-MAY-CHANGE is set to at least one day less than the PASSWORD-MUST-CHANGE value, then users can't change their passwords more than once per day. This prevents them from re-using a password for at least 10 days.

```
Example:
PASSWORD-MUST-CHANGE = 60
PASSWORD-MAY-CHANGE  = 59

PASSWORD-HISTORY = 10
```

In this example, users may change their password for the last 59 days before it expires. This means that they can change it every day, but not more than once per day.

Because PASSWORD-HISTORY is set to 10, they would have to change their password every day for 10 days before they could reuse their initial password.

How PASSWORD-EXPIRES and EXPIRY-GRACE Interact

To minimize the time that someone other than a user knows his password, use the PASSWORD-EXPIRES and the PASSWORD-EXPIRY-GRACE parameters to immediately expire passwords after they are reset by the Help Desk or Security staff.

If each time the password is reset, the PASSWORD-EXPIRATION is set to the current date and time, i.e., then when the user logs on for the first time after the reset, they will be forced to change their password during the logon process. The user has the length of time defined by PASSWORD-EXPIRY-GRACE to logon and enter a new password or the password is frozen.

```
Example:
Before:
PASSWORD-EXPIRY-GRACE = 7
PASSWORD-EXPIRATION = APR 3 2003

After:
PASSWORD-EXPIRY-GRACE = 7
PASSWORD-EXPIRATION = JULY 3 2003 11:50
```

In this example, the user's password was reset on July 3, 2003 and the PASSWORD-EXPIRATION set to July 3, 2003 11:50. The user will be able to logon and choose a new password until July 10, 2003 at 11:50 (7 days).

Password-Expiration With Third Party Products

Some third party products allow the Security staff to delegate the ability to reset passwords to other users, such as a Help Desk. The userids whose passwords can be reset by the Help Desk can be defined, to ensure that privileged userids, such as SUPER.SUPER or Application Owners, cannot be reset by anyone other than the Security staff.

3P-PASSWORD-EXPIRE-01   Some third party products can automatically expire passwords whenever someone other than their own user creates or resets them.

Who Can RESET Passwords

Who is allowed to reset passwords is determined by whether or not Safeguard software or a third party password product is in use on the system.

Without the Safeguard Subsystem

Without Safeguard SUPER.SUPER, the Group Manager, or the user.

With the Safeguard Subsystem

RISK   All of the following users can reset passwords:

The OWNER of the user's Safeguard User Record

The OWNER's Group Manager

Any users granted O(wn) authority in the User Record

The user's Group Manager

SUPER.SUPER (If SUPER.SUPER is configured UNDENIABLE)

BP-USER-OBJTYPE-01   The USER OBJECTTYPE should be created.

With Third Party Password Products

3P-PASSWORD-RESET-O1   Some third party products allow the Security staff to delegate the ability to reset passwords to other users, such as a Help Desk. The userids whose passwords can be reset by the Help Desk can be defined to ensure that privileged userids, such as SUPER.SUPER or Application Owners, cannot be reset by anyone other than the Security staff.

Administering Passwords for Sensitive Userids

RISK   Some userids, such as SUPER.SUPER or Application Owner IDs, are so sensitive that restricted knowledge of their passwords is essential to prevent deliberate or inadvertent damage to systems and applications.

The preferred method of protecting these sensitive passwords is to split the password into two or more parts and have different people create and enter the separate parts.

Seal the password in an envelope, which can be locked up if desired. The passwords can only be retrieved for required activity or emergencies.

AP-PASSWORD-POLICY-03   The Corporate Security Standard should specify the Sensitive userids, how often their passwords must be changed, how the passwords will be protected, and the procedures and documentation required to 'check out' their passwords.

	Discovery Questions	Look here:
PASSWORD-POLICY-01	Does the Corporate Security Policy require the use of passwords?	Policy
PASSWORD-POLICY-02	Does the Corporate Security Policy mandate 'Strong' passwords?	Policy
PASSWORD-POLICY-03	Does the Corporate Security Policy mandate that passwords be encrypted?	Policy
PASSWORD-POLICY-04	Does the Corporate Security Policy mandate how often sensitive passwords must be changed?	Policy
PASSWORD-QUALITY-01	Are passwords to be at least 6 characters in length?	BIND Safecom
PASSWORD-QUALITY-02 to 04	Do passwords conform to the quality rules mandated by the Corporate Security Policy?	BIND Safecom
PASSWORD-CONFIG-01	Is the BLINDPASSWORD parameter bound into the PASSWORD program?	BIND
PASSWORD-CONFIG-04	Is the PROMPTPASSWORD parameter bound into the PASSWORD program?	BIND
PASSWORD-CONFIG-02	Is the ENCRYPTPASSWORD parameter bound into the PASSWORD program?	BIND
PASSWORD-CONFIG-03	Is the MINPASSWORDLEN parameter bound into the PASSWORD program?	BIND
PASSWORD-EXPIRE-01	Are passwords configured to expire at the interval mandated by the Corporate Security Policy?	BIND Safecom
PASSWORD-EXPIRE-02	Are passwords expired immediately after RESETs?	Policy
USER-CONFIG-01	Does the User logon with a unique userid?	Safecom
USER-CONFIG-02	Does the User have a DEFAULT VOLUME?	Safecom
USER-CONFIG-03	Is SUBJECT DEFAULT PROTECTION in User Records set off?	Safecom
USER-CONFIG-04	Does the User Record AUDIT-AUTHENTICATE-PASS = ALL?	Safecom
USER-CONFIG-05	Does the User Record AUDIT-AUTHENTICATE-FAIL = ALL?	Safecom
USER-CONFIG-06	Does the Global or User Record AUDIT-MANAGE-PASS = ALL?	Safecom
USER-CONFIG-07	Does the Global or User Record AUDIT-MANAGE-FAIL = ALL?	Safecom

	Discovery Questions	Look here:
USER-CONFIG-08	Does the User Record AUDIT-USER-ACTION-PASS = NONE?	Safecom
USER-CONFIG-09	Does the User Record AUDIT-USER-ACTION-FAIL = ALL?	Safecom
USER-CONFIG-10	Does the User Record PASSWORD-EXPIRY -GRACE value conform to the Security Policy?	Safecom
USER-CONFIG-11	Does the User Record PASSWORD-MAY-CHANGE value conform to the Security Policy?	Safecom
USER-CONFIG-12	Does the User Record PASSWORD-MUST-CHANGE value conform to the Security Policy?	Safecom
SAFEGARD-GLOBAL-02	Does the Safeguard global AUTHENTICATE-FAIL-TIMEOUT value conform to the Security Policy?	Safecom
SAFEGARD-GLOBAL-03	Does the Safeguard global AUTHENTICATE-FAIL-FREEZE value conform to the Security Policy?	Safecom
SAFEGARD-GLOBAL-04	Does the Safeguard global PASSWORD-REQUIRED value conform to the Security Policy?	Safecom
SAFEGARD-GLOBAL-05	Does the Safeguard global PASSWORD-HISTORY value conform to the Corporate Security Policy or to a value of 10 or greater?	Safecom
SAFEGARD-GLOBAL-06	Does the Safeguard global PASSWORD-ENCRYPT = ON	Safecom
SAFEGARD-GLOBAL-07	Does the Safeguard global PASSWORD-MINIMUM-LENGTH value conform to the Security Policy?	Safecom
SAFEGARD-GLOBAL-08	Does the Safeguard global PASSWORD-MAY-CHANGE value conform to the Security Policy?	Safecom
SAFEGARD-GLOBAL-09	Does the Safeguard global PASSWORD-EXPIRY-GRACE value conform to the Security Policy?	Safecom
SAFEGARD-GLOBAL-53	Does the Safeguard global BLINDLOGON = ON?	Safecom
SAFEGARD-GLOBAL-54	Does the Safeguard global NAMELOGON = ON?	Safecom

4

Authentication, Granting Access to the HP NonStop Server

Now that userids (and Aliases) are organized and created, control must be established over their access to individual nodes and the Expand network.

The authentication sequence depends on four parameters:

Is the access batch or interactive?

What communication medium is being used?

Are Safeguard TERMINAL controls being used?

Which personality of the HP NonStop server is being used?

The combinations of answers to these questions determines which path the user will take through the process of authenticating the user's identity. The following table summarizes the choices:

Type of Access	Connection Medium	Safeguard TERMINAL Records In Use	Personality	TELSERV	LOGIN	LOGON	Command Interpreter
Batch							NetBatch
Interactive	Static terminal	No Safeguard	Guardian				TACL
Interactive	Static terminal	Safeguard	Guardian			Y	TACL
Interactive*	Static TCP/IP	No Safeguard	OSS	Y			*/bin/sh*
Interactive*	Static TCP/IP	Safeguard	OSS	Y		Y	*/bin/sh*
Interactive	Dynamic TCP/IP	No Safeguard	Guardian	Y	Y		TACL

Type of Access	Connection Medium	Safeguard TERMINAL Records In Use	Personality	TELSERV	LOGIN	LOGON	Command Interpreter
Interactive	Dynamic TCP/IP	Safeguard	Guardian	Y	Y	Y	TACL
Interactive	Dynamic TCP/IP	No Safeguard	OSS	Y	Y		/bin/sh
Interactive	Dynamic TCP/IP	Safeguard	OSS	Y	Y	Y	/bin/sh

* Requires third party product to start shell process

The three destination command interpreters are NetBatch, which is the batch processing subsystem, TACL, which is the Guardian personality command interpreter and /bin/sh, which is the command interpreter for the OSS personality. All three pass through the same authentication path, with the following two exceptions:

NetBatch does not prompt for the password; it runs as the user who submitted the job. Note that this is automatically generated by BATCHCOM when the batch job is submitted.

/bin/sh does not communicate with CMON.

Using TACL as the example, the following three diagrams show the TACL initiation process and the authentication sequence for installations that do not use Safeguard software and for those that do use Safeguard to manage User Records (See Figure 4-1).

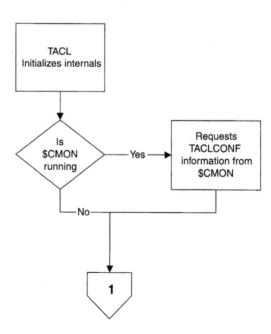

Figure 4-1
Initializing TACL

The initialization of TACL internals uses values that have been bound into TACL:

NAMELOGON

BLINDPASSWORD

If a CMON process is in use, it is also queried for other TACL parameters. Then the first TACL prompt is written (See Figure 4-2).

At that point, the user logs on to the system (See Figure 4-3).

Guardian Authentication

The Guardian system requires that users must logon to the system with a valid userid or alias and a password. TACL is the command interpreter used with the Guardian system.

The logging on process calls the USER_AUTHENTICATE_ routine. During this system call a PRELOGON message is sent to CMON, if it is running. If the PRELOGON request passes the CMON rules, a LOGON request is sent to CMON, if it is running. The USER_AUTHENTICATE_ procedure will utilize the Safeguard facility, $ZSMP, if Safeguard software is on the system. $ZSMP evaluates both the Safeguard configuration and the User Record attributes to determine if the access will be granted. Based on the Safeguard configuration, $ZSMP also determines whether or not the logon will be audited.

If the USER_AUTHENTICATE_ procedure does not exist in the system library, TACL calls the VERIFYUSER system procedure.

There are several ways to control how the user logs on to the system:

TACLCONF parameters

CMON parameters

User-Record parameters

User-Related Safeguard Global parameters

Logon-Related TACLCONF Configuration

The TACLCONF parameters that affect the authentication process are:

CMONREQUIRED

CMONTIMEOUT

REMOTECMONREQUIRED

REMOTECMONTIMEOUT

Figure 4-2
Non-Safeguard
Logon

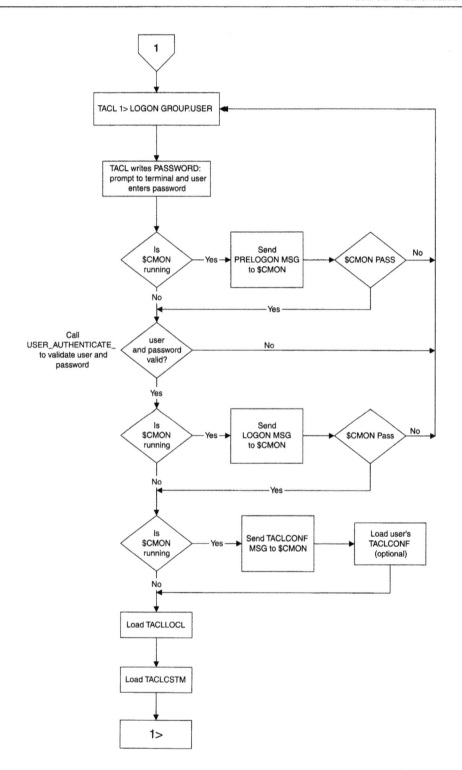

Figure 4-3
*Logon With
Safeguard*

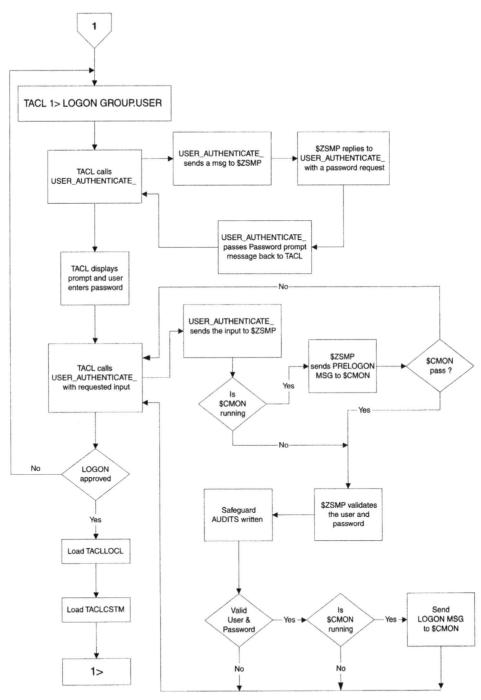

These parameters are discussed in the section on TACL in the Gazette.

The following parameters are discussed in the TACL section in the Gazette:

BLINDLOGON
NAMELOGON

Logon-Related CMON Configuration

If there is a CMON running on the system, see the program's documentation or review the code and configuration files to determine whether or not CMON is handling PRELOGON and LOGON activity and the optional user-specific TACLCONF message.

Logon-Related Password Issues

The logging on process requires the entry of a userid and a valid password. Refer to Passwords in Part Three for additional discussions on passwords.

The following Safeguard Global parameters are discussed in the section on Password Administration and affect the requirements of passwords when logging on:

BP-SAFEGARD-GLOBAL-06   PASSWORD-ENCRYPT = ON

BP-SAFEGARD-GLOBAL-05   PASSWORD-HISTORY = 10

BP-SAFEGARD-GLOBAL-07   PASSWORD-MINIMUM-LENGTH = 6

BP-SAFEGARD-GLOBAL-04   PASSWORD-REQUIRED = OFF

BP-SAFEGARD-GLOBAL-09   PASSWORD-EXPIRY-GRACE = between 7 and 15

BP-SAFEGARD-GLOBAL-08   PASSWORD-MAY-CHANGE = 7 DAYS BEFORE EXPIRE (assuming a 90 days password expiration cycle)

Logon-Related Safeguard Global Parameters

The Safeguard GLOBAL parameters that affect authentication are:

AUTHENTICATE-FAIL-FREEZE
AUTHENTICATE-FAIL-TIMEOUT
AUTHENTICATE-MAXIMUM-ATTEMPTS

AUTHENTICATE-FAIL{-FREEZE | -TIMEOUT }

The AUTHENTICATE-FAIL-FREEZE parameter determines whether or not a userid will be FROZEN when the user enters the wrong password too many times in a row.

If the AUTHENTICATE-FAIL-FREEZE value is ON, when a user exceeds the maximum number of attempts to enter a correct password, the target userid is FROZEN.

RISK   An intruder could easily freeze all the IDs on a system by simply exceeding AUTHENTICATE-MAXIMUM-ATTEMPTS for each user.

RISK   If there are no logged on SUPER.SUPER users or Security Administrators prior to the freeze, the system might have to be reloaded to regain access to the system.

BP-SAFEGARD-GLOBAL-03   AUTHENTICATE-FAIL-FREEZE = OFF

If the AUTHENTICATE-FAIL-TIMEOUT value is n <time interval>>, when a user exceeds the maximum number of attempts to enter a correct password, a delay of the authentication process occurs.

The AUTHENTICATE-FAIL-TIMEOUT determines the length of the delay. The default setting is 60 seconds.

RISK   A longer value slows down an intruder's attempts to break in. However, avoid unreasonably long periods, because a legitimate user who accidentally exceeds AUTHENTICATE-MAXIMUM-ATTEMPTS will be barred from the system for the duration of the delay period.

BP-SAFEGARD-GLOBAL-02   AUTHENTICATE-FAIL-TIMEOUT = 60 seconds

AUTHENTICATE-MAXIMUM-ATTEMPTS

The AUTHENTICATE-MAXIMUM-ATTEMPTS parameter determines the number of times a user can enter an incorrect password before the appropriate AUTHENTICATE-FAIL action takes place.

The default setting is 3.

BP-SAFEGARD-GLOBAL-01   AUTHENTICATE-MAXIMUM-ATTEMPTS = 3

OSS Authentication

OSS requires that users must logon to the system with a valid userid or alias and a password. */bin/sh* is the command interpreter used with OSS.

OSS authentication depends on the USER_AUTHENTICATE_ procedure. It will not use VERIFYUSER, as that operating system procedure does not support aliases.

Safeguard-Controlled Terminals

Safeguard software can be configured to take over control of the logon dialog at specific terminals. Some or all of the terminals on the system can be controlled by Safeguard software. Dynamic TCP/IP terminals are put under Safeguard control by using the LOGON program as the initial authentication program. Static terminals are put under Safeguard control by creating a Safeguard Terminal Definition Record.

Note that this is separate from the Safeguard User Record that is consulted during the logon process for user authentication.

Dynamic Safeguard-Controlled Sessions

Safeguard-controlled terminals can be created dynamically by setting the LOGON program as a service for the TELSERV process for the TCP/IP line. These dynamic terminals will not have Safeguard TERMINAL records, so the TERMINAL record parameters cannot be used to determine which command interpreter will be started after LOGON authenticates the user. Instead, the user's User Record and the Safeguard Globals will be used to determine which command interpreter will be used.

Static Safeguard Terminals

Terminal Definition Records differ from Safeguard Object Protection Records in that there is no Access Control List. To control access to a Safeguard terminal, create a DEVICE (or SUBDEVICE) Protection Record based on the terminal's device name.

NOTE: Any Terminal Definition Records for remote terminals must be completely accessible by SUPER.SUPER:

SUPER.SUPER must have appropriate REMOTEPASSWORDs.

The terminal's DEVICE Protection Record (if any) must not deny access to SUPER.SUPER.

The Terminal Definition Record can be configured to start a Command Interpreter (CI) automatically at the terminal after user authentication.

NOTE: Safeguard software can start a CI only at a Safeguard terminal, that is, one put under Safeguard control with a Terminal Definition Record or dynamic TELSERV services. Though the CI can also be specified in a user authentication record and in the Safeguard Globals, *it is enforced only at terminals controlled by Safeguard software.*

Safeguard-controlled terminals can also be configured for exclusive access, which insures that any user who is logged on to a Safeguard terminal has exclusive access to the terminal until the user logs off.

Two parameters are used to configure Safeguard software to control the authentication process:

TERMINAL DEFINITION RECORD

TERMINAL-EXCLUSIVE-ACCESS

The Terminal Definition Record

When a Terminal Definition Record is added and thawed, Safeguard software takes over control of the logon dialog at that terminal. Terminal Definition Records cannot be used with dynamic terminals.

The Terminal Definition Record can specify that a particular Command Interpreter (CI) be started automatically at the terminal after user authentication.

CIs can be configured in three places:

User Records

Safeguard Terminal Definition Records

Safeguard Global Parameters

Safeguard software searches for a CI specification in the following order: User Record, Terminal Definition Record and Safeguard Globals. The *first* specification found during the search is the CI that is started after user authentication, so *a command interpreter specified in a user authentication record always takes precedence* over one specified in a Terminal Definition Record or the Safeguard Globals.

If no CI is specified in the user authentication record or in the Terminal Definition Record, the CI defined in the Safeguard Globals is used. If no CI is specified globally, then the CI started is $SYSTEM.SYSTEM.TACL.

The Terminal Definition Command Interpreter Attributes are:

PROG

PNAME

LIB

CPU

SWAP

PRI

PARAM-TEXT

Safeguard software does not treat Terminal Definition Records as objects. They are not affected by Warning Mode.

PROG

The PROG parameter specifies the object file of the command interpreter Safeguard software will start after authenticating the user logging onto the defined terminal. The object file must be a local file.

If no object file is specified, the other attributes of the Terminal Definition Record will be ignored.

LIB

The LIB parameter defines the library file to be used with the command interpreter for the terminal after user authentication.

If no library is specified, no library file will be used.

CPU

The CPU parameter determines the number of the CPU the command interpreter will run in. The valid entries are number, representing the CPU or the word "any". If the value is ANY, any available CPU will be used.

If no CPU is specified, any available CPU will be used.

PNAME

The PNAME parameter determines the process name that will be assigned to the command interpreter that is started at the terminal

If no PNAME is specified, Safeguard software will generate a process name when it starts the command interpreter.

The PNAME must be unique for each Safeguard-controlled terminal.

SWAP

The SWAP parameter determines the location of the command interpreter's swap space. The value must be a valid volume name. The subvolume and file names are optional.

If no volume name is entered, the configured system volume will be used.

PRI

The PRI parameter determines the priority at which the command interpreter will be run at this terminal.

If no priority is entered, the Safeguard Global CI-PRI value defaults to the system default priority.

PARAM-TEXT

The PARAM-TEXT determines the data (if any) to be supplied as the startup message for the command interpreter started at this terminal.

The PARAM-TEXT must be the final attribute in the command string.

If no PARAM-TEXT is entered, no startup text is used.

STATUS

The STATUS is either FROZEN or THAWED. If a Terminal Definition Record is frozen, the logon dialog at that terminal is disabled.

TERMINAL-EXCLUSIVE-ACCESS

The TERMINAL-EXCLUSIVE-ACCESS parameter determines whether or not a user who is logged on at a Safeguard terminal has exclusive access to that terminal; no other user can open the terminal during the authenticated user's session.

If TERMINAL-EXCLUSIVE-ACCESS is ON, the user authenticated at a Safeguard terminal has exclusive access to that terminal.

If TERMINAL-EXCLUSIVE-ACCESS is OFF, all users can open the terminal, whether or not another user is currently logged on.

BP-SAFEGARD-GLOBAL-55   TERMINAL-EXCLUSIVE-ACCESS = OFF

NOTE: This attribute applies only to static Safeguard-controlled terminals.

Granting Access to the Remote Nodes

In a secure environment, network access should be evaluated on a user-by-user basis by the Security Administrator, the Application Owners and the System Manager.

Four factors can be used to control whether or not a user can access files or resources on a node remote to the one where that user is currently logged on:

Expand	Can be configured to prevent PASSTHRU access from one node to another. Refer to the section on Expand in Part 2.
CMON	Can be configured to control logons by IP address. Refer to the discussion on CMON later in this section.
File Security	Security on the node where the files reside (whether configured using the Guardian or Safeguard), determine whether or not a remote user can access the files. Refer to Securing Diskfiles in Part Five.
REMOTEPASSWORD	Entries in the user's User Record, whether maintained via RPASSWRD or Safeguard software, determine a specific user's access to remote nodes.

REMOTEPASSWORD

REMOTEPASSWORDs are part of the User Record for each user or alias granted access to more than one node. They are among the first steps used by the Guardian operating system on each HP NonStop server to determine if users will be granted remote access to the node.

REMOTEPASSWORDs for a user must be established for each remote node the user is authorized to access remotely. For a user or alias to be able to access files or resources on a remote node, the REMOTEPASSWORD in the User's Record on both the target node and the user's current (local) node must be identical.

Without the Safeguard Subsystem

By default, a new user is configured as local, without access to other nodes. This default configuration makes all files on remote nodes inaccessible.

REMOTEPASSWORDs are added to a User Record with the TACL REMOTE PASSWORD command or the RPASSWRD program.

The Corporate Security Standards should dictate who is authorized to ADD, ALTER or DELETE REMOTEPASSWORDs for any userids.

With the Safeguard Subsystem

By default, a new user is configured as local, without access to other nodes. This default configuration makes all files on remote nodes inaccessible.

REMOTEPASSWORDs are added to a User Record with the Safeguard ALTER USER or ALTER ALIAS commands.

The Corporate Security Standards should dictate who is authorized to ADD, ALTER or DELETE REMOTEPASSWORDs for any userids or aliases.

With OSS

By default, a new user is configured as local, without access to other nodes. This default configuration makes all files available through the OSS /E directory inaccessible to OSS users.

The Corporate Security Standards should dictate who is authorized to ADD, ALTER or DELETE REMOTEPASSWORDs for any OSS userids or aliases.

CMON

Since its earliest design, the NonStop system has had an interface to a user-supplied Command Monitoring Process. This process, named $CMON, has never been supplied by the NonStop operating systems development groups. Several versions are available, however, such as the one provided by the ITUG user group, that monitor and control different aspects of the system usage.

3P-CMON-PROCESS-01 There are several supported third party CMON products available.

The original CMON specification allows the CMON process to mediate LOGONs, LOGOFFs, NEW PROCESS RUNs, ALTER PRIORITY commands, USER ADDs and USER DELETEs. Since the advent of Safeguard software with the C20 series operating system releases, the USER ADD and USER DELETE functions have become superfluous. Most third party packages allow the security administrator to set rules controlling:

The CPU of a new process

The priority of a new process

Changes to the priority of a running process

User logons based on user's logical port (IP address)

When a CMON process is present on the system and any of the actions above occur, a message is sent to the CMON process. The sending process waits until either CMON responds or the time spent waiting for CMON's response exceeds the timeout parameter defined by the system manager in the TACLCONF or Safeguard software, generally 15–30 seconds. If the CMON message does not block the action or the wait for CMON does not exceed the timeout parameter, processing continues. If the CMON process returns a message blocking the action, the action is denied and an error is returned to the user who originated the action.

CMON Can Control Access To Privileged Ids

If the environment makes it necessary to logon as SUPER.SUPER, users should be forced to logon to the system using their own ID before logging up to SUPER.SUPER. This can be accomplished with a CMON that can force stepped logons.

BP-USER-PRIVLEGE-01   Users should not be able to logon directly as a Privileged ID except for emergencies. They must first logon using their personal userid.

CMON Can Control Remote Access

AP-ADVICE-CMON-01   If the Corporate Security Policy or Standards mandates that access to the HP NonStop server be controlled via IP address or PORT, install a CMON product.

CMON Can Control Access To Utilities Based on Port and Userid

AP-ADVICE-CMON-02   If the Corporate Security Policy or Standards mandates that users can only run certain utilities when logged on from specific PORTs, CMON can restrict the utilities and programs that can be run when a user logs on to a given port.

CMON Can Perform Load Balancing

AP-ADVICE-CMON-03   CMON can be configured to manage which CPU and priority new processes will use.

CMON in a Non-Safeguard Environment

In a Guardian environment, TACL communicates with CMON. The extent of CMON's control is determined by parameters bound into TACL. This is referred to as the TACL configuration or TACLCONF.

The parameters are:

    CMONREQUIRED
    CMONTIMEOUT
    REMOTECMONREQUIRED
    REMOTECMONTIMEOUT

CMONREQUIRED

The CMONREQUIRED parameter determines whether or not CMON must rule on all process requests. The valid entries are:

0 (zero)   A response from CMON is not required. If the CMON-REQUIRED value is 0 (zero) and CMON doesn't respond, TACL will act on the process request.

−1   A response from CMON is required. If the CMONREQUIRED value is −1 and CMON does not respond, TACL will wait for the number of seconds defined by the CMONTIMEOUT value. If the timeout occurs, the action will be denied.

RISK   If the CMONREQUIRED value is −1, the system is at risk for denial of service.

With or without Safeguard software:

BP-TACL-TACLCONF-03   If CMON is running, CMONREQUIRED should be 0, a response is not required.

CMONTIMEOUT

The CMONTIMEOUT parameter determines how long TACL will wait for a response from CMON. A value of −1 will disable timeouts.

−1   If the CMONTIMEOUT is −1, TACL will wait forever for a response from CMON.

<n>   If the CMONTIMEOUT is n <seconds>, TACL will wait n seconds for CMON to respond. If the CMON doesn't respond, TACL will act on the process request. The number of seconds chosen should depend on the speed of the system and the network.

RISK   If the CMONTIMEOUT value is −1, TACL will wait forever for a response. A CMON that isn't running or is running too slow can cause denial of service.

With or without Safeguard software :

> **BP-TACL-TACLCONF-08**   If CMON is running, CMONTIMEOUT should be set to a value that will not seriously inconvenience the user population.

REMOTECMONREQUIRED

The REMOTECMONREQUIRED parameter determines whether or not CMON must rule on all remote process requests. The valid entries are:

0 (zero)   A response from CMON is not required. If the REMOTECMON-REQUIRED value is 0 (zero) and CMON doesn't respond, TACL will act on the process request.

−1   A response from CMON is required. If the REMOTECMON-REQUIRED value is −1 and CMON does not respond, TACL will wait for the number of seconds defined by the REMOTECMON-TIMEOUT value. If the timeout occurs, the action will be denied.

RISK   If the REMOTECMONREQUIRED value is −1, the system is at risk for denial of service.

With or without Safeguard software:

> **BP-TACL-TACLCONF-04**   If CMON is running, REMOTECMONREQUIRED should be 0 (off), a response is not required.

REMOTECMONTIMEOUT

Number of seconds to wait for a response from a remote CMON.

The REMOTECMONTIMEOUT parameter determines how long TACL will wait for the remote CMON to respond:

−1   If the REMOTECMONTIMEOUT is −1, TACL will wait forever for a response from the remote CMON.

\<nn>   If the REMOTECMONTIMEOUT is n \<seconds>, TACL will wait n seconds for the remote CMON to respond. If the CMON doesn't respond, TACL will act on the process request. The number of seconds chosen should depend on the speed of the system and the network.

RISK   If the REMOTECMONTIMEOUT value is −1, TACL will wait forever for a response. A CMON that isn't running or is running too slow can cause denial of service.

With or without Safeguard software:

> **BP-TACL-TACLCONF-09**   If CMON is running,
> REMOTECMONTIMEOUT should be set to a value that will not seriously
> inconvenience the user population.

CMON in a Safeguard Environment

Safeguard software, if configured to do so, will communicate with CMON during the
following events:

> Logons
>
> Process creates of a Command Interpreter at a Safeguard Controlled
> Terminal

CMON

The CMON Global Parameter determines whether or not Safeguard will communicate with CMON in the following events:

> If CMON is ON Safeguard software will communicate with CMON.
>
> If CMON is OFF, Safeguard software will not communicate with CMON.
>
> The default value is OFF.

> **BP-SAFEGARD-GLOBAL-50**   If CMON is running, the CMON parameter
> should be ON

CMONERROR

The CMONERROR parameter determines how Safeguard software will behave when
CMON doesn't respond to Safeguard's communications, for whatever reason.

> If CMONERROR is ACCEPT, failures to communicate with CMON will be
> ignored.

> If CMONERROR is DENY, Safeguard software will deny access requests when
> CMON fails to respond.

> The default value is ACCEPT.

> **BP-SAFEGARDGLOBAL-51**   If CMON is running, the CMONERROR
> parameter should be ACCEPT.

CMONTIMEOUT

Specifies the number of seconds that Safeguard software is to wait for any CMON response. The default is 30 seconds.

> **BP-SAFEGARDGLOBAL-52** If CMON is running, the CMONTIMEOUT parameter value depends on the speed of the system; recommended value is 30 seconds.

Identifier	Questions	Discovery
CMON-PROCESS-01	Is a CMON process running on the system?	Process status
CMON-POLICY-01	Is CMON being used to enforce 'stepped' authentications?	Code review
CMON-POLICY-02	Is CMON being used to control remote access to the system?	Code review
CMON-POLICY-03	Is CMON being used to control access to system resources?	Code review
CMON-POLICY-04	Is CMON being used for load balancing?	Code review
CMON-TACLCONF-03	If CMON is running, is TACL configured CMONREQUIRED 0 (off)?	TACLCONF
CMON-TACLCONF-04	If CMON is running, is TACL configured REMOTECMONREQUIRED 0 (off)?	TACLCONF
CMON-TACLCONF-08	If CMON is running, is TACL configured CMONTIMEOUT <seconds>?	TACLCONF
CMON-TACLCONF-09	If CMON is running, is TACL configured REMOTECMONTIMEOUT <seconds>?	TACLCONF
USER-PRIVLEGE-01	If users are allowed to logon as any Privileged ID, are 'stepped' authentications enforced with CMON?	CMON config

5

Authorization—Object Security

Authorization is the process of controlling access to system resources. Access should be granted based on individual userids and group memberships. Therefore, userids must be carefully assigned based on the principles of Least Privilege, Individual Accountability and Separation of Duties.

User access to system objects (files, processes and devices) should be granted based on job function, mediated by the principles of Least Privilege and Separation of Duties.

Defining User Access to System Resources

This section outlines how to secure a system using the principles of Least Privilege, Separation of Duties and Individual Accountability.

Principles for Granting Access to System Resources

BP-POLICY-USER-01   Userid assignment must be based on the principles of Least Privilege and Separation of Duties.

Least Privilege   Least Privilege dictates that each user has access only to the resources required to perform their job and nothing more.

For example, operators are generally responsible for running the backup program, for managing the batch system and keeping various system devices, such as printers and communication lines, functioning. Individuals performing operations tasks should be assigned userids in the Operations administrative group.

Separation of Duties   Separation of duties dictates that job duties and responsibilities be divided among people or functional groups to a point where collusion is necessary for fraud to occur.

For example, operators should be able to 'bounce' communication lines, but not add new communication lines. Users who generate credit card account numbers should not be responsible for creating PINs for those accounts.

A Typical Access Matrix

The Corporate Security Standard should dictate which user groups have what access to each type of resource. Users should be granted access to only those programs and files necessary to perform their job. Application users are generally authenticated and regulated by the application itself.

	Some Common Task-related User Groups							
	Systems Mgt.	OPS Mgt.	Change Control	Help Desk	App Support	App Data Owner	App Exec ID	Security
Production Data files					R(W)	RWPC	RW	
Production Object Files			RWP		R		E	
Production Log Files	R	R	R	R	R	R	RWP	
Security Utilities and Files	R(E)			(RE)				RWEP
Safeguard and 3RD party Audit Files	R				(R)			R
Op Sys Utilities	RWE	E	E			E	E	E

( ) = access granted via the application, 3rd Party Access Control products or customer-written utilities which provide only limited, audited access to sensitive data or utilities.

Guardian Process Security

A process is defined as "a particular program running within a defined environment that includes an independent set of registers, code-addressing space, and data-addressing space." By default, processes are managed by the Guardian environment. They are created via Guardian procedure calls (See Figure 5-1).

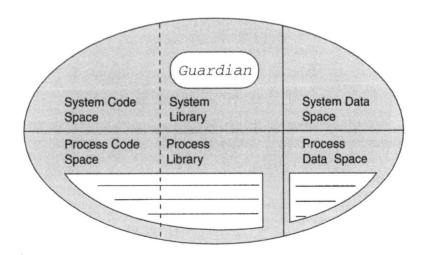

Figure 5-1
*Executing
Process Structure*

A process is created when a user executes a disk file containing object code. The user must have EXECUTE authority for the object file in order to create the process.

To fully protect processes, access to both the object files and the running processes must be protected.

Protecting the object files will be discussed in the chapters on File Security. This chapter concentrates on protecting running processes.

Programs

A program is a sequence of instructions and data that become a process when executed.

A program file is an executable object file. It contains primarily executable code, but may also contain other components such as initial or read-only data and linkage information. Unlike other object files, a program file has a main procedure.

Object files can be produced in two ways:

By compilers that translate the source program, written in a language such as TAL or C, into object code.

By linkers, such as the BINDER and NLD utilities, which link object files together.

Process Identifiers

Each process has multiple attributes:

Creator Accessor ID (CAID)

Process Accessor ID (PAID)

Process Name (optional)

Process Identification Number (PIN)

Process Identifier (PID)

When a process is created, it adopts the creator's userid as its CAID and the PAID of its creator as its PAID. This ensures that processes operate using the creating process's privileges and are able to access only those resources to which that process has been granted access.

> *RISK*   Note that a process' PAID can be altered with USER_AUTHENTICATE_   procedure calls or by executing a PROGID'd object file. Please refer to the Gazette section on PROGID.

> **BP-POLICY-PROCESS-01**   Processes should not run PROGID'd unless authorized by appropriate management and documented by the Security Administration Group.

Process Names

On the HP NonStop server, most objects, including processes, are considered to be files. The file name for a process is known as a process file name. The process name can be used to communicate with the process. Process file names must begin with a dollar sign ($). Subprocess names must begin with a hash or pound sign (#) and be preceded by the parent process name.

```
Example:
$S.#LP
```

Running processes are also identified numerically on a list known as the Process Control Table, which is allocated in the system data space and protected. The numeric value for a process is known as the Process Identification Number (PIN), which is the index to the process in a CPU. The combination of a CPU number and PIN is a Process Identification (PID).

```
Syntax:
<cpu #>,<process #>

Examples:
03,211
12,377
```

The first example shows process number 211 running in CPU 03. The second example shows process number 377 running in CPU 12.

Process Identification Number (PIN)

The PIN can be High or Low:

A Low PIN ranges from 0 through 254.

A High PIN ranges from 256 through the maximum number supported for the CPU.

C-series systems only utilize Low PINs (represented in an 8-bit field).

D-series systems utilize both High and Low

> PIN 255 is a special case low PIN used by high-PIN processes to communicate with an unconverted C-series process. The range of usable low PINs is therefore 0 through 254.

Process Properties

The following properties can be specified for a new process:

Named or unnamed

Waited or nowaited

High PIN or low PIN

Home terminal

Library file to be included in the process, if any

CPU where the process is to run

Priority

Only the following properties are of concern to security administrators:

Unnamed Processes

Priority

Defines

Unnamed Processes

Processes can be named or unnamed.

A NAMED process is one which had a name assigned when it was created.

An UNNAMED process had no name assigned when it was created.

Names can be created by the user or assigned by the operating system.

By default programs like EDIT and FUP run as UNNAMED processes.

RISK Safeguard software can only have one Protection Record for UNNAMED processes, so the same Safeguard security will be applied to *all* UNNAMED processes.

AP-ADVICE-UNNAMED-01   Avoid UNNAMED processes.

BP-POLICY-PROCESS-02 Application programs should not run UNNAMED.

PRIORITY

Processing order is determined by the priority of processes in a READY state.

Application process priorities range from 0 to 199. System priorities range from 200 to 255, so any system processes that are READY will always execute before any application processes.

Processes of the same priority are executed in the order they become ready on the Ready List of the CPU.

New processes with high priorities execute before any processes of lesser priority that were already in the queue.

RISK All processes on a processor, including system processes and application processes, share the same priority structure, so it is very important that each process runs at an appropriate priority, one which permits necessary system operations when needed.

When Priorities Are Set

When priorities are set depends on the type of process:

System process priorities are set during system generation.

I/O processes (but not disk processes) can have their priorities dynamically changed using the Dynamic System Configuration (DSC) utility on D-series systems or SCF on G-series systems.

User and Application process priorities are set during process creation. Processor-bound processes may have their priority reduced automatically to allow other processes to gain access to the processor. This is necessary to lessen the risk of a process taking over a CPU and pre-empting all other activity.

3P-CMON-PROCESS-01   CMON can be configured to manage which CPU and priority new processes will use.

3P-PROCESS-ADVICE-01   Third party process control software can be used to manage which CPU and priority the processes will use.

STATE

During its life, a process will pass back and forth between several process states (See Figure 5-2).

Starting	A temporary state occurring as the process starts up.
Ready	The process is either executing, ready to execute, or waiting for service from the memory manager (because of a page fault).
Suspended	The process has been suspended as a result of the a PROCESS_SUSPEND_call and will remain in this state until the PROCESS_ACTIVATE_ call makes the process runnable again.
Activating	A temporary state occurring as the result of PROCESS_ACTIVATE_ call that makes the process runnable again. Available only for suspended processes.
DEBUG and INSPECT	Either the DEBUG program or the INSPECT debugger has the process open. This state has several substates: Memory Access Breakpoint (MAB) breakpoint (BKPT) trap (TRAP) request (REQ)
Saveabend	The process is waiting for the INSPECT program to create a SAVEABEND file.
Stopping	A temporary state occurring while the process is being deleted.

Only processes that are in the READY state are capable of using the processor and only one process, the ACTIVE process, can use the processor at a time. The ACTIVE process will always be the one with the highest priority that is ready and not waiting for some external event such as a disk IO.

Figure 5-2
Process States

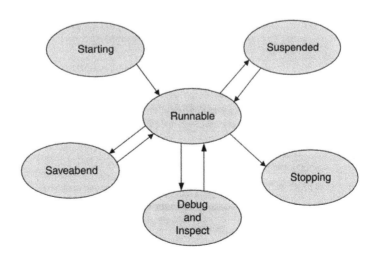

The ACTIVE process will go into a temporary WAIT substate when, during execution, it has to wait for an external event. Processes in the WAIT substate move back to the READY substate when their wait conditions are satisfied.

An ACTIVE process can be preempted by a higher priority process. When this happens, it goes to the READY substate. The highest priority READY process goes into the ACTIVE state immediately if its priority is higher than the current ACTIVE process, otherwise, it becomes ACTIVE when the current ACTIVE process goes into its WAIT substate.

Process Structure

When a process is created, it occupies space in virtual memory.

Each application or system process has physical CPU memory space allocated for object code, libraries, and data. The space where system code exists is separate from the space where application code exists. So, the operating system environment can be thought of as being divided into six sections:

System Code Space
System Data Space
System Library Space
Application Code Space
Application Data Space
Application Library Space

Code Space

The CODE SPACE contains program instructions and constants from the object file. Only READ access is permitted to the object code in the code space of a running process. This prevents modification of code during execution.

To maximize disk space efficiency, multiple copies of a process, even when running in different CPUs, can share the same object code on the disk.

To maximize memory efficiency, if multiple copies of a process are running in the same CPU, the processes all share one code space in memory.

Data Space

DATA SPACE is used by a process to store and manipulate data. Each running process maintains its own private data space, modifying the data as required during execution.

Library Space

LIBRARY SPACE is used by a process to store any routines loaded from libraries.

Securing Processes

The HP NonStop server provides many tools for managing processes on the system, both at the Command-Interpreter level and the procedure-call level. To prevent users from using these tools to interfere with another user's process (for example, to delete someone else's process) or access privileged data, the operating system provides tools for protecting processes from each other and for protecting data from indiscriminate access.

Each Guardian process is assigned a creator access ID (CAID), a process access ID (PAID), and a STOP MODE.

Three levels of process security exist:

Object file security

Process ownership controls

STOP MODE controls

The PAID is used to determine whether restricted actions against a process (such as stopping the process or invoking the debugger) are possible. Normally, the users who can stop a process are:

The process owner

The process owner's Group Manager

SUPER.SUPER

However, the STOP MODE can be set within a program to enforce various levels of security against stopping the process.

STOP MODE can restrict the ability to stop a process to one of the following:

Any process on the system can stop the configured process

A process with a PAID equal to that of SUPER.SUPER, the group manager of the target process, or the target process itself can stop the configured process

Only the configured process can stop itself

Safeguard software can override the first two STOP MODES when Protection Records are in place.

RISK   If a user creates a process configured so that only that process can stop itself, Safeguard software cannot override it. Even SUPER.SUPER cannot stop such processes.

With CMON

CMON can perform load-balancing tasks. If configured, CMON can control:

The CPU a process will start in

The initital process priority

ALTPRI requests

AP-ADVICE-CMON-01   CMON can be configured to manage which CPU and priority new processes will use. See the chapter on CMON for more information.

Without the Safeguard Subsystem

Actions that a process (or user) can attempt on another process:

ABEND

ACTIVATE

ALTPRI

DEBUG

OPEN

STOP

SUSPEND

How the Guardian System Evaluates Process Access Attempts

When a process is created, it adopts the creator's userid as it's the PAID, and the creating process becomes the CAID of the new process.

The PAID of any process attempting to affect another running process is compared with the CAID of the target process. If they do not match, the attempt will be denied.

The only exceptions to this rule are:

RISK   Processes owned by Group Manager IDs can manipulate any processes owned by members of their own groups.

BP-USER-PRIVLEGE-03   No users should be assigned a Group Manager ID as a personal userid.

RISK   Processes owned by SUPER.SUPER can manipulate any other processes.

BP-USER-PRIVLEGE-05   No user should be assigned SUPER.SUPER as a personal userid.

3P-PROCESS-PRIVLEGE-01   Third party process control software should be used to grant granular management of processes running as any Privileged ID for users who require these privileges in order to perform their jobs. These products generally also provide comprehensive auditing of the activities they secure.

Securing Processes With the Safeguard Subsystem

Safeguard software extends process security beyond simple ownership. Using PROCESS or SUBPROCESS Protection Records, it is possible to grant or deny access to processes independent of their ownership.

Safeguard protection replaces Guardian protection. While an object is under Safeguard control, the Guardian security setting becomes inactive.

Safeguard software makes its rulings on PROCESS access attempts based on the Safeguard Global Parameters and the individual PROCESS and SUBPROCESS records.

The following items may affect Safeguard PROCESS security:

Process-related Safeguard OBJECTTYPES

Process-related Safeguard Global Parameters

PROCESS Protection Records

SUBPROCESS Protection Records

Process-Related Safeguard OBJECTTYPES

Safeguard OBJECTTYPEs determine who is allowed to ADD Protection Records for each type of object. Two OBJECTTYPEs affect process security:

PROCESS OBJECTTYPE

SUBPROCESS OBJECTTYPE

Please refer to Safeguard Subsystem in Part One for the complete discussion of Safeguard OBJECTTYPE Records.

Securing NAMED and UNNAMED Processes

Safeguard software provides two special Safeguard Protection Records that can be used to control who can CREATE or STOP any NAMED or UNNAMED process, whether or not the process is otherwise protected by Safeguard software. The PROCESS OBJECTTYPE controls who can create the special Protection Records for NAMED and UNNAMED processes.

This feature is intended to allow a specified group of users, such as system operators, the ability to CREATE or STOP any process on the system.

For NAMED and UNNAMED records, READ and WRITE authorities are not valid; the only valid access authorities are:

CREATE (run)

PURGE (stop)

OWNER

The Safeguard Global parameter COMBINATION-PROCESS must be set to FIRST-RULE for the NAMED and UNNAMED feature to function as intended.

RISK   Without PROCESS OBJECTTYPE or SUBPROCESS OBJECTTYPE records, any user can add a Safeguard Protection Record for a process name (regardless of ownership), thereby gaining control of the process.

RISK   The PROCESS OBJECTTYPE also controls who can create the special Protection Records for NAMED and UNNAMED processes. This is very important because any user granted PURGE authority on both the NAMED and UNNAMED Protection Records can stop any process on the system.

BP-PROCESS-OBJTYPE-01   The PROCESS OBJECTTYPE should be created.

BP-SUBPROC-OBJTYPE-01   The SUBPROCESS OBJECTTYPE should be created.

BP-PROCESS-OBJTYPE-02   The PROCESS OBJECTTYPE should be owned by the Security-Administrator.

BP-SUBPROC-OBJTYPE-02   The SUBPROCESS OBJECTTYPE should be owned by the Security-Administrator.

BP-PROCESS-OBJTYPE-03   The PROCESS OBJECTTYPE should be audited for Access; AUDIT-ACCESS-PASS & AUDIT-ACCESS-FAIL

BP-SUBPROC-OBJTYPE-03   The SUBPROCESS OBJECTTYPE should be audited for Access; AUDIT-ACCESS-PASS & AUDIT-ACCESS-FAIL

BP-PROCESS-OBJTYPE-04 The PROCESS OBJECTTYPE should be audited for Manage; AUDIT-MANAGE-PASS & AUDIT-MANAGE-FAIL

BP-SUBPROC-OBJTYPE-04 The SUBPROCESS OBJECTTYPE should be audited for Manage; AUDIT-MANAGE-PASS & AUDIT-MANAGE-FAIL

UNNAMED Protection Record

RISK When a Protection Record specifying UNNAMED as the process name is created, that record applies to *all unnamed processes.*

In the case of the UNNAMED Protection Record, *only those users specified* on the UNNAMED Protection Record will be able to CREATE and STOP unnamed processes.

RISK Whoever is granted PURGE authority on the UNNAMED Protection Record can stop any UNNAMED process on the system.

Safeguard software can only have one Protection Record for UNNAMED processes, so the same Safeguard security will be applied to *all* UNNAMED processes.

AP-ADVICE-UNNAMED-01 Avoid UNNAMED processes.

BP-POLICY-PROCESS-02 Application programs should not run UNNAMED.

NAMED Protection Record

When a Protection Record specifying NAMED as the process name is created, that record applies to *all* NAMED processes.

RISK In NAMED Protection Records, *only those users specified* on the NAMED Protection Record will be able to create and stop named processes. If no other Protection Records exist for processes, no users will be able to CREATE and STOP named processes except users specified on the NAMED Protection Record.

For NAMED and UNNAMED records, the only valid access authorities are CREATE, PURGE, and OWNER.

BP-POLICY-PROCESS-03 If the company security policy requires that a Protection Record for NAMED processes be created, then create Protection Records for all the named processes on the system, to ensure that the appropriate users can manage them.

The user who CREATES a process is allowed to STOP the process even if a Protection Record prevents it.

How the Safeguard Subsystem Evaluates Process Management Requests

A User Creating a Protected Process

Access to PROCESSES or SUBPROCESSES with protected names is controlled by the Protection Record defined for the name. When a user attempts to CREATE a process with a protected name, Safeguard software checks for a Protection Record for the name.

If the user has CREATE authority, Safeguard software allows the process to be created.

If the user doesn't have CREATE authority, the request is rejected with a security violation error (Error 48).

A Process Opening a Protected Process or Subprocess

When a process attempts to open another process or subprocess with a protected name, Safeguard software checks the record to see if the user identified by the PAID of the requesting process is authorized to open the protected process.

If the open request is for READ/WRITE and the user has READ/WRITE authority, the request is allowed to complete successfully.

If the user does not have the proper authority, Safeguard software rejects the open request with a security violation error (Error 48).

NOTE: If the process is opened for READ, the file system will allow both READ and WRITE operations. Therefore, *the process itself must enforce the distinction between an open for READ and an open for WRITE.*

Stopping a Protected Process

If a user attempts to stop a process with a protected name, Safeguard software checks the Protection Record for the process name to determine whether the user has PURGE authority.

If the user has PURGE authority, Safeguard software allows the process to be stopped.

If the user does not have PURGE authority, the stop request is rejected with a security violation error (Error 48).

Process-Related Safeguard Global Parameters

The following global parameters determine whether or not Safeguard software will rule on attempts to manage PROCESSES and how it will make its ruling:

ACL-REQUIRED-PROCESS
CHECK-PROCESS
CHECK-SUBPROCESS
COMBINATION-PROCESS
DIRECTION-PROCESS

ACL-REQUIRED-PROCESS

The ACL-REQUIRED-PROCESS parameter determines whether or not all processes on the system must have a Safeguard Protection Record.

If ACL-REQUIRED-PROCESS is OFF, and no Protection Record is found, Guardian rules apply.

If ACL-REQUIRED-PROCESS is ON, Safeguard software will deny access to any PROCESS that does not have a Safeguard Protection Record.

The default value is OFF.

RISK   If ACL-REQUIRED-PROCESS is ON, Safeguard will deny access to any PROCESS that does not have a Safeguard Protection Record.

BP-SAFEGARD-GLOBAL-21   ACL-REQUIRED-PROCESS should be OFF unless required by the Corporate Security Policy.

CHECK-PROCESS

The CHECK-PROCESS parameter determines whether or not Safeguard software will check to see if there is a PROCESS Protection Record when a process access attempt is made.

If CHECK-PROCESS is ON, Safeguard software will refer to PROCESS Protection Records to evaluate PROCESS access requests.

If CHECK-PROCESS is OFF, PROCESS Protection Records will not be checked.

The default value is ON.

Safeguard software does not check Safeguard Protection Records for PROCESSes unless it is configured to check them.

BP-SAFEGARD-GLOBAL-18   CHECK-PROCESS should be set to ON.

CHECK-SUBPROCESS

The CHECK-SUBPROCESS parameter determines whether or not Safeguard software will check to see if there is a SUBPROCESS Protection Record when a subprocess access attempt is made.

If CHECK-SUBPROCESS is ON, Safeguard will refer to SUBPROCESS Protection Records to evaluate SUBPROCESS access requests.

If CHECK-SUBPROCESS is OFF, PROCESS Protection Records will not be checked.

The default value is ON.

BP-SAFEGARD-GLOBAL-20   CHECK-SUBPROCESS should be set to ON.

COMBINATION-PROCESS

COMBINATION-PROCESS tells Safeguard how to resolve conflicts when both PROCESS and SUBPROCESS Protection Records exist for the target process, but the records don't grant equal access authority for the user and the attempted operation. The value can be:

FIRST-ACL   The first Protection Record found (based on DIRECTION-PROCESS) determines the access, and whether or not the user and the attempted operation are included in the record.

FIRST-RULE Protection Records are searched until *both* the user and the access requested is explicitly granted or denied.

ALL   Both the PROCESS and SUBPROCESS rules must grant the requested access.

The default value is FIRST-ACL.

BP-SAFEGARD-GLOBAL-19   COMBINATION-PROCESS should be FIRST-ACL

RISK   The Safeguard Global parameter COMBINATION-PROCESS must be set to FIRST-RULE for the special NAMED and UNNAMED Process Protection Records to function correctly.

AP-SAFEGARD-GLOBAL-19   If the NAMED and UNNAMED Protection Records do not exist, then the COMBINATION-PROCESS parameter should be set according to the Corporate Security Policy.

DIRECTION-PROCESS

DIRECTION-PROCESS determines which direction Safeguard software will search for Protection Records when both CHECK-PROCESS and CHECK-SUBPROCESS are ON. This attribute is used in conjunction with COMBINATION-PROCESS. The valid entries are:

PROCESS-FIRST	Safeguard software searches for a PROCESS record first.
SUBPROCESS-FIRST	Safeguard software searches for a SUBPROCESS record first.

The default value is PROCESS-FIRST.

BP-SAFEGARD-GLOBAL-17   DIRECTION-PROCESS should be SUBPROCESS-FIRST.

Process And Subprocess Protection Records

Processes can be protected by two levels of Safeguard Rules: PROCESS and SUBPROCESS. Rules for one or both levels can exist.

Each Safeguard PROCESS Protection Record has three parts:

PRIMARY OWNER	By default the userid that created the Protection Record. Can be altered.
Access Control List (ACL)	The list of Userids that are allowed to access the object and the operations they are allowed to perform on the object.
Audit Settings	Determines whether Safeguard software will audit attempts to access the object.

Each PROCESS and SUBPROCESS Protection Record specifies the users allowed to access the process or subprocess and the operations these users are allowed to perform. The valid operations are:

READ	Refers to the authority to open a PROCESS or SUBPROCESS for input/output
WRITE	Refers to the authority to open a PROCESS or SUBPROCESS for input/output
CREATE	Refers to the authority to CREATE a process with a protected name. (A user must also have Execute authority for the program object file.) *Create does not apply to subprocesses.*

PURGE   Refers to the authority to STOP a process with a protected name. *Does not apply to subprocesses.*

OWNER   Has authority to ALTER the Protection Record.

Only userids or File-Sharing Groups, not aliases, can be included in PROCESS and SUBPROCESS Protection Records. Safeguard aliases gain all the access authority of their underlying userid. See User Administration in Part Three.

If remote access is appropriate for a given process or subprocess, the users must be defined as network users (*.) when granting privileges in the PROCESS or SUBPROCESS ACL, or Safeguard software will deny the OPEN access requests from another node. Users defined as network users are automatically granted the appropriate local access privileges as well.

Process Protection Record Ownership

Every Safeguard Protection Record has an owner. The record owner is the Primary Owner. By default, the owner is the user who created the Protection Record, but that user can give ownership to another userid.

By default, only the Primary Owner of a Protection Record, the owner's group manager, and SUPER.SUPER can manage (ALTER or DELETE) a Protection Record.

In addition, the initial owner can add owners to a Protection Record. Additional ownership is defined by the OWNER authority code for Protection Record entries and is an independent extension of the initial owner. Additional owners can do anything that the initial owner is permitted to do. They are equal, in every way, to the initial owner. For example, they can modify the Safeguard Protection Records for any process they own, and they can access any process they own when that process has been FROZEN. The OWNER authority may be used to deny explicitly a local SUPER.SUPER any of the authorities implicitly granted to SUPER.SUPER, including OWNER. The OWNER authority can always be specified for all processes protected by Safeguard software .

Auditing Process And Subprocess Access and Management

The following Global parameters can be used to configure system-wide process auditing.

AUDIT-PROCESS-ACCESS-PASS
AUDIT-PROCESS-ACCESS-FAIL
AUDIT-PROCESS-MANAGE-PASS

AUDIT-PROCESS-MANAGE-FAIL

AUDIT-PROCESS-ACCESS{ -PASS | -FAIL }

The AUDIT-PROCESS-ACCESS-PASS/FAIL parameters determine whether or not successful attempts to access all processes or subprocesses on the system are audited. The value can be ALL, NONE, LOCAL, or REMOTE.

If AUDIT-PROCESS-ACCESS-PASS value is configured to anything other than NONE, then the appropriate successful process access attempts will be audited.

If AUDIT-PROCESS-ACCESS-FAIL value is configured to anything other than NONE, then the appropriate unsuccessful process access attempts will be audited.

This setting *supplements* the audit settings for individual processes and sub-processes.

If an individual PROCESS or SUBPROCESS Protection Record is configured to audit only LOCAL access attempts, but the Global parameter is REMOTE, then both LOCAL and REMOTE access attempts will be audited.

However, if an individual PROCESS or SUBPROCESS Protection Record is configured to audit only NONE and the Global parameter is ALL, then Safeguard software will not audit either successful or unsuccessful process access attempts.

The default is NONE.

BP-PROCESS-POLICY-04   Whether or not PROCESS access attempts are audited depends on the Corporate Security Policy.

AUDIT-PROCESS-MANAGE { -PASS | -FAIL }

The AUDIT-PROCESS-MANAGE-PASS/FAIL parameters determine whether or not attempts to CREATE, ALTER or DELETE Process Protection Record will be audited. This setting *supplements* the audit settings for individual processes or subprocesses. The value can be ALL, NONE, LOCAL, or REMOTE.

If an individual PROCESS or SUBPROCESS Protection Record is configured to audit only LOCAL management attempts, but the Global parameter is REMOTE, then both LOCAL and REMOTE management attempts will be audited.

However, if an individual PROCESS or SUBPROCESS Protection Record is configured to audit only NONE and the Global parameter is ALL, then Safeguard software will not audit either successful or unsuccessful process management attempts.

The default is NONE.

BP-PROCESS-AUDIT-01 AUDIT-PROCESS-MANAGE-PASS should be ALL.

BP-PROCESS-AUDIT-02 AUDIT-PROCESS-MANAGE-FAIL should be ALL.

Identifier	Question	Look in
POLICY-PROCESS-01	Do any processes run PROGID'd that are not authorized?	Process Status
POLICY-PROCESS-02	Do any application processes run UNNAMED?	Process Status
POLICY-PROCESS-03	Does the Corporate Security Policy require Protection Records for NAMED processes?	Policy
PROCESS-OBJTYPE-01	Does the PROCESS OBJECTTYPE exist?	Safecom
SUBPROC-OBJTYPE-01	Does the SUBPROCESS OBJECTTYPE exist?	Safecom
PROCESS-OBJTYPE-02	Is the PROCESS OBJECTTYPE owned by the SECURITY ADMINISTRATOR?	Safecom
SUBPROC-OBJTYPE-02	Is the SUBPROCESS OBJECTTYPE owned by the SECURITY ADMINISTRATOR?	Safecom
PROCESS-OBJTYPE-03	Is the PROCESS OBJECTTYPE set to audit accesses?	Safecom
SUBPROC-OBJTYPE-03	Is the SUBPROCESS OBJECTTYPE set to audit accesses?	Safecom
PROCESS-OBJTYPE-04	Is the PROCESS OBJECTTYPE set to audit manage attempts?	Safecom
SUBPROC-OBJTYPE-04	Is the SUBPROCESS OBJECTTYPE set to manage attempts?	Safecom
SAFEGARD-GLOBAL-21	Is the Safeguard Global parameter ACL-REQUIRED-PROCESS value OFF?	Safecom
SAFEGARD-GLOBAL-18	Is the Safeguard Global parameter CHECK-PROCESS value ON?	Safecom
SAFEGARD-GLOBAL-20	Is the Safeguard Global parameter CHECK=-SUBPROCESS value ON?	Safecom .
SAFEGARD-GLOBAL-19	Is the Safeguard Global parameter COMBINATION-PROCESS value FIRST-ACL?	Safecom
SAFEGARD-GLOBAL-17	Is the Safeguard Global parameter DIRECTION-PROCESS value SUBPROCESS-FIRST?	Safecom
PROCESS-POLICY-04	Does the Corporate Security Policy mandate auditing of attempts to access PROCESSES?	Policy
PROCESS-POLICY-04	Are all attempts to access PROCESS Protection Records audited?	Safecom
PROCESS-POLICY-05	Does the Corporate Security Policy mandate auditing of attempts to manage PROCESSES?	Policy
PROCESS-AUDIT-01 PROCESS-AUDIT-02	Are all attempts to manage PROCESS Protection Records audited?	Safecom

Device Security

Until a device or subdevice is added to the Safeguard database, any process can open the device for input or output. Once added to Safeguard, only processes executing on behalf of users included in the Protection Record can access the device or subdevice.

Identifying Devices

Devices are identified by either a Device Name or a Logical Device Number. The Subdevice name, or Qualifier, is optional.

Device Name

The DEVICE NAME identifies the device. It can be up to eight characters long. The first character must be a dollar sign ($). The second character must be a letter. The remaining six characters can be numbers or letters.

Qualifier

The QUALIFIER is the optional Subdevice name. It can be up to eight characters long, including the required leading pound or hash sign (#). The first character following the # must be a letter.

Subqualifier

The SUBQUALIFIER is the optional specifier, subordinate to Qualifier. It can be up to eight alphanumeric characters long. The first character must be a letter.

LDEV-Number

The LDEV-NUMBER is the Logical Device Number. Logical Device Numbers consist of a dollar sign ($) followed by one to five numbers.

Without the Safeguard Subsystem

In the Guardian environment, any process can open any device for input or output.

With the Safeguard Subsystem

Safeguard software extends device security beyond simple ownership. It allows creation of Protection Records that grant or deny access to devices.

Safeguard software makes its rulings on DEVICE access attempts, based on the following Safeguard Global Parameters and the individual DEVICE and SUBDEVICE records.

The following items may affect Safeguard DEVICE security:

Device-related Safeguard OBJECTTYPES

Device-related Safeguard Global Parameters

DEVICE Protection Records

SUBDEVICE Protection Records

Safeguard software distinguishes between local and remote open requests. A remote open request is defined as a request made by a process that was started by a network user logged onto a remote system. *When a process is remote, with respect to the device or subdevice that it is attempting to open, the network user must also be granted remote access.* Otherwise, Safeguard software rejects the open request with a security violation error.

DEVICE-Related Safeguard OBJECTTYPES

Safeguard OBJECTTYPEs determine who is allowed to ADD DEVICE or SUBDEVICE Protection Records. Two OBJECTTYPEs affect DEVICE security:

OBJECTTYPE DEVICE

OBJECTTYPE SUBDEVICE

Please refer to the Safeguard Subsystem in Part Three for more information on OBJECTTYPES.

RISK   Without DEVICE OBJECTTYPE or SUBDEVICE OBJECTTYPE records, any local member of the SUPER group can add a Safeguard Protection Record for a device name, thereby gaining control of the device.

BP-DEVICE-OBJTYPE-01   The DEVICE OBJECTTYPE should be created.

BP-SUBDEV-OBJTYPE-01   The SUBDEVICE OBJECTTYPE should be created.

BP-DEVICE-OBJTYPE-02   The DEVICE OBJECTTYPE should be owned by the Security-Administrator.

BP-SUBDEV-OBJTYPE-02   The SUBDEVICE OBJECTTYPE should be owned by the Security-Administrator.

BP-DEVICE-OBJTYPE-03   The DEVICE OBJECTTYPE should be audited for Access; AUDIT-ACCESS-PASS & AUDIT-ACCESS-FAIL

BP-SUBDEV-OBJTYPE-03   The SUBDEVICE OBJECTTYPE should be audited for Access; AUDIT-ACCESS-PASS & AUDIT-ACCESS-FAIL

BP-DEVICE-OBJTYPE-04   The DEVICE OBJECTTYPE should be audited for Manage; AUDIT-MANAGE-PASS & AUDIT-MANAGE-FAIL

BP-SUBDEV-OBJTYPE-04   The SUBDEVICE OBJECTTYPE should be audited for Manage; AUDIT-MANAGE-PASS & AUDIT-MANAGE-FAIL

DEVICE-Related Safeguard Global Parameters

The following Global parameters determine whether or not Safeguard software will rule on attempts to access DEVICES and how it will make its ruling:

ACL-REQUIRED-DEVICE

CHECK-DEVICE

CHECK-SUBDEVICE

COMBINATION-DEVICE

DIRECTION-DEVICE

Devices can be protected by two levels of Safeguard Protection Records: DEVICE rules and SUBDEVICE rules. A device may be protected by any combination of DEVICE and SUBDEVICE rules.

ACL-REQUIRED-DEVICE

The ACL-REQUIRED-DEVICE parameter determines whether of not all DEVICES on the system must have a Safeguard Protection Record.

If ACL-REQUIRED-DEVICE is OFF, and no Protection Record is found, Guardian rules apply.

If ACL-REQUIRED-DEVICE is ON, Safeguard software will deny access to any DEVICE that does not have a Safeguard Protection Record.

The default value is OFF.

RISK   If ACL-REQUIRED-DEVICE is ON, Safeguard software will deny access to any DEVICE that does not have a Safeguard Protection Record.

BP-SAFEGARD-GLOBAL-16   ACL-REQUIRED-DEVICE should be OFF unless required by the Corporate Security Policy.

CHECK-DEVICE

The CHECK-DEVICE parameter determines whether or not Safeguard software will check to see if there is a DEVICE Protection Record when a DEVICE access attempt is made.

If CHECK-DEVICE is ON, Safeguard software will refer to DEVICE Protection Records to evaluate DEVICE access requests.

If CHECK-DEVICE is OFF, DEVICE Protection Records will not be checked.

The default value is ON.

BP-SAFEGARD-GLOBAL-13   CHECK-DEVICE should be ON.

CHECK-SUBDEVICE

The CHECK-SUBDEVICE parameter determines whether or not Safeguard software will check to see if there is a SUBDEVICE Protection Record when a SUBDEVICE access attempt is made.

If CHECK-SUBDEVICE is ON, Safeguard software will refer to SUBDEVICE Protection Records to evaluate SUBDEVICE access requests.

If CHECK-SUBDEVICE is OFF, SUBDEVICE Protection Records will not be checked.

The default value is ON.

BP-SAFEGARD-GLOBAL-15   CHECK-SUBDEVICE should be ON.

COMBINATION-DEVICE

COMBINATION-DEVICE tells Safeguard software how to resolve conflicts when both DEVICE and SUBDEVICE Protection Records exist for the target DEVICE, but the records don't grant equal access authority for the user and the attempted operation. The value can be:

FIRST-ACL	The first Protection Record found (based on DIRECTION-DEVICE) determines the access, whether or not the user and the attempted operation are included in the record.
FIRST-RULE	Protection Records are searched until *both* the user and the access requested is explicitly granted or denied.
ALL	Both the DEVICE and SUBDEVICE rules must grant the requested access.

The default value is FIRST-ACL.

BP-SAFEGARD-GLOBAL-14   COMBINATION-DEVICE should be FIRST-ACL.

DIRECTION-DEVICE

DIRECTION-DEVICE determines which direction Safeguard software will search for a Protection Record when both CHECK-DEVICE and CHECK-SUBDEVICE are ON. This attribute is used in conjunction with COMBINATION-DEVICE. The valid entries are:

DEVICE-FIRST   Safeguard software searches for a DEVICE record first.

SUBDEVICE-FIRST   Safeguard software searches for a SUBDEVICE record first.

The default value is DEVICE-FIRST.

BP-SAFEGARD-GLOBAL-12   DIRECTION-DEVICE should be SUBDEVICE-FIRST.

Device And Subdevice Protection Records

Devices can be protected by two levels of Safeguard Rules: DEVICE and SUBDEVICE Protection Records. One or both levels can exist.

Each Safeguard device and subdevice Protection Record has three parts:

PRIMARY OWNER	By default the userid that created the protection record. Can be altered.
Access Control List (ACL)	The list of Userids that are allowed to access the device and the operations they are allowed to perform on the object.
Audit Settings	Determines whether Safeguard software will audit attempts to access the device.

Each DEVICE and SUBDEVICE Protection Record Access Control List (ACL) specifies the users allowed to access the device or subdevice and the operations these users are allowed to perform. The valid operations are:

READ, WRITE   refers to authority to open a device/subdevice for input/ output

OWNER   refers to authority to ALTER or PURGE the DEVICE or SUBDEVICE Protection Record

Only userids or File-Sharing Groups, not aliases, can be included in DEVICE and SUBDEVICE Protection Records. Safeguard aliases gain all the access authority of their underlying userid.

If remote access, defined as an OPEN attempt made by a user authenticated on a different node, is appropriate for a given device or subdevice, the users must be defined as network users (*.), when granting privileges in the DEVICE or SUBDEVICE Protection Record, otherwise, Safeguard software will deny the OPEN access requests from another node. Users defined as network users are automatically granted the appropriate local access privileges as well.

Device Protection Record Ownership

A device has no owner until a Safeguard Protection Record is created. Every Safeguard Protection Record contains an OWNER attribute. The OWNER attribute contains the userid of the user who can manage the Safeguard access controls for the device.

The user who adds the record can set the OWNER attribute to the userid of any user (by including an OWNER specification in a SET DEVICE or ADD DEVICE command). The owner of a DEVICE Protection Record, the owner's group manager, and SUPER.SUPER can transfer ownership to another user by changing the OWNER attribute through the ALTER DEVICE command.

In addition, the initial owner can add owners to a Protection Record. Additional ownership is defined by the OWNER authority code in the Protection Record. Additional owners can do anything that the initial owner is permitted to do. They are equal, in every way, to the initial owner. For example, they can modify the Safeguard Protection Records for any device they own, and they can access any device they own when that device has been FROZEN. The OWNER authority may be used to deny explicitly a local SUPER.SUPER any of the authorities implicitly granted to SUPER.SUPER, including OWNER. The OWNER authority can always be specified for all devices protected by Safeguard software.

Auditing Device And Subdevice Access and Management

The following Safeguard Global parameters are discussed in Safeguard Configuration in Part Two.

AUDIT-DEVICE-ACCESS-PASS

AUDIT-DEVICE-ACCESS-FAIL

AUDIT-DEVICE-MANAGE-PASS

AUDIT-DEVICE-MANAGE-FAIL

AUDIT-DEVICE-ACCESS{ -PASS | -FAIL }

The AUDIT-DEVICE-ACCESS-PASS/FAIL parameters determine whether or not successful attempts to access all devices or subdevices on the system are audited. The value can be ALL, NONE, LOCAL, or REMOTE.

If the AUDIT-DEVICE-ACCESS-PASS value is configured to anything other than NONE, then the appropriate successful DEVICE access attempts will be audited.

If the AUDIT-DEVICE-ACCESS-FAIL value is configured to anything other than NONE, then the appropriate unsuccessful DEVICE access attempts will be audited.

This setting *supplements* the audit settings for individual devices or subdevices.

If an individual DEVICE or SUBDEVICE Protection Record is configured to audit only LOCAL access attempts, but the Global parameter is REMOTE, then both LOCAL and REMOTE access attempts will be audited.

However, if an individual DEVICE or SUBDEVICE Protection Record is configured to audit only NONE and the Global parameter is ALL, then Safeguard software will not audit either successful or unsuccessful DEVICE access attempts.

The default is NONE.

BP-DEVICE-POLICY-01   Whether or not DEVICE access attempts are audited depends on the Corporate Security Policy.

AUDIT-DEVICE-MANAGE { -PASS | -FAIL }

The AUDIT-DEVICE-MANAGE-PASS/FAIL parameters determine whether or not attempts to CREATE, ALTER or DELETE a DEVICE or SUBDEVICE Protection Record will be audited. This setting *supplements* the audit settings for individual devices or subdevices. The value can be ALL, NONE, LOCAL, or REMOTE.

If an individual DEVICE or SUBDEVICE Protection Record is configured to audit only LOCAL access attempts, but the Global parameter is REMOTE, then both LOCAL and REMOTE access attempts will be audited.

However, if an individual DEVICE or SUBDEVICE Protection Record is configured to audit only NONE and the Global parameter is ALL, then Safeguard software will not audit either successful or unsuccessful DEVICE access attempts.

The default is NONE.

BP-DEVICE-AUDIT-01   AUDIT-DEVICE-MANAGE-PASS should be ALL.

BP-DEVICE-AUDIT-02   AUDIT-DEVICE-MANAGE-FAIL should be
ALL.

Identifier	Question	Look in
DEVICE -OBJTYPE-01	Does the DEVICE OBJECTTYPE exist?	Safecom
SUBDEV -OBJTYPE-01	Does the SUBDEVICE OBJECTTYPE exist?	Safecom
DEVICE -OBJTYPE-02	Is the DEVICE OBJECTTYPE owned by the SECURITY ADMINISTRATOR?	Safecom
SUBDEV -OBJTYPE-02	Is the SUBDEVICE OBJECTTYPE owned by the SECURITY ADMINISTRATOR?	Safecom
DEVICE -OBJTYPE-03	Is the DEVICE OBJECTTYPE set to audit accesses?	Safecom
SUBDEV -OBJTYPE-03	Is the SUBDEVICE OBJECTTYPE set to audit accesses?	Safecom
DEVICE -OBJTYPE-04	Is the DEVICE OBJECTTYPE set to audit manage attempts?	Safecom
SUBDEV -OBJTYPE-04	Is the SUBDEVICE OBJECTTYPE set to manage attempts?	Safecom
SAFEGARD-GLOBAL-16	Is the Safeguard Global parameter ACL-REQUIRED-DEVICE value OFF?	Safecom
SAFEGARD-GLOBAL-13	Is the Safeguard Global parameter CHECK-DEVICE value ON?	Safecom
SAFEGARD-GLOBAL-15	Is the Safeguard Global parameter CHECK-SUBDEVICE value ON?	Safecom
SAFEGARD-GLOBAL-14	Is the Safeguard Global parameter COMBINATION-DEVICE value FIRST-ACL?	Safecom
SAFEGARD-GLOBAL-12	Is the Safeguard Global parameter DIRECTION-DEVICE value SUBDEVICE-FIRST?	Safecom
DEVICE-POLICY-01	Does the Corporate Security Policy mandate auditing of attempts to access DEVICES?	Policy
DEVICE-POLICY-01	Are all attempts to access DEVICES Protection Records audited?	Safecom
DEVICE-POLICY-02	Does the Corporate Security Policy mandate auditing of attempts to manage DEVICES?	Policy
DEVICE-AUDIT-01 DEVICE-AUDIT-02	Are all attempts to manage DEVICES Protection Records audited?	Safecom

The File Subsystem

This chapter discusses files in general and the risks associated with certain files or file
attributes, ways to mitigate these risks, and ways to evaluate the security of these files
on the system.

File Names

Files are always referred to by their names. The user or process that creates the file gives it a name.

A disk file name includes the file's NODE, VOLUME, SUBVOLUME and FILE names. Each part is separated by a period.

The NODE name represents the computer system where the file resides. The name can be one to eight characters long, but must begin with a backslash (\). When referencing a file, the NODE may be omitted if the file resides on the current default system.

The VOLUME name represents the physical or virtual disk where the file resides. The name can be one to eight characters long, but must begin with a dollar sign ($). When referencing a file, the VOLUME name can be omitted if the file resides on the current default VOLUME.

RISK Users on some remote nodes may not be able to use volume names on the local node that have names more than 7 characters long, including the dollar sign.

BP-VOLUME-NAME-01 VOLUME names should not exceed 7 characters in length on any node connected to a network.

The SUBVOLUME name is the equivalent of a directory name on a PC. It represents a set of files. The name can be 1 to 8 characters long, but must begin with a letter. When referencing a file, the SUBVOLUME can be omitted if the file resides on the current VOLUME and SUBVOLUME.

The FILE name represents one individual file. The filename can never be omitted. File names can be one to eight characters long, but must begin with a letter.

Types of Files

Disk files are created to store databases, programs, or text. HP Enscribe database, the NonStop database record manager, supports the following disk file types:

Unstructured

Structured

    Key-sequenced

    Relative

    Entry-sequenced

Enscribe Database

Enscribe software is the database record manager of the Guardian operating system. It supports structured and unstructured files.

Unstructured Enscribe Files

Unstructured Enscribe files are basically just an array of bytes of data. The organization of an unstructured file is determined by its creator. Unstructured files often contain program code or text.

Structured Enscribe Files

Structured files are designed to contain databases. A database contains logical records (individual sets of data about separate items or people). Each type of structured file uses a different structured organization.

When creating a file, FUP is used to specify the structure of the file to match the type of data to be stored in the file. The security string can also be specified.

Structured files are one of:

Key-sequenced files

Entry-sequenced files

Relative files

Key-sequenced Enscribe files

In Key-Sequenced files, the primary key is a field or combination of fields within the record. Records are inserted in sequence based on the primary key and can be updated or deleted.

Relative Enscribe files

In Relative files, the primary key is a record number relative to the beginning of the file. Records are inserted at the end of the file or at the location specified by the relative key, and can be updated or deleted.

Entry-sequenced Enscribe files

In Entry-sequenced files, the primary key is a system generated key value. Records can only be inserted at the end of the file. Records can be updated, but not deleted.

There are two file formats:

Format 1

Format 2

Format 1 Files

Format 1 files are files with a size of up to 2 gigabytes of data.

Format 2 Files

Release Version G06.00 introduced a new Enscribe disk file format called Enscribe Format 2. They are frequently referred to as Type 2 files.

Type 2 or Format 2 files are very large files. They can be up to 1024 gigabytes of data. They are currently limited only by disk size.

Enscribe Format 2 files, are *not* supported for use with:

Object files

Queue files

EDIT files

RISK   Format 2 files should be closely monitored to avoid filling up a disk.

NonStop SQL

HP NonStop SQL database is the HP NonStop server's implementation of the Structured Query Language (SQL). It is a distributed, relational database management system for on-line transaction processing.

NonStop SQL tables are not accessible from the Enform report writer, READ, WRITE commands or FUP commands other than FUP INFO.

Securing Diskfiles In the Guardian Environment

In the Guardian environment, each file has an owner and a security vector. By default, the owner of the file is the userid that created it and the security vector is the owner's default security as defined in their User Record.

By default, a file owner or the owner's group manager can give their files to another user, using the FUP GIVE command, and also change the file's security vector using the FUP SECURE command.

The four file operations controlled by the security vector are:

READ   Determines who can read or copy any kind of file or who can
           execute a macro or OBEY an obey file.

WRITE   Determines who can modify the contents of a file.

EXECUTE   Determines who can execute a code 100 or 700 (object file) with
           the TACL RUN command.

PURGE   Determines who can delete, rename or FUP ALTER a file.

The security settings are always displayed in this order: READ, WRITE, EXECUTE, PURGE (RWEP).

There are seven possible values for each operation. These values reflect who is allowed to perform the operation and whether or not the operation can be performed by someone on a remote node. The value is always a single character. The values are:

	LOCAL	REMOTE (Superset of local)
File Owner	O (owner)	U (user)
File Owner's Group	G (group)	C (community)
Everyone	A (all users)	N (all network users)
Local SUPER.SUPER only	- (hyphen)	

```
Example 1:
AFILE                        255,255            - - - -
SOMEFILE                     200,100            - - - -
```

In Example 1, only SUPER.SUPER can READ, WRITE, EXECUTE or PURGE either of the files. Notice that it does not matter who owns the file, if the security for any or all operations is a hyphen, then only SUPER.SUPER can perform that operation on the file.

```
Example 2:
AFILE                        255,255            UUUU
```

In Example 2, only a network SUPER.SUPER can READ, WRITE, EXECUTE or PURGE the file because SUPER.SUPER owns the file.

```
Example 3:
AFILE                        255,255            GG-G
```

In Example 3, only a local SUPER.SUPER can execute this file, but the rest of the local SUPER group can READ, WRITE, OR PURGE the file.

```
Example 4:
AFILE                        200,100            CC-U
```

In Example 4, only a local SUPER.SUPER can EXECUTE this file, only the owner, 200,100 can PURGE, but the rest of network group 200 can READ and WRITE the file.

```
Example 5:
AFILE                              200,100            OOOO
```

In Example 5, only local user 200,100 can READ, WRITE, EXECUTE or PURGE the file.

```
Example 6:
AFILE                              200,100            NUNU
```

In Example 6, only network user 200,100 can WRITE or PURGE, but all network users can READ or EXECUTE the file.

```
Example 7:
AFILE                              200,100            CUUO
```

In Example 7, user 200,100 can only PURGE the file when logged on locally, but can READ, WRITE or EXECUTE the file remotely. Users in group 200 can only READ the file, whether local or remote.

The Default Program

The DEFAULT program, is used to set the following parameters for User Records:

DEFAULT VOLUME

DEFAULT SECURITY

Please refer to Managing Userids in the Guardian System in Part Three.

Securing Disk Files With the Safeguard Subsystem

Safeguard software provides more versatile disk file security than the Guardian environment. It allows creation of rules, called Protection Records, which grant or deny access to files independent of a file's ownership or Guardian security vector.

Safeguard protection replaces Guardian protection; while an object is under Safeguard control, the Guardian security setting becomes inactive.

The following parameters may affect Safeguard DISKFILE security:

DISKFILE-related User Record Settings

DISKFILE-related Safeguard OBJECTTYPES

DISKFILE-related Safeguard Global Parameters

VOLUME Protection Records

SUBVOLUME Protection Records

DISKFILE Protection Records

Diskfile-Related User Record Settings

There are three fields in Safeguard User Records that affect file security.

Guardian Default Volume

The VOLUME and SUBVOLUME where the user's TACL session will begin. This is the equivalent of the Guardian volume and subvolume set using the DEFAULT program.

Guardian Default Security

The Guardian security vector that will automatically be assigned to every file that the user creates. This is the equivalent of the Guardian security vector set using the DEFAULT program. Please refer to the chapter Managing Userids in the Safeguard Subsystem.

Subject Default-Protection

Defines the Safeguard Diskfile Protection Record that will be created for each file the user creates. Please see the chapter on User Administration for the detailed auditing information relating to this field in Safeguard User Records.

The default Protection Record is defined like any other diskfile Protection Record, specifying an owner and the Access Control List .

Please refer to the chapter Managing Userids in the Safeguard Subsystem.

Disk-Related Safeguard OBJECTTYPES

Safeguard OBJECTTYPEs determine who is allowed to ADD disk file Protection Records. Three OBJECTTYPEs affect disk file security:

OBJECTTYPE VOLUME

OBJECTTYPE SUBVOLUME

OBJECTTYPE DISKFILE

Please refer to the chapter on the Safeguard Subsystem for more information on OBJECTTYPES.

RISK   Without VOLUME or SUBVOLUME and DISKFILE OBJECTTYPE records, any local member of the SUPER group can add a Safeguard Protection Record for a device name, thereby gaining control of diskfiles.

BP-VOLUME-OBJTYPE-01 The VOLUME OBJECTTYPE should be created.

BP-SUBVOL-OBJTYPE-01 The SUBVOLUME OBJECTTYPE should be created.

BP-DISKFILE-OBJTYPE-01 The DISKFILE OBJECTTYPE should be created.

BP-VOLUME-OBJTYPE-02 The VOLUME OBJECTTYPE should be owned by the Security-Administrator.

BP-SUBVOL-OBJTYPE-02 The SUBVOLUME OBJECTTYPE should be owned by the Security-Administrator.

BP-DISKFILE-OBJTYPE-02 The DISKFILE OBJECTTYPE should be owned by the Security-Administrator.

BP-VOLUME-OBJTYPE-03 The VOLUME OBJECTTYPE should be audited for Access; AUDIT-ACCESS-PASS & AUDIT-ACCESS-FAIL

BP-SUBVOL-OBJTYPE-03 The SUBVOLUME OBJECTTYPE should be audited for Access; AUDIT-ACCESS-PASS & AUDIT-ACCESS-FAIL

BP-DISKFILE-OBJTYPE-03 The DISKFILE OBJECTTYPE should be audited for Access; AUDIT-ACCESS-PASS & AUDIT-ACCESS-FAIL

BP-VOLUME-OBJTYPE-04 The VOLUME OBJECTTYPE should be audited for Manage; AUDIT-MANAGE-PASS & AUDIT-MANAGE-FAIL

BP-SUBVOL-OBJTYPE-04 The SUBVOLUME OBJECTTYPE should be audited for Manage; AUDIT-MANAGE-PASS & AUDIT-MANAGE-FAIL

BP-DISKFILE-OBJTYPE-04 The DISKFILE OBJECTTYPE should be audited for Manage; AUDIT-MANAGE-PASS & AUDIT-MANAGE-FAIL

Disk-Related Safeguard Global Settings

Disk files can be protected by three levels of Safeguard Protection Records: VOLUME rules, SUBVOLUME rules and DISKFILE rules. Any combination of VOLUME, SUBVOLUME and DISKFILE rules can exist. The following Safeguard Globals are related to DISKFILEs:

ACL-REQUIRED-DISKFILE

CHECK VOLUME

CHECK SUBVOLUME

CHECK-FILENAME

DIRECTION-DISKFILE

COMBINATION-DISKFILE

CLEARONPURGE-DISKFILE

RISK Any attempt to CREATE a disk file is subject to access checking at all levels, regardless if whether or not CHECK-VOLUME and CHECK-SUBVOLUME are OFF.

ACL-REQUIRED-DISKFILE

The ACL-REQUIRED-DISKFILE parameter determines whether or not Safeguard software will grant access to a file that doesn't have a Protection Record.

If ACL-REQUIRED-DISKFILE is OFF and no Protection Record is found, access is allowed based on Guardian security.

If ACL-REQUIRED-DISKFILE is ON, Safeguard software will deny access to any file that does not have a Safeguard Protection Record.

The default value is OFF.

RISK Use caution in setting the ACL-REQUIRED Safeguard Global attributes. With these attributes set, access is normally denied for any object that does not have a Protection Record, but in warning mode, access to all such objects is granted.

RISK When the ACL-REQUIRED-DISKFILE parameter is changed to ON, a Protection Record for the SAFECOM object file granting EXECUTE authority to the necessary users (including the user making the change) must be created. Otherwise, when the session used to make the change ends, no one will be able to control Safeguard software through the SAFECOM Command Interpreter because they will be unable to run SAFECOM.

BP-SAFEGARD-GLOBAL-26   ACL-REQUIRED-DISKFILE = OFF

CHECK-VOLUME

The CHECK-VOLUME Global Parameter enables or disables the checking of Protection Records at a VOLUME level.

If CHECK-VOLUME is OFF, Safeguard software does not check volume Protection Records for attempts to access a disk file.

If CHECK-VOLUME is ON, Safeguard software enforces any VOLUME Protection Records.

Having CHECK-VOLUME OFF the access result is the same as if that level had No Record

NOTE: Safeguard software reads the Safeguard files three times, once for VOLUME, once for SUBVOLUME and once for DISKFILE Protection Records, *before* evaluating the CHECK-VOLUME setting.

RISK   Any attempt to CREATE a disk file is subject to access checking at all levels, regardless if whether or not CHECK-VOLUME and CHECK-SUBVOLUME are OFF.

BP-SAFEGARD-GLOBAL-23   CHECK-VOLUME should be OFF.

CHECK-SUBVOLUME

The CHECK-SUBVOLUME Global Parameter enables or disables the checking of Protection Records at a SUBVOLUME level.

If CHECK-SUBVOLUME is OFF, Safeguard software does not check SUBVOLUME Protection Records for attempts to access a disk file.

If CHECK-SUBVOLUME is ON, Safeguard software enforces any SUBVOLUME Protection Records.

NOTE: Safeguard software reads the Safeguard files three times, once for VOLUME, once for SUBVOLUME and once for DISKFILE Protection Records, *before* evaluating the CHECK-SUBVOLUME setting.

RISK   Any attempt to CREATE a disk file is subject to access checking at all levels, regardless of whether or not CHECK-VOLUME and CHECK-SUBVOLUME are OFF.

If the VOLUME Protection Record grants the user the authority to create a disk file, Safeguard software then checks for a SUBVOLUME Protection Record for the subvolume on which the disk file is to be created. If found, the Safeguard software checks whether the subvolume Protection Record grants the user the authority to create a disk file. If the subvolume Protection Record grants the user the authority to create a disk file, the user's file-creation request succeeds. However, when the user lacks the authority to create a disk file on the subvolume, the file-creation request is rejected with a security violation error (file error 48).

If no Protection Record exists for the volume, a user's file-creation request is rejected only if both a Protection Record for the subvolume exists and the subvolume Protection Record does not grant the user CREATE authority. If no Protection Record exists for either the volume or subvolume, any user can create a disk file on the subvolume.

The Safeguard software does not restrict the creation of temporary files, such as swap files. Volume and subvolume Protection Records are not checked when a temporary file is created.

BP-SAFEGARD-GLOBAL-25   CHECK-SUBVOLUME = ON

CHECK-FILENAME

The CHECK-FILENAME Global Parameter enables or disables the checking of Protection Records at a DISKFILE level.

If CHECK-FILENAME is OFF, Safeguard software does not rule based on DISKFILE Protection Records for attempts to access a disk file.

If CHECK-FILENAME is ON, Safeguard software enforces any DISKFILE Protection Records.

NOTE: Safeguard software reads the Safeguard files three times, once for VOLUME, once for SUBVOLUME and once for DISKFILE Protection Records, *before* evaluating the CHECK-DISKFILE setting.

BP-SAFEGARD-GLOBAL-27   CHECK-FILENAME should be ON.

CLEARONPURGE-DISKFILE

The CLEARONPURGE-DISKFILE parameter determines whether or not file data space is overwritten with zeros when a file is deleted.

If CLEARONPURGE-DISKFILE is ON, then when diskfiles are deleted, the data is overwritten with zeros.

If CLEARONPURGE-DISKFILE is OFF, the disk space is de-allocated when purged, but the data is not set to zeros.

The default value is OFF.

RISK   If CLEARONPURGE is OFF then sensitive data can be left on the disk and another program could read the data.

RISK   If CLEARONPURGE is ON then very large file deletes could take a long time.

BP-SAFEGARD-GLOBAL-28   CLEARONPURGE-DISKFILE should be OFF.

COMBINATION-DISKFILE

COMBINATION-DISKFILE tells Safeguard software how to resolve conflicts when VOLUME, SUBVOLUME and DISKFILE Protection Records exist for the target DISKFILE. The value can be:

FIRST-ACL   The first record found (based on DIRECTION-DISKFILE) determines the access, whether or not the user and attempted operation is included in the record.

FIRST-RULE Records are searched until both the user and the access requested is explicitly granted or denied,

ALL   The VOLUME, SUBVOLUME and DISKFILE rules must all grant the requested access.

If ALL is selected, Safeguard software grants access only if it is granted by all the rules that exist. If VOLUME, SUBVOLUME and DISKFILE rules exist, then all three rules must agree on both the userid and the attempted operation or the request will be denied.

If FIRST-ACL is selected, Safeguard software uses the first rule it finds, regardless of whether the rule contains the specified userid. If the user is included in the rule, the operations allowed by the rule will be allowed and operations either denied or omitted will be denied. If the user is not included in the rule, access will be denied, Safeguard software will not look for any other rules protecting the file being accessed. The direction that Safeguard software searches for rules depends on the DIRECTION-DISKFILE parameter.

If FIRST-RULE is selected, Safeguard software searches until it finds a Protection Record (Rule) that contains the specified user *and* operation.

If both the user and the attempted operation are found on the first level rule, Safeguard software bases its ruling on the first rule.

If either the user or the attempted operation is missing from the first level rule found, Safeguard software will look for a rule at the next level.

If there is no second level rule, the access will be denied.

If a second level rule exists and both the user and the attempted operation are found on the second level rule, Safeguard software bases its ruling on the second level rule.

If either the user or the attempted operation is missing from the second level rule found, Safeguard software will look for a rule at the next level.

If no third level rule exists, access is denied.

If a third level rule exists and both the user and the attempted operation are found on third level rule, Safeguard software bases its ruling on the third level rule.

If either the user or the attempted operation is missing from the third level rule, Safeguard software denies access.

BP-SAFEGARD-GLOBAL-24   COMBINATION-DISKFILE should be FIRST-ACL.

DIRECTION-DISKFILE

The DIRECTION-DISKFILE setting determines the direction that Safeguard searches for Protection Records if more than one of the CHECK parameters is "ON". The value is FILENAME-FIRST or VOLUME-FIRST.

If DIRECTION-DISKFILE is FILENAME-FIRST, Safeguard looks first for a DISKFILE Protection Record when evaluating access to a disk file, then for a SUBVOLUME Protection Record and, finally, for a VOLUME Protection Record.

If DIRECTION-DISKFILE is VOLUME-FIRST, Safeguard looks first for a VOLUME Protection Record when evaluating access to a disk file, then for a SUBVOLUME Protection Record and, finally, for a DISKFILE Protection Record.

BP-SAFEGARD-GLOBAL-22   DIRECTION-DISKFILE should be FILENAME-FIRST

RISK   If CHECK-SUBVOLUME ON is set and DIRECTION-DISKFILE is set to VOLUME-FIRST and there is no OBJECTTYPE SUBVOLUME record, it is possible for any user to gain access to someone else's files. All files that are in subvolumes that have not been added to the Safeguard database are vulnerable. This situation occurs because any user can add the SUBVOLUME to the database and thereby own it.

Diskfile-related Protection Records

Diskfiles can be protected by rules at any or all of the following three 'levels':

Volume

Subvolume

Diskfile

VOLUME Protection Records

Each Safeguard VOLUME Protection Record has the following parts:

PRIMARY OWNER	By default the userid that created the ACL. Can be altered.
Access Control List (ACL)	The list of userids that are allowed to access the object and the operations they are allowed to perform on the object.
Audit Settings	Determines whether Safeguard software will audit attempts to access the object.

VOLUME Protection Record ACL

Each VOLUME Protection Record Access Control List (ACL) specifies the users allowed to access the volume and the operations these users are allowed to perform. The valid operations are:

READ (R)	refers to the authority to read any file on the VOLUME.
WRITE (W)	refers to the authority to alter any file on the VOLUME.
EXECUTE (E)	refers to the authority to execute any object file on the VOLUME.
PURGE (P)	refers to the authority to purge any file on the VOLUME.
CREATE (C)	refers to the authority to create a SUBVOLUME and/or file on the volume.
OWN (O)	refers to the authority to ALTER or DELETE the VOLUME Protection Record.

If remote access, defined as an access attempt made by a user authenticated on a different node, is appropriate for a given volume, the users must be defined as network users (*.) when granting privileges in the VOLUME Protection Record, or Safeguard software will deny the access requests from another node. Users defined as network users are automatically granted the appropriate local access privileges as well.

VOLUME Protection Record Ownership

A VOLUME has no owner until it is placed under Safeguard control. Then, by default, the user who added the Protection Record becomes its OWNER. Also by default, the OWNER of the Protection Record, the OWNER'S Group Manager, and SUPER.SUPER can ALTER or DELETE the Protection Record.

The OWNER of the Protection Record can 'give' ownership to another userid.

The OWNER can grant ownership privileges with the OWNER (O) authority. The OWNER attribute grants the ability to ALTER or DELETE the Protection Record to the specified users. These additional owners can do anything that the initial owner is permitted to do. They are equal, in every way, to the initial owner.

By denying the OWNER authority, SUPER.SUPER or Group Managers can be explicitly denied any of the authorities implicitly granted to them.

SUBVOLUME Protection Records

Each Safeguard VOLUME Protection Record has the following parts:

PRIMARY OWNER	By default the userid that created the ACL. Can be altered.
Access Control List (ACL)	The list of Userids that are allowed to access the object and the operations they are allowed to perform on the object.
Audit Settings	Determines whether Safeguard software will audit attempts to access the object.

SUBVOLUME Protection Record ACL

Each SUBVOLUME Protection Record's Access Control List (ACL) specifies the users allowed to access the subvolume and the operations these users are allowed to perform. The valid operations are:

READ (R) SUBVOLUME.   refers to the authority to READ any file in the

WRITE (W)   refers to the authority to alter any file in the SUBVOLUME.

EXECUTE (E)   refers to the authority to execute any object file in the SUBVOLUME.

PURGE (P) SUBVOLUME.   refers to the authority to purge any file in the

CREATE (C)   refers to the authority to create a file in the SUBVOLUME.

OWN (O)   refers to the authority to ALTER or DELETE the SUBVOLUME Protection Record.

If remote access, defined as an access attempt made by a user authenticated on a different node, is appropriate for a given subvolume, the users must be defined as network users (*.) when granting privileges in the SUBVOLUME ACL, or Safeguard will deny the access requests from another node. Users defined as network users are automatically granted the appropriate local access privileges as well.

SUBVOLUME Protection Record Ownership

A SUBVOLUME has no owner until it is placed under Safeguard control. Then, by default, the user who added the Protection Record becomes its OWNER. Also by default, the OWNER of the Protection Record, the OWNER'S Group Manager, and SUPER.SUPER can ALTER or DELETE the Protection Record.

The OWNER of the Protection Record can 'give' ownership to another userid.

The OWNER can grant ownership privileges with the OWNER (O) authority. The OWNER attribute grants the ability to ALTER or DELETE the Protection Record to the specified users. These additional owners can do anything that the initial owner is permitted to do. They are equal, in every way, to the initial owner.

By denying the OWNER authority, SUPER.SUPER or Group Managers can be explicitly denied any of the authorities implicitly granted to them.

DISKFILE Protection Records

Each Safeguard Protection Record has the following parameters:

PRIMARY OWNER	By default the userid that created the Protection Record. Primary owner can be altered.
Access Control List (ACL)	The list of Userids that are allowed to access the object and the operations they are allowed to perform on the object.
Audit Settings	Determines whether Safeguard software will audit attempts to access the object.
Disk file Protection Records have four additional parameters:	
LICENSE	Sets the LICENSED bit on the disk file protected by the Protection Record
PROGID	Sets the PROGID bit on the disk file protected by the Protection Record
PERSISTENT	Determines whether or not the Protection Record will remain after the disk file the Protection Record is protecting is deleted.
CLEARONPURGE	Fills the file with zeros when purged. If a file with persistent protection is purged, CLEARONPURGE retains its current setting. Deleting a file Protection Record does not change the clearonpurge flag.
	For disk files not under Safeguard protection, CLEARONPURGE can be set through the FUP SECURE command or by a program using a SETMODE or SETMODENOWAIT procedure call.

RISK   For userids other than SUPER.SUPER, the FUP GIVE, SECURE, LICENSE, and REVOKE commands no longer work for the disk file that has a Safeguard Protection Record, the equivalent Safeguard commands must be used.

DISKFILE Protection Record ACL

Each DISKFILE Protection Record's Access Control List (ACL) specifies the users allowed to access the file and the operations these users are allowed to perform. The valid operations are:

READ (R)   refers to the authority to read the file.

WRITE (W)   refers to the authority to alter the file.

EXECUTE (E)   refers to the authority to execute the file. Applies only if the file is an object file.

PURGE (P)   refers to the authority to purge the file.

OWNER (O)   refers to the authority to ALTER or DELETE the DISKFILE Protection Record.

NOTE: Copies of a file (such as a copy created with the FUP DUP command) are not protected by Safeguard software, unless DEFAULT-PROTECTION has been established for the user copying the file.

If remote access, defined as an access attempt made by a user authenticated on a different node, is appropriate for a given disk file, the users must be defined as network users (*), when granting privileges in the DISKFILE Protection Record, or Safeguard software will deny the OPEN access requests from another node. Users defined as network users are automatically granted the appropriate local access privileges as well.

DISKFILE Protection Record Ownership

By default, the user who added the Protection Record becomes its owner. Also by default, the OWNER of the Protection Record, the OWNER'S Group Manager, and SUPER.SUPER can ALTER or DELETE the Protection Record.

The OWNER of the Protection Record can 'give' ownership to another userid.

The OWNER can grant ownership privileges with the OWNER (O) authority. The OWNER authority grants the ability to ALTER or DELETE the Protection Record to the specified users. These additional owners can do anything that the initial owner is permitted to do. They are equal, in every way, to the initial owner.

NOTE: By denying the OWNER authority, SUPER.SUPER or Group Managers can be explicitly denied any of the authorities implicitly granted to them.

Guardian File Ownership Is Affected by Safeguard Protection Records

RISK Creating DISKFILE Protection Records changes the Guardian ownership of the file. If the Protection Record is deleted, but not the file, the Protection Record's Primary Owner becomes the Guardian owner of the file.

RISK If a Protection Record for a LICENSED file is created, the LICENSE is automatically revoked. It must be re-LICENSED using SAFECOM.

RISK If a Protection Record for a PROGID'd file is created, the PROGID is automatically removed. It must be re-PROGID'd using SAFECOM.

PROGID'd object files still run as the appropriate userid when they are EXECUTED.

How the Safeguard Subsystem Evaluates Diskfile CREATE Attempts

If the VOLUME Protection Record grants the user the authority to CREATE a disk file, Safeguard software checks for a SUBVOLUME Protection Record for the subvolume on which the disk file is to be created. If a Protection Record exists for the subvolume, its Protection Record is checked to see if the user has CREATE authority.

If the SUBVOLUME Protection Record grants the user the authority to CREATE a disk file, the user's file-creation request succeeds.

If the user lacks the authority to CREATE a disk file on the subvolume, the request is rejected with a security violation error(file error 48).

If no VOLUME Protection Record exists for the volume, the CREATE request is rejected only if a SUBVOLUME Protection Record for the subvolume exists and does not grant the user CREATE authority.

If no Protection Records exists for either the VOLUME or SUBVOLUME, any user can create a disk file on the subvolume.

> The Safeguard software does not restrict the creation of temporary files, such as swap files. Volume and subvolume authorization records are not checked when a temporary file is created.

How the Safeguard Subsytem Evaluates File Access Attempts

For DISKFILE access attempts, the DIRECTION-DISKFILE Global Parameter determines the direction that Safeguard software searches for Protection Records if more than one of the CHECK parameters is "ON". The choices are FILENAME-FIRST and VOLUME-FIRST.

Whether or not Protection Records at the remaining 'levels' are checked depends on the COMBINATION-DISKFILE value.

At each level checked, Safeguard software returns one of four results when it evaluates access:

No Record	No Protection Record exists.
No Mention	A Protection Record exists, but the user or operation is not included in the Protection Record.
Deny	Access is denied. There are two types of DENIALS:
	EXPLICIT—The user is included on the Protection Record and the attempted operation is denied.
	IMPLICIT—The user is included in the Protection Record, but the attempted operation is not, or teh user is not icluded.
Permit	Access is granted. The user is included in the Protection Record and the attempted operation is authorized.

Once Safeguard software has determined if the user (identified by the PAID) has the required authority to access the object the requested access is allowed or denied.

The table below shows how disk file access rules are evaluated depending on how Safeguard software applies the Protection Records in DISKFILE, VOLUME, and SUB-VOLUME Protection Records based on DIRECTION-DISKFILE and COMBINATION-DISKFILE.

DISKFILE ACCESS EVALUATION PAGE (PAGE 1 OF 2)

DIRECTION-DISKFILE			COMBINATION_DISKFILE		
1ST	2ND	3RD	1ST-ACL	1ST-RULE	ALL
Y	Y	Y	Permit	Permit	Permit
Y	Y	N	Permit	Permit	Deny
Y	Y	NM	Permit	Permit	Deny
Y	Y	NR	Permit	Permit	Permit
Y	N	Y	Permit	Permit	Deny
Y	N	N	Permit	Permit	Deny
Y	N	NM	Permit	Permit	Deny
Y	N	NR	Permit	Permit	Deny
Y	NM	Y	Permit	Permit	Deny
Y	NM	N	Permit	Permit	Deny
Y	NM	NM	Permit	Permit	Deny
Y	NM	NR	Permit	Permit	Deny
Y	NR	Y	Permit	Permit	Permit
Y	NR	N	Permit	Permit	Deny
Y	NR	NM	Permit	Permit	Deny
Y	NR	NR	Permit	Permit	Permit
N	Y	Y	Deny	Deny	Deny
N	Y	N	Deny	Deny	Deny
N	Y	NM	Deny	Deny	Deny
N	Y	NR	Deny	Deny	Deny
N	N	Y	Deny	Deny	Deny
N	N	N	Deny	Deny	Deny
N	N	NM	Deny	Deny	Deny
N	N	NR	Deny	Deny	Deny
N	NM	Y	Deny	Deny	Deny
N	NM	N	Deny	Deny	Deny
N	NM	NM	Deny	Deny	Deny
N	NM	NR	Deny	Deny	Deny
N	NR	N	Deny	Deny	Deny

DISKFILE ACCESS EVALUATION PAGE (PAGE 1 OF 2)

DIRECTION-DISKFILE			COMBINATION_DISKFILE		
1ST	2ND	3RD	1ST-ACL	1ST-RULE	ALL
N	NR	NR	Deny	Deny	Deny

* Indicates that access is denied if ACL-REQUIRED

DISKFILE ACCESS EVALUATION PAGE (PAGE 2 OF 2)

DIRECTION-DISKFILE			COMBINATION_DISKFILE		
1ST	2ND	3RD	1ST-ACL	1ST-RULE	ALL
NM	Y	Y	Deny	Permit	Deny
NM	Y	N	Deny	Permit	Deny
NM	Y	NM	Deny	Permit	Deny
NM	Y	NR	Deny	Permit	Deny
NM	N	Y	Deny	Deny	Deny
NM	N	N	Deny	Deny	Deny
NM	N	NM	Deny	Deny	Deny
NM	N	NR	Deny	Deny	Deny
NM	NM	Y	Deny	Permit	Deny
NM	NM	N	Deny	Deny	Deny
NM	NM	NM	Deny	Deny	Deny
NM	NM	NR	Deny	Deny	Deny
NM	NR	Y	Deny	Permit	Deny
NM	NR	N	Deny	Deny	Deny
NM	NR	NM	Deny	Deny	Deny
NM	NR	NR	Deny	Deny	Deny
NR	Y	Y	Permit	Permit	Permit
NR	Y	N	Permit	Permit	Deny
NR	Y	NM	Permit	Permit	Deny
NR	Y	NR	Permit	Permit	Permit
NR	N	Y	Deny	Deny	Deny
NR	N	N	Deny	Deny	Deny

DISKFILE ACCESS EVALUATION PAGE (PAGE 2 OF 2)					
DIRECTION-DISKFILE			COMBINATION_DISKFILE		
NR	N	NM	Deny	Deny	Deny
NR	N	NR	Deny	Deny	Deny
NR	NM	Y	Deny	Permit	Deny
NR	NM	N	Deny	Deny	Deny
NR	NM	NM	Deny	Deny	Deny
NR	NM	NR	Deny	Deny	Deny
NR	NR	Y	Permit	Permit	Permit
NR	NR	N	Deny	Deny	Deny
NR	NR	NM	Deny	Deny	Deny
NR	NR	NR	Guardian *	Guardian *	Guardian *

* Indicates that access is denied if ACL-REQUIRED

Auditing Disk File Access and Management Attempts

An open request that passes the Safeguard authorization check can still fail for another reason. For example, if a process attempts to open a file that is already open with exclusive access, the open attempt fails with file error 12 (file in use). Safeguard software records these events in its audit trail with an outcome of FAILED. FAILED means that the access attempt failed but not because of a Safeguard ruling.

Disk File-Related Global Audit Parameters

The following Global parameters are discussed in Part Four, User Administration.

AUDIT-DISKFILE-ACCESS-PASS

AUDIT-DISKFILE-ACCESS-FAIL

AUDIT-DISKFILE-MANAGE-PASS

AUDIT-DISKFILE-MANAGE-FAIL

AUDIT-DISKFILE-ACCESS{ -PASS | -FAIL }

The AUDIT-DISKFILE-ACCESS-PASS/FAIL parameters determine whether or not successful or unsuccessful attempts to access all disk files on the system are audited. The conditions can be ALL, NONE, LOCAL, or REMOTE.

If AUDIT-DISKFILE-ACCESS-PASS value is configured to anything other than NONE, then the appropriate successful disk file access attempts will be audited.

If AUDIT-DISKFILE-ACCESS-FAIL value is configured to anything other than NONE, then the appropriate unsuccessful disk file access attempts will be audited.

This setting *supplements* the audit settings for individual disk files.

If an individual DISKFILE Protection Record is configured to audit only LOCAL access attempts, but the Global parameter is REMOTE, then both LOCAL and REMOTE access attempts will be audited.

However, if an individual DISKFILE Protection Record is configured to audit only NONE and the Global parameter is ALL, then Safeguard software will not audit either successful or unsuccessful disk file access attempts.

The default is NONE.

AUDIT-DISKFILE-MANAGE { -PASS | -FAIL }

The AUDIT-DISKFILE-MANAGE-PASS/FAIL parameters determine whether or not attempts to CREATE, ALTER or DELETE DISKFILE Protection Record will be audited. This setting *supplements* the audit settings for individual disk files. The conditions can be ALL, NONE, LOCAL, or REMOTE.

If an individual DISKFILE Protection Record is configured to audit only LOCAL access attempts, but the Global parameter is REMOTE, then both LOCAL and REMOTE access attempts will be audited.

However, if an individual DISKFILE Protection Record is configured to audit only NONE and the Global parameter is ALL, then Safeguard software will not audit either successful or unsuccessful DISKFILE access attempts.

The default is NONE.

BP-DISKFILE-AUDIT-01   AUDIT-DISKFILE-MANAGE-PASS should be ALL

BP-DISKFILE-AUDIT-02   AUDIT-DISKFILE-MANAGE-FAIL should be ALL

Certain sensitive files, such as TANDUMP, should have successful manage audited.

Disk File-Related Protection Record Audit Parameters

The following Protection Record parameters determine the amount of auditing for individual VOLUMES, SUBVOLUMES and DISKFILES.

AUDIT-ACCESS-PASS

AUDIT-ACCESS-FAIL

AUDIT-MANAGE-PASS

AUDIT-MANAGE-FAIL

AUDIT-ACCESS{ -PASS | -FAIL }

VOLUME, SUBVOLUME and DISKFILE Protection Records each have these two audit parameters.

The AUDIT-ACCESS-PASS/FAIL parameters determine whether or not successful or unsuccessful attempts to access all disk files on the system are audited. The conditions can be ALL, NONE, LOCAL, or REMOTE.

If AUDIT-ACCESS-PASS value is configured to anything other than NONE, then the appropriate successful disk file access attempts will be audited.

If AUDIT-ACCESS-FAIL value is configured to anything other than NONE, then the appropriate unsuccessful disk file access attempts will be audited.

This setting *supplements* the audit settings for global audit parameters disk files.

If an individual DISKFILE Protection Record is configured to audit only LOCAL access attempts, but the Global parameter is REMOTE, then both LOCAL and REMOTE access attempts will be audited.

However, if an individual DISKFILE Protection Record is configured to audit only NONE and the Global parameter is ALL, then Safeguard software will not audit either successful or unsuccessful disk file access attempts.

The default is NONE.

BP-VOLUME-AUDIT-01   AUDIT-ACCESS-PASS should be NONE

BP-VOLUME-AUDIT-02   AUDIT-ACCESS-FAIL should be ALL

BP-SUBVOL-AUDIT-01   AUDIT-ACCESS-PASS should be NONE

BP-SUBVOL-AUDIT-02   AUDIT-ACCESS-FAIL should be ALL

BP-DISKFILE-AUDIT-01   AUDIT-ACCESS-PASS should be NONE

BP-DISKFILE-AUDIT-02   AUDIT-ACCESS-FAIL should be ALL

AUDIT-MANAGE { -PASS | -FAIL }

VOLUME, SUBVOLUME and DISKFILE Protection Records each have these two audit parameters.

The AUDIT-MANAGE-PASS/FAIL parameters determine whether or not attempts to CREATE, ALTER or DELETE Protection Record will be audited. This setting *supplements* the audit settings for global audit parameters. The conditions can be ALL, NONE, LOCAL, or REMOTE.

If an individual DISKFILE or VOLUME or SUBVOLUME Protection Record is configured to audit only LOCAL access attempts, but the Global parameter is REMOTE, then both LOCAL and REMOTE access attempts will be audited.

However, if an individual DISKFILE or VOLUME or SUBVOLUME Protection Record is configured to audit only NONE and the Global parameter is ALL, then Safeguard software will not audit either successful or unsuccessful DISKFILE access attempts.

The default is NONE.

BP-VOLUME-AUDIT-03   AUDIT-MANAGE-PASS should be ALL

BP-VOLUME-AUDIT-04   AUDIT-MANAGE-FAIL should be ALL

BP-SUBVOL-AUDIT-03   AUDIT-MANAGE-PASS should be ALL

BP-SUBVOL-AUDIT-04   AUDIT-MANAGE-FAIL should be ALL

BP-DISKFILE-AUDIT-03   AUDIT-MANAGE-PASS should be ALL

BP-DISKFILE-AUDIT-04   AUDIT-MANAGE-FAIL should be ALL

Certain sensitive files, such as TANDUMP, should have successful manage audited.

Identifier	Question	Look in
VOLUME-OBJTYPE-01	Does the VOLUME OBJECTTYPE exist?	Safecom
SUBVOL-OBJTYPE-01	Does the SUBVOLUME OBJECTTYPE exist?	Safecom
DISKFILE-OBJTYPE-01	Does the DISKFILE OBJECTTYPE exist?	Safecom
VOLUME-OBJTYPE-02	Is the VOLUME OBJECTTYPE owned by the SECURITY ADMINISTRATOR?	Safecom
SUBDEV-OBJTYPE-02	Is the SUBVOLUME OBJECTTYPE owned by the SECURITY ADMINISTRATOR?	Safecom
DISKFILE-OBJTYPE-02	Is the DISKFILE OBJECTTYPE owned by the SECURITY ADMINISTRATOR?	Safecom

Identifier	Question	Look in
VOLUME-OBJTYPE-03	Is the VOLUME OBJECTTYPE set to audit accesses?	Safecom
SUBVOL-OBJTYPE-03	Is the SUBVOLUME OBJECTTYPE set to audit accesses?	Safecom
DISKFILE-OBJTYPE-03	Is the DISKFILE OBJECTTYPE set to audit accesses?	Safecom
VOLUME-OBJTYPE-04	Is the VOLUME OBJECTTYPE set to audit manage attempts?	Safecom
SUBVOL-OBJTYPE-04	Is the SUBVOLUME OBJECTTYPE set to audit manage attempts?	Safecom
DISKFILE -OBJTYPE-04	Is the DISKFILE OBJECTTYPE set to audit manage attempts?	Safecom
SAFEGARD-GLOBAL-26	Is the Safeguard Global parameter ACL-REQUIRED-DISKFILE value OFF?	Safecom
SAFEGARD-GLOBAL-23	Is the Safeguard Global parameter CHECK-VOLUME value OFF?	Safecom
SAFEGARD-GLOBAL-25	Is the Safeguard Global parameter CHECK-SUBVOLUME value ON?	Safecom
SAFEGARD-GLOBAL-27	Is the Safeguard Global parameter CHECK-FILENAME value ON?	Safecom
SAFEGARD-GLOBAL-24	Is the Safeguard Global parameter COMBINATION-DISKFILE value FIRST-ACL?	Safecom
SAFEGARD-GLOBAL-22	Is the Safeguard Global parameter DIRECTION-DISKFILE value DISKFILE-FIRST?	Safecom
DISKFILE-POLICY	Does the Corporate Security Policy mandate auditing of attempts to access Files?	Policy
VOLUME-AUDIT-01	Are all attempts to successful accesses to VOLUMEs Protection Records audited?	Safecom
SUBVOL-AUDIT-01	Are all attempts to successful accesses to SUBVOLs Protection Records audited?	Safecom
DISKFILE-AUDIT-01	Are all attempts to successful accesses to DISKFILEs Protection Records audited?	Safecom
VOLUME-AUDIT-02	Are all attempts to failed accesses to VOLUMEs Protection Records audited?	Safecom

Identifier	Question	Look in
SUBVOL-AUDIT-02	Are all attempts to failed accesses to SUBVOLs Protection Records audited?	Safecom
DISKFILE-AUDIT-02	Are all attempts to failed accesses to DISKFILEs Protection Records audited?	Safecom
VOLUME-AUDIT-03	Are all attempts to manage VOLUME Protection Records audited?	Safecom
SUBVOL-AUDIT-03 SUBVOL-AUDIT-04	Are all attempts to manage SUBVOLUME Protection Records audited?	Safecom
DISKFILE-AUDIT-03 DISKFILE-AUDIT-04	Are all attempts to manage DISKFILES Protection Records audited?	Safecom
DEVICE-AUDIT-01 DEVICE-AUDIT-02	Are all attempts to manage DEVICES Protection Records audited?	Safecom

6

Gazette A to Z

The Gazette consists of a chapter per program, process or subsystem, containing a discussion of the objects, security concerns and best practice recommendations.

The naming conventions are:

User Program   Object files that users can execute.

System Program   Object files that other programs, not users, execute.

System Utility   Object files generally used by system administrators or operators for system-oriented functions.

Configuration File   Text file such as a Library, DLL and *CSTM file which are used by System and User Programs.

Subsystem   A set of System Programs, User Programs and Configuration files such as Safeguard, MEASURE or SQL software.

Application   A subsystem installed and run as an application.

ADDUSER User Program

The ADDUSER program is used to create userids when Safeguard software is not in use. How this program is secured depends on the Corporate Security Policy and whether or not Safeguard is in use.

Securing ADDUSER

RISK   Adding users to the system is a primary gateway through which unauthorized users could gain access.

AP-ADVICE-ADDUSER-01   Control who is allowed to add or delete users at the highest level.

Without the Safeguard Subsystem

If Safeguard software is not in use on the system, then the ADDUSER program is used to create userids.

How the ADDUSER program is secured depends on who is allowed to perform this function as defined by the Corporate Security Policy and Standards.

If only SUPER.SUPER is allowed to ADD users, the ADDUSER program must be secured for SUPER.SUPER access only and the ADDUSER object file need not be LICENSED. This is the most secure methodology to control the function of adding and deleting users.

BP-FILE-ADDUSER-01   ADDUSER should be secured "- - - -".

BP-OPSYS-LICENSE-01   ADDUSER must NOT be LICENSED.

BP-OPSYS-OWNER-01   ADDUSER should be owned by SUPER.SUPER.

BP-OPSYS-FILELOC-01   ADDUSER must reside in $SYSTEM.SYSnn

If the policy authorizes Group Managers to ADD users to their own groups, then all local groups need to be granted EXECUTE access. The Guardian environment will prevent users other than the 255 member of any group from adding users to existing groups. Only SUPER.SUPER will be able to add to a new group or add users to groups other than their own. To grant Group Managers the right to add userids, the ADDUSER object file must be LICENSED.

BP-FILE-ADDUSER-01   ADDUSER should be secured "- - A -".

BP-OPSYS-LICENSE-01   ADDUSER must be LICENSED.

BP-OPSYS-OWNER-01   ADDUSER should be owned by SUPER.SUPER.

BP-OPSYS-FILELOC-01   ADDUSER must reside in $SYSTEM.SYSnn

RISK   Because of ADDUSER's unique function, any old SYSnn locations must be secured so that users cannot use the old program.

BP-FILE-ADDUSER-02   ADDUSER in old $SYSTEM.SYSnn locations must be secured "- - - -"

	Discovery Questions	Look here:
FILE-POLICY	Are Group Managers allowed to add users?	Policy
OPSYS-OWNER-01	Is ADDUSER owned by SUPER.SUPER?	Fileinfo
OPSYS-LICENSE-01	Is the ADDUSER object file licensed?	Fileinfo

	Discovery Questions	Look here:
FILE-POLICY	Does the security of the ADDUSER object file conform to the Security Policy?	Policy
FILE-ADDUSER-01	Is the ADDUSER object file secured correctly?	Fileinfo
FILE-ADDUSER-02	Are old SYSnn copies of ADDUSER secured?	Fileinfo

With the Safeguard Subsystem

If Safeguard software is in use on the system, then ADDUSER will not run. Instead it will display a warning that Safeguard software should be used to add users.

44> ADDUSER oper.bryan

SAFEGUARD IS RUNNING; USE SAFECOM TO ADD NEW USERS

Groups and Users will be added through the Safeguard interface. Reference Part 2 for more information.

AP-ADVICE-ADDUSER-02   If Safeguard software is not running, the ADDUSER object file's Guardian security string should allow only SUPER.SUPER to execute it.

BP-FILE-ADDUSER-01   ADDUSER should be secured "- - - -".

BP-OPSYS-LICENSE-01   ADDUSER must NOT be LICENSED.

BP-OPSYS-OWNER-01   ADDUSER should be owned by SUPER.SUPER.

BP-OPSYS-FILELOC-01   ADDUSER must reside in $SYSTEM.SYSnn

BP-SAFE-ADDUSER-01   If Safeguard software is installed, add a Safeguard Protection Record to prevent execution of the ADDUSER program.

	Discovery Questions	Look here:
OPSYS-OWNER-01	Is ADDUSER owned by SUPER.SUPER?	Fileinfo
OPSYS-LICENSE-01	Is the ADDUSER object file licensed?	Fileinfo
FILE-POLICY	Does the security of the ADDUSER object file conform to the Security Policy?	Policy
FILE-ADDUSER-01 SAFE-ADDUSER-01	Is the ADDUSER object file correctly secured with the Guardian or Safeguard system?	Fileinfo Safecom

Related Topics

User Administration

Safeguard subsystem

AUDSERV System Program

AUDSERV is only used in an SQL environment. It is not an interactive program; it is invoked by the NonStop TMF subsystem. AUDSERV makes it possible for applications to share the use of a table or index during DDL reorganization.

AUDSERV is invoked when re-organization work is happening concurrently with normal data access. Splitting a partition is one situation where this can occur. When a partition is split, it takes some time for the rows in the table to be physically copied from one partition to another and then be deleted from the first partition. During this time, data access is suspended. If the partition is split while the application is running, AUDSERV interleaves the data access and reorganization functions, keeping track of all the "suspense" NonStop TMF audits generated by the data access and then applying them during the "commit" phase. This way, only a short table lock is needed to mark all the "suspensed" data changes being held in NonStop TMF software as applied. If applications couldn't share operations, then all user access would be locked out for the duration of the data reorganization.

RISK   AUDSERV has no risk associated with user intervention.

Securing AUDSERV

BP-FILE-AUDSERV-01   AUDSERV should be secured "UUUU".

BP-OPSYS-LICENSE-02   AUDSERV must be LICENSED.

BP-OPSYS-OWNER-02   AUDSERV should be owned by SUPER.SUPER.

BP-OPSYS-FILELOC-02   AUDSERV must reside in $SYSTEM.SYSTEM.

If available, use Safeguard software or a third party object security product to grant access to AUDSERV only to users who require access in order to perform their jobs.

BP-SAFE-AUDSERV-01   Add a Safeguard Protection Record to grant appropriate access to the AUDSERV object file equivalent to the Guardian file security string listed above.

	Discovery Questions	Look here:
OPSYS-OWNER-02	Who owns the AUDSERV object file?	Fileinfo
OPSYS-LICENSE-02	Is the AUDSERV object file licensed?	Fileinfo
FILE-AUDSERV-01 SAFE-AUDSERV-01	Is the AUDSERV object file correctly secured with the Guardian or Safeguard system?	Fileinfo Safecom

Related Topics

SQL

NonStop TMF software

AXCEL User Program

The Accelerator (AXCEL) program transforms HP NonStop server compiled language object code to produce accelerated object code, which may run faster. How much faster depends on whether or not the code runs on a RISC (TNS/R) system or an older CISC (TNS) system.

AXCEL is used with TNS compilers and not with native compilers. Native languages are already accelerated for performance. Programs consisting mainly of calls on system code do not get much additional performance gain by acceleration because system code has already been native-compiled. Programs consisting of large amount of user code may gain significant performance by the acceleration compilation (See Figure 6-1).

RISK   AXCEL presents no security risks.

Securing AXCEL

BP-FILE-AXCEL-01   AXCEL should be secured "UUNU".

BP-OPSYS-OWNER-02   AXCEL should be owned by SUPER.SUPER.

BP-OPSYS-FILELOC-02   AXCEL must reside in $SYSTEM.SYSTEM.

AP-ADVICE-AXCEL-01   AXCEL is resource intensive and could affect application processing. Code need not be accelerated on the system where the accelerated object file will be executed.

Figure 6-1
Accelerating Code

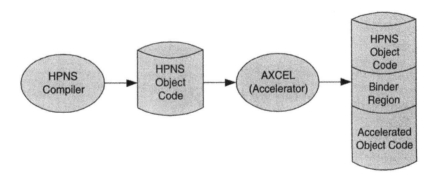

AP-ADVICE-AXCEL-02 To avoid impacting applications, programs should be accelerated on a development or test system and the accelerated program moved to the secure system.

If available, use Safeguard software or a third party object security product to grant access to AXCEL object files only to users who require access in order to perform their jobs.

BP-SAFE-AXCEL-01 Add a Safeguard Protection Record to grant appropriate access to the AXCEL object file.

	Discovery Questions	Look here:
FILE-POLICY	Are accelerations performed on the system?	Policy
OPSYS-OWNER-02	Who owns the AXCEL object file?	Fileinfo
FILE-POLICY	Who is allowed to execute AXCEL on the system?	Policy
FILE-AXCEL-01 SAFE-AXCEL-01	Is the AXCEL object file correctly secured with the Guardian or Safeguard system?	Fileinfo Safecom

Related Topics

Compilers

Securing Applications

BACKCOPY System Utility

The BACKCOPY utility duplicates tape made in the file-mode format for archiving or any duplication reason. The BACKCOPY utility cannot make a copy of a tape backed up using the volume-mode format.

The Corporate Security Policy should detail procedures for physically securing tapes in a tape library.

RISK Tapes can contain sensitive data. Therefore, access to tapes must be controlled physically to ensure security. Copies should only be made by authorized personnel.

Securing BACKCOPY

BP-FILE-BACKCOPY-01 BACKCOPY should be secured "UUCU".

BP-OPSYS-LICENSE-01 BACKCOPY must be LICENSED.

BP-OPSYS-OWNER-01   BACKCOPY should be owned by SUPER.SUPER.

BP-OPSYS-FILELOC-01   BACKCOPY must reside in $SYSTEM.SYSnn.

If available, use Safeguard software or a third party object security product to grant access to BACKCOPY only to users who require access in order to perform their jobs.

BP-SAFE-BACKCOPY-01   Add a Safeguard Protection Record to grant appropriate access to the BACKCOPY object file.

	Discovery Questions	Look here:
OPSYS-OWNER-01	Who owns the BACKCOPY object file?	Fileinfo
OPSYS-LICENSE-01	Is the BACKCOPY object file licensed?	Fileinfo
FILE-POLICY	Who is allowed to copy tapes from the system?	Policy
FILE-BACKCOPY-01 SAFE-BACKCOPY-01	Is the BACKCOPY object file correctly secured with the Guardian or Safeguard system?	Fileinfo Safecom

<u>Related Topics</u>

BACKUP

TAPECOM

BACKUP User Program

The BACKUP utility copies data stored in disk files to magnetic tape for archival purposes. BACKUP is the primary method used to preserve the system's data files and programs. BACKUP is the archival method; RESTORE performs the complementary function to copy the data from tape to disk.

The Corporate Security Policy should detail procedures for physically securing tapes in a tape library.

RISK   Tapes can contain sensitive data. Therefore, access to tapes must be controlled physically to ensure security. Copies should only be made by authorized personnel.

RISK   BACKUP only requires READ access to perform the file read function. If the BACKUP program is accessible to general users, files containing sensitive data could be backed up and restored under their userid.

BACKUP is a privileged program and must be LICENSED to be runnable. Only SUPER.SUPER can run the program if it isn't licensed.

RISK If BACKUP isn't licensed, SQL tables cannot be backed up by anyone (including SUPER.SUPER).

Securing BACKUP

BP-FILE-BACKUP-01   BACKUP should be secured "UUCU".

BP-OPSYS-LICENSE-01   BACKUP must be LICENSED.

BP-OPSYS-OWNER-01   BACKUP should be owned by SUPER.SUPER.

BP-OPSYS-FILELOC-01   BACKUP must reside in $SYSTEM.SYSnn.

If available, use Safeguard software or a third party object security product to grant access to the BACKUP only to users who require access in order to perform their jobs.

BP-SAFE-BACKUP-01   Add a Safeguard Protection Record to grant appropriate access to the BACKUP object file.

Because operators frequently 'run' the backups and because, ideally, operators do not have userids in the SUPER Group, the Corporate Security Policy should mandate how operators will be granted the ability to backup every file on the system. There are two basic choices: with a third party access control product and without one.

With a third party access control product:

3P-ACCESS-BACKUP-01   Use a third-party access control product to allow the users responsible for creating backups the ability to run BACKUP as SUPER.SUPER.

Without a third party access control product:

AP-ADVICE-BACKUP-01   Give those users responsible for running backups EXECUTE access to a PROGID'd *copy* of the BACKUP utility owned by SUPER.SUPER.

RISK Object files PROGID'd to SUPER.SUPER are a security risk.

AP-ADVICE-BACKUP-01A   The PROGID copy of BACKUP should not reside in $SYSTEM.SYSTEM, $SYSTEM.SYSnn or any subvolume in the PMSEARCHLIST that is shared by all users.

AP-ADVICE-BACKUP-01B   The PROGID copy of BACKUP should be secured so that only users authorized to create backup tapes can execute it.

AP-ADVICE-BACKUP-02   Create a job function userid (such as SUPER.BACKUP) that is used only for running BACKUP. Create Safeguard Protection Records to give SUPER.BACKUP READ-only access to all files. Give those users responsible for running backups EXECUTE access to a PROGID *copy* of the BACKUP utility owned by SUPER.BACKUP.

RISK   Anyone logged on as SUPER.BACKUP has read access to every file on the system.

AP-ADVICE-BACKUP-02A   SUPER.BACKUP must be treated as a privileged userid. Users should not be allowed to logon as SUPER.BACKUP.

RISK   This method requires a great deal of Safeguard maintenance.

AP-ADVICE-BACKUP-02B   To reduce the maintenance overhead, Safeguard Protection Records granting READ access to SUPER.BACKUP should be applied at the VOLUME or SUBVOLUME, rather than the DISKFILE level.

	Discovery Questions	Look here:
OPSYS-OWNER-01	Who owns the BACKUP object file?	Fileinfo
OPSYS-LICENSE-01	Is the BACKUP object file licensed?	Fileinfo
FILE-POLICY	Who is allowed to initiate tape backups on the system?	Policy
FILE-BACKUP-01 SAFE-BACKUP-01	Is the BACKUP object file correctly secured with the Guardian or Safeguard system?	Fileinfo Safecom

<u>Related Topics</u>

BACKUP

RESTORE

TAPECOM

Binder Subsystem

Binding (the TNS term) or linking (the native term) is the operation of examining, collecting, and modifying code and data blocks from one or more object files to produce a single object file. Two important aspects of binding or linking a program are validating and resolving references to other routines.

Validating a reference to another routine means determining whether or not the actual parameters of the calling routine correspond to the formal parameters of the called routine.

Resolving a reference to another routine means generating the code that will transfer control from the calling routine to the called routine at execution time.

All Binder operations are performed on program files. Binder uses the following terms when discussing object files:

Block   The smallest unit of code or data that can be relocated as a single entity.

Source File   Code and data blocks, compiled and bound together.

Program   An executable object file. It must contain an entry point with the MAIN attribute.

Target File   BINDER output file, always an object file.

The components of BINDER are:

BINSERV

BIND

VPROC

BINSERV

The BINSERV form of BINDER is only used by language compilers; it cannot be executed by users directly. It executes as a separate process during a compilation, accepts commands from the compiler, builds lists of references that need to be resolved, and finally creates the target file.

BINSERV (See Figure 6-2) builds executable program files for C, COBOL85, FORTRAN, and TAL. (The Pascal compiler uses BINSERV but does not produce an executable program file.)

BIND

BIND is the interactive version of the BINDER. It can be used as an independent, standalone program to query, update and link program files interactively.

BIND can be used to update and link program files written in C, COBOL85, FORTRAN, Pascal, and TAL. BIND is the only form of Binder that produces executable program files for Pascal programs (See Figure 6-3).

BIND is used to:

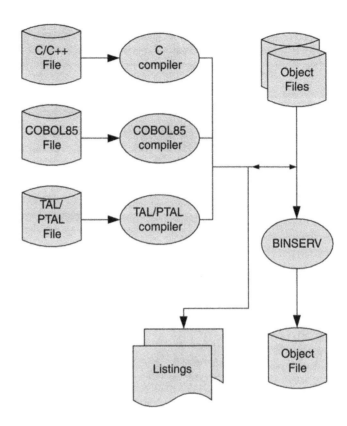

Figure 6-2
BINSERV

Build a single object file from separate object modules.

Build a target file of procedures in a shareable library.

Modify the values of code and data blocks in the target file.

Reorder code blocks in a target file.

Specify a user run-time library.

Display program file contents.

Specify external references not to be resolved by Binder.

Produce load maps and cross-reference listings.

Strip the program file of the BINDER and INSPECT regions.

RISK BIND can be destructive because it can make the following changes to program code files. Programs could be directed to libraries containing malicious procedures and variables and data could be modified.

Build a single object file from separate source files.

Build a target file of procedures in a shareable library.

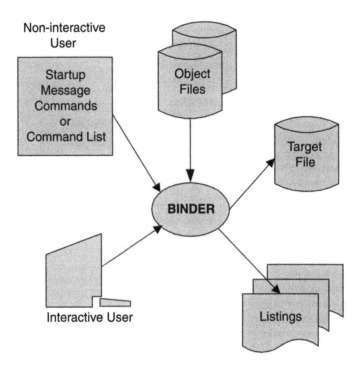

Figure 6-3
BIND

Modify the values in the code and data blocks of the target file.

Reorder code blocks in a target file.

Specify a user run-time library.

The security requirements for BIND and BINSERV differ greatly between a system used for development and a secure environment. The risks for a secure system require stronger security of the BIND command and the compilation function, in general.

VPROC

The VPROC (Version Procedure) program will display the version number for program files developed by HP or third-party vendors and a timestamp that is either the time when the object file was compiled or the time when the object was processed by the BIND program.

VPROC is the generally accepted way to easily determine the version information for an object program.

Securing BINDER Components

BP-FILE-BINDER-01   BIND should be secured "UUNU".

BP-OPSYS-OWNER-02   BIND should be owned by SUPER.SUPER.

BP-OPSYS-FILELOC-02   BIND must reside in $SYSTEM.SYSTEM.

BP-FILE-BINDER-02   BINSERV should be secured "UUNU".

BP-OPSYS-OWNER-02   BINSERV should be owned by SUPER.SUPER.

BP-OPSYS-FILELOC-02   BINSERV must reside in $SYSTEM.SYSTEM.

BP-FILE-BINDER-03   VPROC should be secured "UUNU".

BP-OPSYS-OWNER-02   VPROC should be owned by SUPER.SUPER.

BP-OPSYS-FILELOC-02   VPROC must reside in $SYSTEM.SYSTEM.

If available, use Safeguard software or a third party object security product to grant access to BINDER components only to users who require access in order to perform their jobs.

BP-SAFE-BINDER-01   Add a Safeguard Protection Record to grant appropriate access to the BIND object file.

BIND Commands With Security Implications

This section lists only the BIND commands that pose security risks.

RISK   BIND poses a security risk in a secure environment only if the users authorized to execute BIND have WRITE access to application object files. All of the commands in the list manipulate the creation or contents of a program.

ADD

ALTER

BUILD

CHANGE

DELETE

STRIP

3P-OBJSEC-BINDER-01   If a third party product is used to grant access to BIND running as a privileged userid such as the application object code owner, these commands should be denied to all users other than the system managers.

Application Controls

Only members of the group (if any) responsible for compiling programs on the secure system should have WRITE access to secure object files.

AP-ADVICE-BINDER-01   On secure systems, BIND should be restricted to use by Application Support staff and those responsible for managing object files.

AP-ADVICE-BINDER-02   In secure environments BIND should be used only to research and report on object parameters, not alter them.

BINDER respects file security. If users run BIND under their own userid, they can only BIND object files that they have been granted access to via the Guardian or Safeguard system.

AP-ADVICE-BINDER-03   Users should run BIND under their own userid.

AP-ADVICE-BINDER-04   The application support staff should not have WRITE access to secure object code.

AP-ADVICE-BINDER-05   To safeguard the secure databases, the group (if any) responsible for compiling programs on secure systems should not have READ access to secure database files.

	Discovery Questions	Look here:
OPSYS-OWNER-02	Who owns the BIND object file?	Fileinfo
OPSYS-OWNER-02	Who owns the BINSERV object file?	Fileinfo
OPSYS-OWNER-02	Who owns the VPROC object file?	Fileinfo
OPSYS-OWNER-02	Who is allowed to execute VPROC on the system?	Fileinfo
FILE-POLICY	Who is allowed to execute BIND on the system?	Policy
FILE-BINDER-01 SAFE-BINDER-01	Is the BIND object file correctly secured with the Guardian or Safeguard system?	Fileinfo Safecom
FILE-BINDER-02	Is the BINSERV object file secured correctly?	Fileinfo
FILE-BINDER-03	Is the VPROC object file secured correctly?	Fileinfo

Related Topics

Compilers

Securing Applications

PASSWORD

TACL

BUSCMD System Utility

The BUSCMD program is used to query or change the status of the X or Y interprocessor bus on TNS systems from UP | DOWN and from CPU# to CPU#. BUSCMD is primarily used when some hardware event causes the interprocess path between the CPUs to be faulty.

RISK Because of internal, hard-coded security checks, only members of the SUPER Group can EXECUTE the BUSCMD program. This helps to mitigate the risk of accidental use by users outside the SUPER Group.

RISK BUSCMD is primarily a performance issue, rather than a security risk. The downing of an interprocessor bus could degrade the performance of the system significantly.

This program may be necessary when hardware repair is performed or in emergency situations, requiring access by system operators or a hardware technician. General use of this program is not necessary.

Securing BUSCMD

BP-FILE-BUSCMD-01   BUSCMD should be secured "UUCU".

BP-OPSYS-LICENSE-01   BUSCMD must be LICENSED.

BP-OPSYS-OWNER-01   BUSCMD should be owned by SUPER.SUPER.

BP-OPSYS-FILELOC-01   BUSCMD must reside in $SYSTEM.SYSnn.

If available, use Safeguard software or a third party object security product to grant access to the BUSCMD object file only to users who require access in order to perform their jobs.

BP-SAFE-BUSCMD-01   Add a Safeguard Protection Record to grant appropriate access to the BUSCMD object file.

	Discovery Questions	Look here:
OPSYS-OWNER-01	Who owns the BUSCMD object file?	Fileinfo
OPSYS-LICENSE-01	Is the BUSCMD object file licensed?	Fileinfo
FILE-POLICY	Who is allowed to execute BUSCMD on the system?	Policy
FILE-BUSCMD-01 SAFE-BUSCMD-01	Is the BUSCMD object file correctly secured with the Guardian or Safeguard system?	Fileinfo Safecom

$CMON System Program

The CMON program is not an HP-supplied process, however, when a $CMON process is present on the system messages are sent to the $CMON process to verify logon and process start requests whether or not $CMON exists, a Safeguard protection record should be created for the process name $CMON.

If the $CMON message does not block the action or the wait for $CMON does not exceed the timeout parameter, processing continues. If the $CMON process returns a message blocking the action, the action is denied and an error is returned to whomever originated the action.

The $CMON process can perform many functions for both security reasons and performance reasons, such as:

Control the CPU and priority of the request

Control who can logon to a port

Verify a userid's ability to run a requested program

Log the request

RISK   If a $CMON is not present, an unauthorized $CMON can be added to the system. This $CMON might merely monitor system activity, but it could be designed with malicious intent.

RISK   A 'malicious' $CMON could deny service entirely or force processes into the most inefficient mode in order to slow service, costing both user time and system resources.

RISK   If an authorized $CMON is present and the process is not properly secured, the process can be stopped or debugged by an unauthorized party, causing timeout problems during the period when the process is unavailable.

RISK   If unauthorized users are able to stop $CMON, it could be stopped and an unauthorized version started in its place.

The CMON Program

The CMON program is either customer-written or provided by a third-party vendor.

AP-ADVICE-CMON-01   The object file should not reside in $SYSTEM.SYSTEM or $SYSTEM. SYSnn.

RISK   Because CMON is not an HP NonStop server product; it must be tested with each new Operating System version to ensure that changes to TACL functionality do not cause it to be unable to interact correctly with CMON.

Each company should have procedures and utilities in place to both monitor the presence of $CMON and restart it automatically if it stops unexpectedly.

RISK When CMON is relied upon to rule on logon attempts and process starts, its continuous availability is imperative.

With a third party CMON product:

3P-PROCESS-CMON-01 Use a third party CMON product to perform the following functions:

The CMON program should provide an audit trail detailing its activity

Audit results can be researched and unauthorized access attempts can be captured for review

CMON can deny access to certain ports

CMON can set inactivity timeouts on TACLs

Without a third party CMON product:

AP-ADVICE-CMON-02 Ensure that the source code for the CMON object file is secured appropriately to only those users responsible for making updates and performing compilations of the CMON program.

AP-ADVICE-CMON-03 Perform audit reviews of the CMON source code to verify functionality and correctness.

AP-ADVICE-CMON-04 Put procedures in place to keep CMON up-to-date with new Operating System releases.

CMON and TACL

If the CMON does not support the TACLCONF message, TACL must be configured to effectively work with CMON.

The following parameters must be bound into TACL for communication with CMON. See TACL later in the Gazette for more information on bound parameters.

CMONREQUIRED

REMOTECMONREQUIRED

CMONTIMEOUT

REMOTECMONTIMEOUT

RISK   The TACL program resides in the $SYSTEM.SYSnn subvolume and is replaced with each new operating system upgrade. The parameters must be bound after each operating system upgrade or they will not be applied.

CMON and the Safeguard Subsystem

Safeguard software must be configured to effectively work with CMON. The following Safeguard globals must be set for communication with CMON.

BP-SAFEGARD-GLOBAL-50   The CMON parameter must be ON if CMON is installed on the system.

BP-SAFEGARD-GLOBAL-51   The CMONERROR parameter should be ACCEPT if CMON is installed on the system.

BP-SAFEGARD-GLOBAL-52   The CMONTIMEOUT parameter value depends on the speed of the system. For example, CMONTIMEOUT 30 seconds.

AP-ADVICE-CMON-04   Even if CMON isn't installed on the system, create a Safeguard PROCESS Protection Record to prevent anyone starting a process named $CMON.

Securing CMON

BP-PROCESS-CMON-01   A $CMON process should running.

BP-FILE-CMON-01   CMON should be secured "UUUU".

BP-OPSYS-OWNER-03   CMON object file should be owned by the CMON administrator.

BP-OPSYS-FILELOC-03   CMON object file resides in $<vol>.<svol>

	Discovery Questions	Look here:
PROCESS-CMON-01	Is a $CMON process running on the system?	Status
PROCESS-CMON-02	If $CMON is running, is TACLCONF configured to communicate with it?	TACLCONF
SAFEGARD-GLOBAL-50	If $CMON is running, is Safeguard software configured to communicate with it?	Safeguard
FILE-POLICY	Who is authorized to start and stop the $CMON process?	Policy
OPSYS-FILELOC-03	Where is the object file for the $CMON process located?	Fileinfo

	Discovery Questions	Look here:
OPSYS-OWNER-03	Is CMON owned by the CMON administrator?	Fileinfo
FILE-CMON-01	Is the CMON object file secured correctly?	Fileinfo

Related Topics

User Administration

Safeguard subsystem

TACL

Compilers

Compilers generate object (executable) files from source code files. There are several utilities, libraries and objects used by compilers:

Compiler Languages:

C/C++

COBOL85

FORTRAN

NMC/NMCPLUS

NMCOBOL

Pascal

PTAL

SCOBOL

SQL*

TACL*

TAL

Utilities:

AXCEL*

BINDER*

CROSSREF*

Objects:

System libraries

Common run-time libraries

User libraries

The programs and utilities marked with an asterisk (*) are not covered in this section. Please refer to the appropriate Gazette section.

Compilers and their related utilities are resources whose security varies depending on the Corporate Security Policy concerning compilation on secure systems. Many sites control compilations by enforcing that all compilation be performed on a development system. Application change control policy governs the method and security to update the secure application.

Some sites do not use certain languages, but all sites use at least one language compiler for the secure application. Language compilation controls are a fundamental method that companies can use to control their application.

RISK   Compilers can be destructive because code can be inserted or deleted to circumvent previously implemented controls.

RISK   Language compilers might be used to develop test or hacking programs to access sensitive data.

AP-ADVICE-COMPS-01   On secure systems, languages that are not in active use should be secured from use and other language compilers should be accessible only to necessary personnel.

On secure systems, only members of the group (if any) responsible for compiling programs on the secure system should have access to secure object files.

AP-ADVICE-COMPS-02   To protect applications from inadvertent or malicious changes or outages, compilers and related utilities should be absent or very tightly locked down on secure systems.

AP-ADVICE-COMPS-03   On secure systems, compilers should not be accessible to prevent unauthorized access to secure data.

On development systems, members of the development group responsible for compiling programs should have access according to need.

AP-ADVICE-COMPS-04   Compilers and their associated files should be accessible to the groups needing access.

Securing Compiler Components
C/C++

Access to the C language components is required for compilation. Securing the compiler object file controls the use of the language.

C Compiler Components:

C
CEXTDECS
CFRONT
CPREP
STD* C libraries starting with STD

BP-FILE-C-01   C should be secured "UUNU".

BP-OPSYS-OWNER-02   C should be owned by SUPER.SUPER.

BP-OPSYS-FILELOC-02   C must reside in $SYSTEM.SYSTEM.

BP-FILE-C-02   CFRONT should be secured "UUNU".

BP-OPSYS-OWNER-02   CFRONT should be owned by SUPER.SUPER.

BP-OPSYS-FILELOC-02   CFRONT must reside in $SYSTEM.SYSTEM.

BP-FILE-C-03   CPREP should be secured "UUNU".

BP-OPSYS-OWNER-02   CPREP should be owned by SUPER.SUPER.

BP-OPSYS-FILELOC-02   CPREP must reside in $SYSTEM.SYSTEM.

BP-FILE-C-04   C libraries should be secured "NUNU".

If available, use Safeguard software or a third party object security product to grant access to C object files only to users who require access in order to perform their jobs.

BP-SAFE-C-01   Add a Safeguard Protection Record to grant appropriate access to the C object file.

	Discovery Questions	Look here:
OPSYS-OWNER-02	Who owns the C object file and associated libraries?	Fileinfo
OPSYS-OWNER-02	Who owns the CFRONT object file?	Fileinfo
OPSYS-OWNER-02	Who owns the CPREP object file?	Fileinfo
FILE-POLICY	Who is allowed to use the C compiler on the system?	Policy
FILE-POLICY	Who is allowed to use the CPREP compiler on the system?	Policy
FILE-C-01 SAFE-C-01	Is the C object file correctly secured with the Guardian or Safeguard system?	Fileinfo Safecom

	Discovery Questions	Look here:
FILE-C-02	Is the CFRONT object file secured correctly?	Fileinfo
FILE-C-03	Is the CPREP object file secured correctly?	Fileinfo
FILE-C-04	Are the C libraries secured correctly?	Fileinfo

COBOL85

Access to the COBOL85 language components is required for compilation. Securing the compiler object file controls the use of the language.

COBOL85 Compiler Components:

COBOL85

COBOLEX0

COBOLEX1

COBOLEXT

COBOLFE

COBOLLIB

CLULIB

CBL85UTL

CBLIBEXT

BP-FILE-COBOL-01   COBOL85 should be secured "UUNU".

BP-OPSYS-OWNER-02   COBOL85 should be owned by SUPER.SUPER.

BP-OPSYS-FILELOC-02   COBOL85 must reside in $SYSTEM.SYSTEM.

BP-FILE-COBOL-02   COBOL85 libraries should be secured "NUNU".

If available, use Safeguard software or a third party object security product to grant access to COBOL85 object files only to users who require access in order to perform their jobs.

BP-SAFE-COBOL-01   Add a Safeguard Protection Record to grant appropriate access to the COBOL85 object file.

	Discovery Questions	Look here:
OPSYS-OWNER-02	Who owns the COBOL85 object file?	Fileinfo
FILE-POLICY	Who is allowed to use the COBOL85 compiler on the system?	Policy

	Discovery Questions	Look here:
FILE-COBOL-01 SAFE-COBOL-01	Is the COBOL85 object file correctly secured with Guardian or Safeguard?	Fileinfo Safecom
FILE-COBOL-02	Are the COBOL85 libraries secured correctly?	Fileinfo

FORTRAN

Access to the FORTRAN language components is required for compilation. Securing the compiler object file controls the use of the language.

FORTRAN Compiler Components:

FORTRAN

FORTLIB

FORTERRS

BP-FILE-FORTRAN-01   FORTRAN should be secured "UUNU".

BP-OPSYS-OWNER-02   FORTRAN should be owned by SUPER.SUPER.

BP-OPSYS-FILELOC-02   FORTRAN must reside in $SYSTEM.SYSTEM.

BP-FILE-FORTRAN-02   FORTRAN libraries should be secured "NUNU".

If available, use Safeguard software or a third party object security product to grant access to FORTRAN object files only to users who require access in order to perform their jobs.

BP-SAFE-FORTRAN-01   Add a Safeguard Protection Record to grant appropriate access to the FORTRAN object file.

	Discovery Questions	Look here:
OPSYS-OWNER-02	Who owns the FORTRAN object file?	Fileinfo
FILE-POLICY	Who is allowed to use the FORTRAN compiler on the system?	Policy
FILE-FORTRAN-01 SAFE-FORTRAN-01	Is the FORTRAN object file correctly secured with the Guardian or Safeguard system?	Fileinfo Safecom
FILE-FORTRAN-02	Are the FORTRAN libraries secured correctly?	Fileinfo

NMC/NMCPLUS

Access to the native mode C/C++ language components is required for compilation. Securing the compiler object file controls the use of the language.

NMC/C++ Compiler Components:

NMC

NMCPLUS

NMCMT

BP-FILE-NMC-01   NMC should be secured "UUNU".

BP-OPSYS-OWNER-02   NMC should be owned by SUPER.SUPER.

BP-OPSYS-FILELOC-02   NMC must reside in $SYSTEM.SYSTEM.

BP-FILE-NMC-02   NMCPLUS should be secured "UUNU".

BP-OPSYS-OWNER-02   NMCPLUS should be owned by SUPER.SUPER.

BP-OPSYS-FILELOC-02   NMCPLUS must reside in $SYSTEM.SYSTEM.

BP-FILE-NMC-03   NMC/NMCPLUS libraries should be secured "NUNU".

If available, use Safeguard software or a third party object security product to grant access to NMC/NMCPLUS object files only to users who require access in order to perform their jobs.

BP-SAFE-NMC-01   Add a Safeguard Protection Record to grant appropriate access to the NMC object files.

BP-SAFE-NMC-02   Add a Safeguard Protection Record to grant appropriate access to the NMCPLUS object files.

	Discovery Questions	Look here:
OPSYS-OWNER-02	Who owns the NMC object file?	Fileinfo
OPSYS-OWNER-02	Who owns the NMCPLUS object file?	Fileinfo
FILE-POLICY	Who is allowed to use the NMC compiler on secure system?	Policy
FILE-POLICY	Who is allowed to use the NMCPLUS compiler on the system?	Policy
FILE-NMC-01 SAFE-NMC-01	Is the NMC object file correctly secured with the Guardian or Safeguard system?	Fileinfo Safecom

	Discovery Questions	Look here:
FILE-NMC-02 SAFE-NMC-02	Is the NMCPLUS object file correctly secured with the Guardian or Safeguard system?	Fileinfo Safecom
FILE-NMC-03	Are the NMC libraries secured correctly?	Fileinfo

NMCOBOL

Access to the native mode COBOL language components is required for compilation. Securing the compiler object file controls the use of the language.

NMCOBOL Compiler Components:

NMCOBOL

NMCOBEX0, NMCOBEX1, NMCOBEXT

BP-FILE-NMCOBOL-01   NMCOBOL should be secured "UUNU".

BP-OPSYS-OWNER-02   NMCOBOL should be owned by SUPER.SUPER.

BP-OPSYS-FILELOC-02   NMCOBOL must reside in $SYSTEM.SYSTEM.

BP-FILE-NMCOBOL-02   NMCOBOL libraries should be secured "NUNU".

If available, use Safeguard software or a third party object security product to grant access to NMCOBOL object files only to users who require access in order to perform their jobs.

BP-SAFE-NMCOBOL-01   Add a Safeguard Protection Record to grant appropriate access to the NMCOBOL object file.

	Discovery Questions	Look here:
OPSYS-OWNER-02	Who owns the NMCOBOL object file?	Fileinfo
FILE-POLICY	Who is allowed to use the NMCOBOL compiler on the system?	Policy
FILE-NMCOBOL-01 SAFE-NMCOBOL-01	Is the NMCOBOL object file correctly secured with the Guardian or Safeguard system?	Fileinfo Safecom
FILE-NMCOBOL-02	Are the NMCOBOL libraries secured correctly?	Fileinfo

Pascal

Access to the Pascal language components is required for compilation. Securing the compiler object file controls the use of the language.

Pascal Compiler Components:

Pascal

PASEXT

PASLIB

PASMONO

PASMSG

PASSQA

BP-FILE-PASCAL-01   Pascal should be secured "UUNU".

BP-OPSYS-OWNER-02   Pascal should be owned by SUPER.SUPER.

BP-OPSYS-FILELOC-02   Pascal must reside in $SYSTEM.SYSTEM.

BP-FILE-PASCAL-02   Pascal libraries should be secured "NUNU".

If available, use Safeguard or a third party object security product to grant access to Pascal object files only to users who require access in order to perform their jobs.

BP-SAFE-PASCAL-01   Add a Safeguard Protection Record to grant appropriate access to the Pascal object file.

	Discovery Questions	Look here:
OPSYS-OWNER-02	Who owns the Pascal object file?	Fileinfo
FILE-POLICY	Who is allowed to use the Pascal compiler on the system?	Policy
FILE- PASCAL-01 SAFE-PASCAL-01	Is the Pascal object file correctly secured with Guardian or Safeguard?	Fileinfo Safecom
FILE- PASCAL-02	Are the Pascal libraries secured correctly?	Fileinfo

PTAL

Access to the native TAL language components is required for compilation. Securing the compiler object file controls the use of the language.

PTAL Compiler Components:

PTAL

PTALCOM

BP-FILE-PTAL-01   PTAL should be secured "UUNU".

BP-OPSYS-OWNER-02   PTAL should be owned by SUPER.SUPER.

BP-OPSYS-FILELOC-02   PTAL must reside in $SYSTEM.SYSTEM.

BP-FILE-PTAL-02   PTALCOM should be secured "UUNU".

BP-OPSYS-OWNER-02   PTALCOM should be owned by SUPER.SUPER.

BP-OPSYS-FILELOC-02   PTALCOM must reside in $SYSTEM.SYSTEM.

If available, use Safeguard software or a third party object security product to grant access to PTAL object files only to users who require access in order to perform their jobs.

BP-SAFE-PTAL-01   Add a Safeguard Protection Record to grant appropriate access to the PTAL object file.

	Discovery Questions	Look here:
OPSYS-OWNER-02	Who owns the PTAL object file?	Fileinfo
OPSYS-OWNER-02	Who owns the PTALCOM object file?	Fileinfo
FILE-POLICY	Who is allowed to use the PTAL compiler on the system?	Policy
FILE-PTAL-01 SAFE-PTAL-01	Is the PTAL object file correctly secured with the Guardian or Safeguard system?	Fileinfo Safecom
FILE-PTAL-02	Is the PTALCOM object file secured correctly?	Fileinfo

SCOBOL

Access to the SCOBOL language components is required for compilation. Securing the compiler object file controls the use of the language.

SCOBOL Compiler Components:

SCOBOLX

SCOBOLX2

BP-FILE-SCOBOL-01   SCOBOLX should be secured "UUNU".

BP-OPSYS-OWNER-02   SCOBOLX should be owned by SUPER.SUPER.

BP-OPSYS-FILELOC-02   SCOBOLX must reside in $SYSTEM.SYSTEM.

BP-FILE-SCOBOL-02   SCOBOLX2 should be secured "UUNU".

BP-OPSYS-OWNER-02   SCOBOLX2 should be owned by SUPER.SUPER.

BP-OPSYS-FILELOC-02   SCOBOLX2 must reside in $SYSTEM.SYSTEM.

If available, use Safeguard software or a third party object security product to grant access to SCOBOLX object files only to users who require access in order to perform their jobs.

BP-SAFE-SCOBOL-01   Add a Safeguard Protection Record to grant appropriate access to the SCOBOLX object file.

	Discovery Questions	Look here:
OPSYS-OWNER-02	Who owns the SCOBOLX object file?	Fileinfo
OPSYS-OWNER-02	Who owns the SCOBOLX2 object file?	Fileinfo
FILE-POLICY	Who is allowed to use the SCOBOL compiler on the system?	Policy
FILE-SCOBOL-01 SAFE-SCOBOL-01	Is the SCOBOLX object file correctly secured with the Guardian or Safeguard system?	Fileinfo Safecom
FILE-SCOBOL-02	Is the SCOBOLX2 object file secured correctly?	Fileinfo

SQL

SQL compilation is discussed in the Gazette section on NonStop SQL.

TAL

Access to the TAL language components is required for compilation. Securing the compiler object file controls the use of the language.

TAL Compiler Components:

TAL

TALDECS

TALERROR

TALH

TALLIB

BP-FILE-TAL-01   TAL should be secured "UUNU".

BP-OPSYS-OWNER-02   TAL should be owned by SUPER.SUPER.

BP-OPSYS-FILELOC-02   TAL must reside in $SYSTEM.SYSTEM.

BP-FILE-TAL-02   TAL libraries should be secured "NUNU".

If available, use Safeguard software or a third party object security product to grant access to TAL object files only to users who require access in order to perform their jobs.

BP-SAFE-TAL-01 Add a Safeguard Protection Record to grant appropriate access to the TAL object file.

	Discovery Questions	Look here:
OPSYS-OWNER-02	Who owns the TAL object file?	Fileinfo
FILE-POLICY	Who is allowed to use the TAL compiler on the system?	Policy
FILE-TAL-01 SAFE-TAL-01	Is the TAL object file correctly secured with the Guardian or Safeguard system?	Fileinfo Safecom
FILE-TAL-02	Are the TAL libraries secured correctly?	Fileinfo

Related Topics

Securing Applications

BINDER

Libraries, SRLs & Common Routines

COUP System Utility

The Configuration Utility Program (COUP) is a utility used on D-series and earlier releases to make online changes to the configuration of devices and controllers. COUP is part of the Dynamic-System Configuration (DSC) facility. COUP has been superceded by SCF on G series OS releases.

COUP makes it possible to avoid shutting down and regenerating a system every time a change must be made to the configuration. COUP is used to:

Get information about the system configuration

Add, delete or alter the characteristics of controllers and other devices in the system configuration.

Add and delete disk volumes

Start or Stop devices' I/O processes.

Alter the SYSTEM^ID or SYSTEM^TIME attributes

COUP updates the OSCONFIG file, which stores the current operating system's configuration information.

RISK   COUP is a security risk in its ability to alter the system-generated configuration dynamically. This could alter or disable devices on the system.

RISK   COUP must be run locally to make changes to the system configuration, but queries can be done remotely. Remote execution access should normally not be allowed, forcing the local SUPER user to use this program.

By program default, only members of the SUPER Group can EXECUTE the COUP commands that alter the system configuration. This helps to mitigate the risk of accidental use by users outside the Super Group.

This program is used when system hardware changes are necessary or in emergency situations, requiring access by system operators or a hardware technician. General use of this program is not usually necessary.

AP-ADVICE-COUP-01   Operating System configuration records are recorded in the OSCONFIG file. Access must be prevented to secure it from inadvertent loss or corruption of this file.

On G-series releases, similar functions are performed by SCF, therefore no COUP program should exist.

Securing COUP

BP-FILE-COUP-01   COUP should be secured "UUCU".

BP-OPSYS-OWNER-01   COUP should be owned by SUPER.SUPER.

BP-OPSYS-FILELOC-01   COUP must reside in $SYSTEM.SYSnn.

BP-FILE-COUP-02   OSCONFIG should be secured "CCUU".

BP-OPSYS-OWNER-01   OSCONFIG should be owned by SUPER.SUPER.

BP-OPSYS-FILELOC-01   OSCONFIG must reside in $SYSTEM.SYSnn.

If available, use Safeguard or a third party object security product to grant access to COUP for necessary personnel, and deny access to all other users.

BP-SAFE-COUP-01   Add a Safeguard Protection Record to grant appropriate access to the COUP object file.

BP-SAFE-COUP-02   Add a Safeguard Protection Record to grant appropriate access to the OSCONFIG file.

COUP Commands With Security Implications

COUP has its own 'internal' security; controlling sensitive commands, marked with an asterisk (*) in the list below. These commands can only be run by members of the SUPER Group. All of the commands in the list manipulate the hardware configuration of the system.

ADD*

ALTER*

CONFIG

DELETE*

RENAME*

RUN

START*

STOP*

3P-ACCESS-COUP-01   If a third party product is used to grant access to COUP running as a SUPER Group userid, these commands should be denied to all users other than the system managers.

	Discovery Questions	Look here:
OPSYS-OWNER-01	Who owns the COUP object file?	Fileinfo
OPSYS-OWNER-01	Who owns the OSCONFIG file?	Fileinfo
FILE-POLICY	Who is allowed to execute COUP on the system?	Policy
FILE-COUP-01 SAFE-COUP-01	Is the COUP object file correctly secured with the Guardian or Safeguard system?	Fileinfo Safecom
FILE-COUP-02 SAFE-COUP-02	Is the OSCONFIG object file correctly secured with the Guardian or Safeguard system?	Fileinfo Safecom

Related Topics

SCF

CROSSREF User Program

CROSSREF is a tool used to display symbol reference information. CROSSREF is used on source code files, unlike BINDER, which produces cross-reference information from object files (entry points and common data blocks only).

CROSSREF produces a cross-reference listing of selected identifiers in source code files. It can be used with C, COBOL85, FORTRAN, Pascal, SCOBOL, and TAL.

CROSSREF uses the compiler to scan the source file and gather information about the identifiers, which it then combines, and sorts into a single, alphabetized cross-reference listing. Each entry includes information about:

Identifier name

Identifier type (label, variable, and so forth)

Identifier reference type (for example, a read or write reference)

Identifier location (source file and line number).

The components of CROSSREF are:

CROSSREF

SYMSERV

CROSSREF

Interactive program used to obtain cross-reference data from source files.

RISK   CROSSREF is a reporting utility only, with no destructive commands; it poses minimal risk.

AP-ADVICE-CROSSREF-01   CROSSREF is usually used as a development tool, and may be secured more strictly on a secure system.

SYMSERV

The Compiler-dependent form of CROSSREF, SYMSERV cannot be invoked directly by users.

Securing CROSSREF

BP-FILE-CROSSREF-01   CROSSREF should be secured "UUNU".

BP-OPSYS-OWNER-02   CROSSREF should be owned by SUPER.SUPER.

BP-OPSYS-FILELOC-02   CROSSREF must reside in $SYSTEM.SYSTEM.

BP-FILE-CROSSREF-02   SYMSERV should be secured "UUNU".

BP-OPSYS-OWNER-02   SYMSERV should be owned by SUPER.SUPER.

BP-OPSYS-FILELOC-02   SYMSERV must reside in $SYSTEM.SYSTEM.

If available, use Safeguard software or a third party object security product to grant access to CROSSREF only to users who require access in order to perform their jobs.

BP-SAFE-CROSSREF-01   Add a Safeguard Protection Record to grant appropriate access to the CROSSREF object file.

	Discovery Questions	Look here:
OPSYS-OWNER-02	Who owns the CROSSREF object file?	Fileinfo
OPSYS-OWNER-02	Who owns the SYMSERV object file?	Fileinfo
FILE-POLICY	Who is allowed to execute CROSSREF on the system?	Policy
FILE-CROSSREF-01 SAFE-CROSSREF-01	Is the CROSSREF object file correctly secured with the Guardian or Safeguard system?	Fileinfo Safecom
FILE-CROSSREF-02	Is the SYMSERV object file secured correctly?	Fileinfo

<u>Related Topics</u>

Securing Applications

BINDER

*CSTM Customization Files

Many HP NonStop server utilities create a user-specific custom (CSTM) file. Users can include any of the commands available within the utility in this file. When the user invokes one of these utilities, the utility reads this file before presenting the user with the first prompt.

Some of these utilities also have LOCL files, which reside in the object file's subvolume or in $SYSTEM.SYSTEM. The *LOCL file is read before the CSTM file. The *LOCL file for each utility is addressed in the Gazette section on the specific utility.

The utilities with custom files are:

DSAP

EMSA

FTP **

FUP **

INSPECT

SEEVIEW

SCF **

TACL **

VHS

RISK   The utilities marked by a '**' in the list above pose a higher security risk for their associated *CSTM files, especially if the users are in the SUPER Group and can execute any of the utility's destructive commands within the *CSTM file.

Depending on the utility, the *CSTM files may or not be created automatically:

Automatic	Manual
DSAP	EMSA
FUP	FTP
SCF	INSPECT
TACL	SEEVIEW
	VHS

Depending on the utility, the commands in the files may or not be displayed to the user as they are executing.

RISK   *CSTM files do not automatically move or get removed when a userid is deleted or a user's default subvolume is changed; the old files will remain on the system.

RISK   One command that is allowed within a *CSTM is an assign statement. The assign statement can point to another *CSTM file.

If *CSTM files are shared, then the target *CSTM file must be READ accessible to the referring user.

```
Example:
ASSIGN SCFCSTM, [[[\ system.]$ volume.] subvolume.]SCFCSTM
```

DSAPCSTM Configuration File

DSAP provides the ability to automatically access a command file containing a set of personalized DSAP commands before the start of a DSAP session. DSAP does not use a DSAPLOCL file.

The user can specify any DSAP option(s) in the DSAPCSTM file. Any DSAP options specified in the DSAPCSTM file will be appended to the DSAP command typed at the TACL prompt.

> This file is created automatically the first time the user runs the DSAP program.

RISK DSAP is a reporting program only and has no commands that modify files. There are no inherent risks in having DSAPCSTM files. If the files are not secured to the owner, however, another user could alter the file, changing the default information and format of the owner's DSAP reports.

If users are allowed to manage their own DSAPCSTM files, these controls are suggested:

BP-FILE-DSAPCSTM-01   DSAPCSTMs should be owned by the user.

BP-FILE-DSAPCSTM-03   DSAPCSTMs should be secured "UUUU".

If available, use Safeguard software or a third party object security product to grant access to DSAPCSTM only to users who require access in order to perform their jobs.

BP-SAFE-DSAPCSTM-01   If required by policy, add a Safeguard Protection Record to grant appropriate access to the DSAPCSTM disk files.

	Discovery Questions	Look here:
FILE-POLICY	Does the Security Policy require limiting access to the DSAPCSTM files?	Policy
FILE-DSAPCSTM-01	Are all DSAPCSTM files owned by the appropriate user in their default subvolume?	Fileinfo
FILE-DSAPCSTM-02 SAFE-DSAPCSTM-01	Are the DSAPCSTM file correctly secured with the Guardian or Safeguard system?	Fileinfo Safecom

EMSACSTM Configuration File

EMSA provides the ability to automatically access a command file containing a set of personalized EMSA commands before the start of an EMSA session. EMSA does not use an EMSALOCL file.

The user can specify any EMSA option(s) in the EMSACSTM file. Any EMSA options specified in the EMSACSTM file will be appended to the EMSA command typed at the TACL prompt.

> This file is not automatically created. It must be manually created.

RISK EMSA is a reporting program only and has no commands that modify files.

There are no inherent risks in having EMSACSTM files.

RISK   If the files are not secured against unwanted alterations, another user could add a RUN command to the EMSACSTM. The program started would run as the owner of the altered EMSACSTM file.

If users are allowed to manage their own EMSACSTM files, these controls are suggested:

BP-FILE-EMSACSTM-01   EMSACSTMs should be owned by the user.

BP-FILE-EMSACSTM-03   EMSACSTMs should be secured "UUUU".

If available, use Safeguard or a third party object security product to grant access to EMSACSTM only to users who require access in order to perform their jobs.

BP-SAFE-EMSACSTM-01   If required by policy, add a Safeguard Protection Record to grant appropriate access to the EMSACSTM disk files.

	Discovery Questions	Look here:
FILE-POLICY	Does the Security Policy require limiting access to the EMSACSTM files?	Policy
FILE-EMSACSTM-01	Are all EMSACSTM files owned by the appropriate user in their default subvolume?	Fileinfo
FILE-EMSACSTM-02 SAFE-EMSACSTM-01	Are the EMSACSTM file correctly secured with the Guardian or Safeguard system?	Fileinfo Safecom

FTPCSTM Configuration File

FTP provides the ability to automatically access a command file containing a set of personalized FTP commands before the start of an FTP session. FTP does not use an FTPLOCL file.

The user can specify any FTP option(s) in the FTPCSTM file. Any FTP options specified in the FTPCSTM file will be appended to the FTP command typed at the TACL prompt.

This file is not automatically created. It must be manually created.

RISK   If the security of the FTPCSTM file permits a user WRITE or PURGE access, other than the owner, they could modify the file or PURGE it and replace it with a new one.

RISK   Users often set account passwords to be used to log on to various hosts in the FTPCSTM as a convenience. Passwords appear in the clear in the FTPCSTM files. Anyone with READ access to the files can read the passwords.

BP-FILE-FTPCSTM-03   Passwords should not be included in the FTPCSTM files.

If users are allowed to manage their own FTPCSTM files, these controls are suggested:

BP-FILE-FTPCSTM-01   FTPCSTMs should be owned by the user.

BP-FILE-FTPCSTM-03   FTPCSTMs should be secured "UUUU".

If FTPCSTM files are used to manage the environment, a more stringent control over these files is suggested to mitigate the risks:

FTPCSTMs should be owned by the FTP administrator ID.

Secure the FTPCSTMs files "NUUU"

If available, use Safeguard software or a third party object security product to grant access to FTPCSTM only to users who require access in order to perform their jobs.

BP-SAFE-FTPCSTM-01   If required by policy, add a Safeguard Protection Record to grant appropriate access to the FTPCSTM disk files.

	Discovery Questions	Look here:
FILE-POLICY	Does the Security Policy require limiting access to the FTPCSTM files?	Policy
FILE-POLICY	Does the Security Policy restrict users from embedding passwords in the FTPCSTM files?	Policy
FILE-FTPCSTM-01	Are all FTPCSTM files owned by the appropriate user in their default subvolume?	Fileinfo
FILE-FTPCSTM-02 SAFE-FTPCSTM-01	Are the FTPCSTM files correctly secured with the Guardian or Safeguard system?	Fileinfo Safecom
FILE-FTPCSTM-03	Are embedded passwords accessible in FTPCSTM files?	Review text

FUPCSTM Configuration File

FUP provides the ability to automatically access a command file containing a set of personalized FUP commands before the start of a FUP session. FUP reads two files, if available, FUPLOCL and FUPCSTM before issuing its first prompt. Both files can contain valid FUP commands

The FUPLOCL file resides in the FUP object file's subvolume. This file enables the system manager to customize the system-wide FUP environment. FUPCSTM is located on the user's default volume and subvolume. This file enables the user to customize personal preferences and environments.

> These files are created automatically the first time the user runs the FUP program.

When FUP is run on a remote node, the FUPCSTM in the appropriate subvolume on the remote node is used.

RISK   If the security of the FUPCSTM file permits a user other than the owner WRITE or PURGE access, they could modify the file or PURGE it and replace it with a new one.

RISK   The FUPCSTM commands will override the similar commands in the global FUPLOCL commands.

RISK   The FUPCSTM file is created using the user's default security. The default security may not adequately secure these files.

RISK   SUPER Group members should not be able to alter their FUPCSTM files. They could put destructive commands, such as SECURE, PROGID, in the file that will execute prior to FUP's first prompt.

If users are allowed to manage their own FUPCSTM files, these controls are suggested:

BP-FILE-FUPCSTM-01   FUPCSTMs should be owned by the user.

BP-FILE-FUPCSTM-03   FUPCSTMs should be secured "UUUU".

If FUPCSTM files are used to manage the environment, a more stringent control over these files is suggested to mitigate the risks:

FUPCSTMs should be owned by the FUP administrator ID.

Secure the FTPCSTMs files "NUUU"

If available, use Safeguard software or a third party object security product to grant access to FUPCSTM only to users who require access in order to perform their jobs.

BP-SAFE-FUPCSTM-01   If required by policy, add a Safeguard Protection Record to grant appropriate access to the FUPCSTM disk files.

	Discovery Questions	Look here:
FILE-POLICY	Does the Security Policy require limiting access to the FUPCSTM files?	Policy
FILE-FUPCSTM-01	Are all FUPCSTM files owned by the appropriate user in their default subvolume?	Fileinfo
FILE-FUPCSTM-02 SAFE-FUPCSTM-01	Are the FUPCSTM files correctly secured with the Guardian or Safeguard system?	Fileinfo Safecom

INSPCSTM Configuration File

INSPECT provides the ability to automatically access a command file containing a set of personalized INSPECT commands before the start of an INSPECT session. INSPECT reads two files, if available, INSPLOCL and INSPCSTM before issuing its first prompt. Both files can contain valid INSPECT commands

The INSPLOCL file resides in the INSPECT object file's subvolume. This file enables the system manager to customize the system-wide INSPECT environment. INSPCSTM is located on the user's default volume and subvolume. This file enables the user to customize personal preferences and environments.

This file is not automatically created. It must be manually created.

The user can specify any INSPECT option(s) in the INSPCSTM file. Any INSPECT options specified in the INSPCSTM file will be executed before INSPECT prompts for input.

RISK INSPECT can be used to change data in memory before that data is written to a file. With INSPECT, users can view sensitive data.

There are no inherent risks in having INSPCSTM files. If the files are not secured to the owner, however, another user could alter the file, changing the default information and format of the owner's INSPECT reports.

RISK The INSPCSTM commands will override the similar commands in the global INSPLOCL commands.

If users are allowed to manage their own INSPCSTM files, these controls are suggested:

BP-FILE-INSPCSTM-01   INSPCSTMs should be owned by the user.

BP-FILE-INSPCSTM-03   INSPCSTMs should be secured "UUUU".

If available, use Safeguard software or a third party object security product to grant access to INSPCSTM only to users who require access in order to perform their jobs.

BP-SAFE-INSPCSTM-01   If required by policy, add a Safeguard Protection Record to grant appropriate access to the INSPCSTM disk files.

	Discovery Questions	**Look here:**
FILE-POLICY	Does the Security Policy require limiting access to the INSPCSTM files?	Policy
FILE-INSPCSTM-01	Are all INSPCSTM files owned by the appropriate user in their default subvolume?	Fileinfo
FILE-INSPCSTM-02 SAFE-INSPCSTM-01	Are the INSPCSTM file correctly secured with the Guardian or Safeguard system?	Fileinfo Safecom

SCFCSTM Configuration File

SCFCSTM resides in each user's default subvolume. The file is created automatically in the user's default subvolume the first time the user invokes SCF. The user can then place any SCF commands in the SCFCSTM file.

> The file is created automatically in the user's default subvolume the first time the user invokes SCF.

When SCF is run on a remote node, the SCFCSTM in the appropriate subvolume on the remote node is used.

RISK   If the security of the SCFCSTM file permits a user other than the owner WRITE or PURGE access, they could modify the file or PURGE it and replace it with a new one.

RISK   The SCFCSTM commands will override the similar commands in the global SCFLOCL commands.

RISK   The SCFCSTM file is created using the user's default security. The default security may not adequately secure these files.

RISK   SUPER Group members should not be able to alter their SCFCSTM files. They could put destructive commands in the file that will execute prior to SCF's first prompt.

If users are allowed to manage their own SCFCSTM files, these controls are suggested:

BP-FILE-SCFCSTM-01   SCFCSTMs should be owned by the user.

BP-FILE-SCFCSTM-03   SCFCSTMs should be secured "UUUU".

If SCFCSTM files are used to manage the environment, a more stringent control over these files is suggested to mitigate the risks:

SCFCSTMs should be owned by the SCF administrator ID.

Secure the SCFCSTMs files "NUUU"

If available, use Safeguard software or a third party object security product to grant access to SCFCSTM only to users who require access in order to perform their jobs.

BP-SAFE-SCFCSTM-01   Add a Safeguard Protection Record to grant appropriate access to the SCFCSTM disk files.

	Discovery Questions	Look here:
FILE-POLICY	Does the Security Policy require limiting access to the SCFCSTM files?	Policy
FILE-SCFCSTM-01	Are all SCFCSTM files owned by the appropriate user in their default subvolume?	Fileinfo
FILE-SCFCSTM-02 SAFE-SCFCSTM-01	Are the SCFCSTM files correctly secured with the Guardian or Safeguard system?	Fileinfo Safecom

SEECSTM Configuration File

SEEVIEW provides the ability to automatically access a command file containing a set of personalized SEEVIEW commands before the start of an SEEVIEW session.

The user can specify any SEEVIEW commands in the SEECSTM file to customize their environment.

This file is not automatically created. It must be manually created.

RISK   There are no inherent risks in having SEECSTM files. If the files are not secured to the owner, however, another user could alter the file, changing the programs or macros that are run from the user's menus.

If users are allowed to manage their own SEECSTM files, these controls are suggested:

BP-FILE-SEECSTM-01   SEECSTMs should be owned by the user.

BP-FILE-SEECSTM-3   SEECSTMs should be secured "UUUU".

If available, use Safeguard software or a third party object security product to grant access to SEECSTM only to users who require access in order to perform their jobs.

BP-SAFE-SEECSTM-01   If required by policy, add a Safeguard Protection Record to grant appropriate access to the SEECSTM disk files.

	Discovery Questions	Look here:
FILE-POLICY	Does the Security Policy require limiting access to the SEECSTM files?	Policy
FILE-SEECSTM-01	Are all SEECSTM files owned by the appropriate user in their default subvolume?	Fileinfo
FILE-SEECSTM-02 SAFE-SEECSTM-01	Are the SEECSTM file correctly secured with the Guardian or Safeguard system?	Fileinfo Safecom

TACLCSTM Configuration File

TACLCSTM resides in each user's default subvolume.

RISK   If no Guardian DEFAULT VOLUME is entered when a user record is added, Safeguard software assigns the default value of $SYSTEM.NOSUBVOL.

AP-ADVICE-TACLCSTM-01   Each user should have a unique Guardian DEFAULT VOLUME to prevent the sharing of TACLCSTM and other *CSTM files.

> The file is created automatically in the user's default subvolume when the user first logs onto the system.

RISK   If the security of the TACLCSTM file permits a user other than the owner WRITE or PURGE access, they could modify the file or PURGE it and replace it with a new one.

RISK   The TACLCSTM commands will override the similar commands in the global TACLLOCL commands.

RISK   The TACLCSTM file is created using the user's default security. The default security may not adequately secure these files.

RISK   The TACLCSTM file can contain PMSEARCHLIST commands to alter the location that the TACL software uses to find a program file when a

RUN command is issued in which the file name is not fully qualified, which is the common practice.

RISK   SUPER Group members should not be able to alter their TACLCSTM files. They could put destructive commands in the file that will execute prior to TACL's first prompt.

NOTE: If a macro is executed within a TACLCSTM, the macro file must also be secured so that only authorized users can WRITE or PURGE it. Otherwise, someone could rename it and then install another file with the same name or simply insert commands that execute a Trojan horse program by invoking the macro via the TACLCSTM file.

Sharing TACLCSTM Files

It is sometimes desirable to share macros and functions defined in a particular TACLCSTM. To do so and still meet the requirement that all users have their own TACLCSTM, simply insert the line "RUN $vol.subvol.TACLCSTM" in an individual user's TACLCSTM file, making sure the "secondary" TACLCSTM is secured against WRITE access. READ access is required on the referenced TACLCSTM file.

The Corporate Security Policy should include a written explanation, approved and signed by the appropriate authority, for this type of TACLCSTM sharing.

Some reasons this method might be used are:

The technique of running a "secondary" TACLCSTM can be used to allow different default macros and references to be set by a user for his/her different roles or projects. In this case the "secondary" TACLCSTM should contain a volume command to change the current volume default to the correct volume and subvolume location for the work being done.

If all users in a particular Guardian User Group never have personal files and must share a particular environment, it may be more practical to maintain a single TACLCSTM file rather than propagating required changes to numerous TACLCSTM files in numerous user subvolumes.

Securing TACLCSTM Files

If users are allowed to manage their own TACLCSTM files, these controls are suggested:

BP-FILE-TACLCSTM-01   TACLCSTMs should be owned by the user.

BP-FILE-TACLCSTM-03   TACLCSTMs should be secured "UUUU".

If TACLCSTM files are used to manage the environment, a more stringent control over these files is suggested to mitigate the risks:

TACLCSTMs should be owned by the System Administrator

Secure the TACLCSTMs files "NUUU"

If available, use Safeguard software or a third party object security product to grant access to TACLCSTM only to users who require access in order to perform their jobs.

BP-SAFE-TACLCSTM-01   If required by policy, add a Safeguard Protection Record to grant appropriate access to the TACLCSTM disk files.

	Discovery Questions	Look here:
FILE-POLICY	Does the Security Policy require limiting access to the TACLCSTM files?	Policy
FILE-POLICY	Does the Security Policy allow TACLCSTM file sharing?	Policy
FILE-TACLCSTM-01	Are all TACLCSTM files owned by the appropriate user in their default subvolume?	Fileinfo
FILE-TACLCSTM-02 SAFE-TACLCSTM-01	Are the TACLCSTM file correctly secured with the Guardian or Safeguard system?	Fileinfo Safecom

VHSCSTM Configuration File

VHS provides the ability to automatically access a command file containing a set of personalized VHS commands before the start of a VHSCI session.

The VHSCSTM file is used to customize each user's VHSCI session.

This file is not automatically created. It must be manually created.

RISK   VHS is a reporting program only and has no commands that modify files. There are no inherent risks in having VHS files. If the files are not secured to the owner, however, another user could alter the file, changing the default information and format of the owner's VHS reports.

If users are allowed to manage their own VHS files, these controls are suggested:

BP-FILE-VHSCSTM-01   VHSCSTMs should be owned by the user.

BP-FILE-VHSCSTM-03   VHSCSTMs should be secured "UUUU".

If available, use Safeguard software or a third party object security product to grant access to VHSCSTM only to users who require access in order to perform their jobs.

BP-SAFE-VHSCSTM-01   If required by policy, add a Safeguard Protection Record to grant appropriate access to the VHSCSTM disk files.

	Discovery Questions	Look here:
FILE-POLICY	Does the Security Policy require limiting access to the VHSCSTM files?	Policy
FILE-VHSCSTM-01	Are all VHSCSTM files owned by the appropriate user in their default subvolume?	Fileinfo
FILE-VHSCSTM-02 SAFE-VHSCSTM-01	Are the VHSCSTM file correctly secured with the Guardian or Safeguard system?	Fileinfo Safecom

Related Topics

Related System Utility

Data Build User Program

The Data Build program is used to convert data from a non-HP NonStop system and to load the converted data into a NonStop-system format file. Data Build also loads data from a flat file or an Enscribe file to a NonStop SQL table. Data Build is more efficient than the standard SQL load process.

Data Build creates a COBOL85 conversion program that reads files containing the input data and loads the output data via one of Data Build's conversion procedures. After Data Build creates the COBOL85 conversion program, the COBOL85 conversion program is run to convert and load the input data into NonStop format files.

Data Build uses the concept of a fileset for every input file to be converted. This fileset consists of the following:

Input file

Source Record Descriptions file

DDL Record Descriptions file

Output file (either Enscribe or NonStop SQL table)

Data Build is a Pathway application. The default Pathway name is $DBLD1. Data Build is normally installed to a location as specified in the installation routine. It may be located anywhere on the system. Two subvolumes are created:

Application subvolume

SQL catalog subvolume

Securing Data Build Components

BP-FILE-DATABLD-01   Data Build <subvol >.* should be secured "UUNU".

BP-OPSYS-OWNER-03   Data Build <subvol >.* should be owned by SUPER.SUPER.

BP-OPSYS-FILELOC-03   Data Build <subvol >.* resides in $SYSTEM.<?>.

BP-FILE-DATABLD-02   Data Build SQL<subvol >.* should be secured "UUCU".

BP-OPSYS-OWNER-03   Data Build SQL<subvol >.* should be owned by SUPER.SUPER.

BP-OPSYS-FILELOC-03   Data Build SQL<subvol >.* resides in $SYSTEM.<?>.

If available, use Safeguard software or a third party object security product to grant access to Data Build subvolumes only to users who require access in order to perform their jobs.

BP-SAFE-DATABLD-01   Add a Safeguard Protection Record to grant appropriate access to the Data Build <subvol>.

	Discovery Questions	Look here:
FILE-POLICY	Is Data Build installed on the system?	Fileinfo
FILE-POLICY	Who is allowed to execute Data Build on the system?	Policy
OPSYS-OWNER-03	Who owns the Data Build <subvol>?	Fileinfo
OPSYS-OWNER-03	Who owns the Data Build SQL catalog and database?	Fileinfo SQLCI
FILE-DATABLD-01 SAFE-DATABLD-01	Is the Data Build <subvol> correctly secured with the Guardian or Safeguard system?	Fileinfo Safecom
FILE-DATABLD-02	Is the Data Build SQL <subvol> secured correctly?	Fileinfo SQLCI

<u>Related Topics</u>

DDL

NonStop SQL

DATA Loader/MP User Program

HP DataLoader/MP and NM DataLoader/MP software are applications used to load
Enscribe and NonStop SQL database. They are most commonly used for loading very
large amounts of data.

The Data Loader software is used for:

Loading very large amounts of data

Converting data to various formats

Generation of test data

Extraction of data

Loading data that comes from multiple data sources

System balancing and recovery

RISK   DataLoader/MP software is a utility that poses no risks if the data files
that are accessed are secured properly. If a user has READ access to sensitive data,
DataLoader/MP software provides a tool that can extract data into other
formats.

RISK   By the nature of the function of DataLoader, the program would normally be used by database administrators.

Securing DataLoader/MP Components

BP-FILE-DATALOAD-01   DATALOAD should be secured "UUNU".

BP-OPSYS-OWNER-02   DATALOAD should be owned by
SUPER.SUPER.

BP-OPSYS-FILELOC-02   DATALOAD must reside in $SYSTEM.SYSTEM.

BP-FILE-DATALOAD-02   DataLoader <subvol >.* should be secured
"NUNU".

BP-OPSYS-OWNER-03   DataLoader <subvol >.* should be owned by
SUPER.SUPER.

BP-OPSYS-FILELOC-03   DataLoader <subvol >.* resides in
$SYSTEM.ZDTLOAD.

If available, use Safeguard software or a third party object security product to grant access to DATALOAD object files only to users who require access in order to perform their jobs.

BP-SAFE-DATALOAD-01   Add a Safeguard Protection Record to grant appropriate access to the DATALOAD object file.

	Discovery Questions	Look here:
OPSYS-OWNER-02	Who owns the DATALOAD object file?	Fileinfo
OPSYS-OWNER-03	Who owns the DATALOAD <subvol>?	Fileinfo
FILE-POLICY	Who is allowed to execute DATALOAD on the system?	Policy
FILE-DATALOAD-01 SAFE-DATALOAD-01	Is the DATALOAD object file correctly secured with the Guardian or Safeguard system?	Fileinfo Safecom
FILE-DATALOAD-02	Is the DataLoader <subvol> secured correctly?	Fileinfo

Related Topics

DDL

NonStop SQL

DCOM System Utility

The Disk Compression (DCOM) utility rearranges the extent locations of disk file extents.

DCOM moves allocated file extents (areas reserved for the growth of designated files) and free-space extents (unallocated areas) to different locations on a disk volume.

DCOM consolidates the free-space extents, making larger extents available.

After using DCOM to rearraange disk space, new files with larger extent sizes can be allocated.

DCOM is not a destructive utility, but should only be used by persons responsible for the overall performance of the system. Generally DCOM is used by system operators and system managers.

RISK   By the nature of the function of DCOM, this utility requires excessive disk cycles and is not for use during peak performance hours, as it will degrade the performance of the disks.

Securing DCOM

BP-FILE-DCOM-01   DCOM should be secured "UUCU".

BP-OPSYS-LICENSE-01   DCOM must be LICENSED.

BP-OPSYS-OWNER-01   DCOM should be owned by SUPER.SUPER.

BP-OPSYS-FILELOC-01   DCOM must reside in $SYSTEM.SYSnn.

If available, use Safeguard software or a third party object security product to grant access to DCOM object files only to users who require access in order to do their jobs.

BP-SAFE-DCOM-01   Add a Safeguard Protection Record to grant appropriate access to the DCOM object file.

	Discovery Questions	Look here:
OPSYS-OWNER-01	Who owns the DCOM object file?	Fileinfo
OPSYS-LICENSE-01	Is the DCOM object file licensed?	Fileinfo
FILE-POLICY	Who is allowed to execute DCOM on the system?	Policy
FILE-DCOM-01 SAFE-DCOM-01	Is the DCOM object file correctly secured with the Guardian or Safeguard system?	Fileinfo Safecom

Data Definition Language (DDL) Subsystem

The Data Definition Language (DDL) language enables users to define data objects in Enscribe files and to translate these object definitions into source code definitions for programming languages and other products on HP subsystems.

DDL performs two main functions:

Compiling statements that define data objects

Translating compiled definitions into source code for host languages and FUP

Using DDL Definitions

DDL Statements are used to define, modify, delete or display definitions in the DDL Dictionary and to generate data definition output files for other subsystems and compilers.

DDL Functions	Description
Create a data dictionary	DDL schemas are stored in one or many DDL Dictionaries.
Create a Schema	Using DDL commands, record schema definitions are created and stored into the dictionary

DDL Functions	Description
Generate Schema Definition	Output a record schema as FUP commands
Create a database	The output FUP commands are used to create the database files
Generate source code	Output source code data definitions that are used directly by the programming languages.
Create messages	Define interprocess messages and store them in the dictionary. Like record definitions, these schemas can be output to source code format.
Maintain a dictionary	Dictionary maintenance functions
Examine a dictionary	Dictionary reports

Enscribe DBMS

Enscribe data files are supported by the Guardian file system as one of four structured and one unstructured format.

Key-Sequenced

The Enscribe software uses index blocks to locate primary keys, which are stored in the record. Alternate index files are also key-sequenced. Key-sequenced files are accessible for random and sequential access.

Queue

The Enscribe software uses index blocks to locate primary keys, which are stored in the record. An Enscribe queue file is a special type of key-sequenced file where processes can queue and dequeue records.

Entry-Sequenced

The Enscribe software uses record addresses to find the physical location of a record in a file. Entry-sequenced files are used for sequentially oriented data, such as date oriented log files.

Relative

The Enscribe software uses record number to calculate the physical location of a record in a file. Relative sequenced files are primarily used for positionally oriented data, where the relative record number is unique.

Unstructured

The blocks of data must be programmatically managed. No record structure is available.

Enscribe files are used extensively on HP as the basic DBMS relational structured file. Some of the subsystems that rely upon DDL definitions are:

ENABLE

ENFORM

Programming languages

AP-ADVICE-DDL-01   Generally users should be prevented from creating new DDL schema on secure systems. Secure system applications will contain a pre-created data dictionary that must be secured at the same level as the secure data files.

RISK   DDL poses no direct security risk as long as the data files and application files are secured properly, such that the output of DDL and the dictionary schemas cannot be used to gain unauthorized access the secure data.

Enscribe Application Dictionaries

AP-ADVICE-DDL-02   DDL Dictionaries should be secured to the appropriate group.

AP-ADVICE-DDL-03   DDL Dictionaries should be owned by the appropriate application manager.

AP-ADVICE-DDL-04   DDL Dictionaries can reside anywhere on the system.

Securing DDL Components

BP-FILE-DDL-01   DDL should be secured "UUNU".

BP-OPSYS-OWNER-02   DDL should be owned by SUPER.SUPER.

BP-OPSYS-FILELOC-02   DDL must reside in $SYSTEM.SYSTEM.

BP-FILE-DDL-02   DDQUERYS should be secured "NUNU".

BP-OPSYS-OWNER-02   DDQUERYS should be owned by SUPER.SUPER.

BP-OPSYS-FILELOC-02   DDQUERYS must reside in $SYSTEM.SYSTEM.

BP-FILE-DDL-03   DDSCHEMA should be secured "NUNU".

BP-OPSYS-OWNER-02   DDSCHEMA should be owned by SUPER.SUPER.

BP-OPSYS-FILELOC-02   DDSCHEMA must reside in
$SYSTEM.SYSTEM.

If available, use Safeguard software or a third party object security product to grant access to DDL object files only to users who require access in order to perform their jobs.

BP-SAFE-DDL-01   Add a Safeguard Protection Record to grant appropriate access to the DDL object file.

	Discovery Questions	Look here:
OPSYS-OWNER-02	Who owns the DDL object file?	Fileinfo
OPSYS-OWNER-02	Who owns the DDQUERYS file?	Fileinfo
OPSYS-OWNER-02	Who owns the DDSCHEMA file?	Fileinfo
FILE-POLICY	Who is allowed to execute DDL on the system?	Policy
FILE-DDL-01 SAFE-DDL-01	Is the DDL object file correctly secured with the Guardian or Safeguard system?	Fileinfo Safecom
FILE-DDL-02	Is the DDQUERYS file secured correctly?	Fileinfo
FILE-DDL-03	Is the DDSCHEMA file secured correctly?	Fileinfo
FILE-DDL-04	Are the DDL Dictionaries on the system correctly secured to the application?	Fileinfo

Related Topics

Securing Applications
ENFORM
ENABLE

DEFAULT User Program

The DEFAULT program allows users to set their own default volume/subvolume and default Guardian file security vector.

If users are allowed to run the DEFAULT program, they will be able to set the following parameters:

DEFAULT VOLUME/SUBVOLUME
DEFAULT SECURITY

The Corporate Security Standards should dictate whether or not users are allowed to run the DEFAULT program and the security of the DEFAULT object file required to enforce the standard.

Setting Default Volume

The DEFAULT VOLUME actually determines the subvolume where the user's TACL session will begin. The user's TACLCSTM and FUPCSTM files will be created here.

Notice that the current userid is assumed. The next time the user who invoked DEFAULT enters a VOLUME command with no command options, or logs off and back on, their current volume will be the new volume.

> *RISK*   Generally users are allowed to change their default volume. However, their TACLCSTM and other *CSTM, if used to setup default session controls, do not get moved to the new location. Therefore, changing the default logon subvolume could circumvent these *CSTM files.

> **AP-ADVICE-DEFAULT-01**   Users should be prevented from setting their default subvolume on $SYSTEM, thus requiring access to $SYSTEM to logon. The only exception to this may be SUPER Group members.

Setting Default File Security

The security vector will automatically be assigned to every file that the user creates.

Notice that the current userid is assumed. Changing the default security does not alter the security assigned to previously created files. Users can use the FUP SECURE command to change the security vector of existing files.

> *RISK*   Each time a user creates a new file, it is assigned its default security 'RWEP,' unless otherwise specified. If users set their default security to something less restrictive like 'AAAA,' then their files may not be adequately secured. If a user sets the default security to something more restrictive like 'OOOO', it is possible that other users will not be able to access files that they need. The default security should be set to a level that ensures newly created files meet minimum standard security.

Securing DEFAULT

> **BP-FILE-DEFAULT-01**   DEFAULT should be secured "UUNU".

> **BP-OPSYS-LICENSE-01**   DEFAULT must be LICENSED.

> **BP-OPSYS-OWNER-01**   DEFAULT should be owned by SUPER.SUPER.

> **BP-OPSYS-FILELOC-01**   DEFAULT must reside in $SYSTEM.SYSnn.

BP-USERS-DEFAULT-01   Users should not be allowed to set their default subvolume to the $SYSTEM disk.

BP-USERS-DEFAULT-02   Users must have a default subvolume set.

	Discovery Questions	Look here:
FILE-POLICY	Are users in general allowed to change their default volume and default security?	Policy
OPSYS-OWNER-01	Who owns the DEFAULT object file?	Fileinfo
OPSYS-LICENSE-01	Is the DEFAULT object file licensed?	Fileinfo
FILE-DEFAULT-01	Is the DEFAULT object file secured correctly?	Fileinfo
USER-DEFAULT-01	Do users have defaults set to $SYSTEM?	Userinfo Safecom
USER-DEFAULT-02	Do all users have a default set?	Userinfo Safecom

Related Topics

Users

Safeguard subsytem

DELUSER User Program

The DELUSER program is used to delete userids when Safeguard software is not in use. How this program is secured depends on the Security Policy and whether or not Safeguard software is in use.

Securing DELUSER

RISK   If the DELUSER utility is not controlled, the SUPER.SUPER user or other important userids could be deleted from the system.

Deleting users from the system is recommended when that userid is no longer needed. Deleting a userid stops that user from logging on to the system. Who is allowed to delete users should be controlled at the maximum level.

RISK   When a userid is deleted from the system, the files that are owned by the userid are orphaned. These files should be located and ownership changed to a valid userid.

Without the Safeguard Subsystem

If Safeguard software is not in use on the system, then the DELUSER program is used to delete userids.

How the DELUSER program is secured depends on who is allowed to perform this function as defined by the Corporate Security Policy.

If only SUPER.SUPER is allowed to delete users, then the DELUSER program must be secured to SUPER access only. The DELUSER object file need not be licensed. This is the most secure methodology to control the function of deleting users from the system.

BP-FILE-DELUSER-01   DELUSER should be secured "- - - -".

BP-OPSYS-LICENSE-01   DELUSER must NOT be LICENSED.

BP-OPSYS-OWNER-01   DELUSER should be owned by SUPER.SUPER.

BP-OPSYS-FILELOC-01   DELUSER must reside in $SYSTEM.SYSnn

If the policy authorizes Group Managers to DELETE userids from their own groups, then all groups will have to be granted EXECUTE access. Guardian will prevent users other than the 255 member of any group from deleting users to existing groups. Only SUPER.SUPER will be able delete userids from other groups. To allow Group Managers the right to delete userids, the DELUSER object file must be licensed.

BP*-FILE-DELUSER-01   DELUSER should be secured "- - A -".

BP*-OPSYS-LICENSE-01   DELUSER must be LICENSED.

BP*-OPSYS-OWNER-01   DELUSER should be owned by SUPER.SUPER.

BP*-OPSYS-FILELOC-01   DELUSER must reside in $SYSTEM.SYSnn

RISK   Because of DELUSER's unique function, any old SYSnn locations that may be present on the system must be secured from unauthorized use.

BP-FILE-DELUSER-02   DELUSER in old $SYSTEM.SYSnn locations must be secured "- - - -".

	Discovery Questions	Look here:
FILE-POLICY	Are Group Managers allowed to delete users?	Policy
OPSYS-OWNER-01	Is DELUSER owned by SUPER.SUPER?	Fileinfo
OPSYS-LICENSE-01	Is the DELUSER object file licensed?	Fileinfo
FILE-POLICY	Does the security of the DELUSER object file conform to the Security Policy?	Policy

	Discovery Questions	Look here:
FILE-DELUSER-01	Is the DELUSER object file secured correctly?	Fileinfo
FILE-DELUSER-02	Are old SYSnn copies of DELUSER secured?	Fileinfo

With the Safeguard Subsystem

If Safeguard software is in use on the system, then DELUSER will not run. Instead it will display a warning that Safeguard should be used to delete users.

```
44> deluser oper.bryan
SAFEGUARD IS RUNNING; USE SAFECOM TO DELETE USERS
```

Groups and Users will be deleted through the Safeguard interface. See chapter titled Safeguard Subsystem for more information.

AP-ADVICE-DELUSER-01   The DELUSER object file's Guardian security string and/or a Safeguard Protection Record should prevent any user other than SUPER.SUPER from executing it, in the case that Safeguard software is not running.

BP-FILE-DELUSER-01   DELUSER should be secured "- - - -".

BP-OPSYS-LICENSE-01   DELUSER must NOT be LICENSED.

BP-OPSYS-OWNER-01   DELUSER should be owned by SUPER.SUPER.

BP-OPSYS-FILELOC-01   DELUSER must reside in $SYSTEM.SYSnn

BP-SAFE-DELUSER-01   Add a Safeguard Protection Record to prevent execution of the DELUSER object file directly by any user.

	Discovery Questions	Look here:
OPSYS-OWNER-01	Is DELUSER owned by SUPER.SUPER?	Fileinfo
OPSYS-LICENSE-01	Is the DELUSER object file licensed?	Fileinfo
FILE-POLICY	Does the security of the DELUSER object file conform to the Security Policy?	Policy
FILE-DELUSER-01 SAFE-DELUSER-01	Is the DELUSER object file correctly secured with the Guardian or Safeguard system?	Fileinfo Safecom

Related Topics

Users

Safeguard

Disk Processes

The disk process software is an integral part of the operating system. Each disk volume runs its own copy of the disk process program. Disks can be of one of two types:

A physical disk volume of a specified type and size

A virtual disk volume physically resides on one or more physical volumes. A virtual disk is a software configured disk that has a distinct volume name. Virtual disks are created and managed with the Storage Management Foundation (SMP) software.

There are two distinct Disk Processes that match the above:

TSYSDP2   HP disk process operating system component

OVDP   Disk process used by disks configured as VIRTUAL

The disk volume process is run as the name of the volume, i.e., $DATA1. Volume names are reserved on the system and the processes are run automatically by the operating system.

Disk Process Security

BP-FILE-DISKPROC-01   TSYSDP2 should be secured "UUUU".

BP-OPSYS-OWNER-01   TSYSDP2 should be owned by SUPER.SUPER.

BP-OPSYS-FILELOC-01   TSYSDP2 must reside in $SYSTEM.SYSnn.

BP-FILE-DISKPROC-02   OVDP should be secured "UUUU".

BP-OPSYS-OWNER-01   OVDP should be owned by SUPER.SUPER.

BP-OPSYS-FILELOC-01   OVDP must reside in $SYSTEM.SYSnn.

	Discovery Questions	Look here:
OPSYS-OWNER-01	Who owns the TSYSDP2 object file?	Fileinfo
OPSYS-OWNER-01	Who owns the OVDP object file?	Fileinfo
FILE-DISKPROC-01	Is the TSYSDP2 object file secured correctly?	Fileinfo
FILE-DISKPROC-02	Is the OVDP object file secured correctly?	Fileinfo

<u>Related Topics</u>

SMP

DISKGEN System Utility

DISKGEN is a part of the utilities that are invoked during a SYSGEN that copies the new files to a System Image Disk (SID).

A SYSGENR option invokes the DISKGEN program to copy directly to disk those files necessary to generate an HP NonStop Kernel operating system. DISKGEN can be used instead of a System Image Tape (SIT).

Using DISKGEN for system generation and running SYSGENR outside of DSM/SCM, is an action that is not recommended.

RISK   Using DISKGEN directly is NOT recommended as the normal method of sysgening a system image and should be strictly secured.

RISK   Only those who know how to use DISKGEN properly should use it.

Securing DISKGEN

BP-FILE-DISKGEN-01   DISKGEN should be secured "UUCU".

BP-OPSYS-LICENSE-01   DISKGEN must be LICENSED.

BP-OPSYS-OWNER-01   DISKGEN should be owned by SUPER.SUPER.

BP-OPSYS-FILELOC-01   DISKGEN must reside in $SYSTEM.SYSnn.

If available, use Safeguard software or a third party object security product to grant access to DISKGEN object files only to users who require access in order to perform their jobs.

BP-SAFE-DISKGEN-01   Add a Safeguard Protection Record to grant appropriate access to the DISKGEN object file.

	Discovery Questions	Look here:
OPSYS-OWNER-01	Who owns the DISKGEN object file?	Fileinfo
OPSYS-LICENSE-01	Is the DISKGEN object file licensed?	Fileinfo
FILE-POLICY	Who is allowed to execute DISKGEN on the system?	Policy
FILE-DISKGEN-01	Is the DISKGEN object file correctly secured	Fileinfo
SAFE-DISKGEN-01	with the Guardian or Safeguard system?	Safecom

Related Topics

System Generation

DSMSCM

SYSGEN

Distributed Name Service (DNS) Subsystem

DNS is part of the set of the Distributed Systems Management (DSM) subsystem.

DNS simplifies management of relationships between objects in a NonStop system or an Expand network by managing a distributed and partly replicated name database that models those objects.

DNS provides facilities that:

Maintain names of objects controlled by the HP server and other types of systems

Provide alternative names (aliases) for objects

Translate an alias for subsystem-object names, allowing command interpreters to accept meaningful names

Translate subsystem-object names to aliases, allowing event-processing applications to report meaningful names to operators

Organize objects into groups

Provide a single name for a set of objects

Translate a group name to the names of the members of that group, allowing network management applications (NMAs) to implement group-oriented commands

Almost anything can be defined as an object to DNS: employee names, phone numbers, locations, and departments, for example. The DNS subsystem allows assignment of names to these objects to make object management easier.

The DNS subsystem is generally created and managed by a SUPER Group person responsible for the naming of a system or network. DNS should not be available for write access to general users.

RISK Names must be monitored and maintained to eliminate duplication, which will cause ambiguity and possible errors.

DNS Components

The components of DNS are (See Figure 6-4):

DNSCOM

Figure 6-4
*DNS
Components*

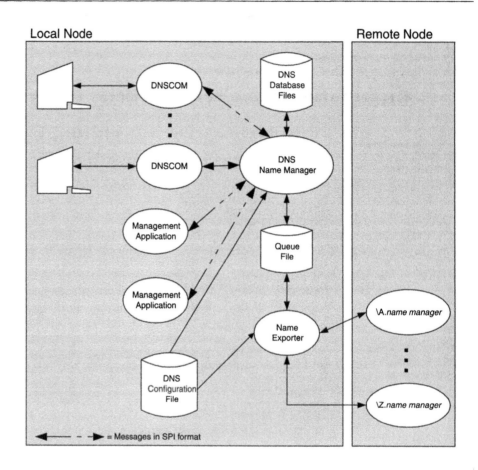

DNSCONF

DNSEXP

DNSHELP

DNSMGR

DBDDLS

LOAD

ENFORM Report and Query Subsystem

DNSCOM

The user interface to the DNS subsystem. It is used to create DNS databases, control the DNS processes, and perform inquiries and updates against DNS databases.

This interface allows one to create the DNS database, control the DNS processes, and perform inquiries and update of names.

DNSCONF

DNS configuration file as defined by the =_DNS_CONFIG system define. The default is $SYSTEM.SYSTEM.DNSCONF.

DNSEXP

DNSEXP is the executable code file for the DNS name exporter. All replication of name definitions from one node to another is handled by the name exporter processes. Each replicated DNS database has its own name exporter; consequently, there may be multiple name exporters running simultaneously on a single system.

DNSHELP

A data file containing DNS help and error and warning messages.

DNSMGR

DNSMGR is the executable name manager for DNS. All interactions between programs (including DNSCOM) and DNS databases are performed by name managers. Each DNS database has its own name manager process. There may be multiple name managers running simultaneously on a single system.

A name manager processes requests from DNSCOM and user applications using Subsystem Programmatic Interface (SPI) requests.

LOAD

The load file is a command file that can be read by DNSCOM to initially load the DNS database with the definitions of some commonly used subsystems and their object types.

DBDDLS & ENFORM Reports

DBDDLS is the DDL source file describing the DNS database. ENFORM uses this file to create a data dictionary capable of generating reports on the DNS database.

DNS Database Configuration

Each DNS database is associated with a DNS configuration created with the INITIALIZE DNS command. Each DNS database consists of 15 key-sequenced files. The files need not reside on the same disk volume.

Securing DNS Components

BP-FILE-DNS-01   DNSCOM should be secured "UUCU".

BP-OPSYS-OWNER-02   DNSCOM should be owned by SUPER.SUPER.

BP-OPSYS-FILELOC-02   DNSCOM must reside in $SYSTEM.SYSTEM.

BP-FILE-DNS-02   DNSCONF should be secured "CCCU".

BP-OPSYS-OWNER-02   DNSCONF should be owned by SUPER.SUPER.

BP-OPSYS-FILELOC-02   DNSCONF must reside in $SYSTEM.SYSTEM.

BP-FILE-DNS-03   DNSEXP should be secured "UUNU".

BP-OPSYS-OWNER-02   DNSEXP should be owned by SUPER.SUPER.

BP-OPSYS-FILELOC-02   DNSEXP must reside in $SYSTEM.SYSTEM.

BP-FILE-DNS-04   DNSHELP should be secured "NUUU".

BP-OPSYS-OWNER-02   DNSHELP should be owned by SUPER.SUPER.

BP-OPSYS-FILELOC-02   DNSHELP must reside in $SYSTEM.SYSTEM.

BP-FILE-DNS-05   DNSMGR should be secured "UUNU".

BP-OPSYS-OWNER-02   DNSMGR should be owned by SUPER.SUPER.

BP-OPSYS-FILELOC-02   DNSMGR must reside in $SYSTEM.SYSTEM.

BP-FILE-DNS-06   LOAD should be secured "CCCU".

BP-OPSYS-OWNER-03   LOAD should be owned by SUPER.SUPER.

BP-OPSYS-FILELOC-03   LOAD resides in $SYSTEM.ZDNS.

BP-FILE-DNS-07   DBDDLS should be secured "CCCU".

BP-OPSYS-OWNER-03   DBDDLS should be owned by SUPER.SUPER.

BP-OPSYS-FILELOC-03   DBDDLS resides in $SYSTEM.ZDNS.

If available, use Safeguard software or a third party object security product to grant access to DNSCOM object files only to users who require access in order to perform their jobs.

BP-SAFE-DNS-01   Add a Safeguard Protection Record to grant appropriate access to the DNSCOM object file.

	Discovery Questions	Look here:
FILE-POLICY	Is DNS used on the system	Fileinfo
OPSYS-OWNER-02	Who owns the DNSCOM file?	Fileinfo
OPSYS-OWNER-02	Who owns the DNSCONF file?	Fileinfo

	Discovery Questions	Look here:
OPSYS-OWNER-02	Who owns the DNSEXP file?	Fileinfo
OPSYS-OWNER-02	Who owns the DNSHELP file?	Fileinfo
OPSYS-OWNER-02	Who owns the DNSMGR file?	Fileinfo
OPSYS-OWNER-03	Who owns the LOAD file?	Fileinfo
OPSYS-OWNER-03	Who owns the DBDDLS file?	Fileinfo
FILE-POLICY	Who is allowed to run DNSCOM on the system?	Policy
FILE-DNS-01 SAFE-DNS-01	Is the DNSCOM object file correctly secured with the Guardian or Safeguard system?	Fileinfo Safecom
FILE-DNS-02	Is the DNSCONF object file secured correctly?	Fileinfo
FILE-DNS-03	Is the DNSEXP object file secured correctly?	Fileinfo
FILE-DNS-04	Is the DNSHELP object file secured correctly?	Fileinfo
FILE-DNS-05	Is the DNSMGR object file secured correctly?	Fileinfo
FILE-DNS-06	Is the LOAD object file secured correctly?	Fileinfo
FILE-DNS-07	Is the DBDDLS object file secured correctly?	Fileinfo

DIVER System Utility

The DIVER program is used to stop a processor, causing all processes and all lines to switch to the backup. The program was created so programmers can down a single CPU to test their NonStop programs. DIVER is never used under normal circumstances.

RISK **DIVER** is a dangerous program. Forcing the system to use the backup processor for any affected devices or programs may affect the performance of the backup processor, particularly if it is already being heavily used when the command is issued.

RISK Processes that are not non-stop and are running in the CPU will terminate abruptly.

AP-ADVICE-DIVER-01 DIVER can be used in emergency circumstances to down a CPU that has programmatically locked up. However, it is better to attempt to stop the suspect processes that may be causing the lock up, rather than downing the CPU.

Securing DIVER

BP-FILE-DIVER-01   DIVER should be secured "- - - -".

BP-OPSYS-LICENSE-01   DIVER must be LICENSED.

BP-OPSYS-OWNER-01   DIVER should be owned by SUPER.SUPER.

BP-OPSYS-FILELOC-01   DIVER must reside in $SYSTEM.SYSnn.

If available, use Safeguard software or a third party object security product to grant access to DIVER object files only to users who require access in order to perform their jobs.

BP-SAFE-DIVER-01   Add a Safeguard Protection Record to grant appropriate access to the DIVER object file.

	Discovery Questions	Look here:
OPSYS-OWNER-01	Who owns the DIVER object file?	Fileinfo
OPSYS-LICENSE-01	Is the DIVER object file licensed?	Fileinfo
FILE-POLICY	Who is allowed to execute DIVER on the system?	Policy
FILE-DIVER-01 SAFE-DIVER-01	Is the DIVER object file correctly secured with the Guardian or Safeguard system?	Fileinfo Safecom

DSAP User Program

The Disk Space Analysis Program (DSAP) is used to analyze how disk space is utilized on a specified volume. DSAP copies the disk directory and free-space table to the current work file. By specifying options, one can manipulate this data to produce several different reports about the use of the disk space for that volume.

The free-space table is limited only by the primary (main) and secondary (contiguous disk space) memory requirements.

RISK   DSAP is strictly a reporting tool and, therefore, poses no security risk. It is most often used to determine the amount of free space available on a disk volume.

RISK   Running DSAP consumes system resources.

AP-ADVICE-DSAP-01   Many system managers prefer that the majority of users be unable to run DSAP. It is up to each company to determine whether or not all users, or only specific users, are allowed to run DSAP. The Corporate Security Policy should dictate who is allowed to run DSAP.

The components of DSAP are:

DSAP
DSAPDDL
DSAPCSTM

DSAP

Disk space analysis program. Space can be queried by parameters, of which some of the common ones are:

Subvol summary
User summary
File details
Free space analysis
Flags; BROKEN, EXPIRED, LICENSED, AUDITED, SQL, etc.
Opened

DSAPDDL

DDL dictionary schema for DSAP output, used by ENFORM custom reports.

DSAPCSTM

Optionally a DSAPCSTM file can be used to perform standard setup commands and shortcuts for DSAP as defined in each user's default subvolume. Please refer to the Gazette section on *CSTM Configuration Files.

Securing DSAP

BP-FILE-DSAP-01   DSAP should be secured "UUNU".

BP-OPSYS-LICENSE-01   DSAP must be LICENSED.

BP-OPSYS-OWNER-01   DSAP should be owned by SUPER.SUPER.

BP-OPSYS-FILELOC-01   DSAP must reside in $SYSTEM.SYSnn.

BP-FILE-DSAP-02   DSAPDDL should be secured "NUNU".

BP-OPSYS-OWNER-02   DSAPDDL should be owned by SUPER.SUPER.

BP-OPSYS-FILELOC-02   DSAPDDL must reside in $SYSTEM.SYSTEM.

If available, use Safeguard software or a third party object security product to grant access to DSAP object files only to users who require access in order to perform their jobs.

BP-SAFE-DSAP-01   Add a Safeguard Protection Record to grant appropriate access to the DSAP object file.

	Discovery Questions	Look here:
OPSYS-OWNER-01	Who owns the DSAP object file?	Fileinfo
OPSYS-OWNER-02	Who owns the DSAPDDL object file?	Fileinfo
OPSYS-LICENSE-01	Is the DSAP object file licensed?	Fileinfo
FILE-POLICY	Does the Security Policy require limiting access to the DSAP program?	Policy
FILE-DSAP-01 SAFE-DSAP-01	Is the DSAP object file correctly secured with the Guardian or Safeguard system?	Fileinfo Safecom
FILE-DSAP-02	Is the DSAPDDL file secured correctly?	Fileinfo

DSM/SCM Subsystem

The Distributed Systems Management/Software Configuration Manager (DSM/SCM) provides centralized planning, management, and installation of software on distributed (target) HP NonStop servers.

DSM/SCM runs on an HP NonStop server (host) and receives, archives, configures, and packages software for distributed (target) systems. From the host system, one uses DSM/SCM to transfer software files to target systems. DSM/SCM also runs on each target system, where it places (or applies) the software received from the host system.

DSM/SCM is a complex, multi-faceted utility that should be used and run by system knowledgeable personnel.

DSM/SCM Methodology

DSM/SCM has several parts:

Receive New Software into Archive

Create a Software Revision

Build new Revision

Apply the new Revision

Activate the new Revision on the Target System

Receive New Software into Archive

The first step in building a software configuration revision is to receive the new software (input) into the DSM/SCM archive. A software input consists of one or more products, which can be HP, customer, or third-party software, on either disk or tape.

When software is received, the files from each product are stored in the archive, and the file attributes are stored in the database.

RISK Once the software has been downloaded or restored from tape, but not received into DSM/SCM, the files are not compressed and therefore vulnerable. Files should be received into DSM/SCM immediately for compression and to mitigate this risk.

RISK The SUT tape should be stored in a secured place for both disaster recovery purposes and to prevent unauthorized access and modification.

Once received into DSM/SCM, the restored files are transitioned into a compressed format used only by the DSM/SCM subsystem.

RISK Generally there is no risk to the use of these files, except by DSM/SCM subsystem users.

Create a Software Revision

After receiving all required inputs into the DSM/SCM archive, plan and create a new software revision for the target system. A software revision is a list of products stored in the archive that together are built into a configuration revision. When creating a software revision, ensure that all products included are compatible with each other and that all requisite SPRs are accounted for.

As each new software revision is archived, it is up to the system administrator to determine when a new operating system upgrade is required. Not all products apply to all systems, and multiple revisions may be applied at one time to minimize impact to the running system.

When the system administrator decides to upgrade the operating system, the inclusion of software for this revision is created with DSM/SCM and defined to DSM/SCM's database.

Build and Apply new Configuration Revision

A new configuration revision is the package that DSM/SCM builds to transfer the products listed in a software revision from the archive to the target system. After the configuration revision is built and transferred to the target system, it is applied to the target system.

The target system can be the local system or a remote system. DSM/SCM can create and build software revisions for multiple systems and multiple software revision levels, as defined by the system administrator.

The activation package is built into a temporary location on $VOL.ZAnnnn.

RISK In some cases the BUILD step is done some period of time prior to the system cold load that brings the new revision on line. These temporary staging areas must be secured from tampering during the staging period.

Activate the new Revision on the Target System

Once an activation package is applied to a target system, the target system operator must activate the software before it can be used. Activating the new software involves preparing the system for the new software, then starting the new software.

Software activation is outlined in operator instructions included with the activation package and viewable through the Target Interface. DSM/SCM generates operator instructions that might vary depending on the software being installed. Also, the planner might have edited the instructions to include site-specific tasks earlier in the configuration process. Only the instructions required for the particular installation are included in the activation package.

Finally, the software revision is activated on the server. In many cases the revision may require a full cold load. In other cases the revision may require the stopping and restarting of subsystems.

A new SYSnn subvolume will be created or updated

A new CSSnn subvolume will be created or updated

Following the activation of new software, the rename function moves software components into their final location. Rename is performed from a TACL running the ZPHIRNM program.

The appropriate files in $SYSTEM.SYSTEM will be replaced

The appropriate files in TSV subvolumes will be replaced

RISK File security is propagated to the new operating system. For instance, if the DIVER object file is owned by 255,255 and secured "UUUU", this security will be propagated into the next operating system

RISK   A default security can be set within DSMSCM for new files. This should be set as "CUCU" and later expanded as determined by the security administrators.

Securing DSMSCM Components

BP-PROCESS-DSMSCM-01   The $YPHI Pathway application should be running.

BP-FILE-DSMSCM-01   DSMSCM* object programs should be secured "UUCU".

BP-OPSYS-OWNER-03   DSMSCM* object programs should be owned by SUPER.SUPER.

BP-OPSYS-FILELOC-03   DSMSCM* object programs reside in $<dsmscm-vol>.ZDSMSCM.

BP-FILE-DSMSCM-02   DSMSCM* non-object files should be secured "CCCU".

BP-OPSYS-OWNER-03   DSMSCM* non-object files should be owned by SUPER.SUPER.

BP-OPSYS-FILELOC-03   DSMSCM* non-object files reside in $<dsmscm-vol>.ZDSMSCM.

BP-OPSYS-LICENSE-03   CBEXE must be LICENSED.

BP-OPSYS-PROGID-03   CBEXE is PROGID'd.

BP-OPSYS-LICENSE-03   TAEXE must be LICENSED.

BP-OPSYS-PROGID-03   TAEXE is PROGID'd.

BP-FILE-DSMSCM-03   DSMSCM SQL Catalog should be secured "CCCU".

BP-OPSYS-OWNER-03   DSMSCM SQL Catalog should be owned by SUPER.SUPER.

BP-OPSYS-FILELOC-03   DSMSCM SQL Catalog resides in $<vol>.<?>.

BP-FILE-DSMSCM-04   DSMSCM SQL Database should be secured "CCCU".

BP-OPSYS-OWNER-03   DSMSCM SQL Database should be owned by SUPER.SUPER.

BP-OPSYS-FILELOC-03   DSMSCM SQL Database resides in $<vol>.<?>.

If available, use Safeguard software or a third party object security product to grant access to DSM/SCM object files and Pathway environment. Access should be granted to users who require access in order to perform their jobs.

BP-SAFE-DSMSCM-01   Add a Safeguard Protection Record to grant appropriate access to the DSMSCM Pathway environment and DSM/SCM files.

	Discovery Questions	Look here:
FILE-POLICY	Who are the users who should have access to the DSM/SCM application?	Policy
PROCESS-DSMSCM-01	Is the $YPHI process running?	Status
OPSYS-OWNER-03	Who owns the DSM/SCM Pathway Objects in $<dsmscm-vol>.ZDSMSCM.?	Fileinfo
OPSYS-OWNER-03	Who owns the DSM/SCM files in $<dsmscm-vol>.ZDSMSCM.?	Fileinfo
OPSYS-OWNER-03	Who owns the DSM/SCM subsystem files in $<dsmscm-vol>.ZDSMSCM.?	Fileinfo
OPSYS-OWNER-03	Who owns the DSM/SCM catalog and databases?	SQLCI
OPSYS-LICENSE-03	Is the CBEXE object file licensed?	Fileinfo
OPSYS-LICENSE-03	Is the TAEXE object file licensed?	Fileinfo
OPSYS-PROGID-03	Is the CBEXE object file PROGID'd?	Fileinfo
OPSYS-PROGID-03	Is the TAEXE object file PROGID'd?	Fileinfo
SAFE-DSMSCM-01	Is the $YPHI Pathway correctly secured with Safeguard?	Safecom
FILE-DSMSCM-01 SAFE-DSMSCM-01	Is the $<dsmscm-vol>.ZDSMSCM.* object files correctly secured with the Guardian or Safeguard system?	Fileinfo Safecom
FILE-DSMSCM-02 SAFE-DSMSCM-01	Is the $<dsmscm-vol>.ZDSMSCM.* files correctly secured with the Guardian or Safeguard system?	Fileinfo Safecom
FILE-DSMSCM-03	Is the DSM/SCM SQL catalog secured correctly?	SQLCI
FILE-DSMSCM-04	Are the DSM/SCM SQL database objects secured correctly?	SQLCI

Related Topics
DSM/TC
SQL
SYSGEN

DSM/TC Subsystem

The Distributed Systems Management Tape Catalog (DSM/TC) subsystem manages tape files for the HP NonStop server systems. The DSM/TC subsystem supports the following functions:

A tape file can be accessed by name

Tape files are protected from being accidentally overwritten

Multiple tape file generations and versions within a generation can be managed

BACKUP tapes are more easily tracked

Scratch tapes can be assigned to users

Tapes can be managed and shared between nodes

Control of tapes can be centralized on one node

Tape catalog is stored in a NonStop SQL/MP database

Database is protected by NonStop TMF software

NonStop SQL/MP software can be used to query the database

The Corporate Security Policy should detail procedures for securing tapes in a tape library.

RISK   Tapes can contain sensitive data. Securing the backup tapes and the utilities that can read or copy the data is imperative.

RISK   Access to DSM/TC and its database facilitates identification of physical tapes. If a general user has access to identifying tapes and those tapes are not physically secure, the tapes are more vulnerable.

RISK   Inappropriate usage of the DSM/TC catalog and the unauthorized manipulation of the catalog can destroy accessibility to physical tapes by the system software. Tapes can become orphaned from the catalog.

The components of DSM/TC are:

MEDIACOM

MEDIADBM

MEDIAMSG

MEDIASRV

MEDDEM

SQL/MP TAPE CATALOG

ZSVRCONF

ZSERVER

MEDIACOM

MEDIACOM is the interactive interface used to manage labeled-tape operations. It can:

Label new tapes and catalog them

Make tape mount requests

Manage the use of uncataloged tapes

Create scratch tapes

MEDIACOM must be enabled before it can be used on a system. It is enabled with a command in CONFTEXT file.

If MEDIACOM is enabled, both labeled and unlabeled tapes can be used.

If MEDIACOM is not enabled, only unlabeled tapes can be used.

Once MEDIACOM is enabled, all tape requests are routed through the tape server process of ZSERVER.

MEDIADBM

MEDIADBM is the SQL database manager process for DSM/TC. MEDIADBM is the interface for DSM/TC's SQL catalog and database tables.

MEDIAMSG

MEDIAMSG is a file containing the DSM/TC error and informative messages.

MEDIASRV

MEDIASRV is the interface between the management application and the other elements that make up the DSM/TC subsystem. MEDIACOM automatically opens a MEDIASRV server process whenever it needs to. One server process accommodates ten MEDIACOM users at a time. The default MEDIASRV process is named $XDMS.

MEDIASRV is also the programmatic interface to the DSM/TC subsystem. Management application control of the DSM/TC subsystem takes place by using procedures to communicate with the DSM/TC programmatic process, MEDIASRV.

MEDDEM

MEDDEM is ZSERVER's automatic tape expiration program. DSM/TC can be configured for this feature or it can be disabled.

SQL Tape Catalog and Database

The DSM/TC tape library is stored in an NonStop SQL/MP database. DSM/TC requires NonStop SQL/MP database to be installed and running. DSM/TC requires a DSM/TC system catalog and a tape database. DSM/TC can share the NonStop SQL/MP system catalog or defines its own.

> **AP-ADVICE-DSMTC-01**   The SQL configuration of DSM/TC can be customized. Consult with the system manager to determine the location of the SQL/MP catalog and database for DSM/TC.

> *RISK*   The security of the DSM/TC SQL catalog and database might allow users with SQLCI access to access the DSM/TC catalog files outside of the DSM/TC controlled interface.

ZSERVER

ZSERVER is the labeled tape server process. There is one ZSERVER process pair for each system, usually named $ZSVR. The $ZSVR process pair is normally started as part of the standard system startup procedure.

Securing DSM/TC Components

> **BP-FILE-DSMTC-01**   MEDIACOM should be secured "UUCU".

> **BP-OPSYS-OWNER-01**   MEDIACOM should be owned by SUPER.SUPER.

> **BP-OPSYS-FILELOC-01**   MEDIACOM must reside in $SYSTEM.SYSnn.

> **BP-FILE-DSMTC-02**   MEDIADBM should be secured "UUCU".

> **BP-OPSYS-LICENSE-01**   MEDIADBM must be LICENSED.

BP-OPSYS-OWNER-01   MEDIADBM should be owned by
SUPER.SUPER.

BP-OPSYS-FILELOC-01   MEDIADBM must reside in $SYSTEM.SYSnn.

BP-FILE-DSMTC-03   MEDIAMSG should be secured "CUCU".

BP-OPSYS-OWNER-01   MEDIAMSG should be owned by
SUPER.SUPER.

BP-OPSYS-FILELOC-01   MEDIAMSG must reside in $SYSTEM.SYSnn.

BP-PROCESS-MEDIASRV-01 $ZDMS process should be running.

BP-FILE-DSMTC-04   MEDIASRV should be secured "UUCU".

BP-OPSYS-LICENSE-01   MEDIASRV must be LICENSED.

BP-OPSYS-OWNER-01   MEDIASRV should be owned by SUPER.SUPER.

BP-OPSYS-FILELOC-01   MEDIASRV must reside in $SYSTEM.SYSnn.

BP-FILE-DSMTC-05   MEDDEM should be secured "UUCU".

BP-OPSYS-OWNER-01   MEDDEM should be owned by SUPER.SUPER.

BP-OPSYS-FILELOC-01   MEDDEM must reside in $SYSTEM.SYSnn.

BP-PROCESS-ZSERVER-01 $ZSVR process should be running.

BP-FILE-DSMTC-06   ZSERVER should be secured "UUCU".

BP-OPSYS-LICENSE-01   ZSERVER must be LICENSED.

BP-OPSYS-OWNER-01   ZSERVER should be owned by SUPER.SUPER.

BP-OPSYS-FILELOC-01   ZSERVER must reside in $SYSTEM.SYSnn.

BP-FILE-DSMTC-07   DSM/TC SQL Catalog should be secured "CCCU".

BP-OPSYS-OWNER-03   DSM/TC SQL Catalog should be owned by
SUPER.SUPER.

BP-OPSYS-FILELOC-03   DSM/TC SQL Catalog resides in $<vol>.?.

BP-FILE-DSMTC-08   DSM/TC SQL Database should be secured "CCCU".

BP-OPSYS-OWNER-03   DSM/TC SQL Database should be owned by
SUPER.SUPER.

BP-OPSYS-FILELOC-03 DSM/TC SQL Database resides in $<vol>.?.

MEDIACOM Commands with Security Implications

MEDIACOM allows users access to copy or destroy sensitive data on tape media and to manipulate the DSM/TC catalog. The following list of commands is controlled by DSM/TC for SUPER Group only.

ADD

ALTER

CREATE

DELETE

DROP

LABEL

TAPEDRIVE

3P-ACCESS-MEDIACOM-01 If a third party product is used to grant access to MEDIACOM running as a SUPER group userid, these commands should be denied to all SUPER users other than the designated SUPER group userid responsible for tapes.

MEDIACOM allows any users access to RECOVER a tape to disk. It is not necessary to be in the SUPER Group to perform the RECOVER command.

RECOVER

3P-ACCESS-MEDIACOM-02 If a third party product is used to grant access to MEDIACOM, secure the RECOVER command should be denied to all users other than the designated SUPER user responsible for tapes.

If available, use Safeguard software or a third party object security product to grant access to MEDIACOM object files only to users who require access in order to perform their jobs.

BP-SAFE-DSMTC-01 Add a Safeguard Protection Record to grant appropriate access to the MEDIACOM object file.

	Discovery Questions	Look here:
FILE-DSMTC	Is DSM/TC used for tape cataloging?	Policy
PROCESS-MEDIASRV-01	Is the $ZDMS process running?	Status

	Discovery Questions	Look here:
PROCESS-ZSERVER-01	Is the $ZSVR process running?	Status
OPSYS-OWNER-01	Who owns the MEDIACOM object file?	Fileinfo
OPSYS-OWNER-01	Who owns the MEDIADBM object file?	Fileinfo
OPSYS-OWNER-01	Who owns the MEDIAMSG object file?	Fileinfo
OPSYS-OWNER-01	Who owns the MEDIASRV object file?	Fileinfo
OPSYS-OWNER-01	Who owns the MEDDEM object file?	Fileinfo
OPSYS-OWNER-01	Who owns the ZSERVER object file?	Fileinfo
OPSYS-OWNER-03	Who owns the DSM/TC tape catalog and databases?	SQLCI
OPSYS-LICENSE-01	Is the MEDIADBM object file licensed?	Fileinfo
OPSYS-LICENSE-01	Is the MEDIASRV object file licensed?	Fileinfo
OPSYS-LICENSE-01	Is the ZSERVER object file licensed?	Fileinfo
FILE-POLICY	Who is allowed to execute MEDIACOM on the system?	Policy
FILE-DSMTC-01 SAFE-DSMTC-01	Is the MEDIACOM object file correctly secured with the Guardian or Safeguard system?	Fileinfo Safecom
FILE-DSMTC-02	Is the MEDIADBM object file secured correctly?	Fileinfo
FILE-DSMTC-03	Is the MEDIAMSG object file secured correctly?	Fileinfo
FILE-DSMTC-04	Is the MEDIASRV object file correctly secured with the Guardian or Safeguard system?	Fileinfo Safecom
FILE-DSMTC-05	Is the MEDDEM file secured correctly?	Fileinfo
FILE-DSMTC-06	Is the ZSERVER file secured correctly?	Fileinfo
FILE-DSMTC-07	Is the DSM/TC tape SQL catalog secured correctly?	SQLCI
FILE-DSMTC-08	Are the DSM/TC tape SQL database objects secured correctly?	SQLCI

Related Topics

DSM/SCM

TAPECOM

NonStop SQL database

ECHO User Program

ECHO is used to test the connection to a remote system by sending data to the ECHO server on that system. If the connection is successful, the server returns the data transmitted in the sequence that the data was entered. HP NonStop server TCP/IP ECHO does not service UDP ports.

The components of ECHO are:

ECHO

ECHOSERV

ECHO

ECHO is the HP NonStop server ECHO client. It is used to interactively test the connection to a remote system. The remote system need not be another NonStop server.

ECHOSERV

ECHOSERV is the HP NonStop server ECHO server. It responds to ECHO requests from remote clients.

Securing ECHO

BP-FILE-ECHO-01   ECHO should be secured "UUNU".

BP-OPSYS-OWNER-01   ECHO should be owned by SUPER.SUPER.

BP-OPSYS-FILELOC-01   ECHO must reside in $SYSTEM.SYSnn.

BP-FILE-ECHO-02   ECHOSERV should be secured "UUNU".

BP-OPSYS-OWNER-03   ECHOSERV should be owned by SUPER.SUPER.

BP-OPSYS-FILELOC-03   ECHOSERV resides in $SYSTEM.ZTCPIP.

	Discovery Questions	Look here:
OPSYS-OWNER-01	Who owns the ECHO file?	Fileinfo
OPSYS-OWNER-03	Who owns the ECHOSERV file?	Fileinfo
FILE-POLICY	Who is allowed to use ECHO on the system?	Policy
FILE-ECHO-01	Is the ECHO object file secured correctly?	Fileinfo

	Discovery Questions	Look here:
FILE-ECHO-02	Is the ECHOSERV object file secured correctly?	Fileinfo

Related Topics

TCP/IP

EDIT User Program

Editors are used to manipulate text files. From an editor program, text can be created, modified, deleted and viewed. Text files on the HP NonStop server reside in unstructured files with a disk file code of 101.

Some types of editor programs are:

EDIT

TEDIT

VS

RISK   Editors can be used to view data or modify text data files.

AP-ADVICE-EDIT-01   Sensitive application data stored in text files should be strictly secured for READ, WRITE and PURGE access to only authorized personnel.

RISK   Most systems contain many text files. Text files are used for configuration files, documents, help file, and many other uses. They are resident on every volume and many subvolumes. It is extremely hard to control the security of the numerous text files.

AP-ADVICE-EDIT-02   System text files, especially those on $SYSTEM.SYSTEM and $SYSTEM.SYSnn should be secured properly to control changing by unauthorized users.

RISK   Once a screen editor program is started, it is impossible to secure the use of internal screen editor commands.

RISK   Editors are often required by most users for every day work. Securing the editor programs to restrict access is often not reasonable, but the risks remain.

EDIT

EDIT and its components provide the ability to manipulate text (file code 101) files on the HP NonStop server. The EDIT program provides a line editor.

The components of EDIT are:

EDIT
EDITTOC
VS

Edit provides a line editor

TEDIT

TEDIT is a screen editor for text files residing on the server.

The components of TEDIT are:

TEDIT
TEDHELP
TEDMSGS
TEDPROFL

VS

VS is a screen editor for T6530-type terminals, initiated from an EDIT session.

Securing **EDITORS**

BP-FILE-EDIT-01   EDIT should be secured "UUNU".
BP-OPSYS-OWNER-02   EDIT should be owned by SUPER.SUPER.
BP-OPSYS-FILELOC-02   EDIT must reside in $SYSTEM.SYSTEM.
BP-FILE-EDIT-02   TEDIT should be secured "UUNU".
BP-OPSYS-OWNER-02   TEDIT should be owned by SUPER.SUPER.
BP-OPSYS-FILELOC-02   TEDIT must reside in $SYSTEM.SYSTEM.
BP-FILE-EDIT-03   VS should be secured "UUNU".
BP-OPSYS-OWNER-02   VS should be owned by SUPER.SUPER.
BP-OPSYS-FILELOC-02   VS must reside in $SYSTEM.SYSTEM.

	Discovery Questions	Look here:
OPSYS-OWNER-02	Who owns the EDIT file?	Fileinfo
OPSYS-OWNER-02	Who owns the TEDIT file?	Fileinfo
OPSYS-OWNER-02	Who owns the VS file?	Fileinfo
FILE-POLICY	Who is allowed to use editors on the system?	Policy
FILE-EDIT-01	Is the EDIT object file secured correctly?	Fileinfo
FILE-EDIT-02	Is the TEDIT object file secured correctly?	Fileinfo
FILE-EDIT-03	Is the VS object file secured correctly?	Fileinfo

EMS Subsystem

The Event Management System (EMS) retrieves and reports on system events. An event is any significant occurrence in the system environment. Event messages are based on tokens that define information about events. The information can be used to:

Monitor the system or network environment

Report and research system problems

Report and analyze changes in the run-time environment

The EMS log is similar to a UNIX syslog.

EMS provides facilities that derive display text from message tokens so that EMS information can be presented both to operators and to applications in the format most appropriate to each.

EMS messages are subsystem specific, so the information they contain can be tailored to provide an exact and complete specification of the event circumstances.

There are three categories of events:

Critical

Action

Informational

Critical Events

A subsystem will designate an event as critical when the consequences of the event might be severe. The subsystem itself cannot accurately determine what conditions should be considered severe for a particular system or network.

Subsystems typically identify these events as critical:

Potential or actual loss of data

Loss of a major subsystem function

Loss of a fault-tolerance capability, such as loss of a redundant resource or loss of a failure-recovery function

Loss of subsystem integrity (for example, an unrecoverable internal error in a subsystem)

Action Events

A subsystem reports an action event when a situation arises that the subsystem cannot resolve without operator intervention. For example, a subsystem might report an action event when it cannot proceed until a tape is mounted or a printer ribbon is replaced.

Action events are reported in pairs of event messages:

The first message, the action-attention message, reports the problem.

The second message, the action-completion message, reports that the appropriate action has been taken.

EMS Components

The EMS Subsystem is made up of the following components (See Figure 6-5):

Event Message Collectors
Event Message Distributors
EMS Filters
EMS Object Files
EMS Utilities

RISK The EMS subsystem is used for reporting only. It does not pose any security risks.

Event Message Collectors

The Collector processes accept event messages from subsystems and logs them.

There is always one primary collector. System managers can define one or more alternate collectors. Both the primary and alternate collectors provide:

Subsystem support

Figure 6-5
EMS
Components

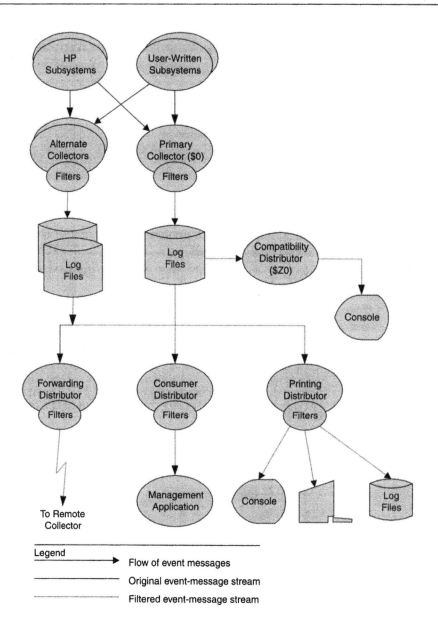

Pre-log filtration (PLF)

Log file management

Distributor support

Pre-log filtration makes it possible to detect and discard all event bursts with specified attributes or specific unwanted events.

Primary Collector ($0)

Each system (or node) has only one primary event message collector, named $0. It is initiated at system generation, and provides a central collection point for all events from all subsystems in a system.

It uses the $ZOPR process to perform waited operations. It has no user interface.

$ZOPR exists on every node and is initiated at cold load.

Alternate Collectors

One or more alternate collectors can be started on a system.

Alternate collectors offer an alternative to the central collection point provided by the primary collector, $0. The separation of events into several log files speeds up event processing because a network application program does not have to read a single large file containing many events unrelated to that application

Each alternate collector maintains its own log files in a structure identical to that of the primary collector.

Alternate collectors are started with a TACL RUN command. They have user-defined process names.

Event Message Distributors

The Distributors filter event messages and return selected messages to the operations environment. Distributors have three basic functions:

Accessing one or more log files

Filtering event messages

Routing the selected event messages to the appropriate destination

Depending on the nature of the destination, one of four types of distributors can be used:

Consumer   Sends selected event messages to a requesting management application.

Forwarding   Sends selected event messages to an EMS collector on another node in the network or to an alternate collector on the same node.

Printing   Obtains formatted text for selected event messages and writes it to a printer or other display device, or to a file. When a routing filter is used, unformatted events can be routed to selected distributor processes.

Compatibility   Filters event messages according to a fixed (rather than a user-specified) criterion, obtains formatted text for the selected primary collector event messages, and writes it to a console device.

Compatibility Distributor ($Z0)

The Compatibility Distributor facilitates viewing console messages during cold loads. $Z0 is the only method available to view these messages.

There is only one Compatibility Distributor per system and it must be configured during SYSGEN.

The Compatibility Distributor has no interactive or programmatic command interface. It is controlled indirectly via commands to the primary collector, which can change certain parameters that affect the Compatibility Distributor. $Z0 can be stopped with the EMSCCTRL facility.

EMS Filters

EMS Filters are used to select the messages that are sent to various EMS Logs. Each EMS collector can use one or more filters, which can be customized to filter out all events of a certain type or from a certain application.

There are three types of filters:

Compiled Filters   Compiled filters are created in EDIT files using the Event Management Service filter (EMF) language and compiled.

Filter Tables   Filter tables are EDIT files that can be loaded into a collector or distributor, which then automatically converts it into an object representation that is then evaluated for each event processed by a collector or distributor.

Burst Filters   Burst filters are used to suppress EMS messages when duplicate messages arrive in a short period of time.

EMS Object Programs

Two object files are used to start EMS:

EMSACOLL   The EMSACOLL (EMS Alternate Collector) starts an alternate collector when invoked by a TACL RUN command.

EMSDIST   The EMSDIST (EMS Distributor) is the object program for starting printing distributors, forwarding distributors, or consumer distributors.

EMS Utilities

These utility programs are provided as part of the EMS Subsystem. They are used for interactive queries and controlling collectors and distributors.

EMSCCTRL   The EMS Collector Control is used to change the parameters that control the primary collectors and the compatibility distributor.

EMSCINFO   Displays event-message statistics and collector status and configuration.

Securing EMS Components

BP-FILE-EMS-01   EMSCCTRL should be secured "UUNU".

BP-OPSYS-OWNER-01   EMSCCTRL should be owned by SUPER.SUPER.

BP-OPSYS-FILELOC-01   EMSCCTRL must reside in $SYSTEM.SYSnn.

BP-PROCESS-EMSACOLL-01 $ZPHI process should be running.

BP-FILE-EMS-02   EMSACOLL should be secured "UUNU".

BP-OPSYS-OWNER-01   EMSACOLL should be owned by SUPER.SUPER.

BP-OPSYS-FILELOC-01   EMSACOLL must reside in $SYSTEM.SYSnn.

BP-FILE-EMS-03   EMSDIST should be secured "UUNU".

BP-OPSYS-OWNER-01   EMSDIST should be owned by SUPER.SUPER.

BP-OPSYS-FILELOC-01   EMSDIST must reside in $SYSTEM.SYSnn.

BP-FILE-EMS-04   EMSCINFO should be secured "UUNU".

BP-OPSYS-OWNER-01   EMSCINFO should be owned by SUPER.SUPER.

BP-OPSYS-FILELOC-01   EMSCINFO must reside in $SYSTEM.SYSnn.

	Discovery Questions	Look here:
PROCESS-EMSACOLL-01	Is the $ZPHI process running?	Status
PROCESS-ZOPR-01	Is the $ZOPR system process running?	Status
OPSYS-OWNER-01	Who owns the EMSCCTRL file?	Fileinfo
OPSYS-OWNER-01	Who owns the EMSACOLL file?	Fileinfo
OPSYS-OWNER-01	Who owns the EMSDIST file?	Fileinfo
OPSYS-OWNER-01	Who owns the EMSCINFO file?	Fileinfo
FILE-POLICY	Who is allowed to use EMS on the system?	Policy
FILE-EMS-01	Is the EMSCCTRL file secured correctly?	Fileinfo

	Discovery Questions	Look here:
FILE-EMS-02	Is the EMSACOLL file secured correctly?	Fileinfo
FILE-EMS-03	Is the EMSDIST file secured correctly?	Fileinfo
FILE-EMS-04	Is the EMSCINFO file secured correctly?	Fileinfo

Related Topics

EMSA

EMSA Subsystem

The EMS Analyzer is used to query the EMS logs and generate reports that can be viewed on a terminal or sent to the spooler, to an Enscribe database or to a Comma Separated Values (CSV) file.

EMSA comes with a default DDL dictionary so that Enform reports can be created based on Enscribe data files.

CSV files can be exported to a PC for analysis and reporting using programs like ACCESS or EXCEL.

The EMS Analyzer's default parameterized filter can be used to specify a set of search criteria.

EMSA comes with tokenized filters that can be customized using a conversational interface. The EMS logs can be searched for events based on: start and stop time, event number, event type, process ID, subsystem ID, logical device, system name, or text string.

EMSA is frequently used to isolate EMS messages generated by application programs, which are then used to help resolve application problems.

Installing EMSA does not require a SYSGEN. It is installed using a TACL routine supplied with the product.

The EMSA Subsystem includes the following components:

EMSA   The EMSA object file.

EMSACSTM   The default EMSACSTM file, created when EMSA is installed.

EMSADDL   The default EMSA DDL for the Enscribe database.

EMSADEF   The default EMSA DEF for the Enscribe database.

EMSAFLTR   The default EMSA filter. Use this as a template for customized filters.

Customized filters may be owned by the users who create them or some other suitable userid and shared by appropriate users.

EMSASSID   File containing the Subsystem ID (SSID) for each of the most common HP NonStop server subsystems.

EMSATEXT   Text file containing EMSA Help and Error messages.

The system manager may also have created one or more alternate collectors specifically for EMSA use.

RISK   The EMSA subsystem is used for reporting only. It does not pose any security risks.

Customizing the EMSA environment

Each time a user invokes EMSA, a file called EMSACSTM is invoked before the first prompt. The EMSACSTM file is an obey file that resides in each user's default subvolume. The file can be used to customize the user's EMSA environment by defining options such as function key/command associations.

The EMSACSTM files should be secured properly. Please refer to Gazette section on *CSTM Configuration Files.

Securing EMSA Components

BP-FILE-EMSA-01   EMSA should be secured "UUNU".

BP-OPSYS-OWNER-02   EMSA should be owned by SUPER.SUPER.

BP-OPSYS-FILELOC-02   EMSA must reside in $SYSTEM.SYSTEM.

BP-FILE-EMSA-02   EMSADDL should be secured "NUNU".

BP-OPSYS-OWNER-02   EMSADDL should be owned by SUPER.SUPER.

BP-OPSYS-FILELOC-02   EMSADDL must reside in $SYSTEM. SYSTEM.

BP-FILE-EMSA-03   EMSADEF should be secured "NUNU".

BP-OPSYS-OWNER-02   EMSADEF should be owned by SUPER.SUPER.

BP-OPSYS-FILELOC-02   EMSADEF must reside in $SYSTEM. SYSTEM.

BP-FILE-EMSA-04   EMSFLTR should be secured "NUNU".

BP-OPSYS-OWNER-02   EMSFLTR should be owned by SUPER.SUPER.

BP-OPSYS-FILELOC-02   EMSFLTR must reside in $SYSTEM. SYSTEM.

BP-FILE-EMSA-05   EMSASSID should be secured "NUNU".

BP-OPSYS-OWNER-02   EMSASSID should be owned by SUPER.SUPER.

BP-OPSYS-FILELOC-02   EMSASSID must reside in $SYSTEM. SYSTEM.

BP-FILE-EMSA-06   EMSATEXT should be secured "NUNU".

BP-OPSYS-OWNER-02   EMSATEXT should be owned by SUPER.SUPER.

BP-OPSYS-FILELOC-02   EMSATEXT must reside in $SYSTEM. SYSTEM.

If available, use Safeguard software or a third party object security product to grant access to EMSA object files only to users who require access in order to perform their jobs.

BP-SAFE-EMSA-01   Add a Safeguard Protection Record to grant appropriate access to the EMSA object file.

	Discovery Questions	Look here:
OPSYS-OWNER-02	Who owns the EMSA file?	Fileinfo
OPSYS-OWNER-02	Who owns the EMSADDL file?	Fileinfo
OPSYS-OWNER-02	Who owns the EMSADEF file?	Fileinfo
OPSYS-OWNER-02	Who owns the EMSFLTR file?	Fileinfo
OPSYS-OWNER-02	Who owns the EMSASSID file?	Fileinfo
OPSYS-OWNER-02	Who owns the EMSATEXT file?	Fileinfo
FILE-POLICY	Who is allowed to use EMSA on the system?	Policy
FILE-EMSA-01 SAFE-EMSA-01	Is the EMSA object file correctly secured with Guardian or Safeguard?	Fileinfo Safecom
FILE-EMSA-02	Is the EMSADDL file correctly secured with Guardian or Safeguard?	Fileinfo Safecom
FILE-EMSA-03	Is the EMSADEF file secured correctly?	Fileinfo
FILE-EMSA-04	Is the EMSFLTR file secured correctly?	Fileinfo
FILE-EMSA-05	Is the EMSASSID file secured correctly?	Fileinfo
FILE-EMSA-06	Is the EMSATEXT file secured correctly?	Fileinfo

Related Topics

EMS

ENABLE User Program

ENABLE can be used to develop a simple application to perform basic data I/O operations, without coding source programs. It allows the user to:

Control the format of the screen displayed by the application

Limit the types of operations (delete, insert, read, or update) that the application can perform on a data base file

Provide an application to view and update databases

The components of ENABLE are:

ENABLE
ENABAPPS
ENABLEGS
ENABLOBJ
ENABPATS

The tasks performed by an ENABLE application, like a Pathway, are divided between requestors and servers.

A requestor displays the data entry screen, accepts the data entered from the terminal, and passes the data to programs that update the database.

A server adds, alters, and retrieves information from the data base.

ENABLE generates a SCREEN COBOL requestor program to manage the display screens and accept requests. ENABLE supplies a server program that accesses the database and performs the requested operations. ENABLE also produces a third component, a command file used to execute the application under a PATHWAY system.

ENABLE is most often used as a developer's tool for testing and modeling application databases. Securing the compiler object file controls the use of the language.

Access to the C language components is required for compilation.

RISK   ENABLE allows anyone with read access to data files and their corresponding dictionary to create an application against the data, with the potential of exposing sensitive information such as account numbers and social security numbers.

RISK   ENABLE also provides a vehicle to update sensitive data in Enscribe databases, to which a user has WRITE access.

Secure databases from unauthorized queries by granting READ access to only those users who need to view secure data to perform their jobs. There is no way to audit or limit the contents of the ENABLE application. ENABLE should not be available on a secure system.

RISK   On development systems, ENABLE can be made available for use by developers by securing it "NUNU". ENABLE will only allow access to data dictionaries to which the individual developer has access.

Securing ENABLE Components

BP-FILE-ENABLE-01   ENABLE should be secured "UUUU".

BP-OPSYS-OWNER-02   ENABLE should be owned by SUPER.SUPER.

BP-OPSYS-FILELOC-02   ENABLE must reside in $SYSTEM.SYSTEM.

BP-FILE-ENABLE-02   ENABAPPS should be secured "NUNU".

BP-OPSYS-OWNER-02   ENABAPPS should be owned by SUPER.SUPER.

BP-OPSYS-FILELOC-02   ENABAPPS must reside in $SYSTEM.SYSTEM.

BP-FILE-ENABLE-03   ENABLEGS should be secured "UUNU".

BP-OPSYS-OWNER-02   ENABLEGS should be owned by SUPER.SUPER.

BP-OPSYS-FILELOC-02   ENABLEGS must reside in $SYSTEM.SYSTEM.

BP-FILE-ENABLE-04   ENABLOBJ should be secured "UUNU".

BP-OPSYS-OWNER-02   ENABLOBJ should be owned by SUPER.SUPER.

BP-OPSYS-FILELOC-02   ENABLOBJ must reside in $SYSTEM.SYSTEM.

BP-FILE-ENABLE-05   ENABPATS should be secured "NUNU".

BP-OPSYS-OWNER-02   ENABPATS should be owned by SUPER.SUPER.

BP-OPSYS-FILELOC-02   ENABPATS must reside in $SYSTEM.SYSTEM.

If available, use Safeguard or a third party object security product to grant access to ENABLE object files only to users who require access in order to perform their jobs.

BP-SAFE-ENABLE-01   Add a Safeguard Protection Record to grant appropriate access to the ENABLE object file.

	Discovery Questions	Look here:
OPSYS-OWNER-02	Who owns the ENABLE object file?	Fileinfo
OPSYS-OWNER-02	Who owns the ENABAPPS file?	Fileinfo
OPSYS-OWNER-02	Who owns the ENABLEGS file?	Fileinfo
OPSYS-OWNER-02	Who owns the ENALOBJ object file?	Fileinfo
OPSYS-OWNER-02	Who owns the ENABPATS file?	Fileinfo
FILE-POLICY	Who is allowed to use the ENABLE compiler on the system?	Policy
FILE-ENABLE-01 SAFE-ENABLE-01	Is the ENABLE object file correctly secured with the Guardian or Safeguard system?	Fileinfo Safecom
FILE-ENABLE-02	Is the ENABAPPS file secured correctly?	Fileinfo
FILE-ENABLE-03	Is the ENABLEGS object file secured correctly?	Fileinfo
FILE-ENABLE-04	Is the ENABLOBJ object file secured correctly?	Fileinfo
FILE-ENABLE-05	Is the ENABPATS file secured correctly?	Fileinfo

ENFORM Subsystem

ENFORM is a reporting tool that retrieves data from Enscribe files. The ENFORM Subsystem is used to:

Retrieve data from databases, sort and group data from databases

Perform calculations and formulas on the retrieved data

Format and print a report containing the retrieved data

Create a new physical file containing the retrieved data

ENFORM is a reporting program. It does not alter any data in the files it queries.

The ENFORM subsystem consists or three sets of components:

1. The user must do the following using the DDL Language:
   Define the Dictionary
   Define the database object(s)
2. The ENFORM subsystem processes are:
   Query compiler/report writer
   Query processor
3. Optional user-provided components:

A host language program

An ENFORM server

A **dictionary** is a collection of files that define the contents of a database. It describes the structure of each record in the database. ENFORM accesses the dictionary before retrieving any data and stores the information in the internal table of the query compiler/report writer.

The **database** is the physical file(s) containing the data. ENFORM searches the database to find the information requested, and then returns it as output.

ENFORM Components

The components of ENFORM are (See Figure 6-6):

BUILDMK

ENFORM

ENFORMMK

ENFORMMT

ENFORMSV

QP

Query Specification with ENFORM

A query is made up of ENFORM statements, clauses, and commands describing the requested information to be retrieved from the database. ENFORM uses the specification to determine:

The query environment

The data to be retrieved

The form in which the retrieved data should be displayed

Using ENFORM statements, ENFORM performs the following functions:

Compiling the query

Formatting and writing a report

RISK: ENFORM allows anyone with READ access to data files and their corresponding dictionary to run ad-hoc reports against the data, with the potential of exposing sensitive information such as account numbers and social security

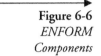

Figure 6-6
ENFORM
Components

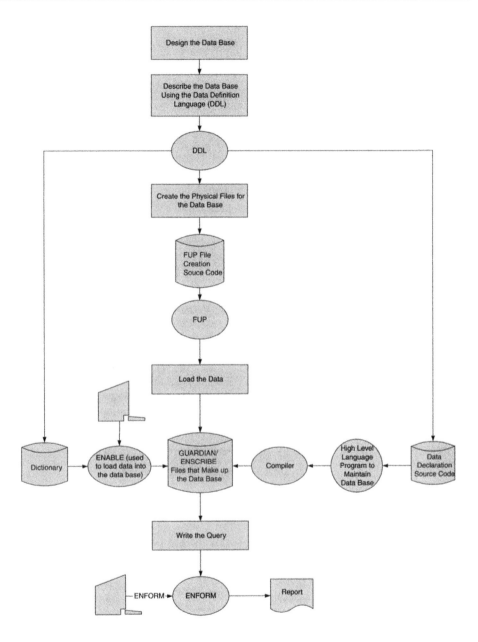

numbers. Running ad hoc reports cannot be audited beyond file opens and process starts. There is no way to audit or limit the report contents.

RISK ENFORM makes intensive use of system resources, CPU, memory space and disk space (for its temporary files). Many companies restrict the use of ENFORM on secure systems to a few select user groups.

RISK ENFORM makes it possible to view sensitive data in Enscribe databases.

Databases should be secured against unauthorized queries by restricting READ access to only those users who must view secure data to perform their jobs.

The Query Processor (QP)

The query processor (QP) receives the query specifications and dictionary information from the query compiler and then gathers the data from the database.

Optional User-provided Components

Companies can also develop application programs and ENFORM servers to access and report on data that might otherwise not be usable by ENFORM.

The following files are supplied by HP to facilitate the creation of custom ENFORM servers.

BUILDMK   A file containing object code that converts the EDIT version of the message table into the special key-sequenced file required by ENFORM.

ENFORMMK   The default version of the message table in a key-sequenced file that contains the ENFORM messages and help text. This file can be customized to suit the environment.

ENFORMMT   An EDIT version of the default message table. This file can be customized. If altered, use BUILDMK to convert the EDIT version of the message table into the special key-sequenced file required by ENFORM.

ENFORMSV   A DDL source file that contains all of the message definitions necessary for a dialogue between the ENFORM query processor and a custom ENFORM server. This can be used to generate message definitions for programs.

Optional ENFORM Plus Components

Companies using Format 2 files (very large files) must use ENFORM Plus servers to access and report on data.

HP provides a TACL macro (ENFPMAC) to switch the ENFORM executables between the 2 types of files. Once the macro is run, the executables are renamed to the same names as Format 1 ENFORM. Only SUPER.SUPER can perform these functions.

Using ENFPMAC to switch from ENFORM to ENFORM Plus:

ENFORM   Renamed to OENFORM

QP   Renamed to OQP

BUILDMK   Renamed to OBUILDMK

ENFORMP   Renamed to ENFORM

QPP   Renamed to QP

BUILDMKP   Renamed to BUILDMK

Using ENFPMAC to switch from ENFORM Plus to ENFORM:

ENFORM   Renamed to ENFORMP

QP   Renamed to QPP

BUILDMK   Renamed to BUILDMKP

OENFORM   Renamed to ENFORM

OQP   Renamed to QP

OBUILDMK   Renamed to BUILDMK

RISK   During conversion, the ENFORM files are renamed but not secured to match the original files. (Therefore, following the conversion, the new files must be secured to match the original files.)

Securing ENFORM Components

Files used only by ENFORM:

BP-FILE-ENFORM-01   ENFORM should be secured "UUNU".

BP-OPSYS-OWNER-02   ENFORM should be owned by SUPER.SUPER.

BP-OPSYS-FILELOC-02   ENFORM must reside in $SYSTEM.SYSTEM.

BP-FILE-ENFORM-02   BUILDMK should be secured "UUNU".

BP-OPSYS-OWNER-02   BUILDMK should be owned by SUPER.SUPER.

BP-OPSYS-FILELOC-02   BUILDMK must reside in $SYSTEM.SYSTEM.

BP-FILE-ENFORM-03   ENFORMMK should be secured "NUNU".

BP-OPSYS-OWNER-02   ENFORMMK should be owned by SUPER.SUPER.

BP-OPSYS-FILELOC-02   ENFORMMK must reside in $SYSTEM.SYSTEM.

BP-FILE-ENFORM-04   ENFORMMT should be secured "NUNU".

BP-OPSYS-OWNER-02   ENFORMMT should be owned by SUPER.SUPER.

BP-OPSYS-FILELOC-02   ENFORMMT must reside in $SYSTEM.SYSTEM.

BP-FILE-ENFORM-05   ENFORMSV should be secured "NUNU".

BP-OPSYS-OWNER-02   ENFORMSV should be owned by SUPER.SUPER.

BP-OPSYS-FILELOC-02   ENFORMSV must reside in $SYSTEM.SYSTEM.

BP-FILE-ENFORM-06   QP should be secured "UUNU".

BP-OPSYS-OWNER-02   QP should be owned by SUPER.SUPER.

BP-OPSYS-FILELOC-02   QP must reside in $SYSTEM.SYSTEM.

Files used only by ENFORM PLUS:

BP-FILE-ENFORM-07   BUILDMKP should be secured "UUNU".

BP-OPSYS-OWNER-02   BUILDMKP should be owned by SUPER.SUPER.

BP-OPSYS-FILELOC-02   BUILDMKP must reside in $SYSTEM.SYSTEM.

BP-FILE-ENFORM-08   ENFORMP should be secured "UUNU".

BP-OPSYS-OWNER-02   ENFORMP should be owned by SUPER.SUPER.

BP-OPSYS-FILELOC-02   ENFORMP must reside in $SYSTEM.SYSTEM.

BP-FILE-ENFORM-09   ENFPMAC should be secured "UUUU".

BP-OPSYS-OWNER-02   ENFPMAC should be owned by SUPER.SUPER.

BP-OPSYS-FILELOC-02   ENFPMAC must reside in $SYSTEM.SYSTEM.

BP-FILE-ENFORM-10   QPP should be secured "UUNU".

BP-OPSYS-OWNER-02   QPP should be owned by SUPER.SUPER.

BP-OPSYS-FILELOC-02   QPP must reside in $SYSTEM.SYSTEM.

Files present only after conversion to ENFORM Plus:

BP-FILE-ENFORM-11   OBUILDMK should be secured "UUNU".

BP-OPSYS-OWNER-02   OBUILDMK should be owned by SUPER.SUPER.

BP-OPSYS-FILELOC-02   OBUILDMK must reside in $SYSTEM.SYSTEM.

BP-FILE-ENFORM-12   OENFORM should be secured "UUNU".

BP-OPSYS-OWNER-02   OENFORM should be owned by SUPER.SUPER.

BP-OPSYS-FILELOC-02   OENFORM must reside in $SYSTEM.SYSTEM.

BP-FILE-ENFORM-13   OQP should be secured "UUNU".

BP-OPSYS-OWNER-02   OQP should be owned by SUPER.SUPER.

BP-OPSYS-FILELOC-02   OQP must reside in $SYSTEM.SYSTEM.

AP-ADVICE-ENFORM-01   Normal application reports should be generated within the application, limiting the data fields retrieved as appropriate to the various users' job functions so that only those users who must view sensitive data can.

AP-ADVICE-ENFORM-02   Separation of duties dictates that no individuals should be able to query, whether via a single report or several, all the data required to commit fraud.

AP-ADVICE-ENFORM-03   ENFORM creates swap files either on $SYSTEM (where the ENFORM object file resides) or in the location specified by NSKCOM or in a user specified location. The disk must have sufficient space for the temporary files.

If available, use Safeguard software or a third party object security product to grant access to ENFORM for necessary personnel, and deny access to all other users.

BP-SAFE-ENFORM-01   Add a Safeguard Protection Record to grant appropriate access to the ENFORM object file.

BP-SAFE-ENFORM-02   Add a Safeguard Protection Record to grant appropriate access to the ENFPMAC disk file.

	Discovery Questions	Look here:
FILE-POLICY	Is ENFORM or ENFORM Plus being used?	Policy
OPSYS-OWNER-02	Who owns the ENFORM object file?	Fileinfo
OPSYS-OWNER-02	Who owns the BUILDMK object file?	Fileinfo
OPSYS-OWNER-02	Who owns the ENFORMMK object file?	Fileinfo
OPSYS-OWNER-02	Who owns the ENFORMMT object file?	Fileinfo
OPSYS-OWNER-02	Who owns the ENFORMSV object file?	Fileinfo
OPSYS-OWNER-02	Who owns the QP object file?	Fileinfo
FILE-POLICY	Is ENFORM Plus used?	Policy
OPSYS-OWNER-02	Who owns the ENFPMAC TACL file?	Fileinfo

	Discovery Questions	Look here:
OPSYS-OWNER-02	Who owns the ENFORMP or OENFORM object file?	Fileinfo
OPSYS-OWNER-02	Who owns the BUILDMKP or OBUILDMK object file?	Fileinfo
OPSYS-OWNER-02	Who owns the QPP or OQP object file?	Fileinfo
FILE-POLICY	Who is allowed to execute ENFORM on the system?	Policy
FILE-ENFORM-01 SAFE-ENFORM-01	Is the ENFORM object file correctly secured with the Guardian or Safeguard system?	Fileinfo Safecom
FILE-ENFORM-02	Is the BUILDMK object file secured correctly?	Fileinfo
FILE-ENFORM-03	Is the ENFORMMK object file secured correctly?	Fileinfo
FILE-ENFORM-04	Is the ENFORMMT file secured correctly?	Fileinfo
FILE-ENFORM-05	Is the ENFORMSV file secured correctly?	Fileinfo
FILE-ENFORM-06	Is the QP object file secured correctly?	Fileinfo
FILE-ENFORM-07	Is the BUILDMKP object file secured correctly?	Fileinfo
FILE-ENFORM-08	Is the ENFORMP object file secured correctly?	Fileinfo
FILE-ENFORM-09 SAFE-ENFORM-02	Is the ENFPMAC file correctly secured with the Guardian or Safeguard sytem?	Fileinfo Safecom
FILE-ENFORM-10	Is the QPP object file secured correctly?	Fileinfo
FILE-ENFORM-11	Is the OBUILDMK object file secured correctly?	Fileinfo
FILE-ENFORM-12	Is the OENFORM object file secured correctly?	Fileinfo
FILE-ENFORM-13	Is the OQP object file secured correctly?	Fileinfo

Related Topics

DDL

ERROR User Program

ERROR is used to return a text message description of an HP Nonstop server error. When an error occurs, the HP NonStop server returns an error number, such as the following example:

```
nn> fup dup esql, esql1
ERROR - $DATAA.TRINA.ESQL1: CREATE ERR 10
*ABEND*
ABENDED: 0,254
```

```
nn> error 10
0010 The new record or file could not be created because a file by that
name or a record with that key already exists.
```

RISK ERROR is a display program only and poses no security risks.

ERROR Security

BP-FILE-ERROR-01   ERROR should be secured "UUNU".

BP-OPSYS-OWNER-01   ERROR should be owned by SUPER.SUPER.

BP-OPSYS-FILELOC-01   ERROR must reside in $SYSTEM.SYSnn.

	Discovery Questions	Look here:
OPSYS-OWNER-01	Who owns the ERROR file?	Fileinfo
FILE-ERROR-01	Is the ERROR object file secured correctly?	Fileinfo

Expand Subsystem

The Expand subsystem enables one to connect as many as 255 geographically dispersed HP NonStop servers to create a network with the same reliability as a single node (See Figure 6-7).

The components of Expand are:

NCPOBJ

OZEXP

$ZNUP

Expand Profile Templates

NCPOBJ

The Expand line handler manager process runs as $NCP and must be running to communicate via Expand. The network control process ($NCP) is responsible for:

Initiating and terminating node-to-node connections

Maintaining the network-related system tables, including routing information

Calculating the most efficient way to transmit data to other nodes in the network

Monitoring and logging changes in the status of the network and its nodes

Figure 6-7
Expand
Network

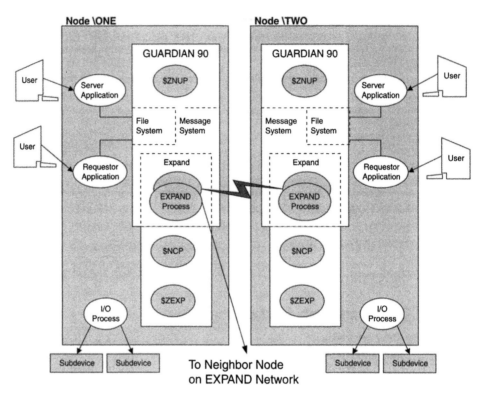

Informing the network control processes at neighbor nodes of changes in line or Expand line-handler process status (for example, lines UP or DOWN)

Informing Expand line-handler processes when all paths are DOWN

The network control process, $NCP, is a process in each node of an Expand network and is always logical device #1.

RISK   The process $NCP must be running for Expand to communicate between systems. Normally it is started when the system is cold loaded and remains running.

AP-ADVICE-EXPAND-01   Only SUPER.SUPER should be allowed to start and stop $NCP.

OZEXP

The Expand line handler manager process runs as $ZEXP and must be running to communicate via Expand software.

The $ZEXP process provides the interface between the Expand subsystem and the Subsystem Control Point (SCP). The Expand manager process directs SCF commands to the appropriate Expand line-handler process and forwards responses from Expand line-handler processes to the appropriate user.

RISK The process $ZEXP must be running for Expand software to communicate between systems. Normally it is started when the system is cold started and remains running.

RISK Only SUPER.SUPER should be allowed to start and stop $ZEXP.

$ZNUP

$NCP uses services provided by the network utility process, $ZNUP. $ZNUP is a part of the NonStop operating system and answers requests for system information, either local or remote. System information may include device, line, processes, traffic and other system status requests.

The network utility process, $ZNUP, is a process in each node of an Expand network and is always logical device #4.

Expand Profile Templates

Expand software stores configuration information in a series of files of named PEXP* and identified by a file code of 832.

RISK Only SUPER.SUPER should be allowed to access these files.

Securing Expand Components

BP-PROCESS-NCPOBJ-01 $NCP process should be running.

BP-FILE-EXPAND-01 NCPOBJ should be secured "UUCU".

BP-OPSYS-OWNER-01 NCPOBJ should be owned by SUPER.SUPER.

BP-OPSYS-FILELOC-01 NCPOBJ must reside in $SYSTEM.SYSnn.

BP-PROCESS-OZEXP-01 $ZEXP process should be running.

BP-FILE-EXPAND-02 OZEXP should be secured "UUCU".

BP-OPSYS-LICENSE-01 OZEXP must be LICENSED.

BP-OPSYS-OWNER-01 OZEXP should be owned by SUPER.SUPER.

BP-OPSYS-FILELOC-01 OZEXP must reside in $SYSTEM.SYSnn.

BP-FILE-EXPAND-03 Files of file code 832 should be secured "CUCU".

BP-OPSYS-OWNER-01 Files of file code 832 should be owned by SUPER.SUPER.

If available, use Safeguard software or a third party object security product to grant access to Expand object files only to users who require access in order to perform their jobs.

BP-SAFE-EXPAND-01 to 02   Add a Safeguard Protection Record to grant appropriate access to the NCPOBJ object file.

	Discovery Questions	**Look Here:**
FILE-POLICY	Is Expand used to network systems together?	Policy
PROCESS-NCPOBJ-01	Is the $NCP process running?	Status
PROCESS-OZEXP-01	Is the $ZEXP process running?	Status
OPSYS-OWNER-01	Who owns the NCPOBJ object file?	Fileinfo
OPSYS-OWNER-01	Who owns the OZEXP object file?	Fileinfo
OPSYS-LICENSE-01	Is the OZEXP object file licensed?	Fileinfo
FILE-POLICY	Who is allowed to manage the Expand network on the system?	Policy
FILE-EXPAND-01 SAFE-EXPAND-01	Is the NCPOBJ object file correctly secured with the Guardian or Safeguard system?	Fileinfo Safecom
FILE-EXPAND-02 SAFE-EXPAND-02	Is the OZEXP object file correctly secured with the Guardian or Safeguard system?	Fileinfo Safecom
FILE-EXPAND-03	Are the configuration files of file code 832 secured correctly?	Fileinfo

FINGER System Utility

FINGER is the HP NonStop server FINGER client. It is used to interactively test the connection to a remote system. The remote system need not be another NonStop server.

FINGER is used to request information about users that are currently logged on to a system on the network. The type of information and the format of the display depend upon the service provided by the FINGER server on the remote system.

FINGER is a part of the TCP/IP subsystem which provides snapshots of running connections.

RISK   Someone familiar with FINGER could use it from a remote machine to get IP addresses and other connection information about a system.

RISK FINGER could be used to obtain a list of user names from a system without logging on to the system, thus giving an attacker a starting point to try to logon.

AP-ADVICE-FINGER-01 To eliminate this risk, FINGER must be removed from the TCP/IP PORTCONF file.

The components of FINGER are:

FINGER

FINGSERV

FINGER

FINGER is the HP Nonstop finger client to request TCP/IP connection information.

FINGSERV

FINGSERV is the HP NonStop server FINGER server. It responds to FINGER requests from remote clients.

Securing FINGER

BP-FILE-FINGER-01 FINGER should be secured "- - - -"

BP-OPSYS-OWNER-01 FINGER should be owned by SUPER.SUPER

BP-OPSYS-FILELOC-01 FINGER must reside in $SYSTEM.SYSnn

BP-FILE-FINGER-02 FINGSERV should be secured "- - - -"

BP-OPSYS-OWNER-03 FINGSERV should be owned by SUPER.SUPER

BP-OPSYS-FILELOC-03 FINGSERV resides in $SYSTEM.ZTCPIP

If available, use Safeguard software or a third party object security product to grant access to FINGER object files only to users who require access in order to perform their jobs.

BP-SAFE-FINGER-01 Add a Safeguard Protection Record to grant appropriate access to the FINGER object file.

BP-SAFE-FINGER-02 Add a Safeguard Protection Record to grant appropriate access to the FINGSERV object file.

	Discovery Questions	Look here:
OPSYS-OWNER-01	Who owns the FINGER client object file?	Fileinfo
OPSYS-OWNER-03	Who owns the FINGSERV server object file?	Fileinfo
FILE-POLICY	Who is allowed to execute FINGER on the system?	Policy
FILE-FINGER-01 SAFE-FINGER-01	Is the FINGER object file correctly secured with the Guardian or Safeguard system?	Fileinfo Safecom
FILE-FINGER-02 SAFE-FINGER-02	Is the FINGSERV object file correctly secured with the Guardian or Safeguard system?	Fileinfo Safecom

Related Topics

TCP/IP

File Transfer Protocols

FTP is widely used for exchanging files between different platforms. For example, Guardian files are transferred between an HP NonStop server and PC-based workstation. Bi-directional binary and text transfers are done by copying exact images of a file.

FTP supports transfer of the following types of files:

ASCII

Unstructured

Structured (key-sequenced, relative, and entry-sequenced)

FTP does not support the transfer of SQL files.

RISK   FTP server has no built in security, it relies entirely on the security native to the resident operating system. If the system hosting the FTP server is not properly secured, users can explore the system at will, copy any files that they have read access to, and place unauthorized files anywhere on the system. It is possible for FTP users to damage applications and databases and steal business data.

RISK   The HP FTP server does not produce audits of its activity.

Safeguard software will audit file accesses by FTP users if configured to do so. Some third party FTP products provide comprehensive auditing of FTP activity on the NonStop server.

RISK FTP is a method that sensitive data can be move from an HP NonStop server to a remote system.

AP-ADVICE-FTP-01 FTP activity must be controlled at a maximum level.

The components are:

FTP

FTPEXTH

FTPSERV

FTPCSTM (FTP Custom Files)

FTP

FTP is the HP NonStop server FTP client. It is used to interactively transfer or manage files on a remote system. The remote system need not be another NonStop server.

FTPSERV

FTP servers respond to file transfer requests from the client FTP. The FTPSERV server is initiated from the LISTNER on the FTP port. The typical port for FTP is 21.

FTP CUSTOM Files

FTP reads the FTPCSTM file before it issues its first prompt. This allows the creation of a customized FTP environment before entering any commands. Please refer to the Gazette section on *CSTM Configuration Files.

FTP Systems

Both local and remote systems can place restrictions on which files can be transferred and where the files can be placed.

FTP Userids

AP-FTP-USERIDS-01 NonStop server users should login to FTP with their own userids to ensure that they only have access to the appropriate files.

Securing the Anonymous FTP Userid and Environment

Anonymous FTP is primarily intended for and supported in the OSS environment, but can be used in the Guardian environment.

The anonymous FTP userid, by convention is named NULL.FTP.

RISK   Only implement Anonymous FTP if it is absolutely necessary. Anonymous FTP opens the system for general access. To mitigate the risks, implement the following precautions:

AP-FTP-USERIDS-02   Create an alias to the NULL.FTP userid, called "anonymous" or "ftp." This alias will be used to log into the FTP subsystem.

BP-FTP-USERIDS-03   Expire NULL.FTP's password. No password is necessary within the FTP subsystem.

BP-FTP-USERIDS-04   Freeze NULL.FTP to prevent users from logging onto the Anonymous userid outside of the FTP subsystem.

RISK   If Safeguard software is down for any reason, the frozen userids (though still frozen) behave as if they are thawed.

Assign NULL.FTP and any of its aliases an appropriate 'home' where any users logging into FTP as anonymous will begin their session:

In the OSS environment, assign an initial directory, for example: /guest/FTP.

In a Guardian environment, assign a default subvolume, for example FTPGUEST.

AP-ADVICE-FTP-02   In the OSS Environment, the NULL.FTP user should not own any directories, especially the initial root directory. Directory owners can alter the security of the directory. Directories should be owned by SUPER.SUPER or another appropriate userid.

RISK   Any references (symbolic links) to directories or files that are outside of the anonymous FTP subtree should be avoided.

> A SYMBOLIC LINK is a file that contains the name of another file. If a system operates on symbolic links, a user can be directed to the file that the symbolic link points to. When the user displays a file that has a symbolic link, the user can see the original file as well as its link, which, depending on the contents of the file, could pose a security risk.

RISK   Any absolute symbolic links (the ones that start with "/") should be avoided within a subtree. Absolute symbolic links will be understood by the system as referring to the Initial-Directory, rather than to the root directory of the OSS fileset.

RISK   Do not grant NULL.FTP write access to any files.

RISK   Files that NULL.FTP or its alias must drop onto the system should be limited to a single 'WRITE only' location. NULL.FTP should not be granted

READ access to the 'WRITE only' location. Requires a lot of user (administrator's) intervention.

RISK NFS file security differs from that of standard files; but the FTP subsystem doesn't have the mechanism to differentiate an NFS file from a standard file.

NULL.FTP should never be allowed to own NFS files, since it'll give the user extended access capabilities.

The following three steps provide a 'safe area' that the Anonymous FTP users can't get out of, while trusted users can easily get at the anonymous mount point's files and drag them wherever they want to without lots of security headaches. The key is containing anonymous users strictly to this OSS mount point.

AP-FTP-USERIDS-05 Set up an OSS partition on one isolated disk pair and make it a separate mount point.

AP-FTP-USERIDS-06 Secure the parent directory of this mount point very tight so the anonymous FTP users can't navigate out of the "root" of this disk.

AP-FTP-USERIDS-07 Use SCF to set up an NFS alias for guest as anonymous (if it is to be NFS mountable from other nodes).

AP-FTP-USERIDS-08 Make sure the NULL.FTP user account is configured the same as the anonymous alias's account so that neither can get at anything except the anonymous OSS file space. The Safeguard initial directory and Guardian default subvolume should both point to this file space.

With CMON

Some CMONs can restrict FTP logon access by PORT and by IP address to limit the IP addresses from which authorized users can logon to a system and access the FTP subsystem.

Please refer to the Gazette section on CMON for more information.

3P-PROCESS-CMON-01 Using a third party CMON product or a modified CMON, restrict the IP addresses that can use the FTP ports.

Without the Safeguard Subsystem

To try to minimize the risks of FTP, grant READ access only those files that FTP users are allowed to GET. This can be difficult because of the large number of files on a system. On a more restricted system, secure the FTP programs or eliminate FTP access through TCP/IP to mitigate the risks.

RISK   In the Guardian environment, there is no way to restrict where FTP users PUT files.

RISK   The HP FTP server does not produce audits of its activity.

With the Safeguard Subsystem

Safeguard provides some support for securing FTP. Use Safeguard VOLUME and SUBVOLUME rules to restrict where FTP users PUT files. To try to minimize the risks of FTP, grant READ access only to those files that FTP users are allowed to GET. This can be difficult because of the large number of files on a system. On a more restricted system, secure the FTP program or eliminate FTP access through TCP/IP to mitigate the risks.

Safeguard software will audit file accesses by FTP users if configured to do so.

AP-SAFE-FTP-01   Add Safeguard VOLUME and SUBVOLUME rules to restrict where FTP users PUT files.

AP-SAFE-FTP-02   Add a Safeguard Protection Record to grant appropriate access to the FTP program.

With Third Party Products

3P-FTP-USERIDS-01   Third party FTP products provide granular access to FTP commands and can provide the following:

Authenticate and authorize users as they logon to the FTP subsystem.

Limit the IP addresses from which authorized users can logon to the FTP subsystem

Limit what FTP users can explore by restricting the use of the FTP DIR and LIST commands.

Limit what files FTP users can retrieve from the system by restricting the use of the FTP GET command

Limit where FTP users write files by restricting the use of the FTP PUT command

Provide auditing of FTP activity.

The NonStop server FTP server provides no control over what users can see once logged in.

AP-FTP-USERIDS-09   They can view the files in any subvolume or directory with the LIST or DIR command.

AP-FTP-USERIDS-10   They can GET (copy) any file that isn't secured against READ access.

RISK HP's implementation of FTP has no encryption capabilities. Sensitive data, userids, and passwords are transferred between remote nodes in the clear and unprotected, vulnerable to capture with a network sniffer.

AP-FTP-USERIDS-11 Some third party products provide encryption for both the Command Channel (port) and the Data transmission Channel (port) between the client FTP software and the server FTP software on the NonStop server.

FTP-USERIDS-11 NFS mounted files [i.e. files whose format is compatible with DOS or UNIX systems. These files are used to manage files on HP Non-Stop server from PC or workstation] are *special case files*. Their security differs from the security of standard files; anonymous FTP, though doesn't have the mechanism to tell them apart from the 'regular' files.

Take extreme caution securing NFS files if they will be accessed by the anonymous FTP userid.

An anonymous user should never be allowed to own NFS files, since it will give the user extended access capabilities.

Securing FTP Components

BP-FILE-FTP-01 FTP should be secured "UUNU".

BP-OPSYS-OWNER-01 FTP should be owned by SUPER.SUPER.

BP-OPSYS-FILELOC-01 FTP must reside in $SYSTEM.SYSnn.

BP-FILE-FTP-02 FTPSERV should be secured "UUNU".

BP-OPSYS-LICENSE-03 FTPSERV must be LICENSED.

BP-OPSYS-OWNER-03 FTPSERV should be owned by SUPER.SUPER.

BP-OPSYS-FILELOC-03 FTPSERV resides in $SYSTEM.ZTCPIP.

With certain exceptions listed above, FTP can only operate on object files that userids have been granted access to via the Guardian or Safeguard system.

AP-ADVICE-FTP-02 Users should run FTP under their own userid.

AP-ADVICE-FTP-03 The databases and other sensitive files should be secured to prevent unauthorized transfer of data via FTP.

If available, use Safeguard software or a third party object security product to grant access to FTP object files only to users who require access in order to perform their jobs.

BP-SAFE-FTP-01   Add a Safeguard Protection Record to grant appropriate access to the FTP object file.

BP-SAFE-FTP-02   Add a Safeguard Protection Record to grant appropriate access to the FTPSERV object file.

	Discovery Questions	Look here:
OPSYS-OWNER-01	Who owns the FTP client object file?	Fileinfo
OPSYS-OWNER-03	Who owns the FTPSERV server object file?	Fileinfo
OPSYS-LICENSE-03	Is the FTPSERV object file licensed?	Fileinfo
FILE-POLICY	Who is allowed to execute FTP on the system?	Policy
FILE-POLICY	Is anonymous FTP used on the system?	Policy
FILE-FTP-01 SAFE-FTP-01	Is the FTP object file correctly secured with the Guardian or Safeguard system?	Fileinfo Safecom
FILE-FTP-02 SAFE-FTP-02	Is the FTPSERV object file correctly secured with the Guardian or Safeguard system?	Fileinfo Safecom

Trivial File Transfer Program (TFTP) User Program

The Trivial File Transfer Protocol (TFTP) is an Internet standard protocol for file transfer that uses minimal capability and minimal overhead. TFTP depends only on the unreliable connectionless datagram delivery service (UDP), so it can be used on machines like diskless workstations that keep such software in ROM and use it to bootstrap themselves.

Remote TFTP clients are used to transfer public files to and from an HP NonStop server host system's TFTP server (TFTPSRV).

The HP TFTP client is used to transfer public files to and from a remote system.

Files can be transferred to or from any system on a network that has a TFTP server that accepts requests from the TFTP client.

RISK   TFTP does not provide any mechanism for users to log on to the remote system with a userid and password and verify which files they can access. The files remote users are allowed to retrieve from a remote system are typically secured for public access; that is, anyone on the network can read the files. The TFTP server on the remote system sets the restrictions on which files users can retrieve, as well as restrictions on storing files.

AP-ADVICE-TFTP-01   Both local and remote systems can each place restrictions on which files that can transferred and where the files can be placed.

Users can GET (retrieve) only files that grant *all users* remote READ access. That is, the files must be secured "Nxxx." TFTP ignores the rest of the security string.

Users can only PUT (drop) files where they have remote WRITE access.

To overwrite a file, the existing file security must grant *all users* remote WRITE access. That is, the files must be secured "xNxx." TFTP ignores the rest of the security string.

Remote users can only create new files in a subvolume specified when the TFTP server was started. If no subvolumes were specified, users can create new files only in $DATA.PUBLIC and only if $DATA.PUBLIC is present on the system.

RISK   TFTP assigns new files PUT onto the system a security string of "NUNU," which allows network access.

TFTP Components

Starting with Release Version Update G06.12, the TFTP server consists of two distinct process types that use the following programs:

TFTP

TFTPSRV

TFTPCHLD

TFTP

TFTP is the HP NonStop server TFTP client. It is used to interactively transfer or manage files on a remote system. The remote system need not be another NonStop server.

TFTPSRV

The TFTPSRV process validates requests and starts the TFTPCHLD processes. For every sixteen TFTP requests, TFTPSRV generates a new TFTPCHLD process.

TFTPCHLD

The TFTPCHLD processes handle data transfers. The individual TFTPCHLD processes terminate when after they've handled sixteen requests and no further request is pending or when they have been idle for 10 minutes.

Securing TFTP Components

TFTP should be managed similarly to FTP. See the discussion on Securing FTP with and without the Safeguard Subsystem above.

> **AP-ADVICE-TFTP-02**   If remote clients are allowed to use TFTP and SWANs are in use on the system, all files in the $SYSTEM.CSSnn subvolume must be secured for network READ access. HP recommends that SWAN users secure these files for network READ and EXECUTE access (NUNU).
>
> **BP-FILE-TFTP-01**   TFTP should be secured "UUNU".
>
> **BP-OPSYS-OWNER-01**   TFTP should be owned by SUPER.SUPER.
>
> **BP-OPSYS-FILELOC-01**   TFTP must reside in $SYSTEM.SYSnn.
>
> **BP-FILE-TFTP-02**   TFTPSRV should be secured "UUNU".
>
> **BP-OPSYS-OWNER-01**   TFTPSRV should be owned by SUPER.SUPER.
>
> **BP-OPSYS-FILELOC-03**   TFTPSRV resides in $SYSTEM.ZTCPIP
>
> **BP-FILE-TFTP-03**   TFTPCHLD should be secured "UUNU".
>
> **BP-OPSYS-OWNER-01**   TFTPCHLD should be owned by SUPER.SUPER.
>
> **BP-OPSYS-FILELOC-03**   TFTPCHLD resides in $SYSTEM.ZTCPIP

If available, use Safeguard software or a third party object security product to grant access to TFTP object files to necessary personnel, and deny access to all other users.

> **BP-SAFE-TFTP-01**   Add a Safeguard Protection Record to grant appropriate access to the TFTP object file.
>
> **BP-SAFE-TFTP-02**   Add a Safeguard Protection Record to grant appropriate access to the TFTPSRV object file.

	Discovery Questions	Look here:
OPSYS-OWNER-01	Who owns the TFTP client object file?	Fileinfo
OPSYS-OWNER-03	Who owns the TFTPSRV server object file?	Fileinfo
OPSYS-OWNER-03	Who owns the TFTPCHLD object file?	Fileinfo
FILE-POLICY	Who is allowed to execute TFTP on the system?	Policy
FILE-TFTP-01 SAFE-TFTP-01	Is the TFTP object file correctly secured with the Guardian or Safeguard system?	Fileinfo Safecom
FILE-TFTP-02 SAFE-TFTP-02	Is the TFTPSRV object file correctly secured with the Guardian or Safeguard system?	Fileinfo Safecom

	Discovery Questions	Look here:
FILE-TFTP-03	Is the TFTPCHLD object file secured correctly?	Fileinfo

Information Exchange Facility (IXF) User Program

The Information Exchange Facility (IXF) is a standard protocol for file transfer support that uses minimal capability and minimal overhead.

Securing IXF Components

IXF should be managed similarly to FTP. See the discussion on Securing FTP with and without the Safeguard Subsystem above.

   BP-FILE-IXF-01   IXF should be secured "UUNU".

   BP-OPSYS-LICENSE-02   IXF must be LICENSED.

   BP-OPSYS-OWNER-02   IXF should be owned by SUPER.SUPER.

   BP-OPSYS-FILELOC-02   IXF must reside in $SYSTEM.SYSTEM.

   If available, use Safeguard software or a third party object security product to grant access to IXF object files to necessary personnel, and deny access to all other users.

BP-SAFE-IXF-01   Add a Safeguard Protection Record to grant appropriate access to the IXF object file.

	Discovery Questions	Look here:
FILE-POLICY	Is IXF allowed to be used to transfer files on the system?	Policy
OPSYS-OWNER-02	Who owns the IXF client object file?	Fileinfo
OPSYS-LICENSE-02	Is the IXF object file licensed?	Fileinfo
FILE-IXF-01 SAFE-IXF-01	Is the IXF object file correctly secured with the Guardian or Safeguard system?	Fileinfo Safecom

Related Topics

Operating System Security
TCP/IP

FUP System Utility

FUP is used to manage disk files. FUP can create, display, and duplicate files, load data into files, alter file characteristics, and purge files. FUP supports these types of Enscribe disk files:

Key sequenced

Entry sequenced

Relative

Unstructured (including text files)

FUP provides information about these types of HP NonStop Kernel Open System Services (OSS) and NonStop SQL/MP files:

Tables

Indexes

Partitions

Views

Object programs

> FUP has limited usage for SQL objects; only file label information can be obtained and SQL program files can be secured with FUP. NonStop SQL/MP files are managed by SQLCI.

FUP supports Storage Management Foundation (SMF) logical file names.

The FUP Subsystem components are:

FUP

ORSERV

FUPCSTM (FUP Custom Files)

FUPLOCL (FUP Local Configuration)

FUP and ORSERV can be accessed interactively from a terminal, or programmatically from a management application written in COBOL85, C, TACL, or TAL. FUP is also available as a keyword from other command interpreters, such as SQLCI.

FUP

A FUP process is created when FUP is invoked by a TACL prompt or with a RUN command. The subsequent FUP commands are interpreted and executed by the FUP process.

RISK If a user has WRITE or PURGE access to sensitive files and EXECUTE authority for the FUP object file, that user can damage or destroy sensitive data.

RISK If a user has READ access to sensitive files and EXECUTE authority for the FUP object file, that user can duplicate or display sensitive data.

AP-ADVICE-FUP-01 The best way to prevent unauthorized use of sensitive FUP commands is to secure the files properly. Because an HP NonStop server can contain a large number of files it may be extremely hard to secure them, therefore, FUP is a very dangerous utility.

ORSERV

The ORSERV process reloads key-sequenced Enscribe files and SQL objects. It can be accessed interactively or programmatically from a management application written in COBOL85, C, TACL, or TAL.

Although key-sequenced files can be reloaded using the interactive FUP RELOAD command, an operator must initiate, SUSPEND (when necessary), or RESUME (when appropriate) the RELOAD operation.

RISK ORSERV should only be accessible to users performing these specialized functions.

FUP Customization Files

FUP reads two files (FUPLOCL and FUPCSTM) before it issues its first prompt. This allows users to customize their FUP environment before entering any commands. Both of these files are standard FUP command OBEY files that contain text with valid FUP commands.

FUPCSTM files are located on each user's default subvolume. Please refer to the Gazette section on *CSTM Configuration Files.

FUPLOCL Files

The FUPLOCL file is generally used to run FUP environment commands such as CONFIGURE and SET for a FUP session.

The FUPLOCL file must reside in the current SYSnn; the FUP object file's sub-volume. The file is 'shared' by all users. Whenever FUP is invoked, each command in the FUPLOCL file is executed. This enables the system administrator to configure a site-standard FUP environment.

When FUP is run on a remote node, the FUPLOCL in the SYSnn subvolume on the remote node is used.

The FUPLOCL file should be treated like a System Configuration File and secured accordingly.

RISK   If the security of the FUPLOCL file permits a user other than the owner WRITE or PURGE access, they could modify the file or purge it and replace it with a new one.

RISK   By default, FUP does not echo the commands so users might not even realize that destructive commands are being executed.

BP-FILE-FUPLOCL-01   Turn on echoing by specifying the CONFIGURE ECHO OBEY command in the FUPLOCL file so that the commands executed in the FUPLOCL file will be displayed.

Securing FUP Components

BP-FILE-FUP-01   FUP should be secured "UUNU".

BP-OPSYS-LICENSE-01   FUP must be LICENSED.

BP-OPSYS-OWNER-01   FUP should be owned by SUPER.SUPER.

BP-OPSYS-FILELOC-01   FUP must reside in $SYSTEM.SYSnn.

BP-FILE-FUP-02   ORSERV should be secured "UUNU".

BP-OPSYS-LICENSE-01   ORSERV must be LICENSED.

BP-OPSYS-OWNER-01   ORSERV should be owned by SUPER.SUPER.

BP-OPSYS-FILELOC-01   ORSERV must reside in $SYSTEM.SYSnn.

BP-FILE-FUP-03   FUPLOCL should be secured "NUUU".

BP-OPSYS-OWNER-01   FUPLOCL should be owned by SUPER.SUPER.

BP-OPSYS-FILELOC-01   FUPLOCL must reside in $SYSTEM.SYSnn.

FUP is used extensively to set the security and run-time options on the system. With certain exceptions listed above, FUP can only operate on object files that userids have been granted access to via the Guardian or Safeguard system. Therefore, to reduce the risks associated with FUP's destructive commands secure (see below):

AP-ADVICE-FUP-02   Users should run FUP under their own userid.

AP-ADVICE-FUP-03   The secure database and other sensitive files should be secured to prevent unauthorized access to the data via FUP.

If a licensed, privileged program is opened with WRITE access, the file becomes unlicensed.

If available, use Safeguard software or a third party object security product to grant access to FUP object files only to users who require access in order to perform their jobs.

BP-SAFE-FUP-01   Add a Safeguard Protection Record to grant appropriate access to the FUP object file.

BP-SAFE-FUP-02   Add a Safeguard Protection Record to grant appropriate access to the ORSERV object file.

BP-SAFE-FUP-03   Add a Safeguard Protection Record to grant appropriate access to the FUPLOCL file.

FUP Commands with Security Implications

The following FUP commands have security implications. If a third party access control product is used to grant selected users access to FUP running as SUPER.SUPER, the sensitive commands listed in the table below should be denied to all users other than the system management or other appropriate groups.

3P-ACCESS-FUP-01   If a third party access control product is used to grant selected users access to FUP running as a SUPER.SUPER or another privileged userid such as the database owner, these sensitive commands should only be granted to the appropriate users and denied to all others.

Protecting Sensitive Data

The data in files that users can access with FUP may be sensitive. The following chart shows the file access required for certain FUP commands to be sensitive.

SUPER.SUPER Only	Owner or SUPER.SUPER[1]	READ Required	PURGE Required	Based on RWEP
LICENSE	GIVE	DUP [2]	GIVE	ALTER
REVOKE	PROGID	COPY	PURGE	LOAD
			RENAME	PURGE
				PURGEDATA
				RELOAD
				RENAME

1 - SUPER.SUPER can only PURGE files owned by other userids if Safeguard software is not installed or is configured SUPER.SUPER UNDENIABLE.
2 - If Safeguard software is installed the user must have CREATE access to the target file's destination volume.

CLEARONPURGE

When a file is PURGED, only the file name is deleted. The extents are marked available but the data in the extents is not erased. Sensitive data could be extracted from the deleted extents. Use the CLEARONPURGE option, which physically destroys the data in the file(s) by overwriting the file space with blank data when the file is purged.

AP-ADVICE-FUP-04   Use CLEARONPURGE option on sensitive files.

Using the NOPURGEUNTIL option with a date in the future ensures that the file cannot be purged until that date even if all other security checks pass.

AP-ADVICE-FUP-05   Use NOPURGEUNTIL option on sensitive files.

RENAME

The RENAME operation requires special evaluation of access authorities when Safeguard software is installed.

Access Authority Required to RENAME a File					
Current File Name			New File Name		Result
Safeguard Record Exists?	Safeguard Purge Allowed?	Guardian Purge Allowed?	Safeguard Vol/Subvol/ Disk Record Exist?	Safeguard Create Allowed?	Rename Allowed?
No	-	Yes	No	-	Yes
No	-	Yes	Yes	Yes	Yes
No	-	Yes	Yes	No	No
No	-	No	-	-	No
Yes	Yes	-	No	-	Yes

Access Authority Required to RENAME a File

Current File Name			New File Name		Result
Safeguard Record Exists?	Safeguard Purge Allowed?	Guardian Purge Allowed?	Safeguard Vol/Subvol/ Disk Record Exist?	Safeguard Create Allowed?	Rename Allowed?
Yes	Yes	-	Yes	Yes	Yes
Yes	Yes	-	Yes	No	No
Yes	No	-	-	-	No

The Safeguard PERSISTENT attribute and RENAMING:

If the original file *does not have* a PERSISTENT Protection Record, the new file *assumes* the original file's Protection Record.

If the original file has a PERSISTENT Protection Record, the new file *does not assume* the original file's Protection Record.

If the new file name *has* a PERSISTENT Protection Record, the new file assumes the PERSISTENT Record.

	Discovery Questions	Look here:
OPSYS-OWNER-01	Who owns the FUP object file?	Fileinfo
OPSYS-OWNER-01	Who owns the ORSERV object file?	Fileinfo
OPSYS-OWNER-01	Who owns the FUPLOCL object file?	Fileinfo
OPSYS-LICENSE-01	Is the FUP object file licensed?	Fileinfo
OPSYS-LICENSE-01	Is the ORSERV object file licensed?	Fileinfo
FILE-POLICY	Who is allowed to execute FUP on the system?	Policy
FILE-POLICY	Is a third party access tool used to secure FUP commands?	Policy
FILE-FUP-01 SAFE-FUP-01	Is the FUP object file correctly secured with the Guardian or Safeguard system?	Fileinfo Safecom
FILE-FUP-02 SAFE-FUP-02	Is the ORSERV object file correctly secured with the Guardian or Safeguard system?	Fileinfo Safecom
FILE-FUP-03 SAFE-FUP-03	Is the FUPLOCL file correctly secured with the Guardian or Safeguard system?	Fileinfo Safecom
FILE-FUPLOCL-01	FUPLOCL file has configure echo obey turned on	Edit

Related Topics

Securing Applications

DDL

GOAWAY System Utility

The GOAWAY utility is used to delete SQL objects or shadow labels, residing in the Guardian environment, which cannot be removed with other commands or utilities. It deletes files or file labels. GOAWAY only works on physical SQL objects, tables, indexes, views and programs.

GOAWAY is a 'last resort' tool, which is made available for sites using SQL to remove orphaned SQL objects in cases where the catalog has been damaged, corrupted, or otherwise disconnected from the SQL objects.

RISK Because GOAWAY does not delete the corresponding catalog entries, misuse of the GOAWAY utility can corrupt files.

RISK   GOAWAY does not verify dependencies on the object it is purging, which can cause additional orphans.

RISK   If GOAWAY is used on valid objects, data will be purged from the system that will be unrecoverable.

RISK   GOAWAY does not invoke NonStop TMF commands that could undo the data on the purged objects. SQL objects purged using GOAWAY are not recoverable.

> GOAWAY should never be used as a substitute for SQL DROP, PURGE, or CLEANUP operations. Always perform these as normal commands.

Securing GOAWAY

BP-FILE-GOAWAY-01   GOAWAY should be secured "UUUU".

BP-OPSYS-LICENSE-02   GOAWAY must be LICENSED.

BP-OPSYS-OWNER-02   GOAWAY should be owned by SUPER.SUPER.

BP-OPSYS-FILELOC-02   GOAWAY must reside in $SYSTEM.SYSTEM

If available, use Safeguard software or a third party object security product to grant access to GOAWAY object files only to users who require access in order to perform their jobs.

BP-SAFE-GOAWAY-01 Add a Safeguard Protection Record to grant appropriate access to the GOAWAY object file.

	Discovery Questions	Look here:
OPSYS-OWNER-02	Who owns the GOAWAY object file?	Fileinfo
OPSYS-LICENSE-02	Is the GOAWAY object file licensed?	Fileinfo
FILE-POLICY	Is SQL used on the system?	Policy
FILE-POLICY	Who is allowed to execute GOAWAY on the system?	Policy
FILE-GOAWAY-01 SAFE-GOAWAY-01	Is the GOAWAY object file correctly secured with the Guardian or Safeguard system?	Fileinfo Safecom

Related Topics

SQL Subsystem

INSPECT Subsystem

INSPECT is an interactive symbolic debugger. It can be used to debug multiple programs at once. Developers specify debugging commands using the same identifiers used in the source code. Because the INSPECT debugger must find symbol tables in the object module to allow this feature, the compilers provide the symbol information to Binder at compile time.

INSPECT makes it possible to look at programs while they are running. It can stop and resume execution of the program selectively, helping a developer find out how the program is malfunctioning.

INSPECT can be used with C/C++, COBOL85, FORTRAN, Pascal, SCREEN COBOL, TAL, PTAL and native languages.

INSPECT can be used in the OSS environment. OSS Programs use the OSS Application interface while interactive users use the OSH shell as the command interpreter. Debugging support includes OSS file descriptors, signals and program IDs (PIDs).

RISK INSPECT provides a mechanism whereby running processes can be modified by human interaction.

AP-ADVICE-INSPECT-01   INSPECT is used extensively on a development system, but should rarely be used on a secure system. Therefore, the security requirements are vastly different.

RISK   A user running INSPECT could capture sensitive data, userids, passwords, etc. as they are used internally in a program.

The INSPECT interactive symbolic debugger consists of the following components:

INSPECT

IMON Process pair

DMON Processes

INSPMSG

INSPEXT Customization Files

INSPSNAP

Saveabend Files

Visual Inspect software

INSPECT User Program

The INSPECT process provides the terminal interface to INSPECT. There is one INSPECT process for each terminal in use for debugging.

INSPECT should run as the user who invoked it.

IMON System Program

The IMON monitors the operation of INSPECT for an entire system. There is one IMON process pair for each system, named $IMON. The $IMON process pair is normally started as part of the standard system startup procedures.

IMON starts the DMON processes and INSPECT. IMON assumes that the object files for the DMON and INSPECT programs also reside in its subvolume.

RISK   INSPECT cannot be started without a running $IMON process.

To stop the INSPECT subsystem, stop the IMON process using the name form of the TACL STOP command. Note that this will stop only the IMON processes, not the DMON processes. So once IMON is stopped, the DMON processes must be stopped individually.

DMON System Program

DMON processes provide the execution control facilities of INSPECT. There is one DMON process for each CPU on a system named $DMnn where the nn is the number of the CPU; i.e. $DM01.

IMON automatically starts the DMON processes, and restarts them if they abend or stop.

INSPECT Customization Files

INSPECT reads two files (INSPLOCL and INSPCSTM) before it issues its first prompt. This allows users to customize their INSPECT environment before entering any commands. Both of these files are standard INSPECT command OBEY files that contain ASCII text with valid INSPECT commands.

Unlike FUP, the INSPLOCL and INSPCSTM files are not automatically created by INSPECT.

INSPCSTM files are located on each user's default subvolume. Please refer to Gazette section on *CSTM Configuration Files.

The INSPLOCL file is generally used to run INSPECT environment commands for an INSPECT session.

The INSPLOCL file must reside in the current SYSnn; the INSPECT object file's subvolume. The file is 'shared' by all users. Whenever INSPECT is invoked, each command in the INSPLOCL file is executed. This enables the system administrator to configure a site-standard INSPECT environment.

When INSPECT is run on a remote node, the INSPLOCL in the SYSnn subvolume on the remote node is used.

The INSPLOCL file should be treated like a System Configuration File and secured accordingly.

RISK   If the security of the INSPLOCL file grants a user other than the owner WRITE or PURGE access, they could modify the file or PURGE it and replace it with a new one.

INSPSNAP

The Inspect Process Snapshot Server (INSPSNAP) creates process snapshot files, also known as save files. INSPSNAP saves information from privileged data segments in save files for processes that run with the SUPER ID (255,255).

INSPECT SAVEABEND Files

When INSPECT creates a save file for a process abend, the disk file code is 130. These files are created in the subvolume where the program file resides. The file name is of the form ZZSA<nnnn>.

VISUAL INSPECT SOFTWARE

HP Visual Inspect software is an optional GUI component for inspecting object code. The server components for Visual Inspect software are:

INSPBRKR

INSPRULE

INSPSVR

INSPSMSG

RISK   If Visual Inspect software is activated, risks detailed in this section are expanded to the PC user.

AP-ADVICE-INSPECT-02   Unless necessary, secure the Visual Inspect server components for limited access.

INSPECT and Pathway

Pathway provides execution controls to the inspect interface for Pathway applications. The Pathway configuration must include SET TCP INSPECT ON command to inspect a requestor and SET SERVER DEBUG ON to inspect a server.

RISK   SET TCP INSPECT ON should not be the default for secure Pathway application requestors or INSPECT can be used.

RISK   SET SERVER DEBUG ON should not be the default for secure Pathway application servers or INSPECT can be used.

Securing INSPECT Components

BP-PROCESS-IMON-01 $IMON process should be running.

BP-FILE-INSPECT-01   IMON should be secured "UUCU".

BP-OPSYS-OWNER-01   IMON should be owned by SUPER.SUPER.

BP-OPSYS-FILELOC-01   IMON must reside in $SYSTEM.SYSnn.

BP-PROCESS-DMON-01 $DM<nn> processes should be running.

BP-FILE-INSPECT-02   DMON should be secured "UUCU".

BP-OPSYS-OWNER-01   DMON should be owned by SUPER.SUPER.

BP-OPSYS-FILELOC-01   DMON must reside in $SYSTEM.SYSnn.

BP-FILE-INSPECT-03   INSPECT should be secured "UUNU".

BP-OPSYS-OWNER-01   INSPECT should be owned by SUPER.SUPER.

BP-OPSYS-FILELOC-01   INSPECT must reside in $SYSTEM.SYSnn.

BP-FILE-INSPECT-04   INSPMSG should be secured "NUNU".

BP-OPSYS-OWNER-01   INSPMSG should be owned by SUPER.SUPER.

BP-OPSYS-FILELOC-01   INSPMSG must reside in $SYSTEM.SYSnn.

BP-PROCESS-INSPSNAP-01 $ZSSnn processes should be running.

BP-FILE-INSPECT-05   INSPSNAP should be secured "UUNU".

BP-OPSYS-OWNER-01   INSPSNAP should be owned by SUPER.SUPER.

BP-OPSYS-FILELOC-01   INSPSNAP must reside in $SYSTEM.SYSnn.

BP-FILE-INSPECT-06   INSPLOCL should be secured "NUNU".

BP-OPSYS-OWNER-01   INSPLOCL should be owned by SUPER.SUPER.

BP-OPSYS-FILELOC-01   INSPLOCL must reside in $SYSTEM.SYSnn.

If available, use Safeguard software or a third party object security product to grant access to INSPECT object files only to users who require access in order to perform their jobs.

BP-SAFE-INSPECT-01   Add a Safeguard Protection Record to grant appropriate access to the IMON object file.

BP-SAFE-INSPECT-02   Add a Safeguard Protection Record to grant appropriate access to the INSPECT object file.

INSPECT Commands With Security Implications

This section lists only the INSPECT commands which pose security risks.

SET PRIV MODE   Enables INSPECT operations requiring privileged system access.

The user must be logged on as SUPER.SUPER to use the SET PRIV MODE command.

M   Modifies data and registers

3P-ACCESS-INSPECT-01   If a third party access control product is used to grant access to INSPECT running as an application owner or other privileged userid, these commands may need to be restricted for certain users.

	Discovery Questions	Look here:
PROCESS-IMON-01	Is the $IMON process running?	Status
PROCESS-DMON-01	Are the $DMnn processes running?	Status
PROCESS-INSPSNAP-01	Are the $ZSSnn process running?	Status
OPSYS-OWNER-01	Who owns the IMON file?	Fileinfo
OPSYS-OWNER-01	Who owns the DMON file?	Fileinfo
OPSYS-OWNER-01	Who owns the INSPECT object file?	Fileinfo
OPSYS-OWNER-01	Who owns the INSPMSG file?	Fileinfo
OPSYS-OWNER-01	Who owns the INSPSNAP file?	Fileinfo
OPSYS-OWNER-01	Who owns the INSPLOCL file?	Fileinfo
FILE-INSPECT-01 SAFE-INSPECT-01	Is the IMON object file correctly secured with the Guardian or Safeguard system?	Fileinfo Safecom
FILE-INSPECT-02	Is the DMON object file secured correctly?	Fileinfo
FILE-POLICY	Who is allowed to execute INSPECT on the system?	Policy
FILE-POLICY	Is Visual Inspect used by PC users?	Policy
FILE-INSPECT-03 SAFE-INSPECT-02	Is the INSPECT object file correctly secured with Guardian or Safeguard?	Fileinfo Safecom
FILE-INSPECT-04	Is the INSPMSG file secured correctly?	Fileinfo
FILE-INSPECT-05	Is the INSPSNAP object file secured correctly?	Fileinfo
FILE-INSPECT-06	Is the INSPLOCL file secured correctly?	Fileinfo

Related Topics

Compilers

Securing Applications

Libraries, SRLs and Common Routines

Libraries are sets of common utility routines that are called by other programs. A library is a set of procedures that the operating system can link to a program file at run time or a set of TACL commands that are loaded via the TACL LOAD command. Libraries are used for the following reasons:

To reduce the storage space required for object code on disk and in main memory

To share a set of common procedures among applications

To extend a single application's code space

TACL command libraries are referenced in TACLLOCL, TACLCSTM and OBEY files. Utility libraries may be referred to in compile macros or OBEY files used to run BIND, NLD or as part of the run command.

> *RISK*   There is a chance that a library of non-authorized routines could be substituted for an existing library of the same name. Unauthorized libraries could also be attached to executable objects. In either case however, an individual must have WRITE access to the library or executable object in question to make the changes.

System Libraries

Each language has system libraries available for standard routines distributed with the language product from HP. These libraries are located in the same subvolume as the language compiler, usually $SYSTEM.SYSTEM. System libraries are included into a user program in whole or part during the BIND phase of the compilation.

> **AP-ADVICE-SYSLIBR-01**   The Security staff should be aware of the languages that are used in the application programs. Each language has system libraries available for standard routines. These libraries are located in the same subvolume as the language compiler. Any system library should be secured for READ access only.

Resolving System Libraries with BINDSERV

Compilers resolve system libraries during the compilation phase of generating executables using the BINSERV utility.

User Libraries

Libraries are attached to objects via the BIND program or via NLD or using a RUN command.

> *RISK*   Changes in the library routines could be used to breach sensitive data or allow unauthorized changes to the program. Run-time binding does not include copying the procedure into the program file; it is a linking function only. Allowing run-time libraries to be linked reduces the ability to monitor potential code changes in the program.

The first time a program is executed after being compiled, the system searches the optional user library to resolve each unresolved external reference, and then it searches the system code and system library. A program file can have one (and only one) user library associated with it. The Guardian environment resolves any external reference by changing the call in the program file to point to either the user library or the system library, as appropriate. Once the external references are resolved in this manner, the program can be run repeatedly without satisfying the references again.

If the operating system cannot find a user or system library procedure to satisfy a run-time external reference, it displays a message as the process starts. When the process makes a call to an unresolved procedure, the process changes the reference into a call to the Debug routine, and the process enters the debug state.

RISK   Processes entering the debug state become vulnerable to run-time modification or stoppage. In either case, the processing is affected.

AP-ADVICE-USERLIBR-01   The Security staff should be aware of any user libraries present on the system. Any user libraries should be secured so that they can only be read, altered or purged by the appropriate users. Only the users responsible for maintaining the libraries should have WRITE and PURGE access.

AP-ADVICE-USERLIBR-02   Each library should be secured so that they are accessible only to the appropriate application(s).

Shared Run-Time Libraries (SRLs)

SRL libraries are special user libraries that contain global system variables. There are two types of SRLs:

Public SRL

Private SRL

Public SRLs

Only HP can supply public SRLs. Users cannot create their own public SRLs. NLD resolves references to the Shared Run-time Libraries that are specified when building an executable program in native languages. Public SRLs are located in the $SYSTEM.SYSnn subvolume.

Private SRLs

Programmers and system managers can create private SRLs. An SRL contains code present in virtual memory at run time, to be shared by processes, rather than linked into object files.

	System Library	Public SRLs	Private SRLs
Who can create?	HP	HP	Users
How many libraries per process?	One	Multiple	Multiple
Can contain global data?	No	Yes	Yes
Does each process get its own copy of the SRL?	No	Yes	Yes

AP-ADVICE-SRLLIBR-01   The Security staff should be aware of any SRLs used on the system.

Resolving SRLs with NLD

NLD resolves references to the SRLs that are specified when building an executable program.

Loading SRLs with LTILT

Run LTILT to determine whether there are any Shared Run-time Libraries (SRLs) in use. If there are SRLs, LTILT displays informational output, as shown below:

TILT Public SRLs were found in CPU 00 \LONDON.$SYSTEM.SYS01:

#	SRL Name Filename	Flags
01	ZATMSRL	ZATMSRL Licensed, CallableProcs
02	ZCMASRL	ZCMASRL HighPin
03	ZCOBSRL	ZCOBSRL HighPin
04	ZCPLGSRL	ZCPLGSRL HighPin
05	ZOSSCSRL	ZOSSCSRL HighPin
06	ZTDM_T9228_FSLIBZOSSF	SRL HighPin
07	ZTDM_T9627_OSSLIBZOSSESRL	HighPin

RISK   LTILT is strictly a reporting tool and, therefore, poses no security risks.

Verifying SRLs with VTILT

The VTILT process verifies the SRLs and determines if any require loading. If any SRLs need loading, they are displayed.

```
$SYSTEM SYS01 106> vtilt
VTilt - Verify TILT Libraries - T7898G09 - (01NOV02) - System \LONDON
```

```
\LONDON.$SYSTEM.SYS01.ZTILT and its subvolume-associated TILT SRLs
should load.
```

RISK   VTILT poses no security risk.

Loading SRLs with ZTILT

The ZTILT process loads the SRLs in each processor at startup (cold load) from the active SYSnn subvolume.

A shared run-time library (SRL) is in many ways similar to the system library. An SRL contains code present in virtual memory at run time, to be shared by processes, rather than linked into object files. Unlike code in the system library, an SRL can also contain global data, and each process using the SRL automatically gets its own run-time copy of the data, called instance data.

RISK   ZTILT is loaded and run automatically by the operating system and presents no risk.

Securing Libraries Components

BP-FILE-LTILT-01   LTILT should be secured "UUNU".

BP-OPSYS-LICENSE-01   LTILT must be LICENSED.

BP-OPSYS-OWNER-01   LTILT should be owned by SUPER.SUPER.

BP-OPSYS-FILELOC-01   LTILT must reside in $SYSTEM.SYSnn.

BP-FILE-VTILT-01   VTILT should be secured "UUNU".

BP-OPSYS-OWNER-01   VTILT should be owned by SUPER.SUPER.

BP-OPSYS-FILELOC-01   VTILT must reside in $SYSTEM.SYSnn.

BP-FILE-ZTILT-02   ZTILT should be secured "UUNU".

BP-OPSYS-OWNER-01   ZTILT should be owned by SUPER.SUPER.

BP-OPSYS-FILELOC-01   ZTILT must reside in $SYSTEM.SYSnn.

BP-FILE-SRLS-01 $SYSTEM.Z*SRL should be secured "NUNU".

BP-OPSYS-OWNER-01 $SYSTEM.Z*SRL should be owned by SUPER.SUPER.

BP-OPSYS-FILELOC-01 $SYSTEM.Z*SRL must reside in $SYSTEM.SYSnn.

Some SRLs have to be licensed. Refer to the section on licensed files.

	Discovery Questions	Look here:
OPSYS-OWNER-01	Who owns the LTILT object file?	Fileinfo
OPSYS-OWNER-01	Who owns the VTILT object file?	Fileinfo
OPSYS-OWNER-01	Who owns the ZTILT object file?	Fileinfo
OPSYS-OWNER-01	Who owns the $SYSTEM.Z*SRL SRL files?	Fileinfo
OPSYS-LICENSE-01	Is the LTILT object file licensed?	Fileinfo
FILE-POLICY	Are private SRLs used on the system?	Policy
FILE-POLICY	Who is allowed to maintain private SRLs on the system?	Policy
FILE-LTILT-01	Is the LTILT object file secured correctly?	Fileinfo
FILE-VTILT-01	Is the VTILT object file secured correctly?	Fileinfo
FILE-ZTILT-01	Is the ZTILT object file secured correctly?	Fileinfo
FILE-SRLS-01	Are the $SYSTEM.Z*SRL SRL files secured correctly?	Fileinfo

Related Topics

Compilers

Securing applications

Operating system

Licensed Files

Operations reserved for Guardian are called privileged operations. They control access to hardware and software resources. The operating system needs some privileged programs.

Guardian prevents application programs and users from directly performing privileged operations. Applications must 'ask' the operating system to perform privileged operations, rather than performing them themselves, this is done with Guardian procedure calls.

Programs running in the privileged mode have complete access to operating system tables and can execute privileged instructions and procedures. Only SUPER.SUPER can execute these programs if they are unlicensed. However, programs containing privileged code can be licensed to enable someone other than SUPER.SUPER to execute them.

Generally, only HP system code should be licensed, but licensing also allows applications to run privileged programs, while preventing users from running unauthorized privileged programs.

Certain third party products may need to license certain of their programs or library files. The necessary documentation should be provided by the vendor.

RISK   Licensing a program has the effect of giving it the privileges of the SUPER.SUPER user. Privileged operations in the program can bypass any ordinary security interface (such as authentication of userids and memory-management protection).

RISK   Licensing can allow a program to execute ordinary instructions but using privileged addressing modes that allow references to system global (SG) data space.

RISK   Licensing a program that uses privileged operations can seriously compromise both system integrity and security, by granting the program access into system spaces that provide the opportunity to alter system tables and data.

RISK   Data and information can be gathered and/or modified anywhere in the system. Execution of privileged instructions can directly access the interprocessor bus and I/O devices. It has the potential to change its PAID in the process control block in order to gain the privileges of other users (including SUPER.SUPER) and then browse and change files or directly manipulate physical hardware resources.

RISK   A licensed program has the potential to bypass any ordinary security interface (such as authentication of userids and memory-management protection)

RISK   If an intruder's program is licensed, the intruder can execute procedures that have either the PRIV or CALLABLE attribute, making the program capable of modifying protected memory areas, including its own or other programs' instructions and data, without leaving evidence of the change.

Securing LICENSED Files

Monitoring the licensed programs on the system is fundamental to the Corporate Security Policy. There are four phases necessary to ensure that the system is not vulnerable to unauthorized licensed programs or unauthorized use of approved licensed programs.

Documentation and authorizing of all licensed programs

Securing licensed files

Controlling the license command

Scheduled review for unauthorized licensed programs

Documentation and Authorization of Licensed Programs

AP-ADVICE-LICENSED-01   Creating in-house licensed programs is not recommended. Licensed programs require review with each new HP operating system release. If in-house licensed programs are used, stringent auditing controls should be performed as described below.

Creating and adhering to procedures to review and document all requests to LICENSE programs is basic to sound security.

The company's HP NonStop server security procedures should include the following instructions for managing license requests for in-house user-written programs.

1. The request for license should include a full explanation of the program's purpose and a justification of the use of privileged procedures.

2. The system manager or a trusted programmer must review the source code. The reviewer should look for possible security violations wherever the program:

    Changes operating system control blocks

    Changes the PAID (especially to 255,255) or effective userid

3. Management must approve the licensing in writing with approved signature(s).

4. To assure that the source code matches the actual object program, the system manager, not the developer, should compile and bind the final program.

5. The program must be tested to ensure that it does not perform or allow any actions that would be considered security violations. This test is usually performed by the Security staff.

6. The above document should be maintained in a file for future reference by auditors.

7. Requests for licensing user programs may be allowed if the following conditions are met:

    a) The function is legitimate and necessary.

    b) The function cannot be achieved using non-privileged programming techniques.

8. Secure LICENSED programs so that only authorized users can execute them.

Securing Licensed Files

LICENSED object files should be tightly secured to prevent security breaches. The following tables list the allowable licensed files that may be present on the HP operating system. Each system will have a subset of these files depending upon the products that are sysgened in the operating system. Review the CUSTFILE to view HP's recommendation for the Operating System files on the nodes.

Licensed Operating System Programs

The following tables list the Operating System files that should be licensed on a Release Version Update G06.18.

Table 1 Lists the only files on $SYSTEM.SYSnn that should be licensed:

Program Name	Program Name	Description
BP-OPSYS-LICENSE-01	ADDUSER	Permits the addition of users records outside of Safeguard controls. Should never be executable if Safeguard software is installed
	BACKCOPY	Copies BACKUP tapes
	BACKUP	Reads every file on the system for backup purposes
	BUSCMD	Queries operating system bus status
	COPYDUMP	Compresses tape dumps, should be restricted to system operations
	DCOM	Compresses disk; severely affects performance. Should be restricted to system manager
	DEFAULT	Sets user's default subvolume outside of Safeguard software. No execution restriction necessary, but PURGE should be restricted to SUPER.SUPER
	DELUSER	Deletes user outside of Safeguard software. Should never be executable if Safeguard software is installed
	DISKGEN	Part of the sysgen process; should only be used by SUPER.SUPER
	DIVER	Crashes CPU for NonStop system testing. Should never be executable
	DSAP	Reports on disk resources. No execution restriction necessary, but PURGE should be restricted to SUPER.SUPER

Program Name	Program Name	Description
	DUSL	Dynamic Update of System Library Should only be used by SUPER.SUPER
	FCHECK	DP2 File Check Program. Should only be used by SUPER.SUPER
	FILCHECK	Reports on system internal physical data structure of files
	FILEMGR	Used for SYSGEN operation. Should be restricted to SUPER.SUPER
	FTAMIOBJ	Part of FTAM (File Transfer) subsystem
	FTAMROBJ	Part of FTAM (File Transfer) subsystem
	FUP	File utility program
	LOGIN	Logon program used by Telnet
	LTILT	Used for SYSGEN operation
	MEASCTL	Part of MEASURE subsystem
	MEASMON	MEASURE subsystem monitor
	MEDIADBM	Used by DSM/TC subsystem
	MEDIASRV	Used by DSM/TC subsystem
	MLSRV	G-series component for NETBIOS communications
	NSKCOM	Manages system swap files
	OMP	Part of SMS subsystem
	OPP	Part of SMS subsystem
	ORSERV	Used for Online File Reloads
	OSMP	The Safeguard Manager Process
	OZEXP	The Expand Line Handler
	OZKRN	Operating System process
	PASSWORD	User password change program
	PEEK	CPU Statistics
	PING	Performs the TCP/IP PING operation
	RELOAD	Reloads a CPU
	RESTORE	Restores files from BACKUP tape

Program Name	Program Name	Description
	RPASSWRD	Permits the addition of remote password to users' records outside of Safeguard controls
	SCP	Part of SCF subsystem
	SCPTC	Part of SCF subsystem
	SCPTCOL	Part of SCF subsystem
	SNOOP	Tool to read NonStop TMF audit trails
	SNOOPDR	Part of SNOOP
	SORTPROG	Sort program
	TAPERDR	Component of DSM/TC subsystem
	TCP/IP	Main interface process for TCP/IP
	TFDS	Tandem Fault Diagnostic System
	TFDSCOM	Tandem Fault Diagnostic System
	TIFSERVE	Part of the GUI NonStop TMF Manager
	TMFBOUT	TMF Backout Process
	TMFCTLG	TMF Catalog Process
	TMFDR	TMF Dump Restore Manager
	TMFFRCV	TMF File Recovery
	TMFFRLS	TMF File Recovery List
	TMFMON2	TMF Monitor Process
	TMFSERVE	TMF Server for programmatic communication with the TMF subsystem
	TMFTMP	TMF Server Master Program
	TMFVRCV	TMF Volume Recovery
	TRACER	Operating system program
	TSC	SYSGENR system program
	TSL	SYSGENR system program
	USERS	Reads user files
	ZATMSRL	Operating system program
	ZFB0005H	Operating system program
	ZLANCSRL	Operating system program
	ZLANDSRL	Operating system program

Program Name	Program Name	Description
	ZLANMSRL	Operating system program
	ZSERVER	NonStop Kernel's operating system's labeled tape server process

Table 2 Lists the files on $SYSTEM.SYSTEM that should be licensed.

	Program Name	Description
BP-OPSYS-LICENSE-02	AUDSERV	System program for SQL reloads
	GOAWAY	Used to remove SQL catalogs that have been corrupted
	IXF	Communication protocol program
	NBT	G-series component for NetBIOS communications
	NBX	G-series component for NetBIOS communications
	NETBATCH	Batch monitor process
	NSSMON	Network Statistics monitor
	RELOCSRV	Operating system program
	SCFLIBOR	Part of SCF subsystem
	SCFLIBXR	Part of SCF subsystem
	SMCONVRT	Part of SMS subsystem
	SMFIXUP	Part of SMS subsystem
	SMREPAIR	Part of SMS subsystem
	SMREVERT	Part of SMS subsystem
	SQLCAT	SQL catalog manager
	SQLCOMP	SQL compiler
	SQLUTIL	Part of SQLCI utilities
	STATSRV	Operating system program
	SWARCLIB	Operating system program
	XLLINK	SYSGENR system program

Table 3 Lists other Operating System files on the $<vol> disk that should be licensed.

	Program Name	Description
BP-OPSYS-LICENSE-03 ($SYSTEM DISK)	ZNBPLUS.PB0010O	Operating system file
	ZNBPLUS.PB9000O	Operating system file
	ZNBPLUS.PS0000O	Operating system file
	ZNBPLUS.PS0130O	Operating system file
	ZTCPIP.FTPSERV	Operating system file
	ZUTIL.LKINFO	Operating system file
BP-OPSYS-LICENSE-04 (other DISK locations)	GENPROG.GBDASQL	Part of NonStop DBA/M
	ZDSMSCM.CBEXE	DSMSCM object file
	ZDSMSCM.TAEXE	DSMSCM object file

Licensed Third Party Programs

When installing third party products, the vendor may require that some of their programs or library files be LICENSED. The necessary documentation should be provided by the vendor.

The vendor of any third party product should provide guidelines for securing the licensed programs included in their software packages as well as the necessary documentation of the program's usage.

Controlling the LICENSE command

RISK Safeguard software does not generate DISKFILE audits based on the LICENSE OPERATION, even when the files are licensed using the Safeguard command. This OPERATION parameter in the Safeguard's Audit Layout is 'reserved for future use'.

In order to audit the LICENSING of a file, all of the following must be true:

The Safeguard ALTER DISKFILE <filename>, LICENSE ON command must be used.

The target file must have a Safeguard DISKFILE ACL

The DISKFILE ACL must have the AUDIT-MANAGE-PASS value set to ALL.

3P-ACCESS-LICENSE-01 Without a third party access control product, there is no way to prevent SUPER.SUPER from using the FUP commands to LICENSE a file.

Scheduled Review for Unauthorized Licensed Files

The Operating System files that require licensing may vary from one release to another. To determine which files need to be licensed, review the CUSTFILE file. The CUSTFILE indicates licensing requirements in section 2 with an "L" in column 62 for modules that must be licensed. (INSTALL uses this information to determine if a module should be licensed when it is moved in the REPSUBSYS phase or restored from a system-image tape (SIT) in the RESTSYS phase.)

Example of CUSTFILE entry:

```
2 R1085F40  OZKRN  ZSYSCFM SYSGEN  COPY   SYSNN   L
```

BP-FILES-LICENSE-01   Routinely monitor the system files, and revoke any unauthorized LICENSES.

BP-FILES-LICENSE-02   Routinely monitor other files, and revoke any unauthorized LICENSES.

BP-FILES-LICENSE-03   Licensed files should be owned by SUPER.SUPER.

BP-FILES-LICENSE-04   Licensed files should be secured correctly. Specific security requirements have been given throughout this section. If not otherwise covered, the security should be "UUUU"

BP-FILES-LICENSE-05   Control the use of the LICENSE command.

	Discovery Questions	Look here:
FILE-POLICY	Are all LICENSED files documented?	Policy
FILES-LICENSE-01	Are the proper Operating System object files LICENSED?	DSAP CUSTFILE
FILES-LICENSE-02	Are the proper third party or user software object files LICENSED?	DSAP CUSTFILE
FILES-LICENSE-03	Are the files owned by SUPER.SUPER?	Fileinfo
FILES-LICENSE-04	Are all the LICENSED files secured correctly?	Fileinfo
FILE-POLICY	Is the LICENSE command audited?	Safecom Third Party
FILES-LICENSE-05	Is the LICENSE command secured from unauthorized use?	Guardian Third Party
FILE-POLICY	Is the system periodically monitored for new or unauthorized LICENSED files?	Policy

Related Topics

FUP

Operating System

LISTNER System Utility

The LISTNER process listens to configured TCP/IP ports, waiting for incoming connection requests from remote clients. LISTNER starts a configured program when a request is made via TCP/IP to a specified port.

The TCP/IP process will notify the configured LISTNER process when a request is received to the port for which it is configured. A port is configured in a <portconf> file along with the server process that will be started when a request is received for the port and any optional startup message. When the LISTNER process receives the notification, it starts the target server process. The target server creates a socket using the hostname and source-port information, then accepts the pending connection request on the newly created socket. Every connection to a single port will generate a unique instantiation of the defined server process for use by each individual remote user.

LISTNER is responsible for starting the ECHO, FINGER, and FTP servers when a client request is received for those processes. LISTNER is used only for TCP/IP processing requests.

Once the connection has been made to the target server process, the LISTNER process is no longer involved in the communication and continues to process new incoming requests.

Multiple LISTNER processes may be running on the system. Each LISTNER has a defined <portconf> file.

> These services do not apply to UDP ports; LISTNER is a TCP-oriented program and listens only to TCP ports.

RISK   The LISTNER process requires privileged access to some TCP/IP ports, so it may need to be started by SUPER Group members. LISTNERs not started by a member of the SUPER Group cannot use ports less than 1024.

Programs started by the LISTNER inherit the CAID and PAID of the LISTNER. Programs started by a LISTNER should always require authentication verification by processing a logon and password sequence.

RISK   Programs started by LISTNER may give SUPER access.

LISTNER is part of the TCP/IP communications subsystem. A program commonly started by LISTNER is FTP, which is used for file transfer.

The components of LISTNER are:

PORTCONF Configuration File

SERVICES Configuration File

PORTCONF

The PORTCONF file is used to designate the usage of specific ports. The PORTCONF file is normally located in the $SYSTEM.ZTCPIP subvolume, but can be located elsewhere as defined to TCP/IP.

The LISTNER process must have a static or continuously available input file, output file and home terminal. $ZHOME or $VHS is recommended.

RISK   If no specific location for the PORTCONF file is specified, the process will load the default PORTCONF in the $SYSTEM.ZTCPIP subvolume, which might not be expected, if alternative locations for the PORTCONF are used.

AP-ADVICE-LISTNER-01   The command to start a LISTNER should explicitly specify the location of the PORTCONF file.

RISK   Discerning which LISTNER is using which <portconf> file is not easily done. This cannot be easily monitored for unauthorized changes.

RISK   Once the LISTNER has read the <portconf> file, the file is closed. If the <portconf> file is modified, the LISTNER will not accept the changes without stopping and restarting the LISTNER.

RISK   If two LISTNER processes are started pointing to the same <portconf>, collisions may occur. Whenever this happens, whichever process is second won't listen at the port. It will issue EMS messages.

The following example shows the <portconf> configuration for ports 7810 and 7820. The '!' is used to designate comments.

```
7810 $DATA5.SECGUI.SECGUIX !test s7400 connect only
7820 $DATA4.SECGUI.KSERVR  !text s7400 connect w/ k expand
```

In the example for port 7810, the program $DATA5.SECGUI.SECGUIX will be started when a request is made of this port via TCP/IP.

Preventing Port Collisions

In the OSS environment, the inetd daemon provides the equivalent function as LISTNER.

> *RISK*   Collisions between the services provided by the LISTNER and the inetd daemon can occur if both processes are assigned to the same TCP/IP process using the same port. When this happens, the second process issues an EMS message and does not listen for a specific service.

To prevent this condition, modify one or both of the configuration files (PORTCONF or inetd.conf):

> In the *inetd.conf* file specify a TCP/IP process (Transport Provider) that doesn't have a LISTNER running on it.

> In the PORTCONF file, take advantage of the fact that LISTNER supports only TCP ports. Comment out the TCP port for the service in the *inetd.conf* file. This will allow the LISTNER process to provide the service (on the TCP port) from the Guardian environment while the *inetd daemon* will provide the service (on the UDP port) from the OSS environment.

TCP/IP Services File

> *RISK*   A process's security via LISTNER is only as secure as the TCP/IP that is supporting it.

Securing LISTNER

> **BP-FILE-LISTNER-01**   LISTNER should be secured "UUCU".

> **BP-OPSYS-OWNER-01**   LISTNER should be owned by SUPER.SUPER.

> **BP-FILE-FILELOC-01**   LISTNER must reside in $SYSTEM.SYSnn.

> **BP-FILE-LISTNER-02**   <portconf> should be secured "NCUU".

> **BP-OPSYS-OWNER-03**   <portconf> should be owned by SUPER.SUPER.

> **BP-FILE-FILELOC-03**   <portconf> resides in $SYSTEM.ZTCPIP.

If available, use Safeguard or a third-party object security product to grant access to LISTNER object files only to users who require access in order to perform their jobs.

> **BP-SAFE-LISTNER–01**   Add a Safeguard Protection Record to grant appropriate access to the LISTNER object file.

> **BP-SAFE-LISTNER-02**   Add a Safeguard Protection Record to grant appropriate access to the PORTCONF disk file.

	Discovery Questions	Look here:
OPSYS-OWNER-01	Who owns the LISTNER object file?	Fileinfo
OPSYS-OWNER-03	Who owns the <portconf> file?	Fileinfo
FILE-POLICY	Who is allowed to start and stop LISTNERs on the system?	Policy
FILE- LISTNER-01 SAFE-LISTNER-01	Is the LISTNER object file correctly secured with the Guardian or Safeguard system?	Fileinfo Safecom
FILE-POLICY	Who can make changes to the <portconf> file?	Policy
FILE- LISTNER-02 SAFE-LISTNER-02	Is the <portconf> file correctly secured with the Guardian or Safeguard system?	Fileinfo Safecom

Related Topics

TCP/IP

LOGIN System Program

The LOGIN program is started by the TELSERV process after a user has specified a service name to TELSERV. The LOGIN program starts the appropriate service and authenticates the user if configured to do so. If the service chosen by the user does not require authentication, the program defined for the service is started and no authentication is done. If authentication is required, the user is prompted for a userid or alias and the password for that userid or alias. If they are valid, the program defined for the service is started already with authentication. If invalid, the user is returned to the userid prompt.

In general, TACL, PATHWAY and LOGON must be started without authentication. /bin/sh must be started with authentication.

NOTE: Services are defined for an individual TELSERV process using the SCF subsystem.

RISK Starting without authentication could allow people to access the system without a password.

Securing LOGIN

BP-FILE-LOGIN-01   LOGIN should be secured "UUNU".

BP-OPSYS-LICENSE-01   LOGIN must be LICENSED.

BP-OPSYS-OWNER-01   LOGIN must be owned by SUPER.SUPER.

BP-OPSYS-FILELOC-01   LOGIN must reside in $SYSTEM.SYSnn.

	Discovery Questions	Look here:
OPSYS-OWNER-01	Who owns the LOGIN object file?	Fileinfo
OPSYS-LICENSE-01	Is the LOGIN object file licensed?	Fileinfo
FILE-POLICY	Who is allowed to execute LOGIN on the system?	Policy
FILE-LOGIN-01	Is the LOGIN object file secured correctly?	Fileinfo

Related Topics

LOGON

Safeguard subsystem

Telnet

LOGON User Program

The LOGON program is used by Safeguard software to manage the user authentication process for Safeguard controlled terminals. LOGON can be started by the LOGIN program if the terminal is connecting to the system via dynamic TCP/IP. Otherwise, it is started directly by Safeguard software . The LOGON program displays the "Safeguard 1>" prompt at which the user enters the userid or alias and the password for that userid or alias.

After authentication, the Safeguard TERMINAL record for the terminal where LOGON is running is used to determine what program will be started. If no values are defined in the TERMINAL record or there is no TERMINAL record, the USER record in Safeguard software will be used. If no values are defined in the USER record, the Safeguard global values will be used. If there are no values in the Safeguard globals, the TACL program located in the active system image will be used.

The program that is started is supplied with all of the user's authentication information so the user is not prompted again for the userid or alias and password.

Securing LOGON

BP-FILE-LOGON-01   LOGON should be secured "UUNU".

BP-OPSYS-LICENSE-01   LOGON should not be LICENSED.

BP-OPSYS-OWNER-01   LOGON must be owned by SUPER.SUPER.

BP-OPSYS-FILELOC-01   LOGON must reside in $SYSTEM.SYSnn.

	Discovery Questions	Look here:
OPSYS-OWNER-01	Who owns the LOGON object file?	Fileinfo
OPSYS-LICENSE-01	Is the LOGON object file licensed?	Fileinfo
FILE-POLICY	Who is allowed to execute LOGON on the system?	Policy
FILE-LOGON-01	Is the LOGON object file secured correctly?	Fileinfo

Related Topics

LOGIN

User Management

Safeguard subsystem

TELSERV

MEASURE Subsystem

MEASURE is a monitoring tool that collects performance statistics about system resources. It gathers data from system components, network components, and applications. This information can be used to tune the system, detect bottlenecks, balance workload, and do capacity planning.

The MEASURE subsystem must be running before any measurement can be made. The subsystem must be started by a SUPER Group member. It is often started as part of the cold-load system start up procedure.

Multiple users can run MEASURE sessions at the same time, and each user can configure and take measurements independently. The performance monitor provides both a command interface and a programmatic interface.

The command interface provides commands that can be entered at a terminal or input from a file. The programmatic interface consists of a set of callable procedures that can be used in application programs to access MEASURE's functions. The procedures allow an application to configure a measurement, start it, stop it, and write the information to the specified output file for analysis.

RISK   MEASURE is strictly a reporting tool and, therefore, poses no security risk. The subsystem itself has minimal impact on performance; it can be started and then allowed to run continuously. However, a MEASURE collection process can consume large amounts of system resources and should not be run on secure system without close supervision to minimize performance issues.

RISK   MEASURE data files can be very large.

Once the data files have been reviewed they should be deleted.

RISK   MEASURE data files can be very large.

Don't store the files on $SYSTEM to avoid affecting system performance.

The following list describes the components that make up the MEASURE Subsystem.

MEASCHMA

MEASCOM

MEASCTL

MEASFH

MEASDDLB

MEASDDLF

MEASDDLS

MEASDECS

MEASIMMU

MEASMON

MEASTCM

MEASZIP

OUTPUT DATA FILES

MEASCOM

MEASCOM is the command interpreter for the MEASURE subsystem. It allows the user who started it to carry on an interactive session with the MEASURE subsystem.

MEASCOM can be used by a SUPER Group member to start the MEASURE subsystem.

Once the subsystem is started, any user can use MEASCOM to configure, run, and examine measurements. Multiple MEASURE sessions can be run simultaneously and multiple measurements may be performed within a single session.

MEASCTL

MEASCTL is Measure's control program. There is one MEASCTL for each CPU on a system named $XMnn where the nn is the number of the CPU; i.e. $XM01. They are created by MEASMON when the MEASURE subsystem is started. MEASMON automatically starts the MEASCTL processes, and restarts them if they abend or stop.

MEASFH

MEASFH processes are the Measure's file handlers. The MEASFH processes are created whenever a measurement is run or a resulting measure data file is examined. There is one MEASFH process per user-designated data file. The process formats the file, adds the data to it, and retrieves the data as needed.

MEASCHMA, MEASDDLB, MEASDDLF, MEASDDLS, MEASDECS

These files contain the record definitions (DDLs) for all the optional structured files produced by the MEASURE commands and procedures that display Measurement results. These files allow users to produce custom reports and programs using measurement data.

MEASDECS

The MEASDECS file contains the structure declarations and literal value definitions used in the MEASURE callable procedures.

MEASIMMU

The MEASIMMU file contains the MEASURE error messages and the online help text accessible through the MEASCOM HELP command.

MEASMON

MEASMON is Measure's Monitor. It creates and coordinates all the MEASCTL processes in each CPU, sending measurement configuration requests and gathering information from them.

There is a single MEASMON process (running as a NonStop process pair) per system. The process is created when the MEASURE subsystem is started.

MEASMON monitors the operation of MEASURE for an entire system. There is one MEASMON process pair for each system, named $XMON or $XMM. The process pair is normally started as part of the standard system startup procedure. MEASMON starts the MEASCTL processes.

RISK   Measurements cannot be performed if the MEASURE Subsystem is not running.

RISK   If the $XMON process is stopped using the name form of the TACL STOP command, only the MEASMON processes are stopped, not the MEASCTL processes. So once MEASMON is stopped, the MEASCTL processes must be stopped individually or they will be left running.

AP-ADVICE-MEASDATA-01   Use MEASCOM to stop the MEASURE subsystem.

MEASTCM

The MEASTCM product is used to summarize measurement data for capacity-planning studies.

MEASZIP

The MEASZIP contains the optional MEASURE GUI application, which can be downloaded to a PC to install the windows client interface.

OUTPUT DATA FILES

MEASURE generates large data files that can reside anywhere on the system. These files are identified with file code 175.

AP-ADVICE-MEASDATA-02   MEASURE data files do not present a security risk, however, they can be very large files. Once reviewed they should be removed.

Securing MEASURE Components

BP-FILE-MEASURE-01   MEASCHMA should be secured "NUNU".

BP-OPSYS-OWNER-01   MEASCHMA should be owned by SUPER.SUPER.

BP-OPSYS-FILELOC-01   MEASCHMA must reside in $SYSTEM.SYSnn.

BP-FILE-MEASURE-02   MEASCOM should be secured "UUNU".

BP-OPSYS-OWNER-01   MEASCOM should be owned by SUPER.SUPER.

BP-OPSYS-FILELOC-01   MEASCOM must reside in $SYSTEM.SYSnn.

BP-PROCESS-MEASCTL-01 $XMnn processes should be running.

BP-FILE-MEASURE-03   MEASCTL should be secured "UUNU".

BP-OPSYS-LICENSE-01   MEASCTL must be LICENSED.

BP-OPSYS-OWNER-01   MEASCTL should be owned by SUPER.SUPER.

BP-OPSYS-FILELOC-01   MEASCTL must reside in $SYSTEM.SYSnn.

BP-FILE-MEASURE-04   MEASFH should be secured "UUNU".

BP-OPSYS-OWNER-01   MEASFH should be owned by SUPER.SUPER.

BP-OPSYS-FILELOC-01   MEASFH must reside in $SYSTEM.SYSnn.

BP-FILE-MEASURE-05   MEASDDLB should be secured "NUNU".

BP-OPSYS-OWNER-01   MEASDDLB should be owned by SUPER.SUPER.

BP-OPSYS-FILELOC-01   MEASDDLB must reside in $SYSTEM.SYSnn.

BP-FILE-MEASURE-06   MEASDDLF should be secured "NUNU".

BP-OPSYS-OWNER-01   MEASDDLF should be owned by SUPER.SUPER.

BP-OPSYS-FILELOC-01   MEASDDLF must reside in $SYSTEM.SYSnn.

BP-FILE-MEASURE-07   MEASDDLS should be secured "NUNU".

BP-OPSYS-OWNER-01   MEASDDLS should be owned by SUPER.SUPER.

BP-OPSYS-FILELOC-01   MEASDDLS must reside in $SYSTEM.SYSnn.

BP-FILE-MEASURE-08   MEASDECS should be secured "NUNU".

BP-OPSYS-OWNER-01   MEASDECS should be owned by SUPER.SUPER.

BP-OPSYS-FILELOC-01   MEASDECS must reside in $SYSTEM.SYSnn.

BP-FILE-MEASURE-09   MEASIMMU should be secured "NUNU".

BP-OPSYS-OWNER-01   MEASIMMU should be owned by
SUPER.SUPER.

BP-OPSYS-FILELOC-01   MEASIMMU must reside in $SYSTEM.SYSnn.

BP-PROCESS-MEASMON-01 $XMM process should be running.

BP-FILE-MEASURE-10   MEASMON should be secured "UUNU".

BP-OPSYS-LICENSE-01   MEASMON must be LICENSED.

BP-OPSYS-OWNER-01   MEASMON should be owned by SUPER.SUPER.

BP-OPSYS-FILELOC-01   MEASMON must reside in $SYSTEM.SYSnn.

BP-FILE-MEASURE-11   MEASTCM should be secured "UUNU".

BP-OPSYS-OWNER-02   MEASTCM should be owned by SUPER.SUPER.

BP-OPSYS-FILELOC-02   MEASTCM must reside in $SYSTEM.SYSTEM.

BP-FILE-MEASURE-12   MEASZIP should be secured "NUNU".

BP-OPSYS-OWNER-01   MEASZIP should be owned by SUPER.SUPER.

BP-OPSYS-FILELOC-01   MEASZIP must reside in $SYSTEM.SYSnn.

If available, use Safeguard software or a third party object security product to grant access to the MEASURE subsystem programs only to users who require access in order to perform their jobs.

BP-SAFE-MEASURE-01   Add a Safeguard Protection Record to grant appropriate access to the MEASMON object file.

BP-SAFE-MEASURE-02   Add a Safeguard Protection Record to grant appropriate access to the MEASCOM object file.

	Discovery Questions	Look here:
PROCESS-MEASMON-01	Is the $XMM process running?	Status
PROCESS-MEASCTL-01	Are the $XMnn processes running?	Status
FILE-POLICY	Who is allowed to run MEASURE queries on the system?	Policy
OPSYS-OWNER-01	Who owns the MEASCHMA file?	Fileinfo
OPSYS-OWNER-01	Who owns the MEASCOM object file?	Fileinfo
OPSYS-OWNER-01	Who owns the MEASCTL object file?	Fileinfo
OPSYS-OWNER-01	Who owns the MEASFH object file?	Fileinfo
OPSYS-OWNER-01	Who owns the MEASDDLB object file?	Fileinfo
OPSYS-OWNER-01	Who owns the MEASDDLF object file?	Fileinfo
OPSYS-OWNER-01	Who owns the MEASDDLS object file?	Fileinfo
OPSYS-OWNER-01	Who owns the MEASDECS object file?	Fileinfo
OPSYS-OWNER-01	Who owns the MEASIMMU object file?	Fileinfo
OPSYS-OWNER-01	Who owns the MEASMON object file?	Fileinfo
OPSYS-OWNER-01	Who owns the MEASZIP object file?	Fileinfo
OPSYS-OWNER-02	Who owns the MEASTCM object file?	Fileinfo
OPSYS-LICENSE-01	Is the MEASCTL object file licensed?	Fileinfo
OPSYS-LICENSE-01	Is the MEASMON object file licensed?	Fileinfo
FILE-MEASURE-01	Is the MEASCHMA file secured correctly?	Fileinfo
FILE-MEASURE-02 SAFE-MEASURE-02	Is the MEASCOM object file correctly secured with the Guardian or Safeguard system?	Fileinfo Safecom
FILE-MEASURE-03	Is the MEASCTL object file secured correctly?	Fileinfo
FILE-MEASURE-04	Is the MEASFH object file secured correctly?	Fileinfo
FILE-MEASURE-05	Is the MEASDDLB file secured correctly?	Fileinfo

	Discovery Questions	Look here:
FILE-MEASURE-06	Is the MEASDDLF file secured correctly?	Fileinfo
FILE-MEASURE-07	Is the MEASDDLS file secured correctly?	Fileinfo
FILE-MEASURE-08	Is the MEASDECS file secured correctly?	Fileinfo
FILE-MEASURE-09	Is the MEASIMMU object file secured correctly?	Fileinfo
FILE-MEASURE-10 SAFE-MEASURE-01	Is the MEASMON object file correctly secured with the Guardian or Safeguard system?	Fileinfo Safecom
FILE-MEASURE-11	Is the MEASTCM object file secured correctly?	Fileinfo
FILE-MEASURE-12	Is the MEASZIP file secured correctly?	Fileinfo

Native Link Editor (NLD) User Program

NLD resolves references to the Shared Run-time Libraries that are specified when building an executable program in native languages.

Native C

Native C++

Native COBOL

Native TAL (PTAL)

The NLD utility links one or more TNS/R object files to produce an executable or non-executable native object file (file code 700). An executable native object file cannot be input to the NLD utility at a later time but a non-executable native object file can.

Link one or more TNS/R native object files to produce a loadfile or linkfile

Modify existing loadfiles

NLD cannot be run interactively. It is run from the native compilers or from a batch obey file containing NLD commands.

Securing NLD

BP-FILE-NLD-01   NLD should be secured "UUNU".

BP-OPSYS-OWNER-02   NLD should be owned by SUPER.SUPER.

BP-OPSYS-FILELOC-02   NLD must reside in $SYSTEM.SYSTEM.

If available, use Safeguard software or a third party object security product to grant access to NLD object files only to users who require access in order to perform their jobs.

BP-SAFE-NLD-01   Add a Safeguard Protection Record to grant appropriate access to the NLD object file.

	Discovery Questions	Look here:
OPSYS-OWNER-02	Who owns the NLD object file?	Fileinfo
FILE-POLICY	Who is allowed to execute NLD on the system?	Policy
FILE-NLD-01 SAFE-NLD-01	Is the NLD object file correctly secured with the Guardian or Safeguard system?	Fileinfo Safecom

Related Topics

Compilers

Securing Applications

Libraries, SRLs & Common Routines

NOFT

Native Object File Tool (NOFT) User Program

NOFT reads and displays information from native object files. It is the native equivalent of BIND for native code programs written in Native C, Native C++, Native COBOL and PTAL.

NOFT can be run interactively from a TACL prompt in the Guardian environment or an OSS shell prompt or as a batch process issuing commands from a terminal or an obey file.

Determine the optimization level of procedures in a file

Display object code with corresponding source code

List shared run-time library (SRL) references in an object file

List unresolved references in an object file

List object file attributes

RISK   NOFT commands are not destructive, but can be used to view native program code.

Securing NOFT

BP-FILE-NOFT-01   NOFT should be secured "UUNU".

BP-OPSYS-OWNER-02   NOFT should be owned by SUPER.SUPER.

BP-OPSYS-FILELOC-02   NOFT must reside in $SYSTEM.SYSTEM.

If available, use Safeguard software or a third party object security product to grant access to NOFT object files only to users who require access in order to perform their jobs.

BP-SAFE-NOFT-01   Add a Safeguard Protection Record to grant appropriate access to the NOFT object file.

	Discovery Questions	Look here:
OPSYS-OWNER-02	Who owns the NOFT object file?	Fileinfo
FILE-POLICY	Who is allowed to execute NOFT on the system?	Policy
FILE-NOFT-01 SAFE-NOFT-01	Is the NOFT object file correctly secured with the Guardian or Safeguard system?	Fileinfo Safecom

<u>Related Topics</u>

Compilers

Securing Applications

Libraries, SRLs & Common Routines

NLD

NETBATCH Subsystem

The NetBatch automates job scheduling, startup, and management on NonStop server systems to provide a method to manage automated job cycles.

The components of the NETBATCH subsystem are:

NETBATCH

BATCHCAL

BATCHCOM

BATCHCTL

BATCHIMU

BATCHLIB

BATCHUTL

NBEXEC

NetBatch Plus Pathway Application Interface

ATTACHMENT-SET

NETBATCH must be installed and started prior to using the NETBATCH subsystem. By default, the NETBATCH process runs non-stop as the named process $ZBAT. The following type of functions can be performed:

Running a job at a specified date/time

Running a job on a cyclical schedule; daily, weekly, or monthly

Running a job dependent upon completion of other jobs

Running a job based upon the outcome of other jobs

Running a job based on a calendar file

RISK NETBATCH provides a method for starting processes on the HP Non-Stop server system. Once a job is defined to NETBATCH, it is started according to the defined schedule without any additional terminal interaction.

RISK Jobs could be setup via NETBATCH that could damage the system integrity for some future date, even for a user that no longer exists.

RISK Jobs start automatically and possibly unexpectedly, based upon the parameters used in the job setup, and not necessarily current information. For instance, a NETBATCH job setup to start at 8:00 PM, starts regardless of the fact that a CPU might be down and causing system performance problems. Jobs are not released by operators.

RISK Once jobs are added to NETBATCH, they must be deleted to preclude subsequent processing.

NETBATCH

The NETBATCH program is the scheduler component. It schedules and starts the jobs, tracks and controls their execution, and records details of their termination. It also controls, through its classes and executors, the distribution of jobs among CPUs in the system.

BATCHCOM

BATCHCOM is NETBATCH's command interpreter. BATCHCOM enables inter-active and non-interactive manipulation of commands for jobs to the scheduler, the scheduler's executors and classes, and attachment sets of jobs.

BATCHCAL

BATCHCAL is the NETBATCH calendar maintenance program. This program allows generation of a calendar file containing a series of dates and times called run times. Schedule a job to run automatically at those times by using the CALENDAR attribute to assign the file to the job. Old calendar files can also be updated or displayed.

BATCHCTL

The BATCHCTL file stores control information for the NETBATCH subsystem. Shutting down a scheduler results in the closure of its database files and log file and the status is stored in the BATCHCTL file so it can restart.

The scheduler keeps details of its configuration at shutdown in its BATCHCTL file for use during a warm start.

NBEXEC

NBEXEC is executor program started by NETBATCH to execute control file com-mands, supplies data to started processes, and logs process output. NBEXEC can run as a process pair and offers a simple job control language that includes error-testing and job-recovery facilities.

NetBatch Plus

NetBatch Plus is an optional Pathway application that is a screen-driven interface for managing NetBatch jobs. If NetBatch Plus is installed, the Pathway application should be secured as a secure application.

AP-SAFE-NETBATCH-01   Add a Safeguard Protection Record to grant appropriate access to the NetBatch Plus Pathway application equivalent to the Guard-ian file security listed below.

ATTACHMENT-SETs

An ATTACHMENT-SET is a named entity containing ASSIGN, DEFINE, and PARAM statements. This information is used as input to a job within NETBATCH.

See Securing Applications Chapter for more information on ASSIGNs, DEFINEs, and PARAMs.

Securing NETBATCH Components

BP-FILE-NETBATCH-01   BATCHCOM should be secured "UUNU".

BP-OPSYS-OWNER-02   BATCHCOM should be owned by SUPER.SUPER.

BP-OPSYS-FILELOC-02   BATCHCOM must reside in $SYSTEM.SYSTEM.

BP-FILE-NETBATCH-02   BATCHCAL should be secured "UUNU".

BP-OPSYS-OWNER-02   BATCHCAL should be owned by SUPER.SUPER.

BP-OPSYS-FILELOC-02   BATCHCAL must reside in $SYSTEM.SYSTEM.

BP-FILE-NETBATCH-03   BATCHCTL should be secured "NUUU".

BP-OPSYS-OWNER-02   BATCHCTL should be owned by SUPER.SUPER.

BP-OPSYS-FILELOC-02   BATCHCTL must reside in $SYSTEM.SYSTEM.

BP-FILE-NETBATCH-04   BATCHIMU should be secured "NUUU".

BP-OPSYS-OWNER-02   BATCHIMU should be owned by SUPER.SUPER.

BP-OPSYS-FILELOC-02   BATCHIMU must reside in $SYSTEM.SYSTEM.

BP-FILE-NETBATCH-05   BATCHLIB should be secured "UUNU".

BP-OPSYS-OWNER-02   BATCHLIB should be owned by SUPER.SUPER.

BP-OPSYS-FILELOC-02   BATCHLIB must reside in $SYSTEM.SYSTEM.

BP-FILE-NETBATCH-06   BATCHUTL should be secured "UUNU".

BP-OPSYS-OWNER-02   BATCHUTL should be owned by SUPER.SUPER.

BP-OPSYS-FILELOC-02   BATCHUTL must reside in $SYSTEM.SYSTEM.

BP-FILE-NETBATCH-07   NBEXEC should be secured "UUNU".

BP-OPSYS-OWNER-02   NBEXEC should be owned by SUPER.SUPER.

BP-OPSYS-FILELOC-02   NBEXEC must reside in $SYSTEM.SYSTEM.

BP-PROCESS-NETBATCH-01 $ZBAT process should be running.

BP-FILE-NETBATCH-08   NETBATCH should be secured "UUNU".

BP-OPSYS-LICENSE-01   NETBATCH is licensed.

BP-OPSYS-OWNER-02   NETBATCH should be owned by SUPER.SUPER.

BP-OPSYS-FILELOC-02   NETBATCH must reside in $SYSTEM.SYSTEM.

If available, use Safeguard software or a third party object security product to grant access to NETBATCH subsystem object files only to users who require access in order to perform their jobs.

BP-SAFE-NETBATCH-01   Add a Safeguard Protection Record to grant appropriate access to the BATCHCOM object file.

BP-SAFE-NETBATCH-02   Add a Safeguard Protection Record to grant appropriate access to the NETBATCH object file.

	Discovery Questions	Look here:
PROCESS-NETBATCH-01	Is the $ZBAT process running?	Status
FILE-POLICY	Is NETBATCH being used as the batch job interface? Is $ZBAT running?	Policy
OPSYS-OWNER-02	Who owns the BATCHCOM object files?	Fileinfo
OPSYS-OWNER-02	Who owns the BATCHCAL object files?	Fileinfo
OPSYS-OWNER-02	Who owns the BATCHCTL object files?	Fileinfo
OPSYS-OWNER-02	Who owns the BATCHIMU object files?	Fileinfo
OPSYS-OWNER-02	Who owns the BATCHLIB object files?	Fileinfo
OPSYS-OWNER-02	Who owns the BATCHUTL object files?	Fileinfo
OPSYS-OWNER-02	Who owns the NBEXEC object files?	Fileinfo
OPSYS-OWNER-02	Who owns the NETBATCH object files?	Fileinfo
OPSYS-LICENSE-02	Is the NETBATCH object file licensed?	Fileinfo
FILE-POLICY	Who is allowed to execute BATCHCOM on the system?	Policy
FILE-NETBATCH-01 SAFE-NETBATCH-01	Is the BATCHCOM object file correctly secured with the Guardian or Safeguard system?	Fileinfo Safecom
FILE-NETBATCH-02	Is the BATCHCAL object file secured correctly?	Fileinfo
FILE-NETBATCH-03	Is the BATCHCTL object file secured correctly?	Fileinfo
FILE-NETBATCH-04	Is the BATCHIMU object file secured correctly?	Fileinfo
FILE-NETBATCH-05	Is the BATCHLIB object file secured correctly?	Fileinfo
FILE-NETBATCH-06	Is the BATCHUTL object file secured correctly?	Fileinfo
FILE-NETBATCH-07	Is the NBEXEC object file secured correctly?	Fileinfo

	Discovery Questions	Look here:
FILE-NETBATCH-08	Is the NETBATCH object file correctly secured with	Fileinfo
SAFE-NETBATCH-02	the Guardian or Safeguard system?	Safecom

NSKCOM System Utility

NSKCOM is the command interface to manage the Kernel-Managed Swap Facility (KMSF).

The KMSF manages virtual memory. When all physical memory has been allocated and more memory is needed, data that is not currently in use is stored on disk. Pages of memory are "swapped," or copied, to disk when there is a shortage of available physical memory and are swapped back to physical memory when the data is accessed. When swapped to disk, the data is stored in "swap files."

The HP NonStop operating system opens one or more swap files for each processor and manages the files for all the processes needing them. A kernel-managed swap file is only opened once and is then available to all the processes running in the processor. Conventional swap files, which are defined by the calling process rather than the system, must be opened and closed by the system monitor on each process creation and deletion.

The components of the KMSF subsystem are:

NSKCOM

ZSYSCFG

Managed Swap Files

NSKCOM

Internal security to NSKCOM allows only SUPER Group members to change the KMSF configuration by adding, stopping use of, or deleting swap space through the NSKCOM interface.

ADD

ALTER

DELETE

START

STOP

RISK   If managed space is used, it should be monitored on a regular basis to ensure appropriate amounts of swap space are made available to processes.

3P-OBJSEC-NSKCOM-01   If a third party product is used to grant access to NSKCOM running as a SUPER Group userid, these commands should be denied to all users other than the system managers.

ZSYSCFG File

The swap files names and characteristics are stored in the ZSYSCFG file. This file is updated using the NSKCOM interface.

Information in the ZSYSCFG file is stored for the volumes that use managed swap space.

RISK   The ZSYSCFG file must be accessible to the users that have the ability to run the NSKCOM program for management purposes. If other users have access to update or delete the ZSYSCFG file the file could be corrupted or deleted.

```
Example:
KMS.SWAPFILE = 0 $SYSTEM.ZSYSSWAP.CPU0A
KMS.SWAPFILE = 1 $SYSTEM.ZSYSSWAP.CPU1A
KMS.SWAPFILE = 1 $DSMSCM.SYSPRSWP.CPU01
KMS.SWAPFILE = 0 $DSMSCM.SYSPRSWP.CPU00
```

Managed SWAP Files

The swap files named in the ZSYSCFG file are created by NSKCOM. Kernel-managed swap files are created with file code of 405.

AP-ADVICE-NSKCOM-01   Any managed swap files should only be accessible to the SUPER Group who manages KMSF.

Securing NSKCOM

BP-FILE-NSKCOM-01   NSKCOM should be secured "UUCU".

BP-OPSYS-LICENSE-01   NSKCOM must be LICENSED.

BP-OPSYS-OWNER-01   NSKCOM should be owned by SUPER.SUPER.

BP-OPSYS-FILELOC-01   NSKCOM must reside in $SYSTEM.SYSnn.

BP-FILE-NSKCOM-02   ZSYSCFG should be secured "NUCU".

BP-OPSYS-OWNER-02   ZSYSCFG should be owned by SUPER.SUPER.

BP-OPSYS-FILELOC-02   ZSYSCFG must reside in $SYSTEM.SYSTEM.

BP-FILE-NSKCOM-03   Files of file code 405 should be secured "OOOO".

BP-OPSYS-OWNER-03   Files of file code 405 should be owned by SUPER.SUPER.

If available, use Safeguard software or a third party object security product to grant access to NSKCOM object files only to users who require access in order to perform their jobs.

BP-SAFE-NSKCOM-01   Add a Safeguard Protection Record to grant appropriate access to the NSKCOM object file.

	Discovery Questions	Look here:
OPSYS-OWNER-01	Who owns the NSKCOM object file?	Fileinfo
OPSYS-OWNER-03	Who owns the ZSYSCFG file?	Fileinfo
OPSYS-LICENSE-01	Is the NSKCOM object file licensed?	Fileinfo
FILE-POLICY	Who is allowed to execute NSKCOM on the system?	Policy
FILE-NSKCOM-01 SAFE-NSKCOM-01	Is the NSKCOM object file correctly secured with the Guardian or Safeguard system?	Fileinfo Safecom
FILE-NSKCOM-02	Is the ZSYSCFG file secured correctly?	Fileinfo
FILE-NSKCOM-03	Are the swap files referenced in the ZSYSCFG secured correctly?	Fileinfo

Operating System

The HP NonStop server operating system (OS) is the foundation for all functions on the system. Sometimes referred to as Guardian or NonStop Kernel operating system, the OS resides on the $SYSTEM volume in several subvolumes:

$SYSTEM.SYSTEM

$SYSTEM.SYSnn

$SYSTEM.CSSnn

$SYSTEM.Z<name> * (* can reside on other disk volumes)

Securing the SYSTEM Disk

AP-ADVICE-SYSDISK-01   All non-HP programs that must reside on $SYSTEM should be documented and moved from the system subvolumes to a separate location. The search list can be updated to include the new subvolume location if these programs are of general interest, but only where there is a genuine need.

AP-ADVICE-SYSDISK-02   The $SYSTEM disk as a whole should be reserved for Operating System files. $SYSTEM resources should be conserved.

AP-ADVICE-SYSDISK-03   Only the group charged with creating and maintaining the operating system installation image and those responsible for maintaining certain of the configuration files, such as PORTCONF, TACLLOCL, etc. should have WRITE access to the system configuration files.

AP-ADVICE-SYSDISK-04   No personal files should reside on the $SYSTEM disk.

AP-ADVICE-SYSDISK-05   The subvolume $SYSTEM.SYSnn is reserved for files created by DSM/SCM. Any other files placed in this subvolume will be lost when a new operating system image is installed.

RISK   By default, Safeguard software creates the current Audit Pool in $SYSTEM.SAFE. The audit pools can create disk space and performance issues on $SYSTEM.

BP-SAFEGARD-CONFIG-07   The Safeguard audit trail should be moved off $SYSTEM to another, less busy, volume.

If Safeguard software's current audit pool becomes unavailable, and RECOVERY Mode is configured to DENY GRANTS, Safeguard software will deny any authorization (object access attempts) and any authentication (logon) requests that require auditing. In this case:

RISK   Only successful access attempts by members of the Security Groups will be granted.

RISK   What auditing occurs will be redirected to $SYSTEM.SAFE. If there is no available space on $SYSTEM, no activity that requires auditing will be allowed. It will not even be possible to switch to another Audit Pool.

BP-SAFEGARD-CONFIG-12   If AUDIT SERVICE is configured to DENY GRANTS, make sure that $SYSTEM always has enough space for 'fallback' auditing or risk disruption of service.

BP-SAFEGARD-CONFIG-13   If AUDIT SERVICE is configured to DENY GRANTS, it is especially important to configure at least one secondary Audit Pool or risk disruption of service.

Temporary Files are files created as temporary workspace for a program. Temporary files are created programmatically and are deleted when the program finishes.

Safeguard software *does not* restrict the creation of temporary files, such as swap files. VOLUME and SUBVOLUME authorization records are not checked when a temporary file with a name beginning with the pound or hash sign (#) is created. Example: #A738902.

Safeguard software *does* restrict the creation of temporary files by the Virtual Screen Editor (XVS or VS), which are created in the subvolume where the user invoked XVS. Example: ZZVS82S.

RISK Audit trails and audit dumps to disk require extensive space and accessibility.

BP-TMF-CONFIG-01 The TMF audit trails should not be located on $SYSTEM to avoid contention. Configure the data files on another, less busy, volume.

RISK The spooler collector's data files requires extensive space and accessibility.

BP-SPOOLER-CONFIG-01 The spooler data files should not be located on $SYSTEM to avoid contention. Configure the data files on another, less busy, volume.

AP-ADVICE-SYSDISK-06 Many other programs, such as ENFORM, may create temporary files in the execution subvolume. Most can be configured to create their temporary files in another location and not on the $SYSTEM disk.

AP-ADVICE-SYSDISK-07 Configure NSKCOM and SORT to use swap space on a disk other than $SYSTEM.

AP-ADVICE-SYSDISK-08 Monitor the $SYSTEM disk for programs that place temporary files on the $SYSTEM disk.

Current Operating System - $SYSTEM.SYSnn

Operating system files located in $SYSTEM.SYSnn get created upon each revision of the operating system to a new SYSnn subvolume. This ensures that the OS set is cohesive and compatible.

Securing the $SYSTEM.SYSnn subvolume determines the accessibility to operating system files for all users. Multiple SYSnn subvolumes can be resident on the $SYSTEM disk at any time. Only one will be currently running the operating system. The other copies can be older or newer versions that are retained for backup or upgrade staging.

RISK Older versions of the OS retained online on as a fallback option following a COLDLOAD to a new OS should be removed or secured as soon as possible. They are not automatically removed by DSM/SCM.

RISK   The current OS subvolume must be owned by SUPER.SUPER. Ownership by any other user might prevent the system from COLD LOADing.

RISK   No personal or system obey files or any other type of file should reside in the SYSnn subvolume. Files in the SYSnn subvolume are assumed to be files belonging to the OS and only for the current version of the OS.

RISK   Only the object programs that are listed in the CUSTFILE or in HP NonStop documentation should be licensed. Please refer to the Gazette section on LICENSED File and references throughout this Gazette.

BP-OPSYS-OWNER-01   Operating System files should be owned by SUPER.SUPER

BP-OPSYS-LICENSE-01   The appropriate object files in the SYSnn should LICENSED; all others should not.

BP-OPSYS-PROGID-01   Only the appropriate object files in $SYSTEM.SYSnn should PROGID'd; all others should not.

BP-SAFE-SYSNN-01   Secure the $SYSTEM.SYSnn subvolume with an appropriate Safeguard Subvolume Protection Record.

BP-SAFE-SYSNN-02   Secure the $SYSTEM.SYSnn files that require tighter security than the SUBVOLUME Protection Record with appropriate DISKFILE Protection Records.

	Discovery Questions	Look here:
FILE-POLICY	What is the name of the current SYSnn subvolume?	FUP
OPSYS-OWNER-01	Who owns the files in the SYSnn subvolume?	Fileinfo
OPSYS-LICENSE-01	Are only the designated files licensed?	DSAP Fileinfo Safecom
OPSYS-PROGID-01	Are only the designated files PROGID'd?	DSAP Fileinfo
SAFE-SYSNN-01 SAFE-SYSNN-02	Is the $SYSTEM.SYSnn subvolume correctly secured with the Guardian or Safeguard system?	Fileinfo Safecom
OPSYS-FILELLOC-01	Are there non-system files in the $SYSTEM.SYSnn subvolume?	Fileinfo

Communication OS - $SYSTEM.CSSnn

The subvolume that contains the files that handle I/O for the 3650/6100 family of communications controllers for the operating system is CSSnn. The numeric portion of the subvolume name is the same as that of the associated SYSnn subvolume.

The CSSnn subvolume is automatically created by the SYSGEN process while installing the operating system. Similar to the SYSnn subvolume, old versions of CSSnn may be present on the system.

> *RISK* As of Release Version Update G06.08, all files in the current CSSnn subvolume need to be secured for network READ and EXECUTE access in order for communication processes to work properly.

> *RISK* The CSSnn subvolume needs to be secured for network READ access for TFTP communications processing.

> *RISK* Older versions of the CSSnn subvolume retained online on as a fallback option following a COLDLOAD to a new OS should be removed or secured as soon as possible. They are not automatically removed by DSM/SCM.

> **BP-FILE-CSSNN-01**   CSSnn.* files should be secured "NUNU".

> **BP-OPSYS-OWNER-03**   CSSnn.* files should be owned by SUPER.SUPER.

> **BP-OPSYS-FILELOC-03**   CSSnn.* files resides on $SYSTEM in a matching CSSnn subvolume to the SYSnn subvolume.

If available, use Safeguard software or a third party object security product to grant appropriate access to $SYSTEM.CSSnn utilities only to users who require access in order to perform their jobs.

> **BP-SAFE-CSSNN-01**   Secure the $SYSTEM.CSSnn with a Safeguard SUBVOLUME Protection Record.

	Discovery Questions	Look here:
OPSYS-OWNER-03	Who owns the current CSSnn.* object files?	Fileinfo
FILE-SYSNN-01 SAFE-SYSNN-01	Is the $SYSTEM.CSSnn subvolume correctly secured with the Guardian or Safeguard system?	Fileinfo Safecom

Old Operating System - $SYSTEM.SYS++

Multiple SYSnn subvolumes can be resident on the $SYSTEM disk at any time. Only one will be currently running the operating system. The other copies can be older or newer versions that are retained for backup or upgrade staging.

In this handbook, the old versions of these two subvolumes will be referred to as:

SYS++

CSS++

RISK   Unless the SYS++ subvolume is strictly secured, users may be able to run old versions of the utilities. The programs can be run manually by users simply by referencing the full pathname of the object file. Assume that SYS02 is an older version of the OS still resident on the system:

```
RUN $SYSTEM.SYS02.FUP
```

BP-FILE-OLDSYS-01   All the files in the entire old SYS++ subvolume (containing old versions of the OS) should be secured so that only SUPER.SUPER can READ, WRITE, EXECUTE or PURGE.

RISK   Unless the CSS++ subvolume is strictly secured, programs can be run manually by users simply by referencing the object file. Assume that SYS02 is an older version of the OS still resident on the system:

BP-FILE-OLDSYS-02   All the files in the entire old CSS++ subvolume (containing old versions of the OS) should be secured so that only SUPER.SUPER can READ, WRITE, EXECUTE or PURGE.

If available, use Safeguard software or a third party product to restrict access to old ++ subvolumes as SUPER.SUPER only, and deny access to all other users.

BP-SAFE-OLDSYS-01   Add a Safeguard SUBVOLUME Protection Record to grant appropriate access to the SYS++ subvolume.

BP-SAFE-OLDSYS-02   Add a Safeguard SUBVOLUME Protection Record to grant appropriate access to the CSS++ subvolume.

	Discovery Questions	Look here:
FILE-OLDSYS-01 FILE-OLDSYS-02	Are old OS SYS++ and CSS++ subvolumes maintained on the $SYSTEM disk?	FUP
FILE-OLDSYS-01 SAFE-OLDSYS-01	Have all the files in any SYS++ subvolumes been secured, with either the Guardian or Safeguard system, so that only SUPER.SUPER can access any of its files?	Fileinfo Safecom
FILE-OLDSYS-02 SAFE-OLDSYS-02	Have all the files in any CSS++ subvolumes been secured, with either the Guardian or Safeguard system, so that only SUPER.SUPER can access any of its files?	Fileinfo Safecom

$SYSTEM.SYSTEM

The $SYSTEM disk as a whole should be reserved for Operating System files.

Operating system files located on the $SYSTEM.SYSTEM subvolume get replaced upon an upgrade of the operating system. Existing files that either are not operating system files or are obsolete do not get replaced or removed.

RISK   No unauthorized and undocumented files, especially object files, should reside in the $SYSTEM.SYSTEM subvolume. Files in the SYSTEM subvolume are assumed to be files belonging to the operating system or system-related files.

RISK   Only the object programs that are listed in the CUSTFILE or in HP NonStop documentation should be LICENSED. Please refer to the Gazette section on LICENSED Files and references throughout this Gazette.

BP-OPSYS-OWNER-02   Operating System files should be owned by SUPER.SUPER

BP-OPSYS-LICENSE-02   Only the appropriate object files in $SYSTEM.SYSTEM should LICENSED; all others should not.

BP-OPSYS-PROGID-02   Only the appropriate object files in $SYSTEM.SYSTEM should PROGID'd; all others should not.

If available, use Safeguard software or a third party object security product to grant access to $SYSTEM.SYSTEM operating system files only to users who require access in order to perform their jobs.

BP-SAFE-SYSTEM-01   Secure the $SYSTEM.SYSTEM subvolume with an appropriate Safeguard Subvolume Protection Record.

BP-SAFE-SYSTEM-02   Secure the $SYSTEM.SYSTEM files that require tighter securing than the SUBVOLUME Protection Record with appropriate DISKFILE Protection Records.

	Discovery Questions	Look here:
OPSYS-OWNER-02	Who owns the files in the SYSTEM subvolume?	Fileinfo
OPSYS-LICENSE-02	Are only the designated files licensed?	DSAP Fileinfo Safecom
OPSYS-PROGID-02	Are only the designated files PROGID'd?	DSAP Fileinfo

	Discovery Questions	Look here:
SAFE-SYSTEM-01 SAFE-SYSTEM-02	Is the $SYSTEM.SYSTEM subvolume correctly secured with the Guardian or Safeguard system?	Safecom

Z Subvolumes

To help keep files organized, HP puts certain files in subvolumes starting with Z<name> on the $SYSTEM disk. (Or other alternate disk name) The <name> corresponds to the subsystem, such as ZMEASURE. The type and usage of these files differs greatly by subsystem. General guidelines are given below, unless otherwise described in this manual.

These subvolumes should all be treated similarly.

BP-FILE-ZNAMED-01   Z<name>.* files should be secured "CUCU".

BP-OPSYS-OWNER-03   Z<name>.* files in $SYSTEM.<Zname> files should be owned by SUPER.SUPER.

BP-OPSYS-OWNER-04   Z<name>.* files in $<vol>.<Zname> files should be owned by SUPER.SUPER.

BP-OPSYS-LICENSE-02   Only the appropriate object files in $SYSTEM.<Zname> should LICENSED; all others should not.

BP-OPSYS-PROGID-02   Only the appropriate object files in $SYSTEM.SYSTEM should PROGID'd; all others should not.

BP-OPSYS-FILELOC-03   Z<name>.* files resides on $SYSTEM.Z<name>

BP-OPSYS-FILELOC-04   Z<name>.* files resides on $<vol>.Z<name>

	Discovery Questions	Look here:
OPSYS-OWNER-03-04	Who owns the current $SYSTEM.Z<name>.* object files?	Fileinfo
OPSYS-LICENSE-03-04	Are only the designated files licensed?	DSAP Fileinfo Safecom
OPSYS-PROGID-03-04	Are only the designated files PROGID'd?	DSAP Fileinfo Safecom
FILE-ZNAMED-01	Are the Z <name>.* object files correctly secured with the Guardian environment?	Fileinfo

<u>Related Topics</u>

DSMSCM Subsystem

Configuration Files

LICENSE

PROGID

PAK/UNPAK User Programs

The PAK and UNPAK utilities perform compression and decompression on HP NonStop server files. Once the data is compressed it can be archived, moved, or downloaded to a remote system.

PAK

PAK compresses files into a single unstructured file of File Code 1729. It can also compress into a self-extracting file and the resultant file is a File Code 700.

BACKUP and PAK require READ access to perform the file read function.

PAK uses the BACKUP program to read and process the files, so the options are similar to BACKUP. Likewise, the risks are similar to BACKUP.

RISK   If the BACKUP program is accessible to general users, files containing sensitive data could be backed up and restored under their userid.

RISK   Compressed files, especially those using the self-extracting option (File Code = 700), are very difficult to distinguish from normal native object files. Therefore, the security of these files is difficult to control.

UNPAK

UNPAK decompresses a paked file or self-extracting file into a subvolume.

UNPAK uses the RESTORE program to read the Paked file and process the file, so the options are similar to RESTORE. Likewise, the risks are similar to RESTORE.

RISK   Compressed files can be moved to a system with less security and uncompressed to allow unauthorized access to the data.

RISK   Compressed files can be restored, overwriting existing files using RESTORE parameters.

RISK   Since Paked files can contain sensitive data, protection of the utilities that can read or copy the data is a security risk.

AP-UNPAK-ADVICE-01   Unpaking should only be done by authorized personnel.

RISK   The RESTORE MYID parameter can be used to change the security of the unpaking files to the userid running UNPAK. This gives that userid full access to the unpaked files.

RISK   If the UNPAK and RESTORE programs are accessible to general users, files containing sensitive data could be retrieved from a tape and restored under their userid.

Securing PAK/UNPAK

BP-FILE-PAK-01   PAK should be secured "UUNU".

BP-OPSYS-OWNER-02   PAK should be owned by SUPER.SUPER.

BP-OPSYS-FILELOC-02   PAK resides in $SYSTEM.SYSTEM.

BP-FILE-PAK-02   UNPAK should be secured "UUNU".

BP-OPSYS-OWNER-02   UNPAK should be owned by SUPER.SUPER.

BP-OPSYS-FILELOC-02   UNPAK must reside in $SYSTEM.SYSTEM.

BP-FILE-PAK-03   File Code 1729 PAK archives should be secured "OOOO".

BP-FILE-PAK-04   File Code 700 PAKed executables should be secured "OOOO".

If available, use Safeguard software or a third party object security product to grant access to PAK/UNPAK object files to necessary personnel, and deny access to all other users.

BP-SAFE-PAK-01   Add a Safeguard Protection Record to grant appropriate access to the PAK object file.

BP-SAFE-PAK-02   Add a Safeguard Protection Record to grant appropriate access to the UNPAK object file.

	Discovery Questions	Look here:
FILE-POLICY	Is there any need to use PAK conversions?	Policy
OPSYS-OWNER-02	Who owns the PAK object file?	Fileinfo
OPSYS-OWNER-02	Who owns the UNPAK object file?	Fileinfo
FILE-POLICY	Who is allowed to execute PAK/UNPAK on the system?	Policy

	Discovery Questions	Look here:
FILE-PAK-01 SAFE-PAK-01	Is the PAK object file correctly secured with the Guardian or Safeguard system?	Fileinfo Safecom
FILE-PAK-02 SAFE-PAK-02	Is the UNPAK object file correctly secured with the Guardian or Safeguard system?	Fileinfo Safecom
FILE-PAK-03	Are the File Code 1729 files secured correctly?	Fileinfo
FILE-PAK-04	Are the File Code 700 PAKed executable files secured correctly?	Fileinfo

Related Topics

BACKUP

RESTORE

Password User Program

The PASSWORD program is used to set or reset user passwords. See the chapter on Password Administration for a more detailed discussion on managing passwords.

Configuring the PASSWORD Program

In the Guardian environment, PASSWORD parameters must be configured by BINDing them to the PASSWORD program.

The parameters that can be bound into the PASSWORD program are:

BLINDPASSWORD

ENCRYPTPASSWORD

MINPASSWORDLEN

PROMPTPASSWORD

These parameters should be bound to the PASSWORD program even if Safeguard software is installed on the system. To determine the current value, see Viewing the PASSWORD BIND Parameters in Appendix A.

The following chart summarizes the settings with and without Safeguard software. The discussion follows.

Parameter Keyword	With Safeguard Subsystem	Without Safeguard Subsystem	Value Returned in BIND*
BLINDPASSWORD	ON	ON	000000 or 000001
ENCRYPTPASSWORD	OFF	ON	000000 or 000001
MINPASSWORDLEN	6-8	6-8	00000n
PROMPTPASSWORD	ON	ON	000000 or 000001

* Value 000000 = OFF, 000001 = ON ·

RISK The PASSWORD program resides in the $SYSTEM.SYSnn subvolume and is replaced upon each new operating system installation.

BP-PASSWORD-SYSGEN-01 The parameters must be bound after each operating system upgrade.

BLINDPASSWORD

The BLINDPASSWORD parameter controls whether the passwords are echoed to the terminal during the change process.

RISK When passwords are entered on the same line as the user name, they are displayed on the screen, in the clear.

If the BLINDPASSWORD value is set to zero (false), the user will see the password displayed as it is entered.

If the BLINDPASSWORD value is set to one (true), the user *will not* see the password displayed as it is entered.

RISK The default is zero (false); the user's password will be displayed on the user's terminal for any passer-by to see.

BLINDPASSWORD should be bound into the PASSWORD program even if Safeguard software is installed and configured with BLINDLOGON ON. The Safeguard setting configures the authentication process, which is used for all authentication attempts. Therefore, always bind BLINDPASSWORD into the PASSWORD program.

With or without Safeguard software:

BP-PASSWORD-CONFIG-01 BLINDPASSWORD should be ON.

With Safeguard software:

> **BP-SAFEGARD-GLOBAL-53**   Safeguard BLINDLOGON global should be ON.

ENCRYPTPASSWORD

The ENCRYPTPASSWORD parameter determines whether or not passwords will be encrypted when they are stored in the userid file. If the passwords are stored in encrypted form, they are unreadable even if someone gains access to the USERID, or LUSERID files.

Without Safeguard software:

> **RISK**   If passwords are not encrypted, anyone with READ access to the USERID file can extract the passwords.

> If the value is set to 1 (true), passwords will be encrypted.

> If the value is set to 0 (false), passwords will not be encrypted.

> The default is zero (false), no encryption.

> Just setting this parameter to 1 does not cause existing passwords to be encrypted; they will be encrypted the next time they are changed. Therefore, all users should change their passwords after setting this parameter.

> **BP-PASSWORD-CONFIG-02**   ENCRYPTPASSWORD should be ON.

With Safeguard software:

> **RISK**   Whether or not Safeguard software can validate that a new password meets its MINIMUM-LENGTH requirement depends on whether or not Safeguard software performs the encryption:

> If the password is encrypted by the PASSWORD program, Safeguard software receives the encrypted version of the password and cannot check for PASSWORD-MINIMUM-LENGTH.

> If the Safeguard software performs the encryption through the PASSWORD-ENCRYPT attribute, it checks PASSWORD-MINIMUM-LENGTH before it encrypts the password.

> **BP-PASSWORD-CONFIG-02**   ENCRYPTPASSWORD should be OFF.

> **BP-SAFEGARD-GLOBAL-06**   Safeguard PASSWORD-ENCRYPT global should be ON.

MINPASSWORDLEN

The MINPASSWORDLEN parameter establishes the minimum number of characters that can make up a password. The maximum length of a password on the HP NonStop Server is eight characters. The more characters a password contains, the harder it is to 'crack'.

RISK   The default is zero, no password required. If no password is required, any userid can be changed to have no password, thus allowing anyone to use the userid.

If the MINPASSWORDLEN value is 0 (zero), no password is required.

If the MINPASSWORDLEN value is set to a number between 1 and 8, a password is required.

If Safeguard is installed, its MINIMUM-LENGTH parameter will take precedence.

With or without Safeguard software:

BP-PASSWORD-CONFIG-03   MINPASSWORDLEN should be at least 6.

With Safeguard software:

BP-SAFEGARD-GLOBAL-07   Safeguard
PASSWORD-MINIMUM-LENGTH global = 6.

PROMPTPASSWORD

The PROMPTPASSWORD parameter determines whether or not the PASSWORD program accepts a command line password change, which displays the new password value on the screen, or goes through a prompting sequence of requiring the old password to be entered with the display suppressed, the new password to be entered, again with display suppressed, and then the new password to be entered again, display suppressed, to ensure that the new password does not contain typing errors.

The default is zero (false), no prompt.

RISK   If the parameter is set to zero, the password change can take place on the command line, which displays the password value and does not require knowledge of the old password, so unauthorized parties are not prohibited from changing the password.

If the PROMPTPASSWORD value is zero (false), the user will be able to set the password without knowledge of the old password and will be able to see the contents of the new password.

If the PROMPTPASSWORD value is set to one (true), the user will be required to know the old password.

With or without Safeguard software:

BP-PASSWORD-CONFIG-04   PROMPTPASSWORD should be ON.

Third Party Password Products

The PASSWORD program's internal Guardian security permits each user to reset their own password, group managers to reset the passwords of members of their group, and SUPER.SUPER to reset any user's password.

3P-PASSWORD-RESET-01   Use a third product that allows for additional controls over resetting passwords.

3P-PASSWORD-EXPIRE-01   Use a third party product that can automatically expire passwords whenever someone other than the user tries to create or reset them.

Third party password products can help to control the password strings set by users so that they conform to certain standards. For instance, the password must contain at least 1 number.

3P-PASSWORD-CONTROL-01   Use a third party product that can control the length, character string and other limitations on the password.

Securing PASSWORD

BP-FILE-PASSWORD-01   PASSWORD should be secured "UUNU".
BP-OPSYS-LICENSE-01   PASSWORD must be LICENSED.
BP-OPSYS-OWNER-01   PASSWORD should be owned by SUPER.SUPER.
BP-OPSYS-FILELOC-01   PASSWORD must reside in $SYSTEM.SYSnn

If available, use Safeguard software or a third party object security product to grant access to the PASSWORD object file only to users who require it in order to perform their jobs.

BP-SAFE-PASSWORD-01   Add a Safeguard Protection Record to grant appropriate access to the PASSWORD object file.

	Discovery Questions	Look here:
OPSYS-OWNER-01	Who owns the PASSWORD object file?	Fileinfo
OPSYS-LICENSE-01	Is the PASSWORD object file licensed?	Fileinfo
FILE-POLICY	Is Safeguard software installed on the system?	Policy
FILE-PASSWORD-01 SAFE-PASSWORD-01	Is the PASSWORD object file correctly secured with the Guardian or Safeguard system?	Fileinfo Safecom
PASSWORD-CONFIG-01	Is the BLINDPASSWORD parameter bound into the PASSWORD program?	Bind
PASSWORD-CONFIG-02	Is the ENCRYPTPASSWORD parameter bound into the PASSWORD program?	Bind
PASSWORD-CONFIG-03	Is the MINPASSWORDLEN parameter bound into the PASSWORD program?	Bind
PASSWORD-CONFIG-04	Is the PROMPTPASSWORD parameter bound into the PASSWORD program?	Bind
SAFEGARD-GLOBAL-06	Is Safeguard global PASSWORD-ENCRYPT = ON	Safecom
SAFEGARD-GLOBAL-07	Is Safeguard global PASSWORD-MINIMUM-LENGTH = 6 or greater	Safecom
SAFEGARD-GLOBAL-53	Is Safeguard global BLINDLOGON = ON	Safecom

Related Topics:

Password Administration

User Administration

BINDER

LICENSE

PROGID

Pathway Subsystem

This section describes securing the components of the Pathway Subsystem itself. Please refer to the chapters on Application Security for a discussion on securing Pathway Applications.

Pathway is an application platform, under which many NonStop server applications run. It is often the pivotal production platform, therefore requiring a wide range of access throughout a company's enterprise.

The Pathway application is the gateway to many production applications, which:

Provides the interface to the company's database

Is the foundation for the availability of the company's enterprise applications

Determines the security methodology for the enterprise databases

Provides multi-threading and configurable components based upon the application

Pathway is a client-server application model. The Pathway monitor provides the interface for the communication layer and the management layer between the client and server. A Pathway application has two major components:

Requestors   A screen program or GUI client component that interacts directly with the terminal. The screen part of the application is written in SCOBOLX or in a GUI language.

Servers   The user program running on the host system that interacts with the databases and performs user calculations, etc. The server part of the application can be written in any available language that functions on the HP NonStop server.

The Pathway subsystem components are:

PATHCOM
PATHMON
PATHTCP2
PATHCTL
PATHTCPL
LINKMON

Components of each Pathway Application:

PATHCTL
POBJDIR/POBJCOD
Server Programs
Assigned files and Databases

PATHCOM

PATHCOM is the interactive interface into a Pathway environment for starting, stopping, and modifying the environment. The designated Pathway owner and security controls the ability to perform commands, via PATHCOM or programmatically to affect the environment.

The owner can perform management commands; start and stop the Pathway objects, alter configuration settings, freeze and thaw terminals, etc.

The designated security attribute specifies the users, relative to the Pathway owner, who can perform management commands. Set the SECURITY parameter using the Guardian security values A, G, O, -, N, C, and U. The internal security attribute does not control the security at which the requestor or server programs run. For instance:

Setting the value to "C", allows anyone in the owner's network group to alter the Pathway or start and stop servers.

Setting the value to "O", allows only the local owner to alter the Pathway or start and stop servers.

Non-dedicated terminals are started via the PATHCOM interface, therefore users responsible for stopping and starting Pathway terminals need EXECUTE access to the PATHCOM object file.

AP-FILE-PATHCOM-01   Starting a terminal through the PATHCOM interface is the method used for non-dedicated terminals, therefore users need EXECUTE access to the PATHCOM object file.

RISK   The PROGRAM security of "N" allows anyone in the network to start the program. Likewise, the security of "A" allows any local user these privileges.

BP-PATHWAY-CONFIG-01   Pathway security should not allow general access or "N" or "A".

3P-ACCESS-PATHWAY-01   Access to PATHCOM commands can be controlled via a third party product that can secure at the command level.

PATHMON

A Pathway monitor program process pair is started for each Pathway system. A Pathway application is started and then configured with the PATHCOM program. PATHCOM commands are used to configure the Pathway application. Each Pathway Monitor has a unique process name, which has been defined during the start of the PATHMON process.

RISK   The Pathway owner is set to the user who starts the Pathway, unless otherwise explicitly set during configuration. Allowing the internal Pathway owner to be defaulted upon startup can configure a Pathway environment to the wrong user.

All TCPs and server processes started by a PATHMON process are run using the PAID of the PATHMON process.

Since the server processes run as the Pathway owner, all databases must be secured to allow appropriate access.

The owner can perform management commands; start and stop the Pathway objects, alter configuration settings, freeze and thaw terminals, etc.

RISK   The default for Pathway security is 'N" unless explicitly set after the START Pathway command is issued, which allows network access by default.

AP-FILE-PATHWAY-02   Ensure that application Pathways have adequate internal security. Internal Pathway security should be set to "O" or "U".

RISK   Pathway reconfiguration may not be successful if the Pathway owner is not also the userid that restarts the Pathway.

RISK   Because PATHCOM defaults to a Pathway named $PM when no other Pathway name is specified, never name a Pathway $PM. Commands from a PATHCOM accidentally started with no name could be applied to the wrong Pathway.

RISK   Running application Pathway systems under SUPER.SUPER is not recommended. It allows access to the system as SUPER.SUPER without the need for a password.

RISK   Pathway does not interact with CMON when starting server processes for authorization, priority, CPU, etc. CPU selection and priority can be set on the Server configuration within Pathway.

RISK   CPU selection and priority can be configured for servers within Pathway. Inappropriate values can harm system performance.

AP-FILE-PATHWAY-03   The Pathway owner should be the same user that started the Pathway environment. PATHMON should not be running as SUPER.SUPER.

AP-FILE-PATHWAY-04   The Pathway owner should always be explicitly set and not defaulted. This does not prevent another user from trying to start the Pathway, but prevents that user from configuring the Pathway after the PATHMON is started. Set the Pathway owner to the user who is designated to start and own the Pathway.

LINKMON

For Pathway applications running via GUI client applications that are remote to the Pathway, Pathway performs the communication via a process called LINKMON. LINKMON establishes communications from the client to the server class. Several methods are in use to perform the communication layer for this function:

Remote Server Call (RSC) software enables personal computers (PCs) and workstations to communicate with Pathway servers and other processes on an HP NonStop server. The security of the access link is not covered in this chapter.

TCP/IP communication channels allow personal computers (PCs) and workstations to communicate with Pathway servers and other processes on an HP NonStop server. The security of the access link is not covered in this chapter.

A typical LINKMON request to Pathway is initiated from a GUI client or Web application via a communication methodology to a PATHMON. Configuration parameters in the PATHMON setup determine accessibility of Pathway to remote clients.

The operating system starts the LINKMON processes (the ROUT program) and names them automatically in each CPU conforming to the name $ZLnn, where nn is the number of the CPU; i.e. $ZL05 is the Linkmon for CPU 5.

LINKMON extended memory is supported by a disk swap file named $SYSTEM.ZLINKMON.ZZLMnn, where nn is the CPU number of the LINKMON process. For example, the LINKMON process $ZL01 in CPU 1 uses the swap file $SYSTEM. ZLINKMON.ZZLM01.

> **AP-FILE-PATHWAY-05**   It is the responsibility of the GUI application and the Pathway server program to successfully handle authorization of the incoming request, both from a security standpoint and a format standpoint.

PATHTCP2

The PATHTCP2 is the terminal control component of the Pathway. This program interprets the POBJCOD and POBJDIR files to run the screen interface. PATHTCP2 is the program for the TCP entity of the Pathway application.

The PATHTCP2 component is often referred to as the TCP. A GUI interface to Pathway does not utilize this component of Pathway. The screen interaction is performed by the GUI application.

The PATHTCPL library is attached to the PATHTCP2 process when it is started. If the PATHTCPL library will be modified for the application, the PATHTCP2 and PATHTCPL files are usually duplicated to an application-specific location so that any other Pathways on the system that use the PATHTCP2 and PATHTCPL code do not get the application-specific code.

AP-FILE-PATHWAY-06   If an application makes extensive use of custom code in the PATHTCPL library, duplicates of PATHTCP2 and PATHTCPL should be made and custom changes permitted only to the duplicates, which will then be used solely for the application.

RISK   Because such duplicated PATHTCP2 and PATHTCPL programs are not stored on the $SYSTEM.SYSnn subvolume, they will not automatically be updated when the sysgen process loads new HP NonStop server software.

PATHCTL

PATHCTL stores the configuration information for the Pathway environment. The Pathway can be shutdown and restarted in a WARM state to return the environment to the previous state. A COLD start initializes the PATHCTL files and it is re-configured from the PATHCOM commands used.

RISK   The Guardian user that starts the Pathway environment must have PURGE access to the PATHCTL and log files that are created during a cold start.

AP-FILE-PATHWAY-07   PATHCTL file should have the same owner and security as the userid running the Pathway.

PATHTCPL

PATHTCPL is a run-time library that is attached to the PATHTCP2 to which user-customized code can be added that will be invoked by SCOBOL routines.

RISK   Code entered into the PATHTCPL library will be invoked by the Pathway requestor. If this file is not secured, unauthorized code modifications can occur.

AP-FILE-PATHWAY-08   PATHTCPL file should have the same owner and security as the userid running the Pathway.

POBJDIR / POBJCOD

For Pathway applications running TCP terminal programs, program object files are stored in Pathway managed component files, by default called POBJCOD and POBJDIR.

SCOBOL is an interpretive language. The POBJCOD and POBJDIR contain the interpretive code. Collectively, these files are called the requestor program. The requestor object configuration is defined to Pathway as a TCLPROG parameter of the TCP entity.

> The prefix for the Pathway terminal programs can be user-defined, but the suffix is always 'COD' and 'DIR'.

The naming convention is <prefix>COD and <prefix>DIR as a matched pair. The name used for the Pathway is defined in the TCP configuration as:

```
Example:
TCLPROG \<node>.$vol.subvolume.POBJT
```

In the example above, the prefix is POBJT, so the files would be created as the POBJTCOD and POBJTDIR files.

The requestor program is accessed by the PROGRAM entity. The PROGRAM entity maintains an OWNER and SECURITY attribute. The SECURITY attribute determines whether a user running the Pathway can run the program.

AP-FILE-PATHWAY-09 The program owner should be the same as the Pathway owner.

AP-FILE-PATHWAY-10 The program security should be set as required by the application.

Server Programs

The Pathway configuration will point to user-written application server programs. Generally these programs need to be secured in relationship to the overall application security. Additional information is discussed about application in Securing Applications.

Securing Pathway Components

BP-FILE-PATHWAY-01   PATHMON should be secured "UUNU".

BP-OPSYS-OWNER-02   PATHMON should be owned by SUPER.SUPER.

BP-OPSYS-FILELOC-02   PATHMON must reside in $SYSTEM.SYSTEM.

BP-FILE-PATHWAY-02   PATHCOM should be secured "UUNU".

BP-OPSYS-OWNER-02   PATHCOM should be owned by SUPER.SUPER.

BP-OPSYS-FILELOC-02   PATHCOM must reside in $SYSTEM.SYSTEM.

BP-FILE-PATHWAY-03   PATHTCP2 should be secured "UUNU".

BP-OPSYS-OWNER-02   PATHTCP2 should be owned by SUPER.SUPER.

BP-OPSYS-FILELOC-02   PATHTCP2 must reside in $SYSTEM.SYSTEM.

BP-FILE-PATHWAY-04   PATHCTL should be secured "NUUU".

BP-OPSYS-OWNER-02   PATHCTL should be owned by the Pathway owner.

BP-OPSYS-FILELOC-02   PATHCTL should reside in $SYSTEM.SYSTEM.

BP-FILE-PATHWAY-09   PATHTCPL should be secured "UUNU".

BP-OPSYS-OWNER-02   PATHTCPL should be owned by SUPER.SUPER.

BP-PROCESS-ROUT-01 $ZLnn processes should be running.

BP-FILE-PATHWAY-05   ROUT should be secured "UUNU".

BP-OPSYS-OWNER-01   ROUT should be owned by SUPER.SUPER.

BP-OPSYS-FILELOC-01   ROUT must reside in $SYSTEM.SYSnn

If available, use Safeguard software or a third party object security product to grant access to Pathway object files to necessary personnel, and deny access to all other users.

BP-SAFE-PATHCOM-01   Add a Safeguard Protection Record to grant appropriate access to the PATHMON object file.

BP-SAFE-PATHCOM-02   Add a Safeguard Protection Record to grant appropriate access to the PATHCOM object file.

BP-SAFE-PATHCOM-03   Add a Safeguard Protection Record to grant appropriate access to the PATHTCP2 object file.

BP-SAFE-PATHCOM-04   Add a Safeguard Protection Record to grant appropriate access to the PATHCTL object file.

BP-SAFE-PATHCOM-05   Add a Safeguard Protection Record to grant appropriate access to the PATHTCPL object file.

BP-SAFE-PATHCOM-06   Update the sysgen process to duplicate PATHTCP2 and PATHTCPL to application specific locations as needed.

	Discovery Questions	Look Here:
FILE-POLICY	Is Pathway used for application interfaces?	Policy
FILE-POLICY	Are GUI Pathways requiring LINKMON run on this system?	Policy
PROCESS-ROUT-01	Are $ZLnn processes running?	Status
OPSYS-OWNER-01	Who owns the ROUT object file?	Fileinfo
OPSYS-OWNER-02	Who owns the PATHMON object file?	Fileinfo
OPSYS-OWNER-02	Who owns the PATHCOM object file?	Fileinfo

	Discovery Questions	Look Here:
OPSYS-OWNER-02	Who owns the PATHTCP2 object file?	Fileinfo
OPSYS-OWNER-02	Who owns the PATHCTL file?	Fileinfo
OPSYS-OWNER-02	Who owns the PATHTCPL object file?	Fileinfo
FILE-POLICY	Who is allowed to execute PATHMON on secure systems to start a Pathway system?	Policy
FILE-PATHWAY-01 SAFE-PATHWAY-01	Is the PATHMON object file correctly secured with the Guardian or Safeguard system?	Fileinfo Safecom
FILE-PATHWAY-02 SAFE-PATHWAY-02	Is the PATHCOM object file correctly secured with the Guardian or Safeguard system?	Fileinfo Safecom
FILE-PATHWAY-03	Is the PATHTCP2 object file secured correctly?	Fileinfo
FILE-PATHWAY-04	Is the PATHTCP2 object file duplicated to an application-specific location?	Fileinfo
FILE-PATHWAY-05	Is the PATHCTL object file secured correctly?	Fileinfo
FILE-PATHWAY-06	Is the PATHTCPL object file secured correctly?	Fileinfo
FILE-PATHWAY-07	Is the PATHTCPL object file duplicated to an application-specific location?	Fileinfo
FILE-PATHWAY-08	Is the ROUT object file secured correctly?	Fileinfo

Related Topics

User Administration

Securing Applications

PCFORMAT User Program

The PCFORMAT program converts Enscribe disk files data into other formats. Once the data is extracted and converted it can be downloaded using IXF or FTP.

The conversion format types that can be done are:

Conversion Format	Description
ASCII	Word processing programs, or any application using ASCII text lines ending with carriage return/line feed (CR/LF) pairs.
BASIC	Microsoft BASIC programs, Lotus 1-2-3, dBASE II, Knowledgeman; each database record is converted to a form acceptable to the INPUT statement of Microsoft BASIC

Conversion Format	Description
DIF	Developed by Software Arts Product Corporation and used by Lotus 1-2-3, Knowledgeman, and many others
SYLK	Developed by Microsoft Corporation for exchanging information between Multi-Tools and application programs

The COPY command of PCFORMAT converts a data file with a record structure defined by <record name> into an unstructured file named <output file> with the specified <format>.

PCFORMAT requires access to the DDL data dictionary record of the file.

RISK PCFORMAT can extract data from sensitive data files and convert it to another format, which can be put on Non HP NonStop server systems. READ access to the Enscribe file is required.

Securing PCFORMAT

BP-FILE-PCFORMAT-01   PCFORMAT should be secured "UUNU".

BP-OPSYS-OWNER-02   PCFORMAT should be owned by SUPER.SUPER.

BP-OPSYS-FILELOC-02   PCFORMAT must reside in $SYSTEM.SYSTEM.

If available, use Safeguard software or a third party object security product to grant access to PCFORMAT object files to necessary personnel, and deny access to all other users.

BP-SAFE-PCFORMAT-01   Add a Safeguard Protection Record to grant appropriate access to the PCFORMAT object file.

	Discovery Questions	Look here:
FILE-POLICY	Is there any need to use PCFORMAT conversions?	Policy
OPSYS-OWNER-02	Who owns the PCFORMAT object file?	Fileinfo
FILE-POLICY	Who is allowed to execute PCFORMAT on the system?	Policy
FILE-PCFORMAT-01 SAFE-PCFORMAT-01	Is the PCFORMAT object file correctly secured with the Guardian or Safeguard system?	Fileinfo Safecom

Related Topics

DDL

TCP/IP

PEEK System Utility

PEEK is a utility that reports statistical information maintained by the operating system. Use PEEK to monitor processor activity for system storage pools, paging activity, message information, send instructions, and interrupt conditions.

RISK PEEK is a reporting program only and does not pose any security risks.

Securing PEEK

BP-FILE-PEEK-01 PEEK should be secured "UUNU".

BP-OPSYS-LICENSE-01 PEEK must be LICENSED.

BP-OPSYS-OWNER-01 PEEK should be owned by SUPER.SUPER.

BP-OPSYS-FILELOC-01 PEEK must reside in $SYSTEM.SYSnn

	Discovery Questions	Look here:
OPSYS-OWNER-01	Who owns the PEEK object file?	Fileinfo
OPSYS-LICENSE-01	Is the PEEK object file licensed?	Fileinfo
FILE-PEEK-01	Is the PEEK object file secured correctly?	Fileinfo

Related Topics

Operating System

PING User Program

The PING program is used to test whether another host is reachable. PING sends an Internet Control Message Protocol (ICMP) echo request message to a host, expecting an ICMP echo reply to be returned. PING measures the round-trip time of the message exchange and monitors any packet loss across network paths.

PING (Packet Internet Groper). The name of a program used in the Internet to test reachability of destinations by sending them an ICMP echo request and wait-

> ing for a reply. The term has survived the original program and is now used like a verb as in, "please ping host A to see if it is alive."

RISK PING is a reporting program only and does not pose any security risks unless a virus or Trojan horse creates a "ping of death" issue.

Securing PING

BP-FILE-PING-01   PING should be secured "UUNU".

BP-OPSYS-LICENSE-01   PING must be LICENSED.

BP-OPSYS-OWNER-01   PING should be owned by SUPER.SUPER.

BP-OPSYS-FILELOC-01   PING must reside in $SYSTEM.SYSnn

	Discovery Questions	Look here:
FILE-POLICY	Is PINGing allowed from this system?	Policy
OPSYS-OWNER-01	Who owns the PING object file?	Fileinfo
OPSYS-LICENSE-01	Is the PING object file licensed?	Fileinfo
FILE-PING-01	Is the PING object file secured correctly?	Fileinfo

<u>Related Topics</u>

TCP/IP

PROGID'd Files

A process's Creator ID (CAID) is the userid of the user who initiated the process's creation.

A process's Accessor ID (PAID) identifies the process and is used to determine if the process has authority to make requests of the system such as accessing a file or stopping another process.

Normally, when a process is created, the PAID of the creator process becomes the new process's CAID and the new process adopts the PAID of its creator. So when a user starts a program, the program runs as the user of the invoking program, with that user's privileges and is able to access those resources to which that user has been granted access.

But PROGIDing the running process's object file causes the running process to take the userid of the *owner* of the program object file instead of the invoker's userid, thus gaining the owner's privileges and access to resources.

PROGID is set using the FUP System Utility program.

PROGID is the equivalent of SETUID on Unix systems.

RISK   When the PROGID attribute of a program is ON, any process created from that PROGID'd program file runs with a PAID equivalent to the program file owner's userid, *not* the PAID of the creating process.

RISK   If the PROGID'd program is owned by SUPER.SUPER, and users can run this program, the running program gains all the privileges of SUPER.SUPER.

Without a third party access control product which can grant audited access to privileged files and data, PROGID is the only way for users to perform certain tasks required by their job or another privileged userid, such as doing system backups or managing application jobs, without either being aliased to or logging on as a SUPER Group member or some other privileged userid.

Certain third party products may require that certain of their programs or library files be PROGID'd. The necessary documentation should be provided by the vendor.

RISK   When a user starts a PROGID'd program, that user temporarily gains another user's privileges without any auditing.

RISK   PROGID is particularly dangerous if the PROGID'd program has a RUN command because any processes started will also run as the owner of the PROGID program file, gaining all that PROGID'd users privileges.

RISK   The input and output files for the PROGID process are opened using the userid that set the PROGID rather than the CAID. Safeguard and Guardian disk security rules will be applied with the PROGID userid rather than the CAID.

Utilities with embedded RUN commands start the subordinate RUN programs using the PROGID userid rather than the CAID. These programs include:

EDIT

TEDIT

SCF

FUP

SAFECOM

SQLCI

ENFORM   (Can only RUN EDIT from within ENFORM)

BATCHCOM   (RUN command and users can queue up batch jobs;
    Another kind of RUN command)

PATHCOM   (Users who can ADD and START a server have a RUN
command)

RISK Without a third party Access Control Product, there is no way to prevent users from using the FUP command to PROGID an object file.

The list of allowable PROGID'd programs must be closely monitored.

Securing PROGID'd Files

Verify that there are policies in place regarding the authorization of PROGID programs and that procedures exist to evaluate the reason for the PROGID and its
function before authorizing the PROGID'd state.

There are four phases necessary to ensure that the system is not vulnerable to
unauthorized PROGID'd programs or unauthorized use of approved PROGID'd
programs:

Documentation and Authorization of PROGID'd programs.

Secure PROGID'd programs.

Controlling the PROGID command

Scheduled Review for Unauthorized PROGID'd Files

Documentation and Authorization

RISK PROGIDing in-house programs can inadvertently grant unwanted
access to application and system objects.

AP-PROGID-POLICY-01   PROGIDing in-house programs is not recommended.

AP-PROGID-POLICY-02   User's actions within programs should be track-
able to their unique userid.

3P-ACCESS-ADVICE   Third party access control products can provide access
to utilities running as appropriate Job Function or Application Owner IDs as
well as granular permission to use certain commands within the utilities. These
products also audit user actions within the utilities.

If in-house PROGID programs are used, the Corporate Security Policy and Standards should include the instructions for managing PROGID requests for in-house programs.

Create procedures to review and document all requests to PROGID programs should include:

1. The request for PROGID should include a full explanation of the program's purpose and a justification of the use.

2. The system manager or a trusted programmer must review the program's function. The reviewer should look for security requirements of the program:

   Verify that the task cannot be achieved without using PROGID.

   Verify that the owner of the PROGID'd program is appropriate for the task.

3. Management must approve the licensing in writing with approved signature(s).

4. To assure that the source code matches the actual object program, the system manager, not the developer, should compile and bind the final program.

5. The program must be tested to ensure that it does not perform or allow any actions that would be considered security violations. This test is usually performed by the Security staff.

6. The above document should be maintained in a file for future reference by auditors.

7. Requests for PROGIDing user programs may be allowed if the following conditions are met:

   a) The function is legitimate and necessary.

   b) The function cannot be achieved using other programming techniques.

Protecting Against Authorized Use

PROGID'd object files must be tightly secured to prevent security breaches.

Secure PROGID'd programs so that only authorized users can execute them.

RISK   If PROGID'd programs reside in $SYSTEM.SYSTEM or $SYSTEM.SYSnn, they will be accessible to the general user population which normally is granted EXECUTE access to the programs in these subvolumes via Safeguard SUBVOLUME Protection Records.

AP-PROGID-POLICY-03   PROGID'd programs should not reside in $SYSTEM.SYSTEM or $SYSTEM.SYSnn.

AP-PROGID-POLICY-04   PROGID'd programs should not reside in sub-volumes that do not have a Safeguard SUBVOLUME Protection record, especially those subvolumes in the PMSEARCHLIST.

PROGID'd Operating System Programs

The following tables list the allowable PROGID'd programs that may be present in the HP NonStop server operating system. According to the CUSTFILE, no HP operating system files require PROGID. However, normal practices of certain subsystems recommend that certain object files be PROGID'd.

The tables are current as of Release Version Update G06.18.

Table 1 Lists the files on the $SYSTEM volume.

PROGID'd Operating System Files on the $SYSTEM volume.		
	Program Name	**Description**
BP-OPSYS-PROGID-01	BACKUP	User program (Should never reside in $SYSTEM.SYSnn)
	RESTORE	User program (Should never reside in $SYSTEM.SYSnn)
BP-OPSYS-PROGID-02	JOB	NetBatch subsystem
	SSGCOM	HP Support interface
	ASAP	ASAP application files
BP-OPSYS-PROGID-04	BACKUP	User program (If Policy allows)
	CBEXE	DSMSCM object file
	RESTORE	User program (If Policy allows))
	TZEXE	DSMSCM object file

PROGID'd Third Party Programs

When installing third party products, the vendor may require that some of their programs or library files be PROGID'd. The necessary documentation should be provided by the vendor.

AP-PROGID-POLICY-05   The vendor of any third party product should provide guidelines for securing the PROGID'd programs included in their software packages as well as the necessary documentation of the program's usage.

Controlling Use of the PROGID Command

Safeguard software does not generate DISKFILE audits based on the PROGID OPERATION, even if the files are PROGID'd using Safeguard software instead of

FUP. This OPERATION parameter in the Safeguard Audit Layout is 'reserved for future use'.

> *RISK*   Without a third party Access Control Product, there is no way to audit the FUP SECURE, PROGID command.

With a third party access control product:

> **3P-ACCESS-PROGID-01**   Use a third party access control product to allow the users responsible for using PROGID the ability to run the command in FUP as SUPER.SUPER.

> **3P-ACCESS-PROGID-02**   Use a third party access control product to give the use of certain FUP PROGID commands to a limited group of users only.

Without a third party access control product:

The only way to audit the PROGIDing of a file is to force Safeguard software to audit all changes to a diskfile's Protection Record. To obtain the audit, all of the following must be true:

The target file must have a Safeguard DISKFILE ACL.

The AUDIT-MANAGE-PASS attribute must be a value other than NONE.

The Safeguard ALTER DISKFILE <filename>, PROGID ON command must be used.

> This method is hardly feasible, as every object program would need a DISKFILE Protection Record.

Scheduled Review for Unauthorized PROGID'd Files

Routinely monitor the system for PROGID'd object files. Catalog authorized PRO-GID'd files and monitor for unauthorized uses of PROGID.

> **BP-POLICY-PROGID-01**   Routinely monitor for unauthorized PROGID'd files.

> **BP-POLICY-PROGID-02**   Remove unauthorized PROGID'd files.

> **BP-POLICY-PROGID-03**   PROGID'd files owned by SUPER.SUPER should be closely monitored.

> **BP-POLICY-PROGID-04**   PROGID'd files should be secured correctly. Specific security requirements have been given throughout this section. If not otherwise covered, the security should be "UUCU"

BP-POLICY-PROGID-05   Control the use of the PROGID command in FUP.

	Discovery Questions	Look here:
FILE-POLICY	Are any PROGID'd files authorized on the system?	Policy
OPSYS-PROGID-01	Do any PROGID'd programs reside in $SYSTEM.SYSnn?	DSAP Fileinfo
OPSYS-PROGID-02	Do any PROGID'd programs reside in $SYSTEM.SYSTEM?	DSAP Fileinfo
OPSYS-PROGID-03	Do any PROGID'd programs reside in $SYSTEM.<svol>?	DSAP Fileinfo
OPSYS-PROGID-04	Do any PROGID'd programs reside in $<vol>.<svol>?	DSAP Fileinfo
OPSYS-OWNER-01	Are any PROGID'd programs in $SYSTEM.SYSnn owned by SUPER.SUPER	Fileinfo
OPSYS-OWNER-02	Are any PROGID'd programs in $SYSTEM.SYSTEM owned by SUPER.SUPER	Fileinfo
OPSYS-OWNER-03	Are any PROGID'd programs in $SYSTEM.<svol> owned by SUPER.SUPER	Fileinfo
OPSYS-OWNER-04	Are any PROGID'd programs in $<vol>.<svol> owned by SUPER.SUPER	Fileinfo
FILE-POLICY	Is each PROGID'd file secured against unauthorized use with either the Guardian or Safeguard system?	Fileinfo
OPSYS-PROGID-01 OPSYS-PROGID-02	The following list of files should not be PROGID'd. Are any of the following object files PROGID'd? EDIT TEDIT SCF FUP SAFECOM SQLCI ENFORM BATCHCOM PATHCOM TACL	Fileinfo Safecom
FILE-POLICY	Are policies and procedures in place to document the PROGID'd programs on the system?	Policy

	Discovery Questions	Look here:
FILE-POLICY	Are policies and procedures in place to periodically review the PROGID'd programs on the system?	Policy

Related Topics:

Securing DISKFILES With Guardian System

Securing DISKFILES With Safeguard Subsystem

FUP

PUP System Utility

The Peripheral Utility Program PUP utility functionality moved into SCF and no longer exists as a stand-alone product on G-series operating systems. This section applies to D-series operating systems only.

PUP manages disks and other peripheral devices such as terminals, printers, and magnetic tape units.

PUP supports the Subsystem Programmatic Interface (SPI) for event management only. Event management is provided by the Event Management Service (EMS).

PUP does not support the Subsystem Programmatic Interface (SPI) command/response interface. PUP cannot be controlled through programmatic commands. PUP event messages can only be retrieved and decoded.

RISK   PUP is a powerful program. If disks and peripheral devices are configured incorrectly, both applications and system programs will be affected.

AP-PUP-ADVICE-01   PUP, or the SCF PUP subsystem commands, should only be used by knowledgeable system personnel.

Securing PUP

PUP Commands With Security Implications

This section lists only the PUP commands that pose security risks. Each of these commands can affect system performance and integrity and therefore can be issued only by a member of the SUPER Group.

ALLOWOPENS

INSERT

RENAME

ALTER

LABEL

REPLACEBOOT

CHECKSUM

REVIVE

CONSOLE

LOADMICROCODE

SETCACHE

DEMOUNT

PRIMARY

SPARE

DOWN

REBUILDDFS

STOPOPENS

EJECT

UP

FORMAT

REMOVE

BP-FILE-PUP-01   PUP should be secured "UUNU".

BP-OPSYS-LICENSE-01   PUP must be LICENSED.

BP-OPSYS-OWNER-01   PUP should be owned by SUPER.SUPER.

BP-OPSYS-FILELOC-01   PUP must reside in $SYSTEM.SYSnn.

With a third party access control product:

3P-ACCESS-PUP-01   Use a third party access control product to allow the users responsible for performing commands the ability to run PUP as SUPER.SUPER.

3P-ACCESS-PUP-02   Use a third party access control product to give the use of certain PUP commands to a limited group of users only.

Without a third party access control product:

If available, use Safeguard software or a third party object security product to grant access to PUP object files to necessary personnel, and deny access to all other users.

BP-SAFE-PUP-01   Add a Safeguard Protection Record to grant appropriate access to the PUP object file.

	Discovery Questions	Look here:
OPSYS-DISCOVER-01	What is the operating system level?	TACL logon
OPSYS-OWNER-01	Who owns the PUP object file?	Fileinfo
OPSYS-LICENSE-01	Is the PUP object file licensed?	Fileinfo
FILE-POLICY	Who is allowed to execute PUP on the system?	Policy
FILE-PUP-01 SAFE-PUP-01	Is the PUP object file correctly secured with the Guardian or Safeguard system?	Fileinfo Safecom

<u>Related Topics:</u>

Operating System

SCF

NonStop RDF Subsystem

The HP NonStop Remote Database Facility (RDF) subsystem works with the TMF components of the NonStop TMF subsystem. The NonStop RDF subsystem replicates one or more local databases to a remote node. The remote database can be used for:

Disaster recovery

Planned outages

Read-only queries on the database to relieve the processing load on the local system.

NonStop RDF software is very flexible. Multiple systems can be replicated to a single system. A single system can be replicated to multiple systems. Systems can be configured as reciprocal backups for each other. It is even possible to replicate one system to two systems, which can then be synchronized to provide full NonStop RDF protection even during outages.

There are three versions of the NonStop RDF product:

1.   NonStop RDF software , RDF/MP and RDF/MPX (matured)

2. NonStop RDF/IMP software, which provides the same functionality as Non-Stop RDF, but with improved performance and on-line product initialization and triple contingency features.

3. NonStop RDF/MPX software, provides the same functionality as NonStop RDF/IMP, with the addition of network transaction support, auxillary audit trail support, and triple contingency.

RDF Components

The RDF components are (See igure 6-8):

    User Programs

    Processes

    Configuration and Control Files

    Image Files

NonStop RDF User Programs

These programs allow users to interact with the NonStop RDF subsystem:

    RDFCHEK

Figure 6-8
RDF and It's
Components

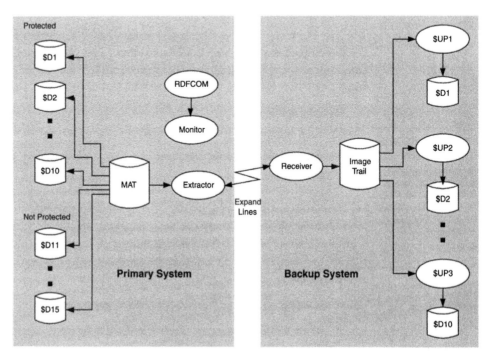

RDFCOM

RDFSCAN

RDFSNOOP

RDFCHEK

RDFCHEK is used to compare two files, subvolumes or volumes. It checks record-for-record equality along with file attribute equality. Enscribe files and SQL tables can be compared, with SQL field definitions driving the comparison—no Enscribe DDL is used.

RISK RDFCHEK is a reporting program only; it does not display any data. It poses no risks.

RDFCOM

RDFCOM is the command interpreter for the NonStop RDF subsystem. Commands are issued to the RDFCOM interface to manage, operate, and control the NonStop RDF subsystem:

Configure and control the NonStop RDF subsystem.

Display status of database activity on the primary system

Display the status of NonStop RDF processing on the backup system.

RISK RDFCOM has many potentially destructive commands, most of which can only be run by a member of the SUPER Group.

RDFSCAN

The RDFSCAN program is used to examine the RDF Log File.

RISK RDFSCAN is a reporting program only; it does not display any data. It poses no risks.

RDFSNOOP

The RDFSNOOP program is used to examine the NonStop RDF Image File records pointed to by RDF exception files.

Only members of the SUPER Group can use RDFSNOOP to READ image files.

RISK RDFSNOOP displays any data contained in the image trails.

AP-RDF-ADVICE-01 RDFSNOOP should only be EXECUTABLE by appropriate users.

NonStop RDF Processes

Five processes carry out the NonStop RDF subsystem's tasks:

Monitor Process

Extractor Process

Purger Process

Receiver Process

Updater Process

Extractor Process

The Extractor Process runs on the primary system. It reads the NonStop TMF Audit Trail which contains all database transactions that affect audited tables and files. The Audit Trail is maintained by the NonStop TMF subsystem.

The Extractor filters out transactions that aren't associated with volumes protected by the NonStop RDF subsystem and sends all the relevant audit information to an NonStop RDF Receiver Process on the backup system. These records on the backup system are called Image Records.

The object file for the Extracter Process is RDFEXTO.

Monitor Process

The Monitor Process runs on the primary system. It coordinates RDF Subsystem starts and stops, messages and NonStop SQL/MP DDL operations using the WITH SHARED ACCESS option on protected volumes, and monitors the other RDF processes.

The object file for the Monitor Process is RDFMONO.

AP-PROCESS-RDF-01   The Monitor Process must run as the same userid that issues the START RDF command.

Purger Process

The Purger Process purges image files as soon as it determines that they are no longer needed.

The object file for the Purger Process is RDFPRGO.

AP-PROCESS-RDF-02   The Purger Process must run as the same userid that issues the START RDF command.

Receiver Process

The Receiver Process runs on the backup system. It accepts the filtered audit information from the Extractor Process, sorts the information and writes it to the appropriate NonStop RDF Image Trail.

The object file for the Receiver Process is RDFRCVO.

AP-PROCESS-RDF-03   The Receiver Process must run as the same userid that issues the START RDF command.

Updater Processes

The Updater Processes run on the backup system. The object file for the Updater Process is RDFUPDO.

Each volume protected by NonStop RDF software on the primary system has its own Updater Process on the backup system. The Updater Process is responsible for applying audit data to partitions corresponding to the volume on the primary system that the Updater Process is protecting. Updates are applied directly to the specific partition, regardless of whether it is a primary or secondary partition. The NonStop RDF subsystem does not use the file system for partition mapping.

Each Updater Process reads its own Image Trail, filters out Image Records for uncommitted transactions, and sends Image Records for all committed transactions to the disk process. The disk process interprets the records and performs the logical REDO operation for each record, updating rows or records in the backup database.

Each updater performs the following functions:

Reads from the NonStop RDF image file and searches for image records associated with the updater's volume on the primary system.

Defines restart points and updates restart information in the Context File.

Sends information to RDFCOM for use in the STATUS RDF command display.

For Enscribe files only, performs the following DDL operations:

CREATE

PURGEDATA

ALTER MAXEXTENTS (used only for increasing MAXEXTENTS)

For SQL files only, the updater performs the PURGEDATA DDL operation.

The updaters are multithreaded processes. The two most prominent threads are:

Read and queue audit for submittal to the disk process.

Handle replies from the disk process and submit audit to it.

AP-PROCESS-RDF-04   The Updater Process must run as the same userid that issues the START RDF command.

Other NonStop RDF Components

The following files are created by the NonStop RDF subsystem and used by NonStop RDF processes:

NonStop RDF Configuration File
NonStop RDF Context File
NonStop RDF Log File
Image Files

Configuration File

The NonStop RDF Configuration File contains all configuration parameters set via RDFCOM. It is a relative file. The file resides on both the primary and backup nodes.

The NonStop RDF Configuration File is named $SYSTEM.<rdf-subvol>.CONFIG

Context file

The RDF Context File is maintained by the RDF processes. It contains information that tells the subsystem where each RDF process stopped.

There is a separate context file on the primary node and the backup node. On both nodes, the context file is named $SYSTEM.<rdf-subvol>.CONTEXT.

NonStop RDF Log File

The NonStop RDF subsystem writes entries to an RDF log file, and also to a log device such as a printer or console. If either the log or the device is unavailable, the messages are logged to $0 as well. RDF messages are generated when:

The NonStop RDF subsystem is initialized

The NonStop RDF subsystem is started or stopped

The NonStop RDF subsystem issues an informational, warning, or error message

A NonStop RDF process takeover occurs

Control switches from the primary to the backup database

An NonStop SQL/MP DDL operation with the WITH SHARED ACCESS option is performed

Image Files

NonStop RDF image files are unstructured files that contain logical audit record images and commit-abort records. Image files exist on the backup node. Image files exist solely for use by the NonStop RDF Receiver and Updater Processes. The files should never be explicitly opened by users for any reason, including backup to tape. Once the Receiver has processed the image file, the file is no longer needed (except in the case of Triple Contingency).

The RDFVOLUME parameter specifies which volume on the backup system will contain the receiver's master image trail.

The file naming convention for image trail files is $volume.<rdf-subvol>.AAnnnnnn, where n is a digit. For example, the first image file might be $DATA01.RDF.AA000001.

> The Image Trail is the collection of Image Files that contain NonStop RDF image data. Each NonStop RDF-protected volume on the primary system has its own Image Trail.

Interaction of NonStop RDF Components

The following table shows the access requirements of the RDF processes.

Primary System Processes

	RDFCOM	RDFMON	RDFSCAN	RDFEXT	Receiver	Updater	RDFSNOOP
Primary System							
Configuration File	RWCP	RW		RW			
Context File	RWCP	RW					
Extractor Object File		E		E			
Extractor Process	RW	RW		E			
RDFCOM Help File	R						
TMF Master Audit File	R			R			
NonStop RDF Log File	RWC	RW	R	RW	R		

Primary System Processes

	RDFCOM	RDFMON	RDFSCAN	RDFEXT	Receiver	Updater	RDFSNOOP
RDFLOCK	RW						
RDFMON Object File	E	E					
RDFMON Process	RW	E			RW		
RDFSCAN Help File			R		R		

Backup System

	RDFCOM	RDFMON	RDFSCAN	RDFEXT	Receiver	Updater	RDFSNOOP
Configuration File	RWC	RW					
Context File	RWCP	RW					
Image Files	P						
NonStop RDF Log File			R				
Receiver Process	RW	RW			RW		
RDFRCV Object File		E					
Updater Process	RW	RW					
RDFUPDO Object File		E					

Backup System Processes

	RDFCOM	RDFMON	RDFSCAN	RDFEXT	Receiver	Updater	RDFSNOOP
Primary System							
NonStop RDF Log File			R				

Backup System

	RDFCOM	RDFMON	RDFSCAN	RDFEXT	Receiver	Updater	RDFSNOOP
Configuration File	RW	R			R	R	
Context File	RW	RW			RW	RW	
Database Files						RWC[1]	
Exception Files	R					WC	R
Image Files	RWPC				RWPC	R	R
NonStop RDF Log File	RW	RW	R		RWC	RW	
RDFCOM Help File	R						

Primary System Processes

	RDFCOM	RDFMON	RDFSCAN	RDFEXT	Receiver	Updater	RDFSNOOP
RDFLOCK	RW						
RDFMON Object File	E	E					
RDFMON Process	RW						
RDFSCAN Help File			R				
Receiver Process	RW	RW				RW	
RDVRCV Object File		E			E		
Updater Processes	RW	RW			RW		
RDFUPD Object File		E					

1 The Updater process logs on as 255.255 before opening the database. CREATE (assumes presence of Safeguard software)

Securing NonStop RDF Components

BP-FILE-RDF-01 $SYSTEM.<rdf-subvol> should be secured "NUUU" unless otherwise noted

BP-OPSYS-OWNER-03 $SYSTEM.<rdf-subvol> should be owned by SUPER.SUPER.

BP-FILE-RDF-02 RDFCHECK should be secured "UUCU".

BP-OPSYS-LICENSE-02 RDFCHECK must be LICENSED.

BP-OPSYS-OWNER-02 RDFCHECK should be owned by SUPER.SUPER.

BP-OPSYS-FILELOC-02 RDFCHECK must reside in $SYSTEM.SYSTEM

BP-FILE-RDF-03 RDFCOM should be secured "UUCU".

BP-OPSYS-OWNER-02 RDFCOM should be owned by SUPER.SUPER.

BP-OPSYS-FILELOC-02 RDFCOM must reside in $SYSTEM.SYSTEM

BP-FILE-RDF-04 RDFEXTO should be secured "UUCU".

BP-OPSYS-OWNER-02 RDFEXTO should be owned by SUPER.SUPER.

BP-OPSYS-FILELOC-02 RDFEXTO must reside in $SYSTEM.SYSTEM

BP-FILE-RDF-05 RDFMONO should be secured "UUCU".

BP-OPSYS-OWNER-02 RDFMONO should be owned by SUPER.SUPER.

BP-OPSYS-FILELOC-02 RDFMONO must reside in $SYSTEM.SYSTEM

BP-FILE-RDF-06 RDFSCAN should be secured "UUCU".

BP-OPSYS-OWNER-02   RDFSCAN should be owned by SUPER.SUPER.

BP-OPSYS-FILELOC-02   RDFSCAN must reside in $SYSTEM.SYSTEM

BP-FILE-RDF-07   RDFSNOOP should be secured "UUUU".

BP-OPSYS-LICENSE-02   RDFSNOOP must be LICENSED.

BP-OPSYS-OWNER-02   RDFSNOOP should be owned by
SUPER.SUPER.

BP-OPSYS-FILELOC-02   RDFSNOOP must reside in $SYSTEM.SYSTEM

BP-FILE-RDF-08   RDFRCVO should be secured "UUCU".

BP-OPSYS-LICENSE-02   RDFRCVO must be LICENSED.

BP-OPSYS-OWNER-02   RDFRCVO should be owned by SUPER.SUPER.

BP-OPSYS-FILELOC-02   RDFRCVO must reside in $SYSTEM.SYSTEM

BP-FILE-RDF-09   RDFUPDO should be secured "UUCU".

BP-OPSYS-LICENSE-02   RDFUPDO must be LICENSED.

BP-OPSYS-OWNER-02   RDFUPDO should be owned by SUPER.SUPER.

BP-OPSYS-FILELOC-02   RDFUPDO must reside in $SYSTEM.SYSTEM

BP-FILE-RDF-10   RDF Image Files should be secured "CUCU".

BP-OPSYS-OWNER-03   RDF Image Files should be owned by
SUPER.SUPER.

BP-OPSYS-FILELOC-03   RDF Image Files reside in $<vol>.<rdf-subvol>

If available, use Safeguard software or a third party object security product to grant access to NonStop RDF components only to users who require the access in order to perform their jobs.

BP-SAFE-RDF -01   Add a Safeguard Protection Record to grant the appropriate access to the RDFCOM object file.

BP-SAFE-RDF -02   Add a Safeguard Protection Record to grant the appropriate access to the RDFMONO object file.

BP-SAFE-RDF -03   Add a Safeguard Protection Record to grant the appropriate access to the RDFSNOOP object file.

BP-SAFE-RDF -04   Add a Safeguard SUBVOLUME Protection Record to grant the appropriate access to the RDF Image Files.

RISK   Unauthorized users of NonStop RDF could copy databases with sensitive data to locations where that data could be read or manipulated.

AP-RDF-ADVICE-02   The NonStop RDF databases, whether local or remote, must be secured at the same or greater level of security than the files being backed up.

AP-RDF-ADVICE-03   The NonStop RDF databases should not be accessible to any but authorized users from on either the local or remote system.

NonStop RDF Commands with Security Implications

This section describes only the RDFCOM commands that pose security risks.

If a third party access control product is used to grant selected users access to RDFCOM running as the NonStop RDF owner the sensitive commands should only be granted to the appropriate users and denied to all others.

ADD* #

ALTER* #

COPYAUDIT* ^

DELETE* #

INITIALIZE* #

RESET* #

SET EXTRACTOR* #

SET MONITOR* #

SET RDF* #

SET RECEIVER* #

SET VOLUME* #

START RDF #

START UPDATE* #

STOP RDF*

STOP UPDATE* #

TAKEOVER* ^

UNPINAUDIT* #

VALIDATE CONFIGURATION* #

In the above list:

*The command can only be executed by a SUPER Group member.

The command can only be run on the primary system.

^ The command can only be run on the backup system.

With a third party access control product

3P-ACCESS-RDF-01   Use a third party access control product to allow the
users responsible for using NonStop RDF commands access as SUPER.SUPER.

	Discovery Questions	Look here:
FILE-POLICY	Is NonStop RDF software used on this system?	Policy
OPSYS-OWNER-02	Who owns the RDFCHEK file?	Fileinfo
OPSYS-OWNER-02	Who owns the RDFCOM file?	Fileinfo
OPSYS-OWNER-02	Who owns the RDFEXTO file?	Fileinfo
OPSYS-OWNER-02	Who owns the RDFMONO object file?	Fileinfo
OPSYS-OWNER-02	Who owns the RDFSCAN file?	Fileinfo
OPSYS-OWNER-02	Who owns the RDFCNOOP file?	Fileinfo
OPSYS-OWNER-02	Who owns the RDFRCVO file?	Fileinfo
OPSYS-OWNER-02	Who owns the RDFUPDO file?	Fileinfo
OPSYS-OWNER-03	Who owns the $SYSTEM.<rdf-subvol> files?	Fileinfo
OPSYS-LICENSE-02	Is the RDFCHEK file licensed?	Fileinfo
OPSYS-LICENSE-02	Is the RDFSNOOP file licensed?	Fileinfo
OPSYS-LICENSE-02	Is the RDFRCVO file licensed?	Fileinfo
OPSYS-LICENSE-02	Is the RDFUPDO file licensed?	Fileinfo
FILE-POLICY	Where are the NonStop RDF Image files on the system?	Fileinfo RDFCOM
FILE-RDF-02	Is the RDFCHEK file secured correctly?	Fileinfo
FILE-RDF-03 SAFE-RDF-01	Is the RDFCOM object file correctly secured with the Guardian or Safeguard system?	Fileinfo Safecom
FILE-RDF-04	Is the RDFEXTO object file secured correctly?	Fileinfo
FILE-RDF-05 SAFE-RDF-02	I Is the RDFMONO object file correctly secured with the Guardian or Safeguard system?	Fileinfo Safecom
FILE-RDF-06	Is the RDFSCAN object file secured correctly?	Fileinfo
FILE-RDF-07 SAFE-RDF-03	Is the RDFSNOOP object file correctly secured with Guardian or Safeguard?	Fileinfo Safecom
FILE-RDF-08	Is the RDFRCVO file secured correctly?	Fileinfo
FILE-RDF-09	Is the RDFUPDO file secured correctly?	Fileinfo

	Discovery Questions	Look here:
FILE-RDF-10	Are the RDF Image files secured correctly using	Fileinfo
SAFE-RDF-04	the Guardian or Safeguard system?	Safecom

Related Topics

NonStop TMF software

Securing Applications

RESTORE User Program

The RESTORE user program copies files from a tape created by BACKUP to disk and displays tape file information. This utility is essential after a disk failure or human error causes disk data to be lost.

AP-RESTORE-POLICY-01 The Corporate Security Policy and Standards should detail procedures for securing and tracking tapes in a tape library.

RISK The security of BACKUP tapes is always based on physical possession of the tape.

AP-RESTORE-POLICY-02 Each organization must have procedures to control access to BACKUP tapes that contain confidential information.

RISK If the RESTORE program is accessible to general users, files containing sensitive data could be retrieved from a tape and restored under their userid.

AP-RESTORE-POLICY-03 Since tapes can contain sensitive data, protection of the tapes and the utilities that can read or copy the data is a security risk.

RISK RESTORE is a privileged program and must be licensed to be runnable. Only SUPER.SUPER can run the program if it isn't licensed.

The RESTORE utility has three modes of operation:

File Mode

Listonly

Volume Mode

File Mode

In File Mode, RESTORE copies individual files to disk from a tape created by file-mode BACKUP.

RISK This mode selectively restores files to the disk. Files can be redirected to new locations and using the MYID option can secure the new files as the userid running RESTORE. Files restored using the userid's security could make accessible sensitive data to unauthorized users.

Listonly Mode

In LISTONLY mode, RESTORE displays information about the files on a backup tape without restoring the files to disk.

RISK This mode has no risk to the data on the tape or files on the system.

Volume Mode

In Volume Mode, RESTORE re-creates an entire disk volume from a tape that was created by a Volume Mode BACKUP. Only SUPER.SUPER can initiate a Volume Mode RESTORE.

AP-RESTORE-POLICY-03 This mode is usually performed for disaster recovery only. Only SUPER.SUPER can perform a volume mode restore.

How RESTORE Interacts With NonStop TMF Software

TMF has its own recovery mechanisms for audited files. However, BACKUP and RESTORE might be used to:

Transport audited files to another system

Archive files and retrieve files that are used infrequently

Keep old versions of files

How RESTORE treats audited files depends on whether or not NonStop TMF software was running when the BACKUP was made and when the RESTORE is performed. It also depends on whether or not the file being restored was an audited file and whether or not the file existed before the RESTORE.

RESTORE Command Used	Conditions	What RESTORE Does
No AUDITED option		Audited file is skipped
AUDITED	NonStop TMF software running	File is restored as an audited file.
AUDITED	NonStop TMF not software running	If file with same name already exists, RESTORE issues Purge Error 82. Otherwise, the file is restored non-audited, and RESTORE issues a warning message.

RESTORE Command Used	Conditions	What RESTORE Does
AUDITED and TURNOFFAUDIT	File does not already exist	File is restored non-audited.
AUDITED and TURNOFFAUDIT	File exists but is not audited	File is restored non-audited.
AUDITED and TURNOFFAUDIT	File exists and is audited	If NonStop TMF software is running, the file is restored non-audited. Otherwise, RESTORE issues Purge Error 82 and does not restore the file.

Securing RESTORE

RESTORE Commands With Security Implications

This list includes only the RESTORE commands, which pose security risks.

KEEP

MYID

NOSAFEGUARD

RISK   If the KEEP option is omitted, and the file on the disk has the same name as the restoring file, the disk file is purged during the RESTORE processing and replaced. For this to happen, the userid running the RESTORE must have purge authority to the file.

RISK   The MYID option sets the ownerid of all of the files that are being restored to that of the userid who is running RESTORE. As each file is restored, it is given the default security of the current user. Applications and operating system utilities may stop functioning because of the change of ownership and Protection Records in Safeguard software may grant or deny based upon the new ownership.

RISK   If the NOSAFEGUARD option is used, files with Safeguard security information are restored but do not retain Safeguard protection. If the option is omitted, the files retain Safeguard protection.

If a third party access control product is used to grant selected users access to RESTORE running as a privileged userid such as SUPER.SUPER or SUPER.OPERATOR, the sensitive commands should only be granted to the appropriate users and denied to all others.

BP-FILE-RESTORE-01   RESTORE should be secured "UUNU".

BP-OPSYS-LICENSE-01   RESTORE must be LICENSED.

BP-OPSYS-OWNER-01   RESTORE should be owned by SUPER.SUPER.

BP-OPSYS-FILELOC-01   RESTORE must reside in $SYSTEM.SYSnn.

If available, use Safeguard software or a third party object security product to grant access to RESTORE only to users who require access in order to perform their jobs.

BP-SAFE-RESTORE-01   Add a Safeguard Protection Record to grant appropriate access to the RESTORE object file.

Because operators frequently 'run' the backups and because operators should not have userids in the SUPER Group, the Corporate Security Policy and Standards should mandate how operators will be granted the ability to backup every file on the system. There are two basic choices: with a third party access control product and without one.

With a third party access control product:

3P-ACCESS-RESTORE-01   Use a third party access control product to allow the users responsible for performing restores the ability to run RESTORE as SUPER.SUPER.

Without a third party access control product:

AP-ADVICE-RESTORE-01   Give those users responsible for running restores EXECUTE access to a PROGID *copy* of the RESTORE utility owned by SUPER.SUPER.

RISK   Object files PROGID'd to SUPER.SUPER are a security risk because anyone executing the program can restore any file.

AP-ADVICE-RESTORE-01A   The PROGID copy of RESTORE should not reside in $SYSTEM.SYSTEM, $SYSTEM.SYSnn or any subvolume in the PMSEARCHLIST that is shared by all users so it cannot be used inadvertently.

AP-ADVICE-RESTORE-01B   The PROGID copy of RESTORE should be secured so that only users authorized to use backup tapes can execute it.

AP-ADVICE-RESTORE-02   Create a job function userid (such as OPER.BACKUP) that is used only for running BACKUP and RESTORE. Create Safeguard Protection Records to give OPER.BACKUP READ-only access to all files. Give those users responsible for running backups EXECUTE access to a PROGID *copy* of the RESTORE utility owned by OPER.BACKUP.

RISK   Anyone logged on as OPER.BACKUP has read access to every file on the system.

AP-ADVICE-RESTORE-02A   OPER.BACKUP must be treated as a privileged userid. Users should not be allowed to logon as OPER.BACKUP.

RISK This method requires a great deal of Safeguard maintenance.

AP-ADVICE-RESTORE-02B To reduce the maintenance overhead, Safeguard Protection Records granting READ access to OPER.BACKUP should be applied at the VOLUME or SUBVOLUME, rather than the DISKFILE level.

	Discovery Questions	Look here:
OPSYS-OWNER-01	Who owns the RESTORE object file?	Fileinfo
OPSYS-LICENSE-01	Is RESTORE licensed?	Fileinfo
FILE-POLICY	Who is allowed to initiate tape functions on the system?	Policy
FILE-RESTORE-01 SAFE-RESTORE-01	Is the RESTORE object file correctly secured with the Guardian or Safeguard system?	Fileinfo Safecom

Related Topics

BACKUP

RPASSWRD User Program

The RPASSWRD program is used to set or reset REMOTE PASSWORDS. Please refer to Password Administration in Part Three for a more detailed discussion on managing REMOTE PASSWORDS.

How this program is secured depends on the Security Policy and whether or not Safeguard software is in use on the systems.

RISK If a user's remote password is not correct, they will not have access to the remote system.

Without Safeguard software:

If Safeguard software is not in use on the system then the RPASSWRD program is used to change users' REMOTEPASSWORDs. The security of RPASSWRD dictates who can perform this function;

To allow only SUPER.SUPER to change remote passwords for all users, the object files EXECUTE access can be set to "-".

If users can change their own remote passwords, the object files EXECUTE access can be set to "N"

BP-FILE-RPASSWRD-01 RPASSWRD should be secured "- - ? -".

With Safeguard software:

If Safeguard software is installed on the system, REMOTE PASSWORDS should be managed through Safeguard software and only users granted the privilege of managing USER Protection Records will be able to configure or modify REMOTEPASSWORDS.

BP-FILE-RPASSWRD-01   RPASSWRD should be secured "- - - -".

Securing RPASSWRD

BP-OPSYS-LICENSE-01   RPASSWRD must be LICENSED.

BP-OPSYS-OWNER-01   RPASSWRD should be owned by SUPER.SUPER.

BP-OPSYS-FILELOC-01   RPASSWRD must reside in $SYSTEM.SYSnn.

If available, use Safeguard software or a third party object security product to grant access to RPASSWRD only to users who require it in order to perform their jobs.

BP-SAFE-RPASSWRD-01   Add a Safeguard Protection Record granting appropriate access to the RPASSWRD object file.

	Discovery Questions	Look here:
OPSYS-OWNER-01	Who owns the RPASSWRD object file?	Fileinfo
OPSYS-LICENSE-01	Is RPASSWRD licensed?	Fileinfo
FILE-POLICY	Who is allowed to change remote passwords on the system?	Policy
FILE-RPASSWRD-01 SAFE-RPASSWRD-01	Is the RPASSWRD object file correctly secured with the Guardian or Safeguard system?	Fileinfo Safecom

Related Topics

User Administration

Password

Safeguard software

Safeguard Subsystem

This section is concerned with securing the Safeguard subsystem itself. See Part 2, Configuring the Safeguard Subsystem for information on using Safeguard to secure the system.

Security Considerations of Safeguard Software Installation

There are two methods of installing Safeguard. The method determines how Safeguard software can be started and stopped once it is installed.

1. Safeguard is manually started after the system is loaded and can be stopped without stopping the system. This method requires that the Safeguard software be configured only in the CONFTEXT file for the current operating system.

    Because the Safeguard subsystem is not included in the OSIMAGE file, the SMP must be manually started.

    RISK Because Safeguard software is not automatically loaded, it is possible for the system to execute without the security rules being enforced.

2. Safeguard software is started automatically and runs continuously from the time the system is loaded until the time it is stopped. This method requires that Safeguard software be configured in the CONFTEXT file and SYSGEN run to include it in the OSIMAGE file.

    RISK If the Safeguard subsystem is included in the OSIMAGE file, it is started automatically when the system is loaded and it *cannot be stopped without stopping the system.*

    If Safeguard software is included in the OSIMAGE file or Safeguard is started as part of the CIIN file, the following precautions must be taken:

    AP-SAFE-CONFIG-01 To recover from an inadvertent security lockout without performing a tape load, keep a 'backup' OSIMAGE file in a backup SYSnn subvolume on $SYSTEM. This backup OSIMAGE file *must not include* either Safeguard software or a CIIN file.

    RISK If Safeguard software is included with system generation and AUDIT SERVICE is configured to DENY GRANTS, auditing might be suspended during the cold load and Safeguard software will deny all access attempts.

    AP-SAFE-CONFIG-02 To prevent auditing from being suspended during a system load, before shutting the system down, ensure that the current audit pool resides on a disk that is connected to the same CPU as the $SYSTEM disk. Once the Cold Load is complete, reconfigure Safeguard software to use the correct audit pool.

    Please refer to the section on Configuring AUDIT SERVICE RECOVERY Mode.

Safeguard Subsystem Components

The Safeguard Subsystem is made up of:

Safeguard Audit files

Safeguard Configuration Files

Safeguard Object Files

Safeguard Audit Files

Safeguard audit files reside in audit pools (subvolumes). These audit pools are managed using the Safeguard AUDIT POOL commands. The filecode of Safeguard audit files is 541.

The Safeguard audit file naming convention is Annnnnnn, where n is an incrementing number between 0 and 999999.

RISK   If users have WRITE or PURGE access to Safeguard audit files, they could potentially alter or delete the files to hide malicious activities.

Safeguard Configuration Files

The Safeguard configuration files are:

File	Filecode	Contents
CONFIG	545	Safeguard global settings
CONFIGA	546	Safeguard global settings, alternate key file
GUARD	542	VOLUME, SUBVOLUME and DISKFILE ACLs
LUSERID	540	Safeguard User File for Aliases
LUSERIDG	540	Safeguard User File for Aliases, alternate key file
USERID	540	User Records, for both Safeguard and non-Safeguard environments, located on $SYSTEM.SYSTEM.
USERIDAK	540	User Records, for both Safeguard and non-Safeguard environments, located on $SYSTEM.SYSTEM.
OTHER	542	Protection Records for all objecttypes other than VOLUME, SUBVOLUME, and DISKFILE

RISK   Safeguard software and only Safeguard software maintains its configuration files. If other users can alter these files, they can override company security settings.

Safeguard Object Files

The Safeguard object files are:

File	Process Name	Contents
OSMON	$ZSnn one per CPU	Security Monitor—authorizes access to protected objects and generates audits
OSMP	$ZSMP	Safeguard Manager—manages databases, performs user authentications and manages OSMON processes
SAFECOM		Safeguard Command Interpreter for Safeguard software
SAFEART		Audit record reporting tool

RISK Only SUPER.SUPER should be able to STOP, ALTPRI or START the $ZSMP process. If other users can STOP Safeguard software either the majority of users will be denied access to objects that they should be able to access or the majority of users will be granted access to objects that they should not be able to access.

RISK Only SUPER.SUPER should be able to STOP, ALTPRI or START the $ZS## processes. If other users can STOP Safeguard software either the majority of users will be denied access to objects that they should be able to access or the majority of users will be granted access to objects that should not be able to access.

Securing Safeguard Components

SAFECOM Command Commands With Security Implications

Several SAFECOM commands pose security risks:

ADD
ALTER
DELETE

If a third party access control product is used to grant selected users access to SAFECOM running as SECURITY.ADMIN or SUPER.SUPER, the sensitive commands should only be granted to the appropriate users and denied to all others.

3P-ACCESS-SAFEGUARD-01   Use a third party access control product to grant access to users responsible for using SAFECOM commands as SUPER.SUPER.

BP-FILE-SAFEGARD-01	Safeguard audit files should be secured "? - - -".
BP-OPSYS-OWNER-03	Safeguard audit files should be owned by SUPER.SUPER.
BP-OPSYS-FILELOC-03	Safeguard audit files resides in $SYSTEM.SAFE.
BP-FILE-SAFEGARD-02	CONFIG should be secured "UUUU".
BP-OPSYS-OWNER-03	CONFIG should be owned by SUPER.SUPER.
BP-OPSYS-FILELOC-03	CONFIG resides in $SYSTEM.SAFE
BP-FILE-SAFEGARD-03	CONFIGA should be secured "UUUU".
BP-OPSYS-OWNER-03	CONFIGA should be owned by SUPER.SUPER.
BP-OPSYS-FILELOC-03	CONFIGA resides in $SYSTEM.SAFE
BP-FILE-SAFEGARD-04	GUARD should be secured "UUUU".
BP-OPSYS-OWNER-03	GUARD should be owned by SUPER.SUPER.
BP-OPSYS-FILELOC-03	GUARD resides in $<volume>.SAFE
BP-FILE-SAFEGARD-05	LUSERID should be secured "- - - -".
BP-OPSYS-OWNER-03	LUSERID should be owned by SUPER.SUPER.
BP-OPSYS-FILELOC-03	LUSERID resides in $SYSTEM.SAFE
BP-FILE-SAFEGARD-06	LUSERIDG should be secured "- - - -".
BP-OPSYS-OWNER-03	LUSERIDG should be owned by SUPER.SUPER.
BP-OPSYS-FILELOC-03	LUSERIDG resides in $SYSTEM.SAFE
BP-FILE-SAFEGARD-07	OTHER should be secured "UUUU".
BP-OPSYS-OWNER-03	OTHER should be owned by SUPER.SUPER.
BP-OPSYS-FILELOC-03	OTHER resides in $SYSTEM.SAFE
BP-PROCESS-OSMP-01	The processes $ZSnn should be running.
BP-FILE-SAFEGARD-08	OSMON should be secured "UUUU".
BP-OPSYS-OWNER-01	OSMON should be owned by SUPER.SUPER.
BP-OPSYS-FILELOC-01	OSMON must reside in $SYSTEM.SYSnn.
BP-PROCESS-OSMP-01	The process $ZSMP should be running.
BP-FILE-SAFEGARD-09	OSMP should be secured "UUUU".
BP-OPSYS-LICENSE-01	OSMP must be LICENSED.
BP-OPSYS-OWNER-01	OSMP should be owned by SUPER.SUPER.
BP-OPSYS-FILELOC-01	OSMP must reside in $SYSTEM.SYSnn.
BP-FILE-SAFEGARD-10	SAFEART should be secured "UUNU".

BP-OPSYS-OWNER-01   SAFEART should be owned by SUPER.SUPER.

BP-OPSYS-FILELOC-01   SAFEART must reside in $SYSTEM.SYSnn.

BP-FILE-SAFEGARD-11   SAFECOM should be secured "UUNU".

BP-OPSYS-OWNER-01   SAFECOM should be owned by SUPER.SUPER.

BP-OPSYS-FILELOC-01   SAFECOM must reside in $SYSTEM.SYSnn.

If available, use Safeguard software or a third party object security product to grant access to Safeguard components only to users who require it in order to perform their jobs.

BP-SAFE-SAFEGARD-01   Add a Safeguard SUBVOLUME Protection Record to grant appropriate access to the $SYSTEM subvolume.

BP-SAFE-SAFEGARD-02   Add a Safeguard Protection Record to grant appropriate access to the SAFEART object file.

BP-SAFE-SAFEGARD-03   Add a Safeguard Protection Record to grant appropriate access to the SAFECOM object file.

	Discovery Questions	Look here:
FILE-POLICY	Is Safeguard software used to protect resources?	Policy
PROCESS-OSMON-01	Are the $ZSnn processes running?	Status
PROCESS-OSMP-01	Is the $ZSMP process running?	Status
OPSYS-OWNER-03	Who owns the Safeguard Audit files?	Fileinfo
OPSYS-OWNER-03	Who owns the CONFIG file?	Fileinfo
OPSYS-OWNER-03	Who owns the CONFIGA file?	Fileinfo
OPSYS-OWNER-03	Who owns the GUARD file?	Fileinfo
OPSYS-OWNER-03	Who owns the LUSERID file?	Fileinfo
OPSYS-OWNER-03	Who owns the LUSERIDG file?	Fileinfo
OPSYS-OWNER-03	Who owns the OTHER object file?	Fileinfo
OPSYS-OWNER-01	Who owns the OSMON object file?	Fileinfo
OPSYS-OWNER-01	Who owns the OSMP object file?	Fileinfo
OPSYS-OWNER-01	Who owns the SAFEART object file?	Fileinfo
OPSYS-OWNER-01	Who owns the SAFECOM object file?	Fileinfo
OPSYS-LICENSE-01	Is the OSMP object file licensed?	Fileinfo

	Discovery Questions	Look here:
FILE-SAFEGARD-01 SAFE-SAFEGARD-01	Are all Safeguard audit files correctly secured with the Guardian or Safeguard system?	Fileinfo Safecom
FILE-SAFEGARD-02	Is the CONFIG file correctly secured with the Guardian or Safeguard system?	Fileinfo Safecom
FILE-SAFEGARD-03	Is the CONFIGA file correctly secured with the Guardian or Safeguard system?	Fileinfo Safecom
FILE-SAFEGARD-04	Is the GUARD file correctly secured with the Guardian or Safeguardsystem?	Fileinfo Safecom
FILE-SAFEGARD-05	Is the LUSERID file correctly secured with the Guardian or Safeguard system?	Fileinfo Safecom
FILE-SAFEGARD-06	Is the LUSERIDG file correctly secured with the Guardian or Safeguard system?	Fileinfo Safecom
FILE-SAFEGARD-07	Is the OTHER file correctly secured with the Guardian or Safeguard system?	Fileinfo Safecom
FILE-SAFEGARD-08	Is the OSMON object file secured correctly?	Fileinfo
FILE-SAFEGARD-09	Is the OSMP object file secured correctly?	Fileinfo
FILE-SAFEGARD-10 SAFE-SAFEGUARD-02	Is the SAFEART object file correctly secured with the Guardian or Safeguard system?	Fileinfo Safecom
FILE-SAFEGARD-11 SAFE-SAFEGUARD-03	Is the SAFECOM object file correctly secured with the Guardian or Safeguard system?	Fileinfo Safecom

Related Topics

User Administration

Safeguard subsystem

Subsystem Control Facility (SCF)

The Subsystem Control Facility (SCF) is used to configure, control, and collect information about many of the HP NonStop server subsystems and their objects. Through SCF, objects such as communication lines are started or stopped. Many of the components of the HP system are controlled via SCF.

RISK   Unauthorized or erroneous use of SCF can cause the starting or stopping of system resources that may be vital to the performance of the system.

AP-ADVICE-SCF-01   SCF should only be used by system knowledgeable personnel.

Subsystems Controlled Via SCF

The subsystems under the SCF umbrella vary depending on the type of NonStop server.

On D-Series Operating Systems

On D-series operating systems, the Subsystem Control Facility (SCF) is only used to configure, control, and collect information about *data communications subsystems*. These subsystems are:

AM3270/TR3271	QIO	SNMP AGENT
ENVOY	SCP	TLAM
EXPAND	SNAX	X25AM
FOX	FTAM	
GDSX	TCPIP	
MULTILAN	OSI	
IPX/SPX	TELSERV	

On G-Series Operating Systems

With the release of G-series operating system, a great many more utilities came under the SCF umbrella. In addition to the subsystems included in D-series, the following subsystems are included in G-series operating systems:

ATM	FOX KERNEL	PUP SCL
ATP6100	MHS	SMN
CMI	NFS	SNAXHLS
COUP	NSC	STORAGE
CP6100	PAM	WAN
ENVOYACX	PTCPIP	

The default SCP process is $ZNET. If $ZNET is not running, SCF starts its own SCP process. The process stops when SCF is stopped.

SCF is made up of the following components:

SCF

SCFLIB

SCFLIBXR

SCFLIBOR

SCFTEXT

Subsystem-specific servers

SCF

SCF is the command interpreter for the Subsystem Control Facility.

SCF Custom Files

Each time a user invokes SCF, a file called SCFCSTM is invoked before the first prompt. The SCFCSTM file is an obey file that resides in each user's default sub-volume. The file can be used to customize the user's SCF environment by defining options such as function key/command associations. See *CSTM Files.

SCF LIBRARIES

The SCFLIB is the default user-library file for the SCF process. Other libraries may be configured. An SCF library can be attached to the SCF process at runtime.

SCFTEXT

The SCFTEXT file contains all the SCF help and error messages. It is a key-sequenced file.

Subsystem-specific servers

SCF has a specific server for each subsystem that it manages. These servers all reside in $SYSTEM.SYSTEM. Each 8-character object file name begins with a Z and ends in SCF, the intervening three characters identify the subsystem:

Subsystem	SCF Server	Subsystem	SCF Server
AM3270	ZAM3SCF	PTCPIP	ZTCPSCF
ATM	ZATMSCF	QIO	ZQIOSCF
ATP6100	ZATPSCF	SCL	ZSCLSCF
CP6100	ZCP6SCF	SCP	ZSCPSCF
ENVOY	ZENVSCF	SCS	ZSCSSCF
ENVOYACF	ZEXFSCF	SLSA	ZLANSCF
EXPAND	ZEXPSCF	SMN	ZSMNSCF
FOX	ZFOXSCF	SNAX	ZSX1SCF

Subsystem	SCF Server	Subsystem	SCF Server
GDS	ZGDSSCF	SNAXAPC	ZAPCSCF
IPXSPX	ZIPXSCF	SNAXCRE	ZCRESCF
KERNEL	ZKRNSCF	SNAXHLS	ZHLSSCF
MHS	ZMHSSCF	SNMP	ZSMPSCF
NFS	ZNFSSCF	STORAGE	ZSTOSCF
NSC	ZNSCSCF	TCPIP	ZTCISCF
NSIM	ZNIMSCF	TDMTALK	ZTLKSCF
OSIAPLMG	ZOSASCF	TELSERV	ZTNTSCF
OSIAS	ZOSISCF	TR3271	ZTR3SCF
OSIFTAM	ZOSFSCF	TSIMS	ZSIMSCF
OSITS	ZOS4SCF	WAN	ZWANSCF
OSS	ZPOSSCF	X25AM	ZX25SCF
PAM	ZPAMSCF		

Securing SCF Components

BP-FILE-SCF-01   SCF should be secured "UUNU".

BP-OPSYS-OWNER-02   SCF should be owned by SUPER.SUPER.

BP-OPSYS-FILELOC-02   SCF must reside in $SYSTEM.SYSTEM.

BP-FILE-SCF-02   SCFLIB should be secured "NUNU".

BP-OPSYS-OWNER-02   SCFLIB should be owned by SUPER.SUPER.

BP-OPSYS-FILELOC-02   SCFLIB must reside in $SYSTEM.SYSTEM.

BP-FILE-SCF-03   SCFLIBOR should be secured "NUNU".

BP-OPSYS-LICENSE-02   SCFLIBOR must be LICENSED.

BP-OPSYS-OWNER-02   SCFLIBOR should be owned by SUPER.SUPER.

BP-OPSYS-FILELOC-02   SCFLIBOR must reside in $SYSTEM.SYSTEM.

BP-FILE-SCF-04   SCFLIBXR should be secured "NUNU".

BP-OPSYS-LICENSE-02   SCFLIBXR must be LICENSED.

BP-OPSYS-OWNER-02   SCFLIBXR should be owned by SUPER.SUPER.

BP-OPSYS-FILELOC-02   SCFLIBXR must reside in $SYSTEM.SYSTEM.

BP-FILE-SCF-05   SCFTEXT should be secured "NUUU".

BP-OPSYS-OWNER-02   SCFTEXT should be owned by SUPER.SUPER.

BP-OPSYS-FILELOC-02   SCFTEXT must reside in $SYSTEM.SYSTEM.

BP-FILE-SCF-06   Z???SCF should be secured "UUNU". (one of subsystem specific servers from the list above)

BP-OPSYS-OWNER-02   Z???SCF should be owned by SUPER.SUPER.

BP-OPSYS-FILELOC-02   Z???SCF reside in $SYSTEM.SYSTEM.

If available, use Safeguard software or a third party object security product to grant access to the SCF components only to users who require access in order to perform their jobs.

BP-SAFE-SCF-01   Add a Safeguard Protection Record to grant appropriate access to the SCF object files.

SCF Commands with Security Implications

SCF processes commands differently, depending on the target subsystem:

If a command is entered that relates only to SCF rather than a subsystem, SCF carries out the required actions.

If a command involving a subsystem is entered, SCF performs syntax checking and validates the object type and object name, then forwards the command to the appropriate subsystem. The subsystem product then validates the command again and translates it into a formatted message for SCP, which then communicates with the appropriate subsystem to perform the specified task.

This list includes only the SCF commands that pose security risks.

ABORT*
ACTIVATE*
ADD*
ALLOCATE*
ALLOWOPENS*
ALTER*
BOOT*
CHECK*
CONNECT*
CONTROL*
COPY*

DELETE*

DIAGNOSE*

DISCONNECT*

DUMP*

INITIALIZE*

LOAD*

MOVE*

PRIMARY*

RELEASE*

RENAME*

REPLACE*

RESET*

RUN

SAVE*

START*

STOP*

STOPOPENS*

SUSPEND*

SWITCH*

TELL*

TRACE*

VERIFY*

Commands marked with an asterisk (*) above, can only be executed by A SUPER Group member

The subsystem owner, i.e. user who started it

A member of the subsystem owner's group

RISK   Indiscriminate use of the DELAY command can have a detrimental effect on the time it takes to process a command file. The DELAY command is intended for use with subsystems that require completion of a command before another can occur and it is possible that SCF may get a 'command completed' message before the command has actually completed.

RISK   Any program started with the SCF RUN command will run as the userid that started the SCF session.

If a third party access control product is used to grant selected users access to SCF running as a SUPER Group member, or a member of a subsystem owners' groups, the sensitive commands should only be granted to the appropriate users and denied to all others.

3P-ACCESS-SCF-01   Use a third party access control product to allow the users responsible for using SCF access to commands as SUPER.SUPER.

	Discovery Questions	Look here:
OPSYS-OWNER-02	Who owns the SCF object file?	Fileinfo
OPSYS-OWNER-02	Who owns the SCFLIB object files?	Fileinfo
OPSYS-OWNER-02	Who owns the SCFLIBOR object files?	Fileinfo
OPSYS-OWNER-02	Who owns the SCFLIBXR object files?	Fileinfo
OPSYS-OWNER-02	Who owns the SCFTEXT object file?	Fileinfo
OPSYS-OWNER-02	Who owns the Z???SCF object file?	Fileinfo
OPSYS-LICENSE-02	Is the SCFLIBOR object file licensed?	Fileinfo
OPSYS-LICENSE-02	Is the SCFLIBXR object file licensed?	Fileinfo
FILE-POLICY	Who is allowed to perform SCF functions on the system?	Policy
FILE-SCF-01 SAFE-SCF-01	Is the SCF object file correctly secured with the Guardian or Safeguard system?	Fileinfo Safecom
FILE-SCF-02	Is the SCFLIB object file secured correctly?	Fileinfo
FILE-SCF-03	Is the SCFLIBOR object file secured correctly?	Fileinfo
FILE-SCF-04	Is the SCFLIBXR object file secured correctly?	Fileinfo
FILE-SCF-05	Is the SCFTEXT file secured correctly?	Fileinfo
FILE-SCF-06	Are the Z???SCF object files secured correctly?	Fileinfo

Related Topics

Operating System
DSMSCM

Subsystem Control Point (SCP)

SCP stands for the Subsystem Control Point. SCP is a part of the DSM architecture. The SCP process is a central point through which management applications and subsystems exchange Subsystem Programmatic Interface (SPI) messages

Management processes send SPI messages to an SCP process, which routes each message to a specified subsystem process. Subsystems return response messages to the SCP process, which sends each response to the originator of the corresponding request.

The SPI standard definitions are provided by HP in files of source declarations in DDL and in the programming languages that support Distributed Systems Management (TAL, C, Pascal, COBOL85, and TACL). They consist of six definition files—one in each language plus the DDL definition file.

RISK   If SCP is not active, SPI messages will not function properly.

SCP is made up of the following components:

SCP

SCPTC

SCPTCOL

SCP

An SCP trace creates a record of an object's activity, such as messages sent and received by SCP. Traces are initiated by the subsystem communicating with SCP, but SCP starts and initializes the collector process that receives the trace records.

SCP is generally run as the process $ZNET.

A tracing environment consists of:

The trace procedure called by the tracing process

The extended data segment to which the trace data is written

A disk file for recording the trace records

A collector process that copies trace data from the extended data segment into the disk file.

SCPTC and SCPTCOL

SCPTC and SCPTCOL are trace collectors.

The older SCP Trace-Collector object file is SCPTC.

The newer SCP Trace-Collector object file is SCPTCOL.

RISK   SCP will not function properly unless the SCPTC and SCPTCOL object files both reside in the same subvolume as SCP and have the same software release version as the SCP object file.

Securing SCP Components

BP-PROCESS-SCP-01 $ZNET process should be running.

BP-FILE-SCP-01   SCP should be secured "UUNU".

BP-OPSYS-LICENSE-01   SCP must be LICENSED.

BP-OPSYS-OWNER-01   SCP should be owned by SUPER.SUPER.

BP-OPSYS-FILELOC-01   SCP must reside in $SYSTEM.SYSnn

BP-FILE-SCP-02   SCPTC should be secured "UUCU".

BP-OPSYS-LICENSE-01   SCPTC must be LICENSED.

BP-OPSYS-OWNER-01   SCPTC should be owned by SUPER.SUPER.

BP-OPSYS-FILELOC-01   SCPTC must reside in $SYSTEM.SYSnn

BP-FILE-SCP-03   SCPTCOL should be secured "UUCU".

BP-OPSYS-LICENSE-01   SCPTCOL must be LICENSED.

BP-OPSYS-OWNER-01   SCPTCOL should be owned by SUPER.SUPER.

BP-OPSYS-FILELOC-01   SCPTCOL must reside in $SYSTEM.SYSnn

If available, use Safeguard software or a third party object security product to grant access to SCP only to users who require it in order to perform their jobs.

BP-SAFE-SCP-01   Add a Safeguard Protection Record to grant appropriate access to the SCP object file.

BP-SAFE-SCP-02   Add a Safeguard Protection Record to grant appropriate access to the SCPTC object file.

BP-SAFE-SCP-03   Add a Safeguard Protection Record to grant appropriate access to the SCPTCOL object file.

	Discovery Questions	Look here:
PROCESS-SCP-01	Is the $ZNET process running?	Status
OPSYS-OWNER-01	Who owns the SCP object file?	Fileinfo
OPSYS-OWNER-01	Who owns the SCPTC object file?	Fileinfo
OPSYS-OWNER-01	Who owns the SCPTCOL object file?	Fileinfo
OPSYS-LICENSE-01	Is the SCP object file licensed?	Fileinfo
OPSYS-LICENSE-01	Is the SCPTC object file licensed?	Fileinfo
OPSYS-LICENSE-01	Is the SCPTCOL object file licensed?	Fileinfo
FILE-POLICY	Who is allowed to run SCP on the system?	Policy

	Discovery Questions	Look here:
FILE-SCP-01 SAFE-SCP-01	Is the SCP object file correctly secured with the Guardian or Safeguard system?	Fileinfo Safecom
FILE-SCP-02	Is the SCPTC object file secured correctly?	Fileinfo
FILE-SCP-03	Is the SCPTCOL object file secured correctly?	Fileinfo

<u>Related Topics</u>

SCF

SEEVIEW User Program

The SEEVIEW product provides multi-windowed capability to 6500-series terminals. SEEVIEW allows the user to view several windows simultaneously, similar to a PC workstation environment. SEEVIEW is only applicable for 65xx terminals. SEEVIEW is not necessary for environments without 6500-series terminal access.

RISK   SEEVIEW is a tool and creates no extra risk. If a user can run an application in one session, then running multiple sessions incurs no risk to the system.

The components of SEEVIEW are:

SEEDIT
SEEGATE
SEELOCL/SEECSTM
SEENET
SEESHELL
SEEVIEW
SEEVIEWS

Securing SEEVIEW

BP-FILE-SEEVIEW–01   SEEVIEW should be secured "UUNU".

BP-OPSYS-OWNER-02   SEEVIEW should be owned by SUPER.SUPER.

BP-OPSYS-FILELOC-02   SEEVIEW must reside in $SYSTEM.SYSTEM.

BP-FILE-SEEVIEW–02   SEESHELL should be secured "NUNU".

BP-OPSYS-OWNER-02   SEESHELL should be owned by SUPER.SUPER.

BP-OPSYS-FILELOC-02   SEESHELL must reside in $SYSTEM.SYSTEM.

BP-FILE-SEEVIEW–03   SEEDIT should be secured "UUNU".

BP-OPSYS-OWNER-02   SEEDIT should be owned by SUPER.SUPER.

BP-OPSYS-FILELOC-02   SEEDIT must reside in $SYSTEM.SYSTEM.

BP-FILE-SEEVIEW–04   SEEGATE should be secured "NUNU".

BP-OPSYS-OWNER-02   SEEGATE should be owned by SUPER.SUPER.

BP-OPSYS-FILELOC-02   SEEGATE must reside in $SYSTEM.SYSTEM.

BP-FILE-SEEVIEW–05   SEELOCL should be secured "NUNU".

BP-OPSYS-OWNER-02   SEELOCL should be owned by SUPER.SUPER.

BP-OPSYS-FILELOC-02   SEELOCL must reside in $SYSTEM.SYSTEM.

BP-FILE-SEEVIEW–06   SEENET should be secured "NUNU".

BP-OPSYS-OWNER-02   SEENET should be owned by SUPER.SUPER.

BP-OPSYS-FILELOC-02   SEENET must reside in $SYSTEM.SYSTEM.

BP-FILE-SEEVIEW–07   SEEVIEWS should be secured "NUNU".

BP-OPSYS-OWNER-02   SEEVIEWS should be owned by SUPER.SUPER.

BP-OPSYS-FILELOC-02   SEEVIEWS must reside in $SYSTEM.SYSTEM.

	Discovery Questions	Look Here:
FILE-POLICY	Are users allowed to use SEEVIEW on their 6500 series terminals?	Policy
OPSYS-OWNER-02	Who owns the SEEVIEW object file?	Fileinfo
OPSYS-OWNER-02	Who owns the SEESHELL object file?	Fileinfo
OPSYS-OWNER-02	Who owns the SEEDIT object file?	Fileinfo
OPSYS-OWNER-02	Who owns the SEEGATE object file?	Fileinfo
OPSYS-OWNER-02	Who owns the SEELOCL object file?	Fileinfo
OPSYS-OWNER-02	Who owns the SEENET object file?	Fileinfo
OPSYS-OWNER-02	Who owns the SEEVIEWS object file?	Fileinfo
FILE-SEEVIEW-01	Is the SEEVIEW object file secured correctly?	Fileinfo
FILE-SEEVIEW-02	Is the SEESHELL object file secured correctly?	Fileinfo
FILE-SEEVIEW-03	Is the SEEDIT object file secured correctly?	Fileinfo
FILE-SEEVIEW-04	Is the SEEGATE object file secured correctly?	Fileinfo

	Discovery Questions	Look Here:
FILE-SEEVIEW-05	Is the SEELOCL object file secured correctly?	Fileinfo
FILE-SEEVIEW-06	Is the SEENET object file secured correctly?	Fileinfo
FILE-SEEVIEW-07	Is the SEEVIEWS object file secured correctly?	Fileinfo

SERVICES Configuration File

The SERVICES file contains information on the known services available on the Internet.

When LISTNER starts, it reads the SERVICES file to resolve the services configured in the PORTCONF file, and checks that the service name and corresponding port are valid. Once the accuracy of the PORTCONF file content is verified against the SERVICES file, the LISTNER process listens to the configured ports, waiting for incoming connection requests from remote clients.

Additionally, the HOSTS file maintains the list of host IP addresses. It is likewise consulted for HOST address information.

RISK   LISTNER resolves services configured in PORTCONF. If the services are not configured properly, programs such as FTP will not function.

RISK   There may be more than one SERVICES and HOSTS file active for separate LISTNER processes. If more than one is used, it can become confusing, because it is sometimes difficult to determine which LISTNER is using which file.

Securing SERVICES/HOSTS Files

BP-FILE-SERVICES-01   SERVICES should be secured "NUUU".

BP-OPSYS-OWNER-03   SERVICES should be owned by SUPER.SUPER.

BP-OPSYS-FILELOC-03   SERVICES resides in $SYSTEM.ZTCPIP

BP-FILE-HOSTS-01   HOSTS should be secured "NUUU".

BP-OPSYS-OWNER-03   HOSTS should be owned by SUPER.SUPER.

BP-OPSYS-FILELOC-03   HOSTS resides in $SYSTEM.ZTCPIP

If available, use Safeguard software or a third party object security product to grant access to SERVICES only to users who require it in order to perform their jobs.

BP-SAFE-SERVICES-01   Add a Safeguard Protection Record to grant appropriate access to the SERVICES file.

BP-SAFE-HOSTS-01   Add a Safeguard Protection Record to grant appropriate access to the HOSTS file.

	Discovery Questions	Look here:
FILE-POLICY	Who is allowed to modify the HOSTS and SERVICES file?	Policy
OPSYS-OWNER-03	Who owns the SERVICES object file?	Fileinfo
OPSYS-OWNER-03	Who owns the HOSTS object file?	Fileinfo
FILE-SERVICES-01 SAFE-SERVICES-01	Is the SERVICES file correctly secured with the Guardian or Safeguard system?	Fileinfo Safecom
FILE-HOSTS-01 SAFE-HOSTS-01	Is the HOSTS file correctly secured with the Guardian or Safeguard system?	Fileinfo Safecom

SORT Subsystem

The sorting function for an HP NonStop server is called FastSort. FastSort is the sort-merge utility and can sort or merge records from one or more input sources:

A sort operation arranges and combines one or more sets of input records into a single set of output records. During a sort operation, FastSort arranges the records in either ascending or descending order, or in a combination of both based on a sequence of key-field values.

A merge operation combines two or more sets of sorted input records into a single set of output records. The records for merging are already sorted in an ascending or descending sequence of key-field values.

FastSort accepts records to sort or merge from these input sources:

1 to 32 disk files

A terminal

An application process

Tape files

RISK   FastSort requires read access from the input sources. If an input source is a disk or tape file containing sensitive data, the output of FastSort could allow unauthorized access to the data.

The components of FastSort are:

RECGEN

SORT

SORTPROG

RECGEN

RECGEN is the record generator process for the parallel creation and loading of partitioned indexes, if NonStop SQL/MP database is installed on the system.

The RECGEN processes read the rows of the base NonStop SQL/MP table. SORTPROG processes the generated rows and writes them to the partitions of the index. RECGEN is invoked implicitly by NonStop SQL/MP database as required.

SORT

SORT is the interactive conversational interface to SORTPROG. SORT can only be used by a user with READ access to an input source. The following describes the source and target specifications for SORT:

FROM   Specifies the name of an input source for a sort or merge run and the exclusion mode to use to open the file, the maximum number of records in the file, the maximum length of records in the file, and whether the records in the file are already sorted.

TO   Specifies an output file for a sort run and parameters for the file including the percentage of data and index slack, whether FastSort should purge and recreate an existing output file, and the type of sort run (record, permutation, or key sort).

RISK   SORT does not have inherent risks. The user must have read access to the input source. More risk may be placed upon input tapes that may contain sensitive data not accessible via disk files.

RISK   SORT has a performance risk if not controlled.

AP-ADVICE-SORT-01   It may be desirable to limit interactive sorts, allowing sorts of application data files to be controlled via application processes.

SORTPROG

The SORTPROG process performs all sort or merge operations. It is initiated interactively from the SORT process or via application requests, however, it runs separately from the application process or the interactive SORT process. To configure and start a SORTPROG process, either:

Issue FastSort interactive commands

Call FastSort system procedures

Products that invoke FastSort systematically:

Application languages invoke sorts via system procedures calls

CROSSREF program sorts a cross-reference listing

ENFORM Database Manager sorts records for a report

File Utility Program (FUP) sorts to loads data into a file

NonStop SQL/MP database sorts entries in a query

NonStop SQL/MP database sorts data to load into a table or index

Peripheral Utility Program (PUP) sorts entries in the free-space table

NonStop TMF software sorts audit trail information

RISK   Although SORTPROG performs the actual sort, no risk is attached to the actual sorting process. SORTPROG must be available to the general users and application for requested sort functions. Any risk associated with sorting is associated with the interactive SORT interface.

AP-ADVICE-SORT-02   Since FastSort is invoked from many subsystems, it is not recommended that a Safeguard protection Record be created that does not include everyone.

Securing SORT Components

BP-FILE-SORT-01   RECGEN should be secured "UUNU".

BP-OPSYS-OWNER-01   RECGEN should be owned by SUPER.SUPER.

BP-OPSYS-FILELOC-01   RECGEN must reside in $SYSTEM.SYSnn.

BP-FILE-SORT-02   SORT should be secured "UUNU".

BP-OPSYS-OWNER-01   SORT should be owned by SUPER.SUPER.

BP-OPSYS-FILELOC-01   SORT must reside in $SYSTEM.SYSnn.

BP-FILE-SORT-03   SORTPROG should be secured "UUNU".

BP-OPSYS-LICENSE-01   SORTPROG must be LICENSED.

BP-OPSYS-OWNER-01   SORTPROG should be owned by SUPER.SUPER.

BP-OPSYS-FILELOC-01   SORTPROG must reside in $SYSTEM.SYSnn.

	Discovery Questions	Look here:
OPSYS-OWNER-01	Who owns the RECGEN object file?	Fileinfo
OPSYS-OWNER-01	Who owns the SORT object file?	Fileinfo
OPSYS-OWNER-01	Who owns the SORTPROG object file?	Fileinfo
OPSYS-LICENSE-01	Is SORTPROG object file licensed?	Fileinfo
FILE-SORT-01	Is the RECGEN object file secured correctly?	Fileinfo
FILE-SORT-02	Is the SORT object file secured correctly?	Fileinfo
FILE-SORT-03	Is the SORTPROG object file secured correctly?	Fileinfo

Related Topics

Securing Applications

Subsystem Programmatic Interface (SPI)

The Subsystem Programmatic Interface (SPI) is the path by which management applications and subsystems exchange command-response messages and event messages.

SPI is designed to allow programmatic management of subsystem objects. An object is a logical or physical entity such as a device, a communications line, logical subdevice, process, processor, file, or transaction. Most objects are controlled by subsystems, and a subsystem itself can be treated as an object.

Normally, subsystem objects are controlled by an HP-supplied management interface that has commands to configure, control, monitor, and report the status of subsystem objects. For example, TMFCOM interfaces with NonStop TMF software to perform these functions.

For third party products and user-written utilities, the SPI interface provides a mechanism to send and receive this level of interaction to HP subsystems programmatically.

For example:

Start or stop an object (such as a Pathway terminal)

Change an object attribute value (such as the speed of a communications line)

Add a new object to the system (such as defining a logical subdevice on a communications line)

Inquire whether an object is stopped or running

AP-ADVICE-SPI-01   User-written programs and third party tools can provide mechanisms to perform both helpful and damaging commands to vital subsystems. These programs and tools must be secured in the same manner as their HP-supplied interface counterpart.

AP-ADVICE-SPI-02   User-written programs and third party tools that provide an interface to modify subsystems, such as downing a line, or bringing up a Pathway terminal should be documented as part of the Corporate Security Policy.

SPI Components

SPI messages have a common structure. Each message has a message header followed by as many tokens as are necessary to convey the relevant information.

A standard message format and protocol

A standard unit of information

The token Procedures for composing and decoding messages

Data definitions for commonly used data structures

Rules and guidelines governing message content and protocol

There are two types of SPI messages:

EMS messages

Control and inquiry messages

Tokens are self-identifying data items. A token's name usually indicates its function or the information contained in the token.

The primary SPI Subsystem components of concern to the Security staff are the contents of the Definition Files.

Definition Files

A set of files containing data declarations for items related to SPI messages and their processing. The core definitions required to use SPI are provided in a DDL file and in several language-specific definition files, one for each programming language that supports SPI. The DDL compiler generates the language-specific files from the DDL file. Subsystems that support SPI provide additional definition files containing subsystem-specific definitions.

The Definition Files typically reside in the $SYSTEM.ZSPIDEF, $SYSTEM.ZSPIEXAM and $SYSTEM.ZSPISEGF subvolumes.

SPI Standard Definitions & Libraries

The standard definitions are available for use with the SPI procedures regardless of the subsystem. There is also a set of subsystem-specific declarations for each subsystem and some sets of declarations that apply to multiple subsystems. An application using SPI needs the SPI standard definitions and also the subsystem definitions for all subsystems with which it communicates.

Securing SPI Components

BP-FILE-SPI-01   ZSPIDEF.* files should be secured "NUUU".

BP-OPSYS-OWNER-03   ZSPIDEF.* files owned by SUPER.SUPER.

BP-OPSYS-FILELOC-03   ZSPIDEF.* files reside in $SYSTEM.ZSPIDEF

BP-FILE-SPI-02   ZSPIEXAM.* files should be secured "NUUU".

BP-OPSYS-OWNER-03   ZSPIEXAM.* files owned by SUPER.SUPER.

BP-OPSYS-FILELOC-03   ZSPIEXAM.* files reside in $SYSTEM.ZSPIEXAM

BP-FILE-SPI-03   ZSPISEGF.* files should be secured "NUUU".

BP-OPSYS-OWNER-03   ZSPISEGF.* files owned by SUPER.SUPER.

BP-OPSYS-FILELOC-03   ZSPISEGF.* files reside in $SYSTEM.ZSPISEGF

If available, use Safeguard software or a third party object security product to grant access to the ZSPIDEF, ZSPIEXAM, and ZSPISEGF subvolumes only to users who require access in order to perform their jobs.

BP-SAFE-SPI-01 TO 03   Add Safeguard SUBVOLUME Protection Records to grant appropriate access to the SPI subvolumes.

	Discovery Questions	Look here:
FILE-POLICY	Is there a Corporate Security Policy in regards to programmatic interface to SPI manipulation of HP subsystems?	Policy
FILE-POLICY	Is there a Corporate Security Policy to review the SPI commands used by programmatic interfaces?	Policy
OPSYS-OWNER-03	Who owns the $SYSTEM.ZSPIDEF files?	Fileinfo

	Discovery Questions	Look here:
OPSYS-OWNER-03	Who owns the $SYSTEM.ZSPIEXAM files?	Fileinfo
OPSYS-OWNER-03	Who owns the $SYSTEM.ZSPISEGF files?	Fileinfo
FILE-SPI-01	Are all files in the $SYSTEM.ZSPIDEF subvolume secured correctly?	Fileinfo
SAFE-SPI-01	Are all files in the $SYSTEM.ZSPIDEF subvolume secured with an equivalent Safeguard SUBVOLUME Protection Record?	Safecom
FILE-SPI-02	Are all files in the $SYSTEM.ZSPIEXAM subvolume secured correctly?	Fileinfo
SAFE-SPI-02	Are all files in the $SYSTEM.ZSPIEXAM subvolume secured with an equivalent Safeguard SUBVOLUME Protection Record?	Safecom
FILE-SPI-03	Are all files in the $SYSTEM.ZSPISEGF subvolume secured correctly?	Fileinfo
SAFE-SPI-03	Are all files in the $SYSTEM.ZSPISEGF subvolume secured with an equivalent Safeguard SUBVOLUME Protection Record?	Safecom

Related Topics

Securing Applications

Spooler Subsystem

The HP NonStop server SpoolerPlus Subsystem is a set of utilities that presents an interface between users and applications and the print devices of a system. The Spooler receives output from applications and stores it on disk. This output can be a report in EDIT format, a compiled listing, or any other data. The data stays on disk and can reviewed before printing. If directed to a print location, when the designated print device becomes available, the output is printed.

RISK   Printed output is an important way that data is reported. It may also provide unwanted access to sensitive data and can be easily distributed to non-authorized personnel.

AP-ADVICE-SPOOLER-01   The Corporate Security Policy should detail procedures for the physical security of printers and printer output.

Spooler Subsystem Components

The Spooler is made up of the following components (See Figure 6-9):

    Collectors

    FONT Utility

    PERUSE

    Print Processes

    RP Setup Utility

    SPOOLCOM

    Supervisors

    Spooler Data Files

Figure 6-9
SPOOLER
Subsystem
Components

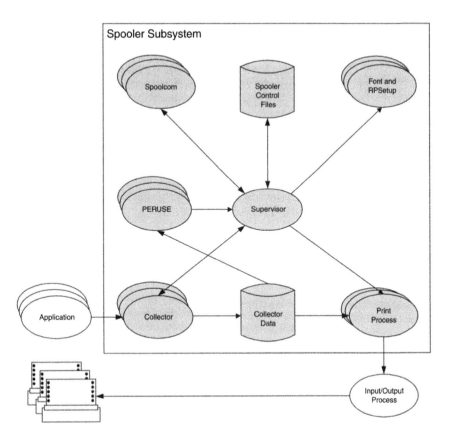

Collectors

Collector processes accept output from applications and store it on disk. There can be up to 15 collectors associated with a given Spooler. Collectors are run in non-stop pairs. The spooler collector object file is $SYSTEM.SYSTEM.CSPOOL. The typical default collector process name is $S.

Applications direct output to a collector by treating the collector as an OUT file.

```
TGAL / IN <file>, OUT $S /
```

An application can open a file to any collector and begin writing its output using the Guardian file system WRITE[X] procedure. Applications can also use the spooler interface procedures to spool their output.

FONT

The FONT utility is used to create FONT jobs. Font job descriptions are created in an EDIT file, called a script file, and then the Font utility is used to configure the selected spooler locations with the indicated font jobs.

Script Files contain commands that can be sent to a printer to control such features as character sets, vertical forms-control specifications, or compressed printing. Such files frequently contain both printable and nonprintable text, but the Font utility makes it possible to enter all font descriptions in plain text; no nonprintable characters are used.

PERUSE

PERUSE is an interactive program that enables users to examine jobs and their attributes while in the spooler subsystem. With PERUSE it is possible to:

View job contents

Display a job while it is being spooled

Monitor changes in job status

Alter job attributes

Redirect jobs to a print location

Copy a job from the spooler queue to an EDIT file or a spooler job file

Copy a spooler job file to the spooler queue

Link/unlink jobs to batches

The internal PERUSE security is as follows:

Users can view and manipulate only their own jobs.

The job creator can always access the job.

A Group Manager can view or manipulate all jobs belonging to that manager's group members.

SUPER Group members can view and manipulate all jobs, regardless of ownership.

RISK Any user with PERUSE access to a job has access to the job output's contents.

PERUSE Commands with Security Implications

This section describes only the PERUSE commands which pose security risks.

BATCH
DEV
FORM
JOB
LINK
LIST*
LOC
OPEN
PURGE
REPORT
UNLINK

RISK The LIST command displays or prints the job output. If the output contains sensitive data, that data is at risk of exposure.

If a third party access control product is used to grant selected users access to PERUSE running as a SUPER Group member or another privileged userid (such as the userid that owns application jobs), access to the sensitive commands should only be granted to the appropriate users and denied to all others.

Print Processes

Print processes retrieve the output stored on disk by a collector and print it to a device. There are multiple print processes. Each print device in the Spooler Subsystem has a print process associated with it.

FASTP

FASTP is the print process that ships with the Spooler. The FASTP print process uses a configuration file named FASTCNFG.

> *RISK*   A FASTCNFG file usually contains information that should not be accessible to all users.

> **AP-ADVICE-SPOOLER-02**   FASTCNFG must be secured for READ access by the FASTP print process only.

RPSETUP Utility

The RPSetup utility configures cross-spooler connections between spoolers in a network allowing users access to printers on remote nodes. The utility makes it possible for print jobs from local applications to be sent to a remote spooler and queued for printing on remote printers.

> *RISK*   Allowing print jobs to be networked may reduce the amount of physical security over the printed materials.

SPOOLCOM

SPOOLCOM is the command interpreter for the Spooler Subsystem. It is used to:

Display the status of collectors.

Display the status of devices.

Display the status of jobs.

Display the status of print processes.

Display the status of the routing structure.

Display the status of the spooler itself.

Change the location, state or any other attribute of a job.

Delete jobs.

Restart devices that have gone offline because of device errors.

SPOOLCOM Commands with Security Implications

This section describes only the SPOOLCOM commands that pose security risks.

BATCH*

COLLECT

DEV*

FONT
JOB*
LOC
OPEN
PRINT
SPOOLER

The commands marked with an asterisk (*) can be used by job owners to alter their own jobs. Members of the SUPER Group can modify any user's jobs.

All users can use the STATUS subcommand to obtain information about Collectors, Devices, Font Jobs, Locations, Printers and Spooler Supervisors, but only members of the SUPER Group can alter the configuration of any of these items.

Any SUPER Group member is allowed to manipulate any jobs and devices.

If a third party access control product is used to grant selected users access to SPOOLCOM only the commands listed above should be granted to general users. All other commands should be restricted.

3P-ACCESS-SPOOLER-01   Use a third party access control product to allow the users responsible for maintaining the Spooler subsystem access to the sensitive commands.

3P-PROCESS-SPOOLER-01   Use a third party access print job manager product that allows for global management of jobs.

3P-PROCESS-SPOOLER-02   Use a third party product that allows a designated user to manage jobs without ownership and without the ability to view the data in the job.

Without a third party access control product:

AP-ADVICE-SPOOLER-01   Spooler processes should run as a job function userid, such as SUPER.SPOOLER, which is not assigned to any individual.

Supervisors

The Spooler Supervisor monitors and communicates with the other programs and determines when and where to print jobs. There is only one Supervisor in each spooler subsystem; but there can be more than one Spooler Subsystem operating at a time.

The spooler object file is $SYSTEM.SYSTEM.SPOOL. The typical default process name is $SPLS.

Spooler Data Files

When a spooler subsystem is configured, an associated datafile is created to store the output on disk until printed or deleted. This file may be located on any disk volume and will be pre-created at its fully allocated size. The default data file name is SPLDATA.

> **BP-SPOOLER-CONFIG-01**   The spooler data file should not be located on $SYSTEM to avoid contention. Configure the data file on another, less busy, volume.

Securing Spooler Components

BP-PROCESS-CSPOOL-01 $S process should be running.

BP-FILE-SPOOLER –01   CSPOOL should be secured "UUNU".

BP-OPSYS-OWNER-02   CSPOOL should be owned by SUPER.SUPER.

BP-OPSYS-FILELOC-02   CSPOOL must reside in $SYSTEM.SYSTEM

BP-FILE-SPOOLER –02   FASTCNFG should be secured "NUUU".

BP-OPSYS-OWNER-02   FASTCNFG should be owned by SUPER.SUPER.

BP-OPSYS-FILELOC-02   FASTCNFG must reside in $SYSTEM.SYSTEM

BP-FILE-SPOOLER –03   FASTP should be secured "UUNU".

BP-OPSYS-OWNER-02   FASTP should be owned by SUPER.SUPER.

BP-OPSYS-FILELOC-02   FASTP must reside in $SYSTEM.SYSTEM

BP-FILE-SPOOLER –04   FONT should be secured "UUNU".

BP-OPSYS-OWNER-02   FONT should be owned by SUPER.SUPER.

BP-OPSYS-FILELOC-02   FONT must reside in $SYSTEM.SYSTEM

BP-FILE-SPOOLER –05   PERUSE should be secured "UUNU".

BP-OPSYS-OWNER-02   PERUSE should be owned by SUPER.SUPER.

BP-OPSYS-FILELOC-02   PERUSE must reside in $SYSTEM.SYSTEM

BP-FILE-SPOOLER –06   PSPOOL / PSPOOLB should be secured "UUNU".

BP-OPSYS-OWNER-02   PSPOOL / PSPOOLB should be owned by SUPER.SUPER.

BP-OPSYS-FILELOC-02   PSPOOL / PSPOOLB must reside in $SYS-TEM.SYSTEM

BP-FILE-SPOOLER –07   RPSETUP should be secured "UUCU".

BP-OPSYS-OWNER-02   RPSETUP should be owned by SUPER.SUPER.

BP-OPSYS-FILELOC-02   RPSETUP must reside in $SYSTEM.SYSTEM

BP-PROCESS-SPOOL-01 $SPLS process should be running.

BP-FILE-SPOOLER-08   SPOOL should be secured "UUNU".

BP-OPSYS-OWNER-02   SPOOL should be owned by SUPER.SUPER.

BP-OPSYS-FILELOC-02   SPOOL must reside in $SYSTEM.SYSTEM

BP-FILE-SPOOLER –09   SPOOLCOM should be secured "UUNU".

BP-OPSYS-OWNER-02   SPOOLCOM should be owned by SUPER.SUPER.

BP-OPSYS-FILELOC-02   SPOOLCOM must reside in $SYSTEM.SYSTEM

BP-PROCESS-SPOOLPA-01 $SPLP process should be running.

BP-FILE-SPOOLER –10   SPOOLP/SPOOLPA should be secured "UUNU".

BP-OPSYS-OWNER-02   SPOOLP/SPOOLPA should be owned by SUPER.SUPER.

BP-OPSYS-FILELOC-02   SPOOLP/SPOOLPA must reside in $SYSTEM.SYSTEM

BP-FILE-SPOOLER –11   SPLDATA should be secured "NUUU".

BP-OPSYS-OWNER-03   SPLDATA should be owned by SUPER.SUPER.

BP-OPSYS-FILELOC-03   SPLDATA resides in $SYSTEM.??

If available, use Safeguard software or a third party object security product to grant access to the SPOOLER object files only to users who require it in order to perform their jobs.

BP-SAFE-SPOOLER-01   Add a Safeguard Protection Record to grant appropriate access to the FASTP object file.

BP-SAFE-SPOOLER-02   Add a Safeguard Protection Record to grant appropriate access to the RPSETUP object file.

BP-SAFE-SPOOLER-03   Add a Safeguard Protection Record to grant appropriate access to the SPOOLCOM object file.

Many corporations are faced with a printing dilemma: there are multiple applications, each producing jobs with spooled output and each with a unique application ownerid, but the operators must manage ALL the jobs, regardless of ownership.

With a third party access control product or print control process:

3P-ACCESS-SPOOLER-03   Use a third party access control product to allow the users responsible for producing jobs with spooled output the ability to run SPOOLCOM as SUPER.SUPER.

3P-OBJSEC-SPOOLER-04   Use a third party access print job manager product that allows for global management of jobs.

Without a third party access control product:

AP-ADVICE-SPOOLER-03   Give operators a userids in the SUPER Group or give aliases to a SUPER Group member.

RISK   SUPER Group members have many inherent privileges that the Operators should not have.

AP-ADVICE-SPOOLER-04   Give those users responsible for managing print jobs EXECUTE access to a PROGID'd *copy* of the SPOOLCOM and PERUSE utility owned by SUPER.SUPER.

RISK   Object files PROGID'd to SUPER.SUPER are a security risk.

AP-ADVICE-SPOOLER-04A   The PROGID'd copies of SPOOLCOM and PERUSE should be secured so that only users authorized for this function can execute them.

	Discovery Questions	Look here:
FILE-POLICY	What is the corporate policy on managing print functions	Policy
PROCESS-CSPOOL-01	Is the $S process running?	Status
PROCESS-SPOOL-01	Is the $SPLS process running?	Status
PROCESS-SPOOLPA-01	Is the $SPLP process running?	Status
OPSYS-OWNER-02	Who owns the CSPOOL object file?	Fileinfo
OPSYS-OWNER-02	Who owns the FASTCNFG object file?	Fileinfo
OPSYS-OWNER-02	Who owns the FASTP object file?	Fileinfo
OPSYS-OWNER-02	Who owns the FONT object file?	Fileinfo
OPSYS-OWNER-02	Who owns the PERUSE object file?	Fileinfo
OPSYS-OWNER-02	Who owns the PSPOOL/PSPOOLB object files?	Fileinfo
OPSYS-OWNER-02	Who owns the RPSETUP object file?	Fileinfo
OPSYS-OWNER-02	Who owns the SPOOL object file?	Fileinfo
OPSYS-OWNER-02	Who owns the SPOOLCOM object file?	Fileinfo
OPSYS-OWNER-02	Who owns the SPOOLP/SPOOLPA object files?	Fileinfo
OPSYS-OWNER-03	Who owns the SPLDATA object file?	Fileinfo
FILE-POLICY	Who is allowed to manage the SPOOLER subsystem on the system?	Policy

	Discovery Questions	Look here:
FILE-SPOOLER-01	Is the CSPOOL object file secured correctly?	Fileinfo
FILE-SPOOLER-02	Is the FASTCNFG file correctly secured?	Fileinfo
FILE-SPOOLER-03 SAFE-SPOOLER-01	Is the FASTP object file correctly secured with the Guardian or Safeguard system?	Fileinfo Safecom
FILE-SPOOLER-04	Is the FONT object file correctly secured ?	Fileinfo
FILE-SPOOLER-05	Is the PERUSE object file correctly secured?	Fileinfo
FILE-SPOOLER-06	Is the PSPOOL/PSPOOLB object files correctly secured?	Fileinfo
FILE-SPOOLER-07 SAFE-SPOOLER-02	Is the RPSETUP object file correctly secured with the Guardian or Safeguard system?	Fileinfo Safecom
FILE-SPOOLER-08	Is the SPOOL object file correctly secured with the Guardian or Safeguard system?	Fileinfo
FILE-SPOOLER-09 SAFE-SPOOLER-03	Is the SPOOLCOM object file correctly secured with the Guardian or Safeguard system?	Fileinfo Safecom
FILE-SPOOLER-10	Is the SPOOLP/SPOOLPA object files correctly secured?	Fileinfo
FILE-SPOOLER-11	Are the SPLDATA data files correctly secured?	Fileinfo

Storage Management Foundation (SMF) Software

HP Storage Management Foundation (SMF) software manages many of the functions with regard to disk volumes and storage tasks. Managing storage pools can include the following tasks:

Changing the physical location of a file on a disk

Coping with disks that are full

Installing and populating new disk volumes

Making disk names independent of physical names

Determining efficient file placement for maximum performance

Once a virtual disk or volume is created, SMF software is transparent to the user.

AP-ADVICE-SMF-01   The SMF configuration and the management of SMF pools should only be performed by the SMF manager.

SMF accomplishes these tasks using the following concepts:

Location-Independent Naming

Location-independent naming means that a distinction now exists between a file's logical name and its physical name on HP NonStop servers. Previously, the file name has always indicated its physical location; that is, the name of each file indicated the node and physical volume on which the file was located. For example, the file name:

> \NODEB.$DATA1.MYAPP.TOLLRDF identifies a file (TOLLRDF) that resides on a node named \NODEB, on a volume named $DATA1, on a sub-volume named MYAPP.

With SMF software, the file \NODEB.$DATA1.MYAPP.TOLLRDF can reside on any physical volume. With the exception of the node name, the name of a file managed by SMF software is independent of its location. SMF software controls the mapping of the logical name to the physical name. This strategy allows the physical name, which identifies the file's physical location, to change when a file is moved to a different location, while the logical name remains the same to applications and users.

Virtual Disks and Physical Volumes

A virtual disk appears to application programs to be a physical volume in almost all respects. The key difference between virtual disks and physical volumes is that, unlike a physical volume, a virtual disk does not correspond to a physical device.

Any number of virtual disks can be associated with any number of physical volumes. Files on virtual disks are not necessarily placed by SMF software on a single physical volume.

> *RISK*   Virtual disks can be changed or made unavailable more easily than a physical drive. They need to be actively managed to ensure that they are available as defined for applications and users.

> **AP-ADVICE-SMF-01**   Virtual disks need to be actively managed to ensure that they are available as defined for applications and users.

Virtual disks can increase the performance of database access. Partitioning files across virtual disks can take advantage of certain performance enhancements of partitioned files.

Storage Pools

A storage pool is a collection of physical disk volumes managed by SMF software. All of the physical disks in a storage pool must be on the same system. Up to 6,144 physical disk volumes may be placed in a pool.

> A physical disk volume can be in only one storage pool at any given time.

There is no fixed limit to the number of storage pools that can be created on a system. As the need arises, new storage pools can be created dynamically.

Mapping Virtual Files

Virtual disk files reside on a physical disk volume. SMF software maps the file labels. The physical tables are mapped from subvolumes residing on the physical disk using the naming convention ZYS<nnnnn>.

```
$DOC1.JAMES.PURGME            23 Jun 2003, 8:28
  ENSCRIBE
  PHYSICAL FILENAME: $DATAE.ZYS00000.A0000DWK

$DOC1 JAMES 92> fup info $DATAE.ZYS00000.A0000DWK
$DOC1 JAMES 92
        CODE          EOF    LAST MODIF OWNER   RWEP   TYPE   REC
$DATAE.ZYS00000
 A0000DWK    101        108    08:27   222,230 NCNC
```

RISK Virtual files cannot be accessed from the physical disk file name, except from FUP for informational review only. Files can only be accessed using the virtual file name.

The components of SMF software are:

  Master Process
  Pool Process
  SMF Catalogs
  SMS Utilities
  Virtual Disk Process

Master Process

The SMF master process manages a catalog of information required to coordinate SMF storage pools and virtual disks. The fixed name of the master process is $ZSMS.

Pool Process

Pool processes are responsible for collection and distributing information about physical volumes associated with a pool of virtual disks. Pool processes also keep statistical information about the pool.

SMF Catalog

SMF software maintains a catalog of information about pools.

SMF Utilities

The following utility programs can be used by the SMF manager:

Utility Name:	Function:
RELOCSRV	Relocation utility to perform offline relocation
SMFIXUP	A powerful tool to perform maintenance tasks not otherwise easily performed. SMFIXUP actions may not be recoverable.
SMREVERT	Component of SMFIXUP
SMREPAIR	Component of SMFIXUP

RISK   The SMF utilities should only be used by the SMF manager. Someactions may not be able to be recovered.

Virtual Disk Process

Virtual disks use a different disk process than physical disks. When virtual disk volumes are created by the operating system, the operating system starts a virtual disk process, $SYSTEM.SYSnn.OVDP, for each virtual volume. The name of this process is the disk name. See Gazette section on Disk Processes for more information.

Securing SMF Components

BP-PROCESS-OMP-01 $ZSMS process should be running.

BP-FILE-SMF-01   OMP should be secured "UUCU".

BP-OPSYS-LICENSE-01   OMP must be LICENSED.

BP-OPSYS-OWNER-01   OMP should be owned by SUPER.SUPER.

BP-OPSYS-FILELOC-01   OMP must reside in $SYSTEM.SYSnn.

BP-PROCESS-OPP-01 $POOLnn processes should be running.

BP-FILE-SMF-02   OPP should be secured "UUCU".

BP-OPSYS-LICENSE-01   OPP must be LICENSED.

BP-OPSYS-OWNER-01   OPP should be owned by SUPER.SUPER.

BP-OPSYS-FILELOC-01   OPP must reside in $SYSTEM.SYSnn.

BP-FILE-SMF-03   RELOCSRV should be secured "UUCU".

BP-OPSYS-LICENSE-02   RELOCSRV must be LICENSED.

BP-OPSYS-OWNER-02   RELOCSRV should be owned by SUPER.SUPER.

BP-OPSYS-FILELOC-02   RELOCSRV must reside in $SYSTEM.SYSTEM.

BP-FILE-SMF-04   SMFIXUP should be secured "UUCU".

BP-OPSYS-LICENSE-02   SMFIXUP must be LICENSED.

BP-OPSYS-OWNER-02   SMFIXUP should be owned by SUPER.SUPER.

BP-OPSYS-FILELOC-02   SMFIXUP must reside in $SYSTEM.SYSTEM.

BP-FILE-SMF-05   SMREVERT should be secured "UUCU".

BP-OPSYS-LICENSE-02   SMREVERT must be LICENSED.

BP-OPSYS-OWNER-02   SMREVERT should be owned by SUPER.SUPER.

BP-OPSYS-FILELOC-02   SMREVERT must reside in $SYSTEM.SYSTEM.

BP-FILE-SMF-06   SMREPAIR should be secured "UUCU".

BP-OPSYS-LICENSE-02   SMREPAIR must be LICENSED.

BP-OPSYS-OWNER-02   SMREPAIR should be owned by SUPER.SUPER.

BP-OPSYS-FILELOC-02   SMREPAIR must reside in $SYSTEM.SYSTEM.

BP-PROCESS-TZSTO-01 $ZZSTO process should be running.

BP-FILE-SMF-07   TZSTO should be secured "UUCU".

BP-OPSYS-OWNER-01   TZSTO should be owned by SUPER.SUPER.

BP-OPSYS-FILELOC-01   TZSTO must reside in $SYSTEM.SYSnn.

BP-FILE-SMF-08   SMF Catalog files should be secured "NUUU".

BP-OPSYS-OWNER-03   SMF Catalog files should be owned by SUPER.SUPER.

BP-OPSYS-FILELOC-03   SMF Catalog files resides in $SYSTEM.<ZSMSPnn>.

If available, use Safeguard software or a third party object security product to grant access to the SMF subsystem files only to users who require access in order to perform their jobs.

BP-SAFE-SMF-01   Add a Safeguard Protection Record to grant appropriate access to the OMP object file.

BP-SAFE-SMF-02   Add a Safeguard Protection Record to grant appropriate access to the SMFIXUP object file.

	Discovery Questions	Look here:
FILE-POLICY	Is SMF software used on the system?	Policy
PROCESS-OMP-01	Is the $ZSMS process running?	Status
PROCESS-OPP-01	Are the $POOLnn processes running?	Status
PROCESS-TZSTO-01	Is the $ZZSTO process running?	Status
OPSYS-OWNER-01	Who owns the OMP object file?	Fileinfo
OPSYS-OWNER-01	Who owns the OPP object file?	Fileinfo
OPSYS-OWNER-01	Who owns the TZSTO object file?	Fileinfo
OPSYS-OWNER-02	Who owns the RELOCSRV object file?	Fileinfo
OPSYS-OWNER-02	Who owns the SMFIXUP object file?	Fileinfo
OPSYS-OWNER-02	Who owns the SMREVERT object file?	Fileinfo
OPSYS-OWNER-02	Who owns the SMREPAIR object file?	Fileinfo
OPSYS-OWNER-03	Who owns the SMF catalog and database?	Fileinfo
OPSYS-LICENSE-01	Is the OMP object file licensed?	Fileinfo
OPSYS-LICENSE-01	Is the OPP object file licensed?	Fileinfo
OPSYS-LICENSE-02	Is the RELOCSRV object file licensed?	Fileinfo
OPSYS-LICENSE-02	Is the SMFIXUP object file licensed?	Fileinfo
OPSYS-LICENSE-02	Is the SMREVERT object file licensed?	Fileinfo
OPSYS-LICENSE-02	Is the SMREPAIR object file licensed?	Fileinfo
FILE-POLICY	Who is allowed to manage SMF volumes on the system?	Policy
FILE-POLICY	Where is the SMF Catalog?	Policy
FILE-SMF-01 SAFE-SMF-01	Is the OMP object file correctly secured with the Guardian or Safeguard system?	Fileinfo Safecom
FILE-SMF-02	Is the OPP object file secured correctly?	Fileinfo
FILE-SMF-03	Is the RELOCSRV object file secured correctly?	Fileinfo
FILE-SMF-04 SAFE-SMF-02	Is the SMFIXUP object file correctly secured with the Guardian or Safeguard system?	Fileinfo Safecom
FILE-SMF-05	Is the SMREVERT object file secured correctly?	Fileinfo
FILE-SMF-06	Is the SMREPAIR object file secured correctly?	Fileinfo
FILE-SMF-07	Is the TZSTO object file secured correctly?	Fileinfo
FILE-SMF-08	Is the SMF catalog and database secured correctly?	Fileinfo SQLCI

Related Topics

Disk Processes

Securing Applications

SQLCI

NonStop SQL Subsystem

NonStop SQL database is the HP NonStop server implementation of an ANSI-standard SQL DBMS supporting relational database management for applications, including ODBC applications.

Two Versions of NonStop SQL Database

NonStop SQL/MP Database

NonStop SQL/MP database is the HP NonStop server's implementation of the Structured Query Language (SQL). It is a distributed, relational database management system for on-line transaction processing and relational database management system (DBMS), based upon the industry ANSI SQL standard. It is ideally suited for database applications requiring easy access to the data, high performance, high availability, and the ability to scale up the database as the business grows. Conforming to industry-standard programming tools and protocols and accessible from popular PC software tools, NonStop SQL/MP database combines open access with the parallel, distributed processing environment made possible by the HP NonStop server's multiprocessor architecture. Parallel query capabilities and ease of management have made NonStop SQL/MP database the preferred database large business running on HP NonStop servers.

NonStop SQL/MX Database

HP's NonStop SQL/MX database is HP's next-generation relational database management system designed for business-critical applications. NonStop SQL/MX software brings the traditional NonStop SQL/MP fundamentals-high availability, scalability, reliability, and distributed database design and incorporated features that allowing creation of applications for open systems platforms.

NonStop SQL/MX database is a relational database management system that allows applications to use the NonStop SQL/MX query compiler and executor to access NonStop SQL/MP database objects. The NonStop SQL/MX query compiler and executor run in the HP NonStop Kernel Open System Services (OSS) environment. To allow ANSI-compliant applications to access NonStop SQL/MP database objects, the NonStop SQL/MX query compiler and executor provide basic logical name support.

For current versions of NonStop SQL/MX database, the query compiler and executor will operate on NonStop SQL/MP database objects only. NonStop SQL/MX database runs in the OSS environment, so OSS must be installed and running on the system. OSS is an open computing interface to the NonStop Kernel operating system.

The SQL subsystem components should be owned by SUPER.SUPER and Guardian secured "UUNU" or "OOAO", so that the components are accessible by local and remote users of SQL.

Two exceptions are $SYSTEM.SYSTEM.SQLMSG and $SYSTEM.SYSTEM. NLCPMSG which should be secured "NUNU" or "AOAO", granting READ access for reporting error messages.

> Safeguard software cannot secure individual SQL catalog or objects even though the object's name is a diskfile name. SQL tables and other objects can only be secured at the VOLUME or SUBVOLUME level. Safeguard can secure the SQL component files and processes, except for the System Catalog. See the Securing Application Chapter for more discussion on SQL objects

NonStop SQL/MP Subsystem Components are:

    SQLCAT
    SQLCFE
    SQLCI
    SQLCI2
    SQLCOMP
    SQLESP
    SQLEXPMG
    SQLH
    SQLMSG
    SQLUTIL
    NLCPCOMP
    NLCPMSG
    AUDSERV

SQLCAT

The SQL catalog manager process is the interface to reading and updating the SQL catalog structure. If remote access is required, the Catalog Manager communicates to a remote Catalog Manager process. The Catalog Manager is initiated by the SQL subsystem.

SQLCI / SQLCI2 / SQLUTIL

SQLCI and its components SQLCI2 and SQLUTIL are the conversational interface to NonStop SQL database. Commands are entered interactively or via macros to perform data access or to create, alter or purge descriptions. Access to SQLCI and its related components, must be closely controlled.

> *RISK* Access to the conversational interface cannot be controlled, except at the base object Guardian access level. If a user has access to SQLCI and READ, WRITE access to a table, the user can effectively add, alter or delete one, many or all rows within the table. If a user has READ access to a table, all data within the table is accessible, regardless of its sensitivity.
>
> **AP-FILE-SQLCI-02** Application users should not have access to SQLCI. They should use the application's interfaces to insert, update and retrieve data from SQL databases.

SQL commands and access requirements are based on Guardian ownership, but have a revised concept of generalized ownership to objects. Userids that are considered to have generalized ownership of SQL objects are:

Local owner

Remote owner if granted PURGE access

Local SUPER.SUPER

Owner's local group manager

SQLCI Commands with Security Implications

This section describes only the SQLCI commands that pose security risks.

The three categories of SQL statements should be appropriately secured.

Data Definition Language (DDL) statements, issued by the database administrator.

Utility commands used to perform database maintenance and general utility functions, as needed.

Data Manipulation Language (DML) & Data Control Language (DCL) statements, generally issued by application users.

Security issues closely follow the use of three categories of SQL statements. These categories and the most frequent users of each category are as follows:

Access Requirements for SQL Objects

Type	Command	Authority Required
Compile Run	SQLCOMP BINDER Program	READ and PURGE authority for the program file.
		READ and WRITE authority for the PROGRAMS, USAGES, and TRANSIDS table of the catalog in which the program will be registered.
		READ and WRITE authority for the USAGES and TRANSIDS catalog tables of any catalog that contains a description of a table or view that the program uses.
	RUN program file	EXECUTE authority for the program file
		For dynamic recompilation, READ authority for any catalog with a description of a table or view used by the program.

Commands "suitable" for Application Users (usually performed programmatically)

Access Requirements for SQL Objects

Type	Command	Authority Required
DCL Statements	FREE RESOURCES	READ authority for affected objects.
App users	LOCK TABLE UNLOCK TABLE	READ authority for the table or view and all underlying tables of the view.
DML Statements App users	DELETE INSERT UPDATE	READ and WRITE authority for the table or protection view being deleted or modified and,
		READ authority for tables, protection views, and underlying tables of shorthand views specified in subqueries of the statement.

Access Requirements for SQL Objects

Type	Command	Authority Required
	SELECT	READ authority for tables, protection views, and underlying tables of shorthand views specified in the statement.

Commands "suitable" for Database Administration Group:

Access Requirements for SQL Objects

Type	Command	Authority Required
DDL Statements DB admin	DDL commands in general	READ and WRITE authority for affected catalogs unless otherwise noted.
	ALTER	Must be the: - local owner of the object - local SUPER.SUPER - local group manager - remote owner with PURGE authority for the object (or for the underlying table if the object is an index).
	To resecure program	READ and WRITE authority for the affected catalog and for the program file.
	To resecure catalog	Must be the: - local owner of the object - remote owner with PURGE authority for the catalog.
	COMMENT	Must be the: - local owner of the referenced table, view, or underlying table of the index described by the comment - local SUPER.SUPER - local group manager - remote owner with PURGE authority for the object.
	CREATE CATALOG	WRITE authority for the SQL.CATALOGS table on the system that contains the catalog.
	CREATE COLLATION	READ and WRITE authority for the catalog in which the collation will be registered and, READ authority for the collation source file.

Access Requirements for SQL Objects

Type	Command	Authority Required
	CREATE CONSTRAINT	Must be the: - local owner of the underlying table - local SUPER.SUPER - local group manager - remote owner with PURGE authority for the table and READ authority for the underlying table.
	CREATE INDEX	Must be the: - local owner of the object - local SUPER.SUPER - local group manager - remote owner with PURGE authority for the table and READ and WRITE authority for the underlying table and WRITE authority for the USAGES table of catalogs that describes the underlying table.
	CREATE TABLE	READ and WRITE authority for all affected catalogs.
	CREATE VIEW Shorthand	WRITE authority for the USAGES and TRANSIDS tables in catalogs that describe the underlying tables and views and WRITE authority for the VIEWS catalog table.
	CREATE VIEW Protection	Must be the: - local owner of the underlying table - local SUPER.SUPER - local group manager - remote owner with PURGE authority for the table
	DROP CATALOG	READ and PURGE authority for the catalog and READ and WRITE authority for the SQL.CATALOGS table.
	DROP CONSTRAINT DROP INDEX	Must be the: - local owner of the underlying table - local SUPER.SUPER - local group manager - remote owner with PURGE authority for the underlying table.
	DROP PROGRAM DROP TABLE DROP VIEW	Purge authority for the object being dropped.

Access Requirements for SQL Objects

Type	Command	Authority Required
	UPDATE STATISTICS	Must be the: - local owner of the underlying table - local SUPER.SUPER - local group manager - remote owner with PURGE authority for the table for which statistics are being updated.

Commands "suitable" for Database Administration Group:

Access Requirements for SQL Objects

Type	Command	Authority Required
Utility Commands	CLEANUP	Must be the: - Local SUPER.SUPER .
	CONVERT	READ authority for the file to be converted and the DDL dictionary and the same authority as for: CREATE TABLE CREATE INDEX LOAD.
	COPY	READ authority for the source file or object and WRITE authority for the target file or object and for objects, READ authority for the catalogs containing the object descriptions.
	DISPLAY USE OF	READ authority for the catalogs containing the object descriptions.
	DUP	READ authority for objects and files being duplicated; read authority for the catalogs containing the object descriptions and The same authority as for CREATE statements for the types of objects being duplicated and PURGE authority for target files and objects if purging is necessary.
	EDIT	READ and WRITE authority for the file to be edited.
	FILEINFO	READ authority for each object or file for which statistics are to be displayed.
	INVOKE	READ authority for the catalogs containing the object descriptions.

Access Requirements for SQL Objects

Type	Command	Authority Required
	LOAD	READ authority for the source file or object; WRITE authority for the target file or object and for objects, READ authority for the catalogs containing the object descriptions. If the target file is a table, then LOAD requires the authority to WRITE to the catalog in which the table is described.
	MODIFY [DICTIONARY]	Must be the: - local SUPER.SUPER unless the CHECKONLY option is specified. For a MODIFY LABEL CHECKONLY request, READ authority for the SQL objects and object programs For a MODIFY CATALOG CHECKONLY request, READ authority for the catalogs.
	PURGE	Must be the: - local owner of the underlying table - local SUPER.SUPER - local group manager and same authority as for DROP for objects being purged or PURGE authority for files being purged.
	PURGEDATA	WRITE authority for the files and for the tables and affected catalogs.
	SECURE	Must be the: - local owner of the file - local SUPER.SUPER - local group manager and same authority as for ALTER for the object being secured.
	TEDIT	READ and WRITE authority for the file to be edited.
	UPGRADE CATALOG	Must be the: - local owner of the catalog - local SUPER.SUPER - local group manager - remote owner with PURGE authority for the catalog tables and WRITE authority for the system CATALOGS table.
	UPGRADE SYSTEM CATALOG	Must be the: - local SUPER.SUPER
	VERIFY	READ authority for the catalogs containing the object descriptions.

Controlling SQLCI

SQLCI provides the interface to not only inquire into SQL objects, but to perform management functions. There is no internal security within SQLCI, except the security ownership requirements listed above to control commands within SQLCI for which a user has Guardian access.

> *RISK* Without a third party Access Control Product, there is no way to control a user's use of unauthorized commands within SQLCI.

With a third party access control product:

3P-ACCESS-SQL-01   Use a third party access control product to allow the users responsible for using sensitive commands the ability to run SQLCI commands as SUPER.SUPER.

3P-ACCESS-SQL-02   Use a third party access control product to give the use of certain SQLCI commands to a limited group of users only.

Licensed SQLCI2

Normally, the SQL catalogs are managed by the SQL subsystem, meaning all entries into the SQL catalogs are performed via the subsystem, rather than by the user. However, SQLCI includes a diagnostic tool that allows SUPER.SUPER to perform direct data manipulation on the SQL Catalogs. This tool has been provided for disaster recovery of corrupted catalogs.

AP-FILE-SQLCI2-01   Inadvertent use of a licensed SQLCI2 can cause corruption of the SQL catalog structure. SQLCI2 should not be licensed on the SYSTEM.SYSTEM location. It should only be licensed, used and unlicensed if necessary by the SUPER.SUPER user.

AP-FILE-SQLCI2-02   Never LICENSE and PROGID SQLCI2 on the system. Use of this file could corrupt the catalogs.

SQLCOMP / NLCPCOMP

NonStop SQL/MP and SQL/MX compilers to verify and register SQL programs.

A compiler prepares SQL statements to be executed by a host language program and registers the program to the SQL catalog. Only programs processed by SQLCOMP can access SQL objects.

SQLCOMP is invoked explicitly or implicitly by SQL. Unlike other compilers, SQLCOMP is normally available on secure systems, as it is an integral piece of the SQL subsystem. Automatic (implicit) recompilation is invoked whenever an object is invalidated. (see SQL object invalidation.) Explicit SQL compilation is used to initially register SQL application programs in the SQL catalogs.

AP-FILE-SQLCOMP-01   SQLCOMP should be available for execution by the SQL subsystem on any system to perform SQL recompilations.

SQLCFE / SQLH

SQL components of the C compiler and C library extensions. These files enable SQL for C language programs. Other languages have libraries available for SQL extensions.

SQLESP / SQLESMG

Program and message file supporting native languages and SQL.

SQLMSG / NLCPMSG

SQL's message files for NonStop SQL/MP and SQL/MX databases. These files should be generally available.

SQLUTIL

SQLUTIL is initiated by SQLCI to perform certain SQL commands that are designated as utility operations, such as DUP, COPY, etc.

AUDSERV

AUDSERV is only used in an SQL environment. Please refer to the Gazette section on AUDSERV.

Securing SQL Components

BP-FILE-SQL-01   SQLCAT should be secured "UUNU".

BP-OPSYS-LICENSE-02   SQLCAT must be LICENSED.

BP-OPSYS-OWNER-02   SQLCAT should be owned by SUPER.SUPER.

BP-OPSYS-FILELOC-02   SQLCAT must reside in $SYSTEM.SYSTEM

BP-FILE-SQL-02   SQLCFE should be secured "UUNU".

BP-OPSYS-OWNER-02   SQLCFE should be owned by SUPER.SUPER.

BP-OPSYS-FILELOC-02   SQLCFE must reside in $SYSTEM.SYSTEM

BP-FILE-SQL-03   SQLCI should be secured "UUNU".

BP-OPSYS-OWNER-02   SQLCI should be owned by SUPER.SUPER.

BP-OPSYS-FILELOC-02   SQLCI must reside in $SYSTEM.SYSTEM

BP-FILE-SQL-04   SQLCI2 should be secured "UUNU".

BP-OPSYS-LICENSE-02   SQLCI2 should NOT be LICENSED.

BP-OPSYS-OWNER-02   SQLCI2 should be owned by SUPER.SUPER.

BP-OPSYS-FILELOC-02   SQLCI2 must reside in $SYSTEM.SYSTEM

BP-FILE-SQL-05   SQLCOMP should be secured "UUNU".

BP-OPSYS-LICENSE-02   SQLCOMP must be LICENSED.

BP-OPSYS-OWNER-02   SQLCOMP should be owned by SUPER.SUPER.

BP-OPSYS-FILELOC-02   SQLCOMP must reside in $SYSTEM.SYSTEM

BP-FILE-SQL-06   SQLESP should be secured "UUNU".

BP-OPSYS-OWNER-02   SQLESP should be owned by SUPER.SUPER.

BP-OPSYS-FILELOC-02   SQLESP must reside in $SYSTEM.SYSTEM

BP-FILE-SQL-07   SQLESPMG should be secured "UUNU".

BP-OPSYS-OWNER-02   SQLESPMG should be owned by SUPER.SUPER.

BP-OPSYS-FILELOC-02   SQLESPMG must reside in $SYSTEM.SYSTEM

BP-FILE-SQL-08   SQLH should be secured "NUNU".

BP-OPSYS-OWNER-02   SQLH should be owned by SUPER.SUPER.

BP-OPSYS-FILELOC-02   SQLH must reside in $SYSTEM.SYSTEM

BP-FILE-SQL-09   SQLMSG should be secured "NUNU".

BP-OPSYS-OWNER-02   SQLMSG should be owned by SUPER.SUPER.

BP-OPSYS-FILELOC-02   SQLMSG must reside in $SYSTEM.SYSTEM

BP-FILE-SQL-10   SQLUTIL should be secured "UUNU".

BP-OPSYS-LICENSE-02   SQLUTIL must be LICENSED.

BP-OPSYS-OWNER-02   SQLUTIL should be owned by SUPER.SUPER.

BP-OPSYS-FILELOC-02   SQLUTIL must reside in $SYSTEM.SYSTEM

BP-FILE-SQL-11   NLCPCOMP should be secured "UUNU".

BP-OPSYS-OWNER-02   NLCPCOMP should be owned by SUPER.SUPER.

BP-OPSYS-FILELOC-02   NLCPCOMP must reside in $SYSTEM.SYSTEM

BP-FILE-SQL-12   NLCPMSG should be secured "NUNU".

BP-OPSYS-OWNER-02   NLCPMSG should be owned by SUPER.SUPER.

BP-OPSYS-FILELOC-02   NLCPMSG must reside in $SYSTEM.SYSTEM

BP-FILE-SQL-13   The System Catalog should be secured "NUCU".

BP-OPSYS-OWNER-03   The System Catalog should be owned by
SUPER.SUPER.

BP-OPSYS-FILELOC-03   The System Catalog resides in $<vol>.<svol>

If available, use Safeguard software or a third party object security product to grant
access to SQL components object files to necessary personnel, and deny access to all
other users.

BP-SAFE-SQL-01   Add a Safeguard Protection Record to grant appropriate
access to the SQLCI object file.

BP-SAFE-SQL-02 to 03   Add a Safeguard Protection Record to grant appropriate access to the SQLCOMP/NLCPCOMP object files.

BP-SAFE-SQL-04   Add a Safeguard Protection Record to grant appropriate
access to the SQL system catalog.

	Discovery Questions	Look here:
FILE-POLICY	Is NonStop SQL/MP or SQL/MX database used for applications?	Policy
FILE-POLICY	Is SQL installed and active on the system for application or subsystem purposes?	Policy
FILE-POLICY	Where is the System Catalog?	SQLCI
OPSYS-OWNER-02	Who owns the SQLCAT object file?	Fileinfo
OPSYS-OWNER-02	Who owns the SQLCFE object file?	Fileinfo
OPSYS-OWNER-02	Who owns the SQLCI object file?	Fileinfo
OPSYS-OWNER-02	Who owns the SQLCI2 object file?	Fileinfo
OPSYS-OWNER-02	Who owns the SQLCOMP object file?	Fileinfo
OPSYS-OWNER-02	Who owns the SQLESP object file?	Fileinfo
OPSYS-OWNER-02	Who owns the SQLESPMG object file?	Fileinfo
OPSYS-OWNER-02	Who owns the SQLH object file?	Fileinfo
OPSYS-OWNER-02	Who owns the SQLMSG object file?	Fileinfo
OPSYS-OWNER-02	Who owns the SQLUTIL object file?	Fileinfo
OPSYS-OWNER-02	Who owns the NLCPCOMP object file?	Fileinfo
OPSYS-OWNER-02	Who owns the NLCPMSG object file?	Fileinfo
FILE-POLICY	Where is the SQL System Catalog	SQLCI
OPSYS-OWNER-03	Who owns the SQL catalog?	Fileinfo SQLCI

	Discovery Questions	Look here:
OPSYS-LICENSE-02	Is the SQLCAT object file licensed?	Fileinfo
OPSYS-LICENSE-02	Is the SQLCI2 object file licensed?	Fileinfo
OPSYS-LICENSE-02	Is the SQLCOMP object file licensed?	Fileinfo
OPSYS-LICENSE-02	Is the SQLUTIL object file licensed?	Fileinfo
FILE-POLICY	Who is responsible for managing the SQL system catalog and SQL environment?	Policy
FILE-POLICY	Who is allowed to create and manage SQL application catalogs ?	Policy
FILE-SQL-01	Is the SQLCAT object file secured correctly?	Fileinfo
FILE-SQL-02	Is the SQLCFE object file secured correctly?	Fileinfo
FILE-SQL-03 SAFE-SQL-01	Is the SQLCI object file correctly secured with the Guardian or Safeguard system?	Fileinfo Safecom
FILE-SQL-04	Is the SQLCI2 object file secured correctly?	Fileinfo
FILE-SQL-05 SAFE-SQL-02	Is the SQLCOMP object file correctly secured with the Guardian or Safeguard system?	Fileinfo Safecom
FILE-SQL-06	Is the SQLESP object file secured correctly?	Fileinfo
FILE-SQL-07	Is the SQLESPMG object file secured correctly?	Fileinfo
FILE-SQL-08	Is the SQLH file secured correctly?	Fileinfo
FILE-SQL-09	Is the SQLMSG file secured correctly?	Fileinfo
FILE-SQL-10	Is the SQLUTIL object file secured correctly?	Fileinfo
FILE-SQL-11 SAFE-SQL-03	Is the NLCPCOMP object file correctly secured with the Guardian or Safeguard system?	Fileinfo Safecom
FILE-SQL-12	Is the NLCPMSG file secured correctly?	Fileinfo
FILE-SQL-13 SAFE-SQL-04	Is the SQL system catalog correctly secured with the Guardian or Safeguard system?	Fileinfo Safecom

SWID System Utility

SWID is part of a new program called HP Software Gateway, and is available as a stand-alone utility. HP Software Gateway represents a group of related software distribution services and products. The purpose of SWID is to provide unique identification of all files distributed by HP.

This unique identifier is known as the "fingerprint" of the file. This fingerprint is used to perform software inventory, software version analysis, and software delivery.

SWID supercedes the VPROC utility. (Please refer to the Gazette section on BINDER Subsystem)

```
$SYSTEM SYSTEM 16> SWID $SYSTEM.SYS01.PEEK
SoftWare Identification Utility - T9298AAH - (05DEC97) System \MEXICO
Copyright Tandem Computers Incorporated 1991-1997
16Jun 3 14:44:54 (Switches: None)

$SYSTEM.SYS01

      Code Original fpts         Current fpts Mismatch
PEEK   700 64bb-8ebf-6589-d292   64bb-8ebf-6589-d292    No
```

The phrase "fingerprint of a file" means a context-free and content-dependent attribute of the file that can be computed by reading the contents of the file such that:

Two identical copies of a file must yield the same fingerprint regardless of the context (for example, filename, location, ownership, creation time, and last-modified time).

Two files with different contents should not yield the same fingerprint. A fingerprint is displayed as a character string of fixed length (16 hex characters). Internally, a fingerprint is stored as a 96-bit number of which 32 bits are used for version and other reserved information, and the other 64 bits are used to store the fingerprint string. SWID reports two types of fingerprints, "Current" and "Original".

The unique fingerprint generated by SWID can form a basis for change management by other software products.

RISK   SWID is a reporting program only and does not pose any risks.

Securing SWID

BP-FILE-SWID-01   SWID should be secured "UUNU".

BP-OPSYS-OWNER-02   SWID should be owned by SUPER.SUPER.

BP-OPSYS-FILELOC-02   SWID must reside in $SYSTEM.SYSTEM

	Discovery Questions	Look here:
OPSYS-OWNER-01	Who owns the SWID object file?	Fileinfo
FILE-SWID-01	Is the SWID object file secured correctly?	Fileinfo

SYSGENR System Utility

The SYSGEN (CISC) and SYSGENR (RISC) program is invoked by the DSM/SCM system generation application to compile the operating system.

SYSGENR uses many subsystems and configuration files to accomplish its work, and generates the OSIMAGE configuration. SYSGEN uses components that are discussed in other parts of this book. Only the components not covered elsewhere are discussed here.

Securing SYSGENR Components

BP-FILE-SYSGEN-01   SYSGENR should be secured "UUCU".

BP-OPSYS-OWNER-03   SYSGENR should be owned by SUPER.SUPER.

BP-OPSYS-FILELOC-03   SYSGENR resides in $<dsmscm>.ZGUARD.

BP-FILE-SYSGEN-02   TSC should be secured "UUCU".

BP-OPSYS-LICENSE-01   TSC should be licensed.

BP-OPSYS-OWNER-01   TSC should be owned by SUPER.SUPER.

BP-OPSYS-FILELOC-01   TSC must reside in $SYSTEM.SYSnn

BP-FILE-SYSGEN-03   TSL should be secured "UUCU".

BP-OPSYS-LICENSE-01   TSL should be licensed.

BP-OPSYS-OWNER-01   TSL should be owned by SUPER.SUPER.

BP-OPSYS-FILELOC-01   TSL must reside in $SYSTEM.SYSnn.

BP-FILE-SYSGEN-04   XLLINK should be secured "UUCU".

BP-OPSYS-LICENSE-02   XLLINK should be licensed.

BP-OPSYS-OWNER-02   XLLINK should be owned by SUPER.SUPER.

BP-OPSYS-FILELOC-02   XLLINK must reside in $SYSTEM.SYSTEM

	Discovery Questions	Look here:
FILE-POLICY	Who are the users who should have access to the DSMSCM application?	Policy
SYSTEM-POLICY	Are operating systems upgraded regularly?	Policy
OPSYS-OWNER-03	Who owns the SYSGENR object file?	Fileinfo
OPSYS-OWNER-01	Who owns the TSC object file?	Fileinfo
OPSYS-OWNER-01	Who owns the TSL object file?	Fileinfo

	Discovery Questions	Look here:
OPSYS-OWNER-02	Who owns the XLLINK components files?	Fileinfo
OPSYS-LICENSE-01	Is the TSC program licensed?	Fileinfo
OPSYS-LICENSE-01	Is the TSL program licensed?	Fileinfo
OPSYS-LICENSE-02	Is the XLLINK program licensed?	Fileinfo
FILE-SYSGEN-01	Is the SYSGENR object file secured correctly?	Fileinfo
FILE-SYSGEN-02	Is the TSC object file secured correctly?	Fileinfo
FILE-SYSGEN-03	Is the TSL object file secured correctly?	Fileinfo
FILE-SYSGEN-04	Is the XLLINK object file secured correctly?	Fileinfo

Related Topics

Operating System

DSMSCM

System Configuration Files

There are a number of system configuration files used as input to a system generation and output by the process of system generation of a RVU.

> The **RVU** is the collection of compatible revisions of NonStop Kernel operating system software products, identified by a RVU ID such as Release Version Update G06.18, and supported as a unit. The RVU is distributed to customers via Site Update Tapes (SUTs). SUTs may include the complete RVU or only selected products.

> A **Site Update Tape (SUT)** is unique to a customer and a system. The tape(s) contain the products purchased by the customer for the target system. The tape(s) include the softdoc and all the necessary files for each product purchased. A SUT can be ordered each time a new release of the system software is made available.

A full SUT contains the current RVU of the operating system and all ordered products.

A partial SUT contains a specific subset of products for the current RVU of the operating system.

The system manger generates the operating system image using the DSM/SCM subsystem or SYSGENR directly.

RISK Normally there is limited risk in allowing the general user READ access to the configuration files.

AP-ADVICE-SYSCNFG-01 WRITE and PURGE access to system configuration files should be controlled.

The files that supply input to SYSGENR are:

CONFAUX file

CONFTEXT

Preexisting files, such as interim product modifications (IPMs) or user application files, loaded from a SUT during the Install process

The files that are output or generated by SYSGENR are:

CONFALT

CONFBASE

CONFLIST

OSCONFIG

The files that are copied as part of the function of SYSGENR are:

CIIN

CUSTFILE

RLSEID

CONFALT File

The CONFALT file stores the active system configuration as generated by the last SYSGENR and possibly modified by COUP. The CONFALT file is used in cold loading the system and maintaining the current configuration.

RISK This file is generated and maintained by the system and should not be modified manually in any manner.

CONFAUX File

The CONFAUX file is an EDIT file provided on HP SUT tapes. It contains a series of statements that define the locations of operating system programs, library codes, and microcode files that are used by the CONFTEXT file to build the new operating-system files during SYSGENs.

This file is initially created by DSM/SCM and contains information supplied by HP. It is rarely necessary to edit the file. However, if SYSGENR is run outside of DSM/SCM, the CONFAUX file must be created manually

RISK   HP recommends that no changes be made to the CONFAUX file because the continuity of the configuration may be in question.

CONFBASE File

The CONFBASE file is placed on the target SYSnn subvolume specified in DSM/SCM. It contains the minimal configuration to load the system. Generally it would be used in disaster recovery situations or very special circumstances.

$SYSTEM.SYSnn.CONFBASE only configures:

$SYSTEM disk volume

$ZZKRN Kernel subsystem manager

$ZZSTO storage subsystem manager

$ZHOME reliable home-terminal process

RISK   Changing the CONFBASE file could negate its ability to perform in a disaster situation.

AP-ADVICE-CONFBASE-01   Needing to load the system from the CONF-BASE file is unlikely. However, if the current configuration file has become corrupted and there is no other configuration file from which to load the system, it may be necessary to use this method. Only extremely knowledgeable personnel should have access to this file.

CONFLIST File

The CONFLIST file is created by SYSGENR. As SYSGENR processes the CONFTEXT file, it writes actions taken, including error and warning messages. The CONFLIST is the equivalent of a language compiler output listing.

AP-ADVICE-CONFLIST-01   HP recommends that no changes be made to the CONFLIST file because the continuity of the configuration may be in question.

CONFTEXT File

The CONFTEXT configuration file is an EDIT file provided on HP SUT tapes which is used as input to the SYSGENR function. It contains a series of statements defining the hardware and software components of the target system. The file is used to create the operating system image (OSIMAGE file) in the new $SYSTEM.SYSnn sub-volume. The file defines the following items:

The hardware configuration of the system, including the number of processors, controllers, devices, and their connecting paths.

The system library, system code, microcode, and other operating system files needed by the system.

The relationship of the system to other systems in a network.

The contents of the CONFTEXT file depend on the architecture of the HP NonStop server. The following categories are included in the CONFTEXT File. CISC-only paragraphs are noted.

CONFTEXT File Categories

Paragraph	Contents
DEFINEs	(optional) Alphanumeric character string and associated macro name. This feature allows specification of a common configuration statement once, which can be referred to thereafter with a macro name.
MULTIFUNCTION CONTROLLERS (CISC only)	Identification of all system names, product numbers, primary and backup processors, and subchannel addresses for each multifunction controller supporting a communications subsystem logical device.
CONTROLLERS (CISC only)	Identification of each controller name in the system and specification of each controller, primary and backup processor, and subchannel address.
PATHS (CISC only)	The path name and controller name for each 3650 CSS.
MICROCODE_FILES (CISC only)	Names of all processor and controller microcode files.
PERIPHERALS (CISC only)	Identification of each I/O device and communications line in the system and specification of the logical device name and controller name and unit number, or path name and LIU number, macro name, and modifiers.
SYSTEM_PROCESS_MODIFIERS (CISC only)	(optional) Parameters for system processes such as $0.
ALLPROCESSORS	Parameters that define the operating-system image for all processors in the system.
PROCESSORS (CISC only)	(optional) Parameters that define the operating-system image for each specific processor in the system.

Typically, there is no need to change the CONFTEXT file on a G-series system.

AP-ADVICE-SYSGENR-01   Do not modify the CONFTEXT file in the SYSnn subvolume; it is the only record of the system configuration within the OSIMAGE file. Instead, make a copy of it in the same subvolume as the INSTALL program and then edit the copy. This ensures that a working CONF-TEXT file can be put back in place in case of difficulties during the SYSGEN or SYSGENR.

If there are several versions of the operating system on the system, the current version of the CONFTEXT file will be in the subvolume where the OSIMAGE file is open.

Command Interpreter Input File (CIIN)

The CIIN is a command file provided on the SUT tape. The CIIN file is initially configured by HP as $DSMSCM.SYS.CIIN. At the customer site, DSM/SCM will automatically copy the CIIN file from the initial location into each SYSnn subvolume created.

The CIIN file contains a limited set of commands that reload the remaining processors and start a TACL process pair on the system console. If a CIIN file is present and enabled, it is automatically invoked by the initial TACL process after the first processor is loaded.

The name of the CIIN file is specified in the INITIAL_COMMAND_FILE entry of the ALLPROCESSORS paragraph of the CONFTEXT configuration file.

RISK   If erroneous commands are added or modified in the CIIN file, the system may fail to be able to be loaded, in which case it would be impossible to fix the CIIN file to correct the problem.

AP-FILE-SYSCONF-01   Even if a CIIN file is not used during coldloads, the system manager should create a 'dummy' CIIN file so that another user can't create one with malicious contents.

AP-FILE-SYSCONF-01   Many companies modify the RELOAD command in the CIIN file to reload only a minimal set of processors (such as processor 1) in order to test for successful startup of a minimal system environment before bringing up the entire system.

HP recommends that only a limited set of commands be included in the CIIN file because adding commands to bring up other devices or processes can cause the startup sequence to fail if any device should malfunction. The system should be brought up in stages that can be verified before moving on to the next stage. This makes it easier to recover should any step fail.

CUSTFILE File

The CUSTFILE is an edit file included on every Release Version Update (RVU). The file will be located on $SYSTEM in a subvolume named "A<nnnnnn>" where <nnnnnn> is the NonStop server's serial number. The system serial number is stored in the RLSEID file on $SYSTEM.SYSnn. The CUSTFILE contains information on the software products on the SUT, their related files, and the destination and use of each file. The CUSTFILE is customized for each customer's system.

```
Example 1:
$SYSTEM.A064421
```

In Example 1, the system number is A064421 and the CUSTFILE resides in $SYSTEM.A064421.

The first part of the CUSTFILE, the lines with the number one (1) in the first column, lists all the products purchased by the customer and included on the SUT.

```
Example 2:
1 A043421    SITE'S SPECIFIC FILES        021213
1 R0021G05   TAPEPROCESS                  861016
1 R0039G03   WAN 3270                     020312
1 R0051G02   CSSLAPB-X21 DRIVER           020611
1 R0058G05   MEASURE GUI                  990222
```

Example 2 shows several lines from the first part of the CUSTFILE. Each line corresponds to a product.

The second part of the file, lines with the number two (2) in the first column, lists the files on the SUT, labeled by subsystem and showing the use of the file and its destination subvolume. These lines also indicate which object files must be LICENSED. This is shown by the 'L' in column 62. See Appendix A for instructions on creating a listing of just those object files that should be licensed.

```
Example 3:
2 A043421    RLSEID    CONFIG    SYSGEN   COPY    SYSNN       021213090128
2 R0010G02   T0010G02  SOFTDOC   DOCPRINT                     021106154305
2 R0010G02   ZLDSTMPL  ZTEMPL    SYSGEN   TEMPLATE            021104225512
2 R0021G05   A0CINFO   ZPHICNFG  CONFIG                       021106154423
2 R0021G05   DTAPEDEF  ZGUARD    INSTALL                      861016191034
2 R0021G05   OTPPROCP  ZGUARD    SYSGEN   COPY    SYSNN       020930161355
2 R0021G05   STAPTMPL  ZTEMPL    USER                         010625114321
2 R0222G06   DUSL      ZGUARD    SYSGEN   COPY    SYSNN   L   981103122248
2 R0039G03   C0039P00  ZWAN3270  SYSGEN   MCODE   CSSNN       020123041035
```

Example 3 shows several lines from the second part of the CUSTFILE. The DUSL program in the ZGUARD subsystem should be licensed. The OTPPROCP program will be copied to the new SYSnn subvolume. The C003P00 macro will be copied to the new CSSnn subvolume. The SYSGEN and INSTALL notations show whether the program is SYSGENed or installed outside of SYSGEN.

AP-ADVICE-CUSTFILE-01   The CUSTFILE provides a record of installed products and, for integrity purposes, should be secured from inadvertent alteration or deletion. It should be secured against WRITE and PURGE access by general users.

The CUSTFILE is usually available for READ access to general users.

RLSEID File

An edit file included on every SUT and placed on the system as $SYSTEM.SYSnn. The system serial number is stored in the RLSEID the current O/S release level.

```
Example 1:
fup copy $system.sys01.RLSEID
R24 045422 G06.18
```

In Example 1, the RLSEID contains the system number '045422", the software release number is G06.18. In this case the CUSTFILE resides in $SYSTEM.A045422.

The CUSTFILE and RLSEID files are output files only. They are references for the subsystems installed on the system and may be of interest to system managers, developers and users in general.

RISK   Security risk for READ access is minimal.

RISK   The CUSTFILE and RLSEID files should be secured from inadvertent alteration or deletion. Security risk for READ access is minimal.

AP-ADVICE-RLSEID-01   The RLSEID file provides a record of installed products and, for integrity purposes, should be secured from inadvertent alteration or deletion. It should be secured against WRITE and PURGE access by general users.

OSCONFIG File

In D-series RVUs, the Configuration Utility Program (COUP) is used for on-line configuration of system components. COUP configuration records are stored in the OSCONFIG file.

In G-series RVUs, the OSCONFIG configuration file built by SYSGENR contains only Software Problem Isolation and Fix Facility (SPIFF) and Software Identification (SWID) tool records.

Securing the SYSTEM CONFIGURATION Files

BP-FILE-SYSCNF-01   CONFALT should be secured "NUUU".

BP-OPSYS-OWNER-01   CONFALT should be owned by SUPER.SUPER.

BP-OPSYS-FILELOC-01   CONFALT must reside in $SYSTEM.SYSnn.

BP-FILE-SYSCNF-02   CONFAUX should be secured "NUUU".

BP-OPSYS-OWNER-01   CONFAUX should be owned by SUPER.SUPER.

BP-OPSYS-FILELOC-01   CONFAUX must reside in $SYSTEM.SYSnn.

BP-FILE-SYSCNF-03   CONFBASE should be secured "NUUU".

BP-OPSYS-OWNER-01   CONFBASE should be owned by SUPER.SUPER.

BP-OPSYS-FILELOC-01   CONFBASE must reside in $SYSTEM.SYSnn.

BP-FILE-SYSCNF-04   CONFLIST should be secured "NUUU".

BP-OPSYS-OWNER-01   CONFLIST should be owned by SUPER.SUPER.

BP-OPSYS-FILELOC-01   CONFLIST must reside in $SYSTEM.SYSnn.

BP-FILE-SYSCNF-05   CONFTEXT should be secured "NUUU".

BP-OPSYS-OWNER-01   CONFTEXT should be owned by SUPER.SUPER.

BP-OPSYS-FILELOC-01   CONFTEXT must reside in $SYSTEM.SYSnn.

BP-FILE-SYSCNF-06   CIIN should be secured "NUUU".

BP-OPSYS-OWNER-01   CIIN should be owned by SUPER.SUPER.

BP-OPSYS-FILELOC-01   CIIN can reside in $SYSTEM.SYSnn.

BP-FILE-SYSCNF-07   CUSTFILE should be secured "NUUU".

BP-OPSYS-OWNER-03   CUSTFILE should be owned by SUPER.SUPER.

BP-OPSYS-FILELOC-03   CUSTFILE resides in $SYSTEM.A<nnnnnn>.

BP-FILE-SYSCNF-08   RLSEID should be secured "NUUU".

BP-OPSYS-OWNER-01   RLSEID should be owned by SUPER.SUPER.

BP-OPSYS-FILELOC-01   RLSEID must reside in $SYSTEM.SYSnn

BP-FILE-SYSCNF-09   OSCONFIG should be secured "NUUU".

BP-OPSYS-OWNER-01   OSCONFIG should be owned by SUPER.SUPER.

BP-OPSYS-FILELOC-01   OSCONFIG must reside in $SYSTEM.SYSnn.

If available, use Safeguard software or a third party object security product to grant access to the Configuration Files to necessary personnel, and deny access to all others.

BP-SAFE-SYSCNF–01 to 09   Add Safeguard Protection Records to grant appropriate access to the configuration files.

	Discovery Questions	Look here:
OPSYS-OWNER-01	Who owns the CONFALT file?	Fileinfo
OPSYS-OWNER-01	Who owns the CONFAUX file?	Fileinfo
OPSYS-OWNER-01	Who owns the CONFBASE file?	Fileinfo
OPSYS-OWNER-01	Who owns the CONFLIST file?	Fileinfo
OPSYS-OWNER-01	Who owns the CONFTEXT file?	Fileinfo
OPSYS-OWNER-01	Who owns the CIIN file?	Fileinfo
OPSYS-OWNER-03	Who owns the CUSTFILE file?	Fileinfo
OPSYS-OWNER-01	Who owns the RLSEID file?	Fileinfo
OPSYS-OWNER-01	Who owns the OSCONFIG file?	Fileinfo
FILE-SYSCNF-01 SAFE-SYSCNF-01	Is the CONFALT file correctly secured with the Guardian or Safeguard system?	Fileinfo Safecom
FILE-SYSCNF-02 SAFE-SYSCNF-02	Is the CONFAUX file correctly secured with the Guardian or Safeguard system?	Fileinfo Safecom
FILE-SYSCNF-03 SAFE-SYSCNF-03	Is the CONFBASE file correctly secured with the Guardian or Safeguard system?	Fileinfo Safecom
FILE-SYSCNF-04 SAFE-SYSCNF-04	Is the CONFLIST file correctly secured with the Guardian or Safeguard system?	Fileinfo Safecom
FILE-SYSCNF-05 SAFE-SYSCNF-05	Is the CONFTEXT file correctly secured with the Guardian or Safeguard system?	Fileinfo Safecom
FILE-SYSCNF-06 SAFE-SYSCNF-06	Is the CIIN file correctly secured with Guardian or Safeguard system?	Fileinfo Safecom
FILE-SYSCNF-07 SAFE-SYSCNF-07	Is the CUSTFILE file correctly secured with the Guardian or Safeguard system?	Fileinfo Safecom
FILE-SYSCNF-08 SAFE-SYSCNF-08	Is the RLSEID file correctly secured with the Guardian or Safeguard system?	Fileinfo Safecom
FILE-SYSCNF-09 SAFE-SYSCNF-09	Is the OSCONFIG file correctly secured with the Guardian or Safeguard system?	Fileinfo Safecom

Related Topics

Operating System
DSM/SCM

System Processes

This section outlines many of the standard process that will be running on an active system. The list that follows uses the defaulted naming convention recommended by HP. (Some processes could be running as a different name.)

Process Name	Description	Object File
$0	Primary event message collector that provides a central collection point for all events from all subsystems in a system	OSIMAGE
$CMON	User command monitor process	$SYSTEM.<svol>.<cmonobj>
$<disk>	Physical Disk Volume, per volume	$SYSTEM.SYSnn.TSYSDP2
$<vdisk>	Virtual Disk Volume, per volume	$SYSTEM.SYSnn.OVDP
$CLCI	Initial TACL process	$SYSTEM.SYSnn.TACL
$DMnn	INSPECT Collectors, one per CPU	$SYSTEM.SYSnn.DMON
$IMON	INSPECT Monitor	$SYSTEM.SYSnn.IMON
$NULL	Null output process	$SYSTEM.SYSTEM.NULL
$NCP	Expand line handler manager process	$SYSTEM.SYSnn.NCPOBJ
$PIPE	OSS pipe server	$SYSTEM.ZRSCHOST.PIPEMAN
$POOLnn	Storage pool processes, one per CPU	$SYSTEM.SYSnn.OPP
$SIMnn	Process per CPU	OSIMAGE
$S	Spooler Collector	$SYSTEM.SYSTEM.CSPOOL
$SPLS	Spooler Supervisor	$SYSTEM.SYSTEM.SPOOL
$SPLP	Spooler print processor	$SYSTEM.SYSTEM.SPOOLPA
$TMP	TMF TMP process	$SYSTEM.SYSnn.TMFTMP
$VHS	Virtual Home Terminal Process	$SYSTEM.VHS.VHS
$XBKn	NonStop TMF backout process	$SYSTEM.SYSnn.TMFBOUT
$XCAT	NonStop TMF catalog manager	$SYSTEM.SYSnn.TMFCTLG
$XDMS	Mediacom Server	$SYSTEM.SYSnn.MEDIASRV
$XMM	Measure Monitor	$SYSTEM.SYSnn.MEASMON
$XMnn	Measure Collectors per CPU	$SYSTEM.SYSnn.MEASCTL
$YMIOP	Interface to the MSP for other subsystems	OSIMAGE

Process Name	Description	Object File
$YPHI	DSM/SCM Pathway Application	$SYSTEM.SYSTEM.PATHMON
$Z0	EMS Compatibility Distributor process for OSIMAGE.	OSIMAGE
$ZBAT	NetBatch Manager	$SYSTEM.SYSTEM.NETBATCH
$ZCDB	Configuration database manager process	$SYSTEM.SYSnn.ZCDB
$ZCNF	Configuration utility process	OSIMAGE
$ZCVPn	TSM event servers, one per CPU	$SYSTEM.SYSnn.CEVSMX
$ZDMP	TFDS process	$SYSTEM.SYSnn.TFDS
$ZEXP	Expand line handler manager process	$SYSTEM.SYSnn.OZEXP
$ZFMnn	OSS File Manager, one per CPU	$SYSTEM.SYSnn.OSSFM
$ZHOME	Virtual output process for system processes	$SYSTEM.SYSnn.ZHOME
$ZLnn	The LINKMON processes, one per CPU	$SYSTEM.SYSnn.ROUT
$ZLMnn	LAN monitor process, one per CPU	$SYSTEM.SYSnn.LANMON
$ZLOG	TMD collector	$SYSTEM.SYSnn.EMSACOLL
$ZMnn	QIO monitor process, one per CPU	$SYSTEM.SYSnn.QIOMON
$ZMSGQ	OSS message queue service	$SYSTEM.SYSnn.ZMSGQ
$ZNET	Subsystem Control Program (SCP) process	$SYSTEM.SYSnn.SCP
$ZNUP	Network utility process	OSIMAGE
$ZOPR	EMS system-level logger	OSIMAGE
$ZPHI	EMS alternate collector and logger	$SYSTEM.SYSnn.EMSACOLL
$ZPLS	OSS sockets local server	$SYSTEM.SYSnn.OSSLS
$ZPM	Persistence manager	$SYSTEM.SYSnn.ZPM
$ZPMON	OSS monitor process	$SYSTEM.SYSnn.OSSMON
$ZPMPn	RPC portmapper process	$SYSTEM.ZRPC.PORTMAP
$ZPNS	OSS name server	$SYSTEM.SYSnn.NS
$ZPPnn	OSS pipes server, one per CPU	$SYSTEM.SYSnn.OSSPS
$ZRSCX	TDP process	$SYSTEM.SYSTEM.TDP
$ZSnn	Safeguard process, one per CPU	$SYSTEM.SYSnn.OSMON

Process Name	Description	Object File
$ZSMP	Safeguard Manager Process	$SYSTEM.SYSnn.OSMP
$ZSMS	Storage Manager Process	$SYSTEM.SYSnn.OMP
$ZSPE	SP to EMS event conversion process	$SYSTEM.SYSnn.ZSPE
$ZSSnn	INSPECT process snapshot, one per CPU	$SYSTEM.SYSnn.INSPSNAP
$ZSVR	Labeled tape server process	$SYSTEM.SYSnn.ZSERVER
$ZTAnn	OSS transport agents, one per CPU	$SYSTEM.SYSnn.OSSTA
$ZTCPn	TCP/IP process, one per CPU	$SYSTEM.SYSnn.TCPIP
$ZTMnn	NonStop TMF monitor processes, one per CPU	$SYSTEM.SYSnn.TMFMON2
$ZTNPn	Telnet server process	$SYSTEM.SYSnn.TELSERV
$ZTSM	TSM service application transfer process	$SYSTEM.SYSnn.SRM
$ZVHS	$VHS Pathway Process	$SYSTEM.SYSTEM.PATHMON
$ZVPT	ViewPoint PATHMON Process	$SYSTEM.SYSTEM.PATHMON
$ZZATM	Async subsystem monitor process	$SYSTEM.SYSnn.ATMASM
$ZZFOX	FOX subsystem monitor process	$SYSTEM.SYSnn.FOXMON
$ZZKRN	HP NonStop Kernel Manager Process	$SYSTEM.SYSnn.OZKRN
$ZZLAN	LAN subsystem manager process	$SYSTEM.SYSnn.LANMAN
$ZZSTO	Storage subsystem manager process	$SYSTEM.SYSnn.TZSTO
$ZZWAN	WAN subsystem manager process	$SYSTEM.SYSnn.WANMGR
$ZZWnn	Concentrator manager, one per CPU	$SYSTEM.SYSnn.CONMGR

Securing System Processes

For system processes not otherwise noted throughout this Gazette, security is described below. For processes in the table above and not listed below, security is described in the appropriate section of the Gazette.

BP-FILE- SYSPROC-01   TSYSDP2 should be secured "UUCU".

BP-OPSYS-OWNER-01   TSYSDP2 should be owned by SUPER.SUPER.

BP-OPSYS-FILELOC-01   TSYSDP2 must reside in $SYSTEM.SYSnn.

BP-FILE-SYSPROC-02   NULL should be secured "UUNU".

BP-OPSYS-OWNER-02   NULL should be owned by SUPER.SUPER.

BP-OPSYS-FILELOC-02   NULL must reside in $SYSTEM.SYSTEM.

BP-FILE-SYSPROC-03   OZKRN should be secured "UUCU".

BP-OPSYS-LICENSE-01   OZKRN must be LICENSED.

BP-OPSYS-OWNER-01   OZKRN should be owned by SUPER.SUPER.

BP-OPSYS-FILELOC-01   OZKRN must reside in $SYSTEM.SYSnn.

BP-FILE-SYSPROC-04   ZHOME should be secured "UUCU".

BP-OPSYS-OWNER-01   ZHOME should be owned by SUPER.SUPER.

BP-OPSYS-FILELOC-01   ZHOME must reside in $SYSTEM.SYSnn.

BP-FILE-SYSPROC-05   CONMGR should be secured "UUCU".

BP-OPSYS-OWNER-01   CONMGR should be owned by SUPER.SUPER.

BP-OPSYS-FILELOC-01   CONMGR must reside in $SYSTEM.SYSnn.

BP-FILE-SYSPROC-06   SRM should be secured "UUCU".

BP-OPSYS-OWNER-01   SRM should be owned by SUPER.SUPER.

BP-OPSYS-FILELOC-01   SRM must reside in $SYSTEM.SYSnn.

BP-FILE-SYSPROC-07   ZSPE should be secured "UUCU".

BP-OPSYS-OWNER-01   ZSPE should be owned by SUPER.SUPER.

BP-OPSYS-FILELOC-01   ZSPE must reside in $SYSTEM.SYSnn.

BP-FILE-SYSPROC-08   ZPM should be secured "UUCU".

BP-OPSYS-OWNER-01   ZPM should be owned by SUPER.SUPER.

BP-OPSYS-FILELOC-01   ZPM must reside in $SYSTEM.SYSnn.

BP-FILE-SYSPROC-09   CEVSMX should be secured "UUCU".

BP-OPSYS-OWNER-01   CEVSMX should be owned by SUPER.SUPER.

BP-OPSYS-FILELOC-01   CEVSMX must reside in $SYSTEM.SYSnn.

BP-FILE-SYSPROC-10   ZCDB should be secured "UUCU".

BP-OPSYS-OWNER-01   ZCDB should be owned by SUPER.SUPER.

BP-OPSYS-FILELOC-01   ZCDB must reside in $SYSTEM.SYSnn.

BP-FILE-SYSPROC-11   QIOMON should be secured "UUCU".

BP-OPSYS-OWNER-01   QIOMON should be owned by SUPER.SUPER.

BP-OPSYS-FILELOC-01   QIOMON must reside in $SYSTEM.SYSnn.

If a third party process control product is used to grant selected users access to process control, only the users allowed to start and stop process should be allowed and all other commands should be restricted.

With a third party access control product

3P-PROCESS-SYSPROCS-01   Use a third party access control product to give the control of certain processes to a limited group of users only.

	Discovery Questions	Look here:
OPSYS-OWNER-01	Who owns the TSYSDP2 object file?	Fileinfo
OPSYS-OWNER-01	Who owns the OZKRN object file?	Fileinfo
OPSYS-OWNER-01	Who owns the ZHOME object file?	Fileinfo
OPSYS-OWNER-01	Who owns the CONMGR object file?	Fileinfo
OPSYS-OWNER-01	Who owns the SRM object file?	Fileinfo
OPSYS-OWNER-01	Who owns the ZSPE object file?	Fileinfo
OPSYS-OWNER-01	Who owns the ZPM object file?	Fileinfo
OPSYS-OWNER-01	Who owns the CEVSMX object file?	Fileinfo
OPSYS-OWNER-01	Who owns the ZCDB object file?	Fileinfo
OPSYS-OWNER-01	Who owns the QIOMON object file?	Fileinfo
OPSYS-OWNER-02	Who owns the NULL object file?	Fileinfo
OPSYS-LICENSE-01	Is the OZKRN object file licensed?	Fileinfo
FILE-SYSPROC-01	Is the TSYSDP2 object file secured correctly?	Fileinfo
FILE-SYSPROC-02	Is the NULL object file secured correctly?	Fileinfo
FILE-SYSPROC-03	Is the OZKRN object file secured correctly?	Fileinfo
FILE-SYSPROC-04	Is the ZHOME object file secured correctly?	Fileinfo
FILE-SYSPROC-05	Is the CONMGR object file secured correctly?	Fileinfo
FILE-SYSPROC-06	Is the SRM object file secured correctly?	Fileinfo
FILE-SYSPROC-07	Is the ZSPE object file secured correctly?	Fileinfo
FILE-SYSPROC-08	Is the ZPM object file secured correctly?	Fileinfo
FILE-SYSPROC-09	Is the CEVSMX object file secured correctly?	Fileinfo
FILE-SYSPROC-10	Is the ZCDB object file secured correctly?	Fileinfo
FILE-SYSPROC-11	Is the QIOMON object file secured correctly?	Fileinfo

System Startup Files

System startup files are developed and used by the system manager and operators to perform startup and shutdown operations. In some cases the files may be centrally located, separated by subsystem or by startup and shutdown functionality. There is no required naming convention for these files.

System Startup Files

The sequence in which startup files are invoked can be important. Some processes require other processes to be running before they can be started. Examples of subsystems that must be started after a coldload are; TMF, TACLs, SPOOLER, TCPIP, CMON, and ODBC.

> *RISK*   The subvolume(s) that contain these files should reside on $SYSTEM in case that is the only volume that can be loaded.

> *RISK*   Only system managers should be allowed to modify startup files. The loss or modification of these files could be destructive to starting the system processes.

Securing the System Startup Files

> **BP-FILE-STARTUP-01**   Startup files should be secured "NUUU".
>
> **BP-OPSYS-OWNER-03**   Startup files should be owned by SUPER.SUPER.
>
> **BP-OPSYS-FILELOC-03**   Startup files should reside on $SYSTEM.<startup>

If available, use Safeguard software or a third party object security product to grant access to the Startup subvolume to necessary personnel, and deny access to all others.

> **BP-SAFE-STARTUP–01**   Add a Safeguard Protection Records to grant appropriate access to the Startup files.

	Discovery Questions	Look here:
FILE-POLICY	Where are the startup files located?	Policy
OPSYS-OWNER-03	Who owns the startup files?	Fileinfo
FILE-STARTUP-01	Are the startup files correctly secured with the	Fileinfo
SAFE-STARTUP-01	Guardian or Safeguard system?	Safecom

Related Topics

Operating System
DSM/SCM

System Utilities

The following programs are system utilities.

TFDS

Failure recovery utilities

TACL tool utilities

TFD Data System

The HP TFDS data system automates tasks associated with data collection and resource recovery in the event of software-related processor or subsystem failure on G-series operating systems. It can be configured to automatically initiate a processor dump and reload the processor if the software failure is a CPU halt. Automating these steps eliminates the time delay of waiting for manual intervention to collect the data and reload the processor.

TFDS can be configured to determine whether the failure is a first-time problem occurrence or the result of a recurring defect. If it is a recurring defect, TFDS will suppress redundant dumps and instead, track the number of occurrences, and notify HP.

TFDS consists of these components:

DUMPUTIL

RCVDUMP

RELOAD

RPDUMP

TFDS

TFDSCOM

TFDSCONF

TFDS gathers information with little or no impact on the production environment. It takes no processor time to constantly monitor the system; it is awakened only when action is necessary.

RISK   TFDS is a reporting program, it poses no security risks.

However, it is not normally run by the general user and should only be run by authorized personnel.

DUMPUTIL

The fixup utility, DUMPUTIL, is part of the Fast Memory Dump to relate the two CPU dumps.

RCVDUMP

The Recovery Engine performs data collection and initiates processor reloads when necessary. The object file for the Recovery Engine is RCVDUMP.

Processing an RCVDUMP does have an impact on system performance.

RISK   TFDS can accept several dump requests simultaneously, but multiple RCVDUMPs running concurrently places an extreme load on a system.

AP-FILE-TFDS-01   Use the MAXCONDUMPS command to indicate the number of concurrent CPU dumps TFDS should be allowed to initiate.

RELOAD

The RELOAD program reloads processors. It is also used to load processors during a cold load of the system.

RPDUMP

The RPDUMP utility is part of the Fast Memory Dump to post-reload the dump.

TFDS monitor

The TFDS monitor constantly watches system messages for notification of software-related processor halts or software failure. TFDS takes no processor time for this monitoring; it is awakened only when action is necessary. The TFDS monitor process is $ZDMP.

RISK   The TFDS process ($ZDMP) must be running when a software failure event occurs to utilize most TFDS services, so it should be running at all times.

AP-ADVICE-TFDS-02   The TFDS process ($ZDMP) should be running at all times.

TFDSCOM

TFDSCOM is the command interpreter for the TFDS Monitor used to display or modify configuration values, to save a specific configuration, to start or cancel activities, and to request help.

TFDSCONF

TFDSCONF is a configuration file used to configure the TFDS system.

Securing TFDS

BP-FILE-TFDS-01   DUMPUTIL should be secured "UUCU".

BP-OPSYS-OWNER-01   DUMPUTIL should be owned by SUPER.SUPER.

BP-OPSYS-FILELOC-01   DUMPUTIL must reside in $SYSTEM.SYSnn

BP-FILE-TFDS-02   RCVDUMP should be secured "UUCU".

BP-OPSYS-OWNER-01   RCVDUMP should be owned by SUPER.SUPER.

BP-OPSYS-FILELOC-01   RCVDUMP must reside in $SYSTEM.SYSnn

BP-FILE-TFDS-03   RELOAD should be secured "UUCU".

BP-OPSYS-LICENSE-01   RELOAD must be LICENSED.

BP-OPSYS-OWNER-01   RELOAD should be owned by SUPER.SUPER.

BP-OPSYS-FILELOC-01   RELOAD must reside in $SYSTEM.SYSnn

BP-FILE-TFDS-04   RPDUMP should be secured "UUCU".

BP-OPSYS-OWNER-01   RPDUMP should be owned by SUPER.SUPER.

BP-OPSYS-FILELOC-01   RPDUMP must reside in $SYSTEM.SYSnn

BP-PROCESS-TFDS-01   The $ZDMP process should be running.

BP-FILE-TFDS-05   TFDS should be secured "UUCU".

BP-OPSYS-LICENSE-01   TFDS must be LICENSED.

BP-OPSYS-OWNER-01   TFDS should be owned by SUPER.SUPER.

BP-OPSYS-FILELOC-01   TFDS must reside in $SYSTEM.SYSnn

BP-FILE-TFDS-06   TFDSCOM should be secured "UUCU".

BP-OPSYS-LICENSE-01   TFDSCOM must be LICENSED.

BP-OPSYS-OWNER-01   TFDSCOM should be owned by SUPER.SUPER.

BP-OPSYS-FILELOC-01   TFDSCOM must reside in $SYSTEM.SYSnn

BP-FILE-TFDS-07   TFDSCONF should be secured "CUUU".

BP-OPSYS-OWNER-03   TFDSCONF should be owned by SUPER.SUPER.

BP-OPSYS-FILELOC-03   TFDSCONF resides in $SYSTEM.ZTFDS

If available, use Safeguard software or a third party object security product to grant access to the TFDS components only to users who require access in order to perform their jobs.

BP-SAFE-TFDS-01 Add a Safeguard Protection Record to grant appropriate access to the TFDS object file.

BP-SAFE-TFDS-02 Add a Safeguard Protection Record to grant appropriate access to the TFDSCOM object file.

BP-SAFE-TFDS-03 Add a Safeguard Protection Record to grant appropriate access to the RELOAD object file.

	Discovery Questions	Look here:
FILE-POLICY	Who is allowed to execute TFDS and related functions on production systems?	Policy
PROCESS-TFDS-01	Is the $ZDMP process running?	Status
OPSYS-OWNER-01	Who owns the DUMPUTIL object file?	Fileinfo
OPSYS-OWNER-01	Who owns the RCVDUMP object file?	Fileinfo
OPSYS-OWNER-01	Who owns the RELOAD object file?	Fileinfo
OPSYS-OWNER-01	Who owns the PRDUMP object file?	Fileinfo
OPSYS-OWNER-01	Who owns the TFDS object file?	Fileinfo
OPSYS-OWNER-01	Who owns the TFDSCOM object file?	Fileinfo
OPSYS-OWNER-03	Who owns the TFDSCONF object file?	Fileinfo
OPSYS-LICENSE-01	Is the RELOAD file licensed?	Fileinfo
OPSYS-LICENSE-01	Is the TFDS file licensed?	Fileinfo
OPSYS-LICENSE-01	Is the TFDSCOM file licensed?	Fileinfo
FILE-TFDS-01	Is the DUMPUTIL object file secured correctly?	Fileinfo
FILE-TFDS-02	Is the RCVDUMP object file secured correctly?	Fileinfo
FILE-TFDS-03 SAFE-TFDS-03	Is the RELOAD file correctly secured with the Guardian or Safeguard system?	Fileinfo Safeguard
FILE-TFDS-04	Is the PRDUMP object file secured correctly?	Fileinfo
FILE-TFDS-05 SAFE-TFDS-01	Is the TFDS file correctly secured with the Guardian or Safeguard system?	Fileinfo Safeguard
FILE-TFDS-06 SAFE-TFDS-02	Is the TFDSCOM file correctly secured with the Guardian or Safeguard system?	Fileinfo Safeguard
FILE-TFDS-07	Is the TFDSCONF object file secured correctly?	Fileinfo

Failure Utilities

The HP NonStop server provides several TACL utilities and utility programs that perform functions when a processor halts and creates a dump file.

These functions should only be performed by qualified personnel, who are normally part of the SUPER Group.

The utilities are:

COPYDUMP
CRUNCH
GARTH
RCVDUMP

COPYDUMP

The COPYDUMP program copies and compresses a tape dump file into a disk dump file.

CRUNCH

A utility program supplied by HP to analyze CPU dumps on pre Release Version G06 operating systems.

GARTH

GARTH is a utility program supplied by HP to analyze CPU dumps on Release version G06 operating systems. The TACL macro GARTH, initiates the GARTHNSK from the ZGARTH subvolume.

RECEIVEDUMP/RCVDUMP

The RECEIVEDUMP TACL command initiates the RCVDUMP program to receive the dump from a halted processor over the interprocessor bus.

Securing Failure Tools

BP-FILE-FTOOLS-01   COPYDUMP should be secured "UUCU".

BP-OPSYS-LICENSE-01   COPYDUMP must be LICENSED.

BP-OPSYS-OWNER-01   COPYDUMP should be owned by SUPER.SUPER.

BP-OPSYS-FILELOC-01   COPYDUMP must reside in $SYSTEM.SYSnn

BP-FILE-FTOOLS-02   CRUNCH should be secured "UUCU".

BP-OPSYS-OWNER-02   CRUNCH should be owned by SUPER.SUPER.

BP-OPSYS-FILELOC-02   CRUNCH must reside in $SYSTEM.SYSTEM

BP-FILE-FTOOLS-03   GARTH should be secured "CUCU".

BP-OPSYS-OWNER-02   GARTH should be owned by SUPER.SUPER.

BP-OPSYS-FILELOC-02   GARTH must reside in $SYSTEM.SYSTEM

BP-FILE-FTOOLS-04   GARTHNSK should be secured "UUCU".

BP-OPSYS-OWNER-03   GARTHNSK should be owned by
SUPER.SUPER.

BP-OPSYS-FILELOC-03   GARTHNSK resides in $SYSTEM.ZGARTH

BP-FILE-FTOOLS-05   RCVDUMP should be secured "UUCU".

BP-OPSYS-OWNER-01   RCVDUMP should be owned by SUPER.SUPER.

BP-OPSYS-FILELOC-01   RCVDUMP must reside in $SYSTEM.SYSnn

	Discovery Questions	Look here:
FILE-POLICY	Who is allowed to manage processor halts and related functions on production systems?	Policy
OPSYS-OWNER-01	Who owns the COPYDUMP object file?	Fileinfo
OPSYS-OWNER-01	Who owns the CRUNCH object file?	Fileinfo
OPSYS-OWNER-01	Who owns the GARTH macro file?	Fileinfo
OPSYS-OWNER-01	Who owns the GARTHNSK object file?	Fileinfo
OPSYS-OWNER-01	Who owns the RCVDUMP object file?	Fileinfo
OPSYS-LICENSE-01	Is the COPYDUMP file licensed?	Fileinfo
FILE-FTOOLS-01	Is the COPYDUMP object file secured correctly?	Fileinfo
FILE-FTOOLS-02	Is the CRUNCH object file secured correctly?	Fileinfo
FILE-FTOOLS-03	Is the GARTH file secured correctly?	Fileinfo
FILE-FTOOLS-04	Is the GARTHNSK file secured correctly?	Fileinfo
FILE-FTOOLS-05	Is the RCVDUMP object file secured correctly?	Fileinfo

TACL Tool Utilities

The HP NonStop server provides several TACL utilities and utility programs that perform specific functions for analyzing internal components.

The utilities are:

FCHECK

FILCHECK

TANDUMP

FCHECK

The FCHECK program reports on the internal consistency of Enscribe files.

FCHECK is most often used to verify the structure and validity of a file. FCHECK cannot be used to alter the physical structure of a file.

RISK FCHECK is strictly a reporting tool and, therefore, poses no security risks.

FILCHECK

The FILCHECK program reports on the internal, physical data structure of objects and verifies that the structure is consistent.

The FILCHECK utility checks the physical structure of a DP2 structured object and reports any errors. The internal checks include the following:

Forward and backward pointers in blocks

Relative sector number and checksum of every block

Correct index levels

Data block and index block linkage and length

Block headers and rows in relative files

Offset pointers and order

Existence of any unreclaimed free space in the object

RISK FILCHECK is strictly a reporting tool and, therefore, poses no security risks.

TANDUMP

TANDUMP is a binary file editor, which can display and/or modify the contents of disk files.

This function should only performed by qualified personnel, who are normally part of the SUPER Group.

RISK   TANDUMP could be used to display or modify sensitive data or programs. It should not be available to the general user, nor should it be used by non-qualified personnel.

BP-FILE-TANDUMP-01   TANDUMP should not be available to the general user, nor should it be used by non-qualified personnel.

Securing TACL Tools

BP-FILE-TACLTOOL-01   FCHECK should be secured "UUNU".

BP-OPSYS-LICENSE-01   FCHECK must be LICENSED.

BP-OPSYS-OWNER-01   FCHECK should be owned by SUPER.SUPER.

BP-OPSYS-FILELOC-01   FCHECK must reside in $SYSTEM.SYSnn.

BP-FILE- TACLTOOL-02   FILCHECK should be secured "UUNU".

BP-OPSYS-LICENSE-01   FILCHECK must be LICENSED.

BP-OPSYS-OWNER-01   FILCHECK should be owned by SUPER.SUPER.

BP-OPSYS-FILELOC-01   FILCHECK must reside in $SYSTEM.SYSnn.

BP-FILE- TACLTOOL-03   TANDUMP should be secured "UUUU".

BP-OPSYS-OWNER-01   TANDUMP should be owned by SUPER.SUPER.

BP-OPSYS-FILELOC-01   TANDUMP must reside in $SYSTEM.SYSnn.

If available, use Safeguard software or a third party object security product to grant access to the TANDUMP components only to users who require access in order to perform their jobs.

BP-SAFE-TACLTOOL-01   Add a Safeguard Protection Record to grant appropriate access of the FCHECK object file.

BP-SAFE-TACLTOOL-02   Add a Safeguard Protection Record to grant appropriate access of the FILCHECK object file.

BP-SAFE-TACLTOOL-03   Add a Safeguard Protection Record to grant appropriate access of the TANDUMP object file.

	Discovery Questions	Look here:
OPSYS-OWNER-01	Who owns the FCHECK object file?	Fileinfo
OPSYS-OWNER-01	Who owns the FILCHECK object file?	Fileinfo
OPSYS-OWNER-01	Who owns the TANDUMP object file?	Fileinfo
OPSYS-LICENSE-01	Is the FCHECK file licensed?	Fileinfo

	Discovery Questions	Look here:
OPSYS-LICENSE-01	Is the FILCHECK file licensed?	Fileinfo
FILE-TACLTOOL-01	Is the FCHECK object file secured correctly?	Fileinfo
FILE-TACLTOOL-02	Is the FILCHECK object file secured correctly?	Fileinfo
FILE-POLICY	Who is allowed to execute TANDUMP on production systems?	Policy
FILE-TACLTOOL-03 SAFE-TACLTOOL-01	Is the TANDUMP file correctly secured with the Guardian or Safeguard system?	Fileinfo Safeguard

TACL Subsystem

The HP TACL command language is the standard command interface to the Guardian operating system. TACL is also a high level programming language capable of generating program components. TACL programs can be used as server processes to Pathway and GUI applications.

However, TACL is most commonly used for interactive work while the built-in functions are used in TACL programs, also called macros. TACL is fundamental to initiating many of the programs and subsystems discussed in this book.

RISK   TACL has so many possible risks associated with it that this discussion will focus on the components and the basic risks that are associated with TACL basic usage.

Each company should develop a security policy for TACL usage.

RISK   Logged on TACL sessions that are left running on unsecured terminals are at risk. This is an open door to an unauthorized user. Logged on TACL sessions running as SUPER.SUPER put the system at extreme risk.

For a detailed explanation of the logging on process, please refer to Part Four, Granting Access to the HP NonStop server.

TACL reads four files (TACLINIT, TACLSEGF, TACLLOCL and TACLCSTM) before it issues its first prompt. This allows for the creation of a customized TACL environment before any commands can be issued. All of these files contain text and valid TACL commands except the TACLSEGF, which is a compiled segment file.

TACL Subsystem Components

The TACL Subsystem Components are:

TACL

TACLBASE

TACLCOLD

TACLCSTM

TACLINIT

TACLLOCL

TACLSEGF

CPRULES0

CPRULES1

Other TACL-Related Utilities

TACL Built-in commands

TACL Sessions

TACL Configuration

The following parameters can be bound to the TACL object file using BIND, depending on the Operating System version running on the HP NonStop server:

Parameter	Definition			
	Positive Value	NegValue	Default	Risk
AUTOLOGOFFDELAY	Determines whether or not a TACL session will be logged off automatically (after a period of inactivity)			
	# of min inactivity	-1 Never logoff	30 MIN	Sessions that remain open and can be used by another user. Lose accountability.
BLINDLOGON	Can include the password as part of the LOGON command (displayed in the clear)			
	0 ok	1 Not ok	1	If passwords are displayed at logon, someone can read it.
CMONREQUIRED	CMON must rule on all requests			
	1 Required	0 Not Required	0	If $CMON isn't running or is running too slow, can cause denial of service.
REMOTECMONREQUIRED	A Remote CMON must rule on all requests			

Parameter	Definition			
	Positive Value	NegValue	Default	Risk
	1 Required	0 Not Required	0	If $CMON isn't running or is running too slow, can cause denial of service.
LOGOFFSCREENCLEAR	Blanks the screen when TACL session is logged off			
	1 Blanks	0 Doesn't	1	Another user can't review old session
NAMELOGON	Can logon using user number			
	0 Yes	1 No	1	Harder for hacker to guess userid when using names rather than numbers, because there are a finite number of user numbers.
NOCHANGEUSER	The ability to log on from one user to another?			
	0 Can	1 Cannot	0	Limited risk if passwords enforced
CMONTIMEOUT	Number of seconds to wait for $CMON response?			
	# mins to Wait	-1 Wait forever	-1	Denial of service risk if waiting forever
REMOTECMONTIMEOUT	Number of seconds to wait for remote $CMON response?			
	# secs to Wait	-1 Wait forever	-1	Denial of service risk if waiting forever
REMOTESUPERID	Remote SUPER access allowed?			
	0 No	-1 Yes	-1	Super access from one system allows Super to another.
STOPONFEMODEMERR	Will session end when a modem error occurs?			
	0 Don't stop	1 Stop	0	Prevent another user dialing up and picking up an old session

BP-TACL-TACLCONF-01 AUTOLOGOFFDELAY should be 15 minutes or less.

BP-TACL-TACLCONF-02 BLINDLOGON should be set to .

BP-TACL-TACLCONF-03 CMONREQUIRED should be set to 0.

BP-TACL-TACLCONF-04 REMOTECMONREQUIRED should be 0.

BP-TACL-TACLCONF-05 LOGOFFSCREENCLEAR should be 1.

BP-TACL-TACLCONF-06   NAMELOGON should be 1 to force a name logon only.

BP-TACL-TACLCONF-07   NOCHANGEUSER can be 0 to allow logon from another userid.

BP-TACL-TACLCONF-08   CMONTIMEOUT should be 30 seconds or less.

BP-TACL-TACLCONF-09   REMOTECMONTIMEOUT should be 30 minutes or less.

BP-TACL-TACLCONF-10   REMOTESUPERID can be 0 to allow remote Super if its password is controlled.

BP-TACL-TACLCONF-11   STOPONFEMODEMERR should be 0.

RISK   The TACL program resides in the $SYSTEM.SYSnn subvolume and is replaced upon each operating system upgrade. The bound parameters will not be retained.

BP-TACL-TACLCONF-12   The parameters must be bound after each operating system upgrade.

TACLBASE File

An edit file that contains the same functionality as TACLSEGF. It must reside on the same subvolume as the TACL object file. The TACLBASE file is read by the install program and is used as the source for TACLSEGF.

RISK   If TACLBASE and TACLSEGF are not present, TACL can operate, but will provide only built-in functions and variables.

TACLCOLD

A segment file that TACL uses when running as the Coldload Command-Interpreter. TACL creates this file or reuses it as a way of reducing the chance that the coldload TACL will fail due to lack of disk space at startup.

TACLCSTM Files

Please refer to the Gazette section on *CSTM Configuration Files.

TACLINIT File

Edit file that resides on the same subvolume as the TACL file and is executed whenever a new TACL is initiated.

TACLLOCL File

The TACLLOCL program is a global startup file that is executed during the logon of every user at a TACL. It is intended to be used to configure the environment that should be uniform for all users.

> **RISK**   If the security of the TACLLOCL file permits a user other than the owner WRITE or PURGE access, they could modify the file or purge it and replace it with a new one.

> If a macro is executed within a TACLCSTM, the macro file must be also secured so that only authorized users can WRITE or PURGE it, otherwise someone could rename it and then install another file with the same name or simply insert commands that execute a Trojan horse program by invoking the macro via the TACLCSTM file.

TACL Segment Files

Segment files are compiled macros that can be loaded into an extended memory segment. When a segment file is attached to a TACL, it is loaded into memory, giving TACL immediate access to the macros, routines, and other variables the segment contains.

> **RISK**   If TACLBASE and TACLSEGF are not present, TACL can operate, but will provide only built-in functions and variables.

Segment files provide efficient storage for commonly used macros and routines.

The Default TACL Segment File

When each TACL session is started, TACL creates a private segment file to hold the variables in the root (:) directory. This segment is called the 'default segment file'. Next, TACL creates the directory UTILS and attaches the segment file TACLSEGF to it for shared access.

The TACLSEGF contains directories for all HP products on the system that have TACL programs. Each TACL command is stored as a :UTILS:TACL: command.

User-Defined Segment Files

To create a segment file, load a library file into a segment. After the contents of the file are in the segment file, the ATTACHSEG and USE commands establish access to the variables in the segment.

CPRULES0 and CPRULES1

Files that define the character set in use by TACL. CPRULES0 is the default set.

Other TACL-Related Utilities

In addition to the preceding list of files, there are utility programs that assist TACL in performing certain operations. Each program is in a separate program file in $SYSTEM.SYSnn or $SYSTEM.SYSTEM. These programs:

Perform privileged operations, such as adding users or reloading processors

Must be licensed for use by nonprivileged users

Can run only on the local system

The utility programs* are:

ADDUSER
ALARMOFF
BUSCMD
COPYDUMP
DEFAULT
DELUSER
LIGHTS
PASSWORD
RCVDUMP
RELOAD
RPASSWRD
USERS

* These utility programs are discussed separately, in other sections of the Gazette.

Built-in TACL Variables with Security Issues

The built-in TACL variables are:

#PMSEARCHLIST
#TACLSECURITY

#PMSEACHLIST

A Search List is a list of subvolumes that the TACL software uses to find a program file when the program is invoked using a file name that is not fully qualified. By default $SYSTEM.SYSTEM is always searched first and $SYSTEM.SYSnn is searched second.

#PMSEARCHLIST is a built-in TACL variable that specifies the subvolumes to be searched for program and macro files and the order in which the subvolumes will be searched.

Programs and macros residing in the subvolumes included in the PMSEARCHLIST need not be fully qualified when they are invoked.

```
Example 1:
19> fileinfo $system.sys*.fup
$SYSTEM.SYS01
         CODE      EOF  LAST MODIFIED OWNER RWEP  PExt  SExt
FUP       100L     2772160 02JUL2002 4:12 255,255 NUNU  252   64
20> fup
File Utility Program - T6553G07 - (01AUG2002)  System \MEXICO
Copyright Tandem Computers Incorporated 1981, 1983, 1985-2001
-
```

This example shows that because FUP resides in $SYSTEM.SYSnn, it can be invoked by simply typing FUP rather than $SYSTEM.SYS01.FUP.

In addition to specific subvolume names, the Search List can include the #DEFAULTS built-in TACL variable, which designates the user's current subvolume. However, including #DEFAULTS in the Search List can lead a user to accidentally execute a Trojan horse program, especially if #DEFAULTS appears before $SYSTEM.SYSTEM in the Search List. If #DEFAULTS must be used in the search list, put it after $SYSTEM.SYSTEM to ensure that users invoke only the distributed versions when they run trusted system programs such as FUP.

RISK   A potential breach of security exists if a TACL user can open another user's TACL process.

#TACLSECURITY

Returns a pair of characters, enclosed in quotes, that represent the current TACL security. The first character represents the criterion that determines whether or not to allow a process to open the TACL process's $RECEIVE for writing. The second character determines whether to allow an opener with a qualifying name to transfer data to or from a #SERVER.

```
Example 2:
13> #TACLSECURITY
#TACLSECURITY expanded to:
"NN"
```

The characters in the security string displayed are the same as the Guardian file security string. In the example above, 'NN' means all users, local or remote, can open the TACLPROCESS in question.

AP-ADVICE-TACL-01   To limit access to TACL process, use the #TACLSE-CURITY built-in variable to set the current TACL security, which indicates who can open this TACL process.

AP-FILE-TACL-01   To secure the TACL process from $RECEIVE access, set the #TACLSECURITY to "UU".

TACL sessions

TACL sessions can be configured in many ways:

ASSIGNs

DEFINEs

PARAMs

Built-in Variables

See Securing Applications Chapter for more information on ASSIGNs, DEFINEs, and PARAMs.

See HP Documentation for more information about additional Built-ins and other TACL capabilities.

Securing TACL Components

BP-FILE-TACL-01   TACL should be secured "UUNU".

BP-OPSYS-OWNER-01   TACL should be owned by SUPER.SUPER.

BP-OPSYS-FILELOC-01   TACL must reside in $SYSTEM.SYSnn.

BP-FILE-TACL-02   TACLBASE should be secured "NUUU".

BP-OPSYS-OWNER-01   TACLBASE should be owned by SUPER.SUPER.

BP-OPSYS-FILELOC-01   TACLBASE must reside in $SYSTEM.SYSnn.

BP-FILE-TACL-03   TACLCOLD should be secured "NUUU".

BP-OPSYS-OWNER-01   TACLCOLD should be owned by SUPER.SUPER.

BP-OPSYS-FILELOC-01   TACLCOLD must reside in $SYSTEM.SYSnn.

BP-FILE-TACL-04   TACLINIT should be secured "NUUU".

BP-OPSYS-OWNER-01   TACLINIT should be owned by SUPER.SUPER.

BP-OPSYS-FILELOC-01   TACLINIT must reside in $SYSTEM.SYSnn.

BP-FILE-TACL-05   TACLLOCL should be secured "NUUU".

BP-OPSYS-OWNER-02   TACLLOCL should be owned by SUPER.SUPER.

BP-OPSYS-FILELOC-02   TACLLOCL must reside in $SYSTEM.SYSTEM.

BP-FILE-TACL-06   TACLSEGF should be secured "NUUU".

BP-OPSYS-OWNER-01   TACLSEGF should be owned by SUPER.SUPER.

BP-OPSYS-FILELOC-01   TACLSEGF must reside in $SYSTEM.SYSnn.

BP-FILE-TACL-07   CPRULES0 should be secured "NUUU".

BP-OPSYS-OWNER-01   CPRULES0 should be owned by SUPER.SUPER.

BP-OPSYS-FILELOC-01   CPRULES0 must reside in $SYSTEM.SYSnn.

BP-FILE-TACL-08   CPRULES1 should be secured "NUUU".

BP-OPSYS-OWNER-01   CPRULES1 should be owned by SUPER.SUPER.

BP-OPSYS-FILELOC-01   CPRULES1 must reside in $SYSTEM.SYSnn.

If a third party access control product is used to grant selected users access to TACL, only the commands listed should be granted to general users. All other commands should be restricted.

3P-ACCESS-TACL-01   Use a third party access control product to allow the users responsible for using TACL commands and functions as SUPER.SUPER.

3P-ACCESS-TACL-02   Use a third party access control product to give the use of certain TACL commands and functions to a limited group of users only.

If available, use Safeguard software or a third party product to grant access to the TACL object file only to users who require it in order to perform their jobs.

BP-SAFE-TACL-01   Add a Safeguard Protection Record to grant appropriate access to the TACL object file.

	Discovery Questions	Look here:
OPSYS-OWNER-01	Who owns the TACL object file?	Fileinfo
OPSYS-OWNER-01	Who owns the TACLBASE file?	Fileinfo
OPSYS-OWNER-01	Who owns the TACLCOLD file?	Fileinfo
OPSYS-OWNER-01	Who owns the TACLINIT file?	Fileinfo
OPSYS-OWNER-01	Who owns the TACLSEGF file?	Fileinfo
OPSYS-OWNER-01	Who owns the CPRULES0 file?	Fileinfo

	Discovery Questions	Look here:
OPSYS-OWNER-01	Who owns the CPRULES1 file?	Fileinfo
OPSYS-OWNER-02	Who owns the TACLLOCL file?	Fileinfo
FILE-POLICY	What is the security policy concerning TACL?	Policy
FILE-TACL-01	Is the TACL object file correctly secured with	Fileinfo
SAFE-TACL-01	the Guardian or Safeguard system?	Safecom
FILE-TACL-02	Is the TACLBASE file secured correctly?	Fileinfo
FILE-TACL-03	Is the TACLCOLD file secured correctly?	Fileinfo
FILE-TACL-04	Is the TACLINIT file secured correctly?	Fileinfo
FILE-TACL-05	Is the TACLLOCL file secured correctly?	Fileinfo
FILE-TACL-06	Is the TACLSEGF file secured correctly?	Fileinfo
FILE-TACL-07	Is the CPRULES0 file secured correctly?	Fileinfo
FILE-TACL-08	Is the CPRULES1 file secured correctly?	Fileinfo

Related Topics

Operating System

TACL Tools

TAPECOM System Utility

TAPECOM labels tapes and handles labeled-tape requests in a labeled-tape environment. TAPECOM processes labeled-tape requests from other utilities such as BACKCOPY, BACKUP, and RESTORE.

A tape label is a record at the beginning of a tape that identifies the tape volume.

The system operators need to use TAPECOM to:

Monitor labeled-tape messages

Display requests to mount tapes or to use tape drives

Accept or reject tape mount requests or requests to use tape drives

Display the status of tape drives

Label or relabel tapes in ANSI or IBM format

Create scratch tapes

Other users use TAPECOM to display:

The status of tape drives

The requests to mount tapes or to use tape drives

On G-series operating system, labeled-tape operations are managed via MEDIACOM, which is part of the Distributed Systems Management/Tape Catalog (DSM/TC) software system.

AP-ADVICE-TAPECOM-01 On G-series operating systems, MEDIACOM must be used for labeled-tape operations.

AP-ADVICE-TAPECOM-02 The Corporate Security Policy should detail procedures for validating requests for backup tapes and securing those tapes in a tape library.

AP-ADVICE-TAPECOM-03 Physical and procedural protection of the backup tapes is vital.

AP-ADVICE-TAPECOM-04 Access to TAPECOM should be the same as access to other tape utilities.

AP-ADVICE-TAPECOM-05 Access to TAPECOM should be restricted to users authorized to manage labeled tapes.

Securing TAPECOM

BP-FILE-TAPECOM-01 TAPECOM should be secured "UUNU".

BP-OPSYS-LICENSE-01 TAPECOM must be LICENSED.

BP-OPSYS-OWNER-01 TAPECOM should be owned by SUPER.SUPER.

BP-OPSYS-FILELOC-01 TAPECOM must reside in $SYSTEM.SYSnn.

If available, use Safeguard software or a third party object security product to grant access to TAPECOM object files to necessary personnel, and deny access to all other users.

BP-SAFE-TAPECOM-01 Add a Safeguard Protection Record to grant appropriate access to the TAPECOM object file.

TAPECOM Commands With Security Implications

TAPECOM allows users access to copy or destroy sensitive data on tape media. All of the commands in the following list manipulate tapes or the tape library.

ACCEPT

CLEAR BLPCHECK

CLEAR NLCHECK

DUMPLABELS

LABEL[IBM]

NEXTTAPE

REJECT

RELABEL[IBM]

SCRATCH

SET BLPCHECK

SET NLCHECK

UNLABEL

USETAPE

If a third party access control product is used to grant selected users access to TAPECOM, only the commands listed should be granted to privileged users. All other commands should be available for general use.

3P-ACCESS-TAPECOM-01   Use a third party access control product to allow the users responsible for using TAPECOM commands access as SUPER.SUPER.

3P-ACCESS-TAPECOM-02   Use a third party access control product to give the use of certain TAPECOM commands to a limited group of users only.

	Discovery Questions	Look Here:
OPSYS-OWNER-01	Who owns the TAPECOM object file?	Fileinfo
OPSYS-LICENSE-01	Is TAPECOM licensed?	Fileinfo
FILE-POLICY	Who is allowed to execute TAPECOM, BACKUP and RESTORE on the system?	Policy
FILE-TAPECOM-01 SAFE-TAPECOM-01	Is the TAPECOM object file correctly secured with the Guardian or Safeguard system?	Fileinfo Safecom

Related Topics

BACKUP

DSM/TC

RESTORE

Telnet Subsystem

The Telnet subsystem is HP's implementation of the Telnet server portion of the Telnet protocol. The Telnet protocol is a general, bi-directional, eight-bit, byte-oriented protocol in the TCP/IP protocol suite that provides a standard method of interfacing terminal devices and terminal-oriented processes to each other. The HP Telnet server provides Telnet services to HP Telnet clients, specifically TN6530 personality.

Telnet is commonly used to service HP terminal-emulators from the PC platforms.

```
Example 1:
$SYSTEM SYSTEM  132> status *, prog $system.sys01.telserv
Process          Pri PFR %WT Userid  Program file              Hometerm
$ZTNP2  1,283    170   015   255,255 $SYSTEM.SYS01.TELSERV     $YMIOP.#CLCI
$ZTNP2  B 0,263 170   001   255,255 $SYSTEM.SYS01.TELSERV     $YMIOP.#CLCI
```

Example 1 displays the TELSERV process.

Each TELSERV session is identified by a #<name>.

```
Example 2:
$SYSTEM SYSTEM 130> who
Home terminal: $ZTNP2.#PT54RL5
```

Example 2 shows a connected Telnet terminal session. When addressing this session, the name of the terminal is $ZTNP2.#PT54RL5.

If the session is terminated, a new id (#<session id>) will be used.

RISK   Telnet sessions are transient. If the session is lost, the process may suspend.

AP-ADVICE-TELNET-01   Telnet sessions should not be used as HOME-TERM devices for processes.

RISK   A Telnet client can connect to any system on the network that has a Telnet server. The services available to any given terminal depends on what the remote system offers. The user will have access to system resources based on the userid used to make the connection.

RISK   Telnet is a common interface used to allow PC terminals to connect to an HP NonStop server system.

AP-ADVICE-TELNET-01   The interface must be secured to require users to logon with their own userid and password, before allowing access to the server or there will be no way to control users' access to system resources.

TELNET Services

A Telnet service is either conversational, block-mode or print. The most commonly used is conversational-mode. Each Telnet service must be explicitly set to accommodate the needs of the communication.

Securing Telnet Components

BP-FILE-TELNET-01   Telnet should be secured "UUNU".

BP-OPSYS-OWNER-01   Telnet should be owned by SUPER.SUPER.

BP-OPSYS-FILELOC-01   Telnet must reside in $SYSTEM.SYSnn.

BP-PROCESS-TELSERV-01 $ZTNPn processes should be running.

BP-FILE-TELNET-02   TELSERV should be secured "UUCU".

BP-OPSYS-OWNER-01   TELSERV should be owned by SUPER.SUPER.

BP-OPSYS-FILELOC-01   TELSERV must reside in $SYSTEM.SYSnn.

	Discovery Questions	Look Here:
FILE-POLICY	Is Telnet run on the system to support terminals?	Policy
PROCESS-TELSERV-01	Are the $ZTNPn process running?	Status
OPSYS-OWNER-01	Who owns the Telnet object file?	Fileinfo
OPSYS-OWNER-01	Who owns the TELSERV object file?	Fileinfo
FILE-TELNET-01	Is the Telnet object file secured correctly?	Fileinfo
FILE-TELNET-02	Is the TELSERV object file secured correctly?	Fileinfo

Related Topics

Securing Applications

SCF

TCP/IP

TGAL User Program

TGAL is a simple text formatter. It is used to format printable documents. It produces a printable-format copy from an EDIT file. The format commands are entered directly into the text file.

Each TGAL command must be entered on its own line, separated from text lines.

Each TGAL command line must begin with a trigger character. The trigger character must be the first character on the line.

The default trigger character for TGAL is a backslash (\), but each user can change it to any character desired other than quotation marks or a blank.

RISK TGAL formats text files, which usually do not contain corporate sensitive data. Unless the system has sensitive data in EDIT files, the TGAL program poses no risks.

Securing TGAL

BP-FILE-TGAL-01 TGAL should be secured "UUNU".

BP-OPSYS-OWNER-02 TGAL should be owned by SUPER.SUPER.

BP-OPSYS-FILELOC-02 TGAL must reside in $SYSTEM.SYSTEM.

	Discovery Questions	Look Here:
OPSYS-OWNER-02	Who owns the TGAL object file?	Fileinfo
FILE-TGAL-01	Is the TGAL object file secured correctly?	Fileinfo

<u>Related Topics</u>

EDIT

NonStop TMF Subsystem

NonStop Transaction Management Facility (TMF) software is the primary component of the Transaction Manager/MP (TM/MP) product.

NonStop TMF software monitors database transactions. The databases can be distributed among many disks on one or more nodes. NonStop TMF software monitors transactions for SQL catalogs, SQL databases and Enscribe files.

Files and tables must be defined as NonStop TMF audited files to be protected. Only audited files have change records logged to the NonStop TMF audit trails. Files that are not protected by NonStop TMF software are referred to as 'non-audited' files and do not have changes logged by NonStop TMF software.

AP-ADVICE-TMF-01 NonStop TMF software is a complex subsystem, which is integrated into many parts of the operating system and other subsystems. It must be configured and managed by knowledgeable personnel in order to avoid filling up disks or impacting application and system performance.

RISK   NonStop TMF software itself is a security product. Relying upon NonStop TMF software to provide recovery of data files is essential to many environments. If NonStop TMF software is not functional or transactions have been suspended, programs, subsystems etc, relying upon NonStop TMF software will not function, thus suspending the production application.

NonStop TMF Software and Database Recovery

The NonStop TMF subsystem protects transactions and performs database recovery in several ways:

Provides database consistency by transitioning a database from one consistent state to another, despite concurrent transactions.

Provides a mechanism whereby transactions on data stored within distinct files can be collectively linked as a single transaction.

Provides the necessary lock management for transactions.

Provides database consistency by protecting transactions from many potential hazards, including program failures, system component failures, and communication failures. Any incomplete transaction is backed out to the last consistent state.

Provides database recovery from its transaction-audit information.

Provides disaster rollback to a consistent state from retained periodic dump files.

RISK   NonStop TMF software's transaction protection is only performed on audited files and SQL objects. If the files are not set for NonStop TMF auditing, none of the recovery functions apply.

AP-ADVICE-TMF-02   It is important that critical data files be audited.

RISK   If files are audited and NonStop TMF is unavailable for some reason, transactions are halted and the application will not be functional.

NonStop TMF software is generally required on every system. Certain subsystems, such as NonStop SQL database rely upon NonStop TMF software to protect SQL catalog tables. Whether NonStop TMF software is used to protect application databases and at what level this protection is used should be part of the Corporate Security Policy and Standards.

NonStop TMF Configuration

NonStop TMF software has numerous configuration parameters. In order for files to be audited, they must reside on audited disk volumes. Normally, the volume on which the NonStop TMF audit trails reside is not audited.

> **RISK** Not all volumes may be audited. The Corporate Security Policy should determine if any volumes are not audited and which files, other than the NonStop TMF audit trails, can reside on these volumes.

> **AP-ADVICE-TMF-01** Volumes that are not audited should be reserved for authorized non-audited activity and for storing NonStop TMF audit trails.

The NonStop TMF configuration also defines the parameters that govern audit trail retention, timeouts, audit dump configuration and other parameters that directly affect the level of NonStop TMF security over data.

> **BP-TMF-CONFIG-01** The NonStop TMF audit trails should not be located on $SYSTEM to avoid contention. Configure the audit trails on another, less busy, volume.

NonStop TMF Auditing

Transaction control is supported by NonStop TMF auditing of before and after images of the data records. Before any I/O is performed, NonStop TMF software saves the before image of the record. When the I/O is successful, NonStop TMF software saves an after image of the record.

Transaction backout reapplies before-images to database records to undo the effects of an aborted transaction.

Take, for example, an ATM transaction. Such a transaction includes the operation of adding the transaction to the bank's database, adding the transaction to the ATM's audit trail, dispensing the cash or accepting the deposit, adding or subtracting the dollars from the customer's account and adjusting the ATM's cash balance if cash was dispensed. If, for example, the money is subtracted from the customer's account but not dispensed, neither the customer's account nor the cash balance of the ATM machine will reflect the correct balances. If the money is dispensed but not subtracted from the ATM's cash balance, then the ATM and audit trail will not balance. The only way to retain the accuracy and consistency of the bank's databases when errors occur is to back out the entire transaction so that the database returns to its pre-failed transaction state, as if the transaction's changes had never occurred.

Before and After Audit Images

Audit images are stored in NonStop TMF's audit trails. Audit trails are configured to NonStop TMF software during the cold load process. Audit trails are cycled automatically as they become full. They may be deleted or dumped to tape or disk, depending upon NonStop TMF's configuration.

Multiple audit trail files will be resident on the system, controlled by the parameter FILESPERVOLUME for each audit trail defined to NonStop TMF software.

RISK   NonStop TMF audit trails contain data from the production files and can, therefore, be used as source of obtaining sensitive information.

AP-ADVICE-TMF-01   NonStop TMF audit trails should be as well secured as the databases being audited.

Database Recovery Methods

NonStop TMF software incorporates several methods of recovery:

ROLLBACK
ROLLFORWARD
ON-LINE DUMPS

ROLLBACK

Transaction rollback (backout) recovers the database after an application or transaction failure. This is an automated function of NonStop TMF software which uses the before images stored in the audit trails. Any audit trail necessary for this function is by default available on the system.

ROLLFORWARD

Transaction rollforward is initiated by a person to recover a file from a given consistent point, reapplying before and after images up to the most recent consistent control point.

Audit trails may be configured for dumping to tape or disk and are cataloged by NonStop TMF software. On-line dumps of data must be performed periodically.

RISK   Audit trail dumping does not need to be configured for ROLLBACK functionality, but must be configured to perform NonStop TMF ROLLFORWARD functionality, if there is a possibility that an audit trail will be "rolled" and purged from disk.

RISK   Tape or disk management of on-line dumps and audit trails dumps is mandatory for the ability to recover files in this method.

RISK   If a needed Audit trail is not available, disaster recovery may not be able to be accomplished.

AP-ADVICE-TMF-02   If Audit trails are not configured for dumping to tape, care must be taken to insure that all of the audit trail files are retained on disk between one on-line dump to the next.

RISK   If a dump tape is unreadable, for any reason, disaster recovery may not be able to be accomplished.

AP-ADVICE-TMF-03   The COPIES "n" and VERIFYTAPE ON features of audit trail dumps should be configured to minimize the risk of a bad tape.

ON-LINE DUMPS

Periodic snapshots of the audited files are called on-line dumps. These snapshots are stored on cataloged tapes to provide a consistent point from which files can be recovered. The frequency of on-line dumps is determined by the NonStop TMF manager and the Corporate Security Policy and Standards. Dumps can alternatively be output to disk instead of tape media.

RISK   If an on-line dump is not available, not readable, or is not current, disaster recovery may not be able to be accomplished.

AP-ADVICE-TMF-03   The COPIES "n" and VERIFYTAPE ON features of the DUMP FILES command should be used to minimize the risk of a bad tape.

RISK   Tape or disk management of on-line dumps and audit trails dumps is mandatory for the ability to recover files by this method.

RISK   If dumps are made to disk, the dump subvolumes must be secured at least at the same level as the audit trails.

NonStop TMF Subsystem Components

NonStop TMF software is a complex product with many components. The basic component or interfaces are:

NonStop TMF programs residing in $SYSTEM.SYSnn

TMFCOM conversational interface

NonStop TMF Audit Trails

NonStop TMF Tapes

TM View optional GUI application

Programmatic Transaction commands (library calls from programs)

SNOOP audit trail reading utility

Subsystem Programmatic Interface (SPI) to NonStop TMF software

There are three primary areas of the TMF subsystem that must be protected:

NonStop TMF Audit Trails

NonStop TMF Configuration

TMFCOM

NonStop TMF Audit Trails

The NonStop TMF audit trails contain before and after images of the sensitive data.

RISK   NonStop TMF audit trails contain data from the production files and, as such, can be used as a backdoor for obtaining sensitive information.

AP-ADVICE-TMF-04   NonStop TMF audit trails should be as well secured as the databases being audited.

SNOOP Utility

The SNOOP utility is a tool that can read and manipulate NonStop TMF audit records.

RISK   The SNOOP utility can be used to manipulate NonStop TMF audit records.

AP-ADVICE-TMF-05   The SNOOP utility should only be available to the NonStop TMF manager and only used in disaster or problem resolution. General users should never have access to SNOOP or the NonStop TMF audit trails.

NonStop TMF Configuration

NonStop TMF software has numerous configuration parameters. In order for files to be audited, they must reside on audited disk volumes. Normally, the volume on which the TMF audit trails reside is not audited.

RISK   Because generally not all volumes are audited, it is possible that critical files might reside on non-audited volumes.

AP-ADVICE-TMF-06   The Corporate Security policy and Standards should determine if any volumes are not audited and which files, other than the TMF audit trails, should reside on these volumes.

AP-ADVICE-TMF-07   Volumes that are not audited should be reserved for authorized, non-audited activity and for storing NonStop TMF audit trails.

The NonStop TMF configuration also defines the parameters that govern audit trail retention, timeouts, audit dump configuration and other parameters that directly affect the level of NonStop TMF security over data.

TMFCOM

TMFCOM is the program through which NonStop TMF software is configured and managed. Generally, NonStop TMF software runs transparently without the need for the general user to have access to the TMFCOM program.

AP-ADVICE-TMF-08   The NonStop TMF configuration and control should only be accessible by persons responsible for the maintenance of the NonStop TMF subsystem.

TMFCOM Commands With Security Implications

TMFCOM has internal security that protects commands with security implications to SUPER Group members only. The following commands can be made available to any user without risk:

ENV

EXIT

FC

HELP

INFO

OUT

STATUS

VOLUME

?

If a third party access control product is used to grant selected users access to TMFCOM, only the commands listed should be granted to general users. All other commands should be restricted.

With a third party access control product

3P-ACCESS-TMF-01   Use a third party access control product to allow the users responsible for using TMFCOM commands access as SUPER.SUPER.

3P-ACCESS-TMF-02   Use a third party access control product to give the use of certain TMFCOM commands to a limited group of users only.

Without a third party access control product

AP-SAFE-TMF-01   Add a Safeguard Protection Record to grant appropriate access to the TMFCOM object file.

Securing NonStop TMF Components

BP-FILE-TMF-01   TMFBOUT should be secured "UUNU".

BP-PROCESS-TMFBOUT-01 $XBXn processes should be running.

BP-OPSYS-LICENSE-01   TMFBOUT must be LICENSED.

BP-OPSYS-OWNER-01   TMFBOUT should be owned by SUPER.SUPER.

BP-OPSYS-FILELOC-01   TMFBOUT must reside in $SYSTEM.SYSnn

BP-FILE-TMF-02   TMFCMMSG should be secured "NUNU".

BP-OPSYS-OWNER-01   TMFCMMSG should be owned by SUPER.SUPER.

BP-OPSYS-FILELOC-01   TMFCMMSG must reside in $SYSTEM.SYSnn

BP-FILE-TMF-03   TMFCOM should be secured "UUNU".

BP-OPSYS-OWNER-01   TMFCOM should be owned by SUPER.SUPER.

BP-OPSYS-FILELOC-01   TMFCOM must reside in $SYSTEM.SYSnn

BP-FILE-TMF-04   TMFCOM1 should be secured "UUNU".

BP-OPSYS-OWNER-01   TMFCOM1 should be owned by SUPER.SUPER.

BP-OPSYS-FILELOC-01   TMFCOM1 must reside in $SYSTEM.SYSnn

BP-PROCESS-TMFCTLG-01 $XCAT process should be running.

BP-FILE-TMF-05   TMFCTLG should be secured "UUNU".

BP-OPSYS-LICENSE-01   TMFCTLG must be LICENSED.

BP-OPSYS-OWNER-01   TMFCTLG should be owned by SUPER.SUPER.

BP-OPSYS-FILELOC-01   TMFCTLG must reside in $SYSTEM.SYSnn

BP-FILE-TMF-06   TMFDFLT should be secured "UUNU".

BP-OPSYS-OWNER-01   TMFDFLT should be owned by SUPER.SUPER.

BP-OPSYS-FILELOC-01   TMFDFLT must reside in $SYSTEM.SYSnn

BP-FILE-TMF-07   TMFDR should be secured "UUNU".

BP-OPSYS-LICENSE-01   TMFDR must be LICENSED.

BP-OPSYS-OWNER-01   TMFDR should be owned by SUPER.SUPER.

BP-OPSYS-FILELOC-01   TMFDR must reside in $SYSTEM.SYSnn

BP-FILE-TMF-08   TMFEXCPL should be secured "NUUU".

BP-OPSYS-OWNER-01   TMFEXCPL should be owned by SUPER.SUPER.

BP-OPSYS-FILELOC-01   TMFEXCPL must reside in $SYSTEM.SYSnn

BP-FILE-TMF-09   TMFFRCV should be secured "UUNU".

BP-OPSYS-LICENSE-01   TMFFRCV must be LICENSED.

BP-OPSYS-OWNER-01   TMFFRCV should be owned by SUPER.SUPER.

BP-OPSYS-FILELOC-01   TMFFRCV must reside in $SYSTEM.SYSnn

BP-FILE-TMF-10   TMFFRLS should be secured "UUNU".

BP-OPSYS-LICENSE-01   TMFFRLS must be LICENSED.

BP-OPSYS-OWNER-01   TMFFRLS should be owned by SUPER.SUPER.

BP-OPSYS-FILELOC-01   TMFFRLS must reside in $SYSTEM.SYSnn

BP-FILE-TMF-11   TMFMESG should be secured "NUNU".

BP-OPSYS-OWNER-01   TMFMESG should be owned by SUPER.SUPER.

BP-OPSYS-FILELOC-01   TMFMESG must reside in $SYSTEM.SYSnn

BP-PROCESS-TMFMON2-01 $ZTMnnn processes should be running.

BP-FILE-TMF-12   TMFMON2 should be secured "UUNU".

BP-OPSYS-LICENSE-01   TMFMON2 must be LICENSED.

BP-OPSYS-OWNER-01   TMFMON2 should be owned by SUPER.SUPER.

BP-OPSYS-FILELOC-01   TMFMON2 must reside in $SYSTEM.SYSnn

BP-FILE-TMF-13   TMFQRY should be secured "UUNU".

BP-OPSYS-OWNER-01   TMFQRY should be owned by SUPER.SUPER.

BP-OPSYS-FILELOC-01   TMFQRY must reside in $SYSTEM.SYSnn

BP-FILE-TMF-14   TMFSERVE should be secured "UUNU".

BP-OPSYS-LICENSE-01   TMFSERVE must be LICENSED.

BP-OPSYS-OWNER-01   TMFSERVE should be owned by SUPER.SUPER.

BP-OPSYS-FILELOC-01   TMFSERVE must reside in $SYSTEM.SYSnn

BP-FILE-TMF-15   TMFTIFIN should be secured "UUNU".

BP-OPSYS-OWNER-01   TMFTIFIN should be owned by SUPER.SUPER.

BP-OPSYS-FILELOC-01   TMFTIFIN must reside in $SYSTEM.SYSnn

BP-PROCESS-TMFTMP-01 $TMP process should be running.

BP-FILE-TMF-16   TMFTMP should be secured "UUNU".

BP-OPSYS-LICENSE-01   TMFTMP must be LICENSED.

BP-OPSYS-OWNER-01   TMFTMP should be owned by SUPER.SUPER.

BP-OPSYS-FILELOC-01   TMFTMP must reside in $SYSTEM.SYSnn

BP-FILE-TMF-17   TMFVRCV should be secured "UUNU".

BP-OPSYS-LICENSE-01   TMFVRCV must be LICENSED.

BP-OPSYS-OWNER-01   TMFVRCV should be owned by SUPER.SUPER.

BP-OPSYS-FILELOC-01   TMFVRCV must reside in $SYSTEM.SYSnn

BP-FILE-SNOOP-01   SNOOP should be secured "OOOO".

BP-OPSYS-LICENSE-01   SNOOP must be LICENSED.

BP-OPSYS-OWNER-01   SNOOP should be owned by SUPER.SUPER.

BP-OPSYS-FILELOC-01   SNOOP must reside in $SYSTEM.SYSnn

BP-FILE-SNOOP-02   SNOOPDOC should be secured "NOOO".

BP-OPSYS-OWNER-01   SNOOPDOC should be owned by
SUPER.SUPER.

BP-OPSYS-FILELOC-01   SNOOPDOC must reside in $SYSTEM.SYSnn

BP-FILE-SNOOP-03   SNOOPDR should be secured "OOOO".

BP-OPSYS-LICENSE-01   SNOOPDR must be LICENSED.

BP-OPSYS-OWNER-01   SNOOPDR should be owned by SUPER.SUPER.

BP-OPSYS-FILELOC-01   SNOOPDR must reside in $SYSTEM.SYSnn

The NonStop TMF audit trails contain all the same data as the production databases. Anyone with read access to the NonStop TMF audit trails has access to production data.

AP-FILE-TMF-01   To prevent unwanted access to production data, the
NonStop TMF audit trails must be secured at least as tightly as the database files
being audited, or as a default the following:

BP-FILE-TMFAUDIT-19   AUDIT TRAILS should be secured "GGGG".

BP-OPSYS-OWNER-03   AUDIT TRAILS should be owned by
SUPER.SUPER.

BP-OPSYS-FILELOC-03   AUDIT TRAILS resides in $<audit vol.<ztmfat>

If available, use Safeguard software or a third party object security product to grant access to TMFCOM components only to users who require it in order to perform their jobs.

BP-SAFE-TMF-01 Add a Safeguard Protection Record to grant appropriate access to the TMFCOM/TMFCOM1 object files.

BP-SAFE-SNOOP-01 Add a Safeguard Protection Record to grant appropriate access to the SNOOP object file.

	Discovery Questions	Look here:
FILE-POLICY	Is NonStop TMF software used on the system for protection of application databases?	Policy
PROCESS-TMFBOUT-01	Are the $XBKn processes running?	Status
PROCESS-TMFCTLG-01	Is the $XCAT process running?	Status
PROCESS-TMFMON2-01	Are the $ZTMnn processes running?	Status
PROCESS-TMFTMP-01	Is the $TMP process running?	Status
OPSYS-OWNER-01	Who owns the TMFBOUT object file?	Fileinfo
OPSYS-OWNER-01	Who owns the TMFCMMSG object file?	Fileinfo
OPSYS-OWNER-01	Who owns the TMFCOM object file?	Fileinfo
OPSYS-OWNER-01	Who owns the TMFCOM1 object file?	Fileinfo
OPSYS-OWNER-01	Who owns the TMFCTLG object file?	Fileinfo
OPSYS-OWNER-01	Who owns the TMFDFLT object file?	Fileinfo
OPSYS-OWNER-01	Who owns the TMFDR object file?	Fileinfo
OPSYS-OWNER-01	Who owns the TMFEXCPL object file?	Fileinfo
OPSYS-OWNER-01	Who owns the TMFFRCV object file?	Fileinfo
OPSYS-OWNER-01	Who owns the TMFFRLS object file?	Fileinfo
OPSYS-OWNER-01	Who owns the TMFMESG object file?	Fileinfo
OPSYS-OWNER-01	Who owns the TMFMON2 object file?	Fileinfo
OPSYS-OWNER-01	Who owns the TMFQRY object file?	Fileinfo
OPSYS-OWNER-01	Who owns the TMFSERVE object file?	Fileinfo
OPSYS-OWNER-01	Who owns the TMFTIFIN object file?	Fileinfo
OPSYS-OWNER-01	Who owns the TMFTMP object file?	Fileinfo
OPSYS-OWNER-01	Who owns the TMFVRCV object file?	Fileinfo
OPSYS-OWNER-01	Who owns the SNOOP object file?	Fileinfo
OPSYS-OWNER-01	Who owns the SNOOPDR object file?	Fileinfo
OPSYS-OWNER-03	Who owns the AUDIT TRAILS files?	Fileinfo
OPSYS-LICENSE-01	Is TMFBOUT licensed?	Fileinfo

	Discovery Questions	Look here:
OPSYS-LICENSE-01	Is TMFCTLG licensed?	Fileinfo
OPSYS-LICENSE-01	Is TMFDR licensed?	Fileinfo
OPSYS-LICENSE-01	Is TMFFRCV licensed?	Fileinfo
OPSYS-LICENSE-01	Is TMFFRLS licensed?	Fileinfo
OPSYS-LICENSE-01	Is TMFMON2 licensed?	Fileinfo
OPSYS-LICENSE-01	Is TMFSERVE licensed?	Fileinfo
OPSYS-LICENSE-01	Is TMFTMP licensed?	Fileinfo
OPSYS-LICENSE-01	Is TMFVRCV licensed?	Fileinfo
OPSYS-LICENSE-01	Is SNOOP licensed?	Fileinfo
OPSYS-LICENSE-01	Is SNOOPDR licensed?	Fileinfo
FILE-TMF-01	Is the TMFBOUT object file secured correctly?	Fileinfo
FILE-TMF-02	Is the TMFCMMSG object file secured correctly?	Fileinfo
FILE-TMF-03 SAFE-TMF-01	Is the TMFCOM object file correctly secured with the Guardian or Safeguard system?	Fileinfo Safecom
FILE-TMF-04 SAFE-TMF-01	Is the TMFCOM1 object file correctly secured with the Guardian or Safeguard system?	Fileinfo Safecom
FILE-TMF-05	Is the TMFCTLG object file secured correctly?	Fileinfo
FILE-TMF-06	Is the TMFDFLT object file secured correctly?	Fileinfo
FILE-TMF-07	Is the TMFDR object file secured correctly?	Fileinfo
FILE-TMF-08	Is the TMFEXCPL object file secured correctly?	Fileinfo
FILE-TMF-09	Is the TMFFRCV object file secured correctly?	Fileinfo
FILE-TMF-10	Is the TMFFRLS object file secured correctly?	Fileinfo
FILE-TMF-11	Is the TMFMESG object file secured correctly?	Fileinfo
FILE-TMF-12	Is TMFMON2 object file secured correctly?	Fileinfo
FILE-TMF-13	Is the TMFQRY object file secured correctly?	Fileinfo
FILE-TMF-14	Is the TMFSERVE object file secured correctly?	Fileinfo
FILE-TMF-15	Is the TMFTIFIN object file secured correctly?	Fileinfo
FILE-TMF-16	Is the TMFTMP object file secured correctly?	Fileinfo
FILE-TMF-17	Is the TMFVRCV object file secured correctly?	Fileinfo
FILE-SNOOP-01 SAFE-SNOOP-01	Is the SNOOP object file correctly secured with the Guardian or Safeguard system?	Fileinfo Safecom
FILE-SNOOP-02	Is the SNOOPDOC file secured correctly?	Fileinfo

	Discovery Questions	Look here:
FILE-SNOOP-03	Is the SNOOPDR object file secured correctly?	Fileinfo
FILE-TMFAUDIT-01	Are the AUDIT TRAIL files secured correctly?	Fileinfo

Related Topics

DSM/SCM

DDL/Enscribe software

Guardian Operating System procedure calls.

NonStop SQL/MP database

Pathway

NonStop SQL database

TRACER (TRACE ROUTE) System Utility

TRACER is used to display the path taken by IP packets to a network host.

RISK   TRACER is a reporting tool only, it poses no security risks.

Securing TRACER

BP-FILE-TRACER-01   TRACER should be secured "UUNU".

BP-OPSYS-LICENSE-01   TRACER must be LICENSED.

BP-OPSYS-OWNER-01   TRACER should be owned by SUPER.SUPER.

BP-OPSYS-FILELOC-01   TRACER resides in $SYSTEM.SYSnn.

If available, use Safeguard software or a third party object security product to grant access to TRACER object files to necessary personnel, and deny access to all other users.

BP-SAFE-TRACER-01   Add a Safeguard Protection Record to grant appropriate access to the TRACER object file.

	Discovery Questions	Look Here:
OPSYS-OWNER-01	Who owns the TRACER object file?	Fileinfo
OPSYS-LICENSE-01	Is the TRACER object file licensed?	Fileinfo
FILE-TRACER -01 SAFE-TRACER -01	Is the TRACER object file correctly secured with the Guardian or Safeguard system?	Fileinfo Safecom

Related Topics

TCP/IP

USERS User Program

The USERS program is used to obtain information about users from the USERID file. The USERS program is used frequently to determine the name of an owner of a file, a user's default security vector or default subvolume. In functionality it has no inherent risks.

The information displayed for each user is:

User Name
User Number
Guardian Default Security Vector
Guardian Default Volume

RISK   Unrestricted use of the USERS program can potentially make it easier for a hacker to launch a denial of service attack, because the hacker can obtain a list of all userids on the system.

Restricting the use of the USERS program must be weighed against the inconvenience for user's who cannot look up the USER NAME when they only know the USER NUMBER and vice versa.

The #USERNAME function in TACL can be used to provide the same translation of USER NAME to USER NUMBER. As a built-in TACL function, #USERNAME cannot be restricted.

Securing USERS

BP-FILE-USERS-01   USERS should be secured "UUNU".
BP-OPSYS-LICENSE-01   USERS should be LICENSED.
BP-OPSYS-OWNER-01   USERS should be owned by SUPER.SUPER.
BP-OPSYS-FILELOC-01   USERS must reside in $SYSTEM.SYSnn.

If available, use Safeguard software or a third party object security product to grant access to USERS object files to necessary personnel, and deny access to all other users.

BP-SAFE-USERS-01   Add a Safeguard Protection Record to grant appropriate access to the USERS object file.

	Discovery Questions	Look Here:
FILE-POLICY	Are all users allowed to use the USERS program?	Policy
OPSYS-OWNER-01	Who owns the USERS object file?	Fileinfo
OPSYS-LICENSE-01	Is the USERS object file licensed?	Fileinfo
FILE-USERS-01 SAFE-USERS-01	Is the USERS object file correctly secured with the Guardian or Safeguard system?	Fileinfo Safecom

Related Topics

User Administration

LOGON

VIEWPOINT Application

The ViewPoint application provides a block-mode interface for displaying network status. ViewPoint displays event messages collected and distributed by EMS from various subsystems throughout a system or network.

ViewPoint is a Pathway application that can be used by multiple users on multiple systems simultaneously. The default name for the ViewPoint Pathway application is $ZVPT.

ViewPoint includes:

Block-mode screens

A TACL screen

Clipboard File

Define Process commands

The block-mode screens display events and system or network status:

It provides the status of a variety of objects in the network on a single block-mode status screen. The status screen allows operators to monitor the availability and usage of objects such as CPUs, disks, terminals, and communications lines.

Messages about current or past events occurring anywhere in the network are displayed on a set of block-mode events screens. The events screens allow operators to monitor significant occurrences or problems in the network as they occur. Critical events or events requiring immediate action are highlighted.

RISK   ViewPoint is a reporting application and poses no security risks. View-Point uses very little system overhead. It is generally run by operations management.

The ViewPoint application consists of numerous components. It normally installs in its own subvolume, not in the $SYSTEM.SYSTEM subvolume. The default sub-volume is $SYSTEM.ZVIEWPT.

Securing VIEWPOINT Components

BP-PROCESS-VIEWPOINT-01 $ZVPT Pathway application should be running.

BP-FILE-ZVEWPT-01   ZVIEWPT* should be secured "NUNU".

BP-OPSYS-OWNER-03   ZVIEWPT* should be owned by SUPER.SUPER.

BP-OPSYS-FILELOC-03   ZVIEWPT* resides in $SYSTEM.ZVIEWPT.

	Discovery Questions	Look Here:
FILE-POLICY	Is ViewPoint used on the system?	Policy
PROCESS-VIEWPOINT-01	Is the $ZVPT application running?	Status
OPSYS-FILELOC-03	Where is the installed ZVIEWPT subvolume?	Fileinfo
OPSYS-OWNER-03	Who owns the ZVIEWPT subvolume?	Fileinfo
FILE-ZVIEWPT-01	Is the ZVIEWPT subvolume secured properly?	Fileinfo

VIEWSYS User Program

VIEWSYS displays system resource use in block mode and bar graph form. It is used to:

Monitor all processors within a system.

Monitor a selected set of processors within a system.

View resource use within a single processor.

View resource use within all processors being monitored.

View the use of a single resource throughout all the processors being monitored.

VIEWSYS accesses the same system tables as MEASURE and PEEK, but VIEWSYS does not write to any of these tables and doesn't affect PEEK statistics. Therefore, VIEWSYS can be run at the same time as MEASURE and PEEK.

RISK VIEWSYS is a report program and poses no security risks. VIEWSYS uses very little system overhead. It is generally run to monitor system performance.

Securing VIEWSYS

BP-FILE-VIEWSYS-01 VIEWSYS should be secured "UUNU".

BP-OPSYS-OWNER-02 VIEWSYS should be owned by SUPER.SUPER.

BP-OPSYS-FILELOC-02 VIEWSYS must reside in $SYSTEM.SYSTEM.

	Discovery Questions	Look Here:
OPSYS-OWNER-02	Who owns the VIEWSYS object file?	Fileinfo
FILE-VIEWSYS-01	Is the VIEWSYS object file secured correctly?	Fileinfo

<u>Related Topics</u>

Operating System

Virtual Hometerm Subsystem (VHS)

VHS acts as a virtual home terminal for applications by emulating a terminal. It runs as a named process, usually $VHS.

VHS receives messages normally sent to the home terminal, such as displays, application prompts, run-time library errors, and Inspect or Debug prompts. VHS uses these messages to generate event messages to the EMS collector to inform operations staff of problems.

VHS can be used with operator console applications, such as ViewPoint or Non-Stop NET/MASTER software, to highlight system or application problems.

VHS improves operations productivity by helping to avoid three known problems related to using dedicated physical home terminals:

Inability of operations staff to find and respond to critical messages because of the large volume of routine messages.

Need for constant monitoring of physical home terminals by operations staff.

Loss of productivity due to a stopped terminal that is waiting for a response. VHS emulates a terminal, but does not have the disadvantages of a single, dedicated physical terminal. VHS gives the following benefits over a physical terminal:

Easy access to critical application messages

Centralized message handling

Freeing up of physical terminals

Automated handling of Inspect or Debug prompts

Improved availability of applications to end users

Highlighted information to expedite problem resolution

RISK $VHS, the Virtual Hometerm Subsystem, is widely used on HP Non-Stop systems. There is no risk associated with this product.

AP-ADVICE-VHS-01   If there are processes relying upon the availability of $VHS, then $VHS should be running.

The VHS Components

The VHS subsystem consists of the following components (See Figure 6-10):

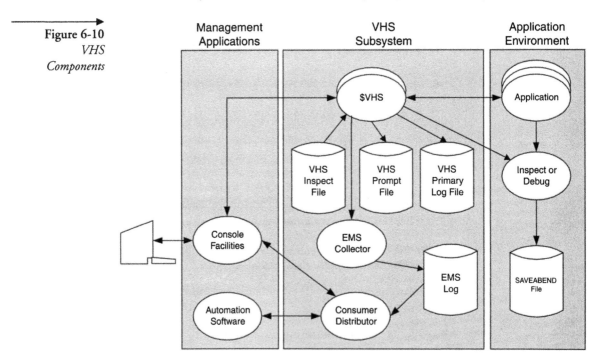

Figure 6-10
VHS
Components

VHS Process

VHS Conversational Interface (VHSCI)

VHS Pathway Browser Application

VHSCSTM

VHS Prompt File

VHS sends event messages to the EMS collector and optionally to a console facility for display only.

VHS

The $VHS process receives messages of many types from many sources. VHS manages six types of messages: open messages, display messages, Inspect prompts, Debug prompts, application prompts, and reply messages. The VHS process emulates a hard-copy terminal.

VHS is an application that is normally run from a separate subvolume on $SYSTEM, usually, $SYSTEM.VHS. The VHS object file is VHS.

VHSCSTM

The VHSCSTM file is used to customize each user's VHSCI session. Please refer to the Gazette section on *CSTM Configuration Files.

VHS Conversational Interface

VHS conversational interface (VHSCI) is used to configure and query the VHS process. This is normally only used by the person responsible for starting, stopping and configuring $VHS.

VHS Primary Log File Set

The VHS Audit Trail contains all of the messages received by VHS . The audit trail is made up of up to five files. The logs are kept in the $SYSTEM.VHS subvolume as ALOGnnn.

VHS Prompt File

VHS stores application prompt messages in the Prompt File.

VHS Browser

The VHS Pathway Browser makes the VHS Audit Trail and Prompt files accessible to general users. Through Pathway screens, messages can be reviewed, searches for specific messages can be requested, and messages can be printed.

The components to the VHS Pathway Browser are:

PATHCTL

POBJDIR

POBJCOD

VHSBCONF

VHSBHELP

VHSBSVR

VHSBTEXT

Securing VHS Components

BP-PROCESS-VHS-01 $VHS process should be running.

BP-FILE-VHS-01   VHS should be secured "UUCU".

BP-OPSYS-OWNER-03   VHS should be owned by SUPER.SUPER.

BP-OPSYS-FILELOC-03   VHS resides in $SYSTEM.VHS.

BP-FILE-VHS-02   VHSCI should be secured "UUNU".

BP-OPSYS-OWNER-03   VHSCI should be owned by SUPER.SUPER.

BP-OPSYS-FILELOC-03   VHSCI resides in $SYSTEM.VHS.

BP-PROCESS-ZVHS-01 $ZVHS process should be running.

BP-FILE-VHS-03   VHS Browser Pathway application should be secured "NUNU".

BP-OPSYS-OWNER-03   VHS Browser components should be owned by SUPER.SUPER.

BP-OPSYS-FILELOC-03   VHS Browser components reside in $SYSTEM.VHS.

If available, use Safeguard software or a third party object security product to grant access to VHS object files to necessary personnel, and deny access to all other VHS .

BP-SAFE-VHS –01   Add a Safeguard Protection Record to grant appropriate access to the VHS object file.

BP-SAFE-VHS –02 Add a Safeguard Protection Record to grant appropriate access to the VHSCI object file.

	Discovery Questions	Look Here:
FILE-POLICY	Is $VHS run on the system as a virtual terminal?	Policy
PROCESS-VHS-01	Is the $VHS process running?	Status
PROCESS-ZVHS-01	Is the $ZVHS Pathway process running?	Status
OPSYS-FILELOC-03	Where is the installed VHS subvolume?	Fileinfo
OPSYS-OWNER-03	Who owns the VHS subvolume files?	Fileinfo
FILE-VHS-01 SAFE-VHS-01	Is the VHS object file correctly secured with the Guardian or Safeguard system?	Fileinfo Safecom
FILE-VHS-02 SAFE-VHS-02	Is the VHSCI object file correctly secured with the Guardian or Safeguard system?	Fileinfo Safecom
FILE-POLICY	Are all users allowed to view the VHS log using the VHS browser?	Policy
FILE-VHS-03	Is the VHS browser subvolume secured correctly?	Fileinfo

Related Topics

Securing Applications

7

Securing Applications

Understanding Application Development

Generally, applications and system tools that run on the HP NonStop server come from the following sources:

In-House application development

Third-party vendor applications

Legacy applications

In-House system tools

Third-party system tools

Regardless of the source, great care must be taken to properly secure an application, its database and its configuration files. First, we will discuss securing applications and later we will deal with system tools.

Applications are the company's business application(s). They are the reason for using the HP NonStop server. In essence, applications are the most important entity on the machine. Everything else that runs on the system supports the application.

In House Application Development

In-house application development is the most mysterious environment of an enterprise; mysterious to everyone other than developers and their managers. To most people, developers are geeks that wear cutoffs, sandals and beanies with propellers. You can hear them talking about the Source, Schemas, Buffers, Parsers and State Machines. How can any normal human communicate with such strange people?

Other than the strange language they speak, developers are no different than the rest of us. The exception is how they perceive computers. Computers are their universe and they take pride in inventing ways to make those electronic devices hum. To developers, there is nothing like a machine obeying their every command. To that extent they strive to learn every computer language on the planet.

Developers DO NOT like to be bogged down with computer security. They would be happiest if they all had access to the SUPER.SUPER password and could do anything they wanted.

But, the fact is that developers have to comply with the Corporate Security Policy and Standards.

The Security Administrator must establish a dialog with the development manager early on in the development cycle to ensure that the following areas comply with the security policy:

Source Control

Application Configuration Source Files

Object Release Control

Application Security Considerations

Source Control

Source Control is the management of a file's change history and the file's relationship to a larger grouping of related files known as a project. Source control is a fundamental part of a well-organized application software development organization.

Source Control is the generic term for tools that manage files (containing program source code) in a multi-developer environment. Most source control tools work something like a traditional public library, maintaining a central repository of files, programs, documents, configuration files or any other related file in a location accessible to all developers. In addition, source control tools include the ability to track the changes that developers make to source files, control simultaneous changes and revert to earlier versions if necessary.

Developers must only have access to submit and extract program source files from the Source Control Foundation.

RISK   If access to the source code is not restricted via a source control product, it is possible that multiple developers could copy a file, each make changes and replace the file, which leaves the validity of the source code questionable.

AP-ADVICE-APPLICATION-01   The source control product and its database must be owned by the responsible job function ID and secured from unauthorized tampering.

Currently HP does not offer a source control product for the HP NonStop server, however there are several third party vendors that do.

3P-SOURCE-ADVICE-01   Use a third party source control product to secure the source code, configuration files, documentation and obey files that the application uses in the production environment.

Application Configuration Source Files

Application configuration source files must be treated the same as the application program source files. Developers must only have access to submit and extract configuration files from the Source Control facility.

Object Release Control

The Object Release Control facility must be owned by the responsible job function ID. Normally the object release utility is part of the source control product.

RISK   At no time should a developer be allowed to submit objects into the release control database.

3P-SOURCE-ADVICE-03   Use a third party source control product to assist in performing and managing change control and versioning.

AP-ADVICE-APPLICATION-02   The Corporate Security Policy and Standards should mandate a periodic review of the system for each application:

The application manager should indicate which programs are being changed and why.

The security department should develop methods to verify that change control procedures are being used properly.

Procedures should be in place for a 'backout' to a prior version if a change causes problems for the application.

Procedures should be in place for verifying the application's security policy for files belonging to the application.

The Corporate Security Policy and Standards should determine the appropriate Job Function ID that will be responsible for performing the following tasks:

Moving the new object code into production.

Giving the files to the designated Application Owner ID.

Securing the files in accordance with the policy.

Application Security Considerations

Security must be considered at all levels of the application; its design, database, maintenance, communications, recovery, etc. This is not an easy task because the application utilizes many facets of the system hardware and system software subsystems.

The security department should work with the application managers to create a mechanism for performing application security reviews.

The Corporate Security Policy and Standards should mandate a periodic review to ensure that application security is in compliance with the policy. Procedures should be put in place to ensure that the reviews take place.

Third-Party Vendor Applications

Third-party vendor applications introduced to HP NonStop servers have the same issues as in-house applications. The difference is that the source code belongs to the third-party vendor.

The following sections described above apply to third-party vendor applications:

Object Release Control

Application Security Considerations

Legacy Applications

Legacy applications are those that are still in use, though many years have passed and the hardware and operating system have changed repeatedly. These applications are kept running in the hope that some day they will be replaced by new state of the art applications being developed in-house or purchased from a third-party vendor.

Legacy applications have a tendency to have a life of their own. Often, employees that were responsible for keeping them running have moved on to other jobs or to opportunities at other companies. Current developers are afraid to attempt updating the code for fear of breaking something else. It might even be the case that the source code for the application no longer exists.

The Security Administrator must inventory the legacy applications; paying close attention to the source code, configuration files, obey files, TACL macros and job streams used to execute the application; to be certain that the application's security conforms with the Corporate Security Policy and Standards.

The following sections described above apply to legacy applications:

Source Control

Application Configuration Source Files

Object Release Control

Application Security Considerations

In-House System Tools

In-house system tools can be obey files, TACL macros, or object programs used to manage databases, update SQL catalogs, partition physical files, add users, change passwords, etc. These tools use many of the HP NonStop server subsystems such as FUP, SCF, BACKUP and SQLCI.

Often the developers of these tools are no longer supporting them because they have moved on and usually there is no documentation available to understand what the tool was designed to accomplish.

The Security Administrator, with the knowledge that these tools are only present to support the application, must evaluate system tools. The Security Administrator must understand the exact function these tools perform in order to determine the appropriate security.

The following sections described above apply to in-house system tools:

Source Control

Application Configuration Source Files

Object Release Control

Application Security Considerations

Third-Party System Tools

The third-party system tools, like the in-house system tools, exist to support the application. The Security Administrator must evaluate each tool to determine which subsystems are being utilized and the appropriate security for the tool according to the security policy.

Usually, third-party tools come well documented and have easy to maintain common user interfaces.

The following sections described above apply to third-party system tools:

Object Release Control

Application Security Considerations

Securing the Production Applications

The production environment applications are the most important entities on the HP NonStop server. If any breach or stoppage occurs to any application, the enterprise will suffer a loss of revenue. Simply put, if the applications aren't running, no revenue is being generated. The entire enterprise suffers when this occurs.

At no time should improper security be the cause of any stoppage or breach. Strict adherence to the Corporate Security Policy and Standards must be enforced without exception. If there are exceptions to the security policy, they must be documented and approved by higher management.

If the Security Administrator is involved in the initial design of the in-house applications or the evaluation of third-party applications there will be fewer surprises at deployment time.

Determining the following will help the Security Administrator to analyze the production applications to see if they comply with the Corporate Security Policy:

Discovery Issues:	Look Here:
Locate where the object files reside.	Fileinfo
Locate where the database files reside.	Fileinfo SQLCI
Determine who owns the object files.	Fileinfo
Determine who owns the database files.	Fileinfo SQLCI
Determine who can execute, add, modify and purge the object files.	Fileinfo Safecom
Determine who can read, write, create and purge the database files.	Fileinfo SQLCI Safecom
Determine which HP utilities are accessed by the application.	Code Review
Review the PORTCONF file to see what object files are being started by the LISTNER process, and how they are secured.	FUP Edit
If any object files are logging on users, make sure some type of encryption is being used to transmit the passwords across the network.	Code Review

Discovery Issues:	Look Here:
Review all Pathway and non-Pathway configuration files for ASSIGNs, DEFINEs and PARAMs; the object files and database files must match the physical location.	PATHCOM Edit Fileinfo
Review the Batch facility by checking what jobs are being started to operate on the production environment.	Batchcom
Review the security of application obey files or TACL macros.	Edit Fileinfo
Review application obey files or TACL macros for embedded passwords.	Edit
Locate the TMF audit trails. Since they contain the before and after images of data from the enterprise database, these files must be owned by the System Administrator.	TMFCOM

Security must be involved in the design to ensure that the production application complies with the Corporate Security Policy and Standards. The following areas must be considered when new applications are designed or existing applications are reviewed.

Platforms

Pathway

Non-Pathway

Batch

Tools

DBMS

SQL Database

Enscribe Database

Communications

System Management

Platforms

Following are application platform descriptions to help the Security Administrator analyze a production environment to determine if the implementation complies with the Corporate Security Policy:

Pathway

Non-Pathway

Batch

Tools

The Pathway Subsystem

Pathway is an application development platform with a client server management system that performs much of the application run-time management.

Pathway is the platform for many HP NonStop server applications. It is often the pivotal production platform, therefore requiring a wide range of access throughout a company's enterprise.

Pathway is a client-server application model. The Pathway monitor provides the interface for the communication layer and the management layer between the client and server. A Pathway application has two major components:

Requestors   A screen program or GUI client component that interacts directly with the terminal. The screen part of the application is written in SCOBOLX or in a GUI language.

Servers   The user program running on the host system that interacts with the databases and performs user calculations and database manipulation, etc. The server part of the application can be written in any language supported by the HP NonStop server.

Terminal Interface

There are three basic ways to run a Pathway environment:

Dedicated Terminals: If a terminal is dedicated to Pathway TACL and terminal logons are not allowed. The terminal is always connected to the Pathway application. The terminals are setup via PATHCOM TERM commands.

Non-dedicated Terminals: The user runs Pathway by starting PATHCOM from a TACL prompt and issuing a RUN PROGRAM command to start the application. Non-dedicated terminals are not configured in Pathway.

PC GUI/Web: A connection is made to an HP NonStop server's TCP/IP interface on a particular port. Communications code must be listening to the port and send the GUI application messages to LINKMON. LINKMON provides the interface that sends and receives messages between the Pathway client and server programs.

RISK   The applications should require logon and logoff mechanisms to ensure that the user at the terminal has a valid logon and is allowed to perform the requested function. The application should also have a timeout facility to prevent someone walking away from a terminal and leaving it open for someone else to walk up to and use.

Dedicated Terminals

RISK Dedicated terminals are always ON. Applications with dedicated terminals must have a user authentication method to control access, otherwise the application is at risk.

Non-Dedicated Terminals

RISK Non-dedicated terminals require access to a TACL and to PATHCOM. If Pathway security allows, the user can make changes using the PATHCOM interface.

RISK If a non-dedicated terminal is left logged on, the application is at risk unless the application times out an inactive session.

RISK If a non-dedicated terminal is left logged on, the application is at risk unless the terminal is timed out via either CMON or TACL configuration.

GUI Terminal Interface

RISK Accessing a Pathway application from a GUI does not enforce any authentication, unless software enforces it. A software mechanism is needed to ensure authorization of users using a GUI interface.

Servers

A Pathway server performs all calculations, disk I/O and communications outside the Pathway environment. Server programs can be written in a variety of application languages to perform many tasks. Servers can perform database I/O to any Enscribe, SQL, OSS or other type of data file on the system. They can also perform communication to devices and other systems.

Servers are started and stopped by the Pathway subsystem as needed. Configuration settings determine how many servers can be started.

The server processes run as the Pathway server owner, regardless of the user who is logged into the terminal or the owner of the Guardian file. It is the Pathway owner's userid that is used to determine the accessibility of system resources such as database objects, etc., unless the program object file is PROGID'd.

AP-ADVICE-APPLICATION-03 Do not PROGID Pathway servers, especially if the server object is owned by a SUPER Group member.

RISK   Pathway does not interact with CMON when starting server processes for priority or CPU settings. CPU selection and priority is set for servers within Pathway.

RISK   The server Owner and Security attributes are ignored by requests from a TCP. They are only valid when LINKMON is the requestor, as discussed separately.

RISK   Pathways running with network security can allow remote access to the application, which should only be allowed when necessary.

RISK   Because Pathway starts servers as the defined userid without requiring user authentication, a poorly secured Pathway interface will permit the malicious addition, removal or substitution of servers.

Configuring Pathways

With Pathway, developers can define the client-server environments using a configuration file. The configuration file contains statements that define the location of the object programs and the location of the database.

Before any Pathway application can be deployed, the Security Administrator should review the security related statements in the configuration file. The Pathway configuration file must be owned by the job function ID responsible for starting, modifying and stopping the Pathway application.

AP-ADVICE-APPLICATION-04   Pathway configuration files must be secured so that the job function ID can read the files but not change them.

AP-ADVICE-APPLICATION-05   Change control staff must be able to manage the Pathway configuration files.

Specifically, the Security Administrator must pay attention to the following statements in the Pathway configuration file:

```
Set Pathway Owner <Owner-Id>
```

The Owner-Id is the userid allowed to issue PATHCOM commands that directly alter the state of the PATHMON-controlled objects. The userid must be known to the system in which the Pathway is running. Use this attribute in conjunction with the SECURITY attribute. The value of ownerid is specified using the following syntax:

```
[\ node. |\ system-number. | \* .] group-name . user-name
Set Pathway Security <security-attribute>
```

The Security-Attribute controls which users can issue PATHCOM commands that directly alter the state of the PATHMON-controlled objects. Before the START PATHWAY command is issued, the owner ID is the process-accessor ID of the

PATHMON process and the security attribute is "O". This security setting controls who can alter the Pathway configuration attributes. The security attribute is the same as the Guardian security attribute. The possible values are:

"A"—All local users

"N"—All network users

"G"—Only local members of the owner's group

"C"—Only network members of the owner's group

"O"—Only the local owner.

"U"—Only the remote or local owner

" - "—Only local SUPER.SUPER

RISK   If the owner of a Pathway system is SUPER.SUPER, allowing the security to default to "N" results in a security risk for the system. In this situation, set the security to "O" or "-", so that only persons logged on as local SUPER.SUPER can add, delete, or modify PATHMON-controlled objects.

```
Set Server Owner <Owner-Id>
```

The Owner-Id specifies the userid that is used to control access from a Pathsend process to a server class. (The TCPs ignore this server attribute.) The userid must be known to the system in which PATHCOM is running. Use this attribute in conjunction with the SERVER SECURITY attribute.

```
Set Server Security < security-attribute>
```

The Security-Attribute controls which users, in relation to the OWNER attribute, can access a server class from a Pathsend requester. (TCPs ignore this attribute.) The security attribute is the same as the Guardian file security attribute.

Communication Between Pathway Environments

Pathway systems can share Pathway server classes, meaning that a client process on Pathway A can send a request to a server within Pathway B.

The userid of the Pathway process controlling the server class has to have corresponding userids and remote passwords with the following systems:

The system where the Pathway process is running

The system where the server class is running

The system where the requesting process is running

The same operations take place whether the Pathway environments are running on the same or on different nodes. If the communication is remote, then the security requirements to allow remote access are:

The Pathway and program security must allow network access.

If the server is on the same system as the database, the databases do not need to be secured for network access.

Securing a Pathway Application

A Pathway application might be the primary mechanism to access the company's sensitive databases. Information is retrieved, added, updated and purged via the application programs.

To enforce separation of duties, database files should be created, configured and owned by the Application Database Owner. The Pathway application executing ID will retrieve, add and update information contained in the database, therefore the Pathway executing ID must have READ and WRITE access to the database.

AP-ADVICE-APPLICATION-06A   If the Database owner and the Pathway/Application Executing ID are in the same administrative group, database files should be secured "GGOO" or, if remote access is appropriate, "CCOO". No userids assigned to actual individuals should be created in the administrative group.

```
Example 1:
Pathway/Application Executing ID = 200,255; BASE24.MGR
Database Owner = 200,1; BASE24.DBASE
```

In Example 1, there should be no individual userids in group 200.

AP-ADVICE-APPLICATION-06B   If the Pathway/Application Executing ID is not in the same group as the Database Owner, then it is strongly recommended that Safeguard software be used to grant granular READ and WRITE access to the Pathway/Application Executing ID.

```
Example 2:
Pathway/Application Executing ID = 200,255; BASE24.MGR
Database Owner = 100,254; DATABASE.OWNER
```

In Example 2, there should be no individual userids in group 200. If the Policy allows, individuals may be given individual userids in the DATABASE administrative group.

AP-SAFE-PATHWAY-02   If Safeguard software is installed, Protection Records should be created to control access to data files for READ only for inquiry, and READ and WRITE for file updates. Access can be granted to a single user if desired.

3P-OBJSEC-ADVICE-01   Safeguard Protection Records do not apply to SQL tables, only to the subvolume or volume that contain the tables. To adequately secure SQL databases, a third party object security module might be required.

The following discovery questions apply to each Pathway environment.

Discovery Questions	Look Here:
Who is allowed to start, stop and modify this Pathway?	Policy
Does the organization have a change control policy?	Policy
Who owns the Pathway environment?	Pathway info
Who owns the POBJCOD and POBJDIR files?	Fileinfo
Who owns the PATHCTL file?	Fileinfo
What is the internal Pathway security vector?	Pathway info
Is the internal owner the same as the running owner?	Pathway info Status
Is the Pathway owner explicitly set?	Pathway conf file
Is there a Safeguard Protection Record to control access to the Pathway application?	Safecom
Who are the Program entity owners?	Pathway info
Are the Program entities secured correctly?	Pathway info
Who are the server entity owners?	Pathway info
Are the server entities secured correctly?	Pathway info
What is the server object files security?	Fileinfo
Are any servers PROGID'd?	Fileinfo DSAP Safecom
Are any servers LICENSED?	Fileinfo DSAP Safecom
Who owns the Pathway configuration files?	Fileinfo
Are the Pathway configuration files secured correctly?	Fileinfo Safecom
Are remote clients used for this Pathway?	Policy
What method is used for remote client access?	Policy
What method of user authorization is used for the incoming request? Is it documented?	Policy

Discovery Questions	Look Here:
Who owns the database files?	Fileinfo
Are the database files secured correctly?	Fileinfo
Is there a Safeguard Protection Record to control access to the database subvolumes?	Safeguard

Binder

The Binder utility must be secured to only those users allowed to create, modify or delete program objects on the production environment. It is a simple task for any user that has gained unauthorized access to an HP NonStop server to use the Binder utility to alter any program object. The altered object is undetectable by Pathway, Safeguard or Guardian security. See Gazette section on BINDER for more information.

AP-ADVICE-APPLICATION-07   Ideally, only system support staff, application support staff and change control staff should be allowed to use BIND on production systems. The person running BIND needs:

READ access to the object file

CREATE and WRITE access to the target file's subvolume

READ access to any libraries that will be bound into the target object.

AP-ADVICE-APPLICATION-08   BIND can be tightly secured if the development system is separate from the production system. Applications can be bound on the development system and moved to the production system. In this scenario, BIND need not be present on the production system.

RISK   To protect proprietary code from the risk of theft from reverse engineering, the DUMP and LMAP commands should also be restricted.

Non-Pathway Applications

While Pathway is the preferred platform to manage enterprise applications, HP Non-Stop servers allow for Requestor-Server programs to execute independent of Pathway. Requestor programs will accept input from terminals, intelligent devices or other processes running on the server or networked server. That input is formulated into data messages then sent to a server program for processing. The server programs perform I/O operations to any database, device or file on the server or network.

The disadvantage of a non-Pathway application is that they are more difficult to code and manage. The programs are not fault tolerant unless special code is added to make them so. Non-Pathway applications perform many of the same features programmatically that are performed by the Pathway monitor.

Securing a non-Pathway application depends on how well the Security administrator understands the purpose and basic functions of the application. The Security Administrator must work with the Application Owner to understand where the object programs and database reside in order to secure those locations. The Security Administrator must develop an application checklist to analyze if the non-Pathway applications comply with the corporate Security Policy.

Batch

The HP NonStop server has a Batch facility capable of scheduling jobs to start at predetermined times. The Batch facility (NetBatch) initiates programs or TACL macros. Generally these programs are functions that are written to perform tasks on the system at predetermined times or under predetermined conditions.

Unlike the applications discussed above, batch jobs do not require human intervention to be started.

RISK   Unauthorized jobs in the batch facility can get started without obvious detection.

Batch Jobs are sometimes used to reorganize large data files during off-hours so as not to impact the production environment during critical hours. Depending on the enterprise, these Batch Jobs will perform special functions to support the main enterprise applications.

AP-ADVICE-APPLICATION-09   The Corporate Security Policy and Standards should mandate a periodic review of the jobs in the Batch facility and make a determination of their use.

AP-ADVICE-APPLICATION-10   Batch jobs should not have embedded passwords.

Tools

Tools come in many different forms and can be developed in-house or obtained from a third party vendor.

Obey files for a utility, such as FUP or SQLCI

TACL macros

Compiled TACL macros

Compiled programs

Pathway Applications

Non-Pathway Applications

Tools should only exist to support the enterprise application and should not interfere with the production environment. These tools are sometimes overlooked by the Security Administrator because they are less easily identified.

AP-ADVICE-APPLICATION-11   All tools must be documented and secured according to the Corporate Security Policy.

Database Management Systems (DBMS)

The following are DBMS subsystem descriptions to help the Security Administrator analyze a production environment to determine if the implementation complies with the Corporate Security Policy:

Enscribe software

NonStop SQL software

Enscribe Databases

An Enscribe database is defined with the Data Definition Language (DDL) facility. DDL enables users to define fields in Enscribe files and translate those object definitions into source code for HP NonStop server languages, such as COBOL, C, TAL and ENFORM.

The Enscribe record manager is integrated into the Guardian file system and provides high level access to records in a database. Many legacy applications running on an HP NonStop server utilize the Enscribe record manager system. Enscribe database security can be managed by the Safeguard Security system and/or Guardian security.

Securing Enscribe Databases With the Guardian System

Enscribe database files can be secured with the Guardian security system. Files will have a designated owner, specified by the groupid and userid. A security vector specifies whether users have READ, WRITE, EXECUTE and PURGE access. The vector controls how other users can access the file. The Guardian system is the fundamental security method to secure any file on the HP NonStop server.

RISK   If Safeguard software is the main security method and not all files are properly secured, the security check defaults to the Guardian system.

AP-ADVICE-APPLICATION-12   Regardless of whether or not the application files are secured with Safeguard, the Guardian security vectors should always be set to provide basic security for the application.

RISK   If backup tapes are not physically secured, application data is not secure.

RISK NonStop TMF audit trails contain sensitive data images. NonStop TMF audit trails must be secured at the same level as the data it protects.

Securing Enscribe Databases With Safeguard

Safeguard software can further secure Enscribe objects at the volume, subvolume and individual diskfile level. With the Safeguard software users can be granted access to objects via Protection Records. The Protection Records can allow or deny READ, WRITE, EXECUTE, CREATE, OWNER and PURGE access to a file for all users or specified users. Sometimes Protection Records can contain allow and deny access to specific users on the same object. Please refer to Securing Diskfiles with Safeguard Subsystem in Part Five for more information.

AP-ADVICE-APPLICATION-13 If Safeguard software is available, sensitive files should have Protection Records to restrict unauthorized access.

RISK If Safeguard software is the main security method and not all files are properly secured, the security check defaults to the Guardian environment.

AP-ADVICE-APPLICATION-14 Regardless of whether or not the application files are secured with Safeguard software, the Guardian security vectors should always be set to provide basic security for the application.

NonStop SQL Databases

Structured Query Language (SQL) is a language used for creating, modifying and accessing relational databases. NonStop SQL is a powerful relational database manager fully integrated with the Guardian operating system and taking full advantage of the distributed processing made possible by the HP NonStop server hardware architecture.

NonStop SQL is thoroughly integrated into the HP NonStop server architecture. It is called an active data dictionary because the NonStop SQL Optimizer queries the application catalogs for statistics for the best access path to the required data at the time the request is made. The Optimizer also updates the access path statistics in the application catalogs for future use.

Catalogs are sets of SQL tables that contain descriptions of the SQL relational objects. Catalog tables can only be modified within SQL, not with FUP. Each Catalog contains:

Table names and descriptions

The column names, data types and sizes in each table

Descriptions of files containing the tables

The names of all the programs that use the tables

Access path statistics

ODBC support tables

There can be one or more catalogs per volume, but only one per subvolume and each catalog must have the same name as the subvolume where it resides. For example, the catalog on $DATA23.APP1 will be named $DATA23.APP1. Each catalog can describe objects in its subvolume or in any other subvolume on any disk.

SQL database objects are created via the SQL Conversational Interface (SQLCI) or programmatically using embedded SQL statements or the Dynamic SQL API facility. Once the database is created, users can access the data from tables or views via the same three methods.

RISK   Access to the SQLCI utility provides access to all SQLCI commands, both informational and destructive.

RISK   Depending on how the relational database was designed and the amount of data being queried, SQLCI can start sort processes that may slow down critical production cycles on the HP NonStop server.

Securing SQL Databases With the Guardian System

NonStop SQL objects such as Catalogs, Tables, Indexes and Views are secured using SQLCI DDL create and alter statements. The ownerid and security vectors are held in the SQL catalog. These can only be altered using SQLCI or programmatically with embedded SQL statements. FUP cannot be used to change the security of any SQL object.

RISK   Change to file security made with SQLCI or programmatic interfaces are immediately applied to the Guardian security vector and may cause a disruption of service if incorrect.

RISK   Safeguard software cannot secure individual SQL catalogs or objects even though the object's name is a disk file name. SQL tables and other objects can only be secured at the VOLUME or SUBVOLUME level with Safeguard.

Securing SQL Databases With the Safeguard Subsystem

Safeguard has limited ability to secure NonStop SQL catalogs and databases.

For SQL catalogs and objects, Safeguard can:

Restrict access to volumes and subvolumes containing SQL tables, views, indexes, collations, and SQL programs stored in Guardian files

Protect an entire catalog by protecting the subvolume that contains the catalog.

NOTE: Every table that requires different access rules must reside in a different subvolume.

For a partitioned table or index, each volume containing a partition of the object should have an identical Protection Record.

Restrict the creation of tables, views, indexes and catalogs on volumes and subvolumes for which it maintains a Protection Record.

Restrict the creation of SQL processes and the execution and purging of SQL program files.

Safeguard software *cannot* protect individual SQL object names, even though names of SQL tables, views, indexes, collations, and programs are disk file names.

Securing Catalogs

The catalog tables compose the data dictionary, a vital part of an application's integrity. The security of a catalog should protect the data dictionary information from unauthorized removal or alteration.

In order to compile a program, users need READ and WRITE access to the USAGES and TRANSIDS tables in any catalog containing descriptions of tables, views, collations, partitions, and indexes the program uses as well as write access to the PROGRAMS table of the catalog in which the program is registered.

RISK When a catalog's security string is altered, the catalog security applies to all of the catalog tables.

Securing the System Catalog

Each node where SQL is used must have at least one catalog, the System Catalog. The System Catalog contains information about all the catalogs on the system. The system catalog is like any other catalog, with the following exceptions:

The system catalog is created during the installation of NonStop SQL database.

The system catalog contains the SQL CATALOGS table in which all catalogs on the node are registered. The system catalog can be used as a catalog directory only or as a general-purpose catalog.

The system catalog must be protected against removal. The PURGE authority must be granted only to the Database Administrator.

RISK   Users must have READ and WRITE access to the System Catalog to create or delete application catalogs.

RISK   Users who need to query the CATALOGS table must have READ access.

AP-ADVICE-APPLICATION-15   The system catalog should not be used as an application catalog. Doing so minimizes the ability to protect the system catalog from corruption or removal.

SQL Objects

NonStop SQL database uses defined SQL Objects to relate to the information stored in the catalog.

The physical SQL objects are:

Tables

Indexes

Views

Programs

Tables

A base table is a physical table, stored in a file. It is made up of rows and columns. Each row is a data record. Each column contains a particular field of data. Data is entered into the table a row at a time. Each row (record) contains a value for each column or null value.

Securing a Base Table

Base tables are the foundation of the database, and base table security ultimately defines much of the security for views, indexes, and DML statements.

The following users have the authority to perform DDL operations on existing tables as the equivalent of the owner:

local owner of an object

remote owner with purge authority

local SUPER.SUPER

local owners group manager

RISK   Anyone with authority to purge a table can drop the table.

RISK   When the security string of a base table is altered, SQL will alter the security of the dependent indexes. The security of dependent protection views might also be altered if the new security of the table violates the system-enforced relationship between these objects, as explained later in "Securing Protection Views."

Indexes

An index is an alternate key to a table. An alternate key is an alternate way to access the data in the table. A NonStop SQL index is stored in a key-sequenced file and includes columns for the primary key and the alternate key.

Securing an INDEX

Indexes must be secured to match its base table to ensure accessibility.

RISK   Purging a base table will automatically purge associated indexes.

SQL Views

Controlled access to base tables can be granted using NonStop SQL views. A view is a logical table derived from one or more base tables. A view can include a projection of columns and a selection of rows from the table or tables. Projected columns and selected rows for a view can come directly from the base tables or indirectly through other views. Views do not store data physically on the disk, but have a disk file label.

There are two types of views:

Protection Views – users can view and enter data

Shorthand Views – users can only view data

Securing Protection Views

A Protection View is a logical view of a table, providing security restrictions so that only certain information can be presented to a user by masking rows and columns of the single underlying table from displays or updates. Protection views are updateable.

Protection views are most commonly used to secure columns or rows of sensitive data from the user. For instance, assume that an employee file contains the name, address, phone number and salary of each employee. A Protection view can eliminate the 'SALARY' column from the view so that the risk of accidental display is minimized.

Protection views can be used to insert, update or delete records.

Securing Shorthand Views

A Shorthand View is a pre-formed query that accesses data to complete the query. Data may be selected from one or more tables or other views and presented to the user as a logical single table. Shorthand views are <u>not</u> updateable.

Shorthand views assist in securing the data by:

The owner of a shorthand view does need not be the owner of any underlying tables or views. Tables and views underlying a shorthand view can have different owners.

Anyone with authority to READ *all* the underlying tables also has authority to READ a shorthand view, but only authorized users can PURGE a shorthand view.

SQL Programs

SQL programs are like any other language program except that they must be SQLCOMPiled to be registered in an SQL catalog and optimized for access.

SQLCOMP / NLCPCOMP

The SQLCOMP or (NLCPCOMP for native mode languages) SQL compilers optimize the SQL statements in the object code file and link the statement to a specific access path determination, then register the program to the SQL catalog. Only programs processed by SQLCOMP can access SQL objects.

Unlike other compilers, SQLCOMP is normally available on secure systems, as an integral piece of the SQL subsystem.

SQLCOMP is invoked explicitly or implicitly (automatic) by SQL.

Explicit Compilation: is used to register SQL application programs to the SQL catalogs. It is demand driven.

Automatic (implicit) Recompilation: is invoked whenever an object is invalidated (see SQL invalidation). When an invalidating event occurs it invalidates the stored optimized access path. While a program is executing, if it discovers an invalid path, the SQL subsystem initiates SQLCOMP for the statement to obtain a new path for access.

AP-FILE-SQLCOMP-01   SQLCOMP should be available for execution by the SQL subsystem on any system to perform SQL recompilations.

AP-FILE-SQLCOMP-02   Automatic SQLCOMPs are valid for the active session of the object's run unit. Once the program has stopped, if it restarts the recompilations will need to be performed again. Only an explicit SQLCOMP can restore the new paths. This has performance implications, as recompiling invalid statements incurs overhead.

SQL Invalidation

A number of SQL and system events can cause invalidation.

Non-DDL events:

Copying the program file. If you copy a program file by using the FUP DUPLICATE command, the original file is unaffected, but the new file is invalid.

Binding the program file. If you explicitly bind a program file by using the Binder program, the original file is unaffected, but the resulting target file is invalid.

Restoring a program file. If you restore a program file (or an underlying table of a protection or shorthand view used by the program) by using the RESTORE program without specifying the SQLCOMPILE ON option, the restored program is invalid. If the SQLCOMPILE ON option is used, an explicit SQL recompile is performed.

Running the Accelerator for the program file. If you run the accelerator to optimize the object code (TNS/R systems only), the program file becomes invalid.

DDL events:

Adding a constraint to a table used by the program.

Adding a column to a table used by the program.

Adding an index to a table used by the program, or to an underlying table of a protection or shorthand view used by the program, unless you specify the NO INVALIDATE option in the CREATE INDEX statement.

Adding a partition to a table or index used by the program.

Changing a collation: dropping and then re-creating the collation, renaming a collation, or changing a DEFINE that points to a collation.

Executing the UPDATE STATISTICS statement unless you specify the NORECOMPILE option.

Dropping a table or view.

Dropping a partition of a table or index.

Dropping an index or constraint on a table.

Restoring a table, including an underlying table of a protection or shorthand view, using the RESTORE program.

Changing the PARTITION ARRAY type associated with the base table.

NOTE: For commands that have options to circumvent the invalidation, the changes may not be utilized by the program until the recompilation is performed. For instance, if a new index is added with the NO INVALIDATE option, the index will not be used by the program until after the subsequent explicit recompilation. Similarly, if the program is compiled with the CHECK INOPERABLE PLANS option and the table and any associated protection views have the similarity check enabled, the invalidation can be circumvented.

Unexpected events:

A node or volume that contains one or more objects involved in the SQL statement is inaccessible.

An event occurs, such as a CPU failure during SQLCOMP or SQL access.

Licensed SQLCI2

Normally, the SQL catalogs are managed by the SQL subsystem, meaning all entries into the SQL catalogs are performed via the subsystem as the commands to add, alter or delete objects is requested. For instance, if the user adds an index, part of the functionality to add the index is to add the appropriate catalog entries. The SQL subsystem makes the appropriate changes to the catalogs, keeping them properly updated.

Under normal conditions a user does not perform direct manipulation to the catalogs. However, SQLCI2 includes a diagnostic tool that allows SUPER.SUPER to perform direct data manipulation on the SQL Catalogs. This tool has been provided for disaster recovery of corrupted catalogs. To facilitate the diagnostic tool, the SQLCI2 object file must be licensed and used by SUPER.SUPER. Using SQLCI2 in this manner makes direct changes to the SQL catalog without affecting the corresponding SQL object.

RISK   Inadvertent use of a licensed SQLCI2 can cause corruption of the SQL catalog structure.

AP-ADVICE-SQLCI2-01   Never leave SQLCI2 licensed on your $SYSTEM.SYSTEM subvolume. If SUPER.SUPER uses this version it will automatically be in the diagnostic mode and could cause corruption.

Sanitizing Test Data

Test data is often overlooked, by those using it as well as those that are charged to protect it. Often test databases are compiled from production data. The production database contains corporate specific if not sensitive data, such as employee information, payroll data, sales forecasts, customer information, etc. This data must be sanitized by whatever means possible before it can be used.

RISK   If sensitive data is extracted from production databases and moved or used as test data, the security of the sensitive data is compromised.

Once data has been moved out of production, security controls are often not as restrictive. Often it is moved to a less restrictive site and access is given to a wide variety of developers and QA personnel.

AP-ADVICE-TESTDATA-01   Test data should be generated from generic data or sanitized to eliminate security issues regarding sensitive data.

DEFINEs, ASSIGNs, PARAMs

Some of the methods of communicating information between processes, applications, within subsystems, etc. are:

DEFINEs

ASSIGNs

PARAMs

DEFINEs

DEFINEs are file-system elements that provide a means for passing information to a process as a logical name instead of a physical name. For example, DEFINEs can be used to pass attributes to a process to provide:

An alternate name for accessing a file

To organize the standard working set of 'pointers' to system resources

A list of subvolumes to search for a file name

A way to set up attributes for processing

A means of passing attributes to the utility subsystem

The operating system (file system or I/O process) usually processes DEFINEs, while application programs or run-time libraries process ASSIGNs.

DEFINEs are added, deleted and altered via:

TACL interactively

TACL MACRO files or OBEY files

Pathway server Configurations

An ATTACHMENT-SET within NETBATCH

The TACLLOCL and TACLCSTM files

A process 'inherits' the working set of DEFINEs upon startup.

RISK   DEFINEs can be 'disabled' by issuing the SET DEFMODE OFF command within TACL or programmatically.

DEFINE Format

DEFINEs are named sets of attributes and associated values. They specify information that is meant to be communicated to a new process in a DEFINE.

A DEFINE has the following components:

NAME   A unique descriptive name starting with '=' and up to 23 characters.

CLASS   A designation of usage class

ATTRIBUTE   A defined attribute of the class

VALUE   The value associated with the attribute; filename, tape name, etc.

There are eight classes (types) of DEFINEs.

DEFINE TYPE	Description
CLASS CATALOG	Used to specify the name of an SQL Catalog
CLASS DEFAULTS	Used to designate a system default DEFINE
CLASS MAP	Used to specify a substitute file name
CLASS SEARCH	Used to specify a list of subvolumes for resolving file names
CLASS SORT and SUBSORT	Used to specify defaults for the FASTSORT utility
CLASS SPOOL	Used to specify the attributes of a spooler job
CLASS TAPE	Used to specify the attributes of a file on a labeled tape
CLASS TAPECATALOG	Used with the tape cataloging facilities of the DSM/TC product

```
Example 1: SQL CATALOG
Define Name          =MY_CATALOG
    CLASS            CATALOG
    SUBVOL           \SYSA.$DISK11.MYCATS
Example 2:  CLASS MAP
Define Name          =MY_CODE_FILE
    CLASS            MAP
    FILE             \SYSA.$TEST21.TESTAPP.CODES
Example 3:  DEFAULTS
Define Name          =_DEFAULTS
```

```
CLASS           DEFAULTS
VOLUME          $DISK21.MYHOMEV
```

RISK   Using DEFINEs can cause erroneous results if the logical DEFINE is changed then referenced. For instance, assume that the DEFINE =MY_CODE_FILE is pointing to a test file. If a TACL command such as FUP PURGEDATA =MY_CODE_FILE is performed, it will purgedata the file \SYSA.$DISK21.MASTER.CODES. If the DEFINE is changed to point to a different file, such as \SYSA.$PROD.PRODAPP.CODES the same command could erroneously purge the data from the production application file (assuming allowable security).

RISK   Using DEFINEs can mask the ultimate file, process, device, etc. that will be affected from the user, which can be desirable and undesirable at the same time.

RISK   Ending a TACL session or logging off of TACL deletes any existing DEFINEs. They must be re-added for each new TACL in order to be in effect for new processes.

_DEFAULTS DEFINE

This is a system DEFINE that specifies the current default node, volume, subvolume and catalog for expanding partially qualified Guardian names throughout the system and subsystems. The _DEFAULTS DEFINE is set with the DEFAULT program.

ASSIGNs

The ASSIGN command within TACL is used to associate the names of a physical file to a logical file name used in a program, and optionally, to specify the attributes of such files. The file attributes are used to describe creation or open mode specifications.

While the operating system (file system or I/O process) usually processes DEFINEs, application programs or run-time libraries process ASSIGNs. The process or run-time library processes the incoming ASSIGNs and uses the information within the code.

Example 1 shows an ASSIGN for an existing file.

```
Example 1:
ASSIGN MASTERFILE, $DATA1.CUSTMR.MSTFILE
```

Example 2 shows an ASSIGN with Create File Characteristics

```
Example 2:
ASSIGN OUTFILE, $DATA2.CUSTMR.NEWMST, EXT 32, CODE 123
```

ASSIGNs are added using TACL or a TACL Macro. TACL stores the assigned values and sends those values to requesting processes in the form of ASSIGN messages. TACL does not interpret the assigned values—that task must be performed by the application program.

RISK ASSIGNs have similar risks to DEFINEs, in that changing the ASSIGN attribute can change the filename or specification that the program using the ASSIGN acts upon.

RISK   Ending a TACL session or logging off of TACL deletes any existing assignments. They must be re-added upon logging on again in order to be in effect when starting new processes.

PARAMs

A PARAM is used to pass any information that the receiving process is expecting. PARAM allows passing parameter names and values to a process.

Example 1 shows a PARAM DEVICE_TYPE.

```
EXAMPLE 1:
SET PARAM DEVICE_TYPE 2
```

The receiving process would be expected to use the PARAM to perform an action based upon the DEVICE_TYPE entered.

PARAMs are added from TACL or a TACL Macro. TACL stores the values of parameters assigned by the PARAM command and sends these values to processes that request parameter values in the form of a PARAM message. TACL does not interpret the assigned values—that task must be performed by the receiving program.

RISK PARAMs can be any type of information including filenames, process names, user names and passwords.

RISK PARAMs have similar risks to DEFINEs, in that changing the PARAM can change the task the receiving program performs.

RISK   Ending a TACL session or logging off of TACL, or executing the CLEAR PARAM command deletes or clears PARAMs. They must be re-added upon logging on again in order to be in effect when starting new processes.

Application Management and Support

System Management

The System Management team is responsible for keeping the HP NonStop servers running efficiently. They are responsible for all aspects of hardware, software and communications that support the enterprise applications.

The System Manager should notify the Security Administration when changes, upgrades or other events could affect the security of the enterprise application.

The System Management methods must also comply with the Corporate Security Policy and Standards, so a good relationship between the systems team and security team is vital.

Database Management

The database management team is responsible for creating and maintaining database organization and integrity. They reorganize databases, partition files as well as install new or updated object programs used by the application. They must keep the Guardian operating system updated and coordinate with the HP site analysts when new hardware components are required.

Communications

There are numerous methods of communicating to and from an HP server system. The communication methods and the security that is necessary to control unauthorized users from getting access to the enterprise application is a joint effort by the System Manager and the Security Manager.

Communication devices, protocols, and methods are not covered in this book.

Protection and Recovery

The HP NonStop server was designed to be fault-tolerant. Depending on the system and enterprise applications, certain functions can be designed to take advantage of the fault-tolerant features of the Guardian operating system. The level of fault-tolerance will ensure the protection of and the ability to recover the application.

RISK   The ability to pick and choose which functions will run as fault-tolerant will control the risk for the enterprise application.

The HP NonStop server hardware and software provide maximum protection against most equipment failures, power failures, and some catastrophic failures. For the enterprise application, the organization should carefully plan how to protect the database and application software.

Methods of Protection and Recovery*:

Mirrored Disk Volumes

Backup and Restore

NonStop Process Pairs

Pathway Applications

NonStop TMF software

NonStop RDF software

* These subsystems are described in more detail in the Gazette part of this book

Mirrored disk volumes

Mirrored disk volumes are a primary protection against disk failures. Fault-tolerant mirrored disk volumes ensure that a single disk failure will not suspend the enterprise application. These volumes also provide the ability to repair and maintain disk volumes online, without interrupting application processing.

BACKUP and RESTORE

The BACKUP utility can copy one or more files or entire volumes to tape. BACKUP is used for database files and SQL programs stored in the Guardian file space. The RESTORE utility is used to retrieve data from the backup tapes.

NonStop Process Pairs

Applications that are written as non-stop process pairs, with application code to checkpoint the running process to its backup, give powerful protection to the enterprise application. If the CPU running the primary copy of the application process fails, the backup copy in the backup CPU takes over and the enterprise application is not affected.

Pathway Applications

Pathway uses the NonStop process pair concept and also uses an automatic load balancing and recovery mechanism. Although Pathway does not run server processes as non-stop pairs, Pathway automatically restarts a server if it fails. Pathway can run dynamic numbers of servers in multiple CPUs, allowing for load balancing and also allowing for CPU failures.

NonStopTMF Subsystem

The NonStop TMF subsystem provides database integrity through transaction control. Transactions can be defined to encompass multiple database updates that must collectively be successful or the transaction is backed out. NonStop TMF ensures that a database is consistently updated.

Remote Duplicate Database Facility (RDF)

Disasters like fires, earthquakes, or flooding can severely damage computer hardware. Catastrophes rarely happen, but when they do, they can take down the entire computer system leaving the company no way to carry on its daily business operations. Even a system shutdown of just a few hours can result in a substantial business loss.

The NonStop RDF subsystem monitors NonStop TMF transaction activity on a designated primary system and applies duplicate updates to an identical copy of the database residing on a remotely located backup system in the same network. The backup database is continually updated by NonStop RDF software, providing a current, online copy of the primary database. The backup database can be located nearby or across the nation, thus, RDF can protect against area-wide or even regional disasters.

Gathering The Audit Information

The following series of commands and examples demonstrates how to gather information to complete the discovery of information from an HP NonStop server.

3P-POLICY-QUERY-01   Use a third party tool to gather and query information about the HP NonStop server to obtain the discovery information.

Legend

Syntax:
Command syntax.

Examples:
Examples will generally follow a Syntax heading.

Output:
Output generated from the examples will be displayed in an outlined box. Text "←" denotes items of interest

Example:

```
SYSINFO - T9268D37 - (27 Nov 97)  SYSTEM \SYDNEY  Date 23 Apr 2003, 16:46:21
COPYRIGHT TANDEM COMPUTERS INCORPORATED 1985, 1987-1997

         System name    \SYDNEY
  EXPAND node number    111
     Current SYSnn       SYS01
     System number      44301                      ←
  Software release ID   G06.18
```

Guardian Wildcarding

These wildcard characters can be used to match characters anywhere in a process name, filename, subvolume or volume name (but not a node name):

* The asterisk matches zero to eight characters.

? The question mark matches a single character.

More than one wildcard can be used in the same command. *If a wildcard is used in the volume name, a dollar sign must be included.*

Wildcards cannot be used to match the periods that separate the elements of a file-name string (system, volume, subvolume, and file names).

Example 1:
```
FILES $SYSTEM.SYS*
```

Example 1 lists all the files in every subvolume on the $SYSTEM disk whose sub-volume name begins with the letters SYS.

Example 2:
```
FILEINFO $DATA*.MN?.*
```

Example 2 lists all files that reside in the subvolume that has a three-character name beginning with MN and volumes beginning with $DATA.

Example 3:
```
FILEINFO $DATA*.MN?.CASH*
```

Example 3 lists all files with names beginning with CASH that reside in the sub-volume that has a three-character name beginning with MN and volumes beginning with $DATA.

Example 4:
```
FILEINFO $DA??01.SAFE*.A00*
```

Example 4 lists all files with names beginning with A00 that reside in the sub-volume with a name beginning with SAFE and all volumes with six character names starting with DA and ending with 01.

CUSTFILE

1. Use the SYSINFO command to get the system number of an HP NonStop server:

```
SYSINFO
```

```
SYSINFO - T9268D37 - (27 Nov 97)  SYSTEM \SYDNEY  Date 23 Apr 2003, 16:46:21
COPYRIGHT TANDEM COMPUTERS INCORPORATED 1985, 1987-1997

          System name      \SYDNEY
  EXPAND node number       111
      Current SYSnn        SYS01
        System number      44301                    ←
  Software release ID      G06.18
```

2. Locate the CUSTFILE located in $SYSTEM.A<system number>

Note that the subvolume name will be the letter A followed by six characters. So, a leading zero (0) may need to be added after the 'A' as shown below.

`FILEINFO $SYSTEM.A044301.*`

```
$SYSTEM.A044301
                CODE            EOF   LAST MODIFIED  OWNER   RWEP   PExt   SExt
CUSTFILE        101          365896 13DEC2002  9:01 255,255 NUNU     20     20
ZMP0000B        961            1536 16DEC2002 17:22 255,255 NCCN      2      2
ZMP0000C        961            1536 30DEC2002 16:33 255,255 NCCC      2      2
ZPHI6030        961             178 02DEC2002 13:36 255,255 NCCN      2      2
ZPHIFI          961            1536 30DEC2002 17:05 255,255 NCCN      2      2
```

3. Use EDIT, in read only mode, to view the contents of the CUSTFILE file. The EDIT Command Interpreter prompt will be an asterisk "*".

`EDIT $SYSTEM.A044301.CUSTFILE R`

```
TEXT EDITOR - T9601D20 - (01JUN93
CURRENT FILE IS $SYSTEM.A044301.CUSTFILE
*
```

4. The EDIT command LC will display the column numbers. Locate the column number where the L (for LICENSE) appears. In this case it is column 62.

`LC`

```
          ....+....1....+....2....+....3....+....4....+....5....+....6....+....7
....+....8....+.
 6814      2 Y9683D43    ZNSSTMPL ZTEMPL    SYSGEN    TEMPLATE
     980130141053
  *
```

5. The EDIT command PUT <output filename>/L/C62 will list all lines in the CUSTFILE where an upper case 'L' appears in column 62 to the output file. In this case, the output file is $DATAA.SECREVU.LICENSED.

`PUT $DATAA.SECREVU.LICENSED /L/C62`

```
CURRENT FILE IS $SYSTEM.A043421.CUSTFILE
```

6. Examine the output file to review all the files for the Operating System Version that HP recommends be LICENSED.

`GET $DATAA.SECREVU.LICENSED`

```
CURRENT FILE IS $DATAA.SECREVU.LICENSED
```

NUMBER ALL
LIST LAST

```
101     2 Y9519D30    TAPERDR ZUTIL    SYSGEN    COPY      SYSNN       L
020624180724
```

In this case there are 101 program files that should LICENSED. The last line is shown above. The copy of TAPERDR residing in $SYSTEM.SYSnn should be LICENSED.

Y9519D30 is the product number.

ZUTIL is the 'installation subvolume' where this program file will be placed during the loading of the SUT tape.

COPY SYSNN means that the program will automatically be copied to the new SYSnn during the SYSGEN process.

SYSGEN means that the program will be copied by SYSGEN.

020624180724 is the compile date of the program.

L (in column 62) means that the program file should be LICENSED.

DSAP Commands

Use the DSAP utility to identify PROGID'd programs. Use EDIT to examine the output file.

```
Syntax:
[RUN] [ \node.]DSAP / out <filename> / [ <volume specification>]
[,<options>]

<volume specification> is of the form:

$<volume name>                — a single volume.
($<vol-name>,$<vol-name>, ..)  — a list of volumes.
$* -or- *                     — ALL volumes.
```

A <volume name> may contain asterisks, which match 0-7 characters, or question marks, which match any single character.

```
Report options:
   TABULAR    — for tabular form of DSAP reports
   BYSUBVOL   — space allocation by subvol
   BYUSER     — space allocation by user-id
   AUDITED    — TMF audited files
   DETAIL     — detailed list of selected files

DETAIL selection options.
   LICENSED
   PROGID
```

To create a listing of all the files and their owner, listed by subvolume:

```
Syntax:
DSAP [ /out <outfile> / ] $*, BYSUBVOL,DETAIL,TABULAR
```

To create a listing of all the files owned by a specific user:

Syntax:
```
DSAP  [ /out <outfile> / ] $*, USER <user name> | <user number>, DETAIL
```

When a file is owned by a userid that no longer exists on the system, the User Number is shown and the User Name is displayed as question marks (?????)

To create a listing of all files that are PROGID or LICENSED:

Syntax:
```
DSAP  [ /out <outfile> / ] $*, DETAIL, LICENSED, PROGID
```

Fileinfo Commands

The FILEINFO command lists information about one or more files. Auditors will use this command to discover the location of certain sensitive files, their owners and their Guardian security string.

To send the output of the FILEINFO command to a file or the SPOOLER, use the OUT command.

Syntax:
```
FILEINFO [ / OUT outfile / ] [ [ wc-vol.] [ wc-subvol.] ] wc-filename ]
```

where WC stands for Wildcarded.

Example 1:
```
FILEINFO $SYSTEM.SYS*.OSMON
```

```
$SYSTEM.SYS00
                CODE            EOF    LAST MODIFIED  OWNER  RWEP    PExt    SExt
OSMON    O     700      477512 16APR2001 10:16 255,255 NUNU     32 .     32
$SYSTEM.SYS06
                CODE            EOF    LAST MODIFIED  OWNER  RWEP    PExt    SExt
OSMON          700      477512 16APR2001 10:16 255,255 NUNU     32       32
```

Example 1 will display all the OSMON object files on any $SYSTEM.SYSnn subvolume.

Example 2:
```
FILEINFO $*.*.APPDEV
```

```
$SYSTEM.APPDEV
                CODE            EOF    LAST MODIFIED  OWNER  RWEP    PExt    SExt
APPDEV  O     100     4763648 24JUN2001 21:51 255,255 UUUU     278       64
```

Example 2 will display the APPDEV object file information.

Example 3:
```
FILEINFO /OUT $USER.BRIAN.SAFELIST/ $*.DATA*.A*
```

Example 3 will display all the files, on any disk, with a subvolume name beginning with the characters DATA and a filename beginning with the letter A. The listing will be sent to a file called SAFELIST in the $USER.BRIAN subvolume.

Example 4:
```
FILEINFO /OUT $S.#WIRELST/ $AUDIT*.WIRE.*
```

Example 4 will display all the files on any disk with a name beginning with the string AUDIT, with a subvolume name of WIRE and send the output to the SPOOLER location $S.#WIRELST.

FUP (File Utility Program) Commands

FUP is designed to manage disk files on the HP NonStop system. Use FUP to create, display, and duplicate files, load data into files, alter file characteristics, and purge files.

Use the FUP INFO command to display summary attributes of a diskfile. To start FUP:

Syntax:
```
FUP
```

The FUP Command Interpreter prompt will be a dash "-".

Example 1:
```
FUP
```

```
File Utility Program - T6553G07 - (01AUG2002)    System  \Toronto
Copyright Tandem Computers Incorporated 1981, 1983, 1985-2001
-
```

```
INFO $DATA01.TEMP.CATDEL
```

```
                CODE          EOF      LAST MODIF OWNER  RWEP    TYPE   REC BL
$DATA01.TEMP
   CATDEL       101          8312   4Feb2002 09:11 22?,11 CCCC
```

Use the INFO DETAIL command to display detail attributes of a diskfile.

Example 2:
```
INFO $DATA01.TEMP.CATDEL, DETAIL
```

```
$DATA01.TEMP.CATDEL                    30 Jun 2003,  8:49
    ENSCRIBE
    TYPE U
    FORMAT 1
    CODE 101
    EXT ( 4 PAGES, 28 PAGES )
    MAXEXTENTS 978
    BUFFERSIZE 4096
    OWNER 222,11
```

```
SECURITY (RWEP): CCCC
DATA MODIF:    4 Feb 2002,  9:11
CREATION DATE:    9 Apr 2003, 11:13
LAST OPEN:    9 May 2003, 11:24
FILE LABEL: 158 (3.8% USED)
EOF: 8312 (0.0% USED)
EXTENTS ALLOCATED: 2
```

Pathway Commands

Use the STATUS command to determine if there are any Pathway applications running and the userids they are running under.

Syntax:
```
STATUS *,PROG $*.*.PATHMON
```

Example 1:
```
STATUS *,PROG $*.*.PATHMON
```

```
Process            Pri PFR %WT Userid  Program file             Hometerm
$BEN       0,100   145 001 222,9   $SYSTEM.SYSTEM.PATHMON   $VHS
$YPHI      0,144   100 005 255,255 $SYSTEM.SYSTEM.PATHMON   $ZHOME
$BMA1      0,146   145 001 222,210 $SYSTEM.SYSTEM.PATHMON   $VHS
$ABOP      0,183   160 005 255,255 $SYSTEM.SYSTEM.PATHMON   $VHS
$QAPQ      0,187   145 001 222,212 $SYSTEM.SYSTEM.PATHMON   $VHS
$DVMA      0,192   145 001 222,9   $SYSTEM.SYSTEM.PATHMON   $VHS
$BFMA   B  0,212   145 001 222,11  $SYSTEM.SYSTEM.PATHMON   $VHS
$AMA       0,222   145 001 222,9   $SYSTEM.SYSTEM.PATHMON   $VHS
$ABOP   B  1,22    160 001 255,255 $SYSTEM.SYSTEM.PATHMON   $VHS
$ZVHS   B  1,31    148 001 255,255 $SYSTEM.SYSTEM.PATHMON   $YMIOP.#CLCI
$XPLP      0,97    145 005 255,255 $SYSTEM.SYSTEM.PATHMON   $VHS
```

For any Pathway applications running under SUPER.SUPER, use the PATHCOM INFO command to determine the internal Pathway security. To start PATHCOM:

Syntax:
```
PATHCOM $<process>.
```

The Pathway Command Interpreter prompt will be an equals sign "="

Example 2:
```
PATHCOM $XPLP
```

```
$Y7D7: PATHCOM - T8344D44 - (02MAY01)
COPYRIGHT HP COMPUTER CORPORATION 1980 - 1985, 1987 - 2001
=
```

Example 3:
```
INFO PATHWAY
```

```
PATHWAY
  MAXASSIGNS 50              [CURRENTLY 0]
  MAXDEFINES 20              [CURRENTLY 0]
```

```
MAXEXTERNALTCPS 0                  [CURRENTLY 0]
MAXLINKMONS 5                      [CURRENTLY 0]
MAXPARAMS 20                       [CURRENTLY 0]
MAXPATHCOMS 5                      [CURRENTLY 2]
MAXPROGRAMS 10                     [CURRENTLY 2]
MAXSERVERCLASSES 50               [CURRENTLY 23]
MAXSERVERPROCESSES 70            [CURRENTLY 23]
MAXSPI 1                           [CURRENTLY 0]
MAXSTARTUPS 20                     [CURRENTLY 0]
MAXTCPS 5                          [CURRENTLY 1]
MAXTELLQUEUE 4
MAXTELLS 32                        [CURRENTLY 0]
MAXTERMS 5                         [CURRENTLY 1]
MAXTMFRESTARTS 5
OWNER \LA.255,255
SECURITY "N"              ←
=
```

Look for any PATHMON process secured "N" or "A".

Status Command

The STATUS command is used to list information about processes running on a
system.

Syntax:
STATUS $<PROCESS NAME>

Example 1:
STATUS $CMON

```
System \LA
Process               Pri PFR %WT Userid  Program file              Hometerm
$CMON        1,171    180     001 255,255 $SYSTEM.APPCM.APPCM        $VHS
                          Swap File Name: $AUDIT.#0
        Current Extended Swap File Name: $AUDIT.#0483691
$CMON     B  0,226    180     001 255,255 $SYSTEM.APPCM.APPCM        $VHS
                          Swap File Name: $AUDIT.#0
        Current Extended Swap File Name: $AUDIT.#0483692
```

Use the FILEINFO $<volume>.<subvolume>.<fileinfo> to list the owner and
RWEP string for the CMON process's object and source files. The STATUS
command shown above, will display the CMON process's object file
$SYSTEM.APPCM.APPCM..

Syntax:
FILEINFO $<volume>.<subvolume>.<filename>

Example 2:
FILEINFO $SYSTEM.APPCM.APPCM

```
$SYSTEM.APPCM

                CODE             EOF    LAST MODIFIED  OWNER   RWEP    PExt    SExt
APPCM   O       100         4763648 24JUN2001 21:51  255,255  0000     278      64
```

Safeguard Commands

The Safeguard commands necessary to gather audit information are provided in the
following table.

Gathering Information about Objects Protected by the Safeguard Subsystem

The following table shows the commands for gathering information about each type of
object.

Information Needed	Safeguard Command
Diskfile access rules	INFO DISKFILE { $<vol name>.<subvol name>.<filename>} ,DETAIL
Subvolume access rules	INFO SUBVOL { $<vol name>.<subvol name> },DETAIL
Volume access rules	INFO VOL { $<volume name > }, DETAIL
Process access rules	INFO PROCESS { $<process name> }, DETAIL
Subprocess access rules	INFO SUBPROCESS {$<subprocess name> },DETAIL
Device access rules	INFO DEVICE { $<device name> }, DETAIL
Subdevice access rules	INFO SUBDEVICE {$<subdevice name> },DETAIL
Safeguard global settings	INFO SAFEGUARD,DETAIL
Groups - Security	INFO SECURITY-GROUP SECURITY-ADMININSTRATOR INFO SECURITY-GROUP SYSTEM-OPERATOR
Groups - File-sharing	INFO GROUP NAME <group name>,DETAIL INFO GROUP NUMBER <group number>,DETAIL
Audit Configuration	INFO AUDIT SERVICE INFO AUDIT POOL <audit pool>
User - Audit parameters	INFO USER {user name | user number},AUDIT
User - Remote passwords	INFO USER {user name | user number}, REMOTEPASSWORD
User - OSS parameters	INFO USER {user name | user number}, OSS
User - CI parameters	INFO USER {user name | user number}, CI
User - Aliases	INFO USER {user name | user number}, ALIAS
User - STATUS	INFO USER {user name | user number}, GENERAL

Information Needed	Safeguard Command
User - File Sharing Groups	INFO USER {user name | user number}, GROUP
User - all parameters	INFO USER {user name | user number}, DETAIL
Alias - Audit parameters	INFO ALIAS {alias }, AUDIT
Alias - Remote passwords	INFO ALIAS {alias}, REMOTEPASSWORD
Alias - OSS parameters	INFO ALIAS {alias}, OSS
Alias - CI parameters	INFO ALIAS {alias}, CI
Alias - STATUS	INFO ALIAS {alias}, GENERAL
Alias- File Sharing Groups	INFO ALIAS {user name | user number}, GROUP
Alias - All fields	INFO ALIAS {alias}, DETAIL
Objecttype settings	INFO OBJECTTYPE {objecttype}, DETAIL

Many Safeguard OBJECTs, such as User Group Name or Number, Volume, Subvolume or Diskfile names can be wildcarded with an asterisk (*).

Use the INFO SAFEGUARD DETAIL command to display all the Global Security attributes of Safeguard software. To start SAFECOM:

Syntax:
`SAFECOM`

The prompt for SAFECOM is an equal sign "=".

Example 1:
`SAFECOM`

```
SAFEGUARD COMMAND INTERPRETER - T9750G06 - (22JUL02)     SYSTEM  \LA
=
```

`INFO SAFEGUARD, DETAIL`

```
SAFEGUARD IS CONFIGURED WITH SUPER.SUPER UNDENIABLE

  AUTHENTICATE-MAXIMUM-ATTEMPTS =       3
  AUTHENTICATE-FAIL-TIMEOUT      =     60 SECONDS
  AUTHENTICATE-FAIL-FREEZE       = OFF

  PASSWORD-REQUIRED = OFF    PASSWORD-HISTORY =  0
  PASSWORD-ENCRYPT  = ON     PASSWORD-MINIMUM-LENGTH = 6
  PASSWORD-MAY-CHANGE    =     1 DAYS BEFORE-EXPIRATION
  PASSWORD-EXPIRY-GRACE =       7 DAYS  AFTER-EXPIRATION

  WARNING-MODE = OFF    WARNING-FALLBACK-SECURITY = GUARDIAN

  DIRECTION-DEVICE       = SUBDEVICE-FIRST    CHECK-DEVICE      = ON
  COMBINATION-DEVICE     = FIRST-ACL          CHECK-SUBDEVICE   = ON
  ACL-REQUIRED-DEVICE    = OFF
```

```
DIRECTION-PROCESS       = SUBPROCESS-FIRST    CHECK-PROCESS     = ON
COMBINATION-PROCESS     = FIRST-ACL           CHECK-SUBPROCESS  = ON
ACL-REQUIRED-PROCESS    = OFF


DIRECTION-DISKFILE      = FILENAME-FIRST       CHECK-VOLUME      = OFF
COMBINATION-DISKFILE    = FIRST-ACL            CHECK-SUBVOLUME   = ON
ACL-REQUIRED-DISKFILE   = OFF                  CHECK-FILENAME    = ON
CLEARONPURGE-DISKFILE   = OFF


AUDIT-OBJECT-ACCESS-PASS = NONE       AUDIT-AUTHENTICATE-PASS    = ALL
AUDIT-OBJECT-ACCESS-FAIL = ALL        AUDIT-AUTHENTICATE-FAIL    = ALL
AUDIT-OBJECT-MANAGE-PASS = ALL        AUDIT-SUBJECT-MANAGE-PASS  = ALL
AUDIT-OBJECT-MANAGE-FAIL = ALL        AUDIT-SUBJECT-MANAGE-FAIL  = ALL


AUDIT-DEVICE-ACCESS-PASS = NONE       AUDIT-PROCESS-ACCESS-PASS  = NONE
AUDIT-DEVICE-ACCESS-FAIL = ALL        AUDIT-PROCESS-ACCESS-FAIL  = ALL
AUDIT-DEVICE-MANAGE-PASS = ALL        AUDIT-PROCESS-MANAGE-PASS  = ALL
AUDIT-DEVICE-MANAGE-FAIL = ALL        AUDIT-PROCESS-MANAGE-FAIL  = ALL


                AUDIT-DISKFILE-ACCESS-PASS = NONE
                AUDIT-DISKFILE-ACCESS-FAIL = ALL
                AUDIT-DISKFILE-MANAGE-PASS = ALL
                AUDIT-DISKFILE-MANAGE-FAIL = ALL


                AUDIT-CLIENT-SERVICE       = OFF

CI-PROG = $SYSTEM.SYSTEM.TACL          CMON        = ON
CI-LIB  = * NONE *                     CMONERROR   = ACCEPT
CI-SWAP = * NONE *                     CMONTIMEOUT =      29 SECONDS
CI-CPU  = * NONE *                     BLINDLOGON  = ON
CI-PRI  =       150                    NAMELOGON   = ON
CI-PARAM-TEXT =
TERMINAL-EXCLUSIVE-ACCESS  = OFF
```

Example 1 shows the Safeguard Globals. Note the first line, which shows that SUPER.SUPER is undeniable.

Example 2:
INFO USER 222,77,DETAIL

```
GROUP.USER      USER-ID    OWNER     LAST-MODIFIED    LAST-LOGON     STATUS
ABCO.PAM        222,77    \*.253,1   12APR02, 11:00   23DEC02,  7:45  THAWED

  UID                        =        56909
  USER-EXPIRES               =     23DEC02,   7:45
  PASSWORD-EXPIRES           =     23DEC02,   7:45
  PASSWORD-MAY-CHANGE        =      * NONE *
  PASSWORD-MUST-CHANGE EVERY =      30 DAYS
  PASSWORD-EXPIRY-GRACE      =      29 DAYS
  LAST-LOGON                 = 23DEC02,   7:45
  LAST-UNSUCCESSFUL-ATTEMPT  =  4DEC02, 13:11
  LAST-MODIFIED              = 12APR02, 11:00
  FROZEN/THAWED              = THAWED
  STATIC FAILED LOGON COUNT  =        4
  GUARDIAN DEFAULT SECURITY  = NCCC
  GUARDIAN DEFAULT VOLUME    = $DATAA.PAM

  AUDIT-AUTHENTICATE-PASS = ALL        AUDIT-MANAGE-PASS = ALL
  AUDIT-AUTHENTICATE-FAIL = ALL        AUDIT-MANAGE-FAIL = ALL
  AUDIT-USER-ACTION-PASS  = NONE
  AUDIT-USER-ACTION-FAIL  = ALL
```

```
CI-PROG = * NONE *
CI-LIB  = * NONE *
CI-NAME = * NONE *
CI-SWAP = * NONE *
CI-CPU  = * NONE *
CI-PRI  = * NONE *
CI-PARAM-TEXT =

INITIAL-PROGTYPE = PROGRAM
INITIAL-PROGRAM  =
INITIAL-DIRECTORY =

PRIMARY-GROUP = ABCO
GROUP         = ABCO

REMOTEPASSWORD = \LA     xxxx
REMOTEPASSWORD = \SYDNEY xxxx
REMOTEPASSWORD = \LONDON   xxxx

ALIAS = pamela
ALIAS = pam1
ALIAS = pam-noseg
ALIAS = plh1a

SUBJECT DEFAULT-PROTECTION SECTION UNDEFINED!
```

Example 2 shows a user record.

Example 3:
INFO USER 222,77,REMOTEPASSWORD

```
GROUP.USER          USER-ID   OWNER      LAST-MODIFIED   LAST-LOGON      STATUS
ABCO.PAM            222,77  \*.253,1   12APR02, 11:00  23DEC02,  7:45   THAWED

  REMOTEPASSWORD = \LA     xxxx
  REMOTEPASSWORD = \SYDNEY xxxx
  REMOTEPASSWORD = \LONDON xxxx
```

Example 3 shows only the remote passwords in a user record.

Example 4:
INFO OBJECTTYPE VOLUME

```
                 LAST-MODIFIED   OWNER    STATUS
VOLUME
                 30SEP02, 15:10  \*.255,255  THAWED
        253,001                 C,O
        \*.253,001              C,O

  AUDIT-ACCESS-PASS = ALL       AUDIT-MANAGE-PASS = ALL
  AUDIT-ACCESS-FAIL = ALL       AUDIT-MANAGE-FAIL = ALL
```

Example 4 shows an OBJECTTYPE VOLUME record.

Example 5:
INFO DISKFILE $DATAA.PAM.*,WARNINGS OFF

```
                      LAST-MODIFIED      OWNER     STATUS
$DATAA.PAM
  MYFILE           13AUG01, 10:08      20,245   THAWED
       \*.020,245        R,W,E,P,C,O
       \*.222,077        R
       \*.222,210        R,W

   AUDIT-ACCESS-PASS = ALL          AUDIT-MANAGE-PASS = ALL
   AUDIT-ACCESS-FAIL = ALL          AUDIT-MANAGE-FAIL = ALL

   LICENSE = OFF  PROGID = OFF  CLEARONPURGE = OFF  PERSISTENT =  ON
```

Example 5 shows a diskfile record.

Example 6:
INFO SECURITY-GROUP SECURITY-ADMINISTRATOR

```
                      LAST-MODIFIED      OWNER     STATUS
SECURITY-ADMINISTRATOR
                   7JAN03, 11:12      255,255   THAWED

        222,233           E,    O
        222,250           E,    O
        253,001           E,    O
```

Example 6 shows a SECURITY-GROUP record.

Example 7:
INFO GROUP NAME TEST,DETAIL

```
GROUP NAME                    NUMBER    OWNER       LAST-MODIFIED
test                            300     255,255     8DEC00, 17:53
   AUTO-DELETE = OFF
   DESCRIPTION = "aaa;bbb"
   MEMBER      = Manuel
   MEMBER      = sec-bryan
   MEMBER      = daryl1
```

Example 7 shows a FILE-SHARING Group record.

Gathering Information about the Safeguard Audit Trail

There are two commands used to display the configuration of Safeguard audit trails:

> INFO AUDIT POOL
>
> INFO AUDIT SERVICE

INFO AUDIT POOL Command

The INFO AUDIT POOL displays parameters that determine the name and size of any Audit Pools.

If the command is entered without a specific Audit Pool name, the Current Audit Pool is assumed.

Example 1:
```
INFO AUDIT POOL
```

```
AUDIT POOL $SYSTEM.SAFE      CONFIGURATION
    MAXFILES                      5
    MAXEXTENTS                    16
    EXTENTSIZE                    128,    128
```

Example 1 shows the configuration of the Current Audit Pool.

Example 2:
```
INFO AUDIT POOL   $DATAA.TEMPPOOL
```

```
AUDIT POOL $DATAA.TEMPPOOL    CONFIGURATION
    MAXFILES                      15
    MAXEXTENTS                    32
    EXTENTSIZE                    256,    256
```

Example 2 shows the configuration of a secondary Audit Pool.

INFO AUDIT SERVICE Command

The INFO AUDIT SERVICE Command displays parameters that determine Safeguard's RECOVERY OPTIONS and the manner in which audit records are written to the Audit Trail.

Example 3:
```
INFO AUDIT SERVICE
```

```
CURRENT AUDIT POOL   $SECURE.SAFE
CURRENT AUDIT FILE   $SECURE.SAFE.A0007739
NEXT AUDIT POOL      $WORK.SFGAUDIT
RECOVERY             RECYCLE FILES
CURRENT STATE        RECYCLING FILES
WRITE-THROUGH CACHE  OFF
EOF REFRESH          OFF
```

Example 3 shows the AUDIT SERVICE parameters. The current Audit Pool is $SECURE.SAFE. The next Audit Pool is $WORK.SFGAUDIT. Audit files are being RECYCLED. Audit records are held in memory before being written to disk and the End of File pointer is not updated until the records are actually written to disk.

SQL Commands

The SQLCI program is used to interact with the SQL database system. To find the SQL system catalog and version, start SQLCI:

SQLCI has two prompt levels. A prompt of two right carets (>>) is displayed when SQLCI is ready to start processing a command. A prompt of a plus sign and a right caret is displayed when SQLCI is in the middle of processing an extended line command. All commands in SQLCI are terminated with a semi-colon; otherwise, SQLCI assumes extended line commands and continues processing for input.

Example 1:
SQLCI

```
SQL Conversational Interface - T9191G07 - (05AUG02)
COPYRIGHT COMPAQ COMPUTER CORPORATION 1987-2002
```

GET CATALOG OF SYSTEM;

```
CATALOG: \LA.$DSMSCM.SQL
-- SQL operation complete.
```

GET VERSION OF CATALOG $DSMSCM.SQL;

```
VERSION: 345
-- SQL operation complete.
```

To view the file label information for SQL objects, use FUP INFO or FILEINFO at the TACL prompt in the same manner as any other file on the system.

FILEINFO $DSMSCM.SQL.*;

```
$DSMSCM.SQL
              CODE      EOF   LAST MODIFIED  OWNER   RWEP    PExt    SExt
  BASETABS  O  572A    6384 06AUG2002 15:49 255,255 NNNU      16     128
  CATALOGS     571A   16384 18JUN2003 14:09 255,255 NNUU      16     128
  CATDEFS   O  900A   12288 12OCT1999 10:08 255,255 AA-A      16      64
  COLUMNS   O  573A  159744 06AUG2002 15:49 255,255 NNNU      16     128
  COMMENTS     574A       0 04DEC1998  7:02 255,255 NNNU      16     128
  CONSTRNT     575A       0 04DEC1998  7:02 255,255 NNNU      16     128
  CPRLSRCE     587A       0 04DEC1998  7:02 255,255 NNNU      16     128
  CPRULES      586A       0 04DEC1998  7:02 255,255 NNNU      16     128
```

Researching SQL catalog information is performed using the SQL query language to execute queries against the SQL catalogs. Generally, research of this type requires extensive knowledge of SQL and SQL query format. A large number of queries can be performed against the SQL catalogs. Some examples are:

To display a list of catalog names from the System Catalog;

Example 2:
```
select * from $dsmscm.sql.catalogs for browse access;
```

```
CATALOGNAME                    SUBSYSTEMNAME                    VERSION
-------------------------------------------------------------------------
VERSIONUPGRADETIME    CATALOGCLASS  CATALOGVERSION
-------------------------------------------------------
\LA.$DATA1.AMACATL    SQL                                       A350

           0  U                        350
\LA.$DATA1.AMATEST    SQL                                       A350

           0  U                        350
\LA.$DATA1.P05AACAT   SQL                                       A350

           0  U                        350
\LA.$DATA1.TAPECAT    SQL                                       A350
```

To display a list of tables from a specified catalog:

Example 3:
```
select * from $dsmscm.tapecat.tables for browse access;
```

```
TABLENAME                           TABLETYPE  TABLECODE  COLCOUNT  GROUPID
--------------------------------------------------------------------------
USERID  CREATETIME          REDEFTIME            SECURITYVECTOR
SECURITYMODE
----------------------------------------------
OBJECTVERSION  SIMILARITYCHECK
-------------------------------

\LA.$DSMSCM.TAPECAT.BASETABS          TA         572        9        255
   255   211793825082668460  211793824964685790  NNCC           G
         1  DISABLED
\LA.$DSMSCM.TAPECAT.COLUMNS           TA         573       26        255
   255   211793825082824170  211793824964685790  NNCC           G
         1  DISABLED
```

To discover the security and owner of catalog tables, query the TABLES table as shown:

Syntax:
```
LOG <log-file> CLEAR;
SELECT TABLENAME, SECURITYVECTOR, GROUPID, USERID
FROM <catalog-name>.TABLES
WHERE TABLENAME = "\SYSTEM.$<VOLUME>.<CATALOG-NAME>.TABLES";
```

To find out the security and owner of the USAGES, TRANSIDS, and PROGRAMS tables:

Syntax:
```
SELECT TABLENAME, SECURITYVECTOR, GROUPID, USERID
FROM <catalog-name>.TABLES
WHERE TABLENAME = "\SYSTEM.$<VOLUME>.<CATALOG-NAME>.USAGES"
OR TABLENAME = "\SYSTEM.$<VOLUME>.<CATALOG-NAME>.TRANSIDS"
OR TABLENAME = "\SYSTEM.$VOLUME.<CATALOG-NAME>.PROGRAMS";
```

Gathering System Information

SYSINFO

To display information such as System Name, Number and Operating System release numbers and the current SYSnn, use the SYSINFO command.

On NonStop K-series servers, the System number displayed using SYSINFO may not be correct. The RLSEID file is a more reliable reference.

<u>**Example 1:**</u>
SYSINFO

```
SYSINFO - T9268D37 - (27 Nov 97)  SYSTEM \LONDON Date 23 Apr 2003, 13:08:28
COPYRIGHT TANDEM COMPUTERS INCORPORATED 1985, 1987-1997

        System name     \LONDON
  EXPAND node number    153
      Current SYSnn     SYS01
      System number     045422
 Software release ID    G06.18
```

Example 1 shows a SYSINFO on a NonStop S-series system.

<u>**Example 2:**</u>
SYSINFO

```
SYSINFO - T9268D37 - (27 Nov 97)  SYSTEM \TORONTO  Date 07 May 2003, 07:07:38
COPYRIGHT TANDEM COMPUTERS INCORPORATED 1985, 1987-1997

        System name     \TORONTO
  EXPAND node number    152
      Current SYSnn     SYS04
      System number     B29625
 Software release ID    D48.03
```

Example 2 shows a SYSINFO on a NonStop K-series system. Note that the System number displayed here differs from that in the RLSEID file shown below.

RLSEID File

The system number and Operating System and Release Version can be found in the file called RLSEID. This file is located in the current $SYSTEM.SYSnn.

<u>**Example 1:**</u>
FUP COPY $SYSTEM.SYS01.RLSEID

```
R24 045422 G06.18
1 RECORDS TRANSFERRED
```

Example 1 shows the RLSEID file on a NonStop S-series server. The system number is '045422''; the software release number is Release Version Update G06.18.

Example 2:
```
FUP COPY $SYSTEM.SYS04.RLSEID
```

```
Q11 064421 D48.03
1 RECORDS TRANSFERRED
```

Example 2 shows the RLSEID file on a NonStop K-series system. The system number is '064421'', the software release number is D48.03.

Researching TACL Configuration

ASSIGNs

In an interactive TACL session:

Enter the keyword **ASSIGN** at a TACL prompt to display ASSIGNs that are added as part of the authentication and TACL initialization process or after the execution of a TACL macro or OBEY file.

In the Pathway Environment:

Enter the command: INFO SERVER *

Manually examine the TACLLOCL file and any TACLCSTM files located for the keyword ASSIGN.

Manually examine all OBEY files for the keyword ASSIGN.

ASSIGNs and DEFINEs In NETBATCH

In the NETBATCH Environment:

Within an ATTACHMENT-SET

Use the BATCHCOM utility to research ATTACHMENT-SETs.

To start BATCHCOM:

Syntax:
```
BATCHCOM
```

The prompt for BATCHCOM is a right curly brace ("}").

Example 1:
```
BATCHCOM
```

First locate a job to examine using the STATUS JOB command:

Example 2:
STATUS JOB *

```
JOB STATUS
JOB  JOBNAME                  USERID  LOG  STATE       CLASSNAME
-----------------------------------------------------------------
  1  AUTOBACKUP               255,255 5487 18:00:00    DEFAULT
  5  INCREMENTAL-BACKUP       255,255 6094 31MAR03     DEFAULT
 29  SETTIME                  255,255 6170 29MAR03     DEFAULT
 45  NIGHTLY-MAINTENANCE      222,250 6163 29MAR03     DEFAULT
```

Then examine the job using the INFO JOB command:

Example 3:
INFO 29

```
JOB ATTRIBUTES for SETTIME
                    jobnumber: 29
                       volume: \LA.$SYSTEM.TIME, "NUNU"
                           in:
                          out: \LA.$S.#BATCH.SETTIME
             executor-program: \LA.$SYSTEM.SYSPROBJ.ADJTIME
                          pfs: 0
                          pri: 120
                       selpri: 3
                 maxprintlines: None
                 maxprintpages: None
                        class: DEFAULT
                         hold: Off
                        stall: Off
                 stop-on-abend: Off
                        every: 1 DAYS
                           at: 14DEC99 04:00:00
                      iffails: On
attachment-set: (SUPER.SUPER)STANDARD                         ←
                      highpin: Of
                       submit: 14DEC99 10:22:04
                        alter: 30APR02 08:41:33
                         user: 255,255
                  next-runtime: 29MAR03 04:00:00
```

Look for an entry such as: "attachment-set: "(SUPER.SUPER)STANDARD"", in the example above.

Finally, to see the contents of the ATTACHMENT-SET, enter the following command:

Example 4:
INFO ATTACHMENT-SET (SUPER.SUPER) STANDARD

```
The items contained in the ATTACHMENT-SET will be displayed

ATTACHMENT-SET ATTRIBUTES for (SUPER.SUPER)STANDARD
     security: "UUUU"
     temporary: Off
```

DEFINEs:

In an interactive TACL session:

Example 1:
`INFO DEFINE =*`

```
    Define Name          =TCPIP^PROCESS^NAME
    CLASS                MAP
    FILE                 \LA.$ZTCP2

    Define Name          =ABOPS_EMS_COLLECTOR
    CLASS                MAP
    FILE                 \LA.$0

    Define Name          =ABOPS_XOUT
    CLASS                MAP
    FILE                 \LA.$XOUT

    Define Name          =_DEFAULTS
    CLASS                DEFAULTS
    VOLUME               $DATAA.MARK
```

Displays all DEFINEs that may have been added as part of the authentication and TACL initialization process or after the execution of a TACL macro or OBEY file.

In the Pathway Environment enter the command:

Example 2:
`INFO SERVER *`

```
SERVER XPLS000
  PROCESSTYPE GUARDIAN
  AUTORESTART 0
  CPUS (1:0)
  CREATEDELAY 1 MINS
  DEBUG OFF
  DELETEDELAY 10 MINS
  HIGHPIN OFF
  HOMETERM \LA.$VHS
  LINKDEPTH 1
  MAXSERVERS 1
  NUMSTATIC 1
  OWNER \LA.255,255
  PRI 120
  PROGRAM \LA.$DATAA.XPLPROBJ.XPLS000
  SECURITY "N"
  TMF OFF
  VOLUME \LA.$DATAA.XPLPRDAT
```

Manually examine the TACLLOCL file and any TACLCSTM files located for the keyword DEFINE.

Manually examine all OBEY files for the keyword DEFINE.

PARAMs:

In an interactive TACL session:

```
Example 1
PARAM
```

Displays PARAMs that may have been added as part of the authentication and TACL initialization process or after the execution of a TACL macro or OBEY file.

In the Pathway Environment enter the command:

```
Example 2:
PATHCOM
INFO SERVER *
```

Manually examine the TACLLOCL file and any TACLCSTM files located.

Manually examine all OBEY files.

Manually examine all ATTACHMENT-SETs

Viewing the TACLCONF Parameters

Use the following TACL commands to display the values of the TACLCONF parameters.

```
Syntax:
#getconfiguration/<parameter>/
```

The parameters are:

```
#getconfiguration/BLINDLOGON/
#getconfiguration/NOCHANGEUSER/
#getconfiguration/AUTOLOGOFFDELAY/
#getconfiguration/LOGOFFSCREENCLEAR/
#getconfiguration/NAMELOGON/
#getconfiguration/CMONTIMEOUT/
#getconfiguration/REMOTECMONTIMEOUT/
#getconfiguration/REMOTESUPERID/
#getconfiguration/CMONREQUIRED/
#getconfiguration/REMOTECMONREQUIRED/
#getconfiguration/STOPONFEMODEMERR /
```

```
Example 1:
#getconfiguration/BLINDLOGON/
```

```
#getconfiguration/BLINDLOGON/ expanded to:
0
```

```
Example 2:
#getconfiguration/NOCHANGEUSER/
```

```
#getconfiguration/NOCHANGEUSER/ expanded to:
0
```

Example 3:
#getconfiguration/AUTOLOGOFFDELAY/

```
#getconfiguration/AUTOLOGOFFDELAY/ expanded to:
-1
```

The value returned from each query is 0 for false, 1 for true or a numeric value for those parameters like CMONTIMEOUT that require a count. A count of −1 for a timeout value means that there is no timeout.

PASSWORD BIND Settings

The BIND program displays values from inside a compiled program. To start BIND:

Syntax:
BIND

The BINDER Command Interpreter prompt will be an "@".

Use the following BIND commands to display the PASSWORD Program parameters.

```
DUMP DATA <PARAMETER-NAME> * FROM $SYSTEM.SYS<NN>.PASSWORD
```

Four parameters control PASSWORD's behavior:

```
PROMPTPASSWORD
BLINDPASSWORD
MINPASSWORDLEN
ENCRYPTPASSWORD
```

Example 1:
BIND

```
BINDER - OBJECT FILE BINDER - T9621D30 - (31MAY02)    SYSTEM \LA
Copyright Compaq Computers Corporation, 1988-2002
```

```
DUMP DATA PROMPTPASSWORD * FROM $SYSTEM.SYS03.PASSWORD
```

```
000000:  000001
```

```
DUMP DATA BLINDPASSWORD * FROM $SYSTEM.SYS03.PASSWORD
```

```
000000:  000001
```

```
DUMP DATA MINPASSWORDLEN * FROM $SYSTEM.SYS03.PASSWORD
```

```
000000:   000006
```

`DUMP DATA ENCRYPTPASSWORD * FROM $SYSTEM.SYS03.PASSWORD`

```
000000:   000001
```

The value returned from each query is either 000000 (false) or 0000001 (true), except for MINPASSWORDLEN, which returns a number between 000000 and 000008, representing the minimum length acceptable.

SCF (Subsystem Control Facility) Commands

Use SCF LISTDEV to display all processes that have a device type and are known to SCF. To start SCF:

SCF Syntax:
`SCF (to enter the SCF command interpreter).`

The SCF command interpreter prompt will be a number, dash, and a greater than sign "n->".

Example 1:
`LISTDEV`

```
LDev   Name      PPID     BPID     Type       RSize Pri Program
   0   $0        0,5      1,5      ( 1,0 )     102 201 \LA.$SYSTEM.SYS01.OSIMAGE
   1   $NCP      0,16     1,13     (62,6 )       1 199 \LA.$SYSTEM.SYS01.NCPOBJ
   3   $YMIOP    0,256    1,256    ( 6,4 )      80 205 \LA.$SYSTEM.SYS01.OSIMAGE
   5   $Z0       0,7      1,7      ( 1,2 )     102 200 \LA.$SYSTEM.SYS01.OSIMAGE
   6   $SYSTEM   0,257    1,257    ( 3,41)    4096 104 \LA.$SYSTEM.SYS01.OSIMAGE
   7   $ZOPR     0,8      1,8      ( 1,0 )     102 201 \LA.$SYSTEM.SYS01.OSIMAGE
  63   $MPATH    0,284    1,284    (63,1 )       0 199 \LA.$SYSTEM.SYS01.LHOBJ
  64   $ZZKRN    0,15     1,23     (66,0 )     132 180 \LA.$SYSTEM.SYS01.OZKRN
  65   $ZZWAN    0,277    1,289    (50,3 )     132 180 \LA.$SYSTEM.SYS01.WANMGR
  66   $ZZW01    1,266    0,0      (50,0 )       0 199 \LA.$SYSTEM.SYS01.CONMGR
 246   $QA0      1,357    0,363    ( 1,0 )    4024 130 \LA.$SYSTEM.SYS01.EMSACOLL…
 247   $DV0      1,358    0,369    ( 1,0 )    4024 130 \LA.$SYSTEM.SYS01.EMSACOLL
 253   $ZPHI     0,375    1,356    ( 1,0 )    4024 130 \LA.$SYSTEM.SYS01.EMSACOLL
 264   $Z03H     0,104    0,0      ( 1,30)     132 150 \LA.$SYSTEM.SYS01.EMSDIST
 270   $NMTRM    1,380    0,0      (46,0 )    6144 150 \LA.$SYSTEM.SYSOPR.ENFORM
 280   $Z6ND     1,390    0,0      (46,0 )    6144 150 \LA.$SYSTEM.SYSOPR.ENFORM
 282   $Z0WY     0,216    0,0      ( 1,30)     132 100 \LA.$SYSTEM.SYS01.EMSDIST
 284   $Z6NJ     1,378    0,0      (46,0 )    6144 150 \LA.$SYSTEM.SYSOPR.ENFORM
 338   $X7MX     1,392    0,0      ( 1,30)     132 130 \LA.$SYSTEM.SYS01.EMSDIST

Total Errors = 0    Total Warnings = 0
```

Use LISTDEV TCPIP to display all TCPIP processes.

Example 2:
`LISTDEV TCPIP`

```
LDev   Name     PPID    BPID   Type     RSize Pri Program
  145  $ZTC0    0,329   1,308  (48,0 )  32000 200 \LA.$SYSTEM.SYS01.TCPIP
  161  $ZTC2    1,54    0,75   (48,0 )  32000 200 \LA.$SYSTEM.SYS01.TCPIP
  164  $ZTC1    1,318   0,334  (48,0 )  32000 200 \LA.$SYSTEM.SYS01.TCPIP
  175  $ZB018   0,345   1,328  (48,0 )  32000 200 \LA.$SYSTEM.SYS01.TCPIP
  176  $ZB01B   0,340   1,322  (48,0 )  32000 200 \LA.$SYSTEM.SYS01.TCPIP
  182  $ZTC3    0,351   1,333  (48,0 )  32000 200 \LA.$SYSTEM.SYS01.TCPIP

Total Errors = 0    Total Warnings = 0
```

Use SCF INFO SUBNET to display TCPIP SUBNET information. This information is particularly useful to determine what TCPIP addresses are configured for access to the system.

Example 3:
`INFO SUBNET $ZTC0.*`

```
TCPIP Info SUBNET \LA.$ZTCP0.*

Name       Devicename      *IPADDRESS      TYPE      *SUBNETMASK  SuName  QIO *R

#LOOP0     \NOSYS.$NOIOP   127.0.0.1       LOOP-BACK %HFF000000          OFF N
#SN1       \LA.LANX        192.168.55.32   ETHERNET  %HFFFFFF00           ON  N
2->
```

Use SCF LISTDEV TELSERV to display all TELSERV processes.

Example 4:
`LISTDEV TELSERV`

```
LDev   Name     PPID    BPID   Type     RSize Pri Program
  147  $ZTN0    0,324   1,293  (46,0 )  6144 170 \LA.$SYSTEM.SYS01.TELSERV
  165  $ZTN1    1,319   0,336  (46,0 )  6144 170 \LA.$SYSTEM.SYS01.TELSERV
  179  $ZN018   0,339   1,330  (46,0 )  6144 150 \LA.$SYSTEM.SYS01.TELSERV
  210  $ZTN2    1,341   0,361  (46,0 )  6144 170 \LA.$SYSTEM.SYS01.TELSERV
  211  $ZTNPX   1,337   0,352  (46,0 )  6144 170 \LA.$SYSTEM.SYS01.TELSERV
```

Use SCF ASSUME and INFO to display a list of services associated with a TELSERV process.

Example 5:
`ASSUME PROCESS $ZTN1`
`INFO SERVICE *`

```
TELSERV Info SERVICE \LA.$ZTN1.*

Name        *Type          *Subtype  *Access *Display *Program
TACL        CONVERSATION   DYNAMIC   ALL     ON       $SYSTEM.SYSTEM.TACL
ZVTL        VTL            STATIC    N/A     OFF      N/A
ZTELNET     CONVERSATION   DYNAMIC   N/A     OFF      N/A
ZBLOCK      BLOCK          STATIC    N/A     OFF      N/A
ZCONV       CONVERSATION   STATIC    N/A     OFF      N/A
ZPRINT      PRINT          STATIC    N/A     OFF      N/A
ZSPI        SPI            STATIC    N/A     OFF      N/A
```

Use SCF INFO SERVICE to display details of a TELSERV service.

Example 6:
`INFO SERVICE TACL,DETAIL`

```
TELSERV Detailed Info SERVICE \LA.$ZTN1.tacl

*Type................. CONVERSATION      *Subtype.............. DYNAMIC
*Display.............. ON                *Autodelete........... OFF
*Owner................ N/A               *Access............... ALL
*CPU.................. N/A               *Pri.................. N/A
*Swap................. N/A
*Program.............. $SYSTEM.SYSTEM.TACL
*Lib.................. N/A
*Resilient............ OFF
*Param................ N/A
*Assigned Window....... OFF
*Default Service....... OFF
```

Use SCF to list all nodes on the network. Compare list to network diagram provided by operations.

Example 7:
`INFO PROCESS $NCP,DETAIL`

```
EXPAND    Detailed Info PROCESS   $NCP        AT \LA (253)

Max System Number..          254  *Aborttimer........        0:02:30.00
Algorithm.........   SPLITHORIZON   AutomaticMaptimer..              ON
*Connecttime........    0:00:00.00   Framesize.........             132
*Maxtimeouts........             3  *Maxconnects........              10
*NetworkDiameter....            15   Type..............          (62,0)
*Message 43.........           OFF   Message 44.........             ON
 Message 45.........            ON  *Message 46.........            OFF
 Message 47.........            ON  *Message 48.........            OFF
*Message 49.........           OFF  *AutoRebal..........            OFF
 Next Rebalance Time   0/00:00:00  *AutoRebalTime......      1/00:00:00
 Trace File Name....   none
```

2. Use SCF maps to list all nodes on the network. Compare this list to a network diagram provided by operations.

Example 8:
`INFO PROCESS $NCP,NETMAP`

```
EXPAND    Info  PROCESS   $NCP, NETMAP

       NETMAP AT \LA (253) #LINESETS=2 TIME:  DEC 13,2002 15:38:01

SYSTEM             TIME       (DISTANCE)  BY   PATH                    INDEX
252 \CHICAGO    190K(01)*  inf(—)                                     [  2]
254 \ABCO        inf(—)    380K(01)*                                  [  2]
-------------------------------------------------------

          LINESETS AT \LA (253) #LINESETS=2

LINESET      NEIGHBOR     LDEV     TF    PID    LINE    LDEV    STATUS  FileErr#
```

```
   1      \CHICAGO      (252)   117  190K ( 0,  330)
                                                       1    117    READY
   2      \ABCO         (254)    63  380K ( 0,  285)
                                                       1    119    READY
                                                       2    118    READY
```

3. Use SCF to check the PASSTHRU setting.

    SCF Syntax:
    INFO PROFILE $ZZWAN.#< profile-name >

    Example 9:
    INFO PROFILE $ZZWAN.#EXPIP

    ```
    WAN MANAGER Info profile \LA.$ZZWAN.#EXPIP

      Devices using this profile

      Device......... 1    : $EXPIP

    DEVICE SPECIFIC MODIFIERS:

    NEXTSYS  253
    L4CONGCTRL_ON
    L4RETRIES  3
    L4TIMEOUT  2000
    COMPRESS_ON
    PASSTHRU_ON                         ←
    L4EXTPACKETS_ON
    SUPERPATH_OFF
    L4SENDWINDOW  254
    PATHBLOCKBYTES  0
    PATHPACKETBYTES  1024
    RXWINDOW  7
    TXWINDOW  7
    ALGORITHM  1
    AUTOMATICMAPTIMER  1
    CONNECTTIME  0
    FRAMESIZE  132
    MAXTIMEOUTS  3
    MAXCONNECTS  5
    NETWORKDIAMETER  15
    ABORTTIMER  15000
    ```

NonStop TMF Software

The TMFCOM program is used to monitor and control NonStop TMF software.
Use the STATUS command to determine current active conditions.

> **TMF Syntax:**
> **TMFCOM**

The NonStop TMF command interpreter prompt will be TMF, a number, and a
right caret "TMF n>".

Example 1:
TMFCOM

```
TMFCOM - T8652G07 - (29NOV2002 - TMF)
COPYRIGHT COMPAQ COMPUTER CORPORATION 2002
TMF 1>
```

Example 2:
STATUS AUDITTRAIL

```
AuditTrail Status:
  Master
    Active audit trail capacity used: 24%
    First pinned file: $AUDIT.ZTMFAT.AA002978
    Reason: Current File
    Current file: $AUDIT.ZTMFAT.AA002978
```

Example 3:
STATUS DATAVOLS

```
Audit  Recovery
```

```
Volume    Trail    Mode     State
-----------------------------------
$DATAA    Mat     Online    Started
$DATAB    Mat     Online    Started
$DATAC    Mat     Online    Started
$DATAD    Mat     Online    Started
$DATAE    Mat     Online    Started
$DSMSCM   Mat     Online    Started
$SYSTEM   Mat     Online    Started
```

Example 4:
STATUS AUDITDUMP

```
AuditDump Status:
Master: State: enabled, Status: inactive
```

Example 4:
STATUS CATALOG

```
Catalog Status:
    Status: active
```

Example 5:
STATUS SERVER

```
TMF Server Status:
    System:      \LA (253)
    Date-Time:   17-Jun-2003 23:55:03
    Process:     $Y5WB  (0,269)
    Creator ID:  (222,230)
    Process ID:  (222,230)
```

```
      Priority:      130
      Object Name:   \LA.$SYSTEM.SYS01.TMFSERVE
      HomeTerm:      \LA.$ZTNP2
      Swap Volume:   $AUDIT
      Version:       TMFSERVE - T8694G07 - (29NOV2002 - TMF)
```

Example 6:
STATUS TMF

```
TMF Status:
System: \LA, Time: 17-Jun-2003 16:53:57
State: started
Transaction Rate: 0.88 TPS
  AuditTrail Status:
Master
    Active audit trail capacity used: 5%
    First pinned file: $AUDIT.ZTMFAT.AA003070
      Reason: Current File
    Current file: $AUDIT.ZTMFAT.AA003070
AuditDump Status:
  Master: State: enabled, Status: inactive
BeginTrans Status: ENABLED
Catalog Status:
      Status: active
```

Example 7:
STATUS TRANSACTIONS

```
   Transaction Identifier       Process      State     Parent  Children
   ------------------------------------------------------------------------
\LA.1.22978248                 $Z5WF (1,454)   Active
\LA.1.22978154                 $Z5WA (1,415)   Active
\CHICAGO.1.3813572             $Y9X6 (1,294)   Active     \CHICAGO
```

Use the INFO command to determine configuration settings.

Example 8:
INFO AUDITTRAIL

```
AuditTrail Configuration:
 Master
   ActiveVols: $AUDIT
   Subvolume ZTMFAT, Prefix AA, filesize 180, filespervolume 4,
   auditdump On, overflowthreshold 80%, begintransdisable 90%
   OverflowVols: $AUDIT
   RestoreVols: $SYSTEM
```

Example 9:
INFO CATALOG

```
Catalog Configuration:
 retaindepth 3, released Off
```

Example 10:
INFO TMF

```
Configuration Volume:
  $SYSTEM
AuditTrail Configuration:
 Master
   ActiveVols: $AUDIT
   Subvolume ZTMFAT, Prefix AA, filesize 180, filespervolume 4,
   auditdump On, overflowthreshold 80%, begintransdisable 90%
   OverflowVols: $AUDIT
   RestoreVols: $SYSTEM
Auditdump Configuration:
 Master:  enabled, medium tape, Copies 1, verifytape Off , blocksize 28,
 system \LA
```

```
Catalog Configuration:
 retaindepth 3, released Off
BeginTrans Configuration:
 TransCountThresh (1500,1600)
 TmfLibMemThresh (85,90)
 TmpMemThresh (90,95)
 TransPerCpu (1024,1024)
 AutoAbort 7200 Seconds
 RecRMCount 256
 RMOpenPerCpu 128
 BranchesPerRM 128
After the next START TMF, the BeginTrans Configuration will be:
 TransPerCpu (1024,1024)
 RecRMCount 256
 RMOpenPerCpu 128
 BranchesPerRM 128
```

NonStop TMF software regularly copies its audit dumps to tape. To display information about the auditdump:

Example 11:
INFO AUDITDUMP

```
Auditdump Configuration:
Master:  enabled, medium tape, Copies 1, verifytape Off ,
blocksize 28,system \LA
```

Example 12:
INFO DUMPS

```
Dump                    Dump   Media
   FileName    Serial   Date-Time      Type   Type    Media Name
-------------------------------------------------------------------
$ZTMFAT.ZTMFAT
  AA003067           66 17-Jun-2003 15:06  audit   tape   TMF001
  AA003068           67 17-Jun-2003 15:49  audit   tape   TMF002
  AA003069           68 17-Jun-2003 16:20  audit   tape   TMF003
```

Example 13:
INFO TAPEMEDIA

```
Media Name   Media Type   Media Status
----------------------------------------
TEST             tape         released
TMF001           tape         assigned
TMF002           tape         assigned
TMF003           tape         assigned
TMF004           tape         assigned
```

NonStop TMF software can also create audit dumps by copying the information to disk:

Example 14:
INFO AUDITDUMP

```
Auditdump Configuration:
 Master:  enabled, medium disk
    DiskMedia \LA.$DATAD.ZT
```

USERS Program

The USERS program lists all or some of the users on the system. Enter an exact user name or user number or replace either the group name or member name with an asterisk (*).

Syntax:
USERS { [groupname. | group#, | *.] [membername. | member#, | *] }

Example:
USERS 222,*

```
GROUP   .USER        I.D. #     SECURITY   DEFAULT VOLUMEID
ABCO    .NOREMOTE    222,001    NNNN       $DATAA.P15QATST
ABCO    .BANKING     222,005    OOOO       $SYSTEM.NOSUBVOL
ABCO    .JULIE       222,007    OOOO       $USERS.JULIEC
ABCO    .STEVE       222,008    CCCC       $DATAA.STEVE
```

The display includes the following information:

User Name and User Number, the user's default security vector and default volume.

SPOOLCOM

The SPOOLCOM program allows management and display of information in a data output spooler. To start SPOOLCOM:

Syntax:
SPOOLCOM

The SPOOLER command interpreter will be a right parenthesis ")"

<u>Example 1:</u>
SPOOLCOM

```
SPOOLCOM - T9101D48 - (25JUL2002)    SYSTEM  \LA
Copyright Tandem Computers Incorporated 1978, 1982, 1983, 1984, 1985, 1986,
1987, 1988, 1989, 1990, 1991
)
```

Use the COLLECT command to display the status of spooler collector configurations.

<u>Example 2:</u>
COLLECT

```
COLLECT   STATE      FLAGS  CPU   PRI  UNIT  DATA FILE                  %FULL
$S        ACTIVE            0 , 1 170  8     $SYSTEM.SYSPRSPL.SPLDATA    56
$TLH      ACTIVE            1 , 0 145  4     $DATAA.P09QATH.SPLDATA      0
```

Use the JOB command to display a list of jobs in the spooler subsystem.

<u>Example 2:</u>
JOB

```
JOB  BATCH STA FLAGS OWNER    TIME  COPY PAGE  REPORT           LOCATION
12   1310  RDY 3     222,210 06/08 1    5     QED ARCH222 210  #REPORT.TARCH
13   1310  RDY 3     222,210 06/08 1    1     ABCO    LEE      #REPORT.TARCH
14   1310  RDY 3     222,210 06/08 1    1     ABCO    LEE      #REPORT.TARCH
15   1310  RDY 3     222,210 06/08 1    1     ABCO    LEE      #REPORT.TARCH
16   1310  RDY 3     222,210 06/08 1    1     ABCO    LEE      #REPORT.TARCH
17   1311  RDY 3     222,210 06/08 1    8     QED ARCH222 210  #REPORT.TADEL
18   1311  RDY 3     222,210 06/08 1    2     ABCO    LEE      #REPORT.TADEL
19   1311  RDY 3     222,210 06/08 1    1     ABCO    LEE      #REPORT.TADEL
20   1311  RDY 3     222,210 06/08 1    1     ABCO    LEE      #REPORT.TADEL
21   1311  RDY 3     222,210 06/08 1    1     ABCO    LEE      #REPORT.TADEL
22   1311  RDY 3     222,210 06/08 1    1     ABCO    LEE      #REPORT.TADEL
23   1311  RDY 3     222,210 06/08 1    1     ABCO    LEE      #REPORT.TADEL
39   1317  RDY 3     222,11  06/09 1    5     BFMA ADD222 11   #BFMA.ADDARC
40   1317  RDY 3     222,11  06/09 1    1     ABCO    MARK     #BFMA.ADDARC
41   1317  RDY 3     222,11  06/09 1    1     ABCO    MARK     #BFMA.ADDARC
```

PERUSE

The PERUSE program is used to display the contents of an output job in the spooler.

<u>Syntax:</u>
PERUSE

The PERUSE command interpreter will be an underscore "_".

<u>Example 1:</u>
PERUSE

```
PERUSE - T9101D48 - (25JUL2002)    SYSTEM  \LA
Copyright Tandem Computers Incorporated 1978, 1982, 1983, 1984, 1985, 1986,
1987, 1988, 1989, 1990, 1991
_
```

Use the JOB command to display a list of spooled jobs.

Example 2:
JOB

```
JOB   BATCH STATE PAGES COPIES PRI HOLD LOCATION          REPORT
39    1317  READY 5     1      3        #BFMA   ADDARC   BFMA ADD222 11
40    1317  READY 1     1      3        #BFMA   ADDARC   ABCO   MARK
41    1317  READY 1     1      3        #BFMA   ADDARC   ABCO   MARK
42    1317  READY 1     1      3        #BFMA   ADDARC   ABCO   MARK
43    1317  READY 1     1      3        #BFMA   ADDARC   ABCO   MARK
46    1319  READY 6     1      3        #BFMA   DELARC   BFMA DEL222 11
47    1319  READY 1     1      3        #BFMA   DELARC   ABCO   MARK
48    1319  READY 1     1      3        #BFMA   DELARC   ABCO   MARK
49    1319  READY 1     1      3        #BFMA   DELARC   ABCO   MARK
50    1319  READY 1     1      3        #BFMA   DELARC   ABCO   MARK
51    1319  READY 1     1      3        #BFMA   DELARC   ABCO   MARK
222   1328  READY 5     1      3        #BFMA   ADDARC   BFMA ADD222 11
```

Use the JOB n command to set the current job.

Example 3:
JOB 7676

Use the LIST n command to display pages from the current job to the screen.

Example 4:
LIST 1

```
                        ABCompany AUDITLOG Report
Date Produced: 05-Jun-2003 at 06:38 AM
Criteria:2003-06-04 00:00 to 2003-06-05 23:59 Subvol:$DATAD.BFMADAT Oper:LOGON,
-------------------------------------------------------------------------------

F 2003-06-04 08:12:31  Subsystem: \LA.SAFEGUARD    Alerted: N
  Subject User: 222,210 ABCO.LEE
  Term: \LA.$VHS             Process: \LA.$X5PX
  Op: AUTHENTICATE    Object: USER        ABCO.LEE
  Result: WRONG-PASSWORD  Wrong-password Authenticate to User ABCO.LEE
```

BATCHCOM

The BATCHCOM program is used to manage the NetBatch subsystem. To start the
BATCHCOM program:

Syntax:
BATCHCOM

The NetBatch command interpreter will be a number and close bracket "n}".

Example 1:
BATCHCOM

Use the STATUS JOB command to display a list of jobs.

Example 2:
STATUS JOB *

```
JOB STATUS

JOB  JOBNAME                       USERID   LOG  STATE      CLASSNAME
-----------------------------------------------------------------------
   1 AUTOBACKUP                    255,255 2264 04JUL03    DEFAULT
   5 INCREMENTAL-BACKUP            255,255 2232 18:00:00   DEFAULT
  29 SETTIME                       255,255 2518 01JUL03    DEFAULT
  45 NIGHTLY-MAINTENANCE           222,250 2504 01JUL03    DEFAULT
2746 QED-ARCH-TST                  222,210 2486 20:00:00   DEFAULT
2747 QED-ARCH-TDEL                 222,210 2491 23:00:00   DEFAULT
2894 QED-ARCH-STEVE                222,9   2481 19:00:00   DEFAULT
2895 QED-ARCHDEL-STEVE             222,9   2498 23:30:00   DEFAULT
3183 BFMA-ADD-ARC                  222,11  2513 01JUL03    DEFAULT
3184 BFMA-DEL-ARC                  222,11  2520 01JUL03    DEFAULT
3246 SW20030610092752-COLLECT      222,233 2459 09:30:00   DEFAULT
3301 TESTJOB                       222,8   1879 06JUL03    DEFAULT
```

Use the INFO JOB command to details about a job.

Example 3:
INFO JOB 1

```
JOB ATTRIBUTES for AUTOBACKUP
                jobnumber: 1
                   volume: \LA.$SYSTEM.OPER, "NUNU"
                       in: \LA.$SYSTEM.OPERBACK.LABACK
                      out: \LA.$S.#BACKUP.RUNLOG
        executor-program: \LA.$SYSTEM.SYSTEM.TACL
                      pfs: 0
                      pri: 10
                   selpri: 3
            maxprintlines: None
            maxprintpages: None
                    class: DEFAULT
                     hold: Off
                  restart: On
                    stall: Off
           stop-on-abend: Off
                 calendar: \LA.$SYSTEM.SYSBATCH.LAFBACKC
                  highpin: Off
                   submit: 23JUN99 08:46:04
                    alter: 03FEB03 10:46:41
                     user: 255,255
             next-runtime: 04JUL03 18:00:00
```

B

HP NonStop File Codes

When viewing files in the FILEINFO utility or FUP utility, each file has a File Code of up to five digits displayed. HP has certain designated file codes that it uses for identification purposes of subsystem files.

File Code	Definition or Subsystem
0-99	Reserved for users
OSS	OSS File
100	TNS executable file
101	EDIT text format
110-111	Edit recovery and VS dump files
115	TEDIT profile files
120-128	Spooler control files
129	Spooler job file
130	Inspect save files
134	NonStop TMF audit trail files
144	CPU dump files
175	Measure data files
176	NonStop SQL/MP surveyor files
180	C data files
210	Pathmaker Installs file
223	Enable log file
230-232	ADA data files
250-299	Transfer subsystem files
300-399	TPS (Pathway) subsystem files

File Code	Definition or Subsystem
400-401	Tape simulator files
405	KMSF subsystem file
410-430	Exercise subsystem
440	TACL saved variable segment file
450	ViewPoint configuration file
451	Event configuration file
500-525	Microcode files
540-549	Safeguard subsystem files
550-599	NonStop SQL/MP subsystem files
600-620	Mumps subsystem files
660-669	Encore subsystem files
700	Native code executable object files
830-835	Data Communications files
832	Expand Profile template files
839	EMS template
840	Snax utility output file
841-842	Coup files
843-845	EMS subsystem files
846	Cover file
847-848	NetBatch file
849-850	DNS subsystem files
851	Snax5 configuration files
852	NonStop CLX shutdown file
853-854	Optical disk file
855	FUP restart file
858	ORSERV status file
863	SysHealth event key file
888	Enform compiled query
904	Exchange trace files
1000-65535	Reserved for users

Third Party HP NonStop Server Security Vendors

XYPRO Technology Corporation
http://www.xypro.com

Insession Technologies
http://www.insession.com

Hewlett-Packard
http://www.hp.com

Gresham Software Labs
http://www.greshamsoftwarelabs.com.au

Greenhouse Software and Consulting
http://www.greenhouse.de

Computer Security Products, Inc.
http://www.compsec.com

Cross-El Software Solutions
http://www.crossel.com

ComForte GmbH
http://www.comforte.com/

Cail Connectivity Solutions

http://www.cail.com

Baker Street Software

http://www.bakerstreetsoftware.com

Unlimited Software Associates, Inc.

http://www.usahero.com

About the Authors

Terri Hill has over 17 years of computer systems experience with expertise in systems security, quality assurance, user documentation and education. As a Security Analyst, she provides Security Review and implementation Services to HP NonStop Server customers. Terri is also a valuable link between customer's business requirements and XYPRO's software development.

Ellen Alvarado has worked in the NonStop industry since 1980. She has been a customer, an analyst, a 3rd party vendor and a consultant. Ellen brings her practical experience and depth of knowledge about exercising the advantages of NonStop server technology to XYPRO as a designer and a developer of security and compliance software solutions.

Index

A

Accelerator (AXCEL) program, 201–2
    defined, 201
    securing, 201–2
Access Control Lists (ACLs), 45–47
    defined, 45
    DEVICE/SUBDEVICE Protection Record,
        167
    DISKFILE Protection Record, 186
    OBJECTTYPE, 51
    SUBVOLUME Protection Record, 184
    user definition in, 46–47
    VOLUME Protection Record, 183
Access controls, 7–10
    accountability, 9
    auditability, 10
    authentication, 9–10
    authorization, 10
    components, 9
    logical, 8–10
    physical, 8
Accountability, 9
ACL-REQUIRED-DEVICE Global parameter,
    165
ACL-REQUIRED-DISKFILE Global parameter,
    178

ACL-REQUIRED-PROCESS Global parameter,
    157
ADDUSER program, 97, 197–99
    defined, 197
    with Safeguard, 199
    without Safeguard, 198–99
    securing, 197
Administrative Groups, 10, 82
Aliases, 83
    case sensitivity, 83
    defined, 83
    userid, 84
Anonymous FTP, 301–3
Application development, 521–26
    configuration source files, 523
    in-house, 521–24
    object release control, 523–24
    security considerations, 524
    source control, 522–23
    third-party vendor, 524
    understanding, 521–26
Application management, 548–51
    communications, 549
    database, 549
    protection and recovery, 549–51
    system, 548–49
Application-owner IDs, 90–91

Applications
in-house, 521–24
legacy, 524–25
non-Pathway, 534–35
Pathway, 532–34, 550
platform, 527–36
production, 526–44
securing, 521–51
third-party vendor, 524
ASSIGNs, 547–48, 570
adding, 548
defined, 547
in NETBATCH, 570–71
risks, 548
ATTACHMENT-SETs, 351–52
Auditability, 10
AUDIT-AUTHENTICATE Global parameter,
108–9
AUDIT-CLIENT-SERVICE Global parameter,
74–75
AUDIT-DEVICE-ACCESS Global parameter,
169
AUDIT-DEVICE-MANAGE Global parameter,
169–70
AUDIT-DISKFILE-ACCESS Global parameter,
191–92
AUDIT-DISKFILE-MANAGE Global parameter,
192
Auditing, 11
configuring for, 73–76
dial access, 25
disk file access/management attempts, 191
events configured for, 73
global, configuring, 73–76
Guardian, 32
NonStop TMF, 501–2
Safeguard, 25, 72–77
Safeguard controls, 40–42
system-wide, configuring, 73–76
third-party key-stroke level, 25
users, 106–10

AUDIT-MANAGE Global parameter, 109
AUDIT-OBJECT-ACCESS Global parameter, 75
AUDIT-OBJECT-MANAGE Global parameter,
75–76
Audit Pools, 54–59
audit file sizing, 55–56
defined, 54
managing, 59
size determination, 54–56
See also Safeguard
AUDIT-PROCESS-ACCESS Global parameter,
161
AUDIT-PROCESS-MANAGE Global parameter,
161–62
Audit(s)
configuring, 73–76
content, 106–7
content determination, 76–77
files, Safeguard, 410
information, gathering, 553–85
OBJECTTYPE attributes, 52–53
reports, generating, 55
write configuration, 56
AUDIT-SUBJECT-MANAGE Global parameter,
108
Audit Trails, 54
Safeguard, information gathering, 565–66
save length, 56
TMF software, 504
VHS, 517
AUDIT-USER-ACTION Global parameter,
109–10
AUDSERV program, 200–201, 456
defined, 200
invocation, 200
securing, 200–201
AUTHENTICATE-FAIL Global parameter, 131
AUTHENTICATE-MAXIMUM-ATTEMPTS
Global parameter, 131
Authentication, 9–10
access to HP NonStop server, 125–42

defined, 9
dial access, 23
Guardian, 31, 127–31
OSS, 132
Safeguard controls, 37
user administration, 81–124
Authorization, 143–96
defined, 10
Guardian, 31–32
licensed programs, 329
PROGID's files, 384–85
Availability, 4
defined, 4
scalability and, 13

B

BACKCOPY utility, 202–3
defined, 202
securing, 202–3
BACKUP program, 203–5, 550
defined, 203
running, 204
securing, 204–5
BATCHCAL, 351
BATCHCOM, 351
defined, 584
INFO JOB command, 585
starting, 584
STATUS JOB command, 585
BATCHCTL, 351
Batch facility, 535
Best Practices
adapting, 3
defined, 2
dial access, 25
/bin/sh, 126
BIND, 206–8
commands with security implications, 209
defined, 206
illustrated, 208

settings, 574–75
uses, 207–8
BINDER, 205–10, 534
BIND, 206–8
BINSERV, 206, 207
components, 206
components, securing, 208–10
file security respect, 210
VPROC, 208
Binding, 205
BINSERV, 206
defined, 206
illustrated, 207
resolving system libraries with, 323
BLINDLOGON Global parameter, 113
BUSCMD utility, 211

C

Catalogs, 537–38
defined, 537
information research, 567
securing, 539
System, securing, 539–40
See also NonStop SQL databases
C/C++ compiler, 216–18
CHECK-DEVICE Global parameter, 166
CHECK-FILENAME Global parameter, 180
CHECK-PROCESS Global parameter, 157
CHECK-SUBPROCESS Global parameter, 158
CHECK-SUBVOLUME Global parameter,
179–80
CHECK-VOLUME Global parameter, 178–79
CLEARONPURGE-DISKFILE Global
parameter, 180
CMON, 137–42, 212–15
can control access to privileged IDs, 138
can control access to utilities, 138
can control remote access, 138
can perform load balancing, 138
defined, 212

CMON (continued)
  FTP with, 303
  load-balancing tasks, 152
  logon-related configuration, 130
  in non-Safeguard environment, 138–41
  processes, 127
  Safeguard controls, 39–40
  in Safeguard environment, 141–42, 214
  securing, 214–15
  specification, 137
  TACL and, 213–14
  TACL communication, 138–39
  third-party product, 213
  user auditing with, 107
CMONERROR Global parameter, 141
CMON Global parameter, 141
CMONREQUIRED Global parameter, 139
CMONTIMEOUT Global parameter, 139–40,
     142
COBOL85 language, 218–19
COMBINATION-DEVICE Global parameter,
     166–67
COMBINATION-DISKFILE Global parameter,
     181–82
COMBINATION-PROCESS Global parameter,
     154–55, 158
Command Interpreter (CI)
  attributes, 100–101
  CI-CPU parameter, 101
  CI-LIB parameter, 100
  CI-NAME parameter, 101
  CI-PARAM-TEXT parameter, 101
  CI-PRI parameter, 101
  CI-PROG parameter, 100
  CI-SWAP parameter, 101
  configuration locations, 100
  controls, 40
  Input (CIIN) file, 466–67
Communications, 549
  control, 24
  operating system, 360

Compilers, 215–25
  C/C++, 216–18
  COBOL85, 218–19
  components, securing, 216–25
  FORTRAN, 219
  languages, 215
  NMCINMCPLUS, 220–21
  NMCOBOL, 221
  objects, 215–16
  Pascal, 222
  PTAL, 222–23
  SCOBOL, 223–24
  SQL, 224
  TAL, 224–25
  utilities, 215
Compliance monitoring, 10–11
  activities, 10
  self, 11
Compliance review frequency, 11
CONFALT file, 463
CONFAUX file, 463–64
CONFBASE file, 464
Confidentiality, 4–5
  defined, 4–5
  information, 5
  risks, 5
  security policy addressing, 5
Configuration Utility Program. See COUP system
     utility
CONFLIST file, 464
CONFTEXT file, 464–66
  categories, 465
  defined, 464
COPYDUMP utility, 481
Corporate Security Policy and Standards
  access matrix, 144
  adapting Best Practice to, 3
  defined, 2
  passwords and, 117
  physical security and, 16
  software security, 33

COUP system utility, 225–27
  command execution, 226
  commands with security implications, 227
  defined, 225
  securing, 226–27
  uses, 225
CPU parameter, 134
Creator access ID (CAID), 151, 382
CROSSREF program, 227–29
  components, 228
  CROSSREF, 228
  cross-reference listing, 228
  defined, 227
  securing, 228–29
  SYMSERV, 228
CRUNCH utility, 481
Cryptographic tokens, 23
*CSTM files, 229–41
  defined, 229
  DSAPCSTM, 230–31
  EMSACSTM, 231–32
  FTPCSTM, 232–33
  FUPCSTM, 233–35
  INSPCSTM, 235–36
  SCFCSTM, 236–37
  SEECSTM, 237–38
  TACLCSTM, 238–40
  VHSCSTM, 240–41
Current operating system, 358–59
CUSTFILE file, 467–68, 554–56

D

Database management, 549
Database Management Systems (DBMS), 536–44
  Enscribe, 536–37
  NonStop SQL, 537–40
Data Build program, 241–43
  components, securing, 242–43
  defined, 241
  fileset, 241

  as Pathway application, 242
Data Definition Language (DDL), 536
  components, securing, 247–48
  definitions, using, 245–46
  functions, 245
  subsystem, 245–48
DataLoader/MP, 243–44
  defined, 243
  securing, 243–44
  uses, 243
DBDDLS, 257
DCOM system utility, 244–45
  defined, 244
  securing, 245
  use of, 244
DEFAULT program, 97–98, 175, 248–50
  DEFAULT SECURITY, 249
  DEFAULT VOLUME, 249
  defined, 248
  parameters, 248
  securing, 249–50
DEFINEs, 545–47, 572
  adding, deleting, altering, 545–46
  _DEFAULTS DEFINE, 547
  defined, 545
  format, 546–47
  in NETBATCH, 570–71
  risks, 547
DELUSER program, 97, 250–52
  defined, 250
  with Safeguard subsystem, 252
  without Safeguard subsystem, 251–52
  securing, 250
DENY GRANTS mode, 58–59
Devices, 30–31
  in Guardian environment, 163
  identifying, 163
  Logical Device Numbers, 163
  names, 163
  Protection Records, 167–68
  with Safeguard, 163–68

Devices (continued)
    Safeguard controls, 38
    security, 163–70
Dial access, 22–25
    auditing, 25
    authentication, 23
    Best Practice recommendations, 25
    communications control, 24
    defined, 22
    dial back modem, 23
    dial port enabling, 23
    encryption, 24
    hardware/software, 22
    interactive, to operating system, 22
    logical port/user restriction, 24
    physical control, 22–23
    See also Networking
DIRECTION-DISKFILE Global parameter, 182
DIRECTION-PROCESS Global parameter, 159
Disk Compression. See DCOM system utility
DISKFILE Protection Records, 185–87
    ACL, 186
    ownership, 186–87
    parameters, 185
Disk files, 27–29
    auditing, access/management attempts, 191
    CREATE attempt evaluation, 187
    Global audit parameters, 191–92
    Global settings, 177–78
    names, 27–28
    OBJECTTYPEs, 176–77
    parameters, 157
    Protection Records, 44, 182–87
    Protection Records with audit parameters,
        193–96
    Safeguard controls, 39
    securing, in Guardian environment, 173–75
    securing, with Safeguard, 175–96
    security string, 28–91
    User Record settings, 176
DISKGEN utility, 254–55

    defined, 254
    securing, 254–55
    using, 254
Disk processes, 253
Disk Space Analysis Program. See DSAP program
Distributed Name Service (DNS) subsystem,
        255–59
    components, 255–57
    components, securing, 258–59
    components illustration, 256
    database configuration, 257
    DBDDLS, 257
    defined, 255
    DNSCOM, 256–57
    DNSCONF, 257
    DNSEXP, 257
    DNSHELP, 257
    DNSMGR, 257
    facilities, 255
    LOAD, 257
Distributed Systems Management/Software
        Configuration Manager. See DSM/SCM
Distributed Systems Management Tape Catalog.
        See DSM/TC
DIVER utility, 259–60
    defined, 259
    securing, 260
DMON program, 319
DNSCOM, 256–57
DNSCONF, 257
DNSEXP, 257
DNSHELP, 257
DNSMGR, 257
DSAPCSTM configuration file, 230–31
    defined, 230
    management controls, 231
DSAP program, 260–62
    commands, 556–57
    components, 261
    defined, 260
    DSAP, 261

DSAPADDL, 261
DSAPCSTM, 261
  securing, 261–62
DSM/SCM subsystem, 262–67
  archive, 263
  components, 265–67
  configuration revision, 263–64
  defined, 262
  methodology, 262–65
  parts, 262–63
  revision on target system, 264–65
DSM/TC subsystem, 267–73
  components, 267–68
  components, securing, 269–73
  defined, 267
  function support, 267
  MEDDEM, 269
  MEDIACOM, 268, 271–73
  MEDIADBM, 268
  MEDIAMSG, 268
  MEDIASRV, 268–69
  tape catalog and database, 269
  ZSERVER, 269
DUMPUTIL utility, 478

E

ECHO program, 273–74
  components, 273
  defined, 273
  ECHO, 273
  ECHOSERV, 273
  securing, 273–74
EDIT, 275
Editors, 274–76
  EDIT, 275
  risks, 274
  securing, 275–76
  TEDIT, 275
  types of, 274
  VS, 275

Emergencies, resolving, 89
EMSACSTM configuration file, 231–32
  defined, 231
  management controls, 232
  options, 231
EMS Analyzer (EMSA) subsystem, 282–84
  components, 282–83
  components, securing, 283–84
  defined, 282
  environment, customizing, 283
  tokenized filters, 282
EMS subsystem, 276–82
  components, 277–81
  components, illustrated, 278
  components, securing, 281–82
  defined, 276
  event categories, 276–77
  Event Message Collectors, 277–79
  Event Message Distributors, 279–80
  filters, 280
  object programs, 280
  utilities, 281
ENABLE program, 285–87
  components, 285
  components, securing, 286–87
  defined, 285
  risks, 285–86
  uses, 285
Encrypting modems, 24
Encryption
  dial access, 24
  session, 24
ENFORM subsystem, 287–94
  components, 288–91
  components, securing, 291–94
  component sets, 287–88
  components illustration, 289
  defined, 287
  files used by, 291–92
  Plus components, 290–91
  query processor (QP), 290

ENFORM subsystem (continued)
   query specification with, 288–90
   user-provided components, 290
   uses, 287
Enscribe databases, 172–73, 536–37
   application dictionaries, 247
   defining, 536
   entry-sequence, 246
   key-sequence, 246
   queue, 246
   relative, 246
   securing, with Guardian, 536–37
   securing, with Safeguard, 537
   unstructured, 247
ERROR program, 294–95
   defined, 294
   security, 295
Event Management System. *See* EMS subsystem
Event Message Collectors, 277–79
Event Message Distributors, 279–80
Expand network, 15–19
   access control with, 17–19
   defined, 15
   illustrated, 296
   max system number, 17
   nodes, 15–16
   PASSTHRU, 19
   security, 18
   unattended sites, 16–17
   understanding, 15–17
   up-to-date diagram, 17
   See also Networking
Expand subsystem, 295–98
   components, 295
   components, securing, 297–98
   defined, 295
   NCPOBJ, 295–96
   OZEXP, 296–97
   profile templates, 297
   $ZNUP, 297

F

FactSort
   components, 426–27
   defined, 426
Failure utilities, 481–82
   COPYDUMP, 481
   CRUNCH, 481
   defined, 481
   GARTH, 481
   RECEIVEDUMP/RCVDUMP, 481
   securing, 481–82
   See also System utilities
FASTP, 436
FCHECK utility, 483
FILCHECK utility, 483
FILEINFO commands, 557–58
Files
   Enscribe, 172–73
   names, 171
   structured, 172–73
   subsystem, 170–73
   types of, 171–73
   unstructured, 172
File-Sharing Groups, 10, 82
File transfer protocols, 300–309
   anonymous, 301–3
   with CMON, 303
   components, securing, 305–6
   custom files, 301
   defined, 300
   file support, 300
   FTP, 301
   FTPSERV, 301
   IXF, 309
   with Safeguard system, 304
   without Safeguard system, 303–4
   systems, 301
   TFTP, 306–9
   with third-party products, 304–5
   userids, 301

FINGER utility, 298–300
   components, 299
   defined, 298
   FINGER, 299
   FINGERSERV, 299
   risks, 298–99
   securing, 299–300
   uses, 298
Firewalls, 24
FONT utility, 434
FORTRAN, 219
FTPCSTM configuration file, 232–33
   defined, 232
   management controls, 233
   option specification, 232
FUPCSTM configuration file, 233–35
   defined, 233–34
   location, 234
   management controls, 234
FUPLOCL files, 311–12
FUP utility, 310–16
   commands, 558–59
   commands with security implications, 313–16
   components, 310
   components, securing, 312–16
   customization files, 311
   defined, 310
   DETAIL command, 558
   FUP, 311
   FUPLOCL files, 311–12
   INFO command, 558
   ORSERV, 311
   RENAME operation, 314–16
   sensitive data protection, 313–14
   SMF support, 310
   uses, 312–13

G

GARTH utility, 481
Global parameters

ACL-REQUIRED-DEVICE, 165
ACL-REQUIRED-DISKFILE, 178
ACL-REQUIRED-PROCESS, 157
AUDIT-DEVICE-ACCESS, 169
AUDIT-DEVICE-MANAGE, 169–70
AUDIT-DISKFILE-ACCESS, 191–92
AUDIT-DISKFILE-MANAGE, 192
AUDIT-PROCESS-ACCESS, 161
AUDIT-PROCESS-MANAGE, 161–62
audit-related, 107–8
AUTHENTICATE-FAIL, 131
AUTHENTICATE-MAXIMUM-
   ATTEMPTS, 131
BLINDLOGON, 113
CHECK-DEVICE, 166
CHECK-FILENAME, 180
CHECK-PROCESS, 157
CHECK-SUBPROCESS, 158
CHECK-SUBVOLUME, 179–80
CHECK-VOLUME, 178–79
CLEARONPURGE-DISKFILE, 180
CMON, 141
CMONERROR, 141
CMONTIMEOUT, 142
COMBINATION-DEVICE, 166–67
COMBINATION-DISKFILE, 181–82
COMBINATION-PROCESS, 154–55, 158
DEVICE-related, 165–67
DIRECTION-DISKFILE, 182
DIRECTION-PROCESS, 159
disk-related, 177–78
logon-related, 130–31
NAMELOGON, 113
PASSWORD-EXPIRY-GRACE, 118
PASSWORD-MAY-CHANGE, 118
PASSWORD-REQUIRED, 114
process-related, 156–59
See also Safeguard
GOAWAY utility, 316–17
   defined, 316
   as 'last resort' tool, 316

GOAWAY utility (continued)
    securing, 316–17
Group Manager IDs, 85
Groups, 81–82
    Administrative, 82
    file-sharing, 82
Guardian, 26–34
    auditing and controls, 32
    authentication, 31, 127–31
    authorization, 31–32
    default security, 176
    default volume, 176
    devices, 30–31, 163
    DISKFILES, 27–28
    DISKFILES security string, 28–29
    in Enscribe database security, 536–37
    objects, 27–31
    Password parameters, 114
    privileged operations, 327
    process access evaluation, 152–53
    processes, 29–30
    process security, 30, 144–53
    Safeguard comparison, 34–35
    securing disk files in, 173–75
    security, 26
    subject default-protection, 176
    userid management in, 97–98
    users, 26–27
    wildcarding, 553–54
    See also Safeguard

H

"Hardened" passwords, 111–12
HP NonStop file codes, 587–88
HP NonStop server
    access control implementation, 2
    application environment, 14
    architecture, 13–15
    authentication, 125–42
    networking, 14, 15–25

operating system (OS), 356–64
personalities, 15
policy, 2
reliability, 16
sorting function, 426
SpoolerPlus subsystem, 432
TCP/IP subsystem, 19–20
Telnet application, 21
third-party security vendors, 589–90
user groups, 10

I

IMON system program, 318
Indexes, 541
Information
    categories, 5–6
    confidential, 5
    internal-use, 6
    non-restricted, 6
    restricted, 6
    securing, 6–7
Information Exchange Facility (IXF) program,
        309
Information security, 3–7
    availability, 4
    confidentiality, 4–5
    integrity, 3–4
    requirements, 3–5
    See also Security
In-house application development, 521–24
In-house system tools, 525
INSPCSTM configuration file, 235–36
    defined, 235
    location, 235
    management controls, 235–36
    options, 235
INSPECT subsystem, 317–22
    commands with security implications, 321–22
    components, 318
    components, securing, 320–22

customization file, 319
defined, 317
DMON system program, 319
IMON system program, 318
INSPECT user program, 318
INSPSNAP, 319
languages with, 317
Pathway and, 320
risks, 317–18
SAVEABEND files, 320
Visual Inspect software, 320
INSPSNAP, 319
Integrity, 3–4
defined, 3
risks, 4
Internal-use information, 6

J

Job-function IDs, 91

K

Kernel-Managed Swap Facility (KMSF), 354

L

Legacy applications, 524–25
LIB parameter, 134
Libraries
components, securing, 326–27
defined, 322
SCF, 416
shared run-time (SRLs), 324–26
system, 323
user, 323–24
uses, 322–23
LICENSE command, 334
Licensed files, 327–36
documentation/authorization of, 329
risks, 328
securing, 328–36

unauthorized, scheduled review for, 335–36
Licensed operating system programs, 330–34
LINKMON, 375
LISTNER utility, 336–39
components, 337
defined, 336
multiple processes, 336
PORTCONF configuration file, 337–38
responsibility, 336
securing, 338–39
TCP/IP service file, 338
LOAD, 257
Location-independent naming, 442
Logical controls, 8–10
Logical Device Numbers, 163
LOGIN program, 339–40
defined, 339
securing, 339–40
Logon
CMON configuration, 130
non-Safeguard, 128
password issues, 130
with Safeguard, 129
Safeguard Global parameters, 130–31
TACLCONF configuration, 127–30
Logon controls
password-related, 112–24
Safeguard, 113–14
settings, 113
LOGON program, 112, 340–41
defined, 340
securing, 340–41

M

Management controls, 7
MAX SYSTEM NUMBER, 17
MEASCOM, 342
MEASCTL, 343
MEASDECS, 343
MEASFH, 343

MEASIMMU, 343
MEASMON, 343–44
MEASTCM, 344
MEASURE subsystem, 341–47
    components, 342
    components, securing, 344–47
    defined, 341
    MEASCOM, 342
    MEASCTL, 343
    MEASDECS, 343
    MEASFH, 343
    MEASIMMU, 343
    MEASMON, 343–44
    MEASTCM, 344
    MEASZIP, 344
    output data files, 344
    risks, 341–42
MEASZIP, 344
MEDDEM, 269
MEDIACOM, 268, 271–73
    defined, 271
    RECOVER access, 271
MEDIADBM, 268
MEDIAMSG, 268
MEDIASRV, 268–69
Mirrored disk volumes, 550

N

NAMELOGON Global parameter, 113
Native Link Editor (NLD) program, 347–48
    defined, 347
    securing, 347–48
Native Object File Tool (NOFT) program,
        348–49
    defined, 348
    interactive use, 348
    securing, 349
NBEXEC, 351
NetBatch command interpreter, 126
NETBATCH subsystem, 349–54

ASSIGNs/DEFINEs in, 570–71
ATTACHMENT-SETs, 351–52
BATCHCAL, 351
BATCHCOM, 351
BATCHCTL, 351
components, 349–50
components, securing, 352–54
defined, 349
NBEXEC, 351
NetBatch Plus, 351
NETBATCH program, 350
risks, 350
Networking, 14, 15–25
    dial access, 22–25
    Expand network, 15–19
    TCP/IP, 19–21
    Telnet, 21
    See also HP NonStop server
NMCINMCPLUS, 220–21
NMCOBOL, 221
Non-Pathway applications, 534–35
Non-restricted information, 6
Nonstop file codes, 587–88
NonStop Remote Database Facility (RDF)
        subsystem, 391–403, 551
NonStop SQL databases, 173, 537–40
    AUDSERV, 456
    components, 448
    components, securing, 456–59
    defined, 537
    securing, with Guardian, 538
    securing, with Safeguard, 538–39
    SQLCAT, 449
    SQLCFE/SQLH, 456
    SQLCI, 449–55
    SQLCI2, 449–55
    SQLCOMP/NLCPCOMP, 45–46
    SQLESP/SQLESMG, 456
    SQL/MP, 447
    SQLMSG/NLCPMSG, 456
    SQL/MX, 447–48

SQLUTIL, 449–55, 456
    versions, 447–48
NonStop SQL subsystem, 447–59
NonStop Transaction Management Facility
        (TMF) software, 499–511, 578–82
NSKCOM utility, 354–56
    defined, 354
    internal security, 354
    managed SWAP files, 355
    securing, 355–56

O

Objects
    files, Safeguard, 411
    Safeguard, 43–44
    SQL, 540–44
OBJECTTYPEs
    ACL, 51
    audit attributes, 52–53
    defined, 48
    DEVICE-related, 164
    disk-related, 176–77
    freezing, 51–52
    OBJECTTYPEs, 48–49
    ownership, 50–51
    process-related, 153–55
    Protection Records, 44, 48, 49–51
    status, 51–52
    thawing, 52
    See also Safeguard
Old operating system, 360–61
Operating system, 356–64
    communications, 36
    current, 358–59
    D-series, 415
    files, reserve system disk for, 33
    G-series, 415–16
    licensed programs, 330–34
    location, 356
    old, 360–61

PROGID'd programs, 386
software, securing, 33
SYSTEM disk security, 356–58
$SYSTEM.SYSTEM, 362–63
Z-subvolumes, 363–64
ORSERV, 311
OSCONFIG file, 468
OSS authentication, 132
Owners
    Primary, 42–43
    Secondary, 43
    types of, 42
Ownership
    device Protection Record, 168
    DISKFILE Protection Record, 186–87
    OBJECTTYPE, 50–51
    process Protection Record, 160
    Safeguard, 42–43
    SUBVOLUME Protection Record, 185
    User Record, 102
    VOLUME Protection Record, 183–84

P

PAK/UNPAK programs, 364–66
    defined, 364
    PAK, 364
    securing, 365–66
    UNPAK, 364–65
PARAMs, 548, 573
PARAM-TEXT Global parameter, 135
Pascal, 222
PASSWORD-ENCRYPT Global parameter, 115
PASSWORD-EXPIRY-GRACE Global
        parameter, 118, 119
PASSWORD-HISTORY Global parameter, 115
PASSWORD-MAY-CHANGE Global parameter,
        118, 119–20
PASSWORD-MINIMUM-LENGTH Global
        parameter, 116
PASSWORD program, 366–71

PASSWORD program (continued)
  BIND settings, 574–75
  BLINDPASSWORD parameter, 367–68
  configuring, 366–70
  defined, 366
  ENCRYPTPASSWORD parameter, 368
  MINPASSWORDLEN parameter, 369
  parameters, 366
  PROMPTPASSWORD parameter, 369–70
  securing, 370–71
Password-related logon controls, 112–24
PASSWORD-REQUIRED Global parameter,
      114
Passwords
  administration, 110–12, 122–24
  Corporate Security Policy and, 117
  encrypted, 115
  expiration, 116–21
  expiration with Safeguard, 117–21
  expiration with third party products, 121
  "hardened," 111–12
  history, 115
  logon-related issues, 130
  minimum number of characters, 116
  quality controls, 114–16
  resetting, 121–22
  Safeguard controls, 37–38
  strong, 116
  third party products, 370
  use of, 110
PATHCOM, 372–73
PATHCTL, 376
PATHMON, 373–74
  defined, 373
  risks, 373–74
PATHTCP2, 375–76
PATHTCPL, 376
Pathway subsystem, 371–79, 528–30
  applications, 550
  applications, securing, 532–33
  as client-server application model, 372

  commands, 559–61
  communication between environments,
      531–32
  components, 372
  components, securing, 377–79
  configuration, 530–31
  dedicated terminals, 529
  defined, 371
  discovery questions, 533–34
  GUI terminal interface, 529
  INSPECT and, 320
  LINKMON, 375
  non-dedicated terminals, 529
  PATHCOM, 372–73
  PATHCTL, 376
  PATHMON, 373–74
  PATHTCP2, 375–76
  PATHTCPL, 376
  POBJDIR/POBJCOD, 376–77
  production application gateway, 372
  server programs, 377
  servers, 529–30
  STATUS command, 559, 560–61
  terminal interface, 528–29
PCFORMAT program, 379–81
  conversion format, 379–80
  defined, 379
  securing, 380–81
PEEK utility, 381
Peripheral Utility Program. See PUP utility
Personal userids, 94–97
PERUSE, 434–35
  command interpreter, 583
  commands with security implications, 435
  defined, 434
  JOB command, 584
  LIST command, 584
  uses, 434–35
Physical controls, 8
  areas, 8
  dial access, 22–23

PING program, 381–82
   defined, 381
   securing, 382
Platforms, 527–36
   Batch, 535
   non-Pathway, 534–35
   Pathway, 528–34
   tools, 535–36
PNAME parameter, 134
POBJDIR/POBJCOD, 376–77
PORTCONF configuration file, 337–38
PRDUMP utility, 478
Primary Owners, 42–43
PRI parameter, 135
Privileged IDs, 84–94
   application-owner, 90–91
   categories, 82
   discovery questions, 93–94
   Group Manager, 85
   with inherent Guardian privileges, 84–90
   job-function, 91
   securing, 92–94
   SUPER Group, 86
   SUPER.SUPER, 86–90
Process access ID (PAID), 151, 382
Processes, 29–30
   ACTIVE, 150
   auditing, access/management, 160–62
   CMON, 127
   CODE SPACE, 150
   DATA SPACE, 150
   disk, 253
   LIBRARY SPACE, 151
   management request evaluation, 156
   managing, 88
   named, 154–55
   names, 146
   owners, 29
   print, 435–36
   processing order, 148
   properties, 147–51

Protection Records, 159–60
RDF, 394–96
running, 29–30
Safeguard controls, 38–39
securing, 151–52
securing, with Safeguard, 153–63
security, 30, 144–53
states, 149–50
structure, 145, 150–51
system, 471–75
unnamed, 147, 154–55
Process identification numbers (PINs), 147
PROGID'd files, 382–89
   authorized use protection, 385–86
   command use, controlling, 386–87
   defined, 383
   documentation and authorization, 384–85
   operating system programs, 386
   securing, 384–89
   third party programs, 386
   unauthorized, scheduled review for, 387–89
PROG parameter, 134
Programs
   ADDUSER, 97, 197–99
   AUDSERV, 200–201
   AXCEL, 201–2
   BACKUP, 203–5
   CMON, 137–42, 212–15
   CROSSREF, 227–29
   Data Build, 241–43
   DataLoader/MP, 243–44
   DEFAULT, 97–98, 175, 248–50
   defined, 145
   DELUSER, 97, 250–52
   DMON, 319
   DSAP, 260–62
   ECHO, 273–74
   EDIT, 274–76
   ENABLE, 285–87
   ERROR, 294–95
   IMON, 318

Programs (continued)
  INSPECT, 318
  IXF, 309
  licensed operating system, 330–34
  LOGIN, 339–40
  LOGON, 112, 340–41
  NETBATCH, 350
  NLD, 347–48
  NOFT, 348–49
  PAK/UNPAK, 364–66
  PASSWORD, 366–71
  PCFORMAT, 379–81
  PING, 381–82
  RESTORE, 403–7
  RPASSWRD, 97, 407–8
  SEEVIEW, 423–25
  SQL, 542–44
  TFTP, 306–9
  TGAL, 498–99
  USERS, 98, 512–13
  VIEWSYS, 514–15
  See also Utilities
Protection Records
  ACL, 45–47
  aliases and, 46
  audit parameters, 47–48
  audit parameters, disk file-related, 193–96
  device/subdevice, 167–68
  DISKFILE, 44, 185–87
  disk file-related, 182–87
  OBJECTTYPE, 44, 48
  operations/privileges granted in, 45
  owners, 42
  PERSISTENT, 46
  process/subprocess, 159–60
  SUBVOLUME, 184–85
  VOLUME, 44, 183
  See also Safeguard
Protection/recovery, 549–51
  BACKUP/RESTORE, 550
  mirrored disk volumes, 550

NonStop process pairs, 550
NonStop TMF subsystem, 550
Pathway applications, 550
RDF, 550
Protection views, 541
PTAL, 222–23
PUP utility, 389–91
  defined, 389
  securing, 389–91
  Subsystem Programmatic Interface (SPI)
      support, 389

R

RCVDUMP utility, 478
RDFCHEK, 393
RDFCOM, 393
RDFSCAN, 383
RDFSNOOP, 393
RECGEN, 427
RECOVERY modes, 57–59
  DENY GRANTS, 58–59
  RECYCLE, 57–58
  SUSPEND AUDIT, 58
RECYCLE mode, 57–58
References
  resolving, 206
  validating, 206
RELOAD utility, 478
REMOTECMONTIMEOUT, 140–41
Remote Database Facility (RDF) subsystem,
      391–403
  commands with security implications, 401–3
  components, 392–99
  components, securing, 399–403
  components illustration, 392
  components interaction, 397–99
  Configuration File, 396
  Context File, 396
  defined, 391
  extractor process, 394

flexibility, 391
image files, 397
log file, 396–97
Monitor Process, 394
processes, 394–96
Purger Process, 394
RDFCHEK, 393
RDFCOM, 393
RDFSCAN, 383
RDFSNOOP, 393
Receiver Process, 395
Updater Processes, 395–96
user programs, 392–93
versions, 391–92
REMOTEPASSWORDs, 136–37
RESTORE program, 403–7, 550
  commands with security implications, 405–7
  defined, 403
  File Mode, 403–4
  Listonly Mode, 404
  operation modes, 403
  securing, 405–7
  TMF software interaction, 404–5
  Volume Mode, 404
Restricted information, 6
RLSEID file, 468, 569–70
RPASSWRD program, 97, 407–8
  defined, 407
  securing, 408
RPSETUP utility, 436

S

SAFECOM commands, 411–14
Safeguard, 408–14
  ADDUSER program with, 199
  audit controls, 40–42
  audit files, 410
  auditing, 25, 72–77
  auditing users with, 107–10
  Audit Pools, 54–59

audit report generation, 55
audit trail information gathering, 565–66
audit write configuration, 56–57
authentication controls, 37
  CMON and, 141–42, 214
  CMON controls, 39–40
  Command Interpreter (CI) controls, 40
  commands, 561–66
  components, 410–11
  components, securing, 411–14
  configuring, 34–79
  control categories, 35
  CREATE attempt evaluation, 187
  defined, 408
  DELUSER program with, 252
  device controls, 38
  devices and, 163–68
  diskfile controls, 39
  in Enscribe database security, 537
  file access attempt evaluation, 188–91
  FTP with, 304
  global configuration, 35–42
  globals/configuration recap, 77–79
  Guardian comparison, 34–35
  INFO AUDIT SERVICE command, 566
  logon controls, 113–14
  non-object entities, 53–68
  object files, 411
  object information gathering, 561–65
  Object Protection Records, 44–48
  objects, 43–44
  OBJECTTYPES, 48–53
  ownership, 42–43
  password controls, 378
  password expiration, 117–21
  Password parameters, 114–16
  password resetting with, 122
  process controls, 38–39
  process management request evaluation, 156
  SAFECOM commands, 411–14
  securing disk files in, 175–96

Safeguard (continued)
  securing processes with, 153–63
  security considerations, 409
  security evaluation, 31
  SECURITY GROUPs, 59–62
  SEEP, 63–68
  Terminal Definition Records, 63
  userid/alias record attributes, 102–6
  userid/alias-related Global parameters, 99–101
  userid management in, 98–106
  Warning Mode, 38, 68–72
  See also Guardian
Safeguard-controlled terminals, 132–35
  dynamic sessions, 132
  static, 132–35
  TERMINAL-EXCLUSIVE-ACCESS Global
      parameter, 135
Sanitizing
  defined, 32
  HP NonStop systems, 32–34
  test data, 544–45
SAVEABEND files, 320
Scalability, availability and, 13
SCFCSTM configuration file, 236–37
  defined, 236
  management controls, 236–37
SCFLIB, 416
SCFTEXT, 416
SCOBOL, 223–24
Secondary Owners, 53
Security
  basics, 1–11
  device, 163–70
  Expand network, 18
  Guardian, 26
  information, 3–7
  physical, 16
  practices, 2
  process, 30, 144–53
  requirements, 3–5
Security Event-Exit Process (SEEP), 63–68

commands, 64
Configuration Records, 64–67
CPU, 67
defined, 63
ENABLE-AUTHENTICATION-EVENT
    parameter, 65
ENABLE-AUTHORIZATION-EVENT
    parameter, 65–66
ENABLED parameter, 65
ENABLE-PASSWORD-EVENT parameter,
    66
EVENT-EXIT-PROCESS parameter, 64
LIB, 66
managing, 67–68
PARAM-TEXT parameter, 67
PNAME parameter, 67
PRI parameter, 67
PROG parameter, 66
RESPONSE-TIMEOUT parameter, 65
SWAP parameter, 67
See also Safeguard
SECURITY GROUPs, 59–62
  defined, 59
  SECURITY-ADMINISTRATOR GROUP,
      60
  SYSTEM-OPERATOR GROUP, 61–62
  valid, 60
Security Policies
  confidentiality and, 5
  Corporate, 2
  defined, 1
  effective, 2
  requirements, 6
SEECSTM configuration file, 237–38
  defined, 237
  management controls, 237–38
SEEVIEW program, 423–25
  components, 423
  defined, 423
  securing, 423–25
Self-monitoring, 11

SERVICES configuration file, 425–26
    defined, 425
    securing, 425–26
Session encryption, 24
Shared run-time libraries (SRLs), 324–26
    defined, 324
    loading, with LTILT, 325
    loading, with ZTILT, 326
    private, 324–25
    public, 324
    resolving, with NLD, 325
    verifying, with VTILT, 325–26
    See also Libraries
Shorthand views, 542
Single SignOn, 84
Site Update Tape (SUT), 462
SNOOP utility, 504
SORTPROG, 427–28
SORT subsystem, 426–29
    components, securing, 428–29
    RECGEN, 427
    SORT, 427
    SORTPROG, 427–28
SPOOLCOM, 436–37
    COLLECT command, 583
    commands with security implications, 436–37
    defined, 436
    JOB command, 583
    starting, 582
    uses, 436
Spooler subsystem, 432–41
    collectors, 434
    components, 433–38
    components, securing, 438–41
    components illustration, 433
    data files, 438
    FASTP, 436
    FONT utility, 434
    PERUSE, 434–35
    print processes, 435–36
    RPSETUP utility, 436

SPOOLCOM, 436–37
SpoolerPlus, 432
supervisors, 437
SQL
    commands, 566–67
    compilation, 224
    defined, 537
    See also NonStop SQL databases
SQLCAT, 449
SQLCFE/SQLH, 456
SQLCI, 449–55
    commands with security implications, 449–54
    controlling, 455
    prompt levels, 567
    starting, 566–67
SQLCI2, 449–55
SQLCOMP/NLCPCOMP, 45–46
SQLESP/SQLESMG, 456
SQLMSG/NLCPMSG, 456
SQL objects, 540–44
    indexes, 541
    licensed SQLCI2, 544
    programs, 542–44
    tables, 540–41
    views, 541–42
SQL programs, 542–44
    SQLCOMP/NLCPCOMP, 542–43
    SQL invalidation, 543–44
SQLUTIL, 449–55, 456
Static Safeguard terminals, 132–35
STATUS parameter, 135
Storage Management Foundation (SMF) logical
        file names, 310
Storage Management Foundation (SMF) software,
        441–47
    catalog, 444
    components, 443–44
    components, securing, 444
    concepts, 441–44
    defined, 441
    location-independent naming, 442

Storage Management Foundation software
        (continued)
    mapping virtual files, 443
    master process, 443
    pool process, 443
    storage pools, 442–43
    utilities, 444
    virtual disk process, 444
    virtual disks, 442
Structured Query Language. *See* SQL
Subsystem Control Facility (SCF), 414–20
    ASSUME command, 576
    commands, 575–78
    commands with security implications, 418–20
    components, securing, 417–20
    custom files, 416
    defined, 414
    on D-series operating systems, 415
    on G-series operating systems, 415–16
    INFO command, 576
    INFO SERVICE command, 577
    INFO SUBNET command, 576
    LISTDEV TELSERV command, 576
    maps, 577–78
    SCF command interpreter, 416
    SCFLIB, 416
    SCFTEXT, 416
    subsystems controlled via, 415–17
    subsystem-specific servers, 416–17
Subsystem Control Point (SCP), 420–23
    components, securing, 422–23
    defined, 420
    SCP, 421
    SCPTC and SCPTCOL, 421
    SPI messages, 420, 421
Subsystem Programmatic Interface (SPI), 429–32
    components, 430–31
    components, securing, 431–32
    defined, 429
    definition files, 430–31
    interface, 429

    messages, 420, 421
SUBVOLUME Protection Records, 184–85
    ACL, 184
    ownership, 185
    parts, 184
SUPER Group IDs, 86
SUPER.SUPER, 36–37, 86–90
    reducing use of, 87–90
    requirement, 87
    for system installation, 90
SUSPEND AUDIT mode, 58
SWAP parameter, 135
SWID utility, 459–60
    defined, 459
    purpose, 459
    securing, 460
    VPROC utility and, 460
SYMSERV, 228
SYSGENR utility, 461–62
    components, securing, 461–62
    defined, 461
SYSINFO command, 554, 569
System configuration files, 462–70
    CIIN, 466–67
    CONFALT, 463
    CONFAUX, 463–64
    CONFBASE, 464
    CONFLIST, 464
    CONFTEXT, 464–66
    CUSTFILE, 467–68
    defined, 462
    OSCONFIG, 468
    RLSEID, 468
    securing, 469–70
SYSTEM disk, 356–58
System libraries, 323
System management, 548–49
System processes, 471–75
    list of, 471–73
    securing, 473–75
System resources

access matrix, 144
access principles, 143–44
defining user access to, 143–96
System startup files, 475–76
  defined, 475
  invocation sequence, 476
  location, 475–76
  securing, 476
$SYSTEM.SYSTEM, 362–63
System tools, 525–26
  in-house, 525
  third-party, 525–26
System utilities, 477–85
  failure utilities, 481–82
  TACL tool utilities, 482–85
  TFDS data system, 477–80
System-wide auditing configuration, 73–76

T

Tables, 540–41
TACLCONF
  logon-related configuration, 127–30
  parameters, 127
  parameters, viewing, 573–74
TACLCSTM configuration file, 238–40
  location, 238
  risks, 238–39
  securing, 239–40
  sharing, 239
TACL subsystem, 485–94
  CMON and, 213–14
  CMON communication, 138–39
  components, 485–86
  components, securing, 492–94
  configuration, 486–88, 570–74
  CPRULES0/CPRULES1, 490
  defined, 26, 485
  initializing, 126
  internals initialization, 127
  #PMSEARCHLIST, 490–91

risks, 485
segment files, 489
sessions, 492
TACLBASE file, 488
TACLCOLD file, 488
TACLCSTM files, 488
TACLINIT file, 488
TACLLOCL file, 489
#TACLSECURITY, 491–92
TACL tool utilities, 482–85
  defined, 482
  FCHECK, 483
  FILCHECK, 483
  securing, 484–85
  TANDUMP, 483–84
  See also System utilities
TAL, 224–25
Tandem Advanced Command Language.
      See TACL subsystem
TANDUMP utility, 483–84
TAPECOM utility, 494–96
  commands with security implications, 495–96
  defined, 494
  securing, 495–96
  uses, 494–95
TCP/IP, 19–21
  configuring, 20–21
  defined, 19
  remote host addressing, 20
Technical measures, 7
TEDIT, 275
Telnet subsystem, 21, 497–98
  components, securing, 498
  defined, 497
  services, 498
  uses, 497
Terminal Definition Records, 63, 132–35
  configuration, 133
  CPU parameter, 134
  defined, 132
  LIB parameter, 134

Terminal Definition Records (continued)
   PARAM-TEXT parameter, 135
   PNAME parameter, 134
   PRI parameter, 135
   PROG parameter, 134
   STATUS parameter, 135
   SWAP parameter, 135
TERMINAL-EXCLUSIVE-ACCESS Global
      parameter, 135
Test data, sanitizing, 544–45
TFDSCOM utility, 478
TFDSCONF utility, 479
TFDS data system, 477–80
   components, 77
   defined, 477
   DUMPUTIL, 478
   monitor, 478
   PRDUMP, 478
   RCVDUMP, 478
   RELOAD, 478
   securing, 479–80
   TFDSCOM, 478
   TFDSCONF, 479
   See also System utilities
TGAL program, 498–99
   defined, 498
   securing, 499
Third party HP NonStop server security vendors,
      589–90
Third party key-stroke level, 25
Third party password products
   password expiration with, 121
   password quality controls with, 116
   resetting passwords with, 122
Third party system tools, 525–26
Third party vendor applications, 524
TMFCOM, 505–6
Tools, 535–36
   in-house system, 525
   third party system, 525–26
TRACER utility, 511–12

defined, 511
   securing, 511–12
Transaction Management Facility (TMF)
      software, 499–511, 550, 578–82
   audit dumps, 581
   auditing, 501–2
   audit trails, 504
   command interpreter prompt, 578
   components, 503–6
   components, securing, 506–11
   configuration, 501, 504–5
   database recovery and, 500–503
   defined, 499
   INFO command, 580–81
   ON-LINE DUMPS, 503
   protection areas, 504
   recovery methods, 502–3
   risks, 500
   ROLLBACK, 502
   ROLLFORWARD, 502–3
   TMFCOM, 505–6
Trivial File Transfer Protocol (TFTP) program,
      306–9
   components, 307
   components, securing, 308–9
   defined, 306
   remote clients, 306
   TFTP, 307
   TFTPCHLD, 307
   TFTPSRV, 307

U

User access, defining, 143–44
User administration, 81–84
User auditing, 106–10
   content, 106–7
   with Safeguard, 107–10
Userids, 81–82
   administering, 95–96
   alias, 84

application-owner, 90–91
categories, 82
defined, 27
deleting, 250
frozen, 103
FTP, 301
groups, 81–82
job-function, 91
management, 96–97
managing, 88, 96–106
managing, in Guardian, 97–98
managing, in Safeguard, 98–106
members, 82
new, procedures to request, 95
obsolete, delete procedures, 95–96
personal, 94–97
privileged, 82, 84–94
privileges, 27, 84–90
PROGID, 383–84
single, 90
SUPER.SUPER, 86–90
thawed, 103
User libraries, 323–24
User management, 33
User Record
    audit-related parameters, 108–10
    Command Interpreter (CI) attributes, 104–5
    DEFAULT PROTECTION parameter, 104
    disk file settings, 176
    Guardian Default Security parameter, 103–4
    Guardian Default Volume parameter, 103
    OSS-specific attributes, 105–6
    ownership, 102
    password-expiration related parameters,
        118–21
    PRIMARY-GROUP attribute, 106
    USER-EXPIRES parameter, 102–3
USERS program, 98, 512–13, 582
    defined, 512
    information display, 512
    securing, 512–13

Utilities
    BACKCOPY, 202–3
    BUSCMD, 211
    COPYDUMP, 481
    COUP, 225–27
    CRUNCH, 481
    DCOM, 244–45
    DISKGEN, 254–55
    DIVER, 259–60
    DUMPUTIL, 478
    EMS, 281
    failure, 481–82
    FCHECK, 483
    FILCHECK, 483
    FINGER, 298–300
    FONT, 434
    FUP, 310–16
    GARTH, 481
    GOAWAY, 316–17
    LISTNER, 336–39
    NSKCOM, 354–56
    PEEK, 381
    PRDUMP, 478
    PUP, 389–91
    RCVDUMP, 478
    RECEIVEDUMP/RCVDUMP, 481
    RELOAD, 478
    RPSETUP, 436
    SNOOP, 504
    SWID, 459–60
    SYSGENR, 461–62
    system, 477–85
    TACL tool, 482–85
    TANDUMP, 483–84
    TAPECOM, 494–96
    TFDSCOM, 478
    TFDSCONF, 479–80
    TFDS data system, 477–80
    TFDS monitor, 478
    TRACER, 511–12
    See also Programs

V

VERIFYUSER system procedure, 127
VHSCSTM configuration file, 240–41, 517
  defined, 240
  management controls, 240–41
ViewPoint application, 513–14
  components, securing, 514
  contents, 513
  defined, 513
Views, 541–42
  protection, 541
  shorthand, 542
  types, 541
VIEWSYS program, 514–15
  defined, 514
  securing, 515
  uses, 514
Virtual disks, 442
Virtual Hometerm Subsystem (VHS), 515–19
  Audit Trail, 517
  benefits, 516
  components, 516–18
  components, securing, 518–19
  components illustration, 516
  conversational interface (VHSCI), 517
  defined, 515
  Pathway Browser, 518

primary log file set, 517
prompt file, 517
uses, 515
VHS, 517
VHSCSTM, 517
Visual Inspect software, 320
VOLUME Protection Records, 183
  ACL, 183
  ownership, 183–84
VPROC, 208
VS, 275

W

Warning Mode, 68–72
  controls, 38
  defined, 68
  disk file access evaluation in, 70–71
  facts, 68
  process access evaluation in, 71–72
  WARNING-FALLBACK-SECURITY, 69–72
  WARNING-MODE, 69
  See also Safeguard

Z

$ZNUP, 297
ZSERVER, 269
ZSYSCFG file, 355